Contemporary Conflict Resolution

Fourth Edition

Contemporary Conflict Resolution

The prevention, management and transformation of deadly conflicts

Fourth Edition

OLIVER RAMSBOTHAM, TOM WOODHOUSE
AND HUGH MIALL

polity

First edition first published in 1999 by Polity Press

This edition first published in 2016 by Polity Press

Polity Press
65 Bridge Street
Cambridge CB2 1UR, UK

Polity Press
350 Main Street
Malden, MA 02148, USA

ISBN-13: 978-0-7456-8721-6
ISBN-13: 978-0-7456-8722-3 (pbk)

A catalogue record for this book is available from the British Library.

Library of Congress Cataloging-in-Publication Data
Ramsbotham, Oliver.
     Contemporary conflict resolution / Oliver Ramsbotham, Tom Woodhouse, Hugh Miall. – Fourth edition.
       pages cm
   Includes bibliographical references and index.
   ISBN 978-0-7456-8721-6 (hardback) – ISBN 978-0-7456-8722-3 (pbk.) 1. Pacific settlement of international disputes. 2. Conflict management. I. Woodhouse, Tom. II. Miall, Hugh. III. Title.
   JZ6010.R26 2016
   327.1'72–dc23
                                                          2015018625

Typeset in 9.5 on 13pt Swift by
Servis Filmsetting Ltd, Stockport, Cheshire

For further information on Polity, visit our website:
politybooks.com

Brief Contents

Detailed Contents

Figures

Tables

Boxes

Maps

Acknowledgements

We want to acknowledge the help of many people in the task of revising this book. We owe special thanks to our publishers at Polity, in particular Louise Knight and Pascal Porcheron, who encouraged us to write this fourth edition and supported us throughout; to Caroline Richmond for her meticulous copy-editing; and to Laina Reynolds Levi for commenting on and helping us to improve the text. The example of those who founded the field continues to provide the inspiration for what we have attempted here. The more we have studied the work of people such as Elise and Kenneth Boulding, Adam Curle, Johan Galtung, John Burton and many other pioneers, the more we realized how wise and prescient they were. We continue to learn from colleagues in the current conflict resolution and transformation field worldwide, whose dynamic responses to a rapidly changing world are another source of inspiration. We hope that this book will help to publicize their work and, above all, to encourage increasing global participation in the conflict resolution enterprise. And we would also like to thank our colleagues, and especially our students, at the Centre for Conflict Resolution, Department of Peace Studies, at the University of Bradford, and at the Conflict Analysis Research Centre at the University of Kent. They have brought a wealth of experience from all parts of the world to our universities, and we have learned from them at least as much as we have imparted. We hope that this book will provide some help to them as they return to their communities and proceed with the work of ridding the world of the scourge of war.

Illustration Acknowledgements

We are grateful to the following for permission to reproduce copyright material:

Figure 1.4 'The conflict tree' from *Working With Conflict* by Simon Fisher et al., Zed Books, 2000, p.29, copyright © Zed Books; Figure 1.7 'Positions, interests and needs' in *Resolving Disputes without Going to Court* by Andrew Floyer-Acland, Century, 1995, p.50, copyright © Andrew Floyer-Acland. Reproduced by permission of the author; Table 1.3 'Three faces of power' from *Three Faces of Power* by Kenneth E. Boulding, Sage Publications, 1989, p.25, copyright © Sage Publications Inc. 1989. Reprinted by permission of SAGE; Figure 1.9 'Transforming asymmetric conflicts (I)' developed from *Preparing for Peace* by John Paul Lederach, Syracuse University Press, Syracuse, New York, 1995. Reproduced with permission; Figure 1.11 'Actors and approaches to peace-building' in *Building Peace: Sustainable Reconciliation in Divided Societies* by John Paul Lederach, Washington, DC: Endowment of the United States Institute of Peace, 1997; Figure 1.12 'Transforming asymmetric conflicts (II)' by Diane Francis, adapted from 'Power and conflict resolution' in *International Alert, Conflict Resolution Training in the North Caucasus, Georgia and the South of Russia*, 1994, copyright © Mrs Diane Francis. Reproduced by permission of the author; Figure 1.14 'William Ury's third side roles' in *The Third Side: Harvard University Global Negotiation Project*, www.thirdside.org, copyright © Dr William Ury. Reproduced by permission of the author; Table 2.1 'The evolution of attempts to create a peaceful postwar international order' from *Peace and War: Armed Conflicts and International Order 1648–1989* by Kalevi J. Holsti, Cambridge University Press, 1991. Reproduced with permission; Figure 3.2 'Number of armed conflicts by type, 1946–2014' from 'Armed Conflicts, 1946–2014' by Thérèse Pettersson and Peter Wallensteen in *Journal of Peace Research*, Vol 52 (4), pp.536–50, SAGE Publications, July 2015, copyright © 2015, Peace Research Institute Oslo. Reprinted by permission of SAGE; Map 3.1 'State fragility and warfare in the global system, 2013' compiled by Dr Monty G. Marshall, July 2014, http://www.systemicpeace.org/warlist/warlist.htm. Reproduced by permission of Center for Systemic Peace, www.systemicpeace.org; Figure 3.4 'Deaths from terrorism, 2000–2013' from the *Global Terrorism Index 2014 highlights*, Institute of Economics and Peace, p.2, http://www.visionofhumanity.org. Reproduced with permission; Box 4.1 from 'Interpretations of the Northern Ireland conflict' in *Interpreting Northern Ireland* by John Whyte, Clarendon Press, 1990, pp.113–205. Reproduced by permission of Oxford University Press; Extracts from *The Rabin Memoirs, 2/e* by Yitzhak Rabin, translated by Dov Goldstein, University of California Press, 1996, copyright © 1979 by General Yitzhak Rabin. Reprinted with the permission of The Orion Publishing Group, London and Little Brown and Company. All rights reserved; Box 8.1 from 'Components of the UN Transition Authority in Cambodia' in *The Blue Helmets: A Review of United Nations Peace-Keeping*, 1996, pp.447–84, copyright © United Nations 1996. Reproduced with permission; Box 10.5 from 'Deliberating the holocaust and the Nakba: disruptive empathy and binationalism in Israel/Palestine' by Bashir Bashir and Amos Goldberg in *Journal of Genocide Research*, Vol 16 (1), pp.77–99, Taylor & Francis, February 2014, copyright © 2014 Routledge; Box 13.3 from 'Women in war and peace: Grassroots peacebuilding' by Donna Ramsey Marshall, in *Peaceworks*, 34, Washington, DC: Endowment of the United States Institute of Peace, August 2000; Box 13.4 adapted from 'Women and peace in the United Nation', by Sarah Poehlman and Felicity Hill, in *New Routes: A Journal of Peace Research and Action*, Vol 6 (3), 2001, p.2, copyright © Life & Peace Institute; Box 16.3 from 'The roles of cultural initiatives in peace-building' in *Fostering Peace through Cultural Initiatives*, Preliminary Research Report by Akiko Fukushima, Joint Research Institute for International Peace and Culture (JRIPEC), Aoyama Gakuin University, 2009, p.ii. Reproduced with permission; Box 17.4 from 'Virtual Peace Education' by Ruth Firer, in *Journal of Peace Education*, Vol 5 (2), pp.193–207, Taylor & Francis, September 2008, copyright © 2008 Routledge; Box 18.2 from *Israeli and Palestinian Narratives of Conflict* ed. Robert I. Rotberg, pp.133, 147–8, 167–8, copyright © 2006 by The World Peace Foundation. All rights reserved. Reprinted with permission of Indiana University Press.

In some instances we have been unable to trace the owners of copyright material and we would appreciate any information that would enable us to do so.

Abbreviations

ACCORD	African Centre for the Constructive Resolution of Disputes
ADR	alternative dispute resolution
AFISMA	African International Support Mission to Mali (ECOWAS-led)
AIAI	Al-Ittihad al-Islamiya (Somalia)
AKUF	Arbeitsgruppe Kriegsursachsforschung (working group on war research, Hamburg University)
AMAR	All Minorities at Risk dataset (University of Maryland, US)
AMISOM	African Union Mission in Somalia
ANC	African National Congress
APEC	Asia-Pacific Economic Cooperation
API	Arab Peace Initiative
AQI	al-Qaeda in Iraq
AQIM	al-Qaeda in the Islamic Maghreb
ARK	Anti-Ratna Kampanja (anti-war campaign, Croatia)
ARPANET	Advanced Research Projects Agency Network, predecessor of the World Wide Web
ASEAN	Association of South-East Asian Nations
ASG	Abu Sayaff Group (Philippines)
AU	African Union
AVU	African Virtual University
BINUB	United Nations Integrated Office in Burundi
CAB	Comprehensive Agreement on the Bangsamoro (Philippines/ Mindanao)
CAR	Central African Republic
CASBS	Center for Advanced Study in the Behavioral Sciences
CBO	community based organization
CCR	cyber conflict resolution
CCR	cosmopolitan (or contemporary) conflict resolution
CEDAW	Convention on the Elimination of All Forms of Discrimination Against Women
CEO	chief executive officer
CETR	Conflict Education and Training Systems, website
CFSP	Common Foreign and Security Policy
CIA	Central Intelligence Agency
CIC	Center on International Cooperation (New York University, US)

CIDCM	Center for International Development and Conflict Management (Maryland, US)
CIS	Commonwealth of Independent States (former Soviet Republics)
CIVPOL	civilian police
CMOC	Civil-Military Operation Centre
CNN	Cable News Network, Major US News Channel
CODESA	Convention for a Democratic South Africa
CONIS	Conflict Information System (University of Heidelberg, Germany)
COW	Correlates of War Project
CPRU	Conflict Prevention and Reconstruction Unit (World Bank)
CSCE	Conference on Security and Cooperation in Europe
CSP	Centre for Systemic Peace
CVE	countering violent extremism
CZM	Centar za Mir (Centre for Peace, Croatia)
DAC	Development Assistance Committee of the OECD
DARPA	Defense Advanced Research Project Agency (US)
DDR	disarmament, demobilization, rehabilitation
DDRRR	disarmament, demobilization, repatriation, resettlement and reintegration
DEVCO	Directorate General for Development and Cooperation – EuropeAid (European Commission)
DFID	Department for International Development (UK)
DFS	Department of Field Support
DPA	Department of Political Affairs (UN)
DPKO	Department of Peacekeeping Operations (UN)
DRC	Democratic Republic of Congo
ECCP	European Centre for Conflict Prevention
ECOMOG	Economic Community of West African States Ceasefire Monitoring Group
ECOWAS	Economic Community of West African States
ECP	Escola de Cultura de Pau (Catalunya)
EEAS	European External Action Service
ELN	National Liberation Army (Colombia)
ETA	Euskadi Ta Askatasuna (Basque Country and Liberty)
EU	European Union
EUBAM	EU Border Assistance Mission in Libya
EUCAP	EU Capacity Assistance Mission
EUJUST LEX	EU Rule of Law Mission for Iraq
EULEX	EU Rule of Law Mission in Kosovo
EUTM	EU Training Mission – Mali
FARC-EP	Revolutionary Armed Forces of the Colombian People's Army
FCO	Foreign and Commonwealth Office

FFCB	Foundation of Football Club Barcelona
FIS	Front Islamique du Salut (Algeria)
G8	Group of Eight
G20	Group of Twenty Finance Ministers and Central Bank Governors
G77	Group of 77 developing nations
GAM	Gerekan Aceh Mereka
GBAV	global burden of armed violence
GCPP	Global Conflict Prevention Pool (UK)
GDI	Gender Development Index
GDP	gross domestic product
GEDS	Global Event-Data System
GEM	Gender Empowerment Measure
GIA	Groupe Islamique Armée (Algeria)
GICM	Moroccan Islamic Combat Group
GIS	Geographic Information System
GPI	Global Peace Index
GRIT	graduated and reciprocated initiatives in tension reduction
GRO	grassroots organization
GSPC	Group for the Call and Combat (Algeria)
GTD	Global Terrorism Database
GTI	Global Terrorism Index
GWOT	global war on terror
HCNM	High Commissioner on National Minorities (OSCE)
HIIK	Heidelberg Institute for International Conflict Research
HUJI	Harakat ul-Jihad-Islami (Pakistan)
HUM	Harakat ul-Mujahidin (Pakistan)
IAA	Islamic Army of Aden
ICC	International Criminal Court
ICG	International Crisis Group
ICISS	International Commission on Intervention and State Sovereignty
ICJ	International Court of Justice
ICM	international conflict mediation
ICRC	International Committee of the Red Cross
ICT	information and communications technologies
ICTR	International Criminal Tribunal for Rwanda
ICTY	International Criminal Tribunal for the Former Yugoslavia
ICU	Islamic Courts Union
IDEA	International Institute for Democracy and Electoral Assistance, Stockholm
IDP	internally displaced person
IDPS	international dialogue on peacebuilding and statebuilding
IEP	Institute for Economics and Peace

IFI	international financial institution
IFOR	Implementation Force (NATO in Bosnia)
IGAD	Intergovernmental Authority on Development (Africa)
IGO	intergovernmental organization
IISS	International Institute for Strategic Studies
IMAT	International Military Advisory Team (Sierra Leone)
IMF	International Monetary Fund
IMT	International Monitoring Team (Philippines)
IMU	Islamic Movement of Uzbekistan
INCAF	International Network on Conflict and Fragility
INCORE	Initiative on Conflict Resolution and Ethnicity (University of Ulster)
INGO	International Nongovernmental Organization
INTERFET	International Force in East Timor
IOC	International Olympic Committee
IPA	International Peace Academy
IPCC	Intergovernmental Panel on Climate Change
IPRA	International Peace Research Association
IR	international relations
IRA	Irish Republican Army
IRENÉ	Institute for Research and Education on Negotiation (ESSEC Business School, France)
IRW	intervention–reconstruction–withdrawal (operation)
IS	Islamic State
ISAF	International Security Assistance Force (Afghanistan)
ISF	Israeli Strategic Forum
ISI	Islamic State of Iraq
ISIL/ISIS	Islamic State of Iraq and the Levant/Syria
JCC	Joint Control Commission (Moldova)
JCR	*Journal of Conflict Resolution*
JEM	Justice and Equality Movement (Darfur, Sudan)
JI	Jemaah Islamiya (South-East Asia)
JIACG	Joint Inter-Agency Cooperation Group (US)
JM	Jaish-e-Mohammed (Pakistan)
JPKF	Joint Peacekeeping Force (Georgia/South Ossetia)
JWP	Joint Warfare Publication (UK Ministry of Defence)
KFOR	Kosovo Force (NATO-led)
KLA	Kosovo Liberation Army
KMM	Kumpulan Mujahidin Malaysia
KNDR	Kenya National Dialogue and Reconciliation
LAS	League of Arab States
LDP	Liberal Democratic Party (Japan)
LICUS	Low Income Countries Under Stress (World Bank)
LNGO	local nongovernmental organization

LRA	Lord's Resistance Army (Uganda)
LT	Lashkar-e-Tayyiba (Pakistan)
LTTE	Liberation Tigers of Tamil Eelam (Sri Lanka)
MAR	Minorities at Risk Project (University of Maryland, US)
MCPMR	Mechanism for Conflict Prevention, Management and Resolution
MDG	Millenium Development Goals
MENA	Middle East and North Africa
MID	militarized international disputes
MILF	Moro Islamic Liberation Front (Philippines)
MINURCAT	United Nations Mission in the Central African Republic and Chad
MINURSO	United Nations Mission for the Referendum in Western Sahara
MINUSCA	UN Multidimensional Integrated Stabilization Mission in Central African Republic
MINUSMA	UN Multidimensional Integrated Stabilization Mission in Mali
MINUSTAH	UN Stabilization Mission in Haiti
MISAHEL	African Union Mission for Mali and the Sahel
MNF-I	Multinational Force in Iraq
MNLA	Mouvement National pour la Libération de l'Azawad (Mali)
MNLF	Moro National Liberation Front (Philippines)
MOD	Ministry of Defence (UK)
MONUSCO	Mission de l'ONU pour la Stabilisation en RD Congo
MOOC	massive open online course
MPC	Myanmar Peace Centre
MUJAO	Mouvement pour L'Unicité et le Jihad en Afrique de l'Ouest (Mali)
NAM	Non-Aligned Movement
NATO	North Atlantic Treaty Organization
NAVCO	Nonviolent and Violent Campaigns and Outcomes (University of Denver, US)
NGO	Nongovernmental Organization
NIWC	Northern Ireland Women's Coalition
NLA	National Liberation Army
NLD	National League for Democracy (Burma)
NP	National Party (South Africa)
NPT	Non-Proliferation Treaty
NSSR	National Security Strategy Report (US)
NSU	Negotiation Support Unit (Palestinian Authority)
OAS	Organization of American States
OAU	Organization of African Unity
ODIHR	Office for Democratic Institutions and Human Rights (OSCE)
OECD	Organization for Economic Cooperation and Development

OIC	Organization of the Islamic Conference
ONUC	UN Peacekeeping Force in Congo
ONUMOZ	UN Operation in Mozambique
ONUSAL	UN Observer Mission in El Salvador
OOTW	operations other than war
OPEC	Organization of the Petroleum Exporting Countries
ORG	Oxford Research Group
ORHA	Office for Reconstruction and Humanitarian Assistance (US/Iraq)
OSCE	Organization for Security and Cooperation in Europe
OTC	Olympic Truce Centre
OTF	Olympic Truce Foundation
P5	Permanent Five members of the UN Security Council
PAM	Peace Accords Matrix (University of Notre Dame, IL, US)
PBC	Peacebuilding Commission (UN)
PBF	Peacebuilding Fund (UN)
PBSO	Peacebuilding Support Office (UN)
PCF	Post-Conflict Fund (World Bank)
PCIA	Peace and Conflict Impact Assessment
PCIG	Palestine Citizens of Israel Group
PCRU	Post-Conflict Reconstruction Unit (UK)
PDD	Presidential Decision Directive (US)
PIOOM	Interdisciplinary Research Project on Root Causes of Human Rights Violations, Centre for the Study of Social Conflict (Leiden University, Netherlands)
PKK	Kurdistan Workers' Party (Turkey)
PLO	Palestine Liberation Army
PRIO	Peace Research Institute Oslo
PSC	protracted social conflict
PSG	Palestine Strategy Group
PSG	peacebuilding and statebuilding goals
PSO	peace support operation
PTSD	post-traumatic stress disorder
PUK	Patriotic Union of Kurdistan (Iraq)
QSIS	al-Qaeda separatists in Iraq and Syria
RDMHQ	Rapidly Deployable Mission HQ
RMA	revolution in military affairs
RPF	Rwanda Patriotic Front
R2P	responsibility to protect
RUF	Revolutionary United Front (Sierra Leone)
SADC	South African Development Council
SALW	small and light weapons
SDLP	Social Democratic and Labour Party
SED	strategic engagement of discourses

SFOR	Stabilization Force (Bosnia)
SHIRBRIG	Stand-by High Readiness Brigade
SIPRI	Stockholm International Peace Research Institute
SLM/A	Sudan Liberation Movement/Army
SPF	State and Peacebuilding Fund (World Bank)
SRSG	special representative of the secretary-general
SSTR	stability, security, transition and reconstruction
SWAPO	South-West Africa People's Organization (Namibia)
TCC	troop-contributing countries
TCG	Tunisian Combat Group
TFG	Transitional Federal Government (Somalia)
TIPH	Temporary International Presence in the City of Hebron (Norway)
TNC	transnational conflict
TRC	Truth and Reconciliation Commission
UAVs	unmanned aerial vehicles
UCDP	Uppsala Conflict Data Programme
ULFA	United Liberation Force of Assam
UN	United Nations
UNAMA	UN Assistance Mission in Afghanistan
UNAMI	UN Assistance Mission in Iraq
UNAMID	United Nations/African Union Hybrid Operation in Darfur
UNAMIR	UN Assistance Mission for Rwanda
UNAMSIL	UN Mission in Sierra Leone
UNAoC	UN Alliance of Civilizations
UNAVEM	UN Angola Verification Mission
UNCTC	UN Counter-Terrorism Committee (of the Security Council)
UNDOF	UN Disengagement Observer Force (Israel/Syria)
UNDP	UN Development Programme
UNDPI	UN Department for Public Information
UNDPKO	UN Department of Peacekeeping Operations
UNEF	UN Emergency Force (Middle East)
UNEPS	UN Emergency Peace Service (proposed)
UNESCO	UN Educational, Scientific and Cultural Organization
UNFICYP	UN Peacekeeping Force in Cyprus
UNGA	UN General Assembly
UNHCR	UN High Commissioner for Refugees
UNICEF	UN Children's Fund
UNIDR	UN Institute for Disarmament Research
UNIF	UN Intervention Force (Somalia)
UNIFIL	UN Interim Force in Lebanon
UNISFA	UN Interim Security Force for Abyei (Sudan)
UNITAF	United Task Force (Somalia)
UNITAR	UN Institute for Training and Research

UNMEE	UN Mission in Eritrea-Ethiopia
UNMIK	UN Mission in Kosovo
UNMIL	UN Mission in Liberia
UNMIN	UN Mission in Nepal
UNMIS	UN Mission in Sudan
UNMISS	UN Mission in South Sudan
UNMIT	UN Integrated Mission in Timor-Leste (East Timor)
UNMOGIP	UN Military Observer Group in India and Pakistan
UNOCI	UN Operation in Côte d'Ivoire (Ivory Coast)
UNODC	UN Office on Drugs and Crime
UNOMIG	UN Observer Mission in Georgia
UNOMIL	UN Observer Mission in Liberia
UNOSOM	UN Operation in Somalia
UNPREDEP	UN Preventive Deployment Force (Macedonia)
UNPROFOR	UN Protection Force (former Yugoslavia)
UNPWG	UN's Policy Working Group on the UN and Terrorism
UNSAS	UN Stand-by Arrangement System
UNSC	UN Security Council
UNSCR	UN Security Council Resolution
UNSG	UN secretary-general
UNSMIL	UN Support Mission in Libya
UNTAC	UN Transitional Authority in Cambodia
UNTAET	UN Transitional Administration in East Timor
UNTAG	UN Transition Assistance Group (Namibia)
UNTSO	United Nations Truce Supervision Organization
UOC	Open University of Catalunya, Barcelona
USAID	US Agency for International Development
USDOD	US Department of Defense
USIP	US Institute of Peace
VERCIC	Virtual European Research Centre in Conflictology
VPE	virtual peace education
WEF	World Economic Forum
WIDER	World Institute for Development Economics Research
WILPF	Women's International League for Peace and Freedom
WOMAD	World of Music, Arts and Dance
WOMP	World Order Models Project
WSIS	World Summit on the Information Society
ZIF	Center for International Peace Operations (Berlin)

PART I

Contemporary Conflict Resolution

CHAPTER ONE

Introduction to Conflict Resolution: Concepts and Definitions

In this fourth edition of our book we bring the survey of conflict resolution up to date in the middle of the second decade of the twenty-first century. All chapters have been adapted, most of them extensively. It is now fifteen years since the first edition came out, so it is worth commenting on the experience of updating every few years in such a rapidly changing field. Each time we begin by thinking that a few relatively minor adjustments need to be made. Each time we find that developments have taken place that demand extensive revision and a considerable amount of rethinking. It has been no different on this occasion. In 2014 alone, the unexpected seizure of territory across the Syria–Iraq border by the self-styled 'Islamic State' and the sudden outbreak of conflict in Ukraine have posed new problems for those hoping to move on from fanatical ideological violence and great power confrontation. This has been symptomatic of other longer-term trends that have recently become more visible. As always, conflict resolution has to adapt to such ongoing changes. So we offer a new assessment of the latest statistical evidence in chapter 3 and a new analysis of what we call prevailing patterns of 'transnational conflict' in chapter 4. These serve as foundations for the updating of chapters 5 to 10 in Part I. In chapter 11 we sum all of this up by outlining the dimensions of what we call 'cosmopolitan conflict resolution', defined reactively as a response to transnational conflict in all its variety, and proactively as the promotion of the cosmopolitan values on which the welfare and life hopes of future generations depend. This is further elaborated in the rest of Part II.

Why a Fourth Edition?

The first edition of the book (1999) was written at a time when, despite setbacks, conflict resolution approaches in peacekeeping, peacemaking and peacebuilding were widely seen for the first time to be central in global politics. International organizations, UN secretary-generals, some world leaders, and many prominent voices in society had come to subscribe broadly to the potential of conflict resolution and tried to promote it. The first edition aimed to explore the application of conflict resolution ideas and practices to the challenging context of contemporary world conflicts.

The second edition of the book (2005) coincided with the apogee of the 'neo-con' reaction, associated particularly with the administration of US President

George W. Bush. The 'global war on terror' had come to dominate the stage, and conflict resolution appeared to have been marginalized and its values either dismissed or co-opted and discredited. The aim of the second edition was to rescue the conflict resolution enterprise from this entanglement and to reassert its distinctive nature and contribution in the first decade of the twenty-first century. The second edition developed the idea of cosmopolitan conflict resolution as an approach not restricted to any particular society, state or culture but offering a constructive and transformative means of handling conflict in the interests of humanity.

The third edition of the book (2011) appeared at a particularly uncertain moment in world history, with the promise of a new US administration once again ready to embrace conflict resolution approaches in wider foreign policy formulation, but with mounting challenges from rising non-western powers (notably China), increasingly complex links between state failure and international terrorism, a severely shaken global economy, and embroilment in Afghanistan and Iraq continuing to wreak a fierce backlash against the whole concept of a 'liberal peace' – in which conflict resolution is often seen to be implicated. The aim of the third edition was to clarify the role of conflict resolution in this uncertain and complex environment. Our central argument was that systemic complexity of this kind may make conflict resolution more difficult but, for the same reason, renders it all the more relevant and urgent.

This fourth edition comes at a time, if anything, of even more rapid change. It seems extraordinary that, in the short space of time since the previous edition, the Arab Spring has erupted into the Arab nightmare. At great power level, Ukraine has become a site for renewed militarized rivalry between Russia and the West, while worsening relations between China and Japan, coupled with ongoing crisis in North Korea, cloud the other side of the Asian landmass. Between the two, the ominous consequences of US withdrawal from Afghanistan have yet to be played out. Meanwhile statistical analysis (chapter 3) seems to have shifted focus, with a greater emphasis now on quantifying state 'fragility' (for example, in Africa) and on the extraordinary scale of 'nonconventional' (criminal) violence (for example, in some Latin American cities). Has the steady decline in levels of recorded large-scale violence since the end of the Cold War now been reversed? Can existing conflict resolution capacity based on the postcolonial state system cope with this lethal mix of rapidly mutating conflicts, associated with ideological fervour, international criminal networks and arms availability, pouring into the increasingly extensive areas in which there is a 'vacuum of authority', where complicated patterns of contested politics give it ample opportunity to lodge and spread? For example, will the entire 'Sykes–Picot' state structure in the Middle East succumb to the swirling forces of the Sunni–Shia confrontation? Has this *de facto* already begun to happen? Does the post-Iraq and post-Afghanistan US have either the will or the capacity to do much about all this? If not, who can? As a key indicator of the increased turbulence and the way it is, above all, the most vulnerable who are affected by it, the figures for refugees and internally displaced people worldwide for 2014 are the worst since 1945 (see chapter 3).

Such is the challenging context to which we try to respond in this fourth edition. We describe the work of what we call the previous four generations of those working in the conflict resolution field – the precursors, the founders, the consolidators and the reconstructors – in chapter 2. But the main focus is on the contemporary generation, whom we call 'cosmopolitans'. In our view, the hallmark of contemporary cosmopolitan conflict resolution is to draw on the rich heritage of the field to rise to these new challenges. What does this require? In brief, we suggest that it requires adequate hybrid local–global responses to tackle the new reality – the hybrid mix of local, regional and global conflicts that we call 'transnational conflict' (chapter 4). Second, it requires an even more determined push to make sure that these efforts are truly intercultural and transcultural. Third, it requires a new emphasis on linking conflict resolution to the 'clusters' of other pools of expertise and enterprise, who may not see themselves as engaged in conflict resolution but are essential allies in this new environment. Fourth, it requires full exploitation of the new cosmopolitan space opened up by the internet. These are some key characteristics of cosmopolitan conflict resolution. To sum this up: human capacity for conflict resolution must learn to be as fast-moving, adaptive and resourceful as the hybrid and mutating forces of violence that it seeks to overcome.

Background

As a defined field of study, conflict resolution started in the 1950s and 1960s. This was at the height of the Cold War, when the development of nuclear weapons and the conflict between the superpowers seemed to threaten human survival. A group of pioneers from different disciplines saw the value of studying conflict as a general phenomenon, with similar properties whether it occurs in international relations, domestic politics, industrial relations, communities or families, or indeed between individuals. They saw the potential of applying approaches that were evolving in industrial relations and community mediation settings to conflicts in general, including civil and international conflicts.

A handful of people in North America and Europe began to establish research groups to develop these new ideas. They were not taken very seriously. The international relations profession had its own categories for understanding international conflict and did not welcome the interlopers. Nor was the combination of analysis and practice implicit in the new ideas easy to reconcile with established scholarly institutions or the traditions of practitioners such as diplomats and politicians.

Nevertheless, the new ideas attracted interest, and the field began to grow and spread. Scholarly journals in conflict resolution were created. Institutions to study the field were established, and their number rapidly increased. The field developed its own subdivisions, with different groups studying international crises, internal wars, social conflicts and approaches ranging from negotiation and mediation to experimental games.

By the 1980s, conflict resolution ideas were increasingly making a difference in real conflicts. In South Africa, for example, the Centre for Intergroup Studies was applying the approaches that had emerged in the field to the developing confrontation between apartheid and its challengers, with impressive results. In the Middle East, a peace process was getting under way in which negotiators on both sides had gained experience both of each other and of conflict resolution through problem-solving workshops. In Northern Ireland, groups inspired by the new approach had set up community relations initiatives that were not only reaching across community divides but also becoming an accepted responsibility of local government. In war-torn regions of Africa and South-East Asia, development workers and humanitarian agencies were seeing the need to take account of conflict and conflict resolution as an integral part of their activities.

By the closing years of the Cold War, the climate for conflict resolution was changing radically. With relations between the superpowers improving, the ideological and military competition that had fuelled many regional conflicts was fading away. Protracted regional conflicts in Southern Africa, Central America and East Asia moved towards settlements. It seemed that the UN could return to play the role its founders expected.

The dissolution of the Soviet Union brought to a close the long period in which a single international conflict dominated the international system. Instead, in the 1990s, internal conflicts, ethnic conflicts, conflicts over secession, and power struggles within countries became the norm. These reflected not so much struggles between competing centres of power, of the kind that had characterized international conflict for most of the 350 years since the peace of Westphalia, as the fragmentation and breakdown of state structures, economies and whole societies. At their extreme, in parts of Africa, the new wars witnessed the return of mercenary armies and underpaid militias, which preyed on civilian populations, and were fed as much by what were meant to be overt flows of international aid as by covert criminal international networks.

In this new climate, the attention of scholars of international relations and comparative politics turned to exactly the type of conflict that had preoccupied the conflict resolution thinkers for many years. A richer cross-fertilization of ideas developed between conflict resolution and these traditional fields. At the same time, practitioners from various backgrounds were attracted to conflict resolution. International statesmen began to use the language, and international organizations such as the Organization for Security and Cooperation in Europe (OSCE) and the Organization of African Unity (OAU) set up conflict resolution mechanisms and conflict prevention centres. A former president of the United States, Jimmy Carter, became one of the most active leaders of a conflict resolution non-governmental organization (NGO). The Nyerere Foundation was established with comparable aims for Africa. Development and aid workers, who had earlier tended to see their function as 'non-political', now became interested in linking their expertise to conflict resolution approaches, because so many of the areas with which they were most concerned were conflict zones – 'complex humanitarian emergencies' were seen also to be 'complex political emergencies'. A similar cross-fertilization took place with international peacekeepers. Overseas development ministries in several countries set up conflict units and began funding conflict prevention and resolution initiatives on a significant scale. International financial institutions such as the International Monetary Fund (IMF) and the World Bank also took on conflict prevention roles. The UN secretary-general declared the prevention of violent conflict to be a central goal for the international community in the new millennium. How to achieve a 'peaceful settlement of disputes' between states was a familiar theme in the international relations and strategic studies literature and had always been part of the stock-in-trade of international diplomacy. Less familiar was the challenge to statist international organizations of managing non-state conflicts.

A greater degree of impact, however, also brought greater scrutiny and the development of searching critiques from different quarters. The second and third editions of our book were largely prompted by these, and this fourth edition continues the engagement. Conflict resolution had always been controversial, both in relation to outside disciplines and internally among its different protagonists and schools. It also drew persistent fire from critics at different points along the political and intellectual spectrum, from neo-realists to neo-Marxists. After the high hopes of the early 1990s, three developments in particular took the gloss off what were no doubt unrealistic expectations of rapid results. First, there were the difficulties that international interveners encountered in chaotic war zones such as in Bosnia (1992–5) and Somalia (1992–3). A number of analysts pointed to the impact of globalization on the weakening of vulnerable states, the provision of cheap weaponry suitable for 'asymmetric war', and the generation of shadow economies that made 'new wars' self-perpetuating and profitable. Conflict resolution was seen to be incapable of addressing this nexus. Second, there was the collapse of the Israeli–Palestinian 'Oslo' peace process with the launch of the second Intifada (Uprising) in September 2000. The Oslo process had been hailed at the time as an example of success for classic conflict resolution approaches. Third came the shock of the destruction of the World Trade Center and the attack on the Pentagon on 11 September 2001, together with the kaleidoscope of events that followed, summed up as the 'global war on terror' (GWOT). Western global hegemony had elicited a global *jihadist* reaction. What possible answer could conflict resolution have to what was seen as the lethal combination of 'rogue' or 'failed' states, trans-border crime, the proliferation of weapons of mass destruction, and the fanatical ideologues of international terrorism?

Behind these political challenges lay more precisely focused intellectual challenges. Three of these in particular will be engaged with in the course of this book. First, a variant of the traditional realist criticism of conflict resolution, in which international politics is seen as a struggle between antagonistic and irreconcilable groups with power and coercion as the ultimate currency, and 'soft power' approaches of conflict resolution dismissed as ineffective and dangerous – the crushing of Tamil military resistance by government forces in Sri Lanka in 2009 was seen as a salutary example here. Second, a variant of the traditional Marxist criticism, which sees 'liberal' conflict resolution as naive and theoretically uncritical, since it attempts to reconcile interests that should not be reconciled, fails to take sides in unequal and unjust struggles, and lacks an analysis within a properly global perspective of the forces of exploitation and oppression. In general, in response to both of these criticisms, whereas realist theory and much Marxist theory sees violence as unavoidable and integral to the nature of conflict, such determinism is rejected in conflict resolution. Here there are always seen to be other options, and direct violence is regarded as an avoidable consequence of human choice. Our third set of critics, exemplified in Paul Salem's 'Critique of western conflict resolution from a non-western perspective' (1993; see also Salem, 1997), argue that the 'western' assumptions on which conflict resolution rests are not applicable universally.

In response to these and other criticisms, this book argues in Part II that, on the contrary, the developing tradition of thinking about conflict and conflict resolution is all the more relevant as the fixed structures of sovereignty and governance breakdown. All over the world, societies are facing stresses from population growth, structural change in the world economy, migration into cities, environmental degradation and rapid social change. Societies with institutions, rules or norms for managing conflict and well-established traditions of governance are generally better able to accommodate peacefully to change; those with weaker governance, fragile social bonds and little consensus on values or traditions are more likely to buckle. This is confirmed, for example, in more comprehensive recent statistical analyses such as the 2015 *Global Peace Index*, as discussed in chapter 3. Strengthening the capacity for conflict resolution within societies and political institutions, especially preventatively, is a vital part of the response to the phenomena of ideological extremism, warlordism and ethno-nationalism. We argue that conflict resolution has a role to play, even in war zones, since building peace constituencies and understandings across divided communities is an essential element of humanitarian engagement. We argue that conflict resolution is an integral part of work for development, social justice and social transformation that aims to tackle the problems of which terrorism, mercenaries and child soldiers are symptoms. We argue for a broad understanding of conflict resolution, to include not only mediation between the parties but also efforts to address the wider context in which international actors, domestic constituencies and intra-party relationships sustain violent conflicts. We maintain that, although many of the recent theories and practices of conflict resolution may have been articulated more vociferously in the West, their deep roots reach into far older world traditions from which they draw their inspiration. Indeed, every culture and society has its own version of what is, after all, a general social and political need. The point is not to abandon conflict resolution because it is western, but to find ways to enrich western and non-western traditions through their mutual encounter. And, finally, this applies all the more urgently to the phenomenon of international terrorism. Conflict resolution teaches that short-term denial strategies on their own (including military force) will fail unless accompanied by and embedded within middle-term persuasion strategies, long-term prevention strategies, and international coordination and legitimation strategies. We will look at this in more detail at the end of chapter 11. And we will discuss the theoretical debate between conflict resolution and its critics more fully in chapter 19.

Conflict Resolution Models

Here we offer a brief initial sketch of the conflict resolution field, followed by an introduction to some of the best-known models that have been found to be useful in it. This introduction is selective and indicative, not systematic, let alone exhaustive. The rest of the book will fill in the gaps.

Conflict is a universal feature of human society. It takes its origins in economic differentiation, social change, cultural formation, psychological development and political organization – all of which are inherently conflictual – and becomes overt through the formation of conflict parties, which come to have, or are perceived to have, mutually incompatible goals. The identity of the conflict parties, the levels at which the conflict is contested, and the issues fought over (scarce resources, unequal relations, competing values) may vary over time and may themselves be disputed. Conflicts are dynamic as they escalate and de-escalate, and are constituted by a complex interplay of attitudes and behaviours that can assume a reality of their own. Third parties are likely to be involved as the conflict develops, and may themselves thereby become parties in an extended conflict. An important point to note from the outset is how early theorists in the field such as Morton Deutsch (1949, 1973) distinguished between *destructive* and *constructive* conflict, suggesting that the former was to be avoided but the latter was a necessary and valuable aspect of human creativity. This remains a key for understanding the normative orientation of the conflict resolution field as a whole, as will be emphasized below.

The new field of conflict resolution in the 1950s defined itself in relation to the challenge of understanding and transforming destructive human conflicts of this kind. In contrast to older established fields, such as international relations, conflict resolution was to be:

- *multi-level*: analysis and resolution had to embrace all levels of conflict: intrapersonal (inner conflict), interpersonal, intergroup (families, neighbourhoods, affiliations), international, regional, global, and the complex interplays between them;
- *multidisciplinary*: in order to learn how to address complex conflict systems adequately, the new field had to draw on many disciplines, including politics, international relations, strategic studies, development studies, individual and social psychology, etc.;
- *multicultural*: since human conflict is a worldwide phenomenon within an increasingly intricate and interconnected local–global cultural web, this had to be a truly cooperative international enterprise, in terms of both the geographical locations where conflict is encountered and the conflict resolution initiatives deployed to address them;
- *both analytic and normative*: the foundation of the study of conflict was to be systematic analysis and interpretation of the 'statistics of deadly quarrels' (polymology), but this was to be combined from the outset with the normative aim of learning how better thereby to transform actually or potentially violent conflict into non-violent processes of social, political and other forms of change;
- *both theoretical and practical*: the conflict resolution field was to be constituted by a constant mutual interplay between theory and practice: only when theoretical understanding and practical experience of what works and what does not work are connected can properly informed experience develop.

We believe that these founding characteristics of the new conflict resolution field remain valid today and can still serve to inspire contemporary versions of cosmopolitan conflict resolution – as argued in chapters 3 and 4.

Conflicts have been variously defined in relation to 'fights, games and debates' (Reading 8; Rapoport, 1960). This remains controversial. For example, some have used 'conflict' to refer both to 'consensual' conflicts over interests (disputants want the same thing) and to 'dissensual' conflicts over values (disputants do not want the same thing) (Aubert, 1963); others, however, have called the former 'disputes' that require settlement and have reserved the term 'conflict' for deeper struggles over unsatisfied human needs that require resolution (Burton, 1990a). We will not enter this discussion here, and are happy to use the term 'conflict' to refer to the widest set of circumstances in which conflict parties perceive that they have mutually incompatible goals – although we do see a difference between conflicts, on the one hand, and sporting encounters, economic competitions and legal cases, in which the rules of contestation are not themselves called into question, on the other.

But we must at the outset address the current debate within the field between *conflict resolution* and *conflict transformation* – although we will then set this aside as well. In this book we see conflict transformation as the deepest level of the conflict resolution tradition rather than as a separate venture, as some would prefer (Väyrynen, 1991; Rupesinghe, 1995; Jabri, 1996; Francis, 2002; Lederach, 2003). John Paul Lederach, for example, downgrades conflict resolution in comparison with conflict transformation on the grounds that it is content-centred rather than relationship-centred, aims at immediate agreement rather than long-term process, and is committed only to de-escalation rather than also including escalation to pursue constructive change (2003: 33). This is something of a caricature of the field and is reminiscent of the way in which, in an earlier period, John Burton caricatured 'dispute settlement' in comparison with the deeper process of 'conflict resolution', which he defined in much the same way as Lederach and others now define conflict transformation. In our view it does not matter in the end which label is used as the umbrella term (candidates have included 'conflict regulation' and 'conflict management', as well as conflict resolution and conflict transformation), so long as the field itself is coherent enough to contain the substance of what is being advocated in each case. We believe that the field does retain its coherence, that it is best left intact, and that conflict resolvers and conflict transformers are essentially engaged in the same enterprise – as shown in titles of books such as Dukes's *Resolving Public Conflict: Transforming Community and Governance* (1996).

We continue to use conflict resolution as the generic term here for four reasons. First, because it was the earliest term used to define the new field (the 1957 *Journal of Conflict Resolution*). Second, because it is still the most widely used term among analysts and practitioners – examples are Morton Deutsch and Peter Coleman's edited volume *The Handbook of Conflict Resolution* (2000), Peter Wallensteen's *Understanding Conflict Resolution* (2007), and *The Sage Handbook of Conflict Resolution* (2009), edited by Jacob Bercovitch, Victor Kremenyuk and William Zartman. Third, because 'conflict resolution' is the term that is most familiar in the media and among the general public. Fourth, because the term 'conflict transformation' is in itself inherently indeterminate unless further qualified – transformation in which direction? As explained in the preface, conflict resolution has from the start encompassed a spectrum that includes peaceful conflict containment at one end, through conflict settlement, and on to conflict transformation at the other end. As is made explicit historically in chapter 2, and theoretically in chapter 19, there have always been tensions between the two.

In this fourth edition – just to add to the complications – it is worth adding that there is now a head of steam behind moves to use the term 'conflict engagement', either as the generic term (for example, Jay Rothman in the second issue of the new *International Journal of Conflict Engagement and Resolution* (2014)) or as the alternative to peaceful containment, settlement and transformation when, so far, conflict resolution fails (for example, Bernard Mayer (2009) and Oliver Ramsbotham (2010; 2014; forthcoming, 2017).

Framework Models

We begin by offering a simplified model of Johan Galtung's seminal think-ing on the relationship between conflict, violence and peace. As described in chapter 2, Galtung was one of the founders of the field, and the breadth of his understanding of the structural and cultural roots of violence is a corrective to those who caricature conflict resolution as purely relational, symmetrical or psychological.

Galtung's models of conflict, violence and peace

In the late 1960s Johan Galtung (1969; see also 1996: 72 and Reading 6) pro-posed an influential model of conflict that encompasses both symmetric and asymmetric conflicts. He suggested that conflict could be viewed as a trian-gle, with contradiction (C), attitude (A) and behaviour (B) at its vertices (see figure 1.1). Here the contradiction refers to the underlying conflict situation, which includes the actual or perceived 'incompatibility of goals' between the conflict parties generated by what Chris Mitchell calls a 'mis-match between social values and social structure' (1981a: 18). In a symmetric conflict, the contradiction is defined by the parties, their interests and the clash of inter-ests between them. In an asymmetric conflict, it is defined by the parties, their relationship and the conflict of interests inherent in the relationship. Attitude includes the parties' perceptions and misperceptions of each other and of themselves. These can be positive or negative, but in violent conflicts parties tend to develop demeaning stereotypes of the other, and attitudes are often influenced by emotions such as fear, anger, bitterness and hatred. Attitude involves emotive (feeling), cognitive (belief) and conative (desire, will) elements. Analysts who emphasize these subjective aspects are said to have an *expressive* view of the sources of conflict (for example: 'a social conflict exists when two or more parties believe they have incompatible objectives'; Kriesberg, 1982: 17). Behaviour is the third component. It can include coop-eration or coercion, gestures signifying conciliation or hostility. Violent con-flict behaviour is characterized by threats, coercion and destructive attacks.

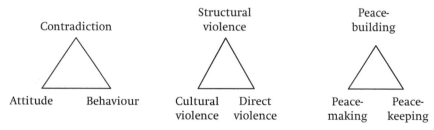

Figure 1.1 *Galtung's models of conflict, violence and peace*

Analysts who emphasize objective aspects such as structural relationships, competing material interests or behaviours are said to have an *instrumental* view of the sources of conflict (for example: there is conflict 'whenever incompatible actions occur ... an action that is incompatible with another action prevents, obstructs, interferes, injures or in some way makes the latter less likely to be effective'; Deutsch, 1973: 10).

Galtung argues that all three components have to be present together in a full conflict. A conflict structure without conflictual attitudes or behaviour is a latent (or structural) one. Galtung sees conflict as a dynamic process in which structure, attitudes and behaviour are constantly changing and influencing one another. As the dynamic develops, it becomes a manifest conflict formation, as parties' interests clash or the relationship they are in becomes oppressive. Parties then organize around this structure to pursue their interests. They develop hostile attitudes and conflictual behaviour. And so the conflict formation starts to grow and intensify. As it does so, it may widen, drawing in other parties, deepen and spread, generating secondary conflicts within the main parties or among outsiders who get sucked in. This often considerably complicates the task of addressing the original, core conflict. Eventually, however, resolving the conflict must involve a set of dynamic changes that mean de-escalation of conflict behaviour, a change in attitudes, and a transformation of the relationships or clashing interests that are at the core of the conflict structure. (For an application of these ideas to a real conflict, see Reading 7.)

A related idea due to Galtung (1990) is the distinction between direct violence (children are murdered), structural violence (children die through poverty) and cultural violence (whatever blinds us to this or seeks to justify it). We end direct violence by changing conflict behaviour, structural violence by removing structural contradictions and injustices, and cultural violence by changing attitudes. These responses relate in turn to broader strategies of peacekeeping, peacebuilding and peacemaking (see figure 1.1).

Galtung defined 'negative peace' as the cessation of direct violence and 'positive peace' as the overcoming of structural and cultural violence as well. These are slightly deceptive terms.

Negative peace is not to be despised (the term 'negative' is a bit unfortunate in this respect). At an intrapersonal level, anyone who has been unable to sleep through grief, remorse (for the past), anxiety (for the future), etc., will know the blessings of a peaceful mind. The same goes at the family level for anyone who has suffered violence or abuse, or, at a community level, discrimination, persecution, 'ethnic cleansing' or genocide, or, at the international level, the terrible destruction of war. Over all of this since 1945 has hung the threat of nuclear holocaust.

On the other hand, negative peace on its own can be coupled with repression, deprivation, exploitation, injustice. Pax Romana, Pax Britannica and Pax Sovietica were all associated with the forcible crushing of legitimate human aspirations. As the Latin historian of the conquest of Britain in the first century AD said of the victorious Roman general: 'he made a wasteland and called it peace'. There was negative peace in Hungary after 1956. There is negative peace today (more or less) in Tibet.

Positive peace, in contrast, includes the key ideas of 'legitimacy' and 'justice'. An unjust structure or relationship in this terminology is not a peaceful one. In order to achieve positive peace, therefore, injustice must be removed. This also operates at all the different levels, from unjust economic relations between 'North' and 'South', though unjust political relations between majority and minority groups within a country, to unjust personal relations between individuals. It applies to all the various types of 'differences' that distinguish sets of human beings: differences of race (the idea that some races are 'superior' to others), gender (male domination), class (perpetuation of socio-economic advantage and disadvantage through birth, not merit), etc. At an intrapersonal level, positive peace goes beyond absence of anxiety and embraces the idea of deep inner peace through integrity (wholeness) of being, physical, emotional, spiritual. Some believe that 'inner' peace of this kind is the ultimate underpinning of lasting world peace.

Positive peace is also deeply problematic, however. For example, 'injustice' usually amounts to 'perceived injustice', and we are immediately plunged into a highly controversial and complicated arena, which virtually includes the whole of politics. Nothing is more characteristic of violent conflict than the fact that all parties genuinely believe that they are victims of injustice, and that therefore 'justice' is on their side. Both pray to God for victory. Linked to this is the well-known paradox that many of those who battle against perceived injustice themselves use force in order to do so. Again, there is a danger here of doctrinaire activists 'forcing people to be free' (Rousseau's phrase). The fact that people may not 'realize' that they are exploited (in the eyes of the activist) is interpreted as 'brainwashing' or 'false consciousness'. It is seen as 'the problem of the happy slave'. The conclusion may then be to try to coerce them into revolt. Behind all of this, the problem of imputation can be seen to be a deep and questionable one. On the other hand, there undoubtedly *is* exploitation and injustice, much of which is institutionalized and also culturally and psychologically internalized. The exploiters may even be as unaware as anyone else of the overall situation and, indeed, genuinely believe that there is no injustice.

A conflict escalation and de-escalation model

Conflicts are dynamic and can develop and change at astonishing speed. They can also take long periods of time to gestate unnoticed before they suddenly erupt into overt violence. The process of conflict escalation is complex and unpredictable. New issues and conflict parties can emerge, internal power struggles can alter tactics and goals, and secondary conflicts and spirals can

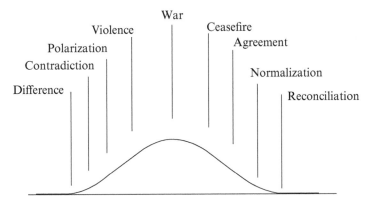

Figure 1.2 *Conflict escalation and de-escalation*

further complicate the situation. The same is true of de-escalation, with unexpected breakthroughs and setbacks changing the dynamics, with advances
in one area or at one level being offset by relapses at others, and with the
actions of third parties influencing the outcome in unforeseen ways. Here we
offer the simplest model, in which escalation phases move along a normal
distribution curve, from the initial *differences* that are part of all social developments, through the emergence of an original *contradiction* that may or
may not remain latent, on up through the process of *polarization* in which
antagonistic parties form and the conflict becomes manifest, and culminating in the outbreak of direct *violence* and *war* (see figure 1.2). As we will see
in chapter 3, escalation models such as this are popular with those who try
to find objective criteria for measuring statistical changes in conflict levels
in different countries from year to year. There has been a renewed focus
here recently on measuring aspects of 'fragility' in those countries seen to
be most vulnerable. Escalation models are also used by those who attempt to
match appropriate conflict resolution strategies to them (Glasl, 1982; Fisher
and Keashly, 1991).

The hourglass model: a spectrum of conflict resolution responses

Here we combine Galtung's ideas on conflict and violence with escalation/
de-escalation phases to produce the 'hourglass' model of conflict resolution
responses (Ramsbotham and Woodhouse, 1999a) (see figure 1.3). The hourglass represents the narrowing of political space that characterizes conflict
escalation (top half of the hourglass model) and the widening of political
space that characterizes conflict de-escalation (bottom half of the hourglass
model). As the space narrows and widens, so different conflict resolution
responses become more or less appropriate or possible. Following Ronald
Fisher and Loraleigh Keashly (1991), this is a *contingency* and *complementarity*
model, in which 'contingency' refers to the nature and phase of the conflict

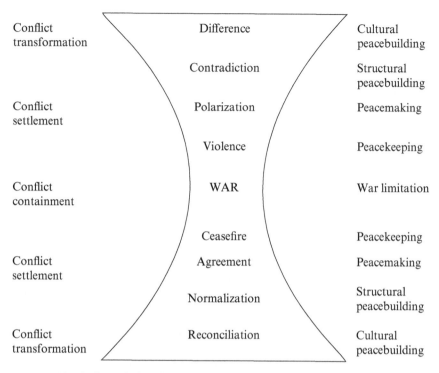

Conflict transformation	Difference	Cultural peacebuilding
Conflict settlement	Contradiction	Structural peacebuilding
	Polarization	Peacemaking
Conflict containment	Violence	Peacekeeping
	WAR	War limitation
Conflict settlement	Ceasefire	Peacekeeping
	Agreement	Peacemaking
Conflict transformation	Normalization	Structural peacebuilding
	Reconciliation	Cultural peacebuilding

Note: In de-escalation phases conflict resolution tasks must be initiated at the same time and are nested. They cannot be undertaken sequentially as may be possible in escalation phases – see chapters 5 and 8. We suggest that what is sometimes called deep peacemaking (which includes reconciliation) is best seen as part of cultural peacebuilding.

Figure 1.3 *The hourglass model: conflict containment, conflict settlement and conflict transformation*

and 'complementarity' to the combination of appropriate responses that need to be worked together to maximize chances of success in conflict resolution. Conflict transformation is seen to encompass the deepest levels of cultural and structural peacebuilding. Conflict settlement (which many critics wrongly identify with conflict resolution) corresponds to what we call 'elite peacemaking' – in other words, negotiation or mediation among the main protagonists with a view to reaching a mutually acceptable agreement. Conflict containment includes preventive peacekeeping, war limitation and post-ceasefire peacekeeping. War limitation is made up of attempts to constrain the fighting geographically, to mitigate and alleviate its intensity, and to bring about its termination at the earliest possible moment. In this model, we distinguish between the elite peacemaking that forms the substance of conflict settlement and the deeper levels of peacemaking (including reconciliation and education) that are better seen as part of cultural peacebuilding.

In chapter 5 ('Preventing Violent Conflict') we will look at the top half of the hourglass model. In chapter 6 ('Containing Violent Conflict: Peacekeeping') we will look at the conflict containment components. In chapter 7 ('Ending Violent Conflict: Peacemaking') we will look at the conflict settlement components. And in chapters 8–10 ('Postwar Reconstruction', 'Peacebuilding', 'Reconciliation') we will look at the bottom half of the hourglass model.

Table 1.1 indicates the range of complementary processes and techniques relevant to the hourglass model of escalation and de-escalation offered in this book and elaborated below.

The conflict tree

Another influential framework model is the 'conflict tree', as developed and applied in particular in the Responding to Conflict Programme at Birmingham (see figure 1.4).

Classical Ideas

Here is a selection of classic conflict resolution models. We have seen above how conflict is an intrinsic and inevitable aspect of social change. It is an expression of the heterogeneity of interests, values and beliefs that arise as new formations generated by social change come up against inherited constraints. But the way we deal with conflict is a matter of habit and choice. It is possible to change habitual responses and exercise intelligent choices.

Conflict approaches

One typical habit in conflict is to give very high priority to defending one's own interests. If Cain's interests clash with Abel's, Cain is inclined to ignore Abel's interests or actively to damage them. Leaders of nations are expected to defend the national interest and to defeat the interests of others if they come into conflict. But this is not the only possible response.

Figure 1.5 illustrates five approaches to conflict, distinguished by whether concern for Self and concern for Other is high or low. Cain has high concern for Self and low concern for Other: this is a 'contending' style. Another alternative is to yield: this implies more concern for the interests of Other than Self. Another is to avoid conflict and withdraw: this suggests low concern for both Self and Other. Another is to balance concern for the interests of Self and Other, leading to a search for accommodation and compromise. And there is a fifth alternative, seen by many in the conflict resolution field as the one to be recommended where possible: high regard for the interests of both Self and Other. This implies strong assertion of one's own interests, but equal awareness of the aspirations and needs of the other, generating energy to search for a creative problem-solving outcome.

Table 1.1 Conflict resolution techniques, complementarity and the hourglass model

Stage of conflict	Strategic response	Examples of responses and capacity

Difference	Cultural peacebuilding	Problem-solving
		Support for indigenous dispute-
		   resolution institutions and CR
		   training
		Fact-finding missions and
		   peace commissions
		Culture of toleration and respect
		Multiple and inclusive identities

Contradiction	Structural peacebuilding	Development assistance Civil society development Governance training and institution building Human rights training Track II mediation and problem-solving Institutional capacity Constitutional and legal provision Legitimacy and social justice
Polarization	Elite peacemaking	Special envoys and official mediation Negotiation Coercive diplomacy Preventive peacekeeping
Violence	Peacekeeping	Interposition Crisis management and containment
War	War limitation	Peace enforcement Peace support and stabilization

Ceasefire	Peacekeeping	Preventive peacekeeping
		Disarmament and security sector
		   reform
		Confidence building and security
		   enhancing measures
		Security in the community through
		   police training

Agreement	Elite peacemaking	Electoral and constitutional reform Power sharing and de-centralization of power Problem-solving

Normalization	Structural peacebuilding	Collective security and cooperation
		   arrangements
		Economic resource cooperation and
		   development
		Alternative defence

Reconciliation	Cultural peacebuilding	Commissions of enquiry/truth and
		   justice commissions
		Peace media development
		Peace and conflict awareness
		   education and training
		Cultural exchanges and initiatives,
		   sport as reconciliation
		Problem-solving as future imaging

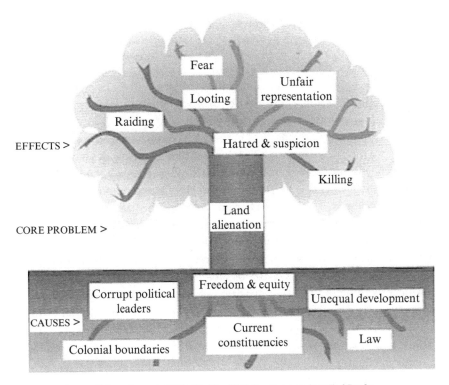

EFFECTS >

CORE PROBLEM >

CAUSES >

Source: Fisher, S., et al. 2000. *Working With Conflict*, London: Zed Books, p. 29

Figure 1.4 *The conflict tree: an example from Kenya*

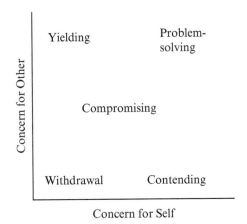

Source: from Katz and Lawyer, 1985

Figure 1.5 *Five approaches to conflict*

Win–lose, lose–lose, win–win outcomes

What happens when the conflict approaches of two parties are considered together? Parties to conflicts are usually inclined to see their interests as diametrically opposed. The possible outcomes are seen to be win–lose (one wins, the other loses) or compromise (they split their difference). But there is a much more common outcome in violent conflicts: both lose. If neither is able to impose an outcome or is prepared to compromise, the conflictants may impose such massive costs on each other that all the parties end up worse off than they would have been had another strategy been adopted. In conflict resolution analysis this is found to be a much more common outcome than is generally supposed. When this becomes clear to the parties (often regrettably late in the day), there is a strong motive based on self-interest for moving towards other outcomes, such as compromise or win–win (defined here not as an ideal future, as is often supposed, but as one in which all parties would be better off). The spectrum of such outcomes may well be wider than conflictants think. But, by then, positions may be so entrenched, passions so strongly aroused, and intransigent leaders so strongly ensconced that change nevertheless proves impossible. This is the all too familiar situation in intractable conflict, a topic we return to at the end of chapter 3 and then address directly in chapter 18.

Traditionally, the task of conflict resolution has been seen as helping parties who perceive their situation as zero-sum[1] (Self's gain is Other's loss) to reperceive it as a non-zero-sum conflict (in which both may gain or both may lose), and then to assist parties to move in the positive-sum direction. Figure 1.6 shows various possible outcomes of the conflict between Cain and Abel. Any point towards the right is better for Abel, any point towards the top is better for Cain. In the Bible, the prize is the Lord's favour. Cain sees the situation as a zero-sum conflict: at point 1 (his best outcome) he gets the Lord's favour, at 2 (his worst) the Lord favours Abel. All the other possibilities lie on the line from 1 to 2 in which the Lord divides his favour, more or less equally, between the two brothers. Point 3 represents a possible compromise position. But it is the other diagonal, representing the non-zero-sum outcomes, that is the more interesting from a conflict resolution perspective: the mutual loss that actually occurred, at 0, when Abel was slain and Cain lost the Lord's favour, and the mutual gain that they missed, at 4, if each had been his brother's keeper.

Prisoner's Dilemma and the evolution of cooperation

Prisoner's Dilemma is a simple representation in game theory that clearly illustrates the tendency for contending strategies to end in lose–lose outcomes. Two players (prisoners accused of a crime) each have two choices: to cooperate with each other (remain silent) or to defect (inform on the other).

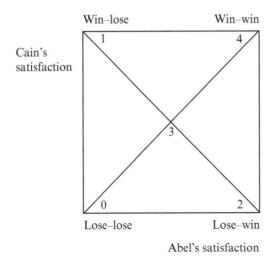

Figure 1.6 *Zero-sum and non-zero-sum outcomes*

Table 1.2 Prisoner's Dilemma

	Cooperate	Defect
Cooperate	3, 3	0, 5
Defect	5, 0	1, 1

The choices must be made in ignorance of what the other will do (they are kept in separate cells). The possible pay-offs are given in table 1.2. On the left are the two choices for player (A) (cooperate or defect). Along the top are the two choices for player (B) (cooperate or defect). In the resulting pay-offs (the four sets of numbers), A's pay-off is the first number and B's pay-off is the second number. In this case, let us say, 5 points may represent freedom and a financial reward, 3 points may represent one year in prison, 1 point may represent ten years in prison, 0 points may represent execution. It can now be seen that, whatever choice the other may make, each player considered singly gains a higher pay-off by choosing to defect (if the other cooperates, defection earns 5 points rather than 3; if the other defects, defection earns 1 point rather than 0). So the only rational course is to defect. But this is not the best outcome for either, since, whereas mutual defection earns 1 point each, mutual cooperation would have earned both of them 3 points. So the individually rational choice turns out to deliver a mutual lose–lose outcome. Let us note here that 'lose–lose' does not mean the worst possible outcome in either case (0): it means that both are worse off than they would have been had they found a route to the more mutually beneficial and available alternative. The collectively rational choice is for both to cooperate, reaching the elusive win–win outcome (point 4 in figure 1.6). But, if both could communicate and agree to go for mutual cooperation, how can each guarantee that the other will not subsequently defect, tempted by the 5-point prize? In this kind of social trap, self-interested parties can readily get stuck at lose–lose outcomes.

The trap depends on the game being played only once. If each move is part of a sequence of repeated games, there are possibilities for cooperative behaviour to evolve. In a well-known series of experiments, Robert Axelrod (1984) invited experts to submit programs for a Prisoner's Dilemma competition run on computer. A spectrum of 'nice' and 'nasty' strategies was submitted and each was tested in pairs against all the others in repeated interactions. The surprise clear overall winner was a simple strategy called 'Tit-for-Tat' (submitted by the conflict resolution analyst Anatol Rapoport), which began by cooperating on the first move and thereafter copied what the other had done on the previous move. The repeated overall success of Tit-for-Tat shows, in Richard Dawkins's phrase, that, contrary to a widely held view about competitive environments of this kind (including Darwinian natural selection), 'nice guys finish first' (Dawkins, 1989: 202–33). Tit-for-Tat is not a pushover. It hits back when the other defects. But, crucially, it initially cooperates (it is 'generous'), and it bears no grudges (it is 'forgiving'). Its responses are also predictable and reliable (it has 'clarity of behaviour'). For the 'evolution of cooperation' to get going in a mêlée of competing strategies, there must be a critical if at first quite small number of initially cooperating strategies, and the 'shadow of the future' must be a long one: interaction must not be confined to just one game (for example, with one player able to wipe out another in one go). But, so long as these conditions operate, even though 'nasty guys' may seem to do well at first, 'nice guys' come out on top in the end.[2] Natural selection favours cooperation.

But even Tit-for-Tat can be locked into mutually destructive conflict if the other persists in competitive play, as happens in intractable conflicts, where mutual suspicion (lack of trust) and the security dilemma (your defence is factored into my worst-case planning as offensive threat and vice versa), as well as ideological commitment and the self-interest of intransigent parties in the continuation of the conflict, perpetuate mutual retaliation. Another way of springing the trap, therefore, is to follow the conflict resolution route and to change the players' perceptions and calculations of gain – and eventually relationship – by reframing the conflict as a shared problem. All key stakeholders must be persuaded that existing strategies lead to a lose–lose impasse and that preferable alternatives are available and will be to their advantage. Remaining irreconcilable spoilers must simply be defeated. Perceived 'pay-off' rules can be altered in ways such as:

- by increasing scarce resources (enlarging the cake);
- by offering bold gestures on less important issues in order to reduce tension and build trust (logrolling and 'graduated reciprocal' strategies);
- by creating new options not included in the original demands (brainstorming);

- by looking for 'superordinate goals' such as mutual economic gains that neither party can achieve on its own – e.g. joint membership of the EU (superordination);
- by compensating those prepared to make concessions (compensation);
- by increasing the penalties for those who are not (penalization).

So taking account of the future relationship (for example, between two communities who will have to live together) is one way out of the trap. Another is to take the social context into account. Imagine, for example, that the prisoners know that there is an agency outside which will punish them if they defect and reward them if they cooperate. This can change their pay-offs and hence the outcome. A similar change occurs if, instead of considering only their own interests, the parties also attach value to the interests of each other: social players are not trapped.

Among recent extensions of game theory is Michael Bacharach's posthumously published *Beyond Individual Choice* (2006), which extends rational actor models to include the different ways in which agents 'frame' the problem and organize themselves into 'teams' to attain common goals (Reading 37).

Positions, interests and needs

How can the parties reframe their positions if they are diametrically opposed, as they often are? One of the classical ideas in conflict resolution is to distinguish between the positions held by the parties and their underlying interests and needs. For example, Egypt and Israel quarrel over Sinai. Each claims sovereignty, and their positions seem incompatible. But in negotiations it turns out that Egypt's main interest is in national territorial integrity and Israel's main interest is in security. So the political space is found for what came to be the Camp David settlement. Interests are often easier to reconcile than positions, since there are usually several positions that might satisfy them. Matters may be more difficult if the conflict is over values, which are often non-negotiable, or relationships, which may need to be changed to resolve the conflict, although the same principle of looking for a deeper level of compatible underlying motives applies.

Some analysts take this to the limit by identifying basic human needs (for example, identity, security, survival) as lying at the root of other motives. Intractable conflicts are seen to result from the denial of such needs, and conflict can only be resolved when such needs are satisfied. Basic human needs are seen to be generic and non-negotiable. But the hopeful argument of these analysts is that, whereas interests may be subject to relative scarcity, basic needs are not (for example, security for one party is reinforced by security for the other). As long as the conflict is translated into the language of needs, an outcome that satisfies both sides' needs can be found (see figure 1.7). A thorough and critical re-examination of the application of human needs theory to conflict resolution can be found in Avruch and Mitchell (2013).

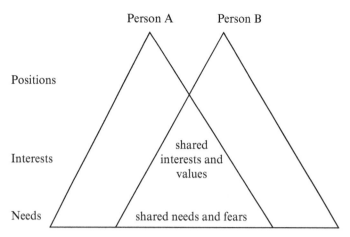

Source: from Floyer Acland, 1995: 50

Figure 1.7 *Positions, interests and needs*

Third-party intervention

Where two parties are reacting to each other's actions, it is easy for a spiral of hostility and escalation to develop through positive feedback. The entry of a third party may change the conflict structure and allow a different pattern of communication, enabling the third party to filter or reflect back the messages, attitudes and behaviour of the conflictants. This intervention may dampen the feedback spiral.

Although all third parties make some difference, 'pure' mediators have traditionally been seen as 'powerless' – their communications are powerful, but they bring to bear no new material resources of their own. In other situations there may also be powerful third parties whose entry alters not only the communication structure but also the power balance. Such third parties may alter the parties' behaviour as well as their communications by judicious use of the carrot and the stick (positive and negative inducement); and they may support one outcome rather than another. Of course, by taking action, powerful third parties may find themselves sucked into the conflict as a full party.

Figure 1.8 illustrates how third parties may act as arbiters (with or without the consent of the conflict parties) or may try to facilitate negotiations or mediate between the parties (coercively or non-coercively).

It may also be helpful to distinguish here between three overlapping classes of third-party intervention in the communicative sphere. There is negotiation/mediation – often at elite and decision-making level – associated with conflict settlement. There is dialogue/facilitation – often at societal level – associated with conflict transformation. And, between the two, there is what is sometimes called 'interactive problem-solving', referred to here by Morton Deutsch as 'the theory of conflict resolution':

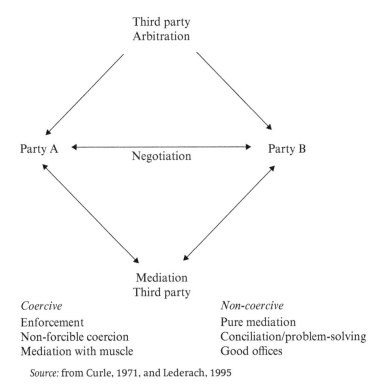

Source: from Curle, 1971, and Lederach, 1995

Figure 1.8 *Coercive and non-coercive third-party intervention*

In brief, the theory equates a constructive process of conflict resolution with an effective cooperative problem-solving process in which the conflict is the mutual problem to be resolved cooperatively. It also equates a destructive process of conflict resolution with a competitive process in which the conflicting parties are involved in a competition or struggle to determine who wins and who loses; often, the outcome of the struggle is a loss for both parties. (Deutsch, 2000: 30)

Here is Ronald Fisher on the difference between problem-solving and dialogue:

Unlike the more focused forms of interactive conflict resolution, such as problem-solving workshops, dialogue interventions tend to involve not influential, informal representatives of the parties, but simply ordinary members of the antagonistic groups. Furthermore, dialogue is primarily directed toward increased understanding and trust among the participants with some eventual positive effects on public opinion, rather than the creation of alternative solutions to the conflict. (Fisher, 1997: 121)[3]

Three faces of power

It may seem strange to call pure mediators powerless when they can often provide the impetus to resolve the conflict. This is because the term 'power' is ambiguous. On the one hand, it means the power to command, order, enforce – coercive or 'hard' power. On the other, it means the power to induce cooperation, to legitimitize, to inspire – persuasive or 'soft' power. Hard power has always been important in violent conflict, but soft power may be more important in conflicts managed peacefully.

Kenneth Boulding (1989) calls the former 'threat power' ('do what I want or I will do what you don't want'). Following earlier theorists of management–labour negotiations, he then further distinguishes between two forms of soft power: 'exchange power', associated with bargaining and the compromising approach ('do what I want and I will do what you want'), and 'integrative power', associated with persuasion and transformative long-term problem-solving ('together we can do something that is better for both of us'). Boulding defines power as the ability to get what you want done. Different forms of power are likely to work better (be more powerful) in different circumstances. So the question in conflict resolution is always: What form of power works best? In general, conflict resolvers try to shift emphasis away from the use of threat power and towards the use of exchange and integrative power (see table 1.3). Over the longer term, it is a principle of cosmopolitan conflict resolution that human societies are in the end held together by integrative power – not by bargaining power, and certainly not by threat power, however great that may seem to be over the shorter term. Boulding argues that none of the three forms of power is found in a pure form but always with admixtures of the others – which is why in table 1.3 the other two aspects are in each case also listed in lower case beneath the predominant aspect.

This also roughly coincides with Joseph Nye's distinction between military, economic and legitimacy power, of which the United States has a huge pre-ponderance of the first, a large share of the second, but only a limited and highly ambiguous measure of the third (Nye, 2002, 2004). Nye concludes that soft power is more important, even from a self-interested perspective, than many unreconstructed realists may suppose.

Third parties such as politicians and governments may use all these forms of power. In terms of third-party intervention (see figure 1.8), it is helpful to distinguish between coercive mediators, or 'mediators with muscle', and non-coercive mediators, whose role is confined to communication and facilita-tion. Track I diplomacy involves official governmental or intergovernmental representatives, who may use good offices, mediation, and sticks and carrots to seek or force an outcome, typically along the win–lose or 'bargaining' line

Table 1.3 Three faces of power

Threat power	Exchange power	Integrative power
Destructive	Productive	Creative
productive	destructive	productive
creative	creative	destructive

Source: from Boulding, 1989: 25

(between the points 1, 3 and 2 in figure 1.6). Track II diplomacy, in contrast, involves unofficial mediators who do not have carrots or sticks. They work with the parties or their constituencies to facilitate agreements, encouraging the parties to see their predicament as lying along the lose–lose to win–win line (between points 0, 3 and 4 in figure 1.6) and to find mutually satisfactory outcomes.

Symmetric and asymmetric conflicts

So far we have been considering conflicts of interest between relatively similar parties. These are examples of *symmetric* conflicts. Conflict may also arise between dissimilar parties, such as between a majority and a minority, an established government and a group of rebels, a master and his servant, an employer and her employees. These are *asymmetric* conflicts. Here the root of the conflict lies not in particular issues or interests that may divide the parties, but in the very structure of who they are and the relationship between them. It may be that this structure of roles and relationships cannot be changed without conflict. In *quantitatively* asymmetric conflicts, conflict parties are dissimilar in resources (for example, one has a bigger army than the other). In *qualitatively* asymmetric conflicts, parties differ in type (for example, one is a state and the other is a rebel faction).

Classical conflict resolution, in some views, applies only to symmetric conflicts. In asymmetric conflicts the structure is such that the top dog always wins, the underdog always loses. The only way to resolve the conflict is to change the structure, but this can never be in the interests of the top dog. So there are no win–win outcomes, and the third party has to join forces with the underdog to bring about a resolution.

From another point of view, however, even asymmetric conflicts impose costs on both parties. It is oppressive to be an oppressor, even if not so oppressive as to be oppressed. There are costs for the top dogs in sustaining themselves in power and keeping the underdogs down. In severe asymmetric conflicts the cost of the relationship becomes unbearable for both sides. This then opens the possibility for conflict resolution through a shift from the existing structure of relationships to another.

The role of the third party is to assist with this transformation, if necessary confronting the top dog. This means transforming what were unpeaceful, unbalanced relationships into peaceful and dynamic ones. Figure 1.9 illustrates how the passage from unpeaceful to peaceful relationships may involve a temporary increase in overt conflict as people become aware of imbalances of power and injustice affecting them (stage 1, education or 'conscientization'), organize themselves and articulate their grievances (stage 2, confrontation), come to terms in a more equal way with those who held a preponderance of power over them (stage 3, negotiation) and finally join in restructuring a more equitable and just relationship (stage 4, peaceful development). There

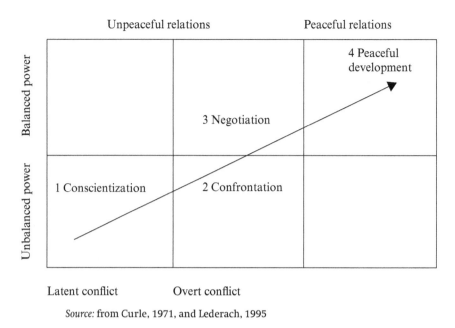

Unpeaceful relations   Peaceful relations

Latent conflict   Overt conflict

Source: from Curle, 1971, and Lederach, 1995

Figure 1.9 *Transforming asymmetric conflicts (I)*

are many ways in which this can be approached without using coercion. There is the Gandhian tactic of 'speaking truth to power', influencing and persuading the power-holders. Then there are the tactics of mobilizing popular movements, increasing solidarity, making demonstrations of resolve, and establishing a demand for change (as in Tunisia and Egypt in 2011). Raising awareness of the conflict among those who are external or internal supporters of the top dog may start to weaken the regime (as did, for example, the opponents of apartheid in South Africa). Here the military power of the top dog is challenged by the 'legitimacy power' of the underdog. The unequal power structure is unbalanced and is held up by props of various kinds; removing the props may make the unbalanced structure collapse. Another tactic is to strengthen and empower the underdogs. The underdogs may withdraw from the unbalanced relationship and start building anew – the parallel institutions approach. Non-violence uses soft power to move towards a more balanced relationship.

New Developments in Conflict Resolution

The new patterns of major armed conflict that became prominent in the 1990s suggested a more nuanced model of conflict emergence and transformation. This model sees conflict formations arising out of social change, leading to a process of violent or non-violent conflict transformation, and resulting in further social change in which hitherto suppressed or marginalized individuals or groups come to articulate their interests and challenge existing norms

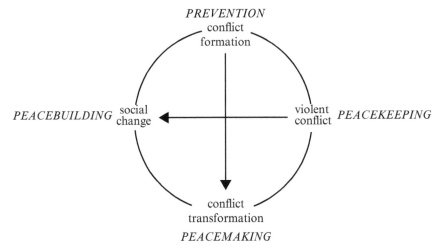

Figure 1.10 *Conflict dynamics and conflict resolution*

and power structures. Figure 1.10 shows a schematic illustration of phases of conflict and forms of intervention that may be feasible at different stages. A schematic life cycle of conflict sees a progression from peaceful social change, to conflict formation, to violent conflict, and then to conflict transformation and back to peaceful social change. But this is not the only path. The sequence can go from conflict formation to conflict transformation and back to social change, avoiding violence. Or it can go from conflict formation to violent conflict and back to the creation of fresh conflicts.

In response, there has been a differentiation and broadening in the scope of third-party intervention. Whereas classical conflict resolution was concerned mainly with entry into the conflict itself and with how to enable parties to violent conflict to resolve the issues between them in non-violent ways, the contemporary approach is to take a wider view of the timing and nature of intervention. In the 1990s came Fisher and Keashly's (1991) complementarity and contingency model of third-party intervention, mentioned earlier, with its attempt to relate appropriate and coordinated resolution strategies (conciliation, mediation, peacekeeping) to conflict phases (segregation, polarization, violence). Lederach's (1997) model of conflict resolution and conflict transformation levels has also been influential, with its emphasis on 'bottom-up' processes and the suggestion that the middle level can serve to link the other two (see figure 1.11).

Francis (1994, 2015) has developed Curle's original asymmetric conflict model, embedding classic conflict resolution strategies within wider strategies for transforming conflicts of this kind (see figure 1.12 for her latest version).

Encarnacion et al. (1990) have elaborated models of third-party intervention in order to stress the way external parties may come to be core parties as their

Source: from Lederach, 1997

Figure 1.11 *Actors and approaches to peacebuilding*

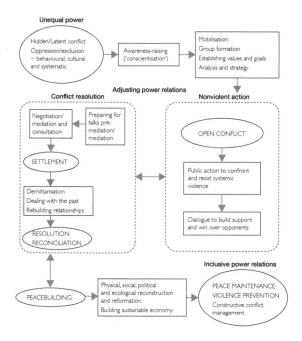

Source: from Francis, 2015

Figure 1.12 *Transforming asymmetric conflicts (II)*

level of involvement increases, and to emphasize the importance of 'embedded parties' from inside the conflict who often play key roles in expediting moves to resolution (see figure 1.13).

William Ury (2000) has developed an influential model, which relates what he terms 'third side roles' in conflict resolution to escalation/de-escalation conflict stages (see figure 1.14). This is discussed further in chapter 14.

In general there has been a shift from seeing third-party intervention as the primary responsibility of external agencies towards appreciating the role of internal 'third parties' or indigenous peacemakers. Instead of outsiders offering the fora for addressing conflicts in one-shot mediation efforts, the

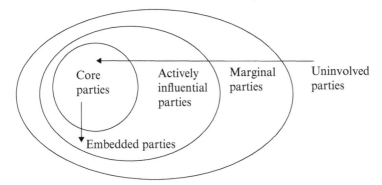

Source: from Encarnacion et al., 1990: 45

Figure 1.13 *The gradient of conflict involvement*

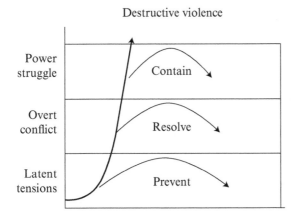

Third side roles to prevent escalation to destructive violence:
Containing roles: Witness, Referee, Peacekeeper
Resolving roles: Mediator, Arbiter Equalizer, Healer
Preventing roles: Provider, Teacher, Bridge-builder

Source: The Third Side: Harvard University Global Negotiation Project: www.thirdside.org

Figure 1.14 *William Ury's third side roles*

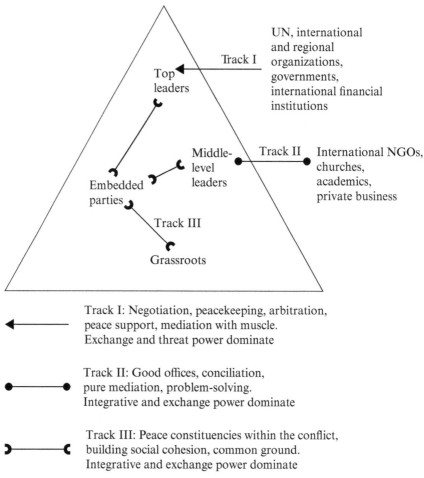

Track I: Negotiation, peacekeeping, arbitration, peace support, mediation with muscle. Exchange and threat power dominate

Track II: Good offices, conciliation, pure mediation, problem-solving. Integrative and exchange power dominate

Track III: Peace constituencies within the conflict, building social cohesion, common ground. Integrative and exchange power dominate

Figure 1.15 *Multitrack conflict resolution*

emphasis is on the need to build constituencies and capacity within societies and to learn from domestic cultures how to manage conflicts in a sustained way over time. This suggests a multitrack model in place of the earlier Track I and Track II models mentioned above, in which emphasis is placed on the importance of indigenous resources and local actors – what we might call Track III (see figure 1.15). There is a shift towards seeing conflict in its context (associated sometimes with structuralist, constructivist or discourse-based views of social reality).

In even broader terms, it is useful to see both triggers for conflict and transformers of conflict operating at the same time across four interrelated spheres. It is this interpenetration of ecological, global, societal and personal space that, in our view, increasingly characterizes the conflict field (Galtung, 1996) (see figure 1.16).

For all these reasons – as indicated at the beginning of this chapter – it is helpful to locate contemporary armed conflicts within a local–global

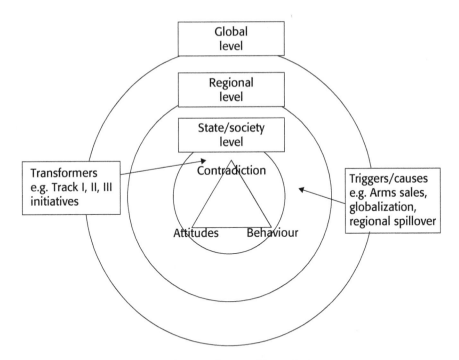

Figure 1.16 *Spheres of cosmopolitan conflict resolution*

cosmopolitan framework that encompasses different levels, from international (global, regional, bilateral), through state, down to societal level (identity groups, individuals). This will be exemplified in chapter 4. Most major armed conflicts today are hybrid struggles that spill across the *international*, *state* and *societal* levels. These are *transnational conflicts*, which is what makes them so hard to resolve or transform. In addition, as noted in the section on 'Conflict Types' in chapter 3, the distinction between interstate conflict, identity conflict, ideological conflict and economic conflict (scarce resources/criminality), although still useful, also needs to accommodate the fact that, in most large-scale contemporary conflicts, these combine and mutate as conditions change. This poses further problems for cosmopolitan conflict resolution.

The 64-year conflict in Kashmir, for example, is seen most simply as an interstate conflict between India and Pakistan going back to the time of partition after 1947. But it is deeply affected by changes at global level (the ending of the Cold War, the *jihadist* reaction against western hegemony, the war on terror) and regional level (the Afghan wars), as well as by economic, political and ideological struggles at sub-state provincial and local levels – including the cross-cutting influence of the wider diasporas. It is at *state level* that in the end these two dimensions (external, internal) mainly impact, because of the ambivalent nature of the state, at the same time the main actor on the international scene and also (at any rate in theory) the main satisfier of internal social needs.

Terminology

Although terminology is often confusing, with the same terms used in different ways both within the academic literature and in general usage, we offer the following definitions of how key terms are used in this book.

By *conflict* we mean the pursuit of incompatible goals by different groups. This suggests a broader span of time and a wider class of struggle than armed conflict. We intend our usage here to apply to any political conflict, whether it is pursued by peaceful means or by the use of force. (Some theorists, notably John Burton, have distinguished between disputes about negotiable interests that can be settled by compromise and more deep-seated conflicts that involve human needs and can only be resolved by removing underlying causes.)

Armed conflict is a narrower category denoting a conflict where parties on both sides resort to the use of force. It is notoriously difficult to define, since it can encompass a continuum of situations ranging from a military overflight or an attack on a civilian by a single soldier to an all-out war with massive casualties. The research community has identified a number of thresholds and rules for deciding what to count. We consider these definitions in chapter 3.

Violent conflict, or *deadly conflict*, is similar to armed conflict, but also includes one-sided violence such as genocides against unarmed civilians and violence associated with domestic and international criminality. There has been a recent trend to return to this wider idea of 'deadly conflict' as originally presented in Lewis Fry Richardson's pioneering work (see chapter 3). We mean direct, physical violence. We acknowledge the strong argument in peace research for broadening the concept of violence to take in exploitative social relations that cause unnecessary suffering, but prefer to use the now well-known term 'structural violence' for this.

Contemporary conflict refers to the prevailing pattern of political and violent conflicts; *contemporary armed conflicts* refer only to those that involve the use of force.

Conflict settlement means the reaching of an agreement between the parties to settle a political conflict, so forestalling or ending an armed conflict. This suggests finality, but in practice conflicts that have reached settlements are often reopened later. Conflict attitudes and underlying structural contradictions may not have been addressed.

Conflict containment incudes peacekeeping and war limitation (geographical constraint, mitigation and alleviation of intensity, and termination at the earliest opportunity).

Conflict management, like the associated term 'conflict regulation', has been used as a generic term to cover the whole gamut of positive conflict handling. Here we understand it to refer in a more limited way to the settlement and containment of violent conflict.

Conflict resolution is a more comprehensive term, which implies that the deep-rooted sources of conflict are addressed and transformed. This implies that behaviour is no longer violent, attitudes are no longer hostile, and the structure of the conflict has been changed. It is difficult to avoid ambiguity, since the term is used to refer both to the process (or the intention) to bring about these changes and to its completion. A further ambiguity is that conflict resolution refers to a particular defined specialist field (as in 'conflict resolution journals'), as well as to an activity carried on by people who may or may not use the term or even be aware of it (as in 'conflict resolution in Central America'). Nevertheless, these two senses of the term are tending to merge.

Conflict transformation is a term which for some analysts is a significant step beyond conflict resolution, but which in our view represents its deepest level. As clarified in figure 1.3, it implies a deep transformation in the institutions and discourses that reproduce violence, as well as in the conflict parties themselves and their relationships. It corresponds to the underlying tasks of structural and cultural peacebuilding. Where this becomes manifest across global cultures, linking the personal, societal, global and ecological spheres (figure 1.16), we call it *cosmopolitan conflict resolution*.

Conflict engagement is increasingly popular, mainly as a term for what can be done when, so far, conflict resolution (settlement, transformation) has not worked.

Negotiation is the process whereby the parties within the conflict seek to settle or resolve their conflicts. *Mediation* involves the intervention of a third party; it is a voluntary process in which the parties retain control over the outcome (pure mediation), although it is sometimes combined with positive and negative inducements (mediation with muscle). *Conciliation* or *facilitation* is close in meaning to pure mediation and refers to intermediary efforts to encourage the parties to move towards negotiations, as does the more minimalist role of providing good offices. *Problem-solving* is a more ambitious undertaking in which conflict parties are invited to reconceptualize the conflict with a view to finding creative, win–win outcomes. *Reconciliation* is a longer-term process of overcoming hostility and mistrust between divided peoples.

We use *peacemaking* in the sense of moving towards settlement of armed conflict, where conflict parties are induced to reach agreement voluntarily – for example, as envisaged in Chapter VI of the UN Charter on the 'Pacific Settlement of Disputes' (Article 33). *Peacekeeping* (traditionally with the consent of the conflict parties) refers to the interposition of international armed forces to separate the armed forces of belligerents, often now associated with civil tasks such as monitoring and policing and supporting humanitarian intervention. *Peace enforcement* is the imposition of a settlement by a powerful third party. *Peacebuilding* underpins the work of peacemaking and peacekeeping by addressing structural issues and the long-term relationships between conflictants. With reference to the conflict triangle (see figure 1.1), it can be suggested that peacemaking aims to change the attitudes of the main protagonists, peacekeeping lowers the level of destructive behaviour, and peacebuilding tries to overcome the contradictions which lie at the root of the conflict (Galtung, 1996: 112).

Finally, following the original lead of Morton Deutsch, as noted above, it is important to recognize that the aim of conflict resolution is not the elimination of conflict, which would be both impossible (conflict is inherent in social change) and, as is made clear in Curle's model of the transformation of asymmetric conflicts (see figure 1.9), often undesirable (there may need to be more, not less, conflict in struggles against injustice). Rather, the aim of conflict resolution is to transform actually or potentially violent conflict into peaceful (non-violent) processes of social and political change. This is an unending task as new forms and sources of conflict arise.

Structure of the Book

The structure of Part I of the book is based on the idea that, having described the evolution of the conflict resolution field (chapter 2), examined the statistical basis for analysis (chapter 3) and characterized the nature of contemporary conflict (chapter 4), broad distinctions can then be made between the tasks of preventing violent conflict (chapter 5), mitigating or alleviating violent conflict once it has broken out while at the same time searching for ways of terminating it (chapter 6), ending violent conflict (chapter 7), and ensuring that conflict does not subsequently regress to violence but is lastingly transformed into peaceful processes of political and social change, including reconstruction (chapter 8), peacebuilding (chapter 9) and reconciliation (chapter 10). We are not suggesting that conflicts necessarily go through these phases, but we think that this is the simplest expository structure to adopt. Part I essentially continues to update and expand the earlier editions of this book. As such, it aims to serve as a comprehensive introduction to the conflict resolution field, showing how it applies across the spectrum in major contemporary conflicts. The aim of this fourth edition is to explore how adequate inherited conflict resolution approaches are to the more recent manifestations of large-scale violence at a time of rapid change in world politics. In this task, as noted in chapter 2, conflict resolution has from the outset recognized the importance of 'learning from failure' (Rothman and Alberstein, 2014). The emphasis has been on 'second-order social learning' and the capacity to adapt to setbacks as well as to consolidate advances. Human violence has deep and manifold roots. Fundamental issues that incubate and breed violence still remain largely unaddressed. The struggle to rid the world of violence is bound to be long, complex and tortuous.

The aim of Part II is to relate what has been described in Part I to the broader issues and challenges that define the transformative task of cosmopolitan conflict resolution in the middle of the second decade of the twenty-first century. This includes the main debates about the whole nature of conflict resolution that are now further defining the field. Conflict resolution remains open to these critiques – from the political right (realist), from the political left (critical, post-structural), from gender perspectives (feminist), from various non-western (sometimes non-liberal) traditions – and wants to go on learning from them. But in Part II the authors also explicitly defend both the 'settlement' and 'transformation' dimensions of the conflict resolution tradition from criticism that seems too sweeping and dismissive. Conflict resolution does not ignore 'hard power' but, rather, argues that hard power on its own is usually in the end ineffective, even counter-productive. And conflict resolution does not uncritically reinforce existing hegemonic exclusions and dominations or turn a blind eye to alterity and difference, but continues to grapple with the perpetual challenge of determining if and how emancipatory struggles can be conducted non-violently. In chapter 11, summing up Part I, we offer a survey of the evolution of the international collectivity from a conflict resolution perspective. In so doing, we suggest that cosmopolitan conflict resolution should be seen as a flexible and comprehensive response to the complexities of prevailing patterns of contemporary transnational conflict, as analysed in Part I, at the same time as a proactive programme that 'promotes a global agenda based on certain values'. One of the main aims of Part II is to clarify what these values are and to claim that they are in the fullest sense *human* values. We believe that, in today's highly complex, uneven and dangerous world, drawn as they are from all the great traditions, they illuminate the best path ahead, however long it may take us to travel down it.

This fourth edition of Contemporary Conflict Resolution is accompanied by a new Contemporary Conflict Resolution Reader that offers a selection of key texts mentioned in the book. Readers may also like to visit the active website at www.politybooks.com/crr.

RECOMMENDED READING

Avruch and Mitchell (2013); Bercovitch and Jackson (2009); Bercovitch, Kremenyuk and Zartman (2009); Burton and Dukes (1990a); Cheldelin et al. (2003); Deutsch and Coleman (2000); Fisher (1997); *International Journal of Conflict Engagement and Resolution* (2013); Jacoby (2008); Kriesberg and Dayton (2011); Mitchell and Banks (1996); Sandole (1999); Wallensteen (2011a); Webel and Galtung (2007).

RELEVANT EXTRACTS IN *THE CONTEMPORARY CONFLICT RESOLUTION READER*

Reading 6: J. Galtung, Conflict Theory and Practice
Reading 7: J. Galtung, The Middle East Conflict
Reading 8: A. Rapoport, Conflict in Man-Made Environment
Reading 37: S. Brams, Negotiation Games

CHAPTER TWO

Conflict Resolution: Origins, Foundations and Development of the Field

In the first issue of the *Journal of Conflict Resolution* (1957: 1), Kenneth Boulding gave the rationale for the new venture:

> The reasons which have led us to this enterprise may be summed up in two propositions. The first is that by far the most important practical problem facing the world today is that of international relations – more specifically the prevention of global war. The second is that if intellectual progress is to be made in this area, the study of international relations must be made an interdisciplinary enterprise, drawing its discourse from all the social sciences and even further.

In the same issue, Quincy Wright argued that the resolution of international conflicts can only proceed through the development of a unified discipline of international relations (Reading 2).

Twenty years later, the remit for the journal had widened considerably:

> The threat of nuclear holocaust remains with us and may well continue to do so for centuries, but other problems are competing with deterrence and disarmament studies for our attention. The journal must also attend to international conflict over justice, equality and human dignity; problems of conflict resolution for ecological balance and control are within our proper scope and especially suited for interdisciplinary attention. (Russell and Kramer, 1973: 5)

These two extracts give a good idea of the way in which conflict resolution, constituted as a distinct field of study through the setting up of formal centres in academic institutions and the publication of professional journals, first defined itself and then expanded its remit during what we are calling its foundational period, in the 1950s and 1960s, and its period of further construction and expansion, in the 1970s and 1980s. In this chapter we describe the historical evolution of the field, some of whose classic concepts we have already outlined in chapter 1. We present conflict resolution as progressing through five stages of intergenerational development and practice. The first, second, third and fourth generations are dealt with in this chapter, which looks at the ideas of the precursors up to 1945, the founders between 1945 and 1965, the consolidators between 1965 and 1985, and the reconstructors between 1985 and 2005. The aim is to give an account of the basis on which the work of the present fifth generation of cosmopolitan conflict resolution – the theme of the rest of the book – is built.

Clearly, these temporal generational categories are not watertight and people and ideas move across them. Many of the founders of the field (Johan Galtung, for example), and those who followed as 'second generation' consolidators, continue to work, and their ideas are still evolving to the present day. Therefore these generations can also be regarded as temporal-intellectual categories, where those in the first and second generations essentially targeted a state-centric approach to conflict resolution; those in the third generation developed an approach which looked to civil society and used a less state-centric lens; while those in the fourth generation then attempted to construct a complex and complementary architecture, which linked levels from civil society to the state and beyond to the regional and international levels. This is a theme that will be developed in Part II, where the current fifth generation of what we call *cosmopolitan conflict resolution*, drawing on the work of the first four generations, is tested in the light of current critiques, and the argument is presented that it still offers the best hope for shaping a context-sensitive global competence which draws on a genuine emancipatory ethic in order to resolve conflict and sustain peace non-violently in the long-term interest of all human beings and generations, not just present power-holders.

Despite the apparent diversity of activity throughout the period covered in this chapter, in what amounted to a wide-ranging pursuit to define both the methods and concepts of conflict resolution, two main concerns predominated. The first was the effort to identify the conditions for a new world order based on conflict analysis, conflict prevention and problem-solving. The second was the effort to mobilize and inspire ever widening and inclusive constituencies based on the promotion of the values of non-violent peacemaking. Putting these two dimensions of activity together, conflict resolution emerged as an enterprise that was normatively associated with the promotion of peace at three levels: first, through a radical reformation of world political systems; second, through the promotion of an inclusive anti-war and pro-peace politics; and, third, through the fashioning of methodologies and processes that provided the opportunity to move through the politics of protest towards a proactive peacemaking project. This proactive peacemaking project was concerned to address the behavioural, attitudinal and structural/objective elements of Galtung's conflict triangle (figure 1.1, p. 12). It also aligned conflict resolution not only with the negative peace goals of preventing war and containing violent conflict but, crucially, with the even more challenging task of building a positive emancipatory peace, in which individuals and groups would, so far as is possible given inevitable ongoing conflict, be able to pursue their life-goals non-violently in ways of their own choosing.

Precursors: The First Generation, 1918–1945

The failure of the variety of peace, socialist and liberal internationalist movements to prevent the outbreak of the First World War motivated many people in the years that followed to develop a 'science' of peace which would provide a firmer basis for preventing future wars than what were in some quarters seen as the frequently sentimental and simplistically moral responses of pacifism.

The study of peace and the quest for world order

Although the institutionalization of peace research did not begin until the years after 1945, a related development took place after 1918 – the establishment of international relations (IR) as a distinct academic discipline. The first chair in international relations was endowed at the University College of Wales, Aberystwyth, in 1919. The initiative sprang from the same anti-war sentiment that inspired the early advocates of peace research. The sponsor of the chair was the Welsh industrialist and Liberal MP David Davies, who conceived the initiative as a memorial to students of the college who were killed in the Great War. During the period 1920–45, international relations courses and institutes were established throughout the UK, Europe and North America, many of them motivated initially by the idealist aspiration to promote peace by study and research into the dynamics of international relations (van den Dungen, 1996: 7). One of the sub-themes in this book is the way in which IR subsequently came to be dominated by realist thinking, perhaps in reaction to the inadequacies of the League of Nations and what were seen as failed attempts at appeasing aggression in the 1930s, thus vacating the intellectual ground that would be occupied by conflict resolution after the Second World War.

As described by van den Dungen (1996), a variety of proposals and initiatives emerged in Europe between 1919 and 1939 which foreshadowed the later institutionalization and development of conflict resolution. Some of these enterprises were associated with an air of optimism surrounding the early years of the League of Nations, such as an International University Federation for the League of Nations formed at Prague in 1924. Another source of influence was from the activities of American internationalists associated with the Carnegie Endowment for International Peace. In 1930 a German Peace Academy was founded, and in 1931 perhaps the first chair of peace research (for the study of international institutions for the organization of peace) was created in France at the University of Lyons. Many of these initiatives foundered in the rising tide of international violence in the 1930s and are easy to dismiss as overly idealistic at the time. But powerful ideas endure and prove capable of inspiring future generations when conditions for their implementation are more propitious. Some of the early advocates identified by van den Dungen were natural scientists, who were aware and critical of the greater contributions made by science and scientists to the causes of war rather than to the causes of peace. Others were medical professionals who had an understanding of the physical and mental costs of war and were struck by the medical analogy: if war was like a disease, then knowledge of symptoms and aetiology should precede diagnosis and therapy or cure. Many proponents of peace research also shared the view that the causes of war and the problems of creating a durable peace were so complex that only a multidisciplinary approach would be adequate and that academic learning needed to spring from broader humanistic and idealistic motivations. These ideas would be drawn on in the foundation of the future field of conflict resolution.

Meanwhile, although not known to many of those calling for a new science of peace, other important pioneering work was being done which would later enrich conflict resolution. Prominent here was the thinking of Mary Parker Follett (1942) in the field of organizational behaviour and labour-management relations. Advocating 'integration' as an alternative conflict resolution mechanism, in contrast to 'domination' and 'compromise' as commonly used, she anticipated much of the later problem-solving agenda as outlined in chapter 1. This was later developed into a 'mutual gains' approach to negotiation associated with what would be called 'integrative bargaining', as against the traditional concession/convergence approach associated with 'distributive bargaining' (Walton and McKersie, 1965).[1] Whereas distributive bargaining assumes concealment, inflated initial demands and zero-sum contexts, the integrative bargaining advocated in the mutual gains approach tries to redefine the negotiation as a shared problem to be resolved. Pooling knowledge and resources and looking to maximize mutual gain is seen to yield greater pay-offs to all parties.

Initiatives in three other fields would also prove of importance to the future interdisciplinary study of conflict resolution – psychology, politics and international studies. For example, in the field of psychology, frustration-aggression theories of human conflict (Dollard et al., 1939) and work on the social psychology of group conflict conducted by Kurt Lewin (1948) would be influential. Similarly, in the field of political studies, Crane Brinton's approach to the analysis of political revolution (1938) – that revolution takes place when the gap between distributed social power and distributed political power reaches a critical point – can be taken as exemplary of what was to prove another significant strand (carried forward later by Dahrendorf (1957), Gurr (1970) and Tilly (1978)). In international studies, David Mitrany's (1943) functionalist approach to overcoming the win–lose dynamic inherent in realist analyses of competitive interstate relations via a progressively denser network of cooperative cross-border frameworks made necessary by the advance of technology – seen by some to have previsaged the evolution of the European Union – would inspire similar ideas for sustaining peace through cross-border institution-building in future conflict resolution circles (complemented by Karl Deutsch's (1957) analysis of the development of 'political community' in the North Atlantic area). Of central significance in all this, and perhaps the critical catalyst in the later emergence of the conflict resolution field, were the early empirical studies of war and conflict conducted in the interwar years by the Russian Pitirim Sorokin, the Englishman Lewis Fry Richardson and the American Quincy Wright.[2] Here at last was a proper statistical foundation upon which to base analysis – so thought the founders of the conflict resolution field when they came across this work in the 1950s.

Against this background of intellectual research and development, and in the context of the failure to prevent the second major world war of the century, the most significant institutional development in this span of first-generation activity came right at the end of the period – with the formation of the United Nations. Representatives of fifty countries met in San Francisco at the United Nations Conference on International Organization to draw up and agree the Charter of the United Nations. The organization officially came into existence on 24 October 1945.

Although it was itself the outcome of the plans of the great powers for a post-Second World War order, and particularly the powers which were the victors in that war, the UN was not merely the creature of those powers, and its formation marked a significant, even if imperfect, development historically in the evolution of world order. Holsti (1991) has looked at peace agreements and security architectures that have shaped the growth of the international system between 1648 and 1945, with significant milestones after the Thirty Years' War (Westphalia 1648), Louis XIV's wars (Utrecht 1713), the Napoleonic Wars (Vienna 1815), World War I (Paris 1919) and World War II (San Francisco 1945) (see table 2.1).

Looking at these epoch-making phases of war and peacemaking, Holsti isolates what he calls eight prerequisites for peace. These are related to:

- *governance* (some system of responsibility for regulating behaviour in terms of the conditions of an agreement);
- *legitimacy* (a new order following war cannot be based on perceived

Table 2.1 The evolution of attempts to create a peaceful postwar international order

Prerequisites for peace	Westphalia	Utrecht	Vienna	Paris	San Francisco
Governance	Yes	Yes	Yes	No*	Yes
Legitimacy	Yes	No	Yes	No	Yes
Assimilation	Yes	Yes	Yes	No	Yes
Deterrence	Yes	No	Yes	No	No**
Conflict resolution	No	No	Yes	Yes	Yes
War as problem	No	No	No	Yes	Yes
Peaceful change	No	No	No	No	No
Future issues	No	No	No	No	No
Conditions satisfied	4/8	2/8	5/8	2/8	5/8

Source: Holsti, 1991: ch.13

* short-lived governance mechanism in League of Nations

** failure to develop deterrent capacity such as proposed Military Staff Committee or UN Standing Forces injustice or repression, and principles of justice have to be embodied into the postwar settlement);

- *assimilation* (linked to legitimacy: the gains of living within a system are greater than the potential advantages of seeking to destroy it);
- *a deterrent system* (victors should create a coalition strong enough to deter defection, by force if necessary, to protect settlement norms, or to change them by peaceful means);
- *conflict-resolving procedures and institutions* (the system of governance should include provision and capacity for identifying, monitoring, managing and resolving major conflict between members of the system, and the norms of the system would include willingness to use such institutions);
- *consensus on war* (a recognition that war is the fundamental problem, acknowledgement of the need to develop and foster strong norms against use of force and clear guiding principles for the legitimate use of force);
- *procedures for peaceful change* (the need to review and adapt when agreements no longer relate to the reality of particular situations: peace agreements need to have built-in mechanisms for review and adaptation); and
- *anticipation of future issues* (peacemakers need to incorporate some ability to anticipate what may constitute conflict causes in the future: institutions and system norms should include provision for identifying, monitoring and handling not just the problems that created the last conflict but future conflicts as well).

Holsti's conclusion from this survey is instructive. The least success has come around developing methods of peaceful change and anticipation of conflict-generating future issues. In general, the more criteria that were met in each agreement, the more stable and peaceful was the ensuing period. The San Francisco meeting which established the UN did a great deal to stabilize interstate relations and provides one explanation at least for the decline of interstate conflict. However, it did not anticipate the forces that would generate future conflicts, which, as we have seen, were civil wars with high levels of civilian casualties; nor did it put in place the mechanisms for peaceful system change. A constant failure of those who have been war leaders has been a failure to 'enlarge the shadow of the future' instead of remaining in the shadow of the past. As Holsti puts it:

> it may be asking too much for wartime leaders to cast their minds more to the future. The immediate war settlements are difficult enough. But in so far as the peacemakers were involved not just in settling a past war but also in constructing the foundations of a new international order, foresight is mandatory. The peace system must not only resolve the old issues that gave rise to previous wars; it must anticipate new issues, new actors, and new problems and it must design institutions, norms and procedures that are appropriate to them. (Holsti, 1991: 347)

In this book we identify cosmopolitan conflict resolution with the full range of factors identified by Holsti for preventing future wars, including elements 'missing' in 1945 such as the 'anticipation of future issues' and the 'capacity to manage peaceful change'. This is a central theme throughout what follows, to be summed up in chapter 20. Somewhat along these lines, the United Nations Intellectual History Project was established at the Ralph Bunche Institute, at the University of New York, to explore the role of the world organization, not as a bureaucratized institution but as creator and disseminator of ideas – for example, around the concept of human security, which, at the level of international organizations, provides a distinctive normative framework to guide future conflict resolution interventions (its first publication was *Ahead of the Curve?* (2001) by Emmerij, Jolly and Weiss).

Non-violence, pacifism and conflict resolution

At this point it is worth clarifying that, despite the tensions between peace researchers and peace activists noted above, the development of conflict resolution as a distinct field of academic enquiry with a strong praxis also owes much to non-violence and pacifist traditions and to the thinkers whose ideas nourished it, although, as discussed in chapter 14, many of those in the conflict resolution field are not pacifists in the strict sense of the term.

The work of non-violence theorists such as Gene Sharp (1973; Reading 34), and the persistence of historical traditions and practices of pacifism such as those contained in the beliefs of Quakers and Mennonites or in the ideas of Gandhi, have cross-fertilized with academic enterprise to enhance understanding of violent political conflict and alternatives to it. The objectives of Gandhi's *satyagraha* ('struggle for truth') were to make latent conflict manifest by challenging social structures which were harmful because they were highly inequitable, but to do this without setting off a spiral of violence – the complementary value was non-violence (*ahimsa*). In the Gandhian model of conflict, which contains within it built-in inhibitors of violence, the objective is not to win but, through what Bondurant called the Gandhian dialectic, 'to achieve a fresh level of social truth and a healthier relationship between antagonists' (Wehr, 1979: 64; Reading 38). In the teachings of the Buddha (the *Dhamma*), on the other hand, McConnell (1995) has shown how the doctrine of the middle way and the four noble truths locate the deepest roots of conflict in the perceptions, values and attitudes of conflictants. While this does not ignore what Gandhi would have seen as oppressive structures, it does direct the peacemaker to focus on changes in self-awareness and the development of self-knowledge.

Weber (1999, 2001) has made a strong case for seeing Gandhian ideas in particular as integral to the normative framework later adopted within conflict resolution. Strong echoes of *satyagraha* can be discerned, for example, in Burton's analysis of conflict as rooted in the denial of ontological human needs and in the uses of the problem-solving method by Burton, Kelman, Mitchell and others to achieve mutually acceptable and self-sustaining outcomes as described. The radical and socially transformative objectives of Gandhian social theory are also echoed in the conflict transformation models associated with peacebuilding from below, which we deal with in chapter 9 (Woodhouse, 1986). Within the 'emancipatory discourse' of a Gandhian framework, conflict resolution techniques are seen as 'tools for transformation' (Curle, 1990), and the field is located within a wider continuum, which includes world order, human security and non-violent peacemaking (Woodhouse, 1991).

More recently, in their book *Why Civil Resistance Works: The Strategic Logic of Nonviolent Conflict*, Erica Chenoweth and Maria Stephan (2011) have shown how the success rate of non-violent and violent campaigns varies according to the objectives pursued. The most successful non-violent campaigns were anti-regime resistance. Non-violent campaigns to expel occupiers or achieve autonomy were marginally more successful than violent campaigns. Violent campaigns aimed at secession were more successful than non-violent campaigns, although the success rate of the former was very low.

There is also a measure of creative tension between conflict resolution and non-violent direct action, however. For example, as we have seen, some argue that conflict resolution is problematic in situations of high asymmetry between adversaries, where more committed strategies associated with non-violent direct action can better raise awareness and make asymmetrical relations more balanced, at which point mediation and other forms of third-party intervention become both more legitimate and more effective (Clark, 2000; Dudouet, 2005, 2014). The remarkable early phases of the 'Arab revolutions' after December 2010 dramatically illustrated the power of non-violent direct action when the time is right – echoing previous achievements such as those that brought down Soviet-backed regimes in Eastern Europe in 1989, prompting widespread use of the term 'Arab Spring' before violence broke out in Libya, Yemen and Syria (see chapter 4). Conversely, the terrible and still spreading violence that has followed makes some advocates of non-violence question whether it is responsible to start revolutions in situations where people have not been adequately prepared in non-violent methods and the means of non-violent communication have not been adequately developed. Some activists and advocates of non-violent direct action have recognized that there are 'spaces' in the hourglass model of conflict (figure 1.3, p. 16), where non-violence (interpreted here as the non-use of military force) may be strategically inappropriate, difficult or counter-productive (Randle, 2002: 11–50).

Foundations: The Second Generation, 1945–1965

The sustained development of peace and conflict research in the form of institutional growth had to wait until the post-1945 world, when the threat of nuclear weapons added a new urgency. The first institutions of peace and conflict research appeared in the twenty-year period between 1945 and 1965. The Peace Research Laboratory was founded by Theodore F. Lentz at St Louis, Missouri, after the bombing of Hiroshima and Nagasaki in 1945. Science, according to Lentz, 'did increase physical power but science did not increase physical harmony ... the power–harmony imbalance has been brought about by science in misorder' (Lentz, 1955: 52–3). Lentz argued not only that people had a capacity to live in harmony, but that 'humatriotism' was a value which would emerge from rigorous research into human attitudes and personality. One of the first attempts to follow up this lead was taken by a group of pioneers of the new conflict resolution field at the University of Michigan.

Kenneth Boulding, Michigan and the Journal of Conflict Resolution

Kenneth Boulding was born in Liverpool in the north of England in 1910. Motivated personally and spiritually as a member of the Society of Friends (Quakers), and professionally as an economist, he moved to America in 1937, married Elise Bjorn-Hansen in 1941, and began with her a partnership that was to make a seminal contribution to the formation of peace and conflict research. After the war he was appointed as professor of economics at the University of Michigan. Here, with a small group of academics, which included the mathematician-biologist Anatol Rapoport, the social psychologist Herbert Kelman and the sociologist Robert Cooley Angell, he initiated the *Journal of Conflict Resolution* (JCR) in 1957 and set up the Center for Research on Conflict Resolution in 1959. Inspirational to what Boulding called the 'Early Church' of the peace research movement (Kerman, 1974: 48) was the work of Lewis Richardson, brought over on microfilm by his son Stephen, and not yet published at that time (Reading 3). In this work Boulding was building on the initiative of the Center for Advanced Study in the Behavioral Sciences (CASBS) at Stanford University.

Boulding's publications focused firmly on the issue of preventing war, because, partly as a result of the failures of the discipline of international relations, 'the international system is by far the most pathological and costly segment of the total social system' (Kerman, 1974: 83). *Conflict and Defense* (1962; Reading 4) advanced the thesis of the decline or obsolescence of the nation-state, while *Perspectives on the Economics of Peace* (1961) argued that conventional prescriptions from international relations were unable even to recognize, let alone analyse, the consequences of this obsolescence. If war was the outcome of inherent characteristics in the sovereign state system, then it might be prevented, in Boulding's view, by a reform of international organization and by the development of a research and information capability. From this capability, data collection and processing could enable the advance of scientific knowledge about the build-up of conflicts to replace the inadequate insights available through standard diplomacy. In the first issue of the JCR in March 1957, Wright had an article proposing a 'project on a world intelligence centre', which showed the influence of Richardson from the past, while anticipating what has more recently come to be called early warning and conflict prevention (see chapter 5). For Boulding, in these formative years of conflict theory, conflict resolution meant the development of a knowledge base in which 'social data stations' would emerge, forming a system analogous to a network of weather stations, which would gather a range of social, political and economic data to produce indicators 'to identify social temperature and pressure and predict cold or warm fronts' (Kerman, 1974: 82).

Johan Galtung and conflict resolution in Northern Europe

While the developments at Michigan and the interest of the Bouldings in peace as well as conflict research provided one polar point for the emergence of peace research, its main elaboration was to be defined in developments in Europe. Lawler (1995) makes a distinction between the more limited agenda of conflict research (seeking to reduce the incidence and extent of war) and the emergence of peace research, whose origins were not in North America but in Scandinavia, and most remarkably in the work of Johan Galtung. We have already introduced Galtung's concept of the conflict triangle, and his distinction between direct violence, structural violence and cultural violence, in chapter 1 (figure 1.1, p. 12), and have commented on his further distinction between negative and positive peace – the former characterized by the absence of direct violence, the latter by the overcoming of structural and cultural violence as well. Negative peace can be associated with the more limited but better defined 'minimalist' conflict resolution agenda of preventing war, and in particular nuclear war, as advocated by what might be called the North American pragmatist school. Positive peace encompasses the broader but vaguer 'maximalist' agenda of conflict resolution insisted upon by the European structuralists. These two poles are reflected in the two quotations from the *Journal of Conflict Resolution* given at the beginning of this chapter.

The medical analogy, which seems to have occurred to so many of the peace science pioneers, was also at work in Galtung's background. His father was a physician, and Galtung absorbed the ethic, transforming it into the notion of the peace researcher as a 'social physician' guided by a body of scientific knowledge. He studied philosophy, sociology and mathematics. In 1958 he became visiting professor of sociology at Columbia University but returned to Oslo in 1960 to help found a unit for research into conflict and peace (the precursor to PRIO, the International Peace Research Institute Oslo), based within the Institute for Social Research at the University of Oslo. The further development of peace research institutions in Europe in the 1960s was vigorous: thus, in 1962 the Polemological Institute was formed in Groningen, the Netherlands; in 1966 the Stockholm International Peace Research Institute (SIPRI) was opened to commemorate Sweden's 150 years of peace; and in 1969 the Tampere Peace Research Institute was formed in Finland. Galtung was also the founding editor of the *Journal of Peace Research*, which was launched in 1964.

This is not the place to attempt a summary of Galtung's work. His output since the early 1960s has been phenomenal and his influence on the institutionalization and ideas of peace research seminal. He saw the range of peace research reaching out far beyond the enterprise of war prevention to encompass study of the conditions for peaceful relations between the dominant and the exploited, rulers and ruled, men and women, western and non-western cultures, humankind and nature. Central here was the search for positive peace in the form of human empathy, solidarity and community, the priority of addressing 'structural violence' in peace research by unveiling and transforming structures of imperialism and oppression, and the importance of searching for alternative values in non-western cosmologies such as Buddhism.[3]

The struggle between European structuralists and North American pragmatists to define the peace research and conflict resolution agenda was at times hard-hitting. In an article in the *Journal of Peace Research* in 1968, for example, Herman Schmid castigated many of those working in the field for failing to engage critically with issues of social justice. Absence of war on its own (negative peace) can obscure deep injustices which make a mockery of peace and, if unaddressed, contain the seeds of future violent conflict. On the other hand, as Lawler's conclusion to his study of Galtung's ideas suggests, although the constant expansion of the peace research and conflict resolution agenda may be seen as a sign of its dynamism, 'it may also be seen as acquiring the qualities of an intellectual black hole wherein something vital, a praxeological edge or purpose, is lost'. This was a criticism made, among others, by Boulding in his 'friendly quarrels' with Galtung (Boulding 1977; Galtung 1987). In our view, the central core of the conflict resolution approach described in this book does represent the 'praxeological edge or purpose' of peace research. As both an analytic and a normative field, conflict resolution takes violent or destructive conflict as its topic and aims to gain an accurate understanding of its nature and aetiology in order to learn how it can best be overcome. This implies not only the treatment of symptoms but work on conflict causes as well.

While we have organized this account of the history of peace and conflict research into chronologies based on generations, the device is, as noted above, artificial. Most of the key thinkers and activists remain active across the 'generations', none more so than Galtung. The 'Galtungian project' for peace research and action has matured into third-generation activity, especially in the TRANSCEND approach formed in 1993 as a teaching, training and research organization to pursue these ideas. In *Searching for Peace*, Galtung and his colleagues define the philosophy and methodologies of TRANSCEND and present an exploration of the case for a new 'forum to address underlying structures and cultures of violence, and the need for new language, dialogue and perspectives such as might offer more creative and viable alternatives for the twenty first century' (Galtung and Jacobsen, 2000: 47; Galtung, 2004).

John Burton and a new paradigm in international studies

At this point we can review the contribution of our third 'founder figure', John Burton. Burton was born in Australia in 1915. He studied from 1938 at the London School of Economics, where he gained a master's degree and, in 1942, a doctorate. He joined the Australian civil service, attended the foundation conference of the United Nations in San Francisco, and served in the Australian Department of External Affairs and as high commissioner in Ceylon. In 1963, following a period on a research fellowship at the Australian National University in Canberra he was appointed to a post at University College London in 1963. This appointment coincided with the formation of the Conflict Research Society in London, of which he became the first honorary secretary. An early product of this initiative was the publication of *Conflict in Society* (de Reuck and Knight, 1966), with contributions from Boulding, Rapoport and Burton. Following soon after the appearance of other important studies of social conflict as a generic phenomenon, whether at community, industrial or other levels (Reading 10; Coser, 1956; Coleman, 1957), and coinciding with a rediscovery of Georg Simmel's pioneering work (1902), this represented a significant step in the drawing together of multidisciplinary insights for the study of conflict at international level from a much broader perspective than was current in the formal international relations field. As seen in chapter 1, whereas some earlier social scientists, such as the Chicago School, regarded conflict as dysfunctional and the job of the sociologist to remove it, most analysts in the conflict resolution tradition, following Morton Deutsch (Reading 13), saw conflict as intrinsic in human relationships so that the task became one of handling it better.

This was linked to attempts to coordinate international study through the formation of an International Peace Research Association (IPRA), which held its first conference at Groningen in the Netherlands in 1965. This built on the work of Walter Isard's formation of the Peace Science Society in 1963. At the same time, during 1965 and 1966, Burton organized the meetings which were to result in the use of controlled communication, or the problem-solving method, in international conflict, to be outlined further in the next section. These meetings were sufficiently impressive for both the provost of University College London and the British Social Science Research Council to support and develop the theoretical and applied techniques, which Burton and his group were pioneering. The result was the formation in 1966 of the Centre for the Analysis of Conflict established under the directorship of Burton and based at University College London.

Burton later spent a period in the mid-1980s at the University of Maryland, where he assisted Edward Azar with the formation of the Center for International Development and Conflict Management and where he worked on the concept of protracted social conflict. This became an important part of an emerging overall theory of international conflict, combining both domestic-social and international dimensions and focused at a hybrid level between interstate war and purely domestic unrest. This model, described more fully through an outline of Azar's analysis in chapter 4, in our view anticipated much of the revaluation of international relations thinking that has taken place since the end of the Cold War. Burton himself did not hold back from making extravagant claims for this new approach in conflict analysis and conflict resolution, describing it as a decisive paradigm shift.

Burton finished his formal academic career as a professor at the Institute for Conflict Analysis and Resolution at George Mason University in Virginia and as a fellow at the United States Institute for Peace in the late 1980s. Here he produced four volumes of the Conflict Series (1990), which offer a good summation of his own work and that of colleagues, associates and others working with him in the field.

Early influences on Burton's intellectual journey away from the conventional wisdom of international relations traditions were systems theory, as a new vocabulary and set of explanations for the cooperative and competitive behaviour of social organisms, and games theory, as a means of analysing the variety of options and orientations available to the conflict parties. The work of Schelling (1960; Reading 11) on irrationality in competitive strategies and Rapoport (Rapoport and Chammah, 1965) on the self-defeating logic of win–lose approaches were influential here. As Rapoport put it, the illusion that increasing losses for the other side is equivalent to winning is *the* reason that the struggles are so prolonged and the conflicting parties play the game to a lose/lose end. We have introduced some of these ideas in chapter 1.

Another source of inspiration for Burton was insight drawn from industrial relations, organizational theory and client-centred social work. Here the legacy of Mary Parker Follett's 'mutual gains' approach was being vigorously carried forward (Blake et al., 1963; Walton and McKersie, 1965) and applied further afield in family conciliation work, community mediation, and the rapidly expanding arena of alternative dispute resolution (ADR) in general, which sought less costly alternatives to formal litigation (Floyer Acland, 1995). The William and Flora Hewlett Foundation provided crucial financial encouragement and support here (Kovick, 2005), an example of the remarkable potential to build critical capacity in a new field that enlightened funders can provide.

Much of this literature, and related literatures on, for example, race and ethnic relations, was based on studies in social psychology and social identity theory, which examined the dynamics of intergroup cooperation and conflict through field-based surveys and small group experimentation. The work of Kurt Lewin was further developed to show how group affiliation and pressure to gain distinctiveness by comparison with other groups can lead to intergroup conflict, and how positive relations can be restored or new relationships negotiated between groups in conflict. Morton Deutsch was among the first to apply this kind of research explicitly to conflict resolution (1949,

1973). Useful surveys of a wide field include Fisher (1990) and Larsen (1993). This research has explored both the negative and positive aspects. Negatively, it has concentrated on processes of selective perception through forms of tunnel vision, prejudice and stereotyping, on malign perceptions of the 'other', on dehumanization and the formation of enemy images, and on the displacement of feelings of fear and hostility through suppression and projection. Positively, it has focused on changing attitudes, on developing mutual understanding and trust, on the development of common or 'superordinate goals', and on the general identification of conditions which promote positive intergroup contact (Sherif, 1966; Deutsch, 1973). These insights were at the same time applied to international conflict, as later summed up in Mitchell (1981a; Reading 14). Linked to this were studies of 'perception and misperception' among decision-makers in international politics, to borrow Jervis's 1976 title. Burton drew on this material in a series of books published in the late 1960s and early 1970s, including *Systems, States, Diplomacy and Rules* (1968), *Conflict and Communication* (1969), and *World Society* (1972).

What made it possible to unlock these intractable conflicts for Burton was above all the application of needs theory (Maslow, 1954; Sites, 1990) through a 'controlled communication' or problem-solving approach (Reading 5). As already indicated in chapter 1 (figure 1.7, p. 24), the positing of a universal drive to satisfy basic needs such as security, identity and recognition provided Burton with the link between causal analysis and modes of resolution precisely because of the differences between interests and needs. Interests, being primarily about material 'goods', can be traded, bargained over and negotiated. Needs, being non-material, cannot be traded or satisfied by power bargaining. However, crucially, non-material human needs are not scarce resources (like territory or oil or minerals might be) and are not necessarily in short supply. With proper understanding, therefore, conflicts based on unsatisfied needs can be resolved. It is possible (in theory) to meet the needs of both parties to a conflict because, 'the more security and recognition one party to a relationship experiences, the more others are likely to experience' (Burton, 1990a: 242). For example, although the question of sovereignty in Northern Ireland or Jerusalem may appear to be intractable, if the conflict can be translated into the underlying basic needs of the conflict parties for security, recognition and development, a space is opened up for the possibility of resolution.

But the problem-solving approach was seen as more than a conflict resolution technique by Burton. It was to become a central concept in his idea of the paradigm shift in thinking about behaviour and conflict in general that he believed was essential if humankind was to avoid future disaster. He was again influenced by some of the concepts in general systems theory here, and in particular the idea of first-order and second-order learning. In systems theory, attention is given to the role of social learning and culture in the way in which social systems change. The theory holds that, although social systems 'learn' through their members, who individually adjust their worldviews according to experience, socio-cultural systems also have underlying assumptions which make the system as a whole more resistant to change than their individual members. These underlying assumptions are defined by Rapoport as 'default values', which, because they are so commonly used, become regarded as immutable, and actors in the system tend to forget that they can exercise choices in order to attain goals. When problems occur, they are addressed by reference to the 'default values', and this kind of reaction is termed first-order learning. Orderly and creative transformation of social systems, however, depends upon a capacity for second-order learning, which requires a willingness and capacity for challenging assumptions. Ideological orientations to social change are regarded as the antithesis of second-order learning, because ideologies are claims to ultimate truth achieved with a predefined set of ends and means, the challenging of which is seen as heretical. For systems theorists such as Rapoport, 'the critical issue of peace and the need to convert conflict to co-operation demand incorporation of second order learning in social systems, and the most effective way to produce social learning is through a participative design process' (Rapoport, 1960: 442).

This idea of second-order learning, or second-order change, is further developed by Burton and Dukes in the third volume of the Conflict series (1990a), where it is seen to be essential for human survival. Burton was influenced here by Norbert Wiener's early use of systems theory to invent the new science of cybernetics, which we comment further on in chapter 17 (Wiener, 1948). The problem-solving approach, given philosophical depth through Charles Sanders Peirce's 'logic of abduction' (1958), is the means of overcoming blockages to second-order learning, thereby becoming a central element in what Burton saw as a new political philosophy, which moves beyond episodic conflict resolution to a new order marked by 'provention' (a neologism that has not been widely adopted):

> conflict provention means deducing from an adequate explanation of the phenomenon of conflict, including its human dimensions, not merely the conditions that create an environment of conflict, and the structural changes required to remove it, but more importantly, the promotion of conditions that create cooperative relationships. (Burton and Dukes, 1990a: 2).

It connotes, in other words, a proactive capability within societies to predict and avoid destructive conflict by the spread of the problem-solving method and philosophy throughout all relevant institutions, discourses and practices. In sum, we can see how far the Burtonian concept of problem-solving and conflict resolution is from the way it is sometimes caricatured in transformationist critiques, where it is wrongly equated with Robert Cox's different use of the term (1981). Indeed, in our view, Burtonian problem-solving, seen as paradigm shift rather than a workshop technique, is itself firmly at the transformationist end of the conflict resolution spectrum (see chapter 1).

Consolidation: The Third Generation, 1965–1985

By the late 1960s and early 1970s, conflict resolution, drawing from a wide range of disciplines and with a reasonably sound institutional base, had defined its specific subject area in relation to the three great projects of avoiding nuclear war, removing glaring inequalities and injustices in the global system, and achieving ecological balance and control. It was attempting to formulate a theoretical understanding of destructive conflict at three levels with a view to refining the most appropriate practical responses.

First, there was the interstate level, where the main effort went into translating détente between the superpowers into formal win–win agreements. Here the processes which produced the 1963 Limited Test Ban Treaty, and later Strategic Arms Limitation Talks and Non-Proliferation Treaty negotiations, were seen to vindicate Osgood's 'graduated and reciprocal initiatives in tension reduction' (GRIT) approach (1962) and to exemplify Axelrod's analysis of the 'evolution of cooperation' described in chapter 1 (table 1.2, p. 21). Similar work went into the formulation of 'alternative defence' strategies in the early 1980s. The expansion of the European Economic Community and of the North Atlantic security area were seen as further confirmation of the ideas of Mitrany and Karl Deutsch.

Second, at the level of domestic politics, a great deal of conflict resolution work, particularly in the United States, went into the building up of expertise in family conciliation, labour and community mediation, and alternative dispute resolution. An important new initiative here was in public policy disputes in general (Susskind, 1987). Here the sub-field of public conflict resolution aims to increase participation in democratic decision-making at all levels (Barber, 1984; Dukes, 1996).

Third, between the two, and for this book the most significant development in the 1970s and 1980s, was the definition, analysis and prescriptive thinking about what were variously described as 'deep-rooted conflicts' (Burton, 1987), 'intractable conflicts' (Kriesberg et al., 1989) or 'protracted social conflicts' (Azar, 1990), in which the distinction between international and domestic-level causes was seen to be elided. Here the emphasis was on defining the elements of 'good governance' at constitutional level and of intergroup relations at community level. Since we will be outlining Edward Azar's thinking about protracted social conflict in chapter 4, we will not elaborate these concepts here. They seem to us to have constituted a significant advance in thinking about what has since become the prevailing pattern of large-scale contemporary conflict. These levels of analysis were brought together from a conflict resolution perspective in studies such as Kriesberg's *The Sociology of Social Conflicts* (1973) and Mitchell's *The Structure of International Conflict* (1981a).

In what follows we select for attention the first systematic attempts to apply the problem-solving approach to real conflicts and the major advances in the analysis of the negotiation and mediation processes, which took place in this

period. We end the section by noting the concomitant expansion of the conflict resolution institutional base worldwide and pay tribute to the role of Elise
Boulding, both in encouraging it and in articulating its wider significance.

Interative problem-solving and principled negotiation

One of the most sustained attempts to wed theory to practice was the attempt
to set up 'problem-solving workshops' to tackle the more intractable conflicts of the day. Initially referred to as 'controlled communication', the first
attempt to apply the problem-solving method was in two workshops in 1965
and 1966, which were designed to address aspects of the conflict between
Malaysia, Singapore and Indonesia and that between the Greek and Turkish
communities in Cyprus. The London Group, among whose members were
Michael Banks, Anthony de Reuck, Chris Mitchell and Michael Nicholson, as
well as Burton, were joined for the second workshop in 1966 by Herb Kelman
and Chad Alger from America. Kelman, who formed at Harvard the Program
on International Conflict Analysis and Resolution, and who had already been
a significant influence in the emergence of conflict resolution research in
the pioneering initiatives at the University of Michigan, went on to become
perhaps the leading practitioner-scholar of the problem-solving method over
the following thirty years, specializing in the Israeli–Palestinian conflict
(Doob, 1970; Kelman, 1996). His background was in the social psychology of
international relations. To anticipate events in the 1990s, Kelman's longstanding 1974–91 'prenegotiation' Arab–Israeli interactive problem-solving workshops, followed by the 'para-negotiation' workshops (1991–3) and (after 1993)
'post-negotiation' workshops (fifty-four workshops in all up to that date),
involved many of the chief negotiators of the 1993 agreement on both sides.
Participants were influential, but non-official, figures; meetings were held in
private academic environments, encouraged by third-party facilitation, but
only in an enabling capacity inasmuch as ground rules were explained and
a problem-solving agenda followed. Information was shared and participants
were encouraged to listen without judging each other's needs, concerns and
perspectives; there was then joint exploration of options, joint analysis of
likely constraints, and a joint search for ways of overcoming those constraints.
These were seen as non-binding non-official micro-processes, which, it was
hoped, would contribute to macro-level negotiations but in no way substitute
for them. One of the chief ways in which they might do this was through the
building of new relationships.

As experience developed among a growing circle of scholar-practitioners
in the 1970s and 1980s, problem-solving workshops were used to pursue a
variety of goals – for example, in some cases they performed a research and
educational or training role – and it became clear that each workshop had
to be designed with some reference to the specific characteristics of the particular conflict. A universal model for the ideal problem-solving process did

not emerge. Nevertheless, there now exists a whole cluster of approaches – known variously as interactive conflict resolution, third-party consultation, process-promoting workshops, facilitated dialogues – which use many of the essential characteristics of the problem-solving approach (Fisher, 1997). This is well explained and illustrated in Mitchell and Banks's *Handbook of Conflict Resolution: The Analytical Problem-Solving Approach* (1996). The difficult questions of methodology and evaluation have been much discussed (Mitchell, 1993), with a view to enhancing the process of hypothesis generation, theory testing and theory use. By the 1980s the study of negotiation in international conflict had also taken on the win–win, problem-solving and mutual gain vocabulary of conflict resolution.

Distinct from this – although also at Harvard – was the work of Roger Fisher and William Ury at the Harvard Program on Negotiation, popularized through their best-selling title *Getting to Yes* (1981) and, more recently, through the quarterly *Negotiation Journal*. Fisher's background was legal and his focus was on improving negotiation practice in general, not with a particular focus at international level. We are indebted to Ronald Fisher, whose distinguished and influential work we acknowledge elsewhere (1990, 1997, 2005), for an important clarification here. We noted in chapter 1 (figure 1.7, p. 24) the distinction between positions and interests, which is central in the 'principled negotiation' approach. As originally presented, this *interest-based negotiation* approach is encapsulated in a number of maxims for negotiators:

- separate the people from the problem and try to build good working relationships;
- facilitate communication and build trust by listening to each other rather than by telling each other what to do;
- focus on underlying interests and core concerns, not demands and superficial positions: this includes concealed interests as well as those yet to be realized;
- avoid zero-sum traps by brainstorming and exploring creative options without commitment to see if legitimate interests on both or all sides can be accommodated;
- use objective criteria for evaluating and prioritizing options in terms of effectiveness and fairness;
- anticipate possible obstacles;
- work out how to overcome the obstacles, including the drafting of clear and attainable commitments.

The aim is to define, and if possible expand, the zone of possible agreement, and to increase its attraction in comparison with the best alternatives to a negotiated agreement as perceived by the negotiating partners individually. It also means assessing the likelihood of the worst alternatives materializing if no agreement is reached. A recent reworking of this process lays stress on 'using emotions as you negotiate' (Fisher and Shapiro, 2005). Building on the

Harvard approach, William Ury has also developed his typology of 'third-side roles' (2000) (figure 1.14, p. 32, and chapter 14).

The Harvard Program involves a consortium of academic centres and, in authentic conflict resolution vein, draws from a range of disciplines, including politics, psychology, anthropology, sociology and international relations, as well as labour relations, community negotiations and public planning. A number of systematic analyses and comparative studies of successful and unsuccessful negotiation approaches and styles are now available, among them Druckman (1977), Zartman (1978), Pruitt (1981), Raiffa (1982), Hall (1993), Pruitt and Carnevale (1993), Zartman and Rubin (1996), Bercovitch and Gartner (2006) and Kydd (2006). This is looked at further in chapter 7.

Adam Curle: the theory and practice of mediation

The practice of mediation has a long history, traceable to Greek and Roman times in the West. By 1945 there were critical studies of state-level diplomacy and international mediation to complement the day-to-day experience acquired by professional diplomats and negotiators (Mitchell and Webb, 1988). The attempt by the international community to convert this into a more formal institutionalized practice following the call in Chapter VI of the United Nations Charter for agreed mechanisms for the peaceful settlement of disputes inspired studies such as that by Oran Young (1967), which included an assessment of the role of the United Nations and its agencies. Nevertheless, a number of scholars in the conflict resolution tradition in the early 1980s agreed with Dean Pruitt that there was a deficit in critical studies of mediation which still lacked systematic analysis (Pruitt and Rubin, 1986: 237). Since then much of the deficit has been made up. In addition to Mitchell and Webb, the literature now includes Touval and Zartman (1985; Reading 41) and Bercovitch and Rubin (1992), as well as Kressell and Pruitt (1989), Bercovitch (1996), Böhmelt (2010), Toft (2010) and a host of individual studies of particular mediations in specific conflicts. This will also be developed in chapter 7. Quite sophisticated comparisons are now being made of different types of mediation, with or without 'muscle', by different types of mediator (official and unofficial, from the UN to individual governments, insider-partial or outsider-neutral) and in different types of conflict situations. A special issue of the *Journal of Peace Research* published in February 1991 first encouraged critical comparison of the efficacy of new paradigm approaches (non-coercive and based broadly on problem-solving) in relation to power–coercion–reward models. This has been followed by continuing efforts to assess the effectiveness of alternative approaches.

As a complement to the emphasis on Track I mediation in many of the studies noted above, we take Adam Curle as our exemplar for the development of 'soft' mediation in the conflict resolution field, particularly what MacDonald and Bendahmane (1987) styled 'unofficial' or Track II mediation. Coming from an academic background in anthropology, psychology and development education, Curle moved from Harvard to take up the first chair of peace studies at the University of Bradford, which, together with the Richardson Institute for Conflict and Peace Research at the University of Lancaster and the Centre for the Analysis of Conflict at the University of Kent (a relocation of the original 1966 centre based at University College London), was to become a focal point for conflict resolution in the UK.

Curle's academic interest in peace was a product of front-line experiences of conflict in Pakistan and in Africa, where he not only witnessed the threats to development from the eruption of violent conflicts but was increasingly drawn into the practice of peacemaking, especially as a mediator. Most importantly, during the intensive and searing experiences of the Biafran War, he felt a compelling need to understand more about why these conflicts happened (Curle, 1971, 1986; Yarrow, 1978). Violence, conflict, processes of social change and the goals of development began to be seen as linked themes. *Making Peace* (1971; Reading 40) defines peace and conflict as a set of peaceful and unpeaceful relationships, so that 'the process of peacemaking consists in making changes to relationships so that they may be brought to a point where development can occur'. Given his academic background, it was natural that Curle should see peace broadly in terms of human development rather than as a set of 'peace-enforcing' rules and organizations. And the purpose of studying social structures was to identify those that enhanced rather than restrained or even suppressed human potential.

In the Middle (Reading 50; Curle 1986) points to the importance of mediation and reconciliation themes in peace research and practice in the conflict-ridden world of the late twentieth century. Curle identified four elements to his mediation process: first, the mediator acts to build, maintain and improve communications; second, to provide information to and between the conflict parties; third, to 'befriend' the conflict parties; and, fourth, to encourage what he refers to as active mediation – that is to say, to cultivate a willingness to engage in cooperative negotiation. His philosophy of mediation is essentially a blend of values and experiences from Quaker practice[4] with the knowledge of humanistic psychology absorbed in his early professional career, both of these influences tempered and modified by his experiences in the field (Reading 49).

Curle's work is an illustration both of the applied nature of conflict resolution and its stress on the crucial link between academic theory and practice. It also provides one example of an approach to Track II or citizens diplomacy (what Diamond and MacDonald (1996) call multitrack diplomacy because they include business contacts, the churches, etc.), and a number of studies have contributed to a fuller understanding of the methods and approaches of mediation and third-party intervention in conflicts at both official-governmental and unofficial-citizens' diplomacy level activity (Berman and Johnson, 1977; MacDonald and Bendahmane, 1987; Berridge, 1995; Aall, 1996; Anderson, 1996b; Davies and Kaufman, 2002). What was loosely called 'unofficial diplomacy' continued to develop in attempts to bridge the East–West divide across the iron curtain, which bore fruit through the inclusion of parliamentary level institutions, as well as government-to-government relations, in the 1975 NATO/Warsaw Pact Conference on Security and Cooperation in Europe (CSCE). This eventually evolved into the 1995 Organization for Security and Cooperation in Europe (OSCE) involving fifty-seven participating states, some of whose work is illustrated in chapter 5. A similar impulse has led to the evolution of what is now called 'national dialogue' at state level (see chapter 10) and the 'dialogue of civilizations' at international level (see chapter 15).

Curle himself continued to evolve his thinking and practice, which did not stay fixed at the point of Track II mediation. During the wars in former Yugoslavia, for example, he broadened his concept and practice of peacemaking to include the empowerment of individuals and civil society groups in a wide variety of roles and developed, along with John Paul Lederach and others, new approaches to peacebuilding from below, based primarily on his work with and support for the Osijek Centre for Peace, Nonviolence and Human Rights, which we examine more fully in chapter 9 (Curle, 1994, 1995, 1999).

Elise Boulding: new voices in conflict resolution

During the 1970s and 1980s the number of peace researchers and conflict resolution specialists worldwide continued to grow, from a few hundred to perhaps thousands, and the institutional bases for conflict resolution expanded accordingly, mainly in Western Europe, North America and Japan, but also increasingly in other parts of the world. Notable centres were established in areas of protracted conflict, such as South Africa, Northern Ireland, the Spanish Basque country and Sri Lanka. In this section we have taken the work of Elise Boulding as exemplary of this process of expansion and of the development of thinking that has accompanied it.

Elise Boulding trained as a sociologist and was involved in the early work of the Michigan Center outlined above, serving as secretary-general of the International Peace Research Association (IPRA) from 1964 and chair of the Women's International League for Peace and Freedom, of which she was subsequently international chair. With the help of UNESCO, the *IPRA Newsletter*, started by Boulding, developed the network, which facilitated the formulation of the association, and she continued to serve as its editor for a number of years. In order to encourage wider participation in peace and conflict resolution processes, she introduced the idea of 'imaging the future' as a powerful way of enabling people to break out of the defensive private shells into which they retreated, often out of fear of what was happening in the public world, and encouraging them to participate in the construction of a peaceful and tolerant global culture. The use of social imagination and the idea of imaging the future was placed within the context of what she called the '200-year present' – that is, the idea that we must understand that we live in a social space which reaches into the past and into the future: 'it is our space, one that we can move around directly in our own lives and indirectly by touching the lives of the young and old around us' (Reading 12; Boulding, 1990: 4). She was also an early exponent of the idea of civil society, of opening up new possibilities for a global civic culture which was receptive to the voices of people who were not part of the traditional discourses of nation-state politics, and in this she anticipated many of the preoccupations of conflict resolution workers today. Women and children were obviously excluded groups, but she added to these the idea that globalism and global civic culture needed to accommodate the many culture communities which were not heard in the existing international order. For Elise Boulding, the next half of our '200-year present' – that is, the next one hundred years from the 1980s – contains within it the basis for a world civic culture and peaceful problem-solving among nations, but also for the possibility of Armageddon. She saw the development of indigenous and international citizens' networks as one way of ensuring that the former prevailed. For her, peacemaking demands specific 'craft and skills', a peace praxis encompassing 'all those activities in which conflict is dealt with in an integrative mode – as choices that lie at the heart of all human interaction' (ibid.: 140). In the intersubjective relationships which make up social and political life, as also in the structures and institutions within which they are embedded, the success with which this is inculcated and encouraged will determine whether, in the end, we are peacemakers or warmakers.

Reconstruction: The Fourth Generation, 1985–2005

During this period the Cold War came to an end, and, as noted in chapter 1, conflict resolution found itself both more central to attempts to redefine a 'new world order' and, at the same time, confronted by the new challenges that followed from the passing of the old order. The summary given in chapter 1 of the background to the three previous editions of this book provides a framework for evaluating success and failure during this period (pp. 3–4).

In a single paragraph outline we would note the increasingly sophisticated efforts of those working in the conflict resolution field during this period to combine the range of approaches in response to new challenges through application of the principles of 'contingency' (the nature of the challenge) and 'complementarity' (the appropriate interconnection of responses) as initiated by Ronald Fisher and Loraleigh Keashly (1991; Reading 62). The argument was that softer forms of intervention are more appropriate when miscommunication and mistrust is high (when the subjective elements are strong), whereas harder forms of intervention are more successful when substantive interests are at the forefront. This involved a clearer and more nuanced understanding of how different interlocking instruments now combine to contain, settle and, where possible, transform conflict at different levels (intergroup, interstate, regional and global), in different sectors (psychological, social, economic, political), using different approaches (prevention, peacemaking, peacekeeping, peacebuilding), in different historico-cultural settings, and at different stages of conflict escalation and de-escalation. The conflict resolution field shares with others a particular concern with what can be done to counter the drivers of destructive conflict and their worst consequences in the poorest societies and most 'fragile' countries. Greater awareness of 'realist' and 'critical' critiques, as also of gender and culture critiques, was recognized and responded to. More professional quantitative and qualitative methodologies for conflict analysis and interpretation were developed, including those for measuring 'emergent conflict and peaceful change', as Hugh Miall (2007) puts it. And criteria for evaluating outcomes and ways of measuring them were improved. As a result of all this, the emphasis in methodology was on what Daniel Druckman describes as 'doing conflict resolution through a multi-method lens' (2009), as echoed in the call to integrate 'multiple paths to knowledge' in conflict management and conflict resolution (Stoll, 2004; Maoz et al., 2004). This reflected the early emphasis in the field on multidisciplinarity but now extended it to newer fields, such as the development of computer-aided methods in international conflict resolution (Trappl, 2006).

The explosion of interest in conflict resolution worldwide during this period also led to a remarkable increase in NGO activity (Ahmed and Potter, 2006). Despite setbacks in some areas, as noted below, this included NGOs which, in the judgement of Andrea Bartoli (2009), had the requisite reputation, trust (confidentiality), legitimacy in the eyes of state actors, and capacity to become successfully involved directly in major 'Track I' peace processes – such as the Community of Sant'Egidio in Mozambique, the Carter Center in Venezuela, the Center for Humanitarian Dialogue in brokering humanitarian ceasefires in Darfur, the Crisis Management Initiative in Aceh, and Sustained Dialogue in Tajikistan. Beyond this, recognition was given to the 'thousands of other global NGOs engaged in excellent work, particularly at the societal level' (Bartoli mentions Search for Common Ground, International Alert, the West African Network for Peacebuilding, the African Centre for the Constructive Resolution of Disputes, the Partnership for the Prevention of Armed Conflict, the European Centre for Conflict Prevention, and the bridging work of the International Crisis Group).

In the third edition of this book we chose four aspects of the post-Cold War conflict scene for special emphasis as cutting-edge issues with which the fourth generation of 'reconstructors' had to grapple – *systemic complexity, asymmetry, cultural diversity* and *intractability*. In each case we illustrated mainly with reference to the communicative and dialogic aspect of conflict resolution (Bohm, 1996; Yankelovich, 1999; Saunders, 2009) (see Box 2.1).

Conflict complexity

The founders of the conflict resolution field were well aware that they were dealing with complex conflict systems. This largely determined the nature

Box 2.1 Dialogue versus debate: a version of David Bohm's analysis

- Dialogue is collaborative: two or more sides work together towards common understanding. Debate is oppositional: two sides oppose each other and attempt to prove each other wrong.
- In dialogue finding common ground is the goal. In debate winning is the goal.
- In dialogue one listens to the other side in order to understand, find meaning, and find agreement. In debate one listens to the other side in order to find flaws and to counter its arguments.
- Dialogue enlarges and possibly changes a participant's point of view. Debate affirms a participant's own point of view.
- Dialogue reveals assumptions for re-evaluation. Debate defends assumptions as truth.
- Dialogue causes introspection into one's own position. Debate causes critique of the other's position.
- Dialogue opens the possibility of reaching a better solution than any of the original solutions. Debate defends one's own positions as the best solution and excludes other solutions.
- Dialogue creates an open-minded attitude – an openness to being wrong and an openness to change. Debate creates a closed-minded attitude, a determination to be right.
- Dialogue calls for temporarily suspending one's beliefs and assumptions. Debate calls for investing wholeheartedly in one's beliefs.
- In dialogue one searches for basic agreements. In debate one searches for differences.
- Dialogue involves a real concern for the other person/s and seeks neither to alienate nor to offend. Debate involves a countering of the other position without focusing on feelings or relationship and often belittles or deprecates the other person.
- Dialogue assumes that many people have pieces of the answer and that together they can put them into a workable solution. Debate assumes that there is a right answer and that someone has it.

Source: developed from Bohm, 1996, by Frank Boulton

of the new study area in comparison, for example, with international relations at the time. But in the post-Cold War world the question of systemic complexity has become even more prominent as a variety of 'new wars' proliferated within a rapidly globalizing world. In his book *Solving Tough Problems* (2007), Adam Kahane identifies three types of complexity, each of which requires a different remedy. Dynamic complexity refers to the fact that links between cause and effect are non-linear and are individually unpredictable. This requires a systemic approach. Social complexity refers to the fact that there are conflicting views about the problem. This requires a participative approach. Generative complexity refers to the fact that former solutions are no longer succeeding. This requires a creative approach.

The analysis of contemporary conflicts as complex systems has recently been greatly enriched by an influx of methodologies from different disciplines, driven particularly by the work of aid and development workers anxious at least to 'do no harm' and at best to 'do some good' (Hendrick, 2009). Peter Coleman has been prominent in the conflict resolution field for his development and application of systemic conflict analysis (Coleman, 2003; Coleman et al., 2005). We will look further at this work at the end of chapter 4.

A complex adaptive system is defined as a group of interrelated elements that exhibit non-linear relations. The more elements and interrelations, the higher the level of complexity in the system. In particular, six features are seen to drive change within a complex system (Moty Cristal, director of NEST Consulting, and Orit Gal, director of the Complexity Hub, unpublished workshop presentation for the Israeli Strategic Forum, Haifa, 2010):

- connectivity and interdependence of elements;
- emergence and self-organization – the system comes out of the accumulated choices of all the individuals operating within it;
- chaos – in the technical sense that simple known changes can produce very different and therefore uncertain results;
- systemic memory and path dependency – today's dynamics are channelled by yesterday's constructions;
- feedback effects – negative feedback dampens or stabilizes the system, while positive fedback amplifies the system;
- evolution and adaptation – the system as a whole responds to a continually changing environment.

These characteristics are exemplified in the case study of the Arab revolutions in chapter 4.

In terms of response, Norbert Ropers at the Berghof Research Center for Constructive Conflict has taken a lead in developing the concept of 'systemic conflict transformation' (Reading 28; Körppen et al., 2008). Rather than solving a problem, in linear style, as in traditional strategic thinking, the aim is to understand a complex ecology and to learn how to operate successfully within it (for an example of a complex systems model, together with explanation of symbols, see Reading 28).

In the communicative sphere, Ropers applies the Buddhist 'tetralemma' ('tetra' is the Greek for 'four') to the linguistic dimension of the Sinhala/Tamil conflict in Sri Lanka by juxtaposing the two 'either–or' mental models of the main antagonists with the 'both–and' and 'neither–nor' alternatives (there is also the fifth possibility: 'none of these'): the tetralemma is 'a tool that has the potential of overcoming the binary logic of these two sets of attitudes and fears' (Ropers, 2008a: 17). This is reminiscent of the contrast between the *win–lose* axis and the *lose–lose/win–win* axis in figure 1.6 in chapter 1 (p. 21). This also features prominently in Johan Galtung's TRANSCEND methodology (Galtung and Jacobsen, 2000). The aim of TRANSCEND is to shift the conflict formation from the former towards the latter.[5]

John-Paul Lederach is also severely critical of reductive either–or frames of reference. He is strongly in favour of acknowledging the complex webs of interactions that make up the real (lived) world and of nurturing what he calls 'the moral imagination' in learning how to navigate and transform them (2005: 172–3):

When we embrace dilemmas and paradoxes, there is the possibility that in conflict we are not dealing with outright incompatibilities. Rather, we are faced with recognizing and responding to different but interdependent aspects of a complex situation. We are not able to handle complexity well if we understand our choices in rigid either/or or contradictory terms. Complexity requires that we develop the capacity to identify the key energies in a situation and hold them up together as *interdependent goals* ... The capacity to live with apparent contradictions and paradoxes lies at the heart of conflict transformation. (Lederach, 2003: 51–3)

Conflict asymmetry

It is in struggling with asymmetric conflicts that some of the most significant advances were made in this period in the communicative sphere. Asymmetric conflicts are those in which conflict parties are unequal in power, either quantitatively (e.g. strong vs. weak states) or qualitatively (e.g. state vs. non-state actors) or both. In these circumstances critics have seen traditional negotiation/mediation, dialogue, and problem-solving approaches as inadequate, if not counter-productive, insofar as they assume equivalence between the conflict parties (Kuttab, 1988; Rouhana and Korper, 1996; Jones, 1999). The result is seen to be to reinforce the relative power of the hegemon:

There is still a military occupation, people are still being killed, imprisoned and denied their rights on a daily basis. The main prerogatives for us Arabs and Palestinians are therefore clear. One: we must struggle to end the occupation. Two: we must struggle even harder to develop our own independent institutions and organizations until we are on a relatively equal footing with the Israelis. Then we can begin to talk seriously about cooperation. In the meantime cooperation can all too easily shade into collaboration with Israeli policy. (Said, 1995: 37)

In these circumstances some in the conflict resolution field, influenced by theorists such as Andrew Linklater (1998), have turned to critical theory in general, and to Jürgen Habermas's discourse ethics in particular, for a transformative approach capable of addressing asymmetry (Hoffman, 1987; Rothman, 1992: 72–3). The result has been the development of *discursive conflict transformation*, which begins from the premise that actions and institutional arrangements can be said to be legitimate only when they result from a process of unconstrained discourse in which all affected parties participate freely. For Habermas, communicative action of this kind appeals to the theory of argumentation itself – the very process of making and redeeming validity claims – to ground its methodology. It is the formal-pragmatic nature of argumentation that dictates why this must be communication free from coercion. Otherwise it is not argument, but merely strategic manipulation or resort to force. The 'ideal speech situation' is defined as such through the very nature of what is thereby appealed to (see Habermas, 1984). This is well exemplified in the work of Vivienne Jabri (1996), who uses Habermas's work to offer a critique of 'discourses of violence' and to construct a theoretical grounding for 'discourses of peace' on this basis. We return to this theme in chapter 19.

Cultural diversity

In this period, controversy about 'religious wars', 'global *jihad*', the 'global war on terror', and so on, have fed controversy about a 'clash of civilizations' (Huntington, 1996) and have stimulated efforts to dispel, expose or overcome it.

An idea of the wide spectrum of dialogic techniques for handling conflict and effecting non-violent social change in conflict resolution can be found in the Pioneers of Change Associates 2006 survey *Mapping Dialogue* (Bojer et al., 2006) (the survey covers approaches such as Appreciative Inquiry, Change Lab, Deep Democracy, Future Search, Open Space, Scenario Planning, Sustained Dialogue, World Café, Bohmian Dialogue, Learning Journeys, etc.). See also the two-volume *Theories of Dialogue* (Sleap and Sener, 2013, 2015) published by the Dialogue Society. In response to the specific challenge of managing conflicts between and across cultural and religious divides, many in the conflict resolution field have been influenced by the philosophy of Hans-Georg Gadamer and its application to intercultural dialogue (Malpas et al., 2002; Ramsbotham, 2015). The Gadamerian approach ultimately sees dialogue as a 'fusion of horizons' across cultural and historical differences. It is called 'hermeneutic dialogue' because it draws a parallel between a conversation and the interpretation of texts. For Gadamer, interpreting an initially unfamiliar text is seen as a form of *conversation* between object and interpreter. In conflict resolution it works the other way. A dialogue or conversation is seen as a mutual *interpretation of texts*. This means a move away from the idea of dialogue as mutual sympathy (getting into each other's shoes: Rogers, 1980: 142) and towards the idea of 'relational empathy', in which a more dynamic and productive process is envisaged whereby, in intense interpersonal exchange that is as much affective as cognitive, participants together generate shared new meaning, sometimes referred to as a 'third culture' (Broome, 1993). This approach reflects Gadamer's insistence in *Truth and Method* that, in the field of interpretation, it is 'a hermeneutical necessity always to go beyond mere reconstruction' in reaching understanding:

> This placing of ourselves is not the empathy of one individual for another, nor is it the application to another person of our own criteria, but it always involves the attainment of a higher universality that overcomes, not only our own particularity, but also that of the other. (Gadamer, [1960] 1975: 272)

These 'dialogic attitudes' are seen as integral to the conflict resolution enterprise by Benjamin Broome:

> The third culture can only develop through interaction in which participants are willing to open themselves to new meanings, to engage in genuine dialogue, and to constantly respond to the new demands emanating from the situation. The emergence of this third culture is the essence of relational empathy and is essential for successful conflict resolution. (Broome, 1993: 104)

Heavy demands are thereby made on participants, who are expected to be able to recognize that they can never escape the universal reach of their own prejudice and that the attempted 'fusion of horizons' or relational empathy will always be the creation of something that did not exist before (a third culture) and an ongoing project, never a completed programme. They are asked to 'decentre' their own identities to the point where – in the words of Stewart and Thomas – instead of seeking 'certainty, closure and control', they welcome the tension between 'irreconcileable horizons' and adopt a 'playfulness' and open-mindedness appropriate to encounter with new experience or the ultimately unabsorbable 'other' (Stewart and Thomas, 2006: 198). This is looked at further in chapter 15.

Conflict intractability

Finally in the communicative sphere, there is the issue of intractability itself. Intractable conflicts are those that continue to defy all efforts at settlement and transformation – often for years (Kriesberg et al., 1989; Crocker et al., 2005). Confronted with the failure of traditional conflict resolution efforts, Guy and Heidi Burgess developed their 'constructive confrontation' methodology (1996, 1997). Their website 'Beyond Intractability: A Free Knowledge Base on More Constructive Approaches to Destructive Conflict' is an excellent resource for deeper understanding of intractability and what can be done about it (www.beyondintractability.org). Bernard Mayer (2009) advises that, in stubborn and enduring conflicts, what is needed is to 'stay with the conflict' – he distinguishes continuing 'conflict engagement' from both conflict resolution and conflict transformation. Peter Coleman's 'Intractable Conflict Lab' studies the 'invisible dynamics' of those conflicts that do not end in settlement and reconciliation or tolerable standoff, but persist in lasting antagonism. Drawing on work done by the International Project on Conflict and Complexity,[6] Coleman's book *The Five Percent* (2011) looks at ways of responding to this (this is discussed further in chapter 4). Faced with intractable conflict such as that between the Israelis and Palestinians in the aftermath of the failure of the 'Oslo process', Oliver Ramsbotham (2010; forthcoming, 2017) traces the roots of what he calls 'linguistic intractability' to the phenomenon of 'radical disagreement'. He suggests that, in these circumstances, what is wanted is not less radical disagreement, as conflict resolution seeks, but more. When negotiation, problem-solving and dialogue do not yet work, promote a 'strategic engagement of discourses' within, across and between conflict parties, including third parties (Ramsbotham, forthcoming, 2017) (this is developed further in chapter 18). Christopher Mitchell (2014) brings the overall study of conflict intractability up to date, and this can serve as a platform for the anaysis of current challenges offered in succeeding chapters.

Conclusion

In this chapter we have noted the diverse nature of the conflict resolution tradition, rooted in different disciplines and encompassing the 'subjectivist' controlled communication and problem-solving approach, the 'objectivist' rational negotiation/mediation approach, and the 'structuralist' social justice approach. We have tentatively suggested that these correspond to attempts to address the 'attitude', 'behaviour' and 'contradiction' vertices of the conflict triangle. Nevertheless, despite this diversity, quite a simple central commitment prevails. Having grown in a number of centres through the pioneering work of a small group of individuals, the enterprise of conflict resolution is now conducted across an international network where scholars and practitioners from many countries share in the common objective of formulating, applying and testing structures and practices for preventing, managing, ending and transforming violent and destructive conflict. Conflict resolution does not prescribe specific solutions or end goals for society, beyond a commitment to the core assumption – challenged by many realists such as Christopher Coker (2014) – that aggressive win–lose styles of engagement in violent conflict usually incur costs that are unacceptably high not only for the conflict parties but also for world society in general. This does not mean endorsing the status quo, since unjust and oppressive systems are seen as some of the chief sources of violence and war. Nor does it mean imposing conflict resolution categories on others. Conflict resolution learns here from critical and post-structural approaches. What it does entail, as the previous chapter suggests, is a search for ways of transforming actually or potentially violent conflict into peaceful processes of political and social change.

We have now carried the story through to what might be said to be the end of the work of the immediate post-Cold War generation. In our view, for reasons given at the beginning of chapter 1, a new phase of challenges is now emerging as the shift of power away from the United States – in terms both of the capacity to control events and the will to intervene – opens the way for a more diversified and complex mix of regional, state, sub-state and trans-state actors to play a sigificant role on the world scene (Schweller, 2014). This comes at a time of intensifying economic, political and ideological change, which spawns new forms of conflict and violence but also new opportunities to strengthen international capacities for engaging and managing change non-violently. The next two chapters examine the nature and sources of contemporary conflict. This will serve as an analytic foundation for the chapters that follow, and especially for chapter 11, where the cosmopolitan conflict resolution response to transnational conflict is more fully defined.

Recommended reading

Avruch (2012); Avruch and Mitchell (2013); Dunn (1995); Kriesberg (1997, 2009); Lawler (1995); Mitchell (2014); Ramsbotham (2010, ch. 3); Sleap and Sener (2013, 2015); Väyrynen (1991); Wallensteen (2011a).

Videos

Parents of the Field Project: video recordings of the recollections and views of some of the individual scholars and practitioners who initiated the field of conflict analysis and peace research in the 1950s and 1960s, conducted by Christopher Mitchell and Johannes Botes, School for Conflict Analysis and Resolution, George Mason University, at http://scar.gmu.edu/parents.

Relevant extracts in *The Contemporary Conflict Resolution Reader*

Reading 2: P. Q. Wright, A General Discipline of International Relations
Reading 3: L. F. Richardson, The Mathematical Psychology of War
Reading 4: K. Boulding, Conflict and Defense: A General Theory
Reading 5: J. Burton, Conflict and Communication
Reading 10: L. Coser, The Functions of Social Conflict
Reading 11: T. Schelling, The Strategy of Conflict
Reading 12: E. Boulding, Building a Global Civic Culture
Reading 13: M. Deutsch, A Brief History of Social Psychological Theorizing about Conflict
Reading 14: C. Mitchell, The Structure of International Conflict
Reading 28: N. Ropers, Systemic Conflict Transformation: Reflection on the Conflict and Peace Process in Sri Lanka
Reading 34: G. Sharp, From Dictatorship to Democracy
Reading 38: M. Gandhi, Nonviolence in Peace and War
Reading 40: A. Curle, Making Peace
Reading 41: S. Touval and I. W. Zartman, International Mediation in Theory and Practice
Reading 49: A. Curle, Peacemaking: Private and Public
Reading 50: A. Curle, In the Middle
Reading 62: R. Fisher and L. Keashly, The Potential Complementarity of Mediation and Consultation within a Contingency Model of Third-Party Intervention

CHAPTER THREE

The Statistics of Deadly Quarrels and the Measurement of Peace

From the beginning the study of conflict resolution has been seen to depend upon prior analysis of conflict data. We have noted how this was clear in the original 1957 issue of the *Journal of Conflict Resolution*, where both Boulding and Wright proposed global conflict data stations to alert the international community to the early onset of situations likely to erupt into full-scale violence. In this chapter we will familiarize ourselves with the 'statistics of deadly quarrels', to borrow the title of Richardson's posthumously published seminal study (1960b) that did so much to excite the interest of the early conflict resolvers. This will serve as the basis for the conflict analysis chapter that follows.

Since the first edition of this book, the nature and scope of statistical analysis has developed dramatically in response to the transformed nature of armed conflict and violence after the end of the Cold War, new methods and sources of data, and the greater capacities opened up by the communications revolution. At the beginning of chapter 1 we noted the 'lethal mix of rapidly mutating conflicts', associated with ideological fervour, international criminal networks and arms availability, pouring into the increasingly extensive areas in which there is a 'vacuum of authority', where the fertile ground of complicated patterns of locally contested politics gives it 'ample opportunity to lodge and spread'. We suggested that, in reply, the efforts of contemporary cosmopolitan conflict resolution need to tackle the new reality of what we call *transnational conflict* (see chapter 4). Following these new patterns of conflict requires new sources of data and renewed efforts to analyse their causes and correlates. In response, analytic tools and datasets have proliferated, encompassing an ever wider range of phenomena related to war, peace, violence and conflict, and innovations have been made in exploiting the new opportunities offered by the internet and modern technology (see chapter 17). In our view, none of this invalidates earlier approaches to quantitative analysis in the conflict resolution field. On the contrary, it rather serves to confirm the prescience of founders such as Pitirim Sorokin and Lewis Fry Richardson, who did not confine their datasets to wars and civil wars, and of those who from the beginning insisted that statistics for direct violence and 'negative peace' must be complemented by an understanding of structural and cultural violence and 'positive peace'. From the outset, as seen in chapter 1, the new conflict resolution field embraced the idea that the study of human conflict had to be multi-level, multidisciplinary, and multicultural.

In the first section of this chapter on the 'conflict domain', we offer a schematic framework to illustrate how different datasets and approaches to statistical conflict analysis are now coming together to provide an increasingly comprehensive record of contemporary peace and conflict. The rest of the chapter then uses this framework to assess current trends.

The Conflict Domain

What are to count as the relevant conflicts? Conflict resolution analysts have traditionally included all levels of conflict, from intrapersonal conflict through to international conflict, and all stages of conflict escalation and de-escalation. At the very beginning of the conflict resolution enterprise, Richardson included both international and domestic conflicts in his dataset of 'deadly quarrels' between 1820 and 1949. By 'deadly quarrel' he meant 'any quarrel which caused death to humans. The term thus includes murders, banditries, mutinies, insurrections, and wars small and large' (1960b). Sorokin included revolutions as well as wars in his study (1937).

In a partial return to this tradition, since the end of the Cold War the relatively simple databases on major armed conflict available at that time have been expanded and elaborated. The result is a bewildering array of overlapping, rapidly proliferating and changing statistical analyses. For example, some ten years ago Kristin Eck identified and commented on sixty major databases (Eck, 2005): the field has further proliferated and diversified since then. In an attempt to clarify this, figure 3.1 offers a schematic framework for understanding the broadening scope of conflict datasets. We hope both that this will help readers see the relationship between the new 'coming together' of datasets and the analysis of negative peace and positive peace given in chapter 1 and that the six 'further tasks from a conflict resolution perspective' listed will give an idea of what we see as some of the cutting-edge issues for the future.

Classic quantitative conflict analysis on *direct violence and war* (for example, the Uppsala Conflict Data Program, which also includes 'one-sided' violence against civilians) is now enriched by data on *terrorism*, on the one hand (for example, the Global Terrorism Index (IEP, 2014c)), and *organized crime*, on the other (for example, the *Global Burden of Armed Violence* report (Krause et al., 2011)).

Moreover, this data is now better calibrated than before in terms of time and space. Episodes of conflict have been precisely dated and no longer have to be aggregated over a calendar year. In addition, progress is under way in providing geo-referenced coordinates for the location of armed violence,[1] so that conflicts can also be analysed in the context of local geography and do not have to be aggregated at the country level (Gleditsch et al., 2013). At an even more fine-grained level, efforts are under way to collect micro-level and household-level data, which has played an important part in the interpretation of the role of violence in civil wars (Kalyvas, 2006). Better data is thus becoming available, from the global to the individual level.

From a conflict resolution perspective, the focus cannot be restricted to armed conflicts alone. We need to understand developments from the formation of a conflict to the dissolution of the conflict formation (see chapter 1). For this purpose, qualitative and quantitative data is increasingly available covering the content, issues and course of political conflicts, including crises, and periods of escalation and de-escalation (for example, the Heidelberg Institute for International Conflict Research (HIIK) *Conflict Barometer* (Hachemer, 2014), the Militarized International Disputes (MID) dataset (Palmer et al., 2015), the International Crisis Behavior database (Brecher and Wilkenfeld, 2010), and qualitative databases on conflict such as the UCDP Conflict Encyclopedia (Uppsala Conflict Data Program, 2015).

A significant new development has been the appearance of datasets about non-violence, which have offered new insights into the widespread nature and significance of non-violent strategies, particularly in challenging governments (Chenoweth and Stephan, 2011).

There is more data about the periods before and after violent conflicts. For example, the degree to which fragile states are at risk of violent conflict is assessed via attempts to quantify *fragility* (see the *Fragile States* report (OECD, 2014)). Similarly, the degree to which minorities are at risk of violence is measured in the *Minorities at Risk* dataset – now extended to include additional socially relevant minority groups and the organizational strategies of minorities (see Birnir et al., 2015). Another important new dataset captures the degree to which political groups are excluded from power, which affects the risk of violent conflict (the *Ethnic Power Relations* dataset, described by Cederman et al., 2010).

There are also new efforts to measure peace as well as violence. For example, the *Global Peace Index Report* (IEP, 2014b) and the *International Peace Institute Report* (2014; see www.ipinst.org) attempt to measure *peacefulness*.

The proliferation of datasets in figure 3.1 makes it possible to merge a variety of data to undertake new analyses. The 2011 *Global Burden of Armed Violence* (GBAV) report offers a persuasive rationale for attempting to mine data from more than one dataset:

> Conventional analyses often compartmentalize armed violence into distinct categories according to a particular context or underlying intentions of the perpetrator. The two most common distinctions are drawn between *organized* (collective) and *interpersonal* (individual) violence, and between *conflict* (politically motivated) and *criminal* (economically motivated) violence ... Governments, multilateral agencies, non-governmental organizations, and research institutes around the world use them to assess overall levels of violence or to plan violence reduction programmes and policies. Yet these distinctions give the misleading impression that different forms and incidents of violence fit into neat

Current attempts to integrate datasets into a comprehensive analytic framework:	
(A) Measuring conflict and conflict resolution	Databases of political conflicts Data on mediation attempts
(B) Measuring direct violence and negative peace	Political violence data (riot, atrocity, war) Terrorism data Organized criminal violence data (homicides) Fragile states
(C) Measuring structural and cultural violence and positive peace	Fragile states and cities Sustainable peace data

Parallel tasks that still need further development:	
(i)	Integrating fuller data on conflicts that are not violent and on early and unofficial mediation attempts in connection with (A).
(ii)	Integrating data on, for example, small and light weapon (SALW) flows in connection with (B).
(iii)	Integrating further data to provide indicators on positive peace in connection with (C).
(iv)	Integrating micro-level data from within conflict localities and developing more systematic methodologies for integrating qualitative data in general.
(v)	Integrating data on conflict escalation/de-escalation (paths to and from violence) that incorporate levels of political contention below the threshold of overt violence (see chapters 4 and 5), both for societies in general and for government/armed resistance interaction.
(vi)	Integrating data on correlations between levels of violence and conflict resolution interventions, such as peacemaking and peacekeeping efforts in response to aspects of (B) (see chapters 6 and 7) and longer-term peacebuilding efforts in response to (C) (see chapters 5 and 8–9). Attempts can then be made to compare these with the measurable effects of other alternatives: for example, doing nothing, forcible intervention, other kinds of intervention (economic, legal), indigenous non-violent direct action, etc.

Figure 3.1a *The proliferation of datasets: towards a comprehensive framework*

and separate categories ... These recurring characteristics – the multiple, simultaneous, and shifting motivations of violent actors, and the links between the different forms of violence – demand more than simple analytical classifications and policy responses. They require new ways of understanding the relationships between what were previously held to be distinct forms of armed violence. (Krause et al., 2011: 4)

The ultimate aim of the GBAV effort, and the Geneva Declaration enterprise from which it came,[2] is to expose the intimate links between 'the global scourge of armed violence and the prospects for sustainable development'. This is seen as a core syndrome that needs to be understood and then tackled in an integrated way by individual states supported by the international community. It has from the start also been a central aim in the conflict resolution

Type of events	Examples of datasets	Dataset description	Sources
CONFLICT AND CONFLICT RESOLUTION			
Disputes, incompatibilities			
International disputes	ICB	International Crisis Behaviour	Brecher and Wilkenfeld (1997)
	COPDAB	Conflict and Peace Data Bank (events data)	Azar (1980)
Intrastate disputes	KOSIMO	Heidelberg Conflict Barometer	Pfetsch and Rohloff (2000)
	MAR	Minorities at Risk	Gurr (1993)
	UCDP	Conflict Encyclopedia	UCDP Conflict Encyclopedia: www.ucdp.uu.se/database
Conflict management			
Conflict prevention	ECPEC	Early Conflict Prevention in Ethnic Crises	Öberg et al. (2009)
Mediation	ICM	International Conflict Mediation	Bercovitch and Jackson (1997)
	CWM	Civil War Mediation	DeRouen et al. (2011)
	MILC	Managing Intrastate Low Intensity Conflict	Melander et al. (2009)
Third-party intervention	TPI	Third-Party intervention in Militarized Interstate Disputes	Frazier and Dixon (2006)
	DI	Diplomatic Interventions	Regan et al. (2009)
Peacekeeping	UNPKO	United Nations peacekeeping personnel commitments	Kathman (2013)
Nonviolence	NAVCO 2.0	Nonviolent and Violent Campaigns	Chenoweth and Stephan (2011)
DIRECT VIOLENCE AND NEGATIVE PEACE			
Direct violence			
Interstate wars	COW	Correlates of War	Singer and Small (1972)
Militarized interstate disputes	MIDS	Militarized Interstate Disputes	Palmer et al. (2015)
Armed conflicts	UCDP-PRIO	Armed Conflicts	Gleditsch and Wallensteen (2001)

Figure 3.1b *The proliferation of datasets: specific examples*

	GED	UCDP Geo-Referenced Events Dataset	www.ucdp.uu.se/ged/
State violence	UCDP	One-Sided Conflict Dataset	UCDP
Non-state violence	UCDP	Non-State Violence	UCDP
Political violence	ACLED	Armed Conflict Locations Events	www.acleddata.com/
	SCAD	Social Conflict in Africa	Salehyan et al. (2012)
Terrorism	GTD	Global Terrorism Database	National Consortium for the Study of Terrorism and Responses to Terrorism, www.start. umd.edu/gtd
Organized criminal violence	GBAV	Global Burden of Armed Violence	Krause et al. (2011)
Negative peace			
Fragile states	Fragile States	Index of State Fragility	OECD (2014)
Peace years	UCDP	Derived from Armed Conflicts data	UCDP
Peace agreements	UCDP	UCDP Peace Agreements Dataset	UCDP
STRUCTURAL AND CULTURAL VIOLENCE AND POSITIVE PEACE			
Structural and cultural violence			
Horizontal inequalities	HI	Geo-referenced horizontal inequalities	Cederman et al. (2013)
Political exclusion	ETH-EPR	Ethnic Power Relations	Cederman et al. (2009)
Positive peace			
Transitional justice	UCDP	Civil War and Transitional Justice	Lie et al. (2007)
Cooperation	GDELT	Global geo-referenced events data	Leetaru and Schrodt (2013)
Quality peace	QP	Based on Peace Accords Matrix	Wallensteen (2013)
Sustainable peace	GPI	Global Peace Index	IEP (2014b)

Figure 3.1b *(continued)*

field. For example, armed violence is seen to be 'a major obstacle to the achievement of the Millennial Development Goals'. Conversely, development in its widest sense is seen to be essential for reducing the prevalence of armed conflict: 'the Geneva Declaration on Armed Violence and Development is a diplomatic initiative aimed at addressing the interrelations between armed conflict and development' (see chapter 4, where this interrelationship can be seen to lie at the heart of Edward Azar's analysis of protracted social conflict).

Before moving on to analyse the contents of these datasets, readers may like to look at the 'challenges of gathering and analysing conflict data' summarized in box 3.1. This will give an idea of the scale of the task now being undertaken.

It is clear from box 3.1 that the information contained in these datasets, while scrupulously collected and checked, is not the product of an exact science. Armed conflicts and their impact are notoriously difficult to measure, and all datasets are contested in one way or another. The thresholds for inclusion (twenty-five battle-related deaths, or 500 battle-related deaths, or

Box 3.1 Challenges of gathering and analysing conflict data

- *Data collection* Collecting data in the midst of armed conflict is a difficult and dangerous task. Researchers are usually reliant on reports in the media, which originate from journalists and, sometimes, from governments and conflict parties. In practice, careful assessments have to be made of multiple sources, including media reports, estimates by scholars, military historians, demographers and country experts, and digests of international news such as Keesing's World News Archive (www.keesings. com). There is usually a wide range between low and high estimates. Distinctions between categories, such as battlefield deaths and civilian deaths, are more easily made by the researcher than by the data gatherer on the ground. Best estimates are based on judgements.
- *Data coding stipulations* Data is usually gathered in a qualitative form at first and then coded (sometimes by junior researchers) according to a scheme prepared by the senior lead researcher. Different ways of coding data impose restrictions on what evidence is counted under different categories, and thus introduce issues of judgement into the foundations of the methodology. Crucial judgements are taken by coders, following coding rules, but such judgements are not always transparent to those who ultimately use the data. This can affect attempts to distinguish conflict 'types' (for example, violence in Mexico is included under conflict data in some datasets but under crime data in others).
- *Quantitative vs. qualitative data* Both quantitative and qualitative information are required to answer different types of questions, but there is always debate about which is appropriate in particular circumstances and how to weigh the claims of studies based on different methodologies. Quantitative scholars develop increasingly sophisticated statistical analyses which many qualitatively trained scholars cannot follow. Qualitative analysts argue that statistical approaches 'reduce the complexity of the social world to what can be measured, thus ignoring the wider body of factors driving human behaviour, such as ideas, meanings, beliefs and reasons' (Clayton, 2014, citing Kurki and Wight, 2007). In our view, Paul Collier and Nicholas Sambanis are right to say that 'quantitative and qualitative research designs are often (mistakenly) considered as substitutes rather than complements in political science' (2003, vol. I: 2). But the challenge is to learn how to integrate them – a challenge that in our opinion is only now beginning to be undertaken in a systematic way.

- *Varying metrics* When attempts are made to 'merge' datasets, a problem arises when different conceptual templates are used by different research communities – for example, categories and criteria used by those analysing organized crime are not the same as those used by military security analysts. It is always important to consider the validity and reliability of indicators and to avoid conceptual mistakes in conducting comparisons.
- *Multiplicity of variables* In an idealized situation it may be possible to determine the impact of a single causal factor by controlling for the impact of other factors. In practice, in conflict studies, multiple variables are at play, and even establishing statistical associations between variables is made difficult by such issues as endogeneity, multicollinearity, selection problems and the rarity of conflict events relative to opportunities for conflicts.
- *Swamping* Interpreting statistical results requires great care, since aggregate statistics – for example, across a number of countries – can be swamped by a 'spike' in numbers from one country or one conflict – for example, global deaths in civil wars would be heavily affected in 2012 by the single case of Syria. Conversely, if one treats armed conflicts as units, it may be necessary to lump together small and large wars.
- *Patchiness of data* Most analysts have to face problems of missing data and discrepancies in the availability of data – for example, government information on homicide rates in different countries (see UNODC, 2013). This may make it difficult to draw accurate transnational comparisons.
- *The involvement of statistics in the conflicts in question* Finally, in intense political conflicts, the statistics – not just concerning human rights violations but also basic estimates of the number and nature of casualties – are themselves part of what is contested.

1,000 battle-related deaths, for example) are arbitrary and there is no agreed universal standard or definition. It is also very difficult to identify clear starting points and termination points, as conflicts go into periods of calm and de-escalation, only to flare up again unpredictably.

Nevertheless, these limitations, which are well recognized by the researchers who employ them, do not invalidate the remarkable cooperative efforts now being made to provide ongoing data on organized violence and conflict as a guide to policy and practice – far from it. These difficulties must simply be borne in mind, and care must be taken to see how they can best be accommodated. Human judgement cannot be excluded from statistical analysis. This is where the mechanics of quantification need to be leavened by qualitative data, and where both in turn need to be informed by the experience and understanding of data-providers and data-users.

Finally, it is also worth noting that it is important to be aware of the particular research aims, assumptions and methodologies of different institutions and approaches, because these determine how research criteria are formulated and therefore what kinds of results can be expected (see box 3.2). For example, Wallensteen (2011b) and Sundberg and Harbom (2011) give interesting accounts of the decisions behind one of the most respected and widely used data programs, the Uppsala Conflict Data Program (UCDP).

Box 3.2 Three approaches to statistical analysis

Most studies since the 1950s in the 'classical' phase of the statistical study of international conflict confined the field to interstate and related wars above a certain measurable threshold. For example, the well-known Correlates of War (COW) Project,[3] initiated at the University of Michigan in the 1960s by Singer and Small, took its start date from 1816. It covered 'interstate wars', defined as conflicts 'involving at least one member of the interstate system on each side of the war, resulting in a total of 1,000 or more battle-deaths', and 'extra-systemic' wars (e.g. imperial war, colonial war and internationalized civil war), defined as international wars 'in which there was a member of the interstate system on only one side of the war, resulting in an average of 1,000 battle deaths per year for system member participants' (Singer and Small, 1972: 381–2). By 2014 the project was directed by Zeev Maoz at the University of California, Davis, and COW had developed thirteen core datasets distributed around a number of universities in the USA under a system termed 'coordinated decentralization'.

Whereas the COW dataset began from a realist state-centric starting point, others have started from entirely different conceptual bases. For example, the criteria for inclusion in the Hamburg University (AKUF) project, initiated by Kende and developed by Gantzel (Gantzel and Schwinghammer, 2000), was not battle-related deaths, because these were seen as unreliable and unduly restrictive since they did not reflect other kinds of suffering. Instead, AKUF 'relates the onset of war to the development of capitalist societies' and sees conflict as 'a result of the new forms of production, monetarization of the economy and the resulting dissolution of traditional forms of social integration' (Wallensteen, 2002b: 22). So here is a dataset whose origin comes from the tradition of Marxist analysis.

Different again is the University of Uppsala Conflict Data Program (UCDP), which from 1989 used the concept of 'armed conflict' and approached the analysis more from a conflict resolution perspective. Unlike COW or AKUF, which are 'satisfied once they have identified the actors and the actions', the Uppsala project 'requires that the conflict should have an issue, an incompatibility' (Wallensteen, 2002b: 24). UCDP now uses the term 'organized violence' and does not formally distinguish between criminal and political organized violence – although its inclusion of data on criminal violence is only partial. Whereas two of its datasets measure global trends in 'state-based conflicts' (involving at least one government) and 'non-state conflicts' (between armed groups), its third database measures 'one-sided violence' by governments and non-state armed groups against unarmed civilians. Nevertheless UCDP's main purpose remains to enable 'systematic studies of the origins of conflict, conflict dynamics and conflict resolution' (quoted in the *Human Security Report* 2013: 56).

It can be seen how, from these divergent conceptual starting points, different statistical patterns and outcomes are likely to emerge.

Other datasets used in this chapter have been equally diverse. For example, the Minorities at Risk (MAR) Project at the Center for International Development and Conflict Management (CIDCM) at the University of Maryland, initiated in 1986 by Ted Robert Gurr, has also been influential in the conflict resolution field because of the work both of Gurr himself and of CIDCM's founder, Edward Azar (see chapter 4). MAR has compared data on the political aspirations of some 250 minority communal groups worldwide and includes measures taken short of the use of armed force.

Within this brief, lists are drawn up of 'ethno-nationalist peoples' who have fought 'sustained or recurrent campaigns of armed force aimed at least in part at securing national independence for a communal group, or their unification with kindred groups in adjoining states', between 1945 and the 1990s. Terrorist and guerrilla strategies have also been counted (Gurr, 1995: 5; Gurr, 2000). This has proved valuable in tracking escalation and de-escalation pathways, as noted further in the next chapter, which few other datasets are able to do. In 2014 this has been adapted to the AMAR dataset, which incorporates a wider range of 'socially relevant ethnic groups' (1,194 groups), not just those that were politically mobilized and could therefore be subject to 'selection bias' towards propensity for conflict (Birnir et al., 2015). The 2014 *Peace and Conflict* biennial flagship publication from CIDCM itself documents trends in national and international conflicts more broadly and includes assessment of future risks of political and social instability along the lines of Azar's own analysis of 'protracted social conflict' (CIDCM, 2014) to be discussed in chapter 4. In the 2014 issue there is a special focus on the hitherto often neglected micro-level study of conflict and peacebuilding data, not only from within states but right down to local level, as emphasized later in this chapter.

Measuring Peace and Peacefulness

Since the first edition of this book, one of the major innovations has been the design of datasets whose purpose is to measure indicators of 'sustainable peace and peacefulness' and indicators of the quality of peace after peace settlements. It is in general more difficult to find adequate quantifiable indicators for peacefulness (positive peace) than for levels of negative peace (absence of direct violence). This will be a recurrent theme in later chapters, particularly on prevention (chapter 5) and postwar reconstruction and peacebuilding (chapters 8 and 9). In this section we look briefly at some of the main resources now available before moving on to consider what short-term and long-term trends seem to emerge from this.

So far as the measurement of levels of *peacefulness* is concerned, the CONIS (Conflict Information System) database developed at the University of Heidelberg offers a good example. Located within the Institute for International Conflict Research (http://hiik.de/), CONIS is linked to their *Conflict Barometer*, which includes data for distinguishing between violent conflicts and those that are non-violently managed. The argument is that, by researching only overtly violent conflict – for example, based on levels of battle-related deaths – crucial data on conflicts that are resolved peacefully is simply missed out (see chapter 5). The inclusion of latent and emergent conflicts and those which have been successfully de-escalated through various forms of non-violent crisis management enables a more sophisticated and nuanced analysis of strategies and policies that might sustain or rebuild peace. The Conflict Barometer distinguishes between disputes, non-violent crises, limited wars and wars, and it tracks these via a large dataset that can be disaggregated at global, regional, national and sub-national levels. The 'Heidelberg approach' also covers 'measures of conflict resolution' (negotiations, international organizations, peacekeeping missions, International Court of Justice rulings).

A second example is the *Global Peace Index* (GPI), produced by the Institute for Economics and Peace (IEP). The GPI first appeared in 2008 and was an attempt to develop a methodology that combined qualitative and quantitative indicators in order to measure both the negative and positive dimensions of Galtung's definition of peace. The objective of the project is to provide data for 'estimating the value of peace to the world economy, and uncovering the social structures and social attitudes that are at the core of peaceful societies'. Using a mixture of twenty-four quantitative and qualitative indicators, the GPI produces a peace index or ranking of 162 countries. In what amounts to probably the most comprehensive of any current database on peace and conflict, the indicators are gathered under eight 'pillars': well-functioning government; sound business environment; equitable distribution of resources; acceptance of the rights of others; good relations with neighbours; free flow of information; high levels of human capital; and low levels of corruption (IEP, 2015: 82–90). These indicators are in turn linked to quantitatively measured potential 'drivers' of peace, such as levels of democracy and transparency, international openness, demographics, education, culture and material well-being. The intention is to use the GPI to strengthen the political economy and culture of peace by enabling governments 'to increase the peacefulness of their nations'. The website of the IEP sums up its mission as an organization 'dedicated to shifting the world's focus to peace as a positive, achievable, and tangible measure of human well-being and progress':

> The Institute for Economics and Peace achieves its goals by developing new conceptual frameworks to define peacefulness; providing metrics for measurement; uncovering the relationship between peace, business and prosperity; and by promoting a better understanding of the cultural, economic and political factors that drive peacefulness. (IEP, 2014b)

A third example is a new programme to develop indicators of 'quality peace', which measure the quality of post-conflict peacebuilding efforts by positive indicators, such as quality of governance, the degree of security, the importance of civil society, the progress of economic reconstruction and reconciliation (Wallensteen, 2013). The Kroc Institute's Peace Accords Matrix (peaceaccords.nd.edu) provides a dataset of peace settlements that can be used in conjunction with the effort to establish 'quality peace' indicators.

For the future, therefore, enhancements in the conceptualization, methodology and technology for measuring fragility and sustainable peace are promising. Conceptually, there is the challenge to design comprehensive indices using deep indicators, both for the drivers of conflict and for the measure of peacefulness, by combining the two poles of the definition of peace, the positive and the negative, or, in United Nations terminology, *freedom from fear* (no direct violence) and *freedom from want* (the positive satisfaction of human rights and needs). There are complex ethical, political and methodological problems involved in how to identify and weight indicators capable of generating such a deep measure of peace and conflict experience in a quantifiable manner, but the knowledge base has evolved in such a way as to make the challenge now seem feasible.

Measuring State Fragility

An important development since the last edition is the appearance of new indicators to measure state fragility. These are taken very seriously by states and international organizations when considering the likelihood of new conflicts, as chapters 5 and 8 show. From the point of view of policy-makers concerned with maintaining the integrity of the international system of states, avoiding state fragility may be the primary goal. From a conflict resolution perspective, state fragility is one of many risk factors that make armed conflicts more likely. There are many others, including low economic growth, political exclusion and horizontal inequalities. Because of the salience that state fragility has taken in international policy discussions, and because of its association with armed conflicts (see Map 3.1, p. 94 below), we treat it on its own here.

A good example of the attempt to measure *fragility* is provided by the annual reports from the Organization for Economic Cooperation and Development (OECD) launched in 2005 by its Development Assistance Committee (DAC) in collaboration with the International Network on Conflict and Fragility (INCAF). INCAF is a 'unique decision-making forum', which brings together diverse stakeholders dealing with conflict and fragility to support development outcomes in the world's most challenging situations. It works with civil society partners, governments, international organizations (UN, NATO, World Bank) and partner countries – in particular, fragile states themselves. The DAC report *Fragile States 2013: Resource Flows and Trends in a Shifting World* offers an ongoing assessment that 'tracks results in the field and globally':

> Addressing fragility as a driver of poverty and instability requires a more robust understanding of fragility, its causes and dimensions. In particular it requires seeing fragility as a deeply political issue centred on the social contract between the state and society, and it requires greater consideration of the role of stress factors (internal and external). (DAC, 2014: 27)

Here is the OECD definition of 'fragility':

> A fragile region or state has weak capacity to carry out basic governance functions, and lacks the ability to develop mutually constructive relations with society. Fragile states are

also more vulnerable to internal or external shocks such as economic crises or natural disasters. More resilient states exhibit the capacity and legitimacy of governing a population and its territory. They can manage and adapt to changing social needs and expectations, shifts in elite and other political agreements, and growing institutional complexity. Fragility and resilience should be seen as shifting points along a spectrum. (Ibid.: 15)

This corresponds to the analysis of 'protracted social conflict' in the conflict resolution field discussed in chapter 4.

Of course, states vary considerably in their form and their context, and state fragility is not a precise or an uncontested concept. There may be pockets outside government control within otherwise robust states, and some societies may be stable while lacking Weberian state structures. Since fragility is conceived as a spectrum, identifying a list of fragile states depends on coding rules and arbitrary cut-off points. Detailed coding rules, and critiques of them, can be found in the literature (for a guide, see Mcloughlin, 2012). Inclusion in such a list may well have policy implications for fragile states, insofar as donors, international financial institutions and major states take them into consideration. Nevertheless, if the coding is done consistently, such listings can give useful information, especially regarding the trends towards greater or lesser state fragility that we consider below.

Conflict Trends

What overall trends emerge from these datasets? We include latest available figures at the time of writing but also material from earlier editions of this book, because, in assessing trends, it is important not just to rely on the latest year's data but to try to set this against longer-term evidence.

This section must begin with a brief assessment of the most important analysis to appear in the field of statistically based measurements of violence since the third edition of our book – Steven Pinker's *The Better Angels of our Nature* (2011; Reading 66). An excellent assessment of the main claims made in Pinker's argument, together with some of the main criticisms of it, can be found in the *Human Security Report* (HSR Project, 2013) produced by Andrew Mack and his colleagues at the School for International Studies, Simon Fraser University, Vancouver. The subtitle of the HSR report is 'The Decline of Global Violence: Evidence, Explanation and Contestation'. This can usefully be read in conjunction with Joshua Goldstein's *Winning the War on War* (2012).

Pinker's magisterial survey is based on comparative measures of violence relative to the size of population. The metric he applies for measuring deadliness of periods of violence is deaths per 100,000 per year. On Pinker's vast canvas, the decline in violence has gone through five phases: the 'pacification process' from hunter-gatherers to agricultural civilizations, the 'civilizing process' from the Middle Ages to nation-states, the 'humanitarian revolution' associated with the abolition of slavery and slow reduction in torture, the 'long peace' after the Second World War, and the 'new peace' after the end of the Cold War. The critics argue that much of the decline Pinker finds is due to his metric of deaths per 100,000 of population. Given rapid population growth, a constant level of violence would look like a rapid decline per capita. We should therefore be cautious in accepting Pinker's claim that 'we may be living in the most peaceable era in our species' existence' (2011: xxi). Certainly many people are living in unprecedented peace, but this is combined with war's unprecedented capacity to destroy all of humanity. So far, however, as Goldstein says, since 1945: 'We have avoided nuclear wars, left behind world war, nearly extinguished interstate war, and reduced civil wars to fewer countries with fewer casualties' (2012: 328).

The 2013 *Human Security Report* attributes much of this to the evolution of a new 'global security governance system' along lines advocated and supported from the outset by the founders of the conflict resolution field:

> In its current stage of development, this continually expanding system of global security remains inchoate, disputatious, inefficient, and prone to tragic mistakes. But as previous *Human Security Reports* have argued, the evidence suggests that it has also been remarkably effective in driving down the number and deadliness of armed conflicts. (HSR Project, 2013: 3)

Evidently, from a conflict resolution perspective this conclusion is encouraging. But many readers may think that the dramatic upsurge in deadly conflicts in 2013–14 that crowded our TV screens and appalled us by their levels of violence – in Ukraine, Syria–Iraq, Gaza and parts of Africa – as well as continuing very high levels of organized violence in Latin America and large-scale war in Afghanistan/Pakistan, together with unprecedented numbers of refugees and internally displaced persons, belie this optimistic view. Is it possible to gain insight into this apparent discrepancy by studying the rich array of statistical data that is now available?

We can begin by reporting a continuation of the main historical trend that is confirmed by the data over a considerable number of years – a decline in the number of interstate wars – the 'scourge' that, in the words of the founders of the United Nations, 'twice in our lifetime has brought untold sorrow to mankind'. Over a longer-term time frame, according to Holsti (1996: 24), the number of interstate wars per year per state has gone down steadily over the past hundred years, comparing the 1918–41 with the 1945–95 periods. In chapter 4 we will suggest that the key transition here came earlier rather than at the end of the Cold War, but since 1989 the decline in the number of interstate wars has approached its limit. There were no interstate wars in 1993 and 1994, only a minor border altercation between Peru and Ecuador in 1995, and a flare-up in the long-running dispute between India and Pakistan over Kashmir in 1996 (Wallensteen and Sollenberg, 1997; SIPRI, 1997: 17). In 2011 the single interstate conflict was the brief low-intensity war between Thailand and Cambodia.

We should no doubt hesitate before celebrating 'the end of interstate war' – for example, the sudden flare-up between Russia and Ukraine in 2014, together with subsequent sanctions and sabre-rattling by NATO, suggests to some commentators a possible return to Cold War rivalry (see the case study in chapter 5). Rising tensions between China and Japan in the East China Sea over the Diaoyu/Senkaku islands (see the case study in chapter 10) also indicate how precarious the restraints on interstate war still are. Above all, looking at the category of 'internationalized civil wars', we can see a high incidence of 'proxy wars', as, for example, in Syria, where struggles for power and influence at the global level between the United States and Russia, and at the regional level between Saudi Arabia and Iran, have fuelled rather than damped down the intensity of the fighting. In this respect, therefore, despite the remarkable decline in the incidence of interstate war, realist insights into the continuing significance of interstate rivalry and balance of power remain valid – a major point that will recur through the rest of the book and be re-emphasized in chapter 20.

What about statistical evidence on non-interstate wars – for example, as analysed since 1989 by the University of Uppsala Conflict Data Program? Figure 3.2 shows the trends. With international (interstate) war in decline, the Uppsala data, consistent with other datasets, reported a 'new pattern of conflict' in the 1990s in which the prime emphasis was on 'challenges to existing state authority', including both secessionist movements which threatened the territorial integrity of the state (former Yugoslavia, Chechnya) and challenges to central control, which may also end in fragmentation with no one actor in overall command (Liberia, Somalia) (Wallensteen and Axell, 1995: 345). By 2009, compared to the peak years of 1988 and 1991, the number of high-intensity armed conflicts (wars) was seen to be down by two-thirds (Harbom and Wallensteen, 2009). In their most recent assessment of armed conflicts between 1946 and 2014, Thérése Pettersson and Peter Wallensteen record forty active conflicts in the world, an increase of six since 2013:

> The number has increased in recent years but is still substantially lower than in 1991, the peak year after the end of the Cold War. 2014 also saw an increase in battle-related deaths. An escalation of several conflicts, and the extremely violent conflict in Syria, resulted in the highest number of battle-related deaths since the end of the Cold War. (Pettersson and Wallensteen, 2015)

Figures from the 2015 *Global Peace Index* suggest that, between 2008 and 2014, numbers of war-related fatalities per year rose from 49,000 to 180,000. In 2014, more than half the number (90,500) came from Syria and Iraq (IEP, 2015).

We can supplement the graph in figure 3.2 of the number of armed conflicts with that in figure 3.3, which shows battle deaths in armed conflicts from 1946 to 2008, based on the PRIO (Peace Research Institute Oslo) battle deaths dataset. UCDP has been collecting similar battle deaths data from 1989. Its estimates are slightly lower than PRIO's but follow similar trend lines (Wischnath and Gleditsch, 2011). There are spikes for the Korean and Vietnam wars and

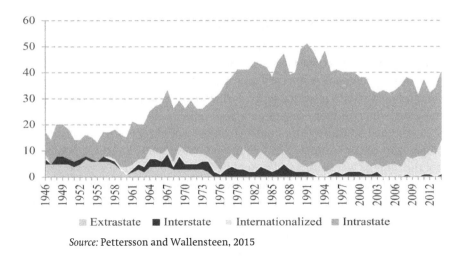

Source: Pettersson and Wallensteen, 2015

Figure 3.2 *Number of armed conflicts by type, 1946–2014*

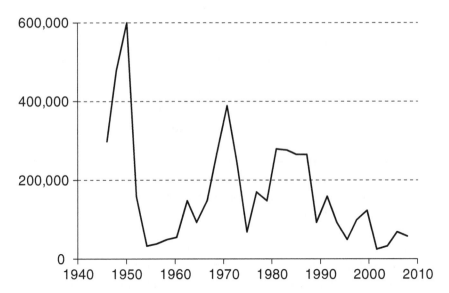

Source: PRIO battle deaths data from www.prio.no/cscw/cross/battledeaths; the PRIO battle deaths dataset, 1946–2008, Version 3.0

Figure 3.3 *Battle deaths, 1946–2008*

the conflicts at the end of the Cold War, but overall the graph shows a downward trend. However, 2014 saw a spike back to the 1997 level.

Battle deaths include fatalities of both combatants and civilians that are directly attributed to combat. The data is subject to two important restrictions. First, it does not take account of secondary deaths due to starvation and disease. Second, it excludes fighting between non-government groups ('non-state violence') and atrocities against civilians ('one-sided violence'), since the armed conflicts are defined as being between combatants with government troops on at least one side. Separate datasets have been compiled on one-sided violence from 1989 and non-state conflicts from 2002, but no comprehensive data is available for earlier years. Comparing the figures for the years when all three sets of data are available, between 2002 and 2006, the combined fatalities from one-sided violence and non-state violence were 55 per cent of the battle deaths toll (Spagat et al., 2009). So battle deaths are not the same as war deaths and cannot necessarily be taken as a proxy for the intensity of warfare. On the one hand, weapons may become more lethal over time; on the other hand, improvements in battlefield medicine may mean that fewer people die of war wounds than in the past (Fazal, 2014).

Turning to other datasets, the HIIK 2013 *Conflict Barometer* (Hachemer, 2014) widens the measure of intensity to include use of weapons, personnel, casualties, refugees/internally displaced persons, and material destruction. It charts a high point of fifty-one high-intensity conflicts in 1992, after which it declines sharply, but rises again to forty-five in 2003. Since then the number has fluctuated between thirty-one and forty-four, reaching forty-five again in 2013 (twenty wars and twenty-five limited wars).

Based on this, and other evidence, the 2014 *Human Security Report* concludes – possibly at variance with the Heidelberg figures – that, although low-intensity state-based armed conflicts rose in 2011, high-intensity conflicts that cause 1,000 or more battle-related deaths a year continued to stay steady or decline through 2013. Non-state armed conflicts (between armed groups), which 'tend to be short-lived and to kill fewer people', also rose in 2011, but no clear trend can yet be discerned over a longer time frame. Deadly assaults on civilians ('one-sided violence') are 'dramatically lower than in the mid-1990s' and about 'half that of 2002 which was the peak year since data started being collected' (HSR, 2013: 89).

Having so far considered what are mainly 'classic' measurements of levels of armed conflict and war, we now move on, first to data on *terrorism* and *organized criminal violence* (i.e. the presence or absence of other forms of direct violence) and then on again to data on *fragile states* and *sustainable peace*.

A good source for data on *terrorism* is the Global Terrorism Database (GTD) (http://www.start.umd.edu/gtd/), which has collected data on 'terrorist events' from around the world (1970–2012). The GTD ranks countries on four indicators weighted over five years: number of terrorist incidents, number of fatalities, number of injuries, and estimated property damage. Based on this data, the Global Terrorism Index (GTI), produced by the Institute for Economics and Peace, offers 'the first index to systematically rank and compare 158 countries worldwide over a ten year period (2002–2012)' in order to 'shed light on the impact of terrorism'. The GTI concludes that the number of successful terrorist attacks has 'steadily increased over the last decade', although 'from 2002 to 2011 over one third of all victims killed in terrorist attacks were Iraqi', showing the highly localized 'swamping' effect that can be produced by a sudden upsurge in one conflict area. To give an idea of the scale of suffering involved, in 2011 the estimate was of '4,564 terrorist incidents globally, resulting in 7,473 deaths and 13,961 injuries' (IEP, 2014c). This rise in incidents seems to go against the downward trend in the number and deadliness of armed conflicts in general. The complex issue of definitions and assessments of terrorism in the light of events in 2013 and 2014 is looked at in a later section of this chapter, and then again in chapter 11. For example, should all the deaths associated with the sudden incursion into Iraq in the summer of 2014 of the grouping which renamed itself as the Islamic State (IS)[4] be classified as terrorism, even when these were battle deaths from clashes between IS forces and the Iraqi national army or Kurdish *peshmerga* militia? Similarly, in the violence in Gaza in July–August 2014, should the six civilian deaths (and eighty-seven civilian injuries) caused by Hamas rockets and incursions be ascribed to terrorism, but the sixty-six deaths (and 469 injuries) to Israel Defense Force soldiers count as battle-related deaths and injuries? And how should the 2,216 Palestinian deaths (1,483 civilians) be classified (UNOCHA, 2015)? The data released in 2014 (covering the period up to and including 2013) is discussed under 'Terrorism and Conflict' (p. 95).

Turning to the category of *organized criminal violence*, this, too, is a complex topic. The importance of widening the statistical analysis of 'deadly conflicts' to include homicides from national and transnational criminal violence is shown by estimates that, in terms of human insecurity, several times more people suffer directly from criminally perpetrated homicides than from armed conflict and war. Here the figures indicate such big discrepancies from region to region that it is difficult to reach an overall global assessment. The World Bank's 2011 *World Development Report* found that Latin America was the sole region in which homicide rates increased between 1999 and 2005. The 2011 *Global Burden of Armed Violence* report calculated that the countries with average annual violent death rates of more than thirty per 100,000 population between 2004 and 2009 were, in order from the highest downwards, El Salvador (over sixty per 100,000), Iraq, Jamaica, Honduras, Colombia, Venezuela, Guatemala, South Africa, Sri Lanka, Lesotho, Central Africa Republic, Sudan, Belize and Democratic Republic of the Congo (Krause et al., 2011: 5). The rate can also fluctuate dramatically – for example, in a benign direction, as in El Salvador after the 2012 peace deal between the main rival gangs (see chapter 7). GBAV estimates that '25% of violent deaths occur in just 14 countries, which are home to less than 5% of the world's population.' But all of this is subject to severe qualification in view of the patchy – often non-existent – official figures from areas such as sub-Saharan Africa. Some of the World Health Organization estimates for Africa are based on extrapolations from other countries because official mortality data is not available. So, as the UN Office on Drugs and Crime (UNODC) acknowledges, some of the reported trends may be more to do with fluctuations in recording than with levels of violence. Having reviewed the evidence, the *Human Security Report 2013* concludes:

> There is plenty of room for debate about the reliability of the global homicide trend data. But we see little evidence to suggest that the dramatic recent increases in homicide rates in parts of Latin America – much of it associated with organized criminal violence – point to a rising global trend. (HSR Project, 2013: 62)

Turning to the measurement of *fragility*, according to the OECD *Fragile States* report, in 2013 fifty-one states were classed as 'fragile' compared with forty-seven the year before. The overall trend is seen to be an increase in fragility even as violent intra- and interstate conflict may be declining (DAC, 2014). On the measurement of *peacefulness*, the 2015 *Global Peace Index* (GPI) concludes that 'the *societal safety and security domain* improved slightly last year [2014], driven by falls in the *homicide rate* and the *likelihood of violent demonstrations*' (2015: 2; original emphasis). The index reports that its overall global 'score' remained stable in 2014 compared with the year before, but that this conceals wide regional discrepancies. Four geographical regions 'experienced an improvement in peace in comparison with 2013, while five became less peaceful', as noted below. Eighty-one countries were measured to be 'more peaceful' in 2014 compared with 2013 and seventy-eight 'less peaceful'. The Institute for Economics and Peace, which produces the GPI, uses both qualitative and quantitative measures, because 'we're covering 162 countries and you cannot always get data from countries on their levels of violence' (IEP, 2014b). Qualitative data comes from some 100 country analysts from the Economist Intelligence Unit, which are then peer-reviewed by an 'expert panel'. A highly significant recent development in the measurement of fragility has been an emphasis not just on fragile states but on fragile cities. The International Peace Institute includes as one of its '2014 top ten issues to watch in peace and security' what it calls 'the urbanization of crisis' or 'fragile cities':

> Alongside the unprecedented urbanization of the last decade, urban fragility has emerged as a central challenge in global security and development. Like the fragile state, fragile cities suffer from rising instability, poverty, and violence and lack the capacities needed to face the magnitude of these challenges. Some analysts believe fragile or 'failing' cities mark 'a new frontier of warfare', whether situated inside a war-torn state or a largely peaceful one. (Mancini, 2014)

Forty-one of the top fifty dangerous cities in 2013 are in Latin America, while 'one third of the world's city dwellers live below the poverty line'. This, therefore, is a theme that will recur through the rest of the book.

Summing up the data on conflict and violence trends in 2014, Dan Smith, producer of the annual *State of the World Atlas*, concludes that the overall situation is still one in which the 'big under-reported good news story' is that 'there are fewer wars than in the 1980s' and that 'the improvement in the state of the world has not come about by accident' (Smith, 2014). He points to the fact that 'there have been more peace agreements and an increasing proportion of them endure for longer' (see chapter 7), and that there 'have also been more peacekeeping operations' (see chapters 6 and 8). However, as the World Bank's *World Development Report* (2011) shows, 'the violent conflicts that are addressed by formal peace agreements and UN peacekeeping operations are only part of the conflict picture.' When looking more broadly ahead to indicators of what may be future trends, Smith (2014) concludes that the main aim 'is not conflict prediction but risk assessment. It's not about which specific conflicts will explode in which places for what reasons, but about their backdrop – the systemic issues that create increased conflict risk.' This will be a central topic in chapters 4 and 5.

Nevertheless, despite both the variations in methodology described above and the challenge to expand the conflict domain to anticipate future trends, there is considerable agreement in the major existing datasets about the major armed conflicts currently in progress. Table 3.1 uses data from the Center for Systemic Peace (CSP), which in turn draws from a wide variety of sources, many of which we have described and summarized in this chapter.[5] In the list there are forty-three cases of major armed conflict. Of these, twenty-four were ongoing in 2014 (marked in table 3.1 by *); eight were diminishing (marked by **); while eleven had terminated over the period 2009–13 (marked by ***). The eleven terminated conflicts were included because they were rated as being at high risk of return to armed conflict (for example, if not adequately supported by a peace agreement and a sustainable peacebuilding process). Since the numbers of deaths for each conflict vary considerably according to sources consulted, the overall casualty figures are indicative rather than definitive. The full list in the dataset gives 332 episodes of armed conflict from 1946 to 2014, defined as consisting of at least 500 directly related fatalities which also 'reach a level of intensity in which political violence is both systematic and sustained' (a base rate of 100 'directly-related deaths per annum'). Marshall and the CSP also include a magnitude score for each conflict on a scale of 1 to 10, according to an 'assessment of the full impact of their violence on the societies that directly experience their effects': 'The effects of political violence and warfare include fatalities and casualties, resource depletion, destruction of infrastructure, and population dislocations, among other things such as the psychological trauma to individuals and adverse changes to the social psychology and political culture of affected social identity groups' (Marshall, 2014). This definition of magnitude provides a powerful indicator of the damage caused by the conflict that takes into account structural, cultural and psychological (trauma) impacts as well as direct fatality from violence. CSP's categories of magnitude run from 1 (sporadic or expressive political violence) to 10 (extermination/annihilation).

Table 3.1 Countries with major armed conflicts in progress, diminishing or recently terminated, 2013

Location	Inception	Conflict parties	Deaths	Magnitude
*Burma/ Myanmar	1948	Ethnic war, Karen, Shan, others	110,000	4
*India	1952	Ethnic war, Assam separatists	25,500	2
**Israel	1965	Arab Palestinians/PLO	22,000	2
**Philippines	1972	Ethnic war, Moros	52,000	3
**Colombia	1975	Civil violence, land reform, drug trafficking, left vs. right guerrilla groups (FARC vs. MAS/AUC)	57,500	4
***Sri Lanka	1983	Ethnic war, Tamils	75,000	5
**Somalia	1988	Civil war	115,000	5
**India	1990	Ethnic war, Kashmiris	43,500	5
**Dem Rep Congo	1996	Civil war, Hutus, Tutsi, Luba/Lunde, Yeki	2,500,000	5
***Nigeria	1997	Delta province, communal violence, Ijaw, Itseken	2,500	1
*Pakistan	1997	Sectarian violence, Sunni, Shia, Ahmadis	4,000	1
*Afghanistan	2001	Civil war, Taliban	42,000	3
*India	2001	Maoist insurgency, People's War Group, Maoist Communist Centre, People's Liberation Guerrilla Army	7,200	2
***Iraq	2003	Regime change post-Saddam, sectarian violence, Sunni, Shia, Kurds, al-Qaeda	150, 000	6
***United States	2003	International war, invasion of Iraq	4,400	2
*Sudan	2003	Communal–separatist violence in Darfur	350,000	5
*Yemen	2004	Followers of al-Huthi in Sanaa	3,000	1
*Pakistan	2004	Pashtuns in federally administered tribal areas	38,250	4
*Thailand	2004	Malay-Muslims in southern border region (Narathiwat, Pattani, Songkhla and Yala provinces)	4,000	1
**Turkey	2004	Kurdish separatism	2,500	1
*Pakistan	2005	Rebellion in Baluchistan	3,000	1
***Chad	2005	Anti-regime, FUC UFDD and others	2,000	2
*Central African Republic	2005	Ethnic war, APRD (northwest), UFDR (northeast) and Seleka rebels	5,000	2
**United States	2005	Stabilization operation in Afghanistan	2,200	1
*Mexico	2006	Govt offensive against drug cartels and corrupt officials in north	75,000	3

Table 3.1 Continued

Location	Inception	Conflict parties	Deaths	Magnitude
***Chad	2006	Communal fighting between Toroboro ('black' sedentary farmer) and Janjawid ('Arab' pastoralist) militias	5,000	2
*Ethiopia	2007	Somali (ONLF) and Oromo (OLF) militants in Ogaden	2,800	1
*Russia	2008	Ethnic violence, Islamist militants in eastern Transcaucasus region: Chechnya, Dagestan, and Ingushetia	4,000	1
*Nigeria	2009	Rebellion by radical Muslim Boko Haram in north border region	8,000	2
*South Sudan	2009	Communal violence, Lue Nuer and Murle	3,500	1
*Nigeria	2010	Communal violence in Jos/Plateau state: Christian and Muslim	3,000	1
***Kyrgyzstan	2010	Ethnic violence, Kyrgyz, Uzbeks, following ousting of Bakiyev	600	2
***Egypt	2011	Popular protests against Mubarak regime	1,000	1
***Ivory Coast	2011	Rejection of December 2010 presidential election results by regime leads to resumption of civil war and ends with arrest of President Gbagbo	3,000	2
*Iraq	2011	Continuing Sunni–Shia sectarian strife	15,500	3
*Syria	2011	Popular protests and regime crackdown trigger warfare with ethnic Sunni militants and Islamist extremists against Assad's ethnic Alawite regime	140,000	5
***Libya	2011	Anti-Gaddhafi elements centred in the eastern coastal region; NATO intervention	25,000	4
*Yemen	2011	Anti-Saleh demonstrations, southern separatists, army mutiny, clan rivalry, and al-Qaeda militants	4,000	1
*Sudan	2011	Armed supporters of the Sudanese People's Liberation Movement (SPLM-North) in South Kordofan and Blue Nile states	3,000	1
***Mali	2012	Islamist Ansar Dine and ethnic Tuareg 'Azawad' separatists	1,000	1
*Egypt	2013	Military ousting of President Morsi and crackdown on Muslim Brotherhood; Islamist rebellion in Sinai and south	2,000	1
*South Sudan	2013	Rebellion by ethnic Nuer supporters of Reik Machar leads to war with ethnic Dinka supporters of President Salva Kiir	10,000	3
*Dem Rep Congo	2013	Ethnic Mai Mai separatist rebellion in Katanga Province	750	1

Notes: * = ongoing; ** = diminishing; *** = recently terminated
Source: Marshall, 2014

Conflict Types

This leads to one of the most testing questions in conflict analysis. Are there different types of conflict that need to be distinguished from each other if effective and discriminate conflict resolution is to be undertaken? This is a controversial topic not only in conflict analysis, but also in international law. For example, international humanitarian law distinguishes between international armed conflict, internationalized armed conflict and non-international armed conflict. But categorizations of this kind are called into question by the hybrid and mutating patterns of transnational conflict today (Wilmshurst, 2012). Nevertheless, despite the proliferation of datasets using different typologies and criteria for inclusion, as noted above, in this section, based on a comparison between some of the better known studies, we venture to offer our own simplified typology. This is summed up in table 3.2 in order to give readers a working conceptual framework for the analysis of contemporary large-scale conflict from a conflict resolution perspective. As suggested in chapter 4, these four conflict types can be related to the four main global level 'drivers' of contemporary transnational conflict (see table 4.2, p. 123).

First, it may be helpful to think more in terms of historically and geographically based 'generations' of conflict rather than in terms of blanket typologies. After all, the roots of all major conflicts reach back into the historical past – often several centuries back. Superimposed on this are clusters of 'enduring rivalries', many still unresolved, going back respectively to the time of the break-up of the Russian, Austro-Hungarian and Ottoman empires at the end of the First World War (we might add Northern Ireland to this list); the political settlements at the end of the Second World War; the period of decolonization (1950s, 1960s); the postcolonial period (1970s, 1980s); and, finally, the break-up of the Soviet bloc (1990s) (see 'Conflict Prevention and the Break-Up of Empires' chapter 5). The early decades of the twenty-first century have seen the superimposition of a new generation of ideological terrorist and anti-terrorist conflicts, linked in general to the *jihadist* challenge to the modern state system and in particular to the complex pattern of emergent Sunni–Shia tensions across the Arab and wider Islamic worlds (see case study in chapter 4, p. 135).

Second, we would do well to heed Singer's advice that a classificatory system should 'remain as atheoretical as possible' lest, 'by accepting conventional labels of certain armed conflicts, we buy into simplistic interpretations, and ultimately embrace disastrous reactions and responses' – although it is unlikely that we will succeed in finding a typology which is 'logically exhaustive, mutually exclusive, operationally explicit, semantically consistent, and substantively comparable' (1996: 40, 48). In previous editions of this book we provided an account of how typologies such as those by Singer, Holsti (1996) and others – including the Uppsala typology employed by the Stockholm International Peace Research Institute (SIPRI) – led to the emergence of a

Table 3.2 A working conflict typology

Conflict type	Example
Interstate	Gulf War 1991
Non-interstate	
revolution/ideology	Egypt
identity/secession	Kurds
economic/resource	Mexico

useful working distinction between four main types of conflict (see table 3.2). Here we omit this explanation, but we think that – with qualifications – these distinctions are still useful

In addition to interstate conflicts, provisional distinctions may usefully be made between three types of predominantly non-interstate conflict. The term 'non-interstate conflict' should not be misunderstood. All it means is that such a conflict is not a classic war between two states. It does not imply that states are not involved either overtly or covertly, or that 'internal wars' do not spill across state borders or draw other states in. The term 'economic/resource conflict' covers *coups d'état*, intra-elite power struggles, brigandage, criminality and warlordism, where the aim is to usurp, seize or retain state power or state resources merely to further economic and other interests. The term 'revolution/ideology conflict' includes the more ambitious aim of changing the nature of government in a state – for example, by (a) changing the system from capitalist to socialist, (b) changing the form of government from dictatorship to democracy, or (c) changing the religious orientation of the state from secular to, say, Islamic (including internal sectarian struggles between branches of the religion in question). In the post-Cold War world it is possible to discern a decline in the incidence of (a) but not in the incidence of (b) and particularly not of (c). The term 'identity/secession conflict' involves the relative status of communities or 'communal groups', however defined, in relation to the state. Depending upon the nature of the group and the contextual situation, this includes struggles for access, for autonomy, for secession or for control (Gurr, 1995: 3–5).[6] In brief, an economic/resource conflict is a struggle to control the resources of the state, a revolution/ideology conflict is in addition a struggle to change the nature of the state, and an identity/secession conflict may well be a threat to the integrity of the state. We might be tempted to see this as roughly coinciding with Zartman's distinction between greed, creed and need conflicts (Zartman, 2000). We continue to have a separate category for terrorism and to treat it mainly as a *means* rather than a *type* of conflict for reasons explained in the section below, although the extraordinary development in 2014 when the Islamic State became *de facto* occupier of large swathes of territory may be seen to break through this conceptual barrier.

At the risk of introducing unnecessary complications, it is worth cross-checking at this point that this working typology roughly corresponds with others, such as the ten categories of 'conflict items' used by the Heidelberg *Conflict Barometer* to classify conflicts (Hachemer, 2014). It might be argued that two of the Heidelberg categories relate particularly to *interstate* conflicts (territory, international power), three to *identity/secession* conflicts (autonomy, secession, national power), two to *revolution/ideology* conflicts (system, ideology) and one to *economic/factional* conflicts (resources). Of the remaining two categories, 'decolonization' is a special case, as seen above, while 'subnational preponderance', defined as 'a focus on the attainment of the de-facto control by a government, a non-state organisation or a population over a territory or a population', spans other categories.

Needless to say, on closer inspection specific conflicts elude neat pigeonholing of this kind. Scholars disagree about categorization, as seen, for example, in the elaborate attempts by Marxist analysts in the 1960s and 1970s to interpret ethnic conflict as class conflict (Munck, 1986), in contrast to the reverse trend on the part of many analysts in the 1990s. More recently we have seen attempts to classify most non-interstate conflicts as economically motivated 'greed' conflicts (Collier and Hoeffler, 2001) (see chapter 4). Moreover, the conflicts themselves often change character over time, are interpreted in different ways by the conflict parties, and can always be captured and manipulated by unscrupulous power-brokers who subsequently justify their depredations by appeal to principle.

Let us end this section by considering a few examples to show how, even when conflicts are hybrid and mutating, the conceptual categories in table 3.2 can offer a useful first analysis to help chart this complexity and track the evolution of conflicts through different phases.

The conflict in Afghanistan in the mid-1990s could be interpreted as a revolution/ideology conflict, to the extent that it was identified with the Taliban's drive to create an Islamic state; as an identity/secession conflict, to the extent that it was seen as a struggle between Pashtuns (Taliban), Uzbeks (Dostum militia) and Tajiks (Masood militia); merely as a factional 'economic/resource' conflict to control resources, if the fighting was seen to be perpetuated simply by the interests of rival warlords and their clients for domination of the opium trade; or even as an interstate conflict by proxy, if the war was seen to be little more than the playing out on Afghan soil of what were essentially rivalries between outside states such as Pakistan, Uzbekistan and Iran. The conflict in Ukraine in 2014 might be classed both as an identity/secession war between the West-leaning and Russian-leaning parts of Ukraine and as an interstate struggle between Russia and the West. Syria in 2014 might be classed as a revolution/ideology war (Islamist war aims), an identity/secession war (status of the Alawite minority), or an international war by proxy at two levels (Saudi Arabia vs. Iran; Russia vs. US). The upsurge of violence in Iraq in 2014 might be coded as a revolution/ideology war (Islamic State aims), an identity/secession war (Sunni resistance to the Shia majority; Kurdish struggle for national self-determination), or an international war by proxy – with resources (oil) a target for control in general. Mali in 2014 might be classed as an identity/secession conflict (Tuareg struggle for autonomy in northern Mali), a revolution/ideology war (al-Qaeda in the Maghreb) that spilled across international borders, or a site for international intervention (France). In the case study of the Arab revolutions in chapter 4 we will see how distinctions of this kind can help to chart the varying outcomes of the Arab revolutions in different Arab countries – offering a useful basis for distinguishing the overlay of appropriate conflict resolution responses that are needed in each case.

To sum up, we think that the simple typology set out in table 3.2 is a useful model from a conflict resolution perspective because it can both give helpful broad-brush-stroke information about what needs to be done in different situations to prevent, contain or end violence and provide a common framework for comparisons. But we advise that all conflict typologies, essential though they are for effective conflict analysis, should be understood as being contested and permanently under review.

Conflict Distribution

Many commentators agree that, with the ending of the Cold War, regional patterns of conflict have become all the more significant. There have, therefore, been efforts to compare characteristics of conflict from region to region.[7]

At the heart of such studies have lain attempts to provide a reliable statistical basis for distinctions such as those between 'zones of peace' and 'zones of war' (Kacowicz, 1995). There are many variations here. For example, Holsti (1996: ch. 7), following Deutsch (1954), Jervis (1982), Väyrynen (1984) and Buzan (1991), distinguished 'pluralistic security communities' in which no serious provisions are made for war between member states, such as North America, the Antipodes and Western Europe; 'zones of peace' between states, such as the Caribbean and the South Pacific; 'no-war zones', such as South-East Asia and (perhaps) East Asia; and 'zones of war', such as Africa, some former Soviet republics, the Middle East, Central America, South Asia and the Balkans. This is discussed further in chapter 4.

It is clearly relevant to conflict resolution to understand the distinctions between regional 'security regimes' with relatively stable interstate relations, such as the Association for South-East Asian Nations (ASEAN) over many years, 'security communities' which avoid large-scale violence, as in Western Europe and North America, and more volatile and conflict-prone regions. There are several quite striking regional variations here, such as the surprising absence of interstate war in South America since 1941 despite its famously turbulent past (Holsti, 1996: 150–82). Why is this?

Map 3.1 shows the distribution of major armed conflict and warfare and the levels of state fragility in mid-2013. In that year the bulk of serious warfare was

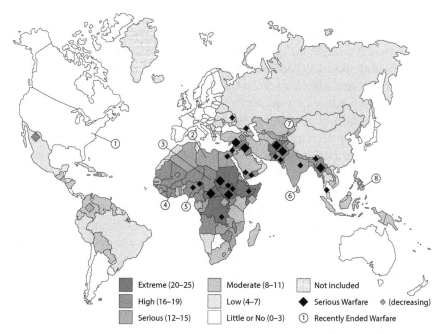

Extreme (20–25)   Moderate (8–11)   Not included

High (16–19)   Low (4–7)   ◆ Serious Warfare   ◇ (decreasing)

Serious (12–15)   Little or No (0–3)   ① Recently Ended Warfare

Source: M. G. Marshall, Centre for Systemic Peace http://www.systemicpeace.org/warlist/warlist.htm

Map 3.1 *State fragility and warfare in the global system, 2013*

located in sub-Saharan Africa, Asia and in the Middle East, with low incidence in Europe and the Americas.

Local variations in conflict are also important and are now being studied using GIS data. Conflict events are geo-referenced to precise places and dates and then related to local geographical factors (mountains, rivers, forests, etc.). This enables analysts to capture regional and micro-level dynamics, thus offering fresh and more nuanced perspectives for conflict research (Buhaug and Gates, 2002; Kalyvas, 2006).

The importance of the question of conflict distribution is now much enhanced by the new focus on 'regionalization' as a key characteristic of post-Cold War transnational conflict. This is carried further in chapter 4, where it is seen to be linked to an enhanced emphasis on the analysis of conflict regions as *complex conflict systems*. For example, the case study on the Arab revolutions in chapter 4 shows the fundamental significance of the regional system as a whole, but also the variations within it and the international forces that sweep across it that together make up the character of prevailing patterns of transnational conflict.

In general, the 2015 *Global Peace Index* (IEP, 2015), reporting data for 2014, noted that the most dramatic change came in the Middle East and North Africa (MENA) region, which for the first time registered as the least peaceful region in the world. The MENA region accounted for a high proportion of the increase in terrorist-caused deaths as noted above, some 100,000 of the overall 180,000 deaths from internal conflicts in 2014, and huge increases in the refugee and internally displaced persons figures (see below). Clearly this has highly significant implications for conflict resolution.

Terrorism and Conflict

As with conflict data in general, there has been significant progress in the development of databases that record and track the development of terrorist attacks over time. In the wake of 9/11 and its profound impact, which encouraged a process of rethinking about the nature of terrorist violence, what had previously been separate datasets, namely armed conflict on the one hand and terrorism on the other, were merged.

Looking first at trends, it is instructive to note the speed with which assessments change in response to events. Much of this is to do with the extraordinary rapidity with which groups using the tactics of terror form, re-form and adapt to the opportunities provided by wider conflict patterns. For example, in the previous edition of this book, we reproduced a graph by LaFree et al. (2010) showing trends in global terrorism between 1970 and 2007. This showed that total terrorist attacks increased from 1970 to a peak in the early 1990s, rose sharply again from 2001 and escalated acutely after the 2003 invasion of Iraq to match the 1992 levels, and indeed to exceed them if incidents in Iraq are included. But the report on terrorist trends from the Human Security Report Project in Canada argues convincingly that, contrary to prevailing opinion and analysis in the intelligence, foreign policy and security communities, the threat from terrorism, including Islamic international terrorism, was declining by 2007–8 (HSR Project, 2013).

Since the third edition of this book, however, the situation has changed dramatically, largely as a result of the civil wars that have broken out in the wake of the 2011 Arab revolutions and the opportunities that this has provided for neo-*jihadist* resurgence. Similar opportunities have arisen in Nigeria and sub-Saharan Africa. It is a complicated and volatile process, as armed groups emerge, vie for pre-eminence, and switch tactics, organization and location. IEP's 2014 Global Terrorism Index, which covers 162 countries, records a 60 per cent increase in deaths from terrorist attacks in 2013 compared with 2012, reaching nearly 18,000 worldwide. The overall trend is sharply upwards since the 9/11 attacks in 2001. But, as figure 3.4 shows, the great majority of fatalities from terrorist incidents have been in just five countries: Iraq, Afghanistan, Pakistan, Nigeria and Syria. There has been a striking growth in terrorism accompanying the 'war on terror' in these five countries, while in the rest of the world the number of fatalities has been fluctuating since the peak of 2001 and has not been rising. The policy implications of this are discussed in chapter 11.

Figure 3.4 shows in the bold line the numbers of global deaths from

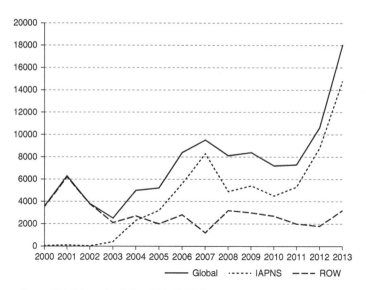

Source: Global Terrorism Index 2014: Highlights

Figure 3.4 *Deaths from terrorism, 2000–2013*

terrorism, in the middle line the deaths from terrorism in Iraq, Afghanistan, Pakistan, Nigeria and Syria, and in the dotted line deaths from terrorism in the rest of the world.

How do typologies of terrorism relate to the typologies of conflict discussed above? In previous editions of this book we traced shifting typologies of terrorism through the period from 2001 to 2010. We omit this explanation here and just present the result – which is to suggest that, with two exceptions, a typology for terrorism can be mapped onto the conflict typology given above in table 3.2. Two main reasons suggest this.

First, however complex and inconsistent definitions of terrorism are – and they are notoriously subject to political manipulation – we will follow those who take terrorism to refer to particular actions and strategies rather than to specific actors or distinct political purposes. In other words, individuals, groups, movements and governments may all adopt terrorist tactics at various times in order to further their political or economic purposes – and then abandon them while still pursuing those purposes. There may be groups that employ only terrorist means and whose purpose does not reach beyond terror itself or is inseparable from it, but these have in the past been very much the exception. Whether this is now changing with the advent of the self-styled Islamic State and Boko Haram will be discussed in chapter 11. Here is the relatively new phenomenon in which radical groups seize the opportunity afforded by local grievances, relative breakdowns in local governmental control, and transnational flows of ideologues and resources to seize control of large swathes of territory together with associated populations. Nevertheless,

Box 3.3 Definitions of terrorism

In line with the approach adopted in this book, Wardlaw's definition of terrorism is focused on the forms of deliberate violence threatened or used, its targets and its wider audience, not on the perpetrators' identity or political, ideological or criminal purpose:

> [Terrorism is] the use, or threat of use, of violence by an individual or a group, whether acting for or in opposition to established authority, when such an act is designed to create extreme anxiety and/or fear-inducing effects in a target group larger than the immediate victims with the purpose of coercing that group into acceding to the political demands of the perpetrators. (Wardlaw, 1982: xx)

After the 9/11 attack, the US government defined terrorism more narrowly by restricting the term to 'subnational groups or clandestine agents' and confining the targets to 'noncombatants':

> The term 'terrorism' means premeditated, politically motivated violence perpetrated against noncombatant targets by subnational groups or clandestine agents, usually intended to influence an audience.
> The term 'international terrorism' means terrorism involving citizens or the territory of more than one country.
> The term 'terrorist group' means any group practicing, or that has significant subgroups which practice, international terrorism. (22 USC 2656f(d))

In contrast are the recurrent requests from Islamic and Arab countries (including the League of Arab States, Gulf Cooperation Council and Organization of the Islamic Conference members) for a comprehensive international agreement on 'the definition of terrorism', which clearly includes 'state terrorism' and distinguishes 'between terrorism and the legitimate struggle of nations against foreign occupation' (League of Arab States' submission to the UN Security Council Counter-Terrorism Committee, February 2003).

The UK Terrorism Act 2000 defines terrorism as the use or threat of action where 'the use or threat is designed to influence the government or to intimidate the public or a section of the public' or 'is made for the purpose of advancing a political, religious or ideological cause' and the action includes 'serious violence against a person', 'serious damage to property' or 'creating a serious risk to the health or safety of the public or a section of the public'.

In its December 2004 report, *A More Secure World*, the UN High-Level Panel defined terrorism as:

> any action . . . that is intended to cause deaths or serious bodily harm to civilians or non-combatants, when the purpose of such an act, by its nature or context, is to intimidate a population or compel a government or an international organisation to do or to abstain from doing something. (p. 49)

in this book, terrorism is taken to be a set of actions or strategies adopted by groups for certain purposes, not the identity of those groups or the nature of those purposes. See box 3.3, which begins with an example of the kind of definition accepted here, then gives contrasting US and Arab/Islamic definitions to illustrate how politically loaded definitions are (which is why, despite twelve UN conventions, no formal international definition of terrorism has yet been agreed), and ends with the definition in the UK Terrorism Act 2000 and that of the UN High-Level Panel (2004).

Box 3.4 Typologies of terrorism

Schmid and Jongman (1988) distinguish between: (a) national/separatist terrorism (such as the Provisional IRA in Ireland, the Tamil Tigers (LTTE) in Sri Lanka, or ETA in Spain); (b) social revolutionary terrorism (such as the Red Army Faction in Germany, or Sendero Luminoso and MRTA in Peru); (c) right-wing terrorism (such as neo-Nazi, racist and anti-government 'survivalist' groups); and (d) religious fundamentalist terrorism (including Jewish, Christian, Islamic and Sikh groups).

Post et al. (2002) accept the Schmid/Jongman typology, although they suggest a fifth category of 'new religion terrorism' to cover groups like the Japanese-based Aum Shinrikyo in their analysis of 'the five principal types of radical groups' most prone to adopting terrorist methods (pp. 110–12).

Martin (2003) has quite similar categories, including various forms of 'communal (e.g. ethno-nationalist) terrorism', 'the terrorist left', 'the terrorist right' and 'religious terrorism', as well as 'criminal terrorism' (pp. 112–215), but also includes 'state terrorism' (pp. 80–111) and 'international terrorism' (pp. 216–42).

Second, consistent with Wardlaw's definition (1982), we will follow a number of terrorism analysts in recognizing a typology of terrorism that accords closely to our own typology of major armed conflict. This strongly suggests that we should correlate national/separatist terrorism with identity/secession conflict, and that we should see 'social revolutionary terrorism', 'right-wing terrorism' and 'religious fundamentalist terrorism' as three manifestations of revolution/ideology conflict (see box 3.4).

We end up, therefore, with a combined terrorism/major armed conflict typology in which types of terrorism approximate to the typology of non-interstate conflicts adopted earlier in this chapter (see table 3.3). There are clear policy implications from this that we will pursue in chapter 11.

That leaves two types of terrorism that do not fit our conflict typology.

First there is 'state terrorism', which includes internal repression as well as external acts of terror and state sponsorship of terrorism. This has historically been by far the largest form of such violence. The US Department

Table 3.3 A conflict resolution terrorism typology

Terrorism type	Conflict type
State terrorism	
Insurgent terrorism	
Ideological	Revolution/ideology
Social revolutionary (SL, FARC)	
Right wing/survivalist	
Radical religious (GIA)	
Nationalist-separatist (LTTE, ETA, KLA)	Identity/secession
Economic/factional (RUF, LRA)	Factional
International terrorism (al-Qaeda)	

of State's *Patterns of Global Terrorism* (2002) report named Cuba, Iran, Iraq, Libya, North Korea, Sudan and Syria as state sponsors of terrorism (with Libya unexpectedly dropping off the list in 2004). More direct is the terrible toll exacted by totalitarian governments both in pursuit of ideological goals and in terrorizing opposition into submission in order to maintain their grip on power. In this sense, by far the greatest number of terrorist atrocities in the past century have been perpetrated by what Walter Laqueur (2004) calls 'terrorism from above'. According to some estimates, repressive governments intentionally killed well over 160 million of their own citizens in the twentieth century. Finally, we have already noted how, in the Arab-Islamic world, 'state terrorism' is a reference to the tactics used by the state of Israel, while western countries in general and the United States in particular are regularly accused of 'state terrorism' in particular cases (for example, the atomic bombing of Hiroshima and Nagasaki). The December 2004 UN High-Level Panel report decided not to include state terrorism in its terms of reference on the grounds that 'the legal and normative framework against state violations is far stronger than in the case of non-state actors' so that the argument was not 'compelling' (paragraph 160). (The panel also recognized the argument about 'the legitimate struggle of nations against occupation' but denied that this legitimized acts of terrorism.)

Second there is 'international terrorism', as noted above. This refers not to the international connections that link most terrorism to trans-border networks, including diaspora support constituencies, internet communications, or criminal supply and money-laundering facilities, but to the groups of dedicated activists who are international in both personnel and purpose and are not rooted in nationally based organizations. This is by no means unprecedented and is akin to previous generations of left-wing terrorism, such as international Bolshevism in the 1920s and 1930s, Che Guevara's strategy for radical global change in the 1960s, and the ambitions for world revolution of Lin Biao in China during the Cultural Revolution. Nevertheless, in the form of 'Islamic radicalism', this has now come to dominate popular perceptions of what terrorism is, because international *jihadis* are involved in other conflicts, such as separatist struggles for national identity in Palestine or Chechnya, and may be disproportionately influential thanks to training, experience, media profile and funding. Above all the sudden eruption of the Islamic State in Syria and Iraq and of Boko Haram in Nigeria have greatly increased the impact of what we are calling international terrorism. The seizure of territory and adoption of the name and rudimentary trappings of 'statehood' clearly introduces a new category that consequently demands new forms of response. We will return to this major issue at the end of chapter 11.

Conflict Costs

Before concluding this chapter we must briefly note human and material costs of contemporary violent conflicts. At least 28 million people have been killed in more than 150 major armed conflicts fought mainly in the Third World since 1945 (IISS, 1997); another estimate puts the total at 40 million civilian and military deaths (Leitenberg, 2003). The proportion of civilian casualties has risen, from only 5 per cent of total casualties in the First World War, to 50 per cent by the Second World War, and to between 80 and 90 per cent, according to some accounts, by the end of the century, of whom the majority were women and children (Grant, 1992: 26; Collier et al., 2003) – although these figures have recently been challenged.

Beyond the toll of direct combat-related deaths, civil wars increase infant and adult mortality as a result of disease, famine, displacement and the collapse of health and other services. The indirect deaths usually outweigh the direct effects of wars (Stewart and Fitzgerald, 2001). Conflicts in developing countries frequently cause food shortages and famines, due either to the deliberate use of hunger as a weapon or to the unplanned effects of fighting on production and distribution (Messer et al., 1998). The land may be mined, the wells may be poisoned. People are forced to flee their homes and abandon their means of livelihood. At their peak in 1990, internal conflicts generated 21 million refugees and 25 million internally displaced people. While refugee numbers had dropped to 16 million by 2009, the total number of displaced people (refugees plus internally displaced persons (IDPs)) remained high and appeared to be rising again towards the historic high of the 1990 figure, showing the costs of conflict being borne by those least able to afford it (UNHCR, 2009).

Since then Syria has moved from being the world's second largest hosting country for refugees to being the second largest source country. Table 3.4 and figure 3.5 show that around 75 to 80 per cent of forcibly displaced people are housed in developing countries. The most recent figures from UNHCR for 2014 (UNHCR, 2015) reveal that the combined global refugee/internally displaced persons figure is still climbing, so that it now reaches the highest number since 1945 (59.5 million compared with 51.2 million in 2013 and 37.5 million a decade earlier). This shocking figure is, in our view, the most alarming indicator of all, combining as it does the outcome of war, persecution, state failure, sectarian violence, and the criminality of 'people trafficking'. This composite tsunami of human suffering is hard to analyse and harder still to manage. It now joins earlier eras of mass migration and challenges the capacity of existing international and regional institutions to cope.

Conflict has catastrophic effects on the economic development of affected countries, generally leading to declining production, collapsing exports, greater indebtedness and falling social expenditure (Stewart and Fitzgerald, 2001). The typical civil war puts development into reverse, reducing pre-war incomes in directly affected countries by 15 per cent on average and growth

Table 3.4 Major refugee-hosting countries and major countries of origin, 2014

Major refugee hosting countries	
Turkey	1,587,374
Pakistan	1,505,525
Lebanon	1,154,040
Iran	982,027
Ethiopia	659,524
Jordan	654,141
Kenya	551,352
Chad	452,897
Uganda	385,513
China	301,052
Main countries of origin	
Syria	3,865,720
Afghanistan	2,593,368
Somalia	1,106,068
Sudan	659,395
South Sudan	616,142
DRC	516,562
CAR	410,787
Iraq	369,904
Eritrea	330,526
Myanmar	223,891

Source: UNHCR, 2015

in neighbouring countries by 0.5 per cent per annum on average (Collier et al., 2003: 2). These effects tend to persist after the fighting is over, and the resulting mal-development and institutional deformation raises the risk of the conflict being renewed.

Among other costs are the opportunity costs involved in the diversion of resources to military purposes and indirect effects such as the export of drugs and AIDS (Collier et al., 2003). There are environmental costs resulting from acts of war, such as plunder of natural resources (for example, forests) and the indirect effects of fighting and forced migration. Cultural costs arise from deliberate or unintended damage to the cultural heritage, and inter-generational costs include the scars of war, abuse, flight and genocide, which continue to traumatize the next generation. The 2015 *Global Peace Index* estimates that, overall, 'the economic impact of violence on the global economy in 2014 was US $14.3 trillion, which represents 13.4 per cent of world GDP' (IEP, 2015: 65).

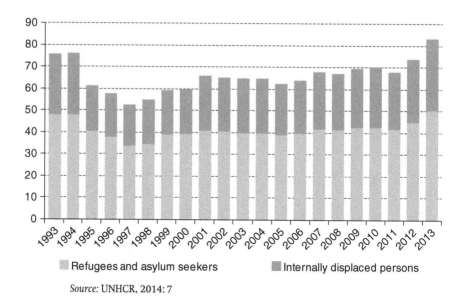

Source: UNHCR, 2014: 7

Figure 3.5 *Global forced displacement, 1993–2013 (in millions)*

Given human suffering and economic costs on this scale, why is more not done to bring conflicts to an end? Despite the widespread social costs, conflicts do have beneficiaries, for whom they can represent a source of livelihood and economic advancement. Warlords, militias, certain sections of governing elites, and rebel groups may profit from opportunities to exploit land, labour or resources, and outside arms manufacturers, traders and corporations sometimes harvest rich pickings from conflict zones (see table 4.2, p. 123). There is, as yet, insufficient effort to regulate such profiteering and to prevent aid from falling into the wrong hands. The human and material costs do, however, provide a very strong impetus for the central aim of conflict resolution: to find means of reconciling differences and achieving social change without the use of violence.

In the welter of data and statistics about peace and conflict indicators that have become available to researchers and policy-makers in the past decade, one striking trend stands out and needs to be noted in the conclusion to this section. Even if we can take some comfort from data which shows declining levels of major armed conflict in recent years, a significant proportion of the world's population do not have the choice to participate in benefits of peace and prosperity. In the case of what he has termed the 'bottom billion', Paul Collier (2008), in a masterly synthesis of his work on civil wars, has defined the conflict and poverty trap where 1 billion people, living in fifty-eight countries mostly in Africa and Central Asia, 'co-exist with the twenty-first century, but their reality is the fourteenth century: civil war, plague, ignorance'. While most of the countries of the developing world have achieved very positive growth rates since the end of the Cold War, Paul Collier's 'bottom billion' were poorer by the turn of the millennium than they had been in the 1970s. These bottom billion people are caught in a set of traps, one of which is conflict, in which there is a clear correlation between economic growth rates and proneness to civil war. In Collier's calculation, there is a 14 per cent risk in any five-year period of a typical bottom billion low-income country undergoing civil war. A typical seven-year civil war leaves a country 15 per cent poorer than it would otherwise have been. Conversely, each percentage point added to the growth rate takes a percentage point off the risk. The big conflict formation for Collier, in this analysis, is that, by 2050, the gulf will not be between the rich 1 billion of the developed world and the 5 billion in developing countries, as assumed in the UN's Millennium Development Goals, but, 'rather, it will be between the trapped one billion and the rest of humankind'. His key point is that the bottom billion in this conflict–poverty cycle or trap can only escape via policies of international action. This is a finding that echoes that of conflict researchers such as Mack and Gurr, who attribute the global decline in armed conflict to concerted programmes of international activism. This strongly supports the 'cosmopolitan conflict resolution' approach, as developed in Part II of this book. Above all, it is the costs of conflict, no matter what its nature, invariably falling mainly on those who are most vulnerable, that drives and inspires the whole enterprise of conflict resolution.

Conflict Mapping and Conflict Tracking

Having concentrated so far on types and patterns of conflict, we conclude the chapter with a brief note on the mapping and tracking of individual conflicts and identify some of the ways in which conflict analysis can be aided by the wealth of data now available on the internet.

Conflict mapping, in Paul Wehr's words, is 'a first step in intervening to manage a particular conflict. It gives both the intervenor and the conflict parties a clearer understanding of the origins, nature, dynamics and possibilities for resolution of the conflict' (1979: 18). It is a method of presenting a structured analysis of a particular conflict at a particular moment in time. It is employed by analysts to give a quick profile of a conflict situation and is also widely used in conflict resolution workshops to elicit from participants a snapshot of their view of the conflict. Any particular map should be understood to represent the views of the author(s) and, as a schematic, to be indicative rather than comprehensive. Wehr himself (ibid.: 18–22) suggested that what was necessary in conflict mapping was:

1 a short summary description (one page maximum);
2 a conflict history;
3 conflict context (geographical boundaries, political structures, communications networks, etc.);
4 conflict parties (primary, secondary, interested third parties), including

power relations (symmetrical or asymmetrical), main goals, potential for coalitions;

5   conflict issues (facts-based, values-based, interests-based, non-realistic);

6   conflict dynamics (precipitating events, issue emergence, polarization, spiralling, stereotyping);

7   alternative routes to a solution of the problem(s); and

8   conflict regulation or resolution potential (internal limiting factors, external limiting factors, interested or neutral third parties, techniques of conflict management).

Wehr's conflict mapping guide was to be applicable to 'the full range of conflict types from interpersonal to international levels'.

Adapting Wehr's conflict mapping guide, we suggest the steps outlined in box 3.5 for preparing an initial profile of a conflict. This can be supplemented by a diagram showing the main parties and third parties, the issues, and the channels of communication and influence between them (Fisher et al., 2000). The Swiss Agency for Development and Cooperation has produced an excellent compendium of seven conflict analysis tools (Reading 26). Another mapping method is the Swisspeace Conflict Analytic Framework (for an application to Angola, see Reading 27).

Box 3.5   A conflict mapping guide

A   Background
  1   Map of the area.
  2   Brief description of the country.
  3   Outline history of the conflict.

B   The conflict parties and issues
  1   Who are the core conflict parties?
     What are their internal sub-groups, on what constituencies do they depend?
  2   What are the conflict issues?
     Is it possible to distinguish between positions, interests (material interests, values, relationships) and needs?
  3   What are the relationships between the conflict parties?
     Are there qualitative and quantitative asymmetries?
  4   What are the different perceptions of the causes and nature of the conflict among the conflict parties?
  5   What is the current behaviour of the parties (is the conflict in an 'escalatory' or 'de-escalatory' phase)?
  6   Who are the leaders of the parties? At the elite/individual level, what are their objectives, policies, interests, and relative strengths and weaknesses?

C   The context: global, regional and state-level factors
  1   At the state level: is the nature of the state contested? How open and accessible is the state apparatus? Are there institutions or fora which could serve as legitimate channels for managing the conflict? How even is economic development and are there economic policies which can have a positive impact?
  2   At the regional level: how do relations with neighbouring states and societies affect the conflict? Do the parties have external regional supporters? Which regional actors might be trusted by the parties?
  3   At the global level: are there outside geopolitical interests in the conflict? What are the external factors that fuel the conflict and what could change them?

Having mapped the structure of the conflict, the next step is to use the information in the map to identify the scope for conflict resolution, preferably with the help of the parties or embedded third parties. A fuller analysis would identify changes in the context which could alter the conflict situation, including the interests and capacities of third parties to influence it; changes within and between the conflict parties, such as internal leadership struggles, varying prospects for military success, and the readiness of general populations to express support for a settlement; possible ways of redefining goals and finding alternative means of resolving differences, such as suggested steps towards settlement and eventual transformation; likely constraints on these; and how these might be overcome. These issues are considered further in the chapters that follow.

A conflict map is an initial snapshot. Analysts may then want to keep updating it by regular 'conflict tracking'. This can now be done increasingly efficiently through the internet. The revolution in communications technology that has occurred over the past few years or so has already had an impact on conflict resolution and post-conflict peacebuilding (Levy, 2004). In particular, high-quality data and information, both quantitative and qualitative in nature, is available on a variety of websites (see box 3.6). In addition, we might begin to see measures of peaceful futures built onto the methodology of conflict mapping and conflict tracking, where transformative energies and scenarios could be simulated through real-world futures workshops and computer-generated virtual alternatives negotiated via powerful ICT gaming and simulation interfaces. Early examples are now emerging of systems that harness the power of the internet and communications technologies in order to develop real-time conflict tracking. One method of doing this is the Ushahidi Mapping Platform (Reading 72), which illustrates the exciting developing potential of the internet as a technology for conflict resolution (a theme that is explored further in chapter 17).

Box 3.6 The Ushahidi mapping platform

USHAHIDI, which means 'testimony' in Swahili, is a website that was initially developed to map reports of violence in Kenya after the post-election fallout at the beginning of 2008 (see box 5.2, p. 160). Its roots are in the collaboration of Kenyan citizen journalists during a time of crisis. The website was used to map incidents of violence and peace efforts throughout the country based on reports submitted via the web and mobile phone. With an initial deployment of 45,000 users in Kenya, it was the catalyst for realizing that there was a need for a platform based on it, which could be used by others around the world.

Because Ushahidi was committed to using open source code, in May of 2008 a group in South Africa used it to map incidents of xenophobic violence. By August 2008, seed funding from Humanity United enabled the platform to be rebuilt, and by October 2008 the alpha version of Ushahidi was completed and deployed to the Democratic Republic of the Congo for testing. In its alpha form, the Ushahidi platform was tested and deployed with eleven different organizations directly, among them the International Center for Transitional Justice, Peace Heroes, and the Kenyan National Commission on Human Rights. Externally, there were four major alpha deployments, including al Jazeera during the war on Gaza, Vote Report India (to monitor the recent local elections) and Pak Voices (to map incidents of violence in Pakistan).

The goal is to create a platform that any person or organization can use to set up in their own way to collect and visualize information. The core platform will allow for plug-ins and extensions so that it can be customized for different locales and needs. The beta version platform is now available as an open source application that users can download and implement and use to bring awareness to crisis situations or other events in their own locales. It is also continually being improved and tested with various partners, primarily in Kenya.

Source: the USHAHIDI website, at www.ushahidi.com; see also iRevolution, the website of Patrick Meier, at http://irevolution.wordpress.com

Box 3.7 below demonstrates the transformation that has taken place for conflict tracking and analysis in the form of the availability of high-capacity, high-speed, searchable and downloadable datasets and related analyses. In particular, the integration of indicators of 'peacefulness' into datasets is a remarkable development of the past few years. The capacity and potential to use these and similar resources as powerful tools for analysis and policy development in the areas of conflict prevention and peacebuilding is one of the most exciting features of working in the field of conflict resolution. We return to these issues in chapter 17, where new developments in crowdsourcing for conflict resolution and peacebuilding are described.

Box 3.7 Sources of information for peace and conflict tracking

Global Peace Index: http://economicsandpeace.org/research/iep-indices-data/global-peace-index

The GPI was launched in 1997 by Steve Killelea, an Australian IT entrepreneur who in 2000 set up the Charitable Foundation, which is one of Australia's largest private funders supporting humanitarian, development and peace projects and initiatives. Killelea was influenced by Tibetan Buddhism and is a trustee of the World Council of Religions for Peace. The GPI has been published annually since 2007 and provides the most sophisticated methodology currently available to measure and rank the peacefulness of nations. In recent years, the Vision of Humanity website has added a number of high-quality datasets and related analyses, including the Global Terrorism Index, the UK Peace Index, the Mexico Peace Index and the US Peace Index. The 'parent' project for the GPI is the Institute for Economics and Peace, which produces reports on a variety of topics related to conflict analysis and peacebuilding, such as Pillars of Peace, Measuring Peace in the Media, Economic Consequences of War on the US Economy, the Economic Cost of Violence Containment – all reports available at http://economicsandpeace.org/publications.

The Heidelberg Institute for International Conflict Research (HIIK): http://hiik. de/en/index.html

Located in the Department of Political Science at the University of Heidelberg in Germany, the HIIK gathers documentation and conducts research and analysis of national and international political conflicts. It was founded in 1991 to continue the work of the research project KOSIMO (Conflict Simulation Model), now called CONIS (Conflict Information System). CONIS records information on political conflicts since 1945 and currently includes information on more than 500 conflicts in over 2,500 phases, according to levels of escalation and de-escalation and violent and non-violent phases. Research results are published in an annual Conflict Barometer.

Autonomous University of Barcelona, School for the Culture of Peace (Escuela de Cultura de Pau), Programme on Conflict and Peacebuilding: http://escola-pau.uab.cat/index.php?lang=en

This programme had its origins in an annual report on arms transfers that began in 1998. The Programme on Conflict and Peacebuilding started in 2001 and conducts daily monitoring and analysis of armed conflicts, situations of tension, peace processes, post-war rehabilitation, humanitarian crises, militarization and disarmament, human rights and international humanitarian law, and gender and peacebuilding. The findings are published in *Semáforo* (fortnightly), *Boletín Mensual* (monthly), *Barómetro* (quarterly) and the comprehensive annual report *Alerta!*.

International Crisis Group: www.icg.org

Based in Brussels, with 100 field analysts on five continents, this organization provides analyses of current conflicts and advocates policy responses. Its *CrisisWatch* bulletin regularly analyses developments in some seventy conflict situations and assesses to what extent the situation has significantly improved, deteriorated or remains the same.

Global Partnership for the Prevention of Armed Conflict: http://www.gppac. net/

The Global Partnership for the Prevention of Armed Conflict (GPPAC) is a member-led network of civil society organizations active in the field of conflict prevention and peacebuilding across the world. Based in The Hague in the Netherlands, it provides information and surveys covering prevention and peacebuilding efforts in the main violent conflicts in the world, with a primary focus on civil society actors. Presented through a searchable database, surveys of conflicts provide background information, detailed descriptions of ongoing activities to transform the conflicts, and assessments of future prospects for conflict prevention and peacebuilding. The database also provides directories leading to local and international organizations working in the field of conflict prevention and peacebuilding in relation to the conflict being researched.

INCORE: www.incore.ulst.ac.uk

Based at the University of Ulster in Northern Ireland, INCORE offers a conflict data service, consisting of a detailed database on conflicts and conflict-related issues worldwide, offering information on conflicts in specific countries and thematic information, as well as interdisciplinary guides on how conflict affects and interacts with other issues and phenomena. The service also provides an online database of peace agreements from around the world. INCORE publishes an *Ethnic Conflict Research Digest*.

Minorities at Risk (MAR): www.cidcm.umd.edu/mar/

The MAR project was initiated by Ted Robert Gurr in 1986 and has been based at the University of Maryland's Center for International Development and Conflict Management (CIDCM) since 1988. It tracks 284 politically active ethnic groups

throughout the world from 1945 to the present and focuses specifically on ethnopolitical groups – non-state communal groups that have 'political significance' – using two
criteria: first, the group collectively suffers, or benefits from, systematic discriminatory
treatment vis-à-vis other groups in a society; second, the group is the basis for political
mobilization and collective action in defence or promotion of its self-defined interests.
The centrepiece of the project is a dataset that tracks groups on political, economic and
cultural dimensions. The project also maintains analytic summaries of group histories,
risk assessments and group chronologies for each group in the dataset.

Uppsala Conflict Data Program (UCDP): www.pcr.uu.se/research/UCDP/
The Department of Peace and Conflict Research at the University of Uppsala in Sweden
has been operating the Uppsala Conflict Data Program (UCDP) for more than twenty
years. The project's dataset is one of the most accurate and well-used datasets on global
intra- and interstate armed conflicts in the world. Data on armed conflict is collected
on an annual basis (calendar year). Until now, comparable data on armed conflicts has
been available for the post-Cold War period – i.e. from 1989 and on. More recently, the
data has been expanded to cover the full post-Second World War period (1946–2001),
as part of a collaborative project between the Uppsala Conflict Data Program and
the International Peace Research Institute in Oslo. Data on armed conflicts has been
published yearly in the report series *States in Armed Conflict* since 1987, in the *SIPRI
Yearbook* (Oxford University Press) since 1988, and in the *Journal of Peace Research*
since 1993. The project's website also gives profiles of individual conflicts. The UCDP
has five main data services: the UCDP-PRIO Armed Conflict Dataset (from 1946 and
updated annually); the UCDP Conflict Termination Dataset, which complements the
main armed conflict dataset with additional information on conflict termination; the
UCDP database, a searchable web-based resource for information on global armed
conflicts since 1989; and the UCDP Non-State Conflict Data and UCDP One-Sided
Violence Data.

Peace Accords Matrix (PAM): https://peaceaccords.nd.edu/about
The Peace Accords Matrix was developed at the University of Notre Dame, Indiana, by
Professor John Derby, and both John Paul Lederach and Peter Wallensteen work on
the project. The PAM database is a unique source of qualitative and quantitative lon-
gitudinal data on the implementation of thirty-four comprehensive peace agreements
negotiated between 1989 and 2012. The population of agreements is 'comprehensive'
in two dimensions: (1) the major parties to the conflict were involved in the negotiations
that led to the written agreement; and (2) the substantive issues underlying the conflict
were included in the negotiations. PAM is a unique source of qualitative and quantitative data on intrastate peace agreements signed since 1989. The database is designed
to allow practitioners, researchers, and policy-makers to understand peace accords by
providing comparative information on accords and their implementation.

**The Nonviolent and Violent Campaigns and Outcomes (NAVCO) Data Project:
www.du.edu/korbel/sie/research/chenow_navco_data.html**
NAVCO is a multi-level data-collection project based at the University of Denver that
catalogues major non-violent and violent resistance campaigns around the globe from
1900 to 2011. Researchers can use the data in order to answer questions about how
tactical choices lead to the success or failure of such political movements, how intergroup relationships among competing insurgent organizations affect their strategic
choices, and how the sequencing of tactical choices influences the overall outcomes
of resistance campaigns. The project produces aggregate-level data on resistance campaigns from 1900 to 2006 (NAVCO 1.1), annual data on campaign behaviour from

1945 to 2006 (NAVCO 2.0) and events data on tactical selection during campaigns from 1987 to 2011 (NAVCO 3.0). Other datasets are under development, such as Building Infrastrucures for Peace and Religion and Social Cohesion.

Source: all project descriptions are from the project websites (see also Eck (2005), which provides a detailed guide to the location, content, methodology and objectives of the main datasets available)

RECOMMENDED READING

Hachemer (2014); HSR Project (2013); Pinker (2011); Smith (2014); Themnér and Wallensteen (2014).

RELEVANT EXTRACTS IN *THE CONTEMPORARY CONFLICT RESOLUTION READER*

Reading 26: S. Mason and S. Rychard, Conflict Analysis Tools
Reading 27: FAST Conflict Analytical Framework Applied to Angola
Reading 66: S. Pinker, The Better Angels of Our Nature: Why Violence Has Declined
Reading 72: Ushahidi: From Crisis Mapping in Kenya to Mapping the Globe

CHAPTER FOUR

Understanding Contemporary Conflict

Having introduced some of the main concepts in conflict resolution theory in chapter 1, described the evolution of the field in chapter 2, and looked at the statistical basis for diagnosis in chapter 3, we begin our survey of conflict resolution in the first quarter of the twenty-first century by considering the way in which major armed conflict has been analysed within the conflict resolution tradition. Adequate conflict analysis – *polemology*, to borrow the French terminology – has from the start been seen as the essential prerequisite for normative conflict resolution. This chapter, therefore, provides the necessary conceptual basis for those that follow.

Theories and Frameworks

In chapter 1 we introduced some well-known general theories of conflict from the conflict resolution tradition. These models are intended to highlight generic aspects of conflict and conflict resolution. At the other end of the spectrum are specific political and historical explanations of particular conflicts. But at the intermediate level, between generic models and individual explanations, is it possible to find what Vasquez calls a 'unified theory of conflict' (1995: 137) sufficient to account for the prevailing patterns of post-Cold War conflict with which we are concerned?

It seems unlikely on the face of it that a single all-encompassing explanation will be adequate for conflicts of different types in all the countries that were listed in table 3.1 (see p. 88). Apart from anything else, since the time when systematic studies were first undertaken in the conflict resolution field, it has been recognized that there are apparently irreducible discrepancies between major schools of analysis.[1] Using figure 4.1 as a schematic model, it is helpful to see how some of these theories are *internal*, because they locate the sources of conflict mainly *within* the nature of the protagonists (e.g. certain ethological and anthropological theories), some are *relational*, because they look for sources mainly in relations *between* conflict parties (e.g. certain theories in behavioural sociology and social psychology), and some are *contextual*, because they look mainly *outside* to the conditioning contexts that structure the conflict and in some versions also generate the conflict parties themselves (e.g. certain neo-realist and Marxist theories).[2]

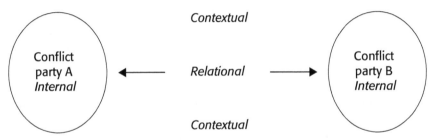

Figure 4.1 *Internal, relational and contextual theories of conflict*

This was already evident in the thinking of the European theorists of the early modern period. For Machiavelli, conflict was a result of the human desire for self-preservation and power. For Hobbes, the three 'principal causes of quarrel' in a state of nature were competition for gain, fear of insecurity, and defence of honour. For Hume, the underlying conditions for human conflict were relative scarcity of resources and limited altruism. For Rousseau, the 'state of war' was born from 'the social state' itself.

Moreover, different types of explanation are more often than not politically compromised, whether propounded by conflict protagonists or by third parties. This was the case during the Cold War[3] and is a common feature of post-Cold War conflicts. For example, in box 4.1 we may note the discrepancy between 'third-party' relational interpretations of the Northern Ireland conflict, such as the 'internal-conflict' model, and the 'traditional nationalist' and 'traditional unionist' interpretations historically espoused by the main conflict parties. This also shows how 'neutral' outside views, including academic theories of various kinds, can become as politically implicated in the struggle as any others.[4]

Nevertheless, there are explanations of conflict at the intermediate level which offer insight into contemporary conflict and help to situate it in the

---

Box 4.1 Interpretations of the Northern Ireland conflict

1 The traditional nationalist interpretation: Britain vs. Ireland
   The Irish people form a single nation and the fault for keeping Ireland divided lies with Britain.

2 The traditional unionist interpretation: Southern Ireland vs. Northern Ireland
   There are two peoples in Ireland who have an equal right to self-determination, Protestant (unionist/loyalist) and Catholic (nationalist/republican), and the fault for perpetuating the conflict lies with the refusal of nationalists to recognize this.

3 Marxist interpretations: capitalist vs. worker
   The cause of the conflict lies in the combination of an unresolved imperial legacy and the attempt by a governing capitalist class to keep the working class repressed and divided.

4 Internal-conflict interpretations: Protestant vs. Catholic within Northern Ireland
   The cause of the conflict lies in the incompatibility between the aspirations of the two divided communities in Northern Ireland.

Source: from Whyte, 1990: 113–205

context of social and international conditions. Here, we will focus on the late Edward Azar's theory of protracted social conflict (PSC) as an example of conflict resolution analysis from the late 1970s and the 1980s, which anticipated much of the current preoccupation with the domestic social roots of conflict and failures of governance (Reading 9). We will then bring Azar's ideas up to date by proposing a framework of analysis for what we call *transnational conflict* (TNC) in the light, first, of the transformed nature of the 'statistics of deadly conflict' looked at in chapter 3; second, of conflict theories that have come to prominence in the years since Azar's death in 1991; and above all, third, of the dramatic changes that have taken place over what is by now the twenty-five-year period since the end of the Cold War. We will illustrate this with reference to the Arab revolutions since December 2010 and their aftermath – all of which have happened since the third edition of this book. We will end with a short section on the analysis of complex conflict systems, because we suggest that this is integral to an understanding of the new pattern of transnational conflict.

The Context for an Evaluation of Conflict Resolution Theory

Within five years of Azar's death, Holsti was writing that wars of the late twentieth century 'are not about foreign policy, security, honor, or status; they are about statehood, governance, and the role and status of nations and communities within states' (1996: 20–1). It may seem strange, therefore, that, '[u]ntil recently, international relations theorists and strategic studies analysts paid comparatively little attention to the causes, effects and international implications of ethnic and other forms of communal conflict' within a context of weak or fragile states (Brown, 1993: vii). By the mid-1990s it had became suddenly fashionable to focus analysis on 'internal conflicts' (Brown, 1996), 'new wars' (Kaldor and Vashee, 1997), 'small wars' (Harding, 1994), 'civil wars' (King, 1997), 'ethnic conflicts' (Stavenhagen, 1996), 'conflict in postcolonial states' (van de Goor et al., 1996), and so on, and for humanitarian and development NGOs and international agencies to refer to 'complex human emergencies' or 'complex political emergencies'. But this had not been the case during Azar's lifetime. Holsti himself, for example, had continued to focus on interstate war in his 1991 study of armed conflict between 1648 and 1989. It was only by 1996 that he had changed his emphasis, diagnosing the status of communities within states and the nature of new and weak states as the 'primary locale of present and future wars' (1996: vii). This may not seem surprising in view of the decline in the relative incidence of interstate as against non-interstate war recorded in annual statistical analyses published in the 1990s, as we saw in the previous chapter. But this trend had been evident long before the 1990s, on some accounts reaching back to 1945,[5] and, although international relations and strategic studies analysts may have paid relatively little attention to the international implications of 'ethnic and other forms of communal conflict' during the Cold War period, a number of scholars in the peace and conflict research field had long been preoccupied with them in their attempts to uncover the sources of what were variously termed 'deep-rooted conflicts' (Burton, 1987), 'intractable conflicts' (Kriesberg et al., 1989) and 'protracted social conflicts'.

It has been popular for some time for analysts to relate accounts of the evolution of modern warfare to accounts of the evolution of the modern state. The key qualitative turning points are seen to have been, first, the emergence of the so-called sovereign dynastic state in Europe, heralded by Machiavelli, Bodin and Hobbes from the sixteenth and seventeenth centuries; second, the coming of the principle of popular sovereignty and national self-determination from the time of the American and French revolutions; and, third, the bipolar stand-off at great power level after 1945. The first is associated with the domestic monopolization and reorganization of military force by sovereigns and its projection outwards to create the relatively formal patterns of early modern interstate warfare in place of earlier more sporadic, localized and ill-disciplined manifestations of organized violence. The second heralded the transition to mass national armies and 'total war' accompanying the first industrial revolution and the romantic movement and reaching its climax in the two world wars. The advent of nuclear weapons and the military stand-off between the Soviet and western blocs rendered major interstate war unviable (with a few exceptions at lower levels). Instead, the prevailing patterns of armed conflict in the 1950s and 1960s became wars of national independence associated with decolonization, and those of the 1970s and 1980s were postcolonial civil wars in which the great powers intervened as part of a continuing geopolitical struggle for power and influence (Howard, 1976; Giddens, 1987; Keegan, 1993). For this reason Rice (1988) called the prevailing pattern of post-1945 wars 'wars of the third kind' (in contrast to the two earlier Clausewitzean phases), a term subsequently endorsed by Holsti and others. These are wars in which communities seek to create their own states in wars of 'national liberation' or which 'involve resistance by various peoples against domination, exclusion, persecution, or dispossession of lands and resources, by the post-colonial state' (Holsti, 1996: 27).

Some detected a further evolution in prevailing patterns of conflict in the 1990s and beyond, a third phase of 'wars of the third kind', as it were, namely a pattern of post-Cold War conflict which was seen to bear little resemblance either to European wars in the era of the dynastic state or to the 'total wars' of the first half of the twentieth century, if anything resembling earlier medieval wars in their lack of differentiation between state and society, soldier and civilian, internal and external transactions across frontiers, war and organized crime (Van Crefeld, 1991). Kaldor characterizes these 'new wars' in terms of political goals (no longer the foreign policy interests of states, but the consolidation of new forms of power based on ethnic homogeneity); ideologies (no longer universal principles such as democracy, fascism or socialism, but tribalist and communalist identity politics); forms of mobilization (no longer conscription or appeals to patriotism, but fear, corruption, religion, magic and the media); external support (no longer superpowers or ex-colonial powers, but diaspora, foreign mercenaries, criminal mafia, regional powers); mode of warfare (no longer formal and organized campaigns with demarcated front lines, bases and heavy weapons, but fragmented and dispersed, involving paramilitary and criminal groups, child soldiers, light weapons, and the use of atrocity, famine, rape and siege); and the war economy (no longer funded by taxation and generated by state mobilization, but sustained by outside emergency assistance and the parallel economy, including unofficial export of timber and precious metals, drug-trafficking, criminal rackets, plunder) (Kaldor and Vashee, 1997: 7–19; Münkler, 2005; Kaldor, 2006; Reading 17).

In fact, both Kaldor and Holsti followed Rice in suggesting that the key turning point in all this was not so much 1989 or 1990 as 1945. For Kaldor, '[s]ince 1945, there have been very few interstate wars' (1999: 29), while, for Holsti:

> The problem is that the Clausewitzean image of war, as well as its theoretical accoutrements, has become increasingly divorced from the characteristics and sources of most armed conflicts since 1945. The key question is: given that most wars since 1945 have been *within* states, of what intellectual and policy relevance are concepts and practices derived from the European and Cold War experiences that diagnosed or prescribed solutions for the problem of war *between* states? (1996: 14; original emphasis)

Does this suggest that the analysis of interstate war, which dominated international relations after 1945, is largely irrelevant to post-1945 conflict? Entire tracts of quantitative research since the Second World War have been devoted to the search for 'correlates of interstate war' which might give a clue to its sources and nature. Analysts have sought to align measurable features of interstate and related wars, such as their incidence, frequency, duration, magnitude, severity, intensity and costs, with empirically verifiable variables, such as structures (e.g. whether the hegemonic system is unipolar, bipolar, multipolar), relations (e.g. patterns of alliances, distribution of relative capabilities, configurations of power and power transition, arms races), national attributes (e.g. levels of domestic unrest, types of domestic regime, levels of economic development), and other aspects of what Mansbach and Vasquez (1981) call the 'paths to war' (e.g. the positive expected utility for decision-makers in initiating hostilities).[6] This vast enterprise is seen to have produced mixed results.[7] But is it possible that, in terms of prevailing patterns of post-1945 conflict, most international relations and strategic studies experts were looking in the wrong direction? Could it be that, mesmerized by the bipolar stand-off at great power level, analysts subsumed both decolonizing wars of national liberation and postcolonial civil wars into traditional Europeanized conceptual categories, failing to notice the qualitative change that had taken place when prevailing patterns of major armed conflict ceased being intra-European interstate wars after 1945? And was it only with the collapse of the Soviet Union that analysts belatedly realized that the 'new' patterns of post-Cold War conflict were in fact not so new, but had been prevalent, albeit under different geopolitical conditions, for nearly half a century?

We do not want to pronounce on these large questions here, beyond noting that this is the context within which Azar's work should be evaluated, because he had been arguing for a radical revision of prevailing Clausewitzean ideas since the 1970s. He was not alone in doing this, of course. He was heavily indebted to other conflict resolution theorists, notably John Burton, with whom he co-published, although we will not try to disentangle credit for contributory ideas here. We should also be careful about unhistorical assumptions about 'new' features of warfare, which can in most cases be shown to have a long ancestry (Newman, 2004). Nevertheless, throughout this period there were still 'Clausewitzean' wars going on (between India and Pakistan, Israel and her neighbours, China and Vietnam, Iraq and Iran), 'mixed civil-international wars' were largely structured by Cold War geopolitics, and at great power level the two main alliances were still strenuously preparing for the possibility, if not likelihood, of a thoroughly Clausewitzean military encounter, despite the nuclear stalemate. It was the latter which largely preoccupied international relations and strategic studies analysts at the time, so that the reconceptualization of prevailing patterns of conflict offered by Azar and other conflict resolution analysts was hardly noticed in the conventional literature.

Edward Azar's Theory of Protracted Social Conflict (PSC)

Edward Azar was born in Lebanon in 1938, moved to the United States as a graduate international relations student, and subsequently specialized in what was at first a mainly quantitative analysis of interstate conflict. His Conflict and Peace Research Data Bank, built up at the University of North Carolina, however, already included internal domestic as well as external international data, and he was progressively drawn to concentrate as much if not more on the former than on the latter, not least as a result of his increasing concern about the condition of his native Lebanon. This was further reinforced by his experience on a number of dialogue and discussion sessions, mainly on the Middle East, including participation in Herbert Kelman's and Stephen Cohen's Harvard University problem-solving workshops. This brought him into the mainstream of the new conflict resolution fraternity, whose attempted reconceptualization of the roots of large-scale contemporary violence he found congenial and confirmatory of his own thinking. In particular, he came to work closely in the 1980s with John Burton, and together they set up the Center for International Development and Conflict Management (CIDCM) at the University of Maryland. When Burton moved on to George Mason University, Azar stayed at Maryland, where he died in 1991 (see Fisher, 1997: ch. 4).

For Edward Azar, in a sustained sequence of studies published from the early 1970s (see References for his main publications), the critical factor in protracted social conflict (PSC), such as persisted in Lebanon (his own particular field of study), Sri Lanka, the Philippines, Northern Ireland, Ethiopia, Israel, Sudan, Cyprus, Iran, Nigeria or South Africa, was that it represented 'the prolonged and often violent struggle by communal groups for such basic needs as security, recognition and acceptance, fair access to political institutions and economic participation' (1991: 93). Traditional preoccupation with relations between states was seen to have obscured a proper understanding of these dynamics. Indeed, in radical contrast to the concerns of international law, the distinction between domestic and international politics was rejected as 'artificial': 'there is really only one social environment and its domestic face is the more compelling' (Azar and Burton, 1986: 33). The role of the state (as also linkages with other states) was to satisfy or frustrate basic communal needs, thus preventing or promoting conflict (Azar, 1990: 10–12; Reading 9; Reading 15).

Drawing upon datasets of PSC compiled from the 1970s at the University of Maryland, Azar systematically developed and refined his understanding of the dynamics which generated violent and persistent conflict of this kind. At the time of his last writings, in the early 1990s, he identified more than sixty examples of this 'new type of conflict', which, 'distinct from traditional disputes over territory, economic resources, or East–West rivalry ... revolves around questions of communal identity' (1991: 93). In the opening chapter of what is perhaps his most succinct summation of a decade and a half's work, *The Management of Protracted Social Conflict: Theory and Cases* (1990), Azar contrasts three aspects of what up until then had been a prevailing orthodoxy in war studies with his own approach. First, there had been a tendency 'to understand conflicts through a rather rigid dichotomy of internal and external dimensions', with sociologists, anthropologists and psychologists preoccupied with the former ('civil wars, insurgencies, revolts, coups, protests, riots, revolutions, etc.') and international relations scholars with the latter ('interstate wars, crises, invasions, border conflicts, blockades, etc.'). Second, prevailing frameworks of analysis had often been based on the functional differentiation of conflict aspects and types into sub-categories of psychological, social, political and economic conflicts and into different 'levels of analysis'. Third, there had been a tendency to focus on overt and violent conflict, while ignoring covert, latent or non-violent conflict, and on an approach to conflict dynamics in terms of conflict cycles in which the 'termination of violent acts is often equated with the state of peace'. In contrast, a study of PSC suggested that:

> many conflicts currently active in the underdeveloped parts of the world are characterized by a blurred demarcation between internal and external sources and actors. Moreover, there are multiple causal factors and dynamics, reflected in changing goals, actors and targets. Finally, these conflicts do not show clear starting and terminating points. (Azar, 1990: 6)

The term 'protracted social conflict' emphasized that the sources of such conflicts lay predominantly within (and across) rather than between states, with four clusters of variables identified as preconditions for their transformation to high levels of intensity.

First, there was the 'communal content', the fact that the 'most useful unit of analysis in protracted social conflict situations is the identity group – racial, religious, ethnic, cultural and others' (Azar, 1986: 31). In contrast to the well-known 'levels of analysis' framework popularized by Kenneth Waltz (1959), which in its classic form distinguished system, state and individual levels, PSC analysis focuses in the first instance on identity groups, however defined, noting that it is the relationship between identity groups and states which is at the core of the problem (what Azar called the 'disarticulation between the state and society as a whole'; 1990: 7), and how individual interests and needs are mediated through membership of social groups ('what is of concern are the *societal needs* of the individual – security, identity, recognition and others'; 1986: 31). Azar links the disjunction between state and society in many parts of the world to a colonial legacy which artificially imposed European ideas of territorial statehood onto 'a multitude of communal groups' on the principle of 'divide and rule'. As a result, in many postcolonial multicommunal societies the state machinery comes to be 'dominated by a single communal group or a coalition of a few communal groups that are unresponsive to the needs of other groups in the society', which 'strains the social fabric and eventually breeds fragmentation and protracted social conflict'. As to the formation of identity groups themselves, as noted in chapter 2, Azar, like other conflict resolution theorists, drew on a rich tradition of research in social psychology and social anthropology to sketch the various ways in which individual needs come to be mediated and articulated through processes of socialization and group identity, themselves culturally conditioned (Lewin, 1948; Kelly, 1955; Sherif, 1966; Deutsch, 1973; Tajfel, 1978; Horowitz, 1985; Reading 16).

Second, following other conflict resolution analysts, notably John Burton, Azar identified deprivation of human needs as the underlying source of PSC ('Grievances resulting from need deprivation are usually expressed collectively. Failure to redress these grievances by the authority cultivates a niche for a protracted social conflict': 1990: 9). Unlike interests, needs are 'ontological' and non-negotiable, so that conflict, if it comes, is likely to be intense, vicious and, from a traditional Clausewitzean perspective, 'irrational'. In particular, Azar cites security needs, development needs, political access needs and identity needs (cultural and religious expression), the first three corresponding to Henry Shue's three 'basic rights' of security, subsistence and freedom (1980). Arguing for a broader understanding of 'security' than was usual in academic circles at the time, Azar linked this to an equally broad understanding of 'development' and 'political access':

> Reducing overt conflict requires reduction in levels of underdevelopment. Groups which seek to satisfy their identity and security needs through conflict are in effect seeking change in the structure of their society. Conflict resolution can truly occur and last if satisfactory amelioration of underdevelopment occurs as well. Studying protracted

conflict leads one to conclude that peace is development in the broadest sense of the term. (1990: 155)

Third, in a world in which the state has been 'endowed with authority to govern and use force where necessary to regulate society, to protect citizens, and to provide collective goods', Azar cited 'governance and the state's role' as the critical factor in the satisfaction or frustration of individual and identity-group needs: 'Most states which experience protracted social conflict tend to be characterized by incompetent, parochial, fragile, and authoritarian governments that fail to satisfy basic human needs' (1990: 10). Here he made three main points. Whereas in western liberal theory the state 'is an aggregate of individuals entrusted to govern effectively and to act as an impartial arbiter of conflicts among the constituent parts', treating all members of the political community as legally equal citizens, this is not empirically what happens in most parts of the world, particularly in newer and less stable states, where political authority 'tends to be monopolized by the dominant identity group or a coalition of hegemonic groups' which use the state to maximize their interests at the expense of others. Both through the mobilization of group interests and identities by ruling elites, and through the reactive counter-identification of excluded 'minorities', the 'communal content of the state' becomes basic to the study of PSC. Next, the monopolizing of power by dominant individuals and groups and the limiting of access to other groups precipitates a 'crisis of legitimacy', so that 'regime type and the level of legitimacy' come to be seen as 'important linkage variables between needs and protracted social conflict' (ibid.: 11). Finally, Azar notes how PSCs tend to be concentrated in developing countries, which are typically characterized by 'rapid population growth and limited resource base' and also have restricted 'political capacity', often linked to a colonial legacy of weak participatory institutions, a hierarchical tradition of imposed bureaucratic rule from metropolitan centres, and inherited instruments of political repression: 'In most protracted social conflict-laden countries, political capacity is limited by a rigid or fragile authority structure which prevents the state from responding to, and meeting, the needs of various constituents.'

Finally, there is the role of what Azar called 'international linkages', in particular political–economic relations of economic dependency within the international economic system and the network of political–military linkages constituting regional and global patterns of clientage and cross-border interest. Modern states, particularly weak states, are porous to the international forces operating within the wider global community: the '[f]ormation of domestic social and political institutions and their impact on the role of the state are greatly influenced by the patterns of linkage within the international system' (1990: 11).

Whether or not in any one case these four clusters of preconditions for PSC in the event activate overt conflict will depend upon the more contingent actions and events of 'process dynamics', which Azar analyses into three groups of determinants: 'communal actions and strategies', 'state actions and strategies' and 'built-in mechanisms of conflict' (1990: 12–15). The first of these involves the various processes of identity-group formation, organization and mobilization, the emergence and nature of leadership, the choice of political goals (access, autonomy, secession, revolutionary political programme) and tactics (civil disobedience, guerrilla war), and the scope and nature of externalities. State actions and strategies form the second main element, with governing individuals and elites at any one time theoretically facing an array of policy choices running from different forms of political accommodation at one end of the spectrum to 'coercive repression' or 'instrumental co-option' at the other. In Azar's view, given the perceived political and economic costs involved in weak and fragmented polities, and because of the 'winner-take-all' norm 'which still prevails in multicommunal societies', it is much more likely to be repression than accommodation. Finally, there are the various self-reinforcing 'built-in mechanisms of conflict' exhaustively studied by conflict resolution analysts once the malign spiral of conflict escalation is triggered.

Azar drew on the work of Sumner (1906), Gurr (1970), Mitchell (1981a) and others to trace the process by which mutually exclusionary 'experiences, fears and belief systems' generate 'reciprocal negative images which perpetuate communal antagonisms and solidify protracted social conflict'. Antagonistic group histories, exclusionist myths, demonizing propaganda and dehumanizing ideologies serve to justify discriminatory policies and legitimize atrocities. In these circumstances, in a dynamic familiar to students of international relations as the 'security dilemma', actions are mutually interpreted in the most threatening light, 'the worst motivations tend to be attributed to the other side', the space for compromise and accommodation shrinks, and 'proposals for political solutions become rare, and tend to be perceived on all sides as mechanisms for gaining relative power and control' (Azar, 1990: 15). All of this intensifies further as political crisis spirals into war, where new vested interests emerge dependent upon the political economy of the war itself, the most violent and unruly elements in society appear in leadership roles, and criminality becomes a political norm. At the limit, disintegration follows. With sustained attrition, political structures buckle and collapse, a social implosion which subsequently sucks everything else in. We reach the scenario of what we call 'disintegrated war zones' and what others have characterized as 'opportunistic' rebellions (Weinstein, 2006) or apparently never-ending and chaotic 'Hobbesian war' (de Waal, 2009, 2014).

Azar saw PSC analysis as an attempt to 'synthesize the realist and structuralist paradigms into a pluralist framework' more suitable for explaining prevalent patterns of conflict than the more limited alternatives (1991: 95). We are not claiming here that Azar's analysis is the last word on the subject, nor that he was alone in pointing to the significance of mobilized identities, exclusionist ideologies, fragile and authoritarian governance, weak states

Table 4.1 Azar's preconditions for protracted social conflict (PSC)

Relevant discipline	Preconditions for PSCs	Correlates
Anthropology, history, sociology	Communal content	Degree of ethnic dominance
Psychology, biology, development studies	Needs	Levels of human development
Politics, political economy	Governance	State capacity and scales of political repression
International relations, strategic studies	International linkages	Volume of arms imports etc.; cross-border fomentation

and disputed sovereignty as chief sources of major armed conflict within an as yet unrepresentative economic and political globalized system in which international arms flows all too easily coalesce with international crime (we have only to think of the work of David Horowitz (1985) and Anthony Smith (1986) in the mid-1980s); we claim only that his approach anticipated many aspects of what has since become orthodoxy and that his ideas deserve more recognition than they have been given.

A further point is worth making. In terms of 'correlates of war', Azar's ideas were also seen to offer a framework for the analysis of prevailing patterns of war, which differed from what was usual when interstate war was the object of analysis (see the kinds of indicator suggested in Esty et al., 1998). Table 4.1 both shows the way in which Azar's 'preconditions' widened the relevance of different disciplines to the study of protracted social conflict beyond what had hitherto been normal in mainstream international relations and suggests indicatively the kinds of correlate that came into view as a result. Such expanded and merged comparative statistical studies of prevailing patterns of conflict are still in their infancy, as chapter 3 has shown. But it might be claimed that Azar's model offered a hopeful beginning.

From Protracted Social Conflict to Transnational Conflict, 1990–2015: An Interpretative Framework

It is now twenty-five years since the end of the Cold War. In previous editions of this book we compared Azar's theory with more recent theories and adapted it accordingly. This time, given the fundamental changes that have taken place in the categorizing of 'statistics of deadly conflicts' as described in chapter 3, and in the prevailing patterns of conflict itself – some becoming evident since the previous edition – we have decided to offer a new interpretative framework to capture and locate the main features of what we call contemporary *transnational conflict*. The framework is not a theory of conflict but an analytic structure where the main theoretical insights – and controversies – can be located. Transnational conflict is an extension of protracted social conflict that takes account of the global changes that have occurred since the end of the Cold War and of the 'regonalization' of conflict that has resulted. The hallmark of transnational conflict is that the global *drivers of conflict* – deeply affected by geopolitical shifts in power – are now linked almost instantaneously to local *sites of confrontation* via *transnational connectors* – flows of people, capital, weapons, criminal networks, money and ideas. These, like a bloodstream passing backwards and forwards through veins and arteries, affect and are affected by what is happening at other levels. In addition to global, regional and local levels, three other intermediate levels of analysis interconnect to make up the nexus of contemporary transnational conflict – state level, identity-group level, and elite/individual level (see table 4.2).[8]

Before commenting on table 4.2, it is worth addressing two influential alternative ways of characterizing prevailing forms of contemporary conflict: first, the attempt in the 'greed versus grievance' debate to refute Azar's central idea that protracted social conflict is rooted in the individual and communal needs of identity groups and the incapacity or unwillingness of states and governments to satisfy them; second, the analysis of contemporary conflict based on the distinction between 'old wars' and 'new wars' noted earlier in this chapter.

On the former, we follow Lars-Erik Cederman, Kristian Gleditsch and Halvard Buhaug's statistically based reaffirmation of the PSC thesis in *Inequality, Grievances and Civil War* (2013), where they argue that 'political and economic inequalities following group lines generate grievances that can motivate civil war' – or, as one of the chapter headings succinctly puts it, 'from horizontal inequality to civil war via grievances' (2013: 30; see also Reading 19). This is a refutation of the claim by Collier and Hoeffler (2001) that civil wars are generated not by the complex intractability of government exclusion and discrimination and resulting group 'grievance' but by more straightforward rebel 'greed' and a contestation over economic resources. It also conflicts with the argument of Fearon and Laitin (2003; Reading 25) that civil wars are caused not by grievances but by opportunities that favour insurgencies. Cederman and his colleagues argue that earlier research is methodologically flawed because it jumps from country-level to individual-level analysis and 'overlooks intermediate levels of aggregation where collective grievances are directly relevant and where inequalities are most easily detected' (2013: 6). In terms of policy recommendations, the significance of this dispute was well explained by Andrew Mack:

> If grievances have nothing to do with the onset of war, then seeking to assuage them via preventive diplomacy, conflict resolution and confidence-building strategies will do nothing to reduce the risk of armed conflicts. If Collier & Hoeffler and Fearon & Laitin are correct, and what counts is not grievance but the relative capabilities of rebels versus the state, the strategies of 'peace through strength', repression and deterrence would appear to be optimal strategies. (2002: 522; quoted in Cederman et al., 2013: 223)

In the event, both Collier (2008) and Fearon and Laitin (2011) have rowed back from their earlier positions. Cederman et al. confirm Azar's argument that 'the best way to break the cycle of violence driven by political exclusion and economic inequality is to involve groups that have been marginalised by giving them a real stake in their country's future' (2013: 7). The element of rapacity and 'greed' is undoubtedly present throughout the phenomenon of transnational conflict – the analysis retains its validity – but it is not sufficiently inclusive or distinct to characterize the prevailing patterns of contemporary conflict as a whole.

Turning to the idea that contemporary conflict is best characterized by a distinction between old wars and new wars, we find this persuasive and highly instructive but, again, not sufficient to capture the wider lineaments of the emergent post-Cold War conflict scene. In the new wars thesis, state decay in some regions has been seen to coincide with the end of Cold War control, rapidly reduced costs, and increased availability of weapons, as well as a change in tactics and the function of war, no longer aimed so much at decisive military victory as at perpetuating the economic and other gains associated with the continuance of violence (Reading 18; Keen, 1998; Kaldor, [1999] 2012; Reno, 1999, 2011; de Waal, 2009). The emphasis is on the way new wars merge into forms of cross-border economic exploitation and criminal networks and are sustained often by the very measures taken to end them (although we have noted above how many or most of these features are far from new). Armed groupings form, merge, shift alliances and mutate depending on local assessments of relative security and gain. We will comment further on this in chapter 6 in relation to what we call 'disintegrated war zones' and in chapter 7 in relation to the challenge in these cases of securing negotiated settlements and building consent from the ground up. In an attempt to distinguish new wars from more traditional civil wars and rebellions, Jeremy Weinstein (2006) contrasts traditional 'activist rebellions', where participation is risky, aims are longer term, and commitment to the cause is high, and 'opportunistic rebellions', where there are fewer immediate risks, gains are short term, and commitment is low. Alex de Waal contrasts traditional 'Schmittian conflicts' between organized conflict parties over sovereignty and power with 'Hobbesan conflicts' made up of a bewildering array of shifting localized struggles and alliances in large, poor and ill-governed countries, a free-for-all where each has to fend for itself in the absence of central government control, which he calls the 'political marketplace' (de Waal, 2014).[9] Insightful and helpful though this is, we find that much of the new wars literature tends to describe symptoms rather than locate causes, and that the dichotomies suggested are too Manichaean to capture the fluid nature of contemporary armed conflict in general.

It is at levels 4 and 5 in table 4.2 in particular that group psychology and individual psychology become prominent. It can be seen that the bottom half of the framework corresponds to Azar's PSC analysis, but the top half is an extension of it. State-level analysis mediates between the two. We now use this interpretative framework to comment on the interlocking features of transnational conflict.

Table 4.2 An interpretative framework for transnational conflict (TNC)

Level	Feature
1 Global	<u>Global drivers</u> Geopolitical transition North–South economic divide Discrepancy between state system and distribution of peoples Global ideological contestation <u>Transnational connectors</u> Movement and exchange (flows) of people, weapons, capital, criminal and terrorist networks, economic resources, and ideas that connect global/local via intermediate levels.
2 Regional	<u>Complex conflict systems</u> E.g., Arab world, West Africa, East Africa, Latin America, former Soviet states, Central Asia, South Asia, East Asia, etc., also including Europe and North America <u>Intra-regional dynamics</u> Regional rivalries, spillover, cross-border demography, contagion, diaspora, etc.
3 State *Social* *Economic* *Political* *Geographical*	<u>Measures of fragility</u> Weak society: cultural divisions, ethnic imbalance Weak economy: poor resource base, relative deprivation Weak polity: partisan government, regime illegitimacy, levels of repression Weak central control
4 Identity group	<u>Nature of conflict parties (bases for group formation)</u> Ethnic/sectarian/clan/family/class <u>Intergroup dynamics (escalation, de-escalation)</u> Group actions and strategies (politicization, militarization) State actions and strategies Built-in mechanisms of conflict (reciprocal dynamics)
5 Elite/ individual	<u>Leadership roles</u> Exclusionist policies, factional interest, rapacity/greed

Global-level analysis

We first identify four main global drivers of transnational conflict. These correspond roughly to the four 'ideal-types' of conflict listed in chapter 3:

- interstate conflict;
- economic/resource conflict;
- identity/secession conflict;
- revolution/ideology conflict.

In the latter three cases, these can also be seen to be associated in turn with 'identity groups', as commented on below, based on class, ethnicity or religious/sectarian differences. Needless to say, as emphasized in chapter 3, these ideal-types intermingle and transmute as they pass across the different levels of transnational conflict – another characteristic feature of the transnational conflict scene. Other global drivers could be added, such as those generated by environmental constraints, but it will be best to look at these later. For the sake of simplicity we do not distinguish the global level from the international level here, but subsume the latter within the global and regional levels.

Global drivers of transnational conflict

Geopolitical transition, a key factor in realist theories, shapes the framework of transnational conflict. The end of the bipolar world saw a number of conflicts become more amenable to settlement in the early 1990s, but others, hitherto suppressed, become more exposed: 'More than anything else, it is the uncertainty following the passing of the old order that allows conflict to break out with such abandon at the end of the millennium' (Zartman, 1997: 6). The brief 'unipolar moment' when the United States seemed the only hyperpower passed with extraordinary rapidity, foundering both on the manifest limitations of US military power to handle transnational conflicts in Afghanistan and Iraq and on the seismic 2008 global economic crisis, which saw the end of the era in which the US economy was strong enough on its own to underpin the world trade system. The advent of Russia, China and India in the international economic system made this unsustainable. It ushered in the current complex multipolar world, where conflicts are regionalized and, for the most part, none of the great powers has the capacity or will to manage them. Interstate rivalries both stoke the antagonisms and neutralize each other, leaving power vacuums into which the unruly forces of transnational conflict rush.

The North–South economic divide is widely recognized as a gobal driver of transnational conflict. This is the locus for the powerful international political economy analysis which argues that 'new wars' in what used to be called the 'Third World' are not symptomatic of local failures in governance but a product of the distortions of late capitalism. The way they are now managed by donor governments, international financial institutions, and aid and development agencies, as well as the United Nations, perpetuates and exacerbates this. Economic development and the penetration of societies by corporate interests may change social development patterns in ways that add to existing social conflicts, regional disparities and grievances and perpetuate structural conflict (Reading 23; Cramer, 2006). Here rapid population rise and mass urbanization within a global capitalist setting have created a global underclass, not only in 'fragile' lower-income states but also in middle-income and upper-income states, where traditional rural communities have been disrupted and predominantly youthful populations of unemployed males in the exploding cities provide fertile soil for radicalization. As noted in chapter 3, 'fragile cities' are now seen as major sites for global concern. The 'transnational connector' of the internet and social media make these discrepancies all too evident to more and more of the global underclass.

Some analysts go further and argue that development has been co-opted into a global security regime that uses conflict resolution and social reconstruction – as well as the more obvious instruments of international military control – to transform target societies in the image of the interveners in order to pacify the unruly periphery and maintain the status quo (see chapters 6 and 8): 'the conflict resolution and post-war reconstruction concerns of liberal governance could be seen as the "riot control" end of a spectrum encompassing a broad range of "global poor relief" activities' (Duffield, 2001: 9; see also Duffield, 2007; Pugh et al., 2008a).

The discrepancy between state borders and the geographical distribution of peoples lies behind the increased prominence of nationalism and ethnicity in explanations for war since the 1990s (van Evera, 1994; Esman, 2004). Although the opening preamble to the UN Charter refers to 'We the peoples', the UN has been seen from the outset as a club of states. The quadrupling of the number of states since 1945 through the process of decolonization has resulted in some 200 states, most of which have been rapidly imposed on the remarkable complexity of the patchwork of underlying groupings. On some estimates, perhaps 5,000 identity groups worldwide could claim independence but find themselves, usually as minorities, in states dominated by other groups or divided by colonially imposed international borders. Beneath this in some parts of the world are innumerable sub-systems of clans, sub-clans and extended families, sometimes identified by religious as well as ethnic and other labels (e.g. sectarian identity groups). These fundamental structural discrepancies impact at regional level (cutting across borders), state level (challenging state capacity) and identity-group level (forming the social basis for both challenger and possessor groups) – demonstrating the characteristic ubiquity of transnational conflict. Ultimately it is the entire postcolonial state system – the foundation of international order – that is challenged, as in the current assault on the 'Sykes–Picot' system in the Middle East.

Global ideological contestation has become if anything more prominent in the post-Cold War world, abetted by the vastly increased capacity for recruitment and radicalization offered by the communications revolution (see chapter 17). Older ideological challenges to the prevailing order, such as Marxism (associated with the second global driver identified above) and ethno-nationalism (associated with the third global driver) – as well as the democratic challenge to autocracy – are still potent. But the 1979 Iranian Revolution ushered in another, and to western academia unexpected, contestant – radical religion – particularly (but not only) in the form of political Islam and its neo-*jihadi* offspring. Some have interpreted historic Muslim *ressentiment* against the West in these terms (Lewis, 2002) or pitted Islamic fundamentalism (*jihad*) against secular consumerist capitalism (McWorld) (Barber, 2001). Others have been more circumspect (Armstrong, 2001; Shadid, 2002). Major sectarian 'fault lines' (Protestant/Catholic in Northern Ireland; Sunni/Shia in Islam) have further complicated and deepened the transnational rifts.

Transnational connectors   We formally locate the transnational connectors in table 4.2 at global level, although they serve to animate and link all the other levels and thereby generate the characteristic 'global/local' aspect of transnational conflict. They are made up of a complex of transnational flows:

- of people (migrants, refugees, diaspora, radicalized *jihadis*);
- of resources (diamonds, timber, drugs, oil, money laundering);
- of corporate investments (which may unbalance and exploit indigenous economies);
- of weapons (small and light weapons (SALW), but also heavier weapons, and even a possible proliferation of chemical, biological, radiological and nuclear material);
- of criminals and terrorist networks (whether or not abetted by governments);
- of images, ideas and movements conveyed by the explosively expanding connector of the global social media.

We retain table 4.3 (primary commodity exports) and box 4.2 (arms exports) from earlier editions of this book to show how this was already a feature in the 1990s.

Although many of these transnational connectors have long existed in a globalized world, their growth and interconnection since the end of the Cold War has been exponential to the point where they are now a defining characteristic of contemporary transnational conflict itself. For example, the struggle between governments and challengers to control the internet is likely to

Table 4.3 Primary commodity exports and the financing of conflict

Combatant	Resource	Period	Est. revenue
Angola rebels (UNITA)	Diamonds	1992–2001	$4–4.2 billion total
Sierra Leone rebels (RUF)	Diamonds	1990s	$25–125 million/year
Liberia government	Timber	Late 1990s	$100–187 million/year
Sudan government	Oil	Since 1999	$400 million/year
Rwanda government	Coltan (from Congo)	1999–2000	$250 million total
Afghanistan (Taliban, Northern Alliance)	Opium, lapis lazuli, emeralds	Mid-1990s–2001	$90–100 million/year
Cambodia government, Khmer Rouge	Timber	Mid-1990s	$230–390 million/year
Myanmar government	Timber	1990s	$112 million/year
Colombia (FARC rebels)	Cocaine	Late 1990s	$140 million/year

Source: Renner, 2002

Box 4.2 Arms exports and conflict

Some $176 billion worth of weaponry was exported to the Third World between 1987 and 1991. Keith Krause (1996) notes three theoretical models of the relation between arms exports and conflict, each of which carries a different policy prescription. Weapon availability can be seen as (a) an independent variable causing conflict, (b) a dependent variable following conflict, or (c) an intervening variable acting as a catalyst in conflicts caused by deeper factors. He favours the third alternative. In fact, many post-Cold War conflicts have been fought with small arms rather than heavy weapons (Boutwell et al., 1995). Moreover, the recipients have increasingly been sub-state groups (Karp, 1994). On one estimate, the trade in small arms has been worth some $10 billion a year (*The Economist*, 12 February 1994: 19–21). Indeed, in many cases, as in Rwanda in 1994, the worst massacres have been perpetrated with machetes.

be critical and to ebb and flow, while the increased capacity of 'asymmetric warfare' to challenge even the most powerful militaries is now reshaping the nature of prevailing patterns of warfare – not only in 'new wars', but more generally.

Regional-level analysis

The end of the Cold War and the resulting 'regionalization' of world politics highlight the importance of the regional level of explanation in contemporary transnational conflict analysis.

Complex regional conflict systems At the centre of this work is the idea of over-lapping complex regional conflict systems, as noted in chapter 3. This is a development of the earlier work on 'regional security complexes' (groups of states with interconnected security concerns) by Barry Buzan and his associates in the 1980s. They found a spectrum ranging from regions in turmoil (marked by numerous conflict formations), through security regimes (where member states remain potential threats to each other but have reduced mutual insecurity by formal and informal arrangements), to pluralistic security communities (where member states no longer feel that they need to make serious provision for a mutual use of force against each other). They originally located the main determinants of regional stability in inter-state factors: the numbers of state players within a given security complex, the patterns of amity and hostility and the distributions of power (Buzan, 1991: ch. 5). Change within a security complex could be measured in terms of four quite simple structural parameters: the maintenance of the status quo, internal change within the complex, external boundary change (states entering or leaving the complex), and 'overlay' – the dominant intrusion of an outside power. By the end of the 1990s this had became a more complex model (Buzan et al., 1997).[10]

Statistical data now suggests that there are marked differences, not only between different levels of conflict across regions (zones of peace and zones of war) but also between different prevailing patterns of conflict. For example, the Afghan conflict must be seen within a complex that includes Pakistan and the neighbouring states involved. Prevailing patterns in West Africa are linked to but also distinct from those in East Africa. Conflict in the former Soviet states is shaped by current attempts to revive a Russian 'homeland' and a Russian 'sphere of influence'. The East Asia complex (which also takes in North Korea) is dominated by the rivalry and historical enmity between China and Japan. Patterns of conflict are distinctive again in Latin America. The main thrust of regional analysis today, informed by the 'merging of datasets' for the measurement of large-scale violence noted in chapter 3 – which includes 'transnational crime' and 'fragile cities' as well as more traditional conflict categories – is to incorporate all of this within the wider analysis of trans-national conflict in general, despite these differences, because of the myriad transnational connectors that now link and shape them. This is illustrated in the case study of the Arab revolutions that follows.

Intra-regional dynamics   This is also the location for the more detailed study of intra-regional dynamics, such as the work of Cederman et al. (2009) on transnational kin groups. Those who emphasize regional dynamics see this as both outwards ('spillover', 'contagion', 'diffusion') and inwards ('influence', 'interference', 'intervention') (Lake and Rothchild, 1997). 'Internal' wars have external effects on the region through the spread of weaponry, economic dis-location, links with terrorism, disruptive floods of refugees, and spillover into regional politics when neighbouring states are dragged in or the same people straddle several states. Conversely, regional instability affects the internal politics of states through patterns of clientage, the actions of outside govern-ments, cross-border movements of people and ideas, black market activities, criminal networks and the spread of small arms. 'Bad neighbours' and 'bad neighbourhoods' may be decisive in overwhelming attempts in fragile states to control these forces (Brown, 1996). Other factors affect intra-regional conflict patterns, as where river basins extend across state boundaries (Gleick, 1995).[11] Alexander Ramsbotham and William Zartman (2011) offer an informed and accessible account of some of these dynamics in their *Paix sans frontières: Building Peace across Borders*, where they note the ways in which 'peacebuilding strategies and capacity must think outside the state: *beyond* it through regional engagement, and *below* it through cross-border community or trade networks.'

State-level analysis

At this point we move from a consideration of *contextual* factors at interna-tional level to *structural* factors at state level. Wherever its other sources may lie, it is at the level of the state that the critical struggle even in transnational conflict is in the end usually played out. Despite predictions of the 'end of the state' under the twin pressures of globalization and what Falk calls 'the local realities of community and sentiment' (1985: 690), the state is nevertheless seen to remain 'the primary locus of identity for most people' (Kennedy, 1993: 134). Clark agrees that the state is still the key mediator in the continually oscillating balance between forces of globalization ('increasingly potent international pressures') and fragmentation ('the heightened levels of domestic discontent that will inevitably be brought in their wake') (1997: 202). Given the juridical monopoly on sovereignty still formally accorded to the state within the current international system, most conflict parties are in the end in any case driven to compete for state control if they want to institute revolutionary programmes (*revolution/ideology conflict*), safeguard communal needs (*identity/secession conflicts*) or merely secure factional interests (*economic/ resource conflicts*). Even in 'failed' states this usually still remains the ultimate prize for the warring elements, as, for example, in Somalia. The apparent exception is the *neo-jihadist* attempt to replace the existing state system by an Islamic caliphate – on a large scale in the case of the unexpected assault on the Sykes–Picot system in Syria and Iraq in June 2014 by Islamic State (IS) forces, and on a smaller scale by Boko Haram in North-East Nigeria. But, even here, acquisition of control over territory and people immediately turns the new possessor into a quasi-state (IS has a shura council, ministers with portfolios, a financial organization with taxing powers, provincial governors, etc.). Unlike classic interstate wars or lower levels of domestic unrest, therefore, the major deadly conflicts with which this book deals are defined as such through their becoming integral crises of the state itself, problematically cast as it still is as chief actor on the international stage and chief satisfier of domestic needs. In the view of 'crisis of governance' analysts, for example, the main emphasis in contemporary conflict should be on the impact of globalization on 'state decay' (Jackson, 1990; Ayoob, 1995). Brzoska (2004) explains how this has been characteristic of 'holistic' German explanations for new wars such as those of Münkler: 'The predominant cause of internal war, in this line of thinking, is the erosion of the capability of the state to govern. This can be the result of the weakening of the legitimacy of the state or of direct challenges to its monopoly of the use of force' (2005: 109).

This relates to other work on 'weak', 'vulnerable' or 'failed' states, such as those forty to sixty states seen by Ashraf Ghani and Clare Lockhart to be 'either sliding backward and teetering on the brink of implosion or have already collapsed (2008: 3). It also links with Paul Collier's analysis of the debilitating effect of the 'conflict trap' on states containing 'the bottom billion' and related policy recommendations for the necessary international response (2008). Chapter 3 emphasized how central this issue of fragile states and fragile cities is now seen to be in UN, OSCE and World Bank analysis of the roots of contemporary conflict, and therefore how important it is for identifying the sites in which there is the greatest need for conflict prevention and postwar peacebuilding – in the words of the report by UN High-Level Panel on the Post-2015 Development Agenda in relation to rapid urbanization and fragile cities: 'cities are where the battle for sustainable development will be won or lost' (UN High-Level Panel, 2013: 4). We return to this issue in chapters 5 and 8.

In assessing state fragility, the interconnection between four sectors is usually seen to be critical – social, economic, political and geographical; in addition, at a certain level of escalation, two other sectors come into play: law and order and security. It is useful to bear these in mind when looking at the issue of 'statebuilding' in prevention (chapter 5) and postwar reconstruction (chapter 8).

In the *social sector* we are concerned with the major types of social division around which conflict fault lines may develop. In recent years the debate between those who emphasize the 'vertical' (ethnic) roots of conflict and those who emphasize the 'horizontal' (class) roots (Munck, 1986) has been further complicated by the advent of other revolutionary ideologies such as Islamist and Hindu nationalist movements (but also Jewish, Christian and even Buddhist). The sectarian divides within these ideologies (e.g. Sunni/Shia) are often more virulent than those between them. On the other hand, others again have noted the inadequacy of western preoccupations with class and ethnicity in determining the social roots of conflict in parts of the world, such as Africa, where social life 'revolves, in the first instance, around a medley of more compact organizations, networks, groupings, associations, and movements that have evolved over the centuries in response to changing circumstances' (Chazan et al., 1992: 73–103). According to the Commonwealth secretary-general, forty-nine of the fifty-three Commonwealth states are ethnically heterogeneous, and, as John Darby notes, given complex settlement patterns and the mismatch between state borders and the distribution of peoples, 'ethnic homogeneity, on past evidence, is almost always unattainable' (Darby, 1998: 2). Statistically, although ethnic heterogeneity does not seem to correlate closely with levels of conflict, ethnic dominance does. This section of 'state-level' analysis overlaps with the analysis of conflict parties in civil wars at 'identity-group level' below.

In the *economic sector* once again there is some measure of agreement that protracted conflict tends to be associated with patterns of underdevelopment or uneven development. This is a much discussed topic, with some evidence, first, that, *contra* certain traditional theories of social and political revolution, there is a correlation between absolute levels of economic underdevelopment and violent conflict (Jongman and Schmid, 1997; Stewart and Fitzgerald, 2001; Collier et al., 2003);[12] second, that conflict is associated with over-fast or uneven development where modernization disrupts traditional patterns, but does not as yet deliver adequate or expected rewards – especially where this is associated with rapid urbanization and population growth with a resulting increase in the relative numbers of untrained and unemployed young males (Newman, 1991); and, third, that, even where there are reasonable levels of development in absolute terms, conflict may still be generated where there is actual or perceived inequity in the distribution of benefits (Lichbach, 1989) and where there are 'horizontal inequalities' between groups (Reading 19; Stewart, 2002). In all three cases mounting discontent offers fertile recruiting ground for ideological extremism and racial exclusionism. One of the main conclusions of the OECD *Fragile States 2013* report is that 'nearly half of all fragile states are now classified as middle-income countries, and pockets of fragility can exist in otherwise stable countries' (DAC, 2014: 1).

For many analysts it is the *government sector* that is the key arena, since social and economic grievances are in the end expressed in political form. Three main patterns may be discerned here. First, conflict can become endemic even in established liberal democratic states when party politics become ascriptively based and one community perceives that state power has been permanently 'captured' by another, and is therefore driven to challenge the legitimacy of the state in order to change the situation, as in Canada, Belgium, Spain (Basques) or Northern Ireland (Lijphart, 1977; Gurr and Harff, 1994: ch. 5). This has also been a feature in a number of non-western countries, such as Sri Lanka (Horowitz, 1991). Second, conflict is likely in countries where authoritarian regimes successfully manipulate the state apparatus in order to cling to power and block political access to all those not part of their own narrow patronage network, eventually becoming little more than exploitative 'kleptocracies', as in some post-Soviet Central Asian and postcolonial African states. Here politics has indeed become 'zero-sum', and change can be effected only through a direct challenge to the incumbent regime. Third, as seen above, there is the atrophy of central state power itself, where, in the absence of adequate means for raising revenue or keeping order, politics succumbs to endemic and chaotic violence. In a report on Africa presented to the UN Security Council in April 1998, Secretary-General Kofi Annan concluded:

> The nature of political power in many African states, together with the real and perceived consequences of capturing and maintaining power, is a key source of conflict across the continent. It is frequently the case that political victory assumes a winner-takes-all form with respect to wealth and resources, patronage, and the prestige and prerogatives of office. Where there is insufficient accountability of leaders, lack of transparency in regimes, inadequate checks and balances, non-adherence to the rule of law, absence of peaceful means to change or replace leadership, or lack of respect for human rights, political control becomes excessively important, and the stakes become dangerously high. (Annan, 1998)

In terms of *geography*, a critical factor is widely seen to hinge on the relation between 'centre' and 'periphery'. In fragile states, the sinews of governance weaken to the point of non-existence in outlying provinces, often characterized by geographical features (mountains, forests). In the worst cases, those living in remote areas gain no benefit from central government and are often subject to spasmodic depradations – sometimes their area is rich in resources, but in these cases revenues go straight into the pockets of outside exploiters, not to local inhabitants.

Finally, we should note how, at a critical stage in conflict escalation, it is the *law and order* and *security sectors* that become increasingly prominent. This is the moment when domestic conflict crosses the Rubicon and becomes a violent struggle for control of the state itself. The two clear indicators are, first, in the *law and order sector*, when the legal system and the civilian police come to be identified with particularist interests and are no longer seen to represent impartial authority, and, second, in the *security sector*, when civil unrest can no longer be controlled by non-military means and armed militia emerge. At this stage, as Barry Posen has noted, the 'security dilemma', familiar to analysts of international relations, now impacts with devastating effect on the inchoate social-state-international scene (1993). Once this genie is out of the bottle and armed factions are organized and active, it is very difficult to put it back again. Gurr is one of those who has charted what is usually the ten-or-more-year period between the manifest onset of conflict and its escalation to military confrontation – the crucial window of opportunity for preventive measures.

Depending how these state-level factors are interpreted, there is some controversy in the conflict resolution field as to whether the aim should be to decentralize state structures or to strengthen them. For example, Azar himself thought that 'highly centralised political structures are sources of conflict'. Instead he advocated 'appropriate decentralised structures' (1986: 33–4). This was at odds with the recommendations of analysts such as Holsti, who advocated, on the contrary, 'the strengthening of states' (1996: xii). The discrepancy may not be as stark as at first appears, however, since Holsti agreed with Azar that 'vertical legitimacy' (political consensus between governers and governed about the institutional 'rules of the game') and 'horizontal legitimacy' (inclusive political community in which individuals and groups have equal access to decisions and allocations) are what ultimately underpin 'the strength of states' (ibid.: 82–98). This is also relevant to recent emphasis on the 'statebuilding' theme that is considered in chapter 8.

Identity-group and conflict party-level analysis

Turning to the societal level and what Azar called the 'disarticulation between the state and society as a whole', contemporary analysis focuses mainly on two features.

The nature of conflict parties (bases for group formation)   The first feature is the study of the social bases on which identity groups and conflict parties are built. Here Benedict Anderson's *Imagined Communities* (1983) has been influential in popularizing the idea that 'communities' are not pre-existing 'givens' but, rather, socially and politically 'constructed' crystallizations of the play of power across the transnational conflict scene. This has already been commented on under *social sector* in the state-level analysis above. These are not fixed categories, because 'sectarian', 'ethnic' and even 'class' identities come to prominence in varying ways – and are politically manipulated – as conditions change. Also, named identity groups are sometimes defined by statehood, as in 'Israelis', sometimes by wider afflilations for stateless peoples, as in 'Palestinians' or 'Kurds', and sometimes by the connotations of their political relations with the regime, as in the case of a dominant minority such as the 'Alawites' in Syria.

Intergroup dynamics (escalation and de-escalation)   Having outlined some of the *contextual* and *structural* sources of contemporary conflict, we move on to consider *relational* sources at conflict party level. This is the focus for Azar's 'process dynamics'. Here Ted Gurr (1993, 1995, 2000), Azar's colleague at Maryland, showed how national peoples, regional autonomists, communal contenders, indigenous peoples, militant sects, ethnoclasses and other groups may move from non-violent protest, through violent protest, to outright rebellion in an uneven escalation that in most cases takes many years. This is the time-lag that gives major incentives for the proactive prevention of violent conflict, as discussed in the next chapter.

> [T]he most common political strategy among the 275 ethnopolitical groups surveyed in the Minorities at Risk study was not rebellion: it was symbolic and organizational politics. … Equally important, the number of groups using armed violence has been declining after decades of increase. The eruption of ethnic warfare that seized observers' attention in the early 1990s was actually the culmination of a long-term general trend of increasing communal-based protest and rebellion that began in the 1950s and peaked immediately after the end of the Cold War. (Gurr, 2000: 275–6)

In the historical sociology tradition, McAdam, Tarrow and Tilly (2001) developed a parallel theory of mobilization and social contention, exploring how political movements frame their grievances and set collective goals (Reading 20). Goals variously include demands for political access, autonomy, secession or control, triggered by historical grievances and contemporary resentments against the socio-cultural, economic and political constraints outlined above. New threats to security, such as those felt by constituent groups in the break-up of former Yugoslavia, and new opportunities, often encouraged by similar demands elsewhere, will encourage mobilization, and the nature of the emergent leadership will often be decisive in determining degrees of militancy. When it comes to demands for secession, usually the most explosive issue, a history of past political autonomy, however long ago, is often critical.

In their study of insurgent identity groups in the 1990s, Lake and Rothchild concluded that ethnic conflict was neither the result of 'ancient hatreds' nor caused by the sudden 'uncorking' of Soviet repression, but

> most often caused by collective fears of the future. As groups begin to fear for their safety, dangerous and difficult-to-resolve strategic dilemmas arise that contain within them the

potential for tremendous violence. As information failures, problems of credible commitment, and the security dilemma take hold, groups become apprehensive, the state weakens, and conflict becomes more likely. Ethnic activists and political entrepreneurs, operating within groups, build upon these fears and polarise society. Political memories and emotions also magnify these anxieties, driving groups further apart. Together these between-group and within-group strategic interactions produce a toxic brew that can explode into murderous violence. (1996: 41)

In her analysis *Insurgent Collective Action and Civil War in El Salvador*, Elizabeth Wood interprets this at macro-level as a 'struggle between classes' and emphasizes the escalatory role of what Azar called 'state actions and strategies': 'Unrest and violence deepened when a coalition of landlords and military hard-liners brutally derailed a reformist government's attempt at limited agrarian reform along the coastal plain' (Wood, 2003: 41). A similar overall conclusion is reached by Nicholas Sambanis: 'government repression increases opposition, and, if that repression is incomplete, it can lead to violence' (Collier and Sambanis, 2003: vol. 2, 318).

As noted earlier in the chapter, *psychological factors* emerge as critical at identity-group and elite/leadership levels. Here individual and group psychology gives crucial insights into the paranoia of authoritarianism, the process of radicalization and recruitment in the formation and mutation of revolutionary groups, the pathology of violence and, decisively, the huge impact of historical trauma and memory – such as the 'victimhood' of the Holocaust and the Nakba in the Israeli–Palestinian conflict (Bashir and Goldberg, 2014).

Elites and individuals

Turning, finally, to the elite/individual level, we will not dwell on the complex arguments about the relative significance of 'agency' or 'structure' in explication of social and political change (itself a lineal descendant of earlier debate about the relative roles of 'great men' and 'vast impersonal forces' in history). The importance of leadership roles seems self-evident if comparison is made between, say, the effect of Slobodan Milošević and Franjo Tudjman in Yugoslavia and F. W. de Klerk and Nelson Mandela in South Africa. For Human Rights Watch, communal violence is rarely the product of 'deepseated hatreds' or 'ancient animosities', as promoted by those with an interest in making out that these are 'natural processes' about which little can be done:

The extensive Human Rights Watch field research summarized here shows that communal tensions per se are not the immediate cause of many violent and persistent communal conflicts. While communal tensions are obviously a necessary ingredient of an explosive mix, they alone are not sufficient to unleash widespread violence. Rather, time after time the proximate cause of communal violence is governmental exploitation of communal differences. (Human Rights Watch, 1995: 1–2)

Michael Brown argued in similar vein in the 1990s that the academic literature 'places great emphasis on mass-level factors' but is 'weak in understanding the role played by elites and leaders in instigating violence'. Most major
conflicts, in his view, are triggered by 'internal, elite-level activities – to put it
simply, bad leaders – contrary to what one would gather from reviewing the
scholarly literature on the subject' (Brown, 1996: 22–3).

Such in outline are the main interlocking features of transnational conflict.
It is a complicated multi-factorial and multi-level phenomenon – as anticipated in the original insights of the founders of the conflict resolution field
in the 1950s and 1960s, as seen in chapter 2. Given this complexity, it may be
helpful to offer a brief illustration.

The Arab Revolutions, 2011–2014: A Case Study

It is extraordinary that the gigantic upheavals of the 2011–14 Arab revolutions have all taken place since the third edition of this book was produced.
These huge, and in many cases tragic, convulsions that have affected the lives
of more than 350 million people (half under the age of twenty-five) in the
twenty-two countries of the Arab League across a very big region – and pulled
in bordering states such as Iran and Turkey – illustrate the size of the challenge posed by prevailing patterns of transnational conflict. The variety, complexity and speed of these mutations leaves both analysts and policy-makers
stumbling in their wake. Here we offer a few selective comments to illustrate
the nature of transnational conflict in action.

The first feature of transnational conflict to be illustrated in the Arab revolutions is the greater prominence of the *regional level* itself in a multipolar world

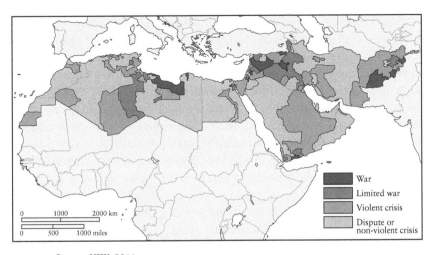

Source: HIIK, 2011

Map 4.1 *The Arab revolutions after one year: intensity of violent conflicts in first-
level sub-national units 2011, Middle East and Maghreb*

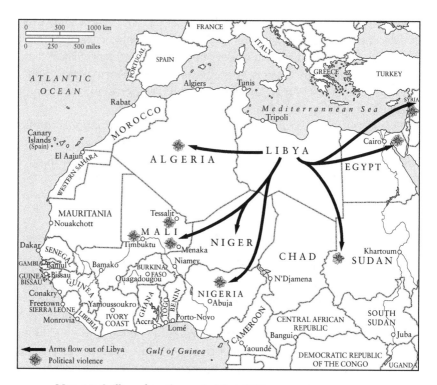

Map 4.2 *Spillover from the war in Libya, 2011*

and the fact that this is best understood as a *complex system* (see maps 4.1 and 4.2 as illustrations of regional and sub-regional dynamics). The US was unable or unwilling to intervene decisively in the wake of the Iraq experience, while contestation with Russia effectively neutralized the UN Security Council (with the exception of the intervention in Libya). As is well known in systems theory, complex systems resist change (see the next section of this chapter). In this case, authoritarian regimes across the Arab world[13] had survived the 'waves of democratization' that swept other regions – Southern Europe in the 1970s, Latin America in the 1980s and Eastern Europe in the 1990s. Systemic resistance to change of this kind is the result of a complex network of factors that reinforce the status quo within the region – including, no doubt, the global prominence of oil supplies. Changing individual factors, or even several factors, does not seem to affect the system as a whole, which falls back into its default pattern. This is discouraging for those who want to change a system.

On the other hand, the Arab revolutions also illustrate how, for linked reasons, when it does come to a complex system, change can be in the form of a sudden collapse of the system as a whole – as mapped in 'catastrophe theory'. An apparently solid system can be progressively 'hollowed out' as the environment changes, to the point where one small shock at a particular point in the system can all at once bring it crashing down. This is nearly always unanticipated even by professional experts – we may think of the unexpected overthrow of the Shah in 1979, or the disintegration of the Soviet Union a decade later, or the near collapse of the capitalist system itself two decades after that (triggered by the apparently small problem of the sub-prime housing market in the US). On Friday 17 December 2010, a 26-year-old fruit vendor in Sidi Bouzid, Tunisia, named Mohamed Bouazizi, the sole provider for his widowed mother and six siblings, refused to pay bribes to corrupt inspectors because he could not afford a licence. They seized his wares. Bouazizi walked to the regional council offices, poured petrol over himself, and lit a match that set the Arab world on fire. He was taken to hospital but died eighteen days later, on 4 January 2011. By the end of the month President Ben Ali and his family had fled from Tunisia – despite his internal security force of 150,000 (he had deliberately kept the army small, at 35,000). On 11 February, after three decades of rule, the Egyptian president, Hosni Mubarak, was overthrown. Nothing could illustrate more graphically the global/local aspect of transnational conflict. The main effects of global drivers of conflict invariably fall on the most vulnerable at the local level. But, conversely – carried at extraordinary speed by transnational connectors – local events can also have global repercussions.

Linked to this illustration of catastrophe theory in transnational conflict, the Arab revolutions in addition demonstrate how 'periods of transition' – for example, from tyranny to democracy – are often more turbulent and unpredictable than either the previous status quo (repressive authoritarianism) or the outcome hoped for (the longer-term stability of mature democracy). This is a theme taken further in chapter 11. Even 'benign' revolutions go through periods of dangerous upheaval that are easily hijacked *en route*. Elections have unpredictable outcomes, and the 'wrong' parties can win, raising fears that this may turn out to be 'one person, one vote, one time'.

Another feature of transnational conflict exhibited through the Arab revolutions is the differential impact of global drivers given the make-up and past history of the region. For example, within the Arab complex system it had been nationalism (pan-Arabism) and socialism that had been the main revolutionary forces at the time of the Nasserite challenge to the postcolonial status quo. These were now spent forces, discredited by the failure of the regimes set up in their name subsequently to meet the needs of their people. This left two main untarnished global ideological drivers – democratization and political Islam. In the words adapted from the teaching of Hasan al-Banna, the founder of the Muslim Brotherhood in Egypt in 1928, 'Islam is the solution' – and so it seemed to many. Although Islamists had won the first stage of the 1991 Algerian elections (Islamic Salvation Front – FIS) and the 2006 Palestinian parliamentary elections (Hamas), in both cases the outcomes were effectively annulled on the grounds that these were considered terrorist organizations. Islamist parties, blocked from power (and therefore also from disillusionment and criticism for subsequent failure in government), built their support locally. In consequence, by 2011 in a number of Arab countries, notably Tunisia and Egypt, they stood to win power at last through the ballot box, not the gun. The result was three waves of revolution in quick succession. First came the democratic revolution of the 'Arab Spring' (so named after the apparent parallels in Eastern Europe during and at the end of the Cold War), which led to the relatively peaceful overthrow of authoritarian regimes in Tunisia and Egypt (closely followed by the more violent demise of regimes in Yemen and Libya, the latter achieved only after foreign military intervention). Then came the counter-revolution, as authoritarian regimes fought back – Saudi Arabia propped up the tottering regime in Bahrain, the Egyptian military overthrew the Islamist government of Morsi, the Syrian regime first survived and then plunged the country into the horrors of civil war. And third came counter-counter revolution in the form of *jihadist* Islam, in both its Shia (Iranian) and Sunni (Saudi Arabian) versions.

It need hardly be said that, as the waves of revolution, counter-revolution, and counter-counter-revolution swept the region, the impact of transnational connectors became evident. The flows of internally displaced people and refugees in their millions tested state, regional and global economic resources and had widespread global political effects (half the population of Syria was displaced). Flows of people in the opposite direction (for example, international neo-*jihadis*) had equally manifest transnational results. Flows of weapons (including seizure of those brought into the region by previous interventions) fuelled the fighting. Transnational flows of resources financed it. Above all the devastating effect of the original democratic revolutions was widely attributed to the power of transnational communication flows via social media operating across all five levels, while the eruption and horrific depredations of Islamic State (IS) were equally shaped by and dependent on manipulation of the global media.

At state level we can discern explanations for the striking differential outcomes of the revolutions in different countries. This was to do not only with the 'actions and strategies' of different regimes but also with the underlying social/political bases on which political power itself rested. Past history was also influential. Perhaps Algeria and Palestine were hardly caught up in the initial upheaval because the long 1991–2000 civil war, in the case of the former, and the two intifadas (1987–93, 2000–5) and Israeli response, in the case of the latter, had exhausted what had earlier been front-runners in popular resistance to the status quo. The two monarchies of Morocco and Jordan have, up to the time of writing, remained relatively unscathed. So has the precarious ethnic/sectarian balance in Lebanon. Saudi Arabia and the Gulf States expended billions of petro-dollars on buying off opposition. The success of the original revolutions in Tunisia and Egypt in 2011 may have been connected, not only to the hollowing out of both regimes (and the refusal of the army in Egypt to back the Mubarak government) but also to the fact that neither country suffered from deep underlying sectarian or politicized ethno-national divisions. Libya was divided historically between the Western (Tripoli) and Eastern (Benghazi – the old Cyrenaica) parts of the country, plus the huge tribal hinterland to the south from which Gaddafi recruited many of the military forces that remained loyal to him. Had it not been for international intervention, Gaddafi may well have survived. In Yemen, superimposed on a previous war between the communist south and the north, the divide is between Iran-backed Shia 'Houthis', in alliance with supporters of ousted President Ali Abdullah Saleh, and Saudi-backed Sunnis. Above all, in Syria there was a fundamental rift between the Sunni majority and the Alawite Shia minority, comprising some 12 per cent of the population, who were concentrated mainly by the Mediterranean and in the coastal mountains, who since the advent of Hafez al-Assad in 1970 had occupied dominant positions in the army and administration. This meant that there was firmly based support for Bashar al-Assad for fear of what would happen if the regime fell. The opposition Free Syria Army was predominantly Sunni. And all of this in turn was deeply affected by what had happened in the opposite direction in neighbouring Iraq, where Saddam Hussein's support had come from the Sunni minority. The introduction of democratic elections after his overthrow had led to the entrenchment of oppressive partisan majority Shia rule, greatly enhancing the influence and power of neighbouring Iran.

Moving to identity-group level, the resulting complex interplay of mutating ethnic (for example, Kurdish), sectarian (for example, Sunni and Shia) and class-based politicized factions can be subsequently mapped, as reflected for instance in the bewildering proliferation of shifting militia in Syria – Michael Lund suggests extreme fragmentation in Syria into some 1,200 armed opposition groups (cited in Themnér and Wallensteen, 2014: 544). The intra-regional rivalry between Saudi Arabia (Sunni) and Iran (Shia), supporting opposed parties, greatly complicated the situation, as did the eruption of al-Qaeda based neo-*jihadis* such as the al-Nusra Front in Syria and its breakaway rival ISIL (later self-styled as the Islamic State) (see chapter 11).

Finally, at the elite/individual level, it was the exclusionist and often brutal actions and strategies of incumbent leaders and their immediate supporters, such as those dependent on Bashar al-Assad in Syria and Nouri al-Maliki in Iraq, which stoked the rapid escalation of violence, together with the actions and strategies espoused by the leaders of opposition factions, most notoriously those espoused by Abu Bakr al-Baghdadi, the self-styled IS caliph.

These brief comments on a massive, highly complicated and volatile example of the impact of transnational conflict (TNC) on a complex regional conflict system may indicate something of the scale of the challenge that TNC poses for conflict resolution. The remaining chapters in Part I address this challenge. The overall conflict resolution response, which we call cosmopolitan conflict resolution (CCR), is summed up in chapter 11. What is clear – daunting though the prospect may be – is that the response must be as multi-faceted and muti-level as the phenomenon it seeks to combat.

The Analysis and Mapping of Complex Conflict Systems

In view of the importance of complex systems for contemporary conflict resolution, it will be useful to revisit the question of conflict mapping at the end of chapter 3 and supplement it with an account of developments in this area. Much of the impetus for more complex or systemic conflict mapping has come from aid and development workers with a view to understanding the interrelationships between the diverse factors that make up the rapidly changing conflict situations with which they have to deal (Körppen et al., 2008). For example, it is now understood that, given the complexity of many conflict contexts, well-intentioned interventions often have unexpected, even paradoxical, outcomes. So it is important to try to understand these interrelations before formulating appropriate responses.

The idea of analysing complex conflict systems has been integral in the conflict resolution field from the outset. The founding theorists – Lewis Fry Richardson before the Second World War, and Kenneth Boulding, Quincy Wright, Johan Galtung, Anatol Rapoport, John Burton, and others from the 1950s – began from the premise that in conflict analysis the sum is greater than the parts, that positive feedback loops reinforce systemic resistance to change, that interventions have unpredictable outcomes, and that at critical moments there can be sudden and abrupt bifurcations as the set of interlocking systems adjusts to changing environments and eco-landscapes in a process of co-adaptation – these are self-organizing and complex adaptive systems.

Chapter 2 noted that Lewis Fry Richardson was an expert on mathematical computations on predictability and turbulence in weather systems. It also mentioned how, in the first issue of the *Journal of Conflict Resolution* (1957), influenced by this, Kenneth Boulding and Quincy Wright proposed global conflict data centres to alert the international community to the upcoming squalls and storms of international conflict. John Burton's thinking was greatly influenced by general systems theory, particularly in the form of the distinction between first- and second-order learning.

More recently – over the past twenty years – the conflict analytic field has been enriched by a further transfer of complex system ideas from the natural to the social sciences, with inputs from sociology, political theory, social psychology, organizational theory and other disciplinary areas influenced by cognate ideas (Hendrick, 2009). This has not been without controversy (Rosenau and Earnest, 2006). There is no single overarching approach here but – as may be fitting, given the topic – a hybrid coming together of different transdisciplinary frameworks.

Contemporary analysts such as Peter Coleman (2003) have recognized that systemic complexity is quite consonant with long-term stability, since, once a complex system has settled into a pattern, no single stimulus or even collection of stimuli may be sufficient to overcome its constantly reinforced inertia. The broad conclusion is that, if the aim is systemic conflict transformation, either the complex must be affected as a whole, or the system must be displaced to another environment, which is more benign. Those working in the conflict transformation field must, therefore, be patient and well informed in their selection and sequencing of entry points and must expect setbacks and apparent regression. It is also understood why the process of transition may be less stable, more turbulent and, potentially, perhaps more dangerous than the original more familiar concatenation. All of these features have been amply demonstrated in the sudden 'catastrophe' or collapse of the interlocking system of governance and control in the Arab world after 2011, as well as in the subsequent turmoil of what is still an onging period of complex transition towards whatever the next *stasis* may be. Coleman's dynamical systems approach to conflict analysis and conflict transformation, together with the similar work of others, represents a significant step forward and provides much needed tools for understanding and managing complex conflicts (Coleman et al., 2005; Coleman, 2011).

Within this framework it is also worth noting how the linguistic dimension of conflict is mapped. This is usually done in terms of 'mental models' and the roles that they are seen to play in perpetuating complex and intractable conflicts. These are seen as the conceptual frames or cognitive structures, largely unconscious, that shape our tacit knowledge and beliefs and adapt us to conform to prevailing social norms – what Lakoff and Johnson have called 'the metaphors we live by' (1980). For example, as David Stroh put it in a private communication, 'systemic thinking is mental models made visible'. Norbert Ropers, building on the work of Oliver Wils et al. (2006), takes thinking in mental models as one of the defining 'characteristics of "systemic thinking"':

> *Thinking in (mental) models yet acknowledging perspective-dependency*: Accepting that all analytical models are a reduction of the complex reality (and are necessarily perspective-dependent) and are therefore only ever a tool and not 'the reality' as such. (Ropers, 2008a: 13; original emphasis)

This idea recurs, albeit not in name, in attempts to accommodate 'beliefs, feelings, and behaviors' in the dynamical-systems approach (Coleman, et al., 2005: 6). 'Mental models' are included as distinct elements in systems perspective maps (Woodrow, 2006). Mental models are identified with 'widely held beliefs and norms' in systemic conflict analysis maps within the 'attitude' dimension of the (SAT) model of peacebuilding (Ricigliano, 2011). 'Mind maps', encompassing stakeholder and evaluator perceptions and interpretations, are used for testing resonances and exploring collective dialogue in the emergent evaluations of large-scale system action research (Burns, 2006: 189). For a critique of the 'mental model' approach in systems mapping in relation to the most intense political conflicts and the 'radical disagreements' associated with them, see Oliver Ramsbotham (2010: 45–51; 2013). Ramsbotham argues that what he calls 'linguistic intractability' is not captured adequately in systems perspective mapping.

See Reading 28 for an example of systems perspective mapping applied to the Sri Lanka conflict. This would be adapted and refined in the light of input from different conflict parties and third parties, changing circumstances, and outcomes from resulting interventions themselves.

Conclusion

This chapter has outlined a framework for the analysis of contemporary conflict that draws on Edward Azar's account of protracted social conflict and then updates it in the light of recent developments in statistical analysis and interpretation. As has been seen, the framework for interpreting transnational conflict offered in table 4.2 is not a theory of conflict but a model for locating the chief sources of contemporary conflict and the controversies associated with them. The main lesson for the rest of the book is that, given the complexity of much contemporary conflict, attempts at conflict resolution have to be equally comprehensive and need to operate – if possible in a coordinated manner – at all five levels.

Although peacemakers striving to maximize humanitarian space and the scope for peace initiatives in the middle of ongoing wars (chapter 6) or aiming to bring the violent phase of conflict to an end (chapter 7) usually have to work within quite narrow power constraints, long-term peacebuilders who aspire to prevent violent conflict (chapter 5) or to ensure that settlements are transformed into lasting peace (chapters 8, 9 and 10) have to address the deeper sources of conflict. This is likely to involve *contextual* change at international level (for example, via more equitable and accountable global and regional arrangements), *structural* change at state level (for example, via appropriate constitutional adaptations and the promotion of good governance – including statebuilding in critical cases), *relational* change at conflict party level (for example, via community relations and reconciliation work), and *cultural* change at all levels (for example, via the transformation of discourses and institutions which sustain and reproduce violence; see Reading 24). In some cases, cultural change means directly opposing egregious ideologies of violence that are not amenable to such transformation. This is taken further in chapters 12 and 15. In 'disintegrated war zones', where structures of civil governance have collapsed and complex and shifting local struggles for influence and control have replaced formal politics, consensus and legitimacy must be built up from the base in the absence of 'institutional and rule-bound governement' or central capacity to offer basic protection or control. This is discussed further under 'War Zones, War Economies and Cultures of Violence', in chapter 6, and in the first part of chapter 7.

RECOMMENDED READING

Berdal and Malone (2000); Brown (1996); Cederman et al. (2013); Coleman (2011); Collier and Sambanis (2003); Duffield (2007); Kaldor (2012); Körppen et al. (2008); Martin (2003); Münkler (2005); Reno (2011).

RELEVANT EXTRACTS IN *THE CONTEMPORARY CONFLICT RESOLUTION READER*

Reading 9: E. Azar, The Management of Protracted Social Conflict
Reading 15: D. Sandole, Extending the Reach of Basic Human Needs
Reading 16: D. Horowitz, Ethnic Groups in Conflict
Reading 17: M. Kaldor, New and Old Wars: Organized Violence in a Global Era
Reading 18: D. Keen, The Economic Functions of Violence in Civil Wars
Reading 19: F. Stewart, Horizontal Inequalities: A Neglected Dimension of Development
Reading 20: D. McAdam, S. Tarrow and C. Tilly, Dynamics of Contention
Reading 23: R. Rubinstein, Conflict Resolution and the Structural Sources of Conflict
Reading 24: J. Demmers, Telling Each Other Apart: A Discursive Approach to Violent Conflict
Reading 25: J. Fearon and D. Laitin, Ethnicity, Insurgency and Civil War
Reading 28: N. Ropers, Systemic Conflict Transformation: Reflections on the Conflict and Peace Process in Sri Lanka

CHAPTER FIVE

Preventing Violent Conflict

From the start, it has been a central purpose of conflict resolution to seek to prevent violent conflicts. As Max van der Stoel, then OSCE High Commissioner on National Minorities, said in 1994, violent conflicts, including ethnic conflicts, are 'not unavoidable but can indeed be prevented'. In order to do this, the 'potential sources of conflict need to be identified and analysed with a view to their early resolution, and concrete steps must be taken to forestall armed confrontation' (van der Stoel, 1994). His words echo those of Kenneth Boulding and Quincy Wright in the first issue of the *Journal of Conflict Resolution*. Fifty years after their call for early warning centres, the UN, the OSCE and most of the major regional international organizations seem to have reached a consensus on the importance of prevention.

This was partly a reaction to the catastrophes in Rwanda, Yugoslavia and elsewhere, and partly a realization that it may be easier to tackle conflicts early, before they reach the point of armed conflict or mass violence. Major-General Romeo Dallaire's assertion that a mechanized brigade group of five thousand soldiers could have saved hundreds of thousands of lives in Rwanda in the spring and summer of 1994 has reverberated throughout the international community. So has a realization that prevention may be cost-effective compared with the exorbitant bill for post-conflict relief and reconstruction (Chalmers, 2004; IEP, 2014a). What can be done to avert violent conflict in cases like these, and also the potential deadly struggles in the decades to come?

In his *Agenda for Peace*, UN Secretary-General Boutros-Ghali defined conflict prevention as the avoidance of new armed conflicts, containment of existing armed conflicts and non-recurrence of ended armed conflicts (Boutros-Ghali, 1992). The influential Carnegie Commission on Preventing Deadly Conflict similarly identified three broad aims: to prevent the emergence of violent conflict, to prevent ongoing conflicts from spreading, and to prevent the re-emergence of violence (Carnegie Commission, 1997; Reading 33). In this chapter we will consider the first and third of these. We also deal with the prevention of genocide and mass atrocities. Other aspects of containment are considered in chapter 6. We deal with prevention of recurrence briefly here and in more depth in chapters 8, 9 and 10. Figure 5.1 shows how the various aspects of prevention engage with different phases of the conflict cycle.

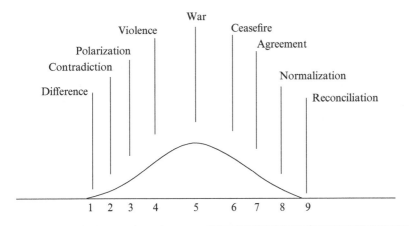

1–3 Preventing violent conflict (deep prevention, light prevention, crisis management)
4–6 Preventing the intensification, prolongation and spread of violent conflict
7–9 Preventing relapse into violent conflict

Figure 5.1 *Conflict prevention and the conflict cycle*

The first part of the chapter deals with how conflicts form and how they can be handled peacefully and constructively, creating a second-order capacity to handle further conflicts. We briefly discuss non-violence as a means of pursuing conflict without violence when agreement cannot be achieved. We then consider the background, proximate and trigger causes of wars and the corresponding factors that can prevent violent conflicts. This leads on to an examination of the progress in developing early warning indicators of impending conflicts. After that we turn to the means of early response and discuss structural and direct conflict prevention. We then consider the extent of the international community's engagement with the concept and practice of conflict prevention, exploring the rise to prominence of preventive diplomacy in the 1990s, its relationship to the new doctrine of Responsibility to Protect in the early 2000s, and the development of a new doctrine of prevention of mass atrocities in the 2010s. We finally offer two case studies to illustrate the scope and challenges of the concept: Kenya at the time of the 2008 elections and the crisis over Ukraine in 2014–15. We conclude by discussing criteria for evaluating the success of conflict prevention efforts.

The aim of conflict prevention is not to avoid conflict altogether but to avert violent conflicts. Conflicts pursued constructively are creative and form a necessary means of bringing about change. We adopt Kriesberg's (1998a: 22) definition of constructive conflict: 'Conflict outcomes are constructive insofar as the parties [eventually come to] regard them as mutually acceptable. Moreover, they are constructive insofar as they provide a basis for an ongoing relationship in which future conflicts tend to be waged constructively.' One might add that constructive outcomes should contribute to well-being and the flourishing of the people affected (Pogge, 2002; Carney, 2005; Harris, 2010).

A difficult underlying question here is whether it is a good thing to try to prevent violent conflict in the first place: may violence not be the only way to remedy injustice? We have addressed this question in general terms in earlier chapters, where we argued, first, that violent conflicts often result in lose–lose outcomes for all parties and the population at large and, second, that attempts to prevent violence must also involve the satisfaction of needs, the accommodation of legitimate aspirations and the remedy of manifest injustices.

Emergent Conflict and Peaceful Change

One of the aims of the conflict resolution endeavour is to increase the range of situations where violence is not a possibility – that is, to create conditions where there are stable expectations of peaceful change. What we might dub 'preventive conflict resolution' is concerned with resolving conflicts before they become violent and creating *contexts*, *structures* and *relations* between parties that make violence less likely, and eventually inconceivable.

Let us consider first how new conflict formations emerge. Typically some social change creates a basis for conflict: for example, an economic change reverses the relative fortunes of two ethnic groups, a new resource makes a previously unclear boundary strategically significant, a new belief system makes the views of some people incompatible with others. In response to such changes, people collectively define their interests, formulate goals and act together, mobilizing support and sometimes forming new groups or parties in order to pursue these goals. If the goals are incompatible with those of other groups, then a conflict forms. If the incompatibility is so severe that the parties' relationship is broken and the structure of institutions and the context in which they live cannot contain the conflict, violence becomes possible.

A crucial part of this process is the definition of goals (Reading 29). Here the parties have their first opportunity for pursuing conflict constructively or destructively. They may choose whether or not to take the goals of others into account, and whether or not to define their goals in a way that can be made compatible with other goals. To take account of others' goals is more likely in a political community where parties are in communication with each other, when the political system gives incentives to cooperate, and where there is some shared political culture or a sense of collective values, making it likely at least that parties frame their goals in terms of collective as well as individual interests. In short, the first element of the capacity to prevent conflict is the degree to which goals are coordinated or, at least, have a capacity to complement the goals of others.

A second element that defines the development of the conflict is the choice of strategies and behaviour that parties adopt in seeking to achieve their aims and their choice of communications (Mitchell, 1981a). These too are shaped by the existing relationships and context and will be moderated in settings where parties expect to have to work together.

A third element is the relationship of the conflict to other conflict formations and, in particular, the implications of the conflict for other parties, which may involve how much it spreads, how it reshapes other issues, and what potential it has for polarization.

In all these respects, the parties themselves, and the social and cultural setting they are in, have the most immediate impact on the development of the conflict. They, and the governing authorities of their societies, are in the best position to prevent conflicts becoming violent. All parties have the choice between destructive and constructive means of pursuing their aspirations. Governments and societies have in their hands choices between a just and unjust social order and an inclusive or exclusive political system.

Negotiations are the main method by which parties try to resolve conflicts peacefully (Starkey et al., 2005). A crucial aspect here is the approach that parties take to negotiations and the range of negotiating options available. Issues may be more negotiable if parties accept the possibility that their goals might be met in different ways, or linked to other goals, or if they are willing to redefine their goals, in ways suggested in chapter 1. A rich literature on negotiations and preventive negotiation is relevant here (Fisher and Ury, 1981; Pruitt and Carnevale, 1993; Raiffa et al., 2002; Zartman, 1982, 2001; Zartman and Faure, 2005). The cultural setting and context also shape the process of negotiations and the approach of the parties (Gulliver, 1979 (Reading 53); Faure and Rubin, 1993).

In ethnic conflicts, for example, many options for preventing and managing conflicts can be considered (McGarry and O'Leary, 1993; Gurr, 1998; Cordell and Wolff, 2009). The possibilities include minority rights, autonomy, voting systems and legislative assemblies that give incentives to ethnic groups to work together, various types of power-sharing and consociational systems, confederal and federal systems, and inter-ethnic associations and similar types of bridging social capital (O'Leary and McEvoy, 2010; Hannum, 1990; Rothchild and Hartzell, 1999; Horowitz, 1985; Burgess, 2006; Reading 31). The South Tyrol conflict, which lasted from the cession of this province, with its German-speakers, to Italy in the Treaty of St Germain, up to the autonomy agreement in 1969, is a good example of a peacefully settled ethnic conflict (Alcock, 1970). The negotiations were protracted and difficult, and at times agreements broke down and had to be renegotiated; at one point a Tyrolese extremist group launched attacks on electricity pylons to further the cause. But the two sides avoided any more violent responses. Negotiations continued and, in the end, were successful. Important ingredients in their success were the diplomatic protection offered by the neighbouring state, Germany, and the recognition of this by the host state, Italy. The autonomy agreement gave the minority guarantees of cultural and economic rights and a right to bring grievances to the Council of Ministers in Rome through a permanent commission. The European Convention for the Peaceful Settlement of Disputes was modified to recognize Austria's right to monitor the internal guarantees.

The peaceful settlement of the South Tyrol case is now frequently cited as a model for other ethnic conflicts in Europe, and South Tyrolese experts advise the Council of Europe on autonomy arrangements elsewhere. In this case, not only was the dispute peacefully settled, but the settlement itself became the basis for further dispute settlement systems – a key aspect in the development of preventive capacity (Ury, 1993).

To take another example of an intrastate conflict, consider the bitter and protracted but peacefully settled conflict between the labour unions and company owners in Sweden in the 1930s. This pitted the communists, who saw Sweden as a 'bourgeois state in unholy alliance with the capitalist class', against the managers, who refused to recognize the unions and were willing to hire strike-breakers to destroy the power of the working class (Rothstein, 2005: 167–200). The clash reached a climax at Ådalen in May 1931, when soldiers fired into a protesting crowd and killed five workers. Rothstein (2005: 183) quotes a communist, who said, 'the bullets that killed our comrades also killed our illusions of consensus and reconciliation with our class enemy.' On both sides of the industrial divide, an internal struggle followed these events. Union leaders needed to improve the workers' immediate conditions. For the managers, protracted strikes and lockouts were too costly to continue. The right-wing political party that had supported intransigence was seen to stand outside the social consensus. In the end the conflict was resolved by the formation of a social democratic government which championed the rights of the unions to represent their members, within a framework of law and rights, and gained the cooperation of the managers in this enterprise. The outcome institutionalized a measure of restraint and, at the same time, laid the basis for social trust and a wider dispute settlement system which became the basis of the Swedish social welfare model.

A third example can be found at the level of international negotiations over resources in the talks which led to the UN Convention on the Law of the Sea (Sebenius, 1984). Although the final convention can be criticized both for legitimating the interests of the multinational mineral companies and coastal states and for lacking enforcement powers, it was a remarkable negotiation leading to wide international agreement on the delineation of coastal waters, rights to the seabed and rights to fisheries. The agreement created a regime for settling maritime disputes and a source of lessons for later international resource and environmental agreements.

A common characteristic of all these conflicts was the statement of incompatible positions at the outset, followed by long and difficult negotiations, which sometimes broke down but eventually, either through the negotiation process or some transformative development in the context of the conflict, led to the discovery of a way forward. Preventive conflict resolution accepts limits, but it is rarely easy or quick.

Non-violence

In the event that negotiations fail to find an agreed way of resolving the dispute, parties have the option of pursuing conflict but limiting their behaviour to avoid violence. A wide range of means is available in civil conflicts, including institutionalized practices such as the law, parliamentary decisions, elections and general political campaigning, as well as more informal methods. Similarly, in international conflicts, a wide range of dispute settlement methods are open to states, as recommended by the UN Charter (Merrills, 2005). Even if agreements cannot be reached, parties can still prosecute conflict by non-violent means.

As Chenoweth and Cunningham (2013) say, 'unarmed civilians routinely prosecute conflicts without resorting to arms – and they do so extremely forcefully and to great effect at times.' Chenoweth and Stephan (2011) claim that, between 1900 and 2006, non-violent campaigns were twice as effective in changing regimes as their violent counterparts. Chenoweth argues that non-violent campaigns derive their effectiveness from mass participation. Large-scale campaigns, such as that of Solidarity in Poland, which represented 10 million people, can mobilize so many people that state organs may be unable to resist (Reading 37). When 3.5 per cent of a society can be mobilized, Chenoweth argues, the campaign is likely to be won. No campaigns with this level of support failed, and some non-violent campaigns with less support also succeeded. Violent repression against non-violent resistance generally causes a backlash that may increase public support for the non-violent campaign, and defections by security forces and personnel from the regime can then further strengthen it. Cases such as the overthrow of Marcos in the Philippines, the colour revolutions in the former Soviet Union, the students' campaign in Serbia, and the largely non-violent resistance in the early phases of the revolutions in Tunisia and Egypt indicate what a powerful, indeed unstoppable, movement a large campaign of civil resistance can be.

Sharp (1973) has documented and analysed the non-violent campaigns of the twentieth century. His guide to would-be non-violent rebels was taken as a manual by the student activists in the Arab Spring (Reading 34). It is clear from the way the Arab Spring developed, however, that a non-violent movement that becomes violent can readily turn into a bloody and protracted armed conflict. Moreover, when a movement has limited public support it can be ruthlessly overpowered, as in Tiananmen Square in China in 1989. As an instrument for seizing power, non-violence is dangerous, because of this risk of triggering civil war. For this reason, non-violence purists stress 'principled non-violence' and urge thorough training in non-violent techniques and non-violent mobilization of the population before and during a campaign of resistance. They stress the importance of maintaining communications with the adversary and building a 'constructive programme' of positive alternatives to repression (Reading 32).

Constructive conflict, peaceful change and non-violence are ways to avoid violent conflict that place a premium on actors deciding to use peaceful rather than violent means. We now turn to ways of preventing conflicts that put the premium on the better management of conflicts by the societies in which they occur and by the international community.

Causes and Prevention of Wars

It is helpful first to say something about the background, proximate and immediate causes of wars and about actions to prevent wars at these three levels. As A. J. P. Taylor noted:

> Wars are much like road accidents. They have a general and a particular cause at the same time. Every road accident is caused in the last resort by the invention of the internal combustion engine ... [But] the police and the courts do not weigh profound causes. They seek a specific cause for each accident – driver's error, excessive speed, drunkenness, faulty brakes, bad road service. So it is with wars. (Quoted in Davies, 1996: 896)

If Taylor is right, perhaps we can learn something about the prevention of wars from the prevention of traffic accidents. It is usually possible to point to particular factors that might have prevented an individual accident. If the driver had not been inebriated, if the weather had not been foggy, if the road had been better lit, the accident might not have happened. But it is hard to be sure of the influence of any particular cause in a single incident. Only when we have a large number of traffic accidents to study can we hope to establish a relationship between accidents and the factors associated with them. This may suggest generic measures that can make roads in general safer. For example, driving tests and road lighting have a measurable impact on accident figures. They are 'preventers' of accidents.

Preventing wars is similar. We need to look for general conditions that reduce the likelihood of conflict. And we have to look at specific interventions that may prevent a conflict turning to war. Structural (or deep) prevention aims to address the root causes of conflicts, such as economic grievances, political exclusion and group discrimination. Positive policies such as equitable economic development, political inclusion and pluralism can thus be 'preventers' of wars. Direct (or light) prevention aims to prevent an existing conflict from becoming violent – for example, through mediation, confidence-building measures and crisis management. The capacity to manage conflict in these ways is thus a preventer.

Suganami, in his incisive analysis *On The Causes of War* (1996), puts three questions which can help us to think about conflict prevention. First, 'What are the conditions which must be present for wars to occur?' This is a question about the necessary causes of wars. Second, 'Under what sorts of circumstances have wars occurred most frequently?' This is a question about the correlates and proximate causes of wars. Third, 'How did this particular war come about?' This is a question about the history of a particular war and its trigger events. We can reformulate these in terms of conflict prevention. First, can war be prevented by removing its necessary conditions? Second, can the incidence of wars be reduced by controlling the circumstances under which they arise? And, third, can a particular conflict be influenced to avoid it becoming violent?

The first question could be reformulated in a less demanding way as follows. Under what conditions is war not considered a serious possibility? This is so when there are stable expectations of peaceful change within states and when states have lost their fear of attack by other states – that is, when there is a pluralistic security community (Deutsch, 1957). These conditions are sufficiently common to make it clear that peaceful change is a realistic and attainable aim.

The second question is addressed by the research literature on the correlates of war. Geller and Singer (1998) and Dixon (2009) have summarized some of its findings. Statistical analysis has identified many structural factors that reduce the incidence of interstate and non-interstate wars.

The third question requires political analysis, judgement and evidence about a particular conflict. We can ask the same type of questions that historians ask about what makes a peaceful settlement possible. It may seem challenging to assess what factors prevented a particular war, but in principle this is no more challenging than when we consider which factors caused a particular war (Goertz and Levy, 2007).

Early Warning

One of the aims of the founders of the conflict resolution field was to develop a conflict early warning system. There are two tasks involved here: first, identification of the type and location of the conflicts that could become violent; and, second, monitoring and assessing their progress with a view to assessing how close to violence they are (Reading 30).

The statistical studies that identify factors that cause or prevent wars can also be used for early warning. We can take Ted Gurr's work as an example of this approach. Using data from his Minorities at Risk project, he identifies three factors that affect the proneness of a communal group to rebel: collective incentives, capacity for joint action, and external opportunities. Each concept is represented by indicators constructed from data coded for the project and justified by correlations with the magnitude of ethnic rebellions in previous years. The resulting table makes it possible to rank the minorities according to their risk-proneness (Gurr, 2000). The assumption is that the more risk-prone are those with high scores on incentives both for rebellion and for capacity/opportunity. Using this type of risk assessment Gurr was able to anticipate a relatively high probability that the Kosovo Albanians and East Timorese would rebel, and that other disadvantaged groups would not. Similarly, Cederman, Gleditsch and Buhaug (2013) showed the significance of political exclusion and horizontal inequalities in the risk of civil wars, developing an out-of-sample prediction of states that are vulnerable to civil war.

Econometric forecasting takes a similar approach. For example, Collier et al. (2003: 53) find that 'countries with low, stagnant and unequally distributed per capita incomes that have remained dependent on primary commodities for their exports face dangerously high risks of prolonged conflict.' Others have developed indicators of genocide (Davies et al., 1997), human rights abuse (Schmid, 1997: 74), state failure (Esty et al., 1998), refugee flows, food crises, and environmental conflicts (Davies and Gurr, 1998). Goldstone (2008) claimed that just four indicators were able to predict 80 per cent of the countries which will have political crises in two years' time: regime type, infant mortality, high levels of discrimination, and presence of armed conflicts in neighbouring states.

It is sometimes possible to anticipate likely conflicts simply because existing conflicts are recurrent and protracted, and because conflicts tend to spill over in conflict regions. 'Enduring rivalries' – that is, protracted disputes between pairs of states or peoples – have accounted for half the wars between 1816 and 1992. These may be expected to be sources of further disputes. As noted in chapter 3, it is not difficult to point to regions – such as West Africa, the Great Lakes region of Africa, the Caucasus, the India–Pakistan border and parts of Indonesia, and now many of the states affected by the Arab Spring – where future violent conflicts can be expected. We also know from economic indicators that the risk of civil war in poor states is far higher than it is in more developed states (Collier et al., 2003). There are therefore plentiful indicators of areas where a preventive response is needed.

Over the last ten years, the US, the UK and some international organizations who have taken up the challenge of developing early warning systems have converged on state fragility as their main indicator of early warning. The UK, for example, undertook to set up 'an Early Warning System that will take a global view of countries in which political, economic and security shocks over the next 12 months could trigger violence' (DFID, 2011). Drawing on intelligence information and diplomatic reports, scholarly analyses, media reports and quantitative indicators, the Department for International Development has prepared its own registers of states at risk. Government early warning experts express confidence in their ability to identify structural factors that contribute to the risk of state fragility. They are less confident of proximate indicators intended to give warnings twelve months ahead, and still less confident of shorter-term warnings.

Qualitative conflict monitoring comprises the mass of reports, news stories, academic analyses and general information that is available about particular situations (see, for example, Guéhenno, 2015). In the public domain it includes the reports of humanitarian agencies (linked together on the ReliefWeb site) and analyses of conflicts and countries at risk (such as those of the International Crisis Group). Governments also rely on their diplomatic services and intelligence agencies. Qualitative monitoring offers vastly more content-rich and contextual information than quantitative statistical analysis but presents problems of noise and information overload. Given the current state of the art, qualitative monitoring is currently likely to be most useful for early warning in the short term and in particular cases: the expertise of the area scholar and the local observer, steeped in situational knowledge, is difficult to beat. Networks of country experts, policy-makers and analysts pool this information, although there is still ample scope for strategic surprise (Austin, 2004).

Finally, still largely at the research stage is an ongoing effort to develop machine-reading of real-time data and events data to monitor the escalation of conflicts. However, new techniques, such as crowdsourcing and relying on mobile phone data and messages from people in areas of conflict, are starting to transform the scope for early warning and early response. For the case of the Ushahidi initiative, which began in Kenya, see the Kenya case study below (Reading 72).

Even when observers issue 'early warnings', it is by no means certain that there will be a response. For some time it has been realized that the key issue is not, in fact, providing early warning but, rather, mustering the political resources to make an appropriate early response when a warning has been issued. Governments and international organizations may be distracted by other crises (as in the case of Yugoslavia) or unwilling to change existing policies (as in the case of Rwanda). The governments of countries vulnerable to conflict may resist external interference. Nevertheless, some governments have recognized the need for an integrated system of early warning and early response, combining structural and direct prevention (DFID, 2011).

Structural Prevention

We referred in chapter 1 to the hourglass model of conflict resolution (see figure 1.3, p. 16). In this model, freedom of action to deal with conflict is at its widest at the early stage of pre-violence prevention and at the late stage of post-violence peacebuilding. At these stages, the issues of conflict management, which narrow down to a few critical choices at the point of crisis, widen out to embrace the broader political context. Here the question of how to prevent and manage conflict becomes very similar to the classical questions political theory asks about how any polity should be governed. How are resources and roles to be allocated in a way that is legitimate and accepted? How are public goods to be provided? What is the basis of political community? How are relationships to be conducted between individuals and groups within and between political communities? What are the values, norms and rules of the community and how are they to be upheld?

When there is an agreed and legitimate basis for a political community and the community provides public goods and secures the accepted values of its members, violent conflict is likely to be avoided. When coercion is used as the basis for the allocation of resources and roles, and when this allocation is uneven, illegitimate and unacceptable to people, violent conflict is more likely to occur.

This applies at the level of global society as well as at the national level and in sub-national communities. Although most current effort in conflict prevention goes into avoiding civil wars in developing countries, in principle a cosmopolitan conflict prevention agenda should address interlinked conflict formations at the international, national and sub-national levels. If we see the context of conflict as forming a vital element of conflict transformation, there is no possibility of addressing local and regional conflicts without also taking the international setting into account (see the analysis of transnational conflict in chapter 4).

We will touch first on structural prevention at the international level before dealing with structural prevention of civil wars. Researchers have identified a range of structural factors that prevent interstate wars. For example, Wallensteen (1984) notes the concerted efforts of states to prevent major wars in 'universalistic' periods where there is a common interest in system maintenance. Security communities have well-established pacifying effects (Adler and Barnett, 1998). Keohane and Nye (1989) argue that complex bonds of interdependence tend to create a set of interlocking issue areas in which security concerns are not necessarily privileged over others. Russett and Oneal (2001) maintain that involvement in international organizations reduces the risk of war. Hegre (2003) contends that development tends to be a preventive factor. As noted further in chapter 11, the 'democratic peace' literature suggests that the risk of war between pairs of states is reduced when both are democracies, though the opposite is the case in pairs of states where one is a democracy and one an autocracy (Raknerud and Hegre, 1997).

Common trade, common democracy, development, and participation in international organizations and security communities form a complex of linked conditions which contribute to the remarkable phenomenon of the 'liberal peace' as seen in the group of mostly western and developed states which have for a long period avoided major wars among themselves. Rasmussen (2003) argues convincingly that these conditions did not develop by accident but were constructed deliberately as part of a historical process. The close political relationships fostered between Britain and America formed the nucleus of an evolving set of political ties. As Rasmussen puts it, 'peace is not a fact, it is a policy.' The liberal peace was made because it suited the interests of the liberal states, which benefited from mutual trade, interdependence and avoidance of war between themselves. The victors of the world wars deliberately embedded liberal principles in the postwar orders. The success of the liberal order then led to its expansion. Democracies tended to win wars, and defeated states then ousted autocracies and installed democracies. As a consequence, there was a systematic growth in the number of liberal states, and these states were incorporated in the western-dominated liberal system. As Mitchell, Gates and Hegre (1999) argue, 'democratization tends to follow war, democratization decreases the systemic amount of war, and the substantive and pacific impact of democracy on war increases over time.' Thus the spread of liberal democracies has been associated with a liberal peace (see dicussion in chapter 11).

However, a less benign element of the liberal peace has been its effects on developing countries. First, the exposure of weaker economies to international competition has resulted in an uneven process of development, which has contributed to global inequalities. Differences inside developing countries in living standards and access to power have widened, and western companies have wittingly or unwittingly contributed to the conditions of conflict (Cramer, 2006). Thus, while they are starting to adopt conflict prevention policies in the developing world, western states are in many ways continuing to shape conflicts, through their decisions over foreign policy, economic and commercial policy and arms sales.

Another vehicle for exacerbating conflict may be democracy promotion, which is now a conscious adjunct of development, peacebuilding and conflict prevention policy, as discussed further in chapter 8. Democratization may become an instrument of conflict prevention when democratic institutions flourish in ways that are appropriate to local conditions. The danger is that, when it is applied as a veneer, democracy may tend to legitimize one-party rule, entrench the dominance of the largest ethnic group, and pose a security threat to autocratic rulers in the region. Then democratization can indeed be a factor which exacerbates conflicts.

The 'liberal peace' has been in many ways a huge achievement in preventing wars among the states that participate in it. If it is to fulfil its potential and overcome the wider historical rivalries with the states which lie outside, a much more inclusive approach is needed. The institutions at its core would need to serve as a basis for creating a legitimate and equitable order that serves human needs broadly rather than entrenching the political and economic interests of a global elite. The Ukrainian crisis, which we deal with below, sharply illustrates the need for a more inclusive European order.

With these general observations about conflict prevention in interstate conflicts, we turn to the structural prevention of civil wars, which has occupied most of the attention of researchers and policy-makers in this field. In the last twenty years, researchers have amassed a host of findings about the factors that are correlated with the onset of civil wars, as noted in chapter 4. From this, it is possible to identify some of the main factors that are likely to reduce the risk of civil wars. These are stable governance, economic development, political and economic inclusiveness, the mitigation of horizontal inequalities, and the protection of human rights.

Turning to governance first, there has been a clear finding that changes of regime tend to be associated with violent conflict, so political stability is a preventive factor. There is evidence that settled democracies are less prone to civil wars than other regime types. Stable autocracies also experience relatively few civil wars. It is semi-democracies and transitional regimes that exhibit the highest incidence (Hegre et al., 2001). Appropriate institutions also contribute to conflict prevention. For example, locally adapted proportional voting systems appear to have been strikingly successful in preventing violent conflicts (Reynal-Querol, 2002).

With regard to economic factors, a strong relationship has been found between low per capita income and the risk of civil war, indicating that inclusive development and a sufficient level of prosperity help to prevent violent conflict. As noted in chapter 3, mal-development creates a 'conflict trap' that the poorest countries find difficult to escape (Collier et al., 2003). The poorest group of countries, with stagnant economies and a history of past conflicts, are most at risk of violent conflict. Middle-income countries have a lower risk of civil war, and this risk is diminishing over time as development proceeds. OECD countries have an almost negligible risk of civil war. Lifting countries out of poverty is thus likely to prevent civil wars as a side effect.

As we saw in chapter 4, Azar theorized that armed conflict degrades governance, deforms institutions and destroys development. The statistical evidence suggests that the opposite is also true: good governance, sound institutions and effective development inhibit the incidence of armed conflict (Miall, 2003).

Similarly, abuse of human rights is widely recognized as an early warning indicator of incipient conflict. Human rights violations are both a trigger for escalation (as, for example, in Kosovo in 1998) and a result of protracted fighting. In contrast, high levels of observance of human rights tend to go with other related factors, such as democratic governance, development and stable governance.

We conclude by highlighting the links between these findings and Azar's theory of protracted social conflict. Direct preventers of non-interstate war correspond roughly to Azar's 'process dynamic' variables in protracted social conflict, among them flexible and accommodating state actions and strategies, moderate communal actions and strategies on the part of the leaders of challenging groups, and mutually de-escalatory 'built-in mechanisms' of conflict management. Structural preventers address Azar's 'preconditions' for protracted social conflict. They include adequate political institutions and good governance, cohesive social structures, opportunities for groups to develop economically and culturally, and the presence of accepted legal or social norms capable of accommodating and peacefully transforming these formations. A stable and peaceful wider regional setting is also important. As table 5.1 shows, preventers of internal conflict operate at a number of different levels.

Table 5.1 Preventers of intrastate conflict

Factors generating conflict	Possible preventers
Global level	
Inappropriate systemic structures	Changes in international order
Regional level	
Regional diasporas	Regional security arrangements
State level	
Ethnic stratification	Power-sharing/federalism/autonomy
Weak economies	Appropriate development
Authoritarian rule	Legitimacy, democratization
Human rights abuse	Rule of law, human rights monitoring/protection
Societal level	
Weak societies	Strengthening civic society, institutions
Weak communications	Round tables, workshops, community relations
Polarized attitudes	Cross-cultural work
Poverty, inequality	Poverty reduction and social reforms
Elite/individual level	
Exclusionist policies	Stronger moderates

Direct Prevention

When disputes are close to the point of violence, direct (or operational) prevention comes into play. The literature tends to focus mainly on external interveners in direct conflict prevention, but, as we have seen, the protagonists themselves and their societies often play the most decisive role by pursuing moderate and constructive strategies (Kriesberg, 1998a). Direct negotiations between the contending parties may limit the risk of conflict escalation at an early stage (Zartman, 2001). In some of the most cited cases of external conflict prevention, such as Macedonia and Estonia, internal and external actors combined together to limit potential conflicts.

A wide range of policy options are in principle available for direct prevention (Creative Associates, 1997: 3–6). They range from official diplomacy (mediation, conciliation, fact-finding, good offices, peace conferences, envoys, conflict prevention centres, hot lines) through non-official diplomacy (private mediation, message-carrying and the creation of back-channels, peace commissions, problem-solving workshops, conflict resolution training, round tables) to peacemaking efforts by local actors (church-facilitated talks, debates between politicians, cross-party discussions). In some cases exploratory talks and trust-building by respected mediators are crucial. In others, positive and negative inducements by relevant states are significant. The literature (Carnegie Commission, 1997; Wallensteen, 1998; Leatherman et al., 1999;

Zartman, 2001; Hampson and Malone, 2002) explores a range of political measures (mediation with muscle, mobilization through regional and global organizations, attempts to influence the media), economic measures (sanctions, emergency aid, conditional offers of financial support) and military measures (preventive peacekeeping, arms embargoes, demilitarization).

Direct prevention thus goes wider than conflict resolution, if that is conceived as bringing parties together to analyse and transform a dispute. However, the effort to resolve conflict at an early stage is at the heart of prevention. It involves identifying the key issues, clearing mistrust and misperceptions, and exploring feasible outcomes that bridge the opposing positions of the parties. Finding ways to negotiate agreements and agree procedures and channels for dispute resolution and transforming contentious relationships is central to the enterprise. These were characteristic of the work of Max van der Stoel, the OSCE High Commissioner for National Minorities, whose intervention in Estonia is noted in box 5.1, and whose work in Central and Eastern Europe in the 1990s is one of the beacons of quiet preventive diplomacy in practice (Khrychikov and

Box 5.1 Conflict prevention in Estonia

In 1993 the citizens of Narva voted by an overwhelming majority to secede from Estonia. They were almost all Russians who had been dismayed to become what they saw as second-class citizens in their own country. The Estonian government declared that the referendum was illegal and threatened to use force if necessary to prevent the break-up of Estonia. Russian vigilante groups began to arm themselves, and in Russia the president warned that he would intervene if necessary to protect the rights of Russian speakers. At a time when it appeared that this deadlock could lead to the outbreak of fighting, the OSCE high commissioner on national minorities, Max van der Stoel, interceded. After meeting with representatives of the Narva city council and the government, he suggested that the Narva council should regard the referendum as a declaration of aspiration without immediate effect. At the same time he suggested to the Estonian government that they abandon their threat to use force against the city. His suggestions were adopted and no armed conflict took place.

In assessing the influence of the high commissioner in the Estonia case, we have to weigh the importance of other factors: the lack of mobilization of the Russian-speaking identity, the unwillingness of Russia to get involved at a stage when it was dependent on western support, and the capacity of the Estonian political system to manage its own disputes. Estonia had adopted a voting system which gave political parties an incentive to seek broad-based support, and the Centre Party became a vehicle for Russian-speakers to express their interests. This, together with the exercise of local government, helped to provide capacity for managing the conflict, even though it did not resolve it. Structural prevention, in the form of some constitutional capacity for managing conflict, together with the presence in the OSCE of an institution which was allowed to monitor minorities, combined with operational and direct diplomacy of Max van der Stoel's diplomatic intervention to head off a potential conflict.

Source: Khrychikov and Miall, 2002

Miall, 2002; Kemp, 2001; Reading 35). They are also the hallmarks of efforts by internal and external non-governmental peacemakers.

In some cases quite protracted conflicts continue at a political level, with successive negotiations, breakdowns, agreements and disagreements, but the conflict is eventually settled or suspended without violence breaking out. The long struggle over South Tyrol was negotiated between the Austrian and Italian governments and the local parties in Alto Adige. In other cases a negotiation process prevents a political conflict reaching any risk of violence. Examples are the peaceful divorce of the Czech and Slovak republics and the negotiations between Moscow and the Tatar government over the status of Tatarstan within the Russian Federation (Hopmann, 2001: 151–6).

Non-governmental organizations, development agencies and social actors also take significant steps to address conflict and attempt to prevent violence at an early stage. It is difficult to evaluate the impact of this kind of 'preventive peacebuilding', especially when the main intended impact may be to improve relations between specific groups or address needs at a community or regional level. It is only when there is an obvious relationship between programmes at the local and community level and impact on the elite level that conflict impact assessment is clear. NGOs work with enormous energy in many conflict hot spots all over the world – for example, Search for Common Ground has fifty-three local offices and works with 1,477 local partners in more than thirty countries. The work can sometimes be very challenging. Conciliation Resources supported a Citizens' Constitutional Forum in Fiji which contributed to the adoption in 1997 of a power-sharing system. This was intended to address the domination of the indigenous Fijians over the Indian-Fijian group. But following the coup, which overthrew the constitution in 2000, the situation became more polarized than ever. Conciliation Resources continues to work with partners to encourage multiculturalism and respect for human rights – for instance, through its support for Fiji Dialogue, which brings people together across the ethnic divide, and the Fiji Women's Rights Movement.

Development agencies have a significant role to play in conflict prevention, especially in the poorest countries, which are most vulnerable to the 'conflict trap'. They have a range of impacts, some positive, some highly negative (Muscat, 2002). Large government donors typically work with the local government and may have negative impacts on local communities when centrally financed development programmes impact on them. For example, EU support for irrigation schemes in the Awash valley in Ethiopia have led to the intensification of latent conflict between local Afar clans and the central government, although this has been partly offset by a small-scale local project with the regional government (of which the central government disapproved). Development agencies bring substantial resources into poor countries, and it is difficult for them to avoid enmeshment in local conflicts. On the other hand, conflict-sensitive work by development agencies can contribute both to development and to the prevention of conflicts.

We close this section with a case study (box 5.2) which illustrates how the UN, regional states, national dialogue, NGOs and crowdsourcing came together to track and avert further escalation of conflict in Kenya in 2008.

Box 5.2 Conflict prevention in Kenya

Kenya has suffered from inter-ethnic conflicts associated with the control of the state by dominant ethnic groups. Stagnant or declining economic growth in the 1990s, combined with conflicts in peripheral areas (such as among the pastoralists in the north-east), seemed to threaten the country's stability. However, the elections of 2002 brought an opposition to power peacefully – unusual in African circumstances. The government's policy of providing free education, encouraging agricultural cooperatives and tackling corruption gained dividends initially in economic progress and international support. Notwithstanding its ethnic and economic divisions, Kenya had avoided large-scale internal conflict until violence erupted again sparked by disputed election results in January 2008. What happened next can be seen as a demonstration of the effectiveness of the combination of factors noted in this chapter: well-directed immediate crisis action linked to deeper national conflict management structures and regionalized capacity, backed up by remarkable local initiatives.

In the initial violence in 2008, over 1,500 people were killed in communal fighting. This threatened to escalate further and destroy the achievements of the preceding period. But, in the event, the situation was rescued following mediation by former UN Secretary-General Kofi Annan, who moved fast to broker talks between the Kenyan president, Mwai Kibaki, and the leader of the opposition Orange Democratic Movement, Raila Odinga. The talks led to a power-sharing agreement which, despite the persistence of intercommunal tensions, succeeded in stabilizing the situation and creating space for preventive actions and programmes. Here rapid international response was able to build on existing power-sharing arrangements at the national level.

This in turn related to the wider prevention capacities of the African Union. In this case, the head of the African Union (President John Kufour of Ghana), Archbishop Tutu of South Africa, and representatives of the Forum of Former African Heads of State and Government all visited the country to encourage political leaders to seek a negotiated solution. Kofi Annan was chosen to lead an African Union-mandated Panel of Eminent African Personalities. A power-sharing agreement was reached on 28 January 2008, and on the following day a Kenya National Dialogue and Reconciliation initiative was launched.

While the focus of the initial response was on stabilizing the political situation, conflict prevention initiatives were also launched as part of a comprehensive programme of peacebuilding to address the causes of conflict at communal and grassroots levels, along the lines we explore further in chapter 9. As noted in box 3.1, Kenyan citizens took the initiative to develop the Ushahidi platform to map incidents of violence via mobile phone, SMS (text messaging), email and the web so that crisis information could be gathered in real time by citizens and NGOs. The data is then matched and analysed through geographic information and mapping tools. The system was designed explicitly to create an effective grassroots early warning system. It was an open source technology, which meant that it could be adapted and developed for a variety of uses and contexts. The philosophy was that 'the Ushahidi engine is there for "everyday" people to link with each other and to let the world know what is happening in their area during a crisis, emergency or other situation. Bringing awareness, linking those in need to those who can assist, and providing the framework for better visualization of information graphically' (www.ushahidi.com).

This kind of analysis was complemented by a variety of community-based peacebuilding activities organized by UNDP Kenya. For example, a 'Tuelewane' Youth Exchange Programme was initiated and, from October 2007 to December 2009, six Tuelewane activities were organized to provide training and education on peace and conflict resolution within six major communities affected by the conflict. Activities included football and other sporting events used for peacebuilding, and local radio was employed to promote mutual understanding and reconciliation.

All of this may be seen to support the evidence, cited in chapter 3, that some progress is being made in reducing the incidence of violent conflict – including evidence that African wars now last significantly less long than the average elsewhere.

Prevention of Conflict Recurrence

Direct prevention is relevant to averting armed conflicts before they occur, but it is also relevant in preventing further escalation after violence has started, as in the Kenya case, and in preventing conflict recurrence. A significant number of armed conflicts recur, so preventing their recurrence has come to be seen as part of conflict prevention, although this task clearly overlaps with ending conflicts and post-conflict peacebuilding. We will discuss prevention of recurrence briefly here while giving our main treatment of this topic in chapters 7, 8, 9 and 10.

According to the Correlates of War project (Sarkees and Schaffer, 2000), 104 civil wars (defined as wars with a threshold of 1,000 battle deaths) took place in fifty-four countries between 1945 and 1997. In other words, half of the countries which experienced civil wars between those years experienced more than one. If we take the lower threshold of twenty-five battle deaths in the Uppsala Conflict Data and the slightly longer time span of 1945 to 2009, 57 per cent of countries experienced more than one civil war. Moreover, as the time since 1945 has passed, an increasing proportion of civil wars are in countries that have had previous civil wars (Walter, 2011). This does not necessarily mean that half of all the civil wars recurred – different conflict parties and different issues may have been involved. But it does mean that civil wars are increasingly likely to be in countries which have experienced civil war before.

Call (2012) argues that the main factor in conflict recurrence is political exclusion and, conversely, that inclusive settlements form the main way of avoiding recurrence. If we interpret the recurrence of war as due to the security dilemma in which unreconciled groups find themselves, it is clear that, if excluded groups can come to be included in governing and security institutions, the security dilemma is likely to be mitigated. Similarly, Walter (2014) maintains that strong institutions are negatively associated with civil war recurrence and suggests that strengthening legal and political institutions is a primary route to getting countries out of the 'conflict trap'. Others argue for the importance of raising income levels (Collier et al., 2003; Collier 2008) and reducing horizontal inequalities (Cederman et al., 2013).

Probably most of the effort directed towards conflict prevention by international organizations, governments and NGOs is actually put into prevention of conflict recurrence. For example, the UN secretary-general's report *Preventive Diplomacy: Delivering Results* (United Nations, 2011) highlights the UN Peacebuilding Commission's efforts to prevent relapse into conflict in the six countries where it was working at the time (Burundi, the Central African Republic, Guinea, Guinea-Bissau, Liberia and Sierra Leone). The report cites other instances of direct prevention which are aimed mainly at preventing recurrence. For example, in 2008, Ban Ki-moon appointed the former Nigerian president General Olusegun Obasanjo as a special envoy to the Great Lakes, following up with a mediation mission which led to demobilization of rebel groups in 2009 and an agreement between Rwanda and the DRC. Similarly, in 2010, the UN Office of Preventive Diplomacy in Kyrgyzstan helped to promote dialogue, political talks and reconciliation after a previous outbreak of ethnic violence. The report also cites examples of interventions that are preventive and do not follow a war (such as the UN role in helping Guinea towards constitutional rule in 2009–10, in partnership with ECOWAS, the African Union and an International Contact Group). But prevention of recurrence has become the main theme.

Prevention of Genocide and Mass Atrocities

President Obama introduced a new theme in 2012 when he announced, in a speech at the US Holocaust Museum, that the US would adopt a policy of prevention of mass atrocities. This has led to the creation of an Atrocities Prevention Board in the White House national security system and the development of a handbook on *Mass Atrocity Response Operations* for the US Army (Sewall et al., 2013). The UN had previously created an office of the Special Adviser on the Prevention of Genocide, which was merged with the office of the Special Adviser for Responsibility to Protect in 2010. This office is attempting to develop a mass atrocities early warning system. Similarly, the EU has established its Task Force on the Prevention of Genocide and Mass Atrocities in Budapest (Smith and Meyer, 2013).

Mass atrocities are taken to be episodes in which at least 5,000 civilians are killed intentionally. There have been 103 such episodes since 1945, the majority of them associated with armed conflict. Since 1945, 67 per cent of the cases and, since 1980, 85 per cent of the cases have occurred within armed conflicts (Bellamy, 2011). Measures which are designed to prevent conflicts, if effective, should therefore also prevent the majority of mass atrocities, although special warning systems and measures are required for the small number of episodes which occur in peacetime.

What steps can be taken to prevent mass atrocities? The most important mirror conflict prevention priorities. There needs to be an early warning system. Structural prevention and, particularly, efforts to reduce the level of political exclusiveness, to improve governance, to reduce discrimination and to protect security and human rights are the priority. Direct prevention includes measures such as fact-finding missions, envoys, and support for indigenous conflict resolution efforts. Non-violent witnesses and accompaniers may help to protect civilians. Mass atrocities are crimes, and there is a strong case for responding with local or international police forces, which should be capable of carrying out investigations and making arrests. Peacekeepers may ultimately be necessary to provide protection in extreme cases.

In practice, conflict prevention, civilian protection and prevention of genocide and mass atrocities are largely overlapping and mutually reinforcing policies, although each also requires its own distinctive lens.

The Adoption of Conflict Prevention by International Organizations

Fifty years after the idea was first examined by the pioneers of the conflict resolution field, it is remarkable how the idea of conflict prevention came to be adopted as the leading edge of international and multilateral conflict management policy. Mechanisms for peaceful change and systems for anticipation of future issues, two of the key perquisites for international peace and security which were absent from all of the historic peace treaties noted by Holsti in chapter 2 of this book (see table 2.1, p. 42), started to be designed into the security architectures of regional and international organizations through the commitment to programmes of conflict prevention. The UN, the OSCE, the EU, the OECD, the AU, ECOWAS, SADC, IGAD, ASEAN, the G8, the IMF and the World Bank all adopted some type of commitment to conflict prevention.

But it would be an overstatement to say that conflict prevention has taken a central place in the policies of international institutions and major states. While international organizations and some major states now deploy agencies with a conflict prevention remit, in practice the focus of policy-makers' attention is on short-term crisis management. The 1990s was perhaps the high water mark of international interest in conflict prevention. After 9/11, the tide turned towards the prevention of terrorism, while the Bush administration adopted a policy of pre-emptive war that alarmed many UN member states. The Responsibility to Protect doctrine, developed from 2005 onwards, gave a distinct new impetus, with an emphasis on preventive action to protect civilians but also a call for military intervention if other measures failed. This was put into practice in the western military intervention in Libya in 2011, which aimed to protect the citizens of Benghazi. But the ferocious civil war that followed, and the spread of Libyan arms to Mali, Sudan and Syria, reduced enthusiasm for R2P operations, as did the waning public support for intervention in the light of Iraq and Afghanistan. When the Obama administration came to power, it became more cautious about intervention, renouncing Bush's doctrine of pre-emption, and made a rhetorical return to prevention. Vice-President Biden said that 'we will strive to act preventively, and not pre-emptively, to avoid where possible a choice of last resort between the risks of war and the dangers of inaction' (Woocher, 2009).

The UN's concern with conflict prevention evolved from *An Agenda for Peace* (Boutros-Ghali, 1992), through the Brahimi Report (Brahimi, 2000), to the Secretary-General's report *The Prevention of Armed Conflict*, presented at the 55th Session of the General Assembly (United Nations, 2001), which made conflict prevention a priority of the organization. Kofi Annan urged his staff to develop a 'culture of prevention'. Similarly, UN Security Council Resolution 1366 of August 2001 identified a key role for the Security Council in the prevention of armed conflict. A Trust Fund for Preventive Action was established and a system-wide training programme on early warning and preventive measures initiated. Within the UN family, the UNDP defined its role in post-conflict peacebuilding through a conflict prevention strategy adopted in November 2000, and 20 per cent of UNDP Track III funding was set aside for 'preventive and curative activities'.

The UN made further commitments in 2004 with the adoption of the High Level Report and the acceptance of a 'responsibility to prevent' (Bellamy, 2008). It was hoped that the Peacebuilding Commission could take on these responsibilities. But, in the event, the member states were divided over accepting Kofi Annan's call for a 'culture of prevention' and made it clear that they would not accept this proposal. The commitment of UN funds to conflict prevention has remained quite limited, and responsibility for prevention has not been concentrated in a particular agency in the Secretariat; rather, the UN Department of Political Affairs, together with resident UN missions, special envoys and groups of friends, play the main roles. Some states favoured a larger UN role, but developing states that might have become recipients of conflict prevention measures were nervous of great power interference. Others, notably China and Russia, argued that the principle of sovereignty remained the best basis for protecting states. Nevertheless, UN Secretary-General Ban Ki-moon pressed ahead with a 'UN year of prevention' in 2012 and published a significant report on conflict prevention in the same year (United Nations, 2012).

If there has been resistance to the principle of conflict prevention among some UN member states, it is in the regional organizations and, above all, in Europe, where progress has been most noticeable.

The Organization for Security and Cooperation in Europe (OSCE) has fifty-five participating states, spanning the world from Vancouver to Vladivostok, and has evolved as a primary regional organization for early warning, conflict prevention, crisis management and post-conflict rehabilitation. Member states agree a set of principles and norms which permit a collective interest in their internal conflicts. The OSCE has a Conflict Prevention Centre, an Office for Democratic Institutions and Human Rights (ODIHR) and, as we have seen, a High Commissioner for National Minorities (HCNM) charged with identifying and seeking early resolution of ethnic tensions that might endanger peace, stability or friendly relations between the participating states. The HCNM gathers information, mediates, promotes dialogue, makes recommendations and informs OSCE members of potential conflicts; significantly, the HCNM does not require approval by member states before becoming involved. This was an impressive innovation, and acceptance of a right of other members of the organization to monitor their internal affairs set an important precedent. The OSCE faces perhaps its greatest challenge in the Ukraine crisis, which has set its western and eastern members at loggerheads (see the case study later in this chapter). Nevertheless, all the OSCE institutions have been in play. The HCNM highlighted the sensitivity of language legislation. The ODIHR conducted its biggest ever observation mission at the presidential elections in May 2014, which helped to de-escalate tensions at a significant moment. The OSCE Permanent Council in Vienna provided a forum for participating states to exchange views, even if these sometimes came close to breaking the normal diplomatic niceties. In addition, the OSCE has supplied missions to monitor ceasefires and negotiate with local commanders. These are all essential conflict preventing roles and serve to underline the importance of having such a body even when its members are deadlocked.

The European Union has developed perhaps the deepest commitment to conflict prevention of any international organization. At the Gothenburg Summit in June 2001, the European Council declared:

> Conflict prevention calls for a cooperative approach to facilitate peaceful solutions to disputes, and implies addressing the root causes of conflicts. The EU underlines its political commitment to pursue conflict prevention as one of the main objectives of the EU's external relations. It resolves to continue to improve its capacity to prevent violent conflicts and to contribute to a global culture of prevention.

The EU has developed a comprehensive set of policies and policy instruments, drawing together human rights programmes, measures to combat the spread of small arms, support for security sector reform, governance reforms and economic support. The Commission aims to foster 'structural stability', defined as developing 'the capacity to manage change without resort to [armed] conflict'. The post-Lisbon reforms have to some extent created bureaucratic obstacles for conflict prevention, which cuts across the EU's pillar structure, dividing the foreign-policy-oriented European External Action Service (EEAS) from the Commission's Directorate General dealing with conflict prevention in a development context (DEVCO). The State Fragility and Crisis Response Unit, created in 2011, aims to ameliorate the lack of coordination between these two arms. The EU sometimes fails both to be proactive in using mediation and dialogue in early phases of conflict and to apply its own conflict analysis tools. Nevertheless, it has a range of instruments and funds that are relevant to conflict prevention and is active in funding conflict prevention efforts by other regional organizations and by NGOs. The EU has sent Conflict Prevention Assessment Missions to such areas of conflict as Papua New Guinea, the Solomon Islands, Fiji, Indonesia and Nepal, and it created a Rapid Reaction Mechanism in 2001 for missions to areas in acute crisis (Kronenberger and Wouters, 2004).

The Organization for Economic Cooperation and Development (OECD), through its Development Assistance Committee, has also produced guidelines for conflict prevention which depend on long-term structural preventive measures built into developmental assistance programmes (Ackermann, 2003).

The G8 countries produced their Rome Initiative on Conflict Prevention in July 2001, concentrating on small arms and light weapons, conflict diamonds, children in conflict, civilian policing, conflict and development, the role of women, and the contribution of the private sector in conflict prevention.

ASEAN's Regional Forum, established in 1994, brings together twenty-seven states of South-East Asia to discuss common security issues. It has a work plan on preventive diplomacy and sponsors second-track diplomacy on regional security issues – for example, on the Spratly Islands dispute – as well as confidence-building measures and Track I consultations on security issues in the South China Sea and elsewhere between the region's states.

The African Union has a Conflict Prevention and Early Warning System with a Continental Early Warning System, a Panel of the Wise – bringing together respected leaders to advise AU conflict prevention efforts – and a Border Programme concerned with border security issues.

The regional organizations have therefore taken conflict prevention on board, and a similar story can be told of many individual states. To take only one example, the UK government launched its Global Conflict Prevention Pool (now known as the Conflict, Security and Stability Fund) in 2001, combining three key departments (the Ministry of Defence, the Department for International Development and the Foreign Office) in an attempt to coordinate strategy around policy development and programme delivery (Kapila and Wermester, 2002). The initial budget of £74 million in 2004 was limited, but the rhetorical commitment was clear. After various reorganizations, the Stabilization Unit is the agency that now coordinates government activity in this field, on the basis of the 'Building Stability Overseas Strategy' (DFID, 2011). The strategy commits the UK 'to helping states build capacity to protect their populations from genocide, war crimes, ethnic cleansing and crimes against humanity and to assisting those who are under stress before crises and conflicts break out.' The means of action envisaged are political engagement, peace support operations, humanitarian action and state capacity-building.

On the ground, NGOs continue to research, advocate and implement conflict prevention activities and work with local partners, a low-level 'sprinkler' system that contrasts with the more public and sometimes more forceful intervention of states.

Conflict Prevention and the Break-Up of Empires: Ukraine – A Case Study

We end this chapter with perhaps the most dangerous failure to prevent the outbreak of violence since the third edition of this book. It is instructive to set it within the wider context of the break-up of states and empires in general. In fact, the overall picture is mixed – and at the time of writing there is still some hope that the crisis in Ukraine can be contained and that some semblance of post-Cold War cooperation within the OSCE area might be restored.

After the First World War, one of main aims of US President Woodrow Wilson's Fourteen Points at the Peace of Paris in 1919 had been to dismantle the defeated empires (Austro-Hungarian, Ottoman Turkish, to a lesser extent German) into their constituent 'nations' (MacMillan, 2001). Russia had already been dismembered by the earlier Treaty of Brest-Litovsk between the new Soviet Union and Germany. The assumption was that the principle of self-determination would remove a major cause of future war. But, because of the endless proliferation and scattered distribution of the constituent 'peoples' on whom the new system was to be imposed, putting this into practice proved highly challenging. President Wilson brought experts from the US National Geographic Society with him, but delegates, such as the large Italian foreign minister Orlando, were seen crawling in puzzlement across huge maps laid out on the floor that charted the ethnic distribution of many peoples of whom most delegates (including Woodrow Wilson himself) had never heard (Moynihan, 1993). However finely tuned, there was no way to redraw borders without cutting across some ethnic groups or imprisoning others as minorities. In the event, a former imperial people such as the Hungarians, for example, found itself scattered around the periphery of the new diminutive 'Hungary' as minorities in other surrounding countries.

This was a harbinger of what was to come.

After the Second World War, it was the turn of the European overseas empires to be broken up. The result was a quadrupling of the membership of the United Nations, with some 150 new states. The resulting incompatibilities were to be accommodated by new constitutions, elected representatives, power-sharing and minority rights. Not surprisingly, these attempts at conflict prevention had mixed success in parts of the world where they were unfamiliar, and some of them continue to baffle those trying to contain the resulting 'intractable' conflicts to this day. For example, the break-up of the British Empire between 1947 and the 1960s led to colossal upheavals, often accompanied by mass violence, which left problems that still persist unresolved, such as the partition of India (Kashmir), the cutting off of the Tamil minority in Sri Lanka from mainland fellow Tamil Hindus, the artificial borders of Iraq as agreed after the 1917 Sykes–Picot agreement, the implementation of the 1917 Balfour Declaration in Palestine, the earlier division of the Pashtun lands in Afghanistan/Pakistan (the Durand Line), innumerable new borders in Africa – including independence for South Africa that did not safeguard the rights of the majority – and comparable problems in Burma/Myanmar and Malaysia. To this we can add the partition of Ireland in 1922.

With the end of the Cold War, in addition to the bloodstained break-up of former Yugoslavia (and the peaceful separation of Slovakia from the Czech Republic), came the at first remarkably non-violent dismemberment of the fifteen former Soviet republics, many artificially adapted under Stalin to contain large Russian minorities in order to strengthen central control; there was no suspicion that these might eventually become independent states. On the western side of Europe, in contrast, the EU and NATO pursued an expansionist programme of eastern enlargement that brought their borders to the edge of Russia.

Under Vladimir Putin, the Russian government has been attempting a *rassemblement* of the ancient Russian lands (see map 5.1).

The challenge for conflict prevention is whether these colliding geopolitical aspirations, together with the internal conflict that has developed in Ukraine, can be managed non-violently. The former Baltic republics (Estonia, Latvia, Lithuania) had never been internationally recognized as part of the Soviet Union, and accommodation was eventually made with the Russian minorities, as illustrated with reference to Estonia earlier in this chapter. They subsequently joined NATO and the EU. In contrast, the threat of a further break-up of the Russian Federation itself was ferociously suppressed in the Chechen wars of 1994–6 and 1999–2009. Most of the former Central Asian republics (Kazakhstan, Kyrgyzstan, Tajikistan, Turkmenistan, Uzbekistan) were left in the hands of Russian-leaning authoritarian rulers supported by economic

Map 5.1 *Russia and the former Soviet Republics*

and military inducements. Kazakhstan was persuaded to join a new customs union with Russia.

That left the former 'heartland' republics, above all Ukraine, cradle of Russian history itself in the era before the Mongol invasions and the eventual rise of Moscow (Sakwa, 2014). This is a deeply resonant theme for Russians, and for Putin, associated as it is with the conversion to Christianity by St Cyril and St Methodius, the subsequent adoption of the Cyrillic script, and the foundation of the 'third Rome' – embodied in the holy Russian Orthodox Church.[1] Here a recognizable pattern could be discerned in Moldova, Georgia and (with variations) Azerbaijan. Russia supported the separatist ambitions of minorities in Transdniestr (Moldova), Abkhazia and South Ossetia (Georgia), and Nagorno-Karabakh (Azerbaijan/Armenia) but held back from annexation, content with a Russian military presence (some 1,500 troops apiece in Transdniestr, Abkhazia and South Ossetia, and 5,000 in Armenia) and *de facto* autonomy within the Russian sphere of influence. A flare-up in Georgia in 2008 (resulting in 8,000 deaths) was ended by a similar arrangement. The resulting 'frozen' conflicts remained dangerous and unresolved but were quite widely seen to 'contain' the danger below a level that would trigger major western involvement.

This changed with the Russian occupation and annexation of the Crimean peninsula in February and March 2014. The Russian grand plan had become one of creating a 'Eurasian Union' of former Soviet republics along the lines of the EU to be formally launched in 2015. Kazakhstan and Belarus had agreed to join, and Armenia, Kyrgyzstan and Tajikistan were considering following suit. But the enterprise would amount to little without Ukraine. So the EU invitation for Ukraine to sign an association agreement in November 2013 was seen as a threat to Russia's political and economic interests. Pressure was put on the Ukrainian president, Viktor Yanukovych, not to sign. He agreed, but was then deposed by an uprising centred in Kiev on 21 March 2014. A new interim government signed the deal with the EU. Now it was the turn of Russian nationalists in Eastern Ukraine to revolt, casting the Kiev authorities as fascist wartime collaborators with Germany. Russia occupied and then annexed Crimea, and massed troops along the border with Eastern Ukraine. The newly elected Ukrainian president, Petro Poroshenko, launched a determined military campaign to crush the rebellions in Donetsk and Luhansk.

How can further escalation be prevented? Two opposite 'lessons from history' have been drawn from a western perspective. One, based on analogy with the First World War, argues that the danger is 'sleepwalking' into a catastrophic confrontation and that the West must not be provocative – as it was when it offered to draw Ukraine westwards through an association agreement with the EU. The other lesson, based on analogy with the Second World War, argues that appeasement does not work with aggressors and that the best way to prevent escalation is by vigorous demonstration of the costs of proceeding with the aggression. Russia is seen to have supplied weapons and troops to the separatists in a classic instance of 'hybrid war' and, in some eyes, a deliberate attempt to divert attention from the Russian government's domestic short-comings. From a Russian perspective, it is the West that has been the aggressor ever since the end of the Cold War, humiliating Russia, excluding it from European institutions, and subverting governments that were formerly in the Russian sphere. Putin and the Russian nationalists who support him assert Russia's legitimate and historic interests as leader of the 'Russian world' and, beyond that, as a great power with huge resources, military capabilities, and permanent membership of the UN Security Council. President Putin is always aware that, if he softens his stance, he will be outflanked and blamed by even more nationalistic ambitious rivals in Russia.

Here is a crucial – indeed momentous – example of the importance of preventing violent conflict. By the beginning of 2015 the number of deaths (6,400 according to UN sources, although some other estimates are higher) was lower than that in many other conflicts, so indicators such as those discussed in chapter 3 would not identify this as an especially major conflict – compared, say, with the war in Syria. But, if mishandled, the crisis could portend a 'new cold war' (Lucas, 2008), with catastrophic consequences at global as well as at regional and local levels. Conflict resolution suggests the swift establishment of a verifiable ceasefire, including border checks, to prevent incursion from outside; genuine power-sharing for regional governments within Ukraine as already promised by Kiev, including locally elected officers; and a binding agreement between the EU and Russia (the planned Eurasian Union) that Ukraine will remain 'neutral' and the divergent orientations of western and eastern Ukraine will be mutually recognized and accommodated.[2] Russia will have to be persuaded that to persist with further annexations would lead to the loss rather than gain of Russian influence in the region. The EU states (particularly those nearer Russia) will have to be persuaded that this is a better way to ensure security than by trying to extend EU/NATO influence eastwards. Beyond this is the problem of the *fait accompli* in Crimea, hugely popular as it is in Russia (queues formed to buy T-shirts with pictures of Putin at the time). Above all, there is the need to revitalize institutions for the wider Europe that give European states from east and west a common stake in preserving a cooperative order.

In the event, the two sides in the Ukrainian civil war agreed a peace deal in Minsk on 5 September 2014. It had become clear that the West would not intervene militarily on the Ukrainian side and that Russia would not allow the rebels to lose. The agreement provided for a ceasefire, monitoring of the border by the OSCE, and decentralized governance for the rebel-held regions within Ukraine. However, the ceasefire broke down and heavy fighting continued around Donetsk and Luhansk. By the end of 2014 the 'second Cold War' seemed to be under way, as western sanctions and falling oil prices took a grip on the faltering Russian economy. In early 2015 a second major effort to establish a ceasefire led by Germany and France led to precarious agreement.

By the time this book is published, readers will know something of the outcome. Failure will cause huge and highly dangerous reverberations across the world, possibly extending to the loss of the economic, political and cultural cooperation – or, at any rate, mutual accommodation – at global level that has been so remarkably built up since the end of the Cold War. Success will not only avert danger but could even pave the way for joint efforts to restore stability in the Middle East and beyond, including the defeat of the vicious groups that have been able to seize the initiative by battening onto the unresolved tensions in other parts of the world where lack of cooperation between the great powers has left a debilitating vacuum.

Such is the grand, if highly challenging, context for the conflict resolution ambition to learn how to prevent violent conflict and transform it into mutually advantageous cooperation when states and empires break up.

Conclusion

In this chapter we have looked at the causes and preventers of contemporary armed conflicts. If, as A. J. P. Taylor suggests, wars have both general and specific causes, then systems of conflict prevention should address both the generic conditions which make societies prone to armed conflicts and the potential triggers which translate war-proneness into armed conflict. If structural conflict prevention is successful in providing capacity to manage emergent conflicts peacefully at an early stage, it should make societies less conflict-prone. If direct conflict prevention is successful, it should avert armed conflicts, without necessarily removing the underlying conditions of proneness to armed conflict (see table 5.2). Both direct and structural approaches to conflict prevention are clearly necessary.

Assessing the effectiveness of conflict prevention evidently depends considerably on the frame of analysis chosen and the criteria used to assess proneness to conflict. Wallensteen (2002b) offers a list of thirty candidates for conflict prevention analysis since the end of the Cold War where direct conflict prevention of some kind took place. Öberg, Möller and Wallensteen (2009) produced the first major large-N study on the impact of early conflict prevention measures. Analysing conflicts where ethnic groups were challenging governments in the 1990s, they showed that diplomatic interventions and relief efforts dampened the likelihood of conflict, although carrots tended to increase the prospect of escalation. We still need more systematic research to

Table 5.2 Success and failure in conflict prevention

	Success	Failure
Direct measures	Armed conflict averted	Armed conflict
Structural measures	Peaceful change	Conflict-prone situation

be in a position to assess more comprehensively the effects of the conflict prevention measures undertaken to date. Until this has been done, it is difficult to be sure to what extent the decline in the number of armed conflicts since the peak in 1991 can be attributed to conflict prevention.

In some respects the geopolitical environment of the 2010s is making the task of conflict prevention harder than it was. The discord between great powers affects their capacity to concert their efforts. There is less willingness to accept international norms. In a more fragmented security environment, states tend to struggle for influence over international organizations rather than using them for common purposes. The weakening of the state removes a bulwark to violence and exposes peoples to competing armed groups and violent ideologies.

Nevertheless, significant progress has been made in learning how to develop instruments and policies to prevent violent conflict and in realizing the importance of resolving conflict at an early stage. The challenge now is to consolidate and extend this progress, to learn from failures as well as successes, and to apply conflict prevention principles not only in poor and developing countries but also to the international and global issues in which the developed countries are conflict parties. In short, while strengthening the capacity for prevention, the challenge is to foster a global culture of preventive conflict resolution, aiming at early identification, discussion and non-violent transformation of emergent conflicts.

RECOMMENDED READING

Call (2012); Engel and Porto (2010); Hampson and Malone (2002); Leatherman et al. (1999); Lund (1996); Miall (2007); Rubin and Jones (2007); Wallensteen (1998); Woocher (2009); Zartman (2001).

RELEVANT EXTRACTS IN *THE CONTEMPORARY CONFLICT RESOLUTION READER*

Reading 29: L. Kriesberg and B. Dayton, Constructive Conflict: From Escalation to Resolution

Reading 30: J. Leatherman et al., Breaking Cycles of Violence: Conflict Prevention in Intrastate Conflicts

Reading 31: A. Varshney, Ethnic Conflict and Civic Life: Hindus and Muslims in India

Reading 32: V. Dudouet, Nonviolent Resistance and Conflict Transformation in Power Asymmetries

Reading 33: Report of the Carnegie Commission on Preventing Deadly Conflict

Reading 34: G. Sharp, From Dictatorship to Democracy

Reading 35: Conflict Prevention in the Baltic States: The OSCE High Commissioner on National Minorities in Estonia, Latvia and Lithuania

Reading 37: S. Brams, Negotiation Games

Reading 72: Ushahidi

CHAPTER SIX

Containing Violent Conflict: Peacekeeping

In this chapter we examine the role for conflict resolution in the most challenging of environments – in areas of heated conflict where violence has become routine and the prevention of violent conflict has failed. In terms of the hourglass model in figure 1.3, we noted how higher levels of violence need more robust forms of intervention. We suggested that peacekeeping is appropriate at three points on the escalation scale: to contain violence and prevent it from escalating to war; to limit the intensity, geographical spread and duration of war once it has broken out; and to consolidate a ceasefire and create space for reconstruction after the end of a war. The first of these relates to topics covered in chapter 5, the third to topics covered in chapter 8, so in this chapter we look at the second: intervention to limit and contain the terrible effects of ongoing war. Here we are examining options at the narrowest part of the hourglass, where political and humanitarian space is most severely constrained. We focus on the changing role of UN and other peacekeepers in these situations (creating security space) and identify that this peacekeeping role is integrally linked to the role of NGOs, UN civil agencies and aid agencies in responding to humanitarian needs (creating humanitarian space). There is a growing recognition that these agencies need to work together to link mitigation and relief to the political tasks that are necessary to settle the conflict and resolve it within a sustainable peace process (creating political space). The central argument in this chapter is that peacekeepers and the various humanitarian and development agencies working in war zones need to be aware of the conflict resolution dimension of their work. In short, there is a vital conflict resolution role for peacekeeping to play even during the most intense period of destruction (see table 6.1).

Table 6.1 Conflict containment and peacekeeping

Phase	Mode of peacekeeping	Negative role	Positive role
Violence	Prevention (see ch. 5)		
War	Limitation	Limit spread	Create security space
		Limit intensity	Create humanitarian space
		Limit duration	Create political space
Ceasefire	Stabilization (see ch. 8)		

We begin by looking at the emergence and development of peacekeeping as a conflict resolution mechanism, outlining the principles and practices which defined it as it evolved through two phases, generally termed *first-generation* and *second-generation* peacekeeping missions. We then look at the results of research into the dynamics of war zones (the targeting of civilians, the destruction of social and cultural institutions, the persistence of warlords), which challenged second-generation peacekeeping missions in the 1990s to the point where they were seen, by some critics at least, as inadequate to protect civilians and restore peace. In the light of this, we look at the ways in which peacekeeping has been adapted and reformed as a more robust conflict resolution intervention mechanism appropriate to the challenges of the twenty-first century. These *third-generation operations* are sometimes called 'peace support operations' (PSOs), or, more commonly, just 'peace operations', to distinguish them from the more circumscribed nature of traditional peacekeeping. For example, Alex Bellamy and Paul Williams now use 'peacekeeping' and 'peace operations' interchangeably:

> We conclude by reflecting on the likely future trajectory of peace operations. Five years on from the first edition of *Understanding Peacekeeping*, it remains our conviction that peace operations play a vitally important role in managing armed conflict, supporting stable peace and – increasingly – protecting endangered populations. (2010: 10)

One trouble with this is that peace operations are, as a result, much less clearly circumscribed than was the case with traditional peacekeeping. Not only has the boundary line between peacekeeping and peace enforcement been blurred – as also between UN and non-UN peacekeeping – but in some cases, in Orwellian manner, operations listed in some quarters as peace operations have virtually become conflated with war-fighting (Afghanistan and Iraq). A major task in this chapter from a conflict resolution perspective, therefore, is to attain sufficient analytic clarity to be able to re-establish the genuine sense in which third-generation peace operations continue to merit that name. The chapter includes two brief case studies of international intervention, both from Africa. One is about Somalia in East Africa, a country where efforts to contain violent conflict in the absence of a sustainable peace agreement have gone on for over twenty years, which provides a salutary lesson in humility for would-be conflict resolution workers and peacekeepers in war zones. The other case study, Mali in West Africa, provides a contrasting example of a recently deployed (2013) peacekeeping mission (MINUSMA) that shows signs of adapting well to tackle the complex conflict that threatened to tear the country apart, but which also reveals new challenges and complexities caused by the effects of the Arab Spring and the uneasy relationship between UN peacekeeping and counter-terrorism in the region, as outlined in chapter 4. The chapter concludes with an outline of the spectrum of current political views on peacekeeping in order to identify the particular contribution that conflict resolution can make. This gives an overview of debates and scenarios that define the options for the evolution of new modes of peacekeeping in the coming decade. It argues for a cosmopolitan model, which may afford the best combination of military capability, political legitimacy, conflict resolution capacity and inclusive cosmopolitan cultural values.

First- and Second-Generation UN Peacekeeping, 1956–1995

United Nations peacekeeping and academic conflict resolution have much in common conceptually, and both emerged as distinct areas of theory and practice at about the same time – in the mid-1950s. When the first conflict resolution centres and journals were being established (see chapter 2), UN Secretary-General Dag Hammarskjöld and UN General Assembly President Lester Pearson were defining the basic principles of peacekeeping in order to guide the work of the United Nations Emergency Force (UNEF I), created in response to the Suez crisis in the Middle East in 1956. Peacekeeping is not mentioned in the UN Charter, prompting the suggestion that it operated somewhere between Chapter VI (the peaceful settlement of disputes) and Chapter VII (enforcement) – chapter 'six-and-a half'. Although *An Agenda for Peace* in the early 1990s attempted to override the principle of consent and the minimum use of force in certain circumstances, the UNEF I principles served to define the essence of UN peacekeeping at least until the mid-1990s. They were based on:

- the consent of the conflict parties;
- political neutrality (not taking sides);
- impartiality (commitment to the mandate);
- the non-use of force except in self-defence;
- legitimacy (sanctioned by and accountable to the Security Council advised by the secretary-general).

During the period of the Cold War, thirteen peacekeeping operations were established, mostly deployed in interstate conflicts (although ONUC in the Congo 1960–4 was an exception). Their main function was to monitor borders and establish buffer zones after the agreement of ceasefires. The missions were typically composed of lightly armed national troop contingents from small and neutral UN member states. This was *first-generation peacekeeping*.

Immediately after the end of the Cold War, however, UN peacekeeping underwent a swift, unexpected and remarkable expansion, as the international community sought to respond to a range of challenges and opportunities that went well beyond first-generation peacekeeping norms, while the habitual paralysis in the UN Security Council was suddenly released (see table 6.2, which shows the growth of peacekeeping missions and the balance between civilian and military elements). It seemed to many that all at once everything became possible.

Table 6.2 The growth of UN peacekeeping, 1988–2014

	1988	1994	2000	2004	2014
Number of missions	5	17	14	16	16
Military and police	9,605	75,523	37,338	62,271	98,071
Civilian personnel	1,516	2,260	3,243	3,949	17,277
Annual UN budget	$266 m	$3.3 bn	$2.2 bn	$3.61 bn	$7.06 bn
Number of contributing countries	26	76	89	103	122

Source: UNDPKO, 2015a

The numerical growth of peacekeeping operations during the 1990s was accompanied by a fundamental change in their nature, their function and their composition. This was *second-generation peacekeeping*. The single ceasefire maintenance function associated with traditional operations evolved into a multiplicity of tasks involving security, humanitarian and political objectives. At the same time, the composition of post-Cold War peacekeeping operations became more diverse and complex: peacekeepers were drawn from a wider variety of sources (military, civilian police and diplomatic), nations and cultures. Second-generation peacekeeping was multilateral, multidimensional and multinational/multicultural. By the mid-1990s the number of countries contributing to peacekeeping missions had almost tripled, from twenty-six in the late 1980s, and this trend continued to the point where more than half the member states of the United Nations were contributing forces to UN peacekeeping missions. The dominant contributors were no longer the small neutral nations traditionally associated with peacekeeping (Canadians, Irish and Scandinavians, for example), but increasingly some of the Security Council P5 countries and, above all, nations in Asia (Bangladesh, Pakistan, India) and Africa (Nigeria, Ethiopia, Ghana). Altogether, '[s]ince the early days of UN peace operations, over 130 member states have contributed military and police personnel' and 'in total 1 million personnel have served under the UN flag' (Bellamy and Williams, 2010: 58). Many hoped that the UN could now at last fulfil its original potential.

However, as table 6.2 also shows, the confidence in peacekeeping, at its height in the mid-1990s, began to wane in the closing years of the decade and into the early years of the twenty-first century. The number of troops deployed, the number of deployments and the budget committed to peacekeeping all declined (although not the number of troop-providing countries). Peacekeepers faced seemingly insurmountable problems and were frequently exposed as powerless to protect civilians, humanitarian workers and even themselves, in the civil wars in former Yugoslavia, in the genocide in Rwanda and in Somalia.

The debacle in October 1993, when eighteen US soldiers were killed and publicly humiliated as part of the UNOSOM II mission in Somalia, effectively ended any possibility of US troops participating integrally and in significant numbers in UN-led missions. At the end of the decade the UN published the reports of inquiries into two other events which marked the nadir of its experience in trying to resolve conflicts. Approximately 800,000 people were killed during the 1994 genocide in Rwanda between April and July 1994. A UN peacekeeping mission (UNAMIR) already in Rwanda, but with its force numbers severely reduced, was largely powerless to prevent the killings, despite the pleas of its force commander, because the Security Council was reluctant to intervene so soon after the Somalia disaster. A year later, in one of the worst war crimes committed in Europe since the end of the Second World War, the Bosnian Muslim town of Srebrenica fell to a siege by Serb militias, during which 8,000 Muslims were killed under the eyes of the UN peacekeeping contingent deployed when Srebrenica had been declared the world's first civilian safe area in 1993 (UNSC, 1993). Two UN reports concluded that, faced with attempts to murder, expel or terrorize entire populations, the neutral, impartial and mediating role of the United Nations was inadequate. Both also called for a process of reflection to clarify and to improve the capacity of the United Nations to respond to various forms of conflict, and especially to 'address the mistakes of peacekeeping at the end of this century and to meet the challenges of the next one' (United Nations, 1999a, 1999b).

When a new set of security challenges manifested themselves in the form of the attack on the US on 11 September 2001, followed by the invasions of Afghanistan and Iraq, the world organization appeared even more marginalized.

War Zones, War Economies and Cultures of Violence

Among the most challenging situations which confront those wishing to engage in conflict resolution are those where warlords and militias have come to establish their power over civilian populations. In such situations, 'not only is there little recognition of the distinction between combatant and civilian, or of any obligation to spare women, children and the elderly, but the valued institutions and way of life of a whole population can be targeted', with the objective of creating 'states of terror which penetrate the entire fabric of grass-roots social relations ... as a means of social control' (Summerfield, 1996: 1). Civilians and humanitarian staff are the targets in these wars, not the accidental victims of it. In the First World War, over 80 per cent of battlefield deaths were combatants; by the 1990s, most were civilians, killed in their own homes and communities, which have become the battlefields of many contemporary wars. As Nordstrom has remarked, the least dangerous place to be in most contemporary wars is in the military (1992: 271). 'Dirty war' strategies, originally identified with state-sponsored terrorism, are now a feature of a widening band of militias, paramilitaries, warlords and armies seeking control of resources through depredation, terror and force. The threat posed to civilians is perceived to be greater still following the events of 11 September 2001, when global mass casualty terrorism and the actions of suicide bombers became a new, or at least a more persistent, concern for the international community (for the most recent available figures, see chapter 3).

Are these behaviours in contemporary wars senseless and irrational convulsions of violence, expressions of ancient hatreds and regressions to tribal war and neo-medieval warlords, as some argue (Kaplan, 1994)? Or are there more systematic explanations, as those writing from an anthropological and radical political economy perspective suggest? An appropriate conflict resolution response will depend upon what answers are given to these questions.

In a pattern that has been well documented since the 1990s – for example, in parts of Africa such as Tigray, Eritrea, Southern and Western Sudan, Northern Uganda, Angola and Somalia – scorched earth tactics have been common, with livestock seized, grain stores attacked and looted, wells and watering places poisoned. Forced population movements have been engineered to perpetuate dependency and control. Actors such as the international drug cartels in Central and South America, the Taliban in Afghanistan and rebel groups in West Africa had effectively set up parallel economies, trading in precious resources such as hardwoods, diamonds, drugs, and so on. The same is true in Burma (Myanmar). In Cambodia the Khmer Rouge leadership profited so much from the smuggling of timber and gems across the Thai border that it saw little incentive to demobilize its forces as agreed under the Paris Peace Accords of 1991, while there was evidence of collusion between the Khmer Rouge and the Cambodian Army in mutual profiteering from this trade (Keen, 1995). Although this does not apply to all internal conflicts, there are war-zone economies where civilians are seen as 'a resource base to be either corralled, plundered, or cleansed' (Duffield, 1997: 103). Humanitarian and development aid is captured, and humanitarian workers kidnapped, held hostage and killed. These wars can be seen to be both lucrative and rational for those who can take advantage and are prepared to act violently to gain power (Keen, 2008; Reading 18).

This is the point at which to re-engage with the economic analyses of what perpetuates endemic wars of this kind – what are sometimes, in some eyes wrongly (Newman, 2004), called 'new wars' – as discussed in chapter 4 (Münkler, 2005; Kaldor, 2006, 2012). We saw how, through the project on 'The Economics of Civil War, Crime and Violence', Collier and his colleagues at the World Bank offered important new insights into the difficulties faced by peacekeepers and other agencies active in areas of conflict (Collier et al., 2003). From this perspective, most civil wars are driven not by ideology or grievance, but by greed and predation. In chapters 3 and 4, we argued that there are genuine identity-based and ideology-based conflicts that are fuelled by failures of existing government structures to accommodate legitimate political aspirations or to satisfy needs, and that economic motives do not explain the deeper dynamics of most major armed conflicts. Nevertheless, in fragile 'quasi-states', particularly where formal structures have hollowed out and war economies have become endemic, such analysis is compelling (de Waal, 2014). Cooper (2001) argued that the trade in conflict goods, generating opportunities to acquire wealth and the means to continue financing arms acquisition, has significant implications for peacekeeping and peacebuilding activities in areas of conflict of this kind. He suggested that the development of strategies for restricting the trade in conflict goods (such as the controls placed on trade in Sierra Leone's conflict diamonds) may be as significant as programmes which prioritize arms control and disarmament in peace processes. The development of conflict goods control programmes is still at a rudimentary stage in war-zone conflict management, although it is becoming increasingly recognized that those who benefit from, and who are therefore motivated to perpetuate, war economies need to be addressed in the early stages of conflict stabilization in peacekeeping.

Strategies to achieve this are now identified in the form of a range of policies that can be pursued by governments, regional organizations and the UN. In identifying some of these strategies and policies, researchers have pointed to important implications for the role of peacekeeping forces. Thus it has been suggested that UN peace operation mandates need to be formulated with an awareness of the economic reality of particular conflicts, especially so that peacekeeping forces can be deployed to establish control over resource-rich areas in order to prevent illicit exploitation and smuggling by factions which wish to use the proceeds to perpetuate conflict. For example, the UN operation in Sierra Leone (UNAMSIL), deployed in the Kono diamond district, had some success in curtailing such activities (Wilton Park Conference, 2003).

For analysts such as Outram, however, in his account of the civil war in Liberia in the 1990s, theories of economic predation of this kind do not go far enough, because they do not explain the extent and absurdity of the violence involved. The violence goes beyond rational expectations of what can be gained economically, for a rational warlord would not kill the goose that lays the golden egg. To explain it, we have to take into account socio-psychological considerations as well as economic motivations. In Liberia, accumulated fears drove people beyond killing the 'ethnic enemy' into factions which practised a general and undirected vengeance (Outram, 1997: 368). We can understand this phenomenon further by considering the pioneering work of Nordstrom at about the same time. While Outram concentrated on the experience of the warring factions and the political economy which they constructed, Nordstrom has worked on the experiences of the victims of the violence. Following field research in Mozambique and Sri Lanka, she explained the many stories of absurd destruction and the use of terror in warfare as deliberate efforts to destroy the normal meanings that define and guide daily life (Nordstrom, 1992: 269). This is the process whereby dirty war becomes the means through which economies of violence merge with what Nordstrom called 'cultures of violence'. As she put it, 'violence parallels power', and people come to have no alternative but to accept 'fundamental knowledge constructs that are based on force' (ibid.). So this is yet another dimension of endemic war zones that peacekeepers and conflict resolvers have to try to understand if they venture to intervene in active combat areas. From a political science perspective, Stathis Kalyvas (2006: 17) argues that a civil war is a 'violent physical division of the sovereign entity into rival armed camps'. Each camp is engaged in a rival statebuilding project in which it strives to rule the citizens. Violent attacks on the citizens are part of the struggle to gain control of territory. Kalyvas relates geographical variations in the level of violence to each camp's degree of control over territory, testing his theory against micro-level findings from the Greek civil war and other conflicts. He maintains that the greatest violence against civilians is found not in the base area, where one camp has undisputed control, or at the front lines, where neither has control, but in the intermediate areas, where the dominant side's control is partial. Each camp uses selective violence to deter civilians from joining the other in areas close to the base where control is partial. Civilians are also complicit in the violence, using the forces of rival camps to settle their scores and sometimes incriminating others in order to save their own skins, as micro-level security dilemmas proliferate. Indiscriminate violence, which gives citizens few incentives to comply with the perpetrator's wishes, tends to take place in areas where the perpetrator has no control. As Kalyvas (ibid.: 389) notes, 'collective and individual preferences, strategies, values and identities are continuously shaped and reshaped in the course of a war.' In the recent transmutation of *jihadist* attempts to control territory as part of the long-term ambition to establish caliphates, similar processes can be observed – for example, in Syria, Iraq and North-East Nigeria. All of this goes a long way towards explaining the catastrophic increase in external refugees and internally displaced persons that seems, if anything, still to be gathering force (see chapter 3).

Working in war zones, then, clearly does create serious challenges for conflict resolution and requires the analyst or intervener to be aware of their particular dynamics. We have commented elsewhere, with reference to humanitarian intervention, how principles of humanity, impartiality, neutrality and universality are necessary to guide action, but also how they are unavoidably compromised in the intensely politicized environment of active conflict (Ramsbotham and Woodhouse, 1996). Conflict resolvers have to be aware of this, while nevertheless continuing to search for an effective and internationally legitimate antidote to the untold misery inflicted on so many by ongoing war.

Third-Generation Peacekeeping: What Counts as Peace Operations?

In response to such challenges, the search for a doctrine for third-generation peacekeeping begins from a prior question: Can there be any role for conflict resolution activities, or indeed for UN peacekeeping, in these circumstances?

May it not even be counter-productive? Providing a negative response to these questions, a series of highly critical accounts appeared in the academic literature from the mid-1990s, questioning both the efficacy of UN peacekeeping and the conflict resolution model with which it was associated.

From one direction came criticism of the ineffectiveness of impartial and non-forcible intervention in war zones (Rieff, 1994). The alternatives of either letting the conflicts 'burn themselves out' or intervening decisively on one side were seen as better options (Luttwak, 1999; Betts, 1994). From the other direction came criticism of the inappropriateness of what were seen to be attempts to impose western interests and western values on non-western countries (Clapham, 1996; Cunliffe, 2013). The requirement for an effective and internationally legitimate third generation of peacekeeping had to meet both these criticisms, somehow combining greater military robustness with commitment to genuine international norms.

Nevertheless, despite these difficulties, another look at table 6.2 shows how, after a severe retraction, a strong revival followed that was already evident when the second edition of this book appeared, and has continued up to the present. But this revival was accompanied by another marked change in the nature of peacekeeping that now raises key questions about the very definition of *third-generation peacekeeping*, and peace operations in general, from a conflict resolution perspective.

During the early 1990s, in the first flush of the expansion of second-generation peacekeeping, it had seemed that UN peacekeeping nevertheless retained its essential character as defined by the Hammarskjöld/Pearson principles cited above:

- the context was one of supporting already achieved peace agreements, and it was assumed that they would be short term;
- the operations were non-forcible;
- the missions were integrated under the UN;
- they were seen to be clearly distinct from UN *peace enforcement*, as exemplified in the 1991 reversal of Iraq's occupation of Kuwait.

Not one of these criteria has survived into third-generation peacekeeping unscathed:

- *First*, in the context of 'new wars', the situation is no longer one of clear-cut post-agreement consensus, nor are many of the interventions short term.
- *Second*, in response to the weakness of most second-generation missions, the UN Brahimi Report asked for much more 'robust' forces capable of deterring aggression (Brahimi, 2000: x), and a number of national defence academies also planned accordingly (UK MOD, 2004).
- *Third*, third-generation peace operations came increasingly to be mounted not under a UN aegis, but by regional security organizations or coalitions of the 'willing and capable', such as NATO forces in Bosnia and Kosovo

(IFOR, SFOR and KFOR); Nigerian peacekeeping forces (ECOMOG) in West Africa; a British-led IMAT (International Military Advisory Team) in Sierra Leone working alongside but independently of the UNAMSIL force; and the Australian military providing the leadership of the force in East Timor (INTERFET/ UNTAET).

- *Fourth*, even the distinction between UN-authorized and UN-managed non-forcible peacekeeping operations, on the one hand (for example, the ONUMOZ mission to support a peace agreement in Mozambique in 1992), and UN authorized but non-UN-managed peace enforcement operations, on the other (for example, operation Desert Storm in the liberation of Kuwait in 1991), was eroded, as in Kosovo (1999), Afghanistan (2001) and Iraq (2003) (Coleman, 2007; Pugh, 2007). In some cases forcible interveners sought no more than posthumous UN endorsement, sometimes retrospectively.

This raises the key question: What count as peace operations from a conflict resolution perspective? A review of operations currently listed as peace operations by international analysts highlights the problem.

The UN Department of Peacekeeping Operations (DPKO) listed sixteen 'current DPKO-led missions' in September 2014, mobilizing 98,071 troops, military advisers and police. But other data sources now include a much wider range of interventions under 'peace operations'. When, in 2006, the Center on International Cooperation (CIC) produced its first *Annual Review of Global Peace Operations*, its 'data sections concentrated heavily on the United Nations'. In 2007, however, after criticism, the dataset was expanded to take in figures on EU, AU, NATO and 'other peace operations'. This resulted in a further thirty 'non-UN missions' being added, giving 'a richer picture of the evolving international architecture for peace operations, within and beyond the UN' (CIC, 2008: ix). This has been followed by other peace operations lists, such as those updated regularly by the ZIF Center for International Peace Operations, from which data for 2014–15 is given in box 6.1. The result of all this is that, in marked contrast to the situation in the early 1990s, when a single mission such as the UN Transitional Authority in Cambodia (UNTAC) could in itself be seen as a comprehensive peace operation (see box 8.1, p. 251), in the more complicated and varied contemporary combinations, several of the missions listed separately (together with others not listed) combine, often indeterminately, in a single undertaking. Table 6.2 shows current UN peacekeeping operations as of 2014. Box 6.1 shows all peacekeeping/peace support operations as of 2014–15.

It can be seen from the figures in table 6.2 that UN peacekeeping has grown enormously since the late 1980s: missions have increased by a factor of three; military and police numbers tenfold; civilians on mission elevenfold; and countries contributing to UN peacekeeping fivefold. The annual budget for UN peacekeeping has also grown significantly over time, but even the 2014 level, at about $7 billion, is less than half of 1 per cent of world military

Box 6.1 Ongoing peace operations, 2014–2015

	International military	*International police*	*International civilian*
UN peacekeeping*	85,227	12,026	5,135
UN political and peacebuilding**	923	28	1,164
European Union***	3,205	993	906
OSCE****	0	0	635
Others (with or without UN mandate)*****	81,472	725	109
Total personnel strength all organizations	170,827	13,772	7,949

* UN peacekeeping missions (16)

UNMIK: UN Interim Administration Mission in Kosovo; UNFICYP: UN Peacekeeping Force in Cyprus; UNSMIL: UN Support Mission in Libya; MINURSO: Misión de las Naciones Unidas para el Referéndum del Sáhara Occidental; UNOMIL/UNMIL: UN Mission in Liberia; UNOCI: UN Operation in Côte d'Ivoire; MINUSMA: UN Multidimensional Integrated Stabilization Mission in Mali; MINUSCA: UN Multidimensional Integrated Stabilization Mission in the Central African Republic; MONUSCO: Mission de l'ONU pour la Stabilisation en RD Congo; UNMISS: UN Mission in the Republic of South Sudan; UNISFA: UN Interim Security Force for Abyei (Sudan); UNAMID: African Union United Nations Hybrid Operation in Darfur; UNMOGIP: UN Military Observer Group in India and Pakistan; UNIFIL: UN Interim Force in Lebanon; UNTSO: UN Truce Supervision Organization; UNDOF: UN Disengagement Observer Force (Israel–Syria)

** UN political and peacebuilding missions (11)

UN Support Mission in Libya; UN Office for West Africa; UN Integrated Peacebuilding Office in Guinea-Bissau; UN Regional Office for Central Africa; UN Regional Centre for Preventive Diplomacy for Central Asia (Turkmenistan); Bureau des Nations Unies au Burundi; UN Assistance Mission in Somalia; Office of the UN Special Coordinator for Lebanon; Office of the UN Special Coordinator for the Middle East Peace Process; UN Assistance Mission for Iraq; UN Assistance Mission in Afghanistan

*** EU missions (17)

EU Border Assistance Mission to Moldova and Ukraine; EU Advisory Mission for Civilian Security Sector Reform Ukraine; EU Military Operation in Bosnia and Herzegovina; EULEX Kosovo – EU Rule of Law Mission in Kosovo; EUBAM Libya – EU Border Assistance Mission in Libya; European Monitoring Mission in Georgia; EU Force en République Centrafricaine; EU Capacity Building Mission in Niger; EU Training Mission in Mali; EU Capacity Building Mission in Mali; EU Advisory and Assistance Mission for Security Sector Reform in the DRC; EU Naval Operation Against Piracy; EU Mission on Regional Maritime Capacity Building; EU Military Mission to Contribute to the Training of Somali Security Forces; EU Border Assistance Mission for the Rafah Crossing Point; EU Police Coordinating Office for Palestinian Police Support; EU Police Mission in Afghanistan

**** OSCE missions (16)

Mission to Bosnia and Herzegovina; Mission to Serbia; Mission to Montenegro; Presence in Albania; Mission in Kosovo; Mission to Skopje; Mission to Moldova; Project Coordinator in Ukraine; OSCE Special Monitoring Mission to Ukraine; Office

Box 6.1 (continued)

in Yerevan (Armenia); Project Coordinator in Baku (Azerbaijan); Centre in Ashgabat (Turkmenistan); Centre in Astana (Kazakhstan); Project Coordinator in Uzbekistan; Centre in Bishkek (Kyrgyzstan); Office in Tajikistan

***** Others (regional and single nation-led missions, with or without UN mandate (14)

Operation Unicorn/Licorne Ivory Coast (France); African Union Mission to Mali and the Sahel; Operation Sangaris Central African Republic (France); Regional Task Force of the Regional Cooperation Initiative for the Elimination of the Lord's Resistance Army Uganda (African Union); Misión de Apoyo al Proceso de Paz en Colombia, Colombia (Organization of American States); ECOWAS Mission in Guinea-Bissau; African Union/ UN Hybrid Mission in Darfur; International Monitoring Team, Philippines (Malaysia); African Union Mission in Somalia; TIPH Temporary International Presence in the City of Hebron (Norway); Multinational Force and Observers Egypt–Israel; International Security Assistance Force, Afghanistan (NATO) withdrawn end 2014 (49,902 troops); replaced by Operation Resolute Support (NATO) from 2015 (non-combat training and assistance to Army of Afghanistan); Regional Assistance Mission to Solomon Islands (fifteen nations from the Pacific region)

(*Source:* www.zif-berlin.org/en/ – Centre for International Peace Operations Berlin)

expenditures (estimated at $1,747 billion in 2013). This increase is a confirmation that UN peacekeeping remains and has enhanced its capacity as a primary tool of choice for international conflict resolution.

Box 6.1 illustrates the ambivalent way in which what were originally the clearly defined principles that defined UN peacekeeping have been blurred to the point where it is possible to use the terms 'peacekeeping operations' and 'peace operations' interchangeably, and then to include under the latter elements that would earlier have distinctly defined the separate venture of peace enforcement – if not war-fighting.

Does this matter? The argument in the rest of the chapter is that, for those in the conflict resolution field, it does matter. We first briefly discuss recent attempts to redefine UN peacekeeping and peace operations and then, by summing up what peace operations imply from a conflict resolution perspective, try to 'recapture' the concept and practice of peacekeeping and peace operations from association with interventions that do not qualify for such description.

To set the scene, we offer a case study of international response to the 2012–15 crisis in Mali, which shows how nuanced assessments need to be made about peacekeeping and peace operations in complex war zones.

Case Study: Mali, 2012–2015

Mali provides an example of some of the difficulties involved in attempts to improve peacekeeping capacity in hybrid transnational war zones.

The insurgency, which broke out in in the north of the country in the early part of 2012, presented hard challenges from a mix of ethnic separatists and Islamic militant groups linked with al-Qaeda, echoing many other conflicts which emerged in the course of the Arab Spring as outlined in chapter 4. The peacekeeping intervention there from 2013 was similarly hybrid – a blend of lead-nation military strength (France) and a robust UN mission mandated to protect civilians, complemented by European Union and African Union support. The range of involvement reached from imaginative efforts to deploy a distinctive use of positive cultural energy and music to unite the country and resist its violent disintegration, at one end of the spectrum, to war-fighting and counter-terrorist actions, at the other. This involvement in the 'New Frontier' of global counter-terrorism and counter-insurgency in the region may be seen to remove such operations even further from the standard practices of peacekeeping.

By 2014 the UN (MINUSMA), the EU (EUTM Mali, and EUCAP Sahel Mali) and the African Union (MISAHEL) all had missions in Mali. The MINUSMA

Source: www.bbc.co.uk/news/world-africa-21054946

Map 6.1 *Conflict positions in Mali, January 2013*

mission (United Nations Multidimensional Integrated Stabilization Mission in Mali) exemplifies the way in which peacekeeping in the second decade of the twenty-first century is continuing to develop to deal with the complexities of contemporary conflict.

MINUSMA was established under UNSCR 2100 of April 2013 with a mandate to help stabilize the country, following a rebellion and *coup d'état* in northern Mali in January 2012 led by a Tuareg liberation movement, the Mouvement National pour la Libération de l'Azawad (MNLA). Taking advantage of this opportunity, Islamic armed groups attempted to seize control, among them Ansar Dine, AQIM (al-Qaeda in the Islamic Maghreb), the Mouvement pour L'Unicité et le Jihad en Afrique de l'Ouest (MUJAO), and battle-hardened combatants returning from Libya following the fall of the Gaddafi regime. The insurrection in the north resulted in the declaration of an independent State of Azawad on 6 April 2012.

From January 2013 the crisis deepened as the *jihadi* groups marginalized the Tuareg MNLA and advanced south towards the capital, Bamako. At this point, the Government of National Unity of Mali, established in August 2012 to stabilize the country and oppose the insurgent groups, asked for the assistance of France to help Malian defence forces restore stability. Operation Serval, led by France, was deployed on 11 January 2013; by the end of January Malian state control had been restored, and *jihadi* groups withdrew north. In addition to the French intervention, an ECOWAS African-led International Support Mission to Mali (AFISMA), authorized under UNSCR 2085 of December 2012, was sent to support the government against the Islamist rebels. Led by a Nigerian general, the main contingent was composed of 1,800 troops from Chad. These troops pursued the Islamist groups into the mountains in the north of Mali, near the border with Algeria, engaged them in combat in February 2013, and took control of the area in which they had based themselves (UNDPKO, 2015b).

In this context, from the beginning of its deployment, MINUSMA operated with robust rules of engagement, authorized to use all necessary force to defend against threats to its mandate and its personnel and to protect civilians. By September 2014, MINUSMA had taken over authority from the AFISMA mission and was deployed with an authorized mission strength of 11,200 military personnel and 1,440 police. From February 2013 a European Union Training Mission in Mali (EUTM) operated to train Malian armed forces, and from April 2014 EUCAP Sahel Mali was deployed as a civilian mission under the Common Defence and Security Policy of the European Union to help Mali's security forces to restore security and establish the conditions for long-lasting peace (EEAS, 2015). Finally, in this hybrid mix of peacekeeping and peace support operations, in August 2013 the African Union Mission for Mali and the Sahel (MISAHEL), a political mission headquartered in Bamako, was established with a mandate to support the country in its recovery process. MISAHEL is also part of a wider African Union strategy for the Sahel region to help the countries of the Sahel face security, governance and development challenges (ISS Africa, 2014).

This case study of peacekeeping and peace operations in Mali contains elements of peacekeeping that are clearly unrecognizable from what would have been characteristics of classical or first-generation peacekeeping. Peacekeeping operations led by coalitions of the willing and capable (here, France) and involving a mixture of actors contributing specific expertise and knowledge (here, EU, ECOWAS and AU) became common in most third-generation missions (for example, UNAMSIL in Sierra Leone) (Curran and Woodhouse, 2007; Curran, 2012). The Mali case highlights not only the complexity of conflict but also the creative flexibilities needed to respond to it in contemporary peacekeeping operations, where political, military security, human security (protection of civilians), humanitarian, development and cultural roles (which we explore in chapter 16) are all vital components for a mission to be effective in this kind of conflict (UN News Service, 2014).

For these reasons, while Mali can and should be seen as a successful case of restoring unity and relative stability to the country, there are concerns that peacekeeping may become too closely allied to the unaccountable activities of counter-insurgency and counter-terrorism strategies. But this is the reality on the ground. The force commander of the MINUSMA mission, at a briefing of force commanders in New York towards the end of 2014, described the dilemma as follows:

> The reality on the ground today is that MINUSMA, which is supposed to be a peacekeeping mission, is facing a terrorist network that is combining patience, intelligence, coercion and brutality to design and direct its attacks when and where it wants. MINUSMA is in a terrorist-fighting situation without an anti-terrorist mandate or adequate training, equipment, logistics or intelligence to deal with such a situation. (UNSC, 2014)

His conclusion was that MINUSMA, if it was to remain effective, would need to develop counter-terrorist capability and authority in its mandate. These are clearly big questions for both peacekeeping and conflict resolution, to which we return in chapters 11 and 14 (Hunt, 2015).[1] All of this illustrates the challenges for defining appropriate cosmopolitan conflict resolution responses to the current multi-faceted and rapidly mutating patterns of transnational conflict.

Redefining Peace Operations

In the light of experiences such as those described in the Mali study, the concluding part of this chapter looks at debates currently under way about the nature of emerging reforms and desirable scenarios for effective peacekeeping in the coming decade. Given the pace of change of conflict and the consequent responses required from peacekeeping, we begin by considering ways in which peace operations can best be defined and understood as a strategic instrument for conflict resolution.

The UN Department of Peacekeeping Operations, established in 1992, with its Office of Planning and Support, Field Missions Procurement Section, permanent Situation Room, and Lessons Learned Unit (later Best Practices Section), was a major attempt to replace earlier ad hoc arrangements. Galvanized by the Brahimi Report (Brahimi, 2000), having undergone severe stresses in the mid-1990s as noted above, further changes were made, including an attempt to set up Integrated Mission Task Forces in specific cases and, eventually (2007), the splitting off of a Department of Field Support (DFS) under a separate under-secretary-general as a base for logistical backing that would in each case be able to deliver an effective supply chain to the UN special representative, the resident coordinator and the military force commander. In addition, instead of CIVPOL (civilian police) being part of the military division, policing was transferred to a separate office that would oversee the 'Rule of Law and Security Institutions'. Some were concerned that what looked like a splitting up of DPKO would lead not to greater cohesion, but to more confusion.

In the absence of a clear definition of UN peacekeeping in changed circumstances, or of an updated inventory of the meaning of terms such as 'impartiality' or 'the minimum use of force', a strong attempt was also made from within DPKO to develop an overall 'capstone doctrine' that would clarify principles and guidelines for third-generation peacekeeping operations. In draft form, the traditional principles of consent, impartiality and non-use of force except in self-defence ('the holy trinity') were to be modified – for example, 'UN peacekeepers should be impartial in their dealings with the parties to conflict, but not neutral in the execution of their mandate' (UNDPKO, 2007: § 66), while, 'although force must be used in a restrained fashion, it may be employed in circumstances other than self-defence; peacekeepers may use force to protect themselves, their mandate and groups identified by the mandate (e.g. civilians, humanitarian workers)' (ibid.: § 69). Three other principles were also envisaged: credibility in swift deployment and capacity to deter spoilers; legitimacy in firm and fair exercise of a legal mandate; and promotion of national and local ownership of the peace process. In the final version, however, as a result of resistance from some member states, much of this was lost. For example, on the use of force, the final version read: 'non-use of force except in self-defence and defence of the mandate' (UNDPKO, 2008). This was no longer called a 'capstone doctrine', the last three principles were watered down to 'success factors', and, instead of being said to give authoritative 'strategic guidance' for UN peacekeeping, the document itself was described as merely 'internal' to DPKO (Bellamy and Williams, 2010: 142–4).

This absence of clear international agreement, together with the fact that peace operations also involve a range of non-UN contributions, means that at the moment there is no authoritative guidance. So perhaps, given its great complexity and variability and the magnitude of the different interlocking tasks currently undertaken by such a diverse range of actors, the best we can do in the circumstances is to contrast 'third-generation' peace operations

Table 6.3 Traditional peacekeeping, peace operations and war

Traditional peacekeeping	Peace operations	War
Universal consent	Consent of target populations, and where possible governments, not of spoilers	No consent
Political neutrality between main conflict parties	No neutrality if a conflict party opposes the mandate	No neutrality
Impartiality in fulfilling mandate	Impartiality in fulfilling mandate	No impartiality
Non-use of force except in self-defence	Full spectrum of force needed to fulfil mandate	Full spectrum of force
International mandate	Uphold UN Charter purposes and principles, where possible with an explicit mandate	National interest

as they have developed with traditional 'first-generation' peacekeeping, on the one hand, and with traditional war fighting, on the other. Then we can briefly sum up from a conflict resolution perspective what distinguishes third-generation peace operations from war (see table 6.3).

Third-Generation Peacekeeping and Human Security

Perhaps the key question here from a conflict resolution perspective, therefore, is whether third-generation peacekeeping is an attempt to combine what cannot be combined – greater military robustness with the service of genuinely cosmopolitan international norms. The key danger is that those with the military capacity will take on such intervention roles entirely outside the ambit of the United Nations, leading to highly ambivalent results in terms of loss of international legitimacy – on which, in the end, the effectiveness of such operations depend:

> The transformation of the UN's peacekeeping role to that of the civilian rather than military tasks of peace operations will confirm the position of the UN as the handmaiden to NATO ... the pre-eminent 'coalition of the willing', rather than the authorizing authority. While NATO powers will have an increasingly free hand to define the limits of sovereignty in the non-Western world, and intervene when they consider it necessary, the UN will have the task of cleaning up afterwards and will have to take responsibility for the unrealistic expectations raised by the growing internationalization of conflict situations. (Chandler, 2001: 17)

For this reason, a concerted attempt was made to expand the traditional concept of military *collective security*, as envisaged in UN Charter Chapter VII, into an international commitment to use military force, where required, ultimately under a UN aegis, to uphold the wider concept of *human security*. The Millennium Report, *We the Peoples: The Role of the United Nations in the Twenty-First Century* (United Nations, 2000), for example, was organized around the themes

Box 6.2 Human security

The meaning and scope of the concept of security have become much broader since the UN Charter was signed in 1945. Human security means the security of people – their physical safety, their economic and social well-being, respect for their dignity and worth as human beings, and the protection of their human rights and fundamental freedoms. The growing recognition worldwide that concepts of security must include people as well as states has marked an important shift in international thinking during the past decade. Secretary-General Kofi Annan himself put the issue of human security at the centre of the current debate, when in his statement to the 54th session of the General Assembly he announced his intention to 'address the prospects for human security and intervention in the new century'.

The traditional, narrow perception of security leaves out the most elementary and legitimate concerns of ordinary people regarding security in their daily lives. It also diverts enormous amounts of national wealth and human resources into armaments and armed forces, while countries fail to protect their citizens from chronic insecurities of hunger, disease, inadequate shelter, crime, unemployment, social conflict and environmental hazard. When rape is used as an instrument of war and ethnic cleansing, when thousands are killed by floods resulting from a ravaged countryside and when citizens are killed by their own security forces, then it is entirely insufficient to think of security in terms of national or territorial security alone. The concept of human security can and does embrace such diverse circumstances.

Source: ICISS, 2001: 15

of the quest for freedom from fear (through conflict management and resolution), freedom from want (through economic development and growth) and sustaining the future (through careful husbanding of the earth's resources and ecosystem). According to Thakur, freedom from fear was central to the other two elements in Kofi Annan's trinity of objectives for the UN in the new century, putting peacekeeping and peacebuilding 'at the cutting edge of the UN's core function in the contemporary world' (Thakur, 2001: 117). This was to provide the normative basis for future peace operations. Although subsequently eclipsed by the furor surrounding the 2001 attack on the World Trade Center and the Pentagon and the subsequent 'global war on terror', this agenda was not lost, emerging, for example, in the title of an edited book containing contributions by leading UN managers to commemorate the life of Sergio Vieira de Mello, UN commissioner for human rights, after his violent death in Baghdad in 2003: *Human Security for All* (Cahill, 2004). Similar conclusions were reached by the International Commission on Intervention and State Sovereignty (ICISS), initiated by the government of Canada at the UN General Assembly in September 2000, as discussed further in chapters 8 and 9 (see box 6.2).

Conflict Resolution and the Theoretical Debate about Peace Operations

In view of the difficulties outlined above, we can now anticipate some of the theoretical issues discussed in Part II by distinguishing *pluralist* concepts of

Table 6.4 A spectrum of current peacekeeping models and levels of conflict resolution (CR) capacity

	1	2	3	4
Theory	Quasi-realist	Pluralist	Solidarist	Cosmopolitan
Practice	Stabilization forces	Traditional peacekeeping	Peace operations	UN emergency peace service
CR capacity	Zero or low CR capacity	Limited passive CR capacity	High military/ low civilian CR capacity	High military/ high civilian CR capacity

(first-generation) 'traditional peacekeeping' and *solidarist* concepts of (third-generation) 'peace operations', from the *realist* concept of 'stabilization forces', on the one hand, and a possible future *cosmopolitan* 'UN emergency peace service', on the other (see table 6.4).

At one end of this spectrum is a neo-realist position that is dismissive of the UN, shows scant interest in international law, and refuses to use 'peace' language at all. The US version looks instead to coalitions of the willing led by the United States in defeating international terrorism. What is needed from this perspective is not peace operations, but *stabilization forces* – 'military support for stability, security, transition and reconstruction' operations in cases where regimes that threaten international peace and security have been overthrown or where failing states are seen as actual or potential havens for terrorism (USDOD, 2005). There are Russian equivalents (which do at times call themselves 'peacekeeping forces') associated with stability operations in the CIS (Commonwealth of Independent States) area (JCC in Moldova, JPKF in South Ossetia, CIS forces in Georgia). Chinese security forces play much the same role in Tibet and elsewhere.

Next come those, such as David Chandler (2004, 2006) who interpret contemporary world politics as no more than a limited society of states with a common interest in preserving collective order, but not enough to underpin universal interventionary principles. Sovereignty preserves plural values and is best left to do just that. The alternative, by breaching non-interventionary norms, distorts local development and invariably leads to great power abuse. First-generation *traditional UN peacekeeping* principles are still seen to be the most appropriate, and peacekeeping should be left to the UN.

Then there is the position of those who take a more extended view of international society along Grotian lines, such as Nicholas Wheeler in the humanitarian intervention debate (2000). Here the society of states is interpreted in a more expansive manner to include universal humanitarian values that trump state sovereignty, either when civil government is contested to the point of breakdown or if it proves incapable of fulfilling its prime task of protecting citizens' basic rights. Wider international society is then seen to have a legitimate interest in intervening, so long as this is ultimately interpreted as 'human security' and can be seen to be internationally sanctioned. This would define genuine third-generation *peace operations*. It is probably true to say that most current specialists writing on peace operations are located somewhere within this broad category.

Beyond this again are those who see the logic behind peace operations being properly met only when a further stage is reached – as it were, *fourth-generation* peacekeeping – in which the universal principles that lie behind genuine peace operations are reflected in global politics (cosmopolitan democracy, global civil society, equitable economic arrangements, universal values that are recognized cross-culturally) as well as operational capability and practice. The conceptual underpinning is provided by theorists such as Richard Falk (1995), David Held (1995) and Mary Kaldor (2003), who advocate a decisive evolution of global order towards cosmopolitan governance, as discussed further in chapter 11. At the operational level this implies a move in the direction of what Woodhouse and Ramsbotham call 'cosmopolitan peace operations' (2005). Among the most innovative ideas here are the quite detailed proposals now on the table for the development of a military intervention capability specifically owned by the United Nations in which designated forces will train and serve entirely as UN forces, not national troops. Plans for a United Nations Emergency Peace Service (UNEPS) were presented to the UN in 2006 (Langille, 2000a; Johansen, 2006), and Michael Codner has elaborated requirements for a United Nations Intervention Force (UNIF) of some 10,000 troops in the first instance (2008).[2] More will be said about this below. Our own research suggests that these apparently 'blue skies' ideas now command much more support from serving military forces currently engaged in peace operations than might be supposed (Woodhouse and Ramsbotham, 2005; Curran and Woodhouse, 2007).

As set out in the bottom line of table 6.4, it is possible to see a steady enhancement of conflict resolution capacity associated with this progression, from no such capacity in the first category to enhanced military and civilian capacity in the fourth category. Current discussion within the conflict resolution field is conducted across the pluralist, solidarist and cosmopolitan spectrum within the broader framework of theoretic debate that will be discussed further in chapters 11 and 19.

Finally it is important to note the force of an even more radical critique, not included in table 6.4 because not yet articulated into clear policy recommendations for peacekeeping or peace operations in general, short of a much wider transformation of global power structures themselves. This is a *critical theoretic* approach to peacekeeping that comes from an international political economy vantage point (Pugh et al., 2008a) and encompasses post-structural Foucauldian views (Duffield, 2001, 2007; see also Bellamy and Williams, 2004). The critical agenda criticizes existing practice as objectivist, non-reflexive and instrumentalist. All existing versions of peacekeeping are seen to lack critical awareness of their own epistemological and ontological assumptions, condemned to reproduce existing power imbalances and inequalities even when they think that they are acting impartially. In contrast, radical critical theory sees its own stance as constructivist, reflexive and normative, conscious of the epistemological and ontological institutions and discourses that underpin existing exclusions and therefore able to serve genuinely emancipatory purposes (Fetherston, 2000). This introduces a fundamental debate between traditional conflict resolution and critical theory that will be pursued further in Part II and will be summed up in chapter 19. In *Legions of Peace: UN Peacekeepers from the Global South* (2013), Philip Cunliffe dismisses UN peacekeeping as 'the highest form of liberal imperialism' and regards peacekeepers from the 'global South' as modern-day '*askaris*' (2013: 217). Although there is truth in this indictment, wholesale condemnation seems too sweeping. We do not think that abandonment of the precarious sixty-year-old UN peacekeeping experiment would lead to a more equal or a safer world.

The few concrete suggestions about peacekeeping that are made from a critical perspective overlap with some of the pragmatic and cosmopolitan conflict resolution proposals discussed above. For example, mention is made of the possibility of purely civilian peacekeepers (non-military peacekeeping); that peacekeepers should be released from an overly state-centric control system; that they should be made 'answerable to a more transparent, democratic and accountable institutional arrangement' based on 'a permanent military volunteer force recruited directly among individuals predisposed to cosmopolitan rather than patriotic values' (post-Westphalian or democratic peacekeeping); and that, 'in so far as a goal of transformation is to remove the injustices that give rise to conflict, the need for military-civilian interventions might be expected to fade' (Bellamy and Williams, 2004). In the end the underlying implication is that, if critical criteria were properly met, peace operations themselves would no longer be needed: 'For critical theory, structural transformation based on social struggles immanent in globalization processes will introduce new forms of democratic peacekeeping in the short term if not rendering it largely obsolete in the long run' (Pugh, 2004: 53–4).

We end the chapter with a case study of Somalia because, over a twenty-five-year period of almost continuous warfare, it shows the very mixed record of international intervention and neglect and the importance of seeing that, as far as is possible, such interventions should recognize, build on and support remarkable indigenous survival and peacemaking capacities. This will also serve as a bridge to the next chapter.

Case Study: Somalia, 1991–2015

The story of international intervention in Somalia over the past twenty-five years exemplifies some of the most harrowing challenges that face peacekeepers in ongoing civil wars. Peacekeepers have been deployed at both ends of this period. Following the overthrow of dictator Siad Barre in 1991, the Somali state collapsed, weapons were widely dispersed, and factional warlordism

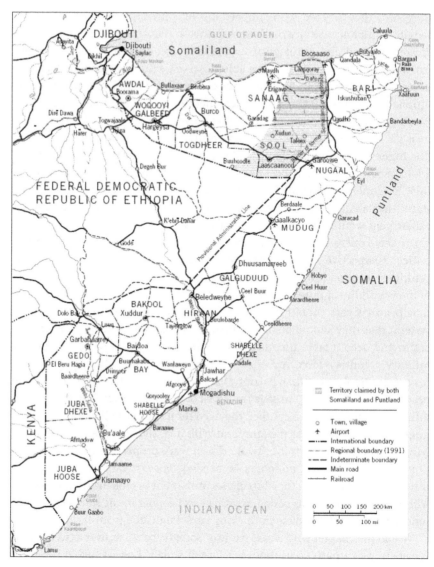

Source: Bradbury and Healy, 2010

Map 6.2 *Somalia showing Somaliland, Puntland, etc.*

reduced the country to chaos. Famine was added to violence, and between
December 1991 and March 1992 perhaps 250,000 Somalis died. In response,
a lightly armed 'second-generation' UN peacekeeping force (UNOSOM I) was
deployed from April 1992 under special UN envoy Mohamed Sahnoun. In
some accounts, Sahnoun's approach, which was to encourage negotiations
between all parties utilizing indigenous Somali methods, was about to pay
off (Sahnoun, 1994; Ramsbotham and Woodhouse, 1996: 193–226), when it
was abruptly terminated by the decision of US President George Bush senior

to send in a large, mainly American United Task Force (UNITAF), endorsed by the UN Security Council in December 1992, to enforce control. In April 1993 UNITAF handed over to the 28,000-strong UNOSOM II, which became embroiled in the war. The death of eighteen US rangers in the 'Black Hawk Down' action in October 1993 led to the withdrawal of US forces in March 1994 and of UNOSOM II by March 1995.

More than ten years later, in December 2006, the UN again authorized a peacekeeping force – this time the deployment of up to 8,000 African Union peacekeepers (AMISOM) in the aftermath of a western-backed Ethiopian intervention to drive out the Islamic Courts Union forces, which had seized control of most of south-central Somalia earlier that summer. In response, the Islamists regrouped around the more militant Harakat Al-Shabaab (youth movement), and the equally militant Hizbul Islamiya (Islamist Party), and declared *jihad* on both the Transitional Federal Government (TFG) and AMISOM, which was protecting it. By September 2009, 1.3 million Somalis had been displaced by the fighting, aid agencies estimated that a third of the population was dependent on food aid, and 60,000 a year were leaving the country. Peacekeepers had again become embroiled in war.

There are no easy lessons from this twenty-five-year experience. The conflict itself transmuted rapidly, from clan-based civil war into warlordism, into proxy war between neighbouring states such as Ethiopia and Eritrea, and now perhaps into globalized religious and ideological struggle. In May 1991 a conference of mainly Isaac clans in the northern part of the country declared an independent Republic of Somaliland. In the adjacent, mainly Harti, area, a non-secessionist Puntland State of Somalia was set up in 1998. International efforts at peacemaking were complicated by the problematic nature of representation and legitimacy in Somali society: 'Representation in Somalia is characterized by multiple affiliations, shifting alliances and transferable identities based on nation, clan and religion. Somali representatives in peace processes commonly wear several "hats", transferring affiliation as appropriate to whichever role suits their personal interests or those of their patrons' (Hoehne, 2010: 37).

Behind this lies the fact that the idea of the state itself has been a European colonial import, during which time Somali territory was divided into five artificial sections, only two of which form modern Somalia (Lewis, 2002). Somalis want peace, but a centralized state does not have positive associations. Power is diffused in Somali pastoral culture. So US-led demands for 'fixing failed states' in order to stabilize regions, eliminate piracy, and deny a haven to terrorists is deeply at odds with indigenous traditions:

> Normal forms of international mediation do not deal easily with the apparent contradiction between a centralized state-based authority and a traditionally egalitarian political culture, in which the legitimacy of force is not vested in a centralized institution of a state but in a diffuse lineage system, regulated by customary law and other institutions. Somalis have been experimenting with alternative state models that are a hybrid of

> Somali and Western democratic traditions. Consequently in Somaliland and Puntland at least, Somalis are experiencing localized forms of government that are more participatory than they have been for decades and will be reluctant to part with them. (Bradbury and Healy, 2010: 106)

All of this poses a major challenge to currently fashionable ideas on the primacy of 'stability' and 'statebuilding', as discussed in chapter 8, and therefore to the success of international peacekeeping deployments sent in accordingly.

Finally, in marked contrast to the experience and frame of reference of many of the international power-brokers, including official UN and other diplomats, domiciled during most of this period mainly in Nairobi, is the remarkably rich variety of indigenous peacemaking and reconciliation resources demonstrated by Somalis during the long years of international neglect. For example, more than ninety examples since 2001 have been catalogued and mapped by Somali centres in south-central Somalia, Somaliland and Puntland facilitated by Interpeace (Bradbury and Healy, 2010: 45–74). This was made possible by a mixture of unwritten customary law (*xeer*), Somali shari'a law within the Islamic Sunni Shafi'i school, traditional values (*caado*), and local codes of social conduct (*dhagan*) by clan elders, Muslim *ulema* (scholars), and women's groups. As will be emphasized in chapter 9, local capacities and resources such as these are usually greatly underestimated and largely misunderstood in mainstream discussion.

By October 2014, the AMISON mission was reporting that the situation in Mogadishu had reached a state of relative peace, so that its civil affairs division was able to organize football matches to provide a sense of normality for the children of the country, and programmes were run on child protection and gender audit workshops. On the other hand, there were reports of abuses against local populations by mission personnel in Somalia resulting in a planned enquiry (Human Rights Watch, 2014). And al-Shabaab *jihadis* were at the same time mounting vicious attacks across the border in Kenya in an attempt to provoke inter-clan conflict in revenge for earlier Kenyan intervention.

Conclusion

It is worth concluding this chapter by recalling the words of one of the creators of UN peacekeeping, Lester Pearson, in his 1957 Nobel Lecture:

> Certainly the idea of an international police force effective against a big disturber of the peace seems today unrealizable to the point of absurdity. We did, however, take at least a step in the direction of putting international force behind an international decision a year ago in the Suez crisis. The birth of this force was sudden and it was surgical. The arrangements for the reception of the infant were rudimentary and the midwives ... had no precedents or experience to guide them. Nevertheless, UNEF, the first genuinely international police force of its kind, came into being and into action ... We made at least a beginning then. If, on that foundation, we do not build something more permanent and stronger, we will once again have ignored realities, rejected opportunities, and betrayed our trust. Will we never learn? (Pearson, 1957)

This dream is not dead. A report published in 2012 by the Berlin-based think tank and research centre ZIF (Center for International Peace Operations) attempted future scenario modelling of what peacekeeping/peace operations might look like in ten years' time. Four possible scenarios or options were presented: National Interests, Erratic Progress, Regional Diversity and Global Cooperation. The first scenario envisages the complete collapse of international peace operations and reversion to the use of military force only in the national interest as narrowly defined. The fourth scenario envisages further advance in a cosmopolitan direction to the point where an imagined 'Beijing Conference' in 2021 creates a global peace operations system (Gienanth et al., 2012). The cosmopolitan model continues to attract the attention of serious analysts. For example, Peter Langille, an early advocate of the United Nations Peace Service model, elaborates both the theory and the operational requirements of such a model in a report that specifies a series of fourteen recommendations to improve UN rapid deployment (Langille, 2014).

Whether or not a cosmopolitan future is ever attained, we have argued that a conflict resolution approach continues in the meantime both to clarify what distinguishes genuine peace operations from other forms of intervention and to indicate the direction in which 'pragmatic' incremental improvements need to develop if these operations are to fulfil the tasks assigned to them. Despite some spectacular failures, particularly in the mid-1990s, we agree with the overall assessment of Alex Bellamy and Paul Williams:

> Since the first edition of this book there is much more conclusive evidence that peace operations can help to manage conflicts and lay the foundations for stable peace. We have a better idea of the conditions that breed success and the factors that lead to failure. We also have a more comprehensive understanding of how peace operations should be organized. (2010: 402)

Peacekeeping for all its faults continues to evolve. Fifteen years after the publication of the first comprehensive review of UN peacekeeping (the Brahimi Report, 2000), UN Secretary-General Ban Ki-moon, in an open debate of the Security Council in June 2014 on trends in peacekeeping, initiated a new comprehensive review (UNSG, 2014). The composition of the review group, known as the High-Level Independent Panel on Peace Operations, was announced on 31 October 2014, under the chairmanship of José Ramos-Horta, Nobel Peace Laureate and former president of Timor-Leste. The recommendations of the panel are likely to have significant implications for the ways in which peacekeeping will function and how effective it will be as a conflict resolving mechanism.[3]

Summing up this chapter, we reiterate that the new field of conflict resolution and the new enterprise of UN peacekeeping were born in the same decade – the 1950s – and from the outset shared a similar agenda. The central aim of peacekeepers has been not to defeat a national enemy, but to support peace processes, protect civilians and fulfil legitimate international mandates. Even when traditional military combat capabilities are required, and indeed when these capabilities include counter-terrorism and counter-insurgency, as is possible in the case of Mali, the overall use and intention of such capabilities is to enhance peace. Similarly, classic conflict resolution approaches have seen violent conflict itself, not particular conflict parties, as the enemy. The main aim of conflict resolution is to transform violent conflict into non-violent forms of political and other kinds of change. For these reasons, as we will argue in chapter 14, similar ethical principles should guide and define both conflict resolution interventions and genuine peace operations. Above all, peace operations must genuinely serve the interests of those in whose name the intervention is carried out, not the interests of the interveners. If they do not, then the central argument in this chapter is that they should not be called peace operations. How is it possible to determine what is, and what is not, in the interests of those in whose name interventions are carried out? That is a question for chapter 9.

RECOMMENDED READING

Bellamy et al. (2004); Bellamy and Williams (2010); Bradbury and Healy (2010); Cunliffe (2013); Diehl (2008); Durch (2007); Gienanth et al. (2012); Langille (2014); Pouligny (2006); Woodhouse and Ramsbotham (2000, 2005).

RELEVANT EXTRACTS IN *THE CONTEMPORARY CONFLICT RESOLUTION READER*

Reading 18: D. Keen, The Economic Functions of Violence in Civil Wars

CHAPTER SEVEN

Ending Violent Conflict: Peacemaking

In this chapter we turn from the question of the role of conflict resolution in ongoing wars to the question of war endings. We will focus especially on efforts to bring armed conflicts to an end in the post-Cold War era and on the factors that have contributed to their success and failure. Having examined the nature and difficulties of ending violent conflict, we will move on to explore 'transformers' of conflict and the place of de-escalation, pre-negotiations, mediation, negotiations and peace talks in ending violence and restoring peace. We illustrate these themes with examples of successful peace processes and of peace processes that have failed or coexisted uneasily with protracted conflict.

On his release from prison on 11 February 1990, Nelson Mandela surprised the waiting world with the expansiveness of his opening words: 'Friends, comrades, and fellow South Africans. I greet you all, in the name of peace, democracy and freedom for all.' In contrast, not long afterwards, with reference to shaking hands with Yasser Arafat on 13 September 1993 on the White House lawn, Israeli Prime Minister Yitzhak Rabin was more grudging:

> I knew that the hand outstretched to me from the far side of the podium was the same hand that held the knife, that held the gun, the hand that gave the order to shoot, to kill. Of all the hands in the world, it was not the hand that I wanted or dreamed of touching. I would have liked to sign a peace agreement with Holland, or Luxembourg, or New Zealand. But there was no need to. That is why, on that podium, I stood as the representative of a nation that wants peace with the most bitter and odious of its foes. (Address by Prime Minister Rabin to the General Assembly of the Council of Jewish Federations, Montreal, 18 November 1993)

Conflict resolution is broader than conflict termination. Ending a violent conflict does not necessarily resolve the issues that were root causes. Nor does resolving the issues in conflict necessarily end violence. It is possible that efforts to resolve a conflict may not end a war and that efforts to end a war may not resolve the underlying conflict. Conflict resolution aims for both a transformation of the conflict and the elimination of violence, but, as we shall see, these are not always achieved.

The Challenge of Ending Violent Conflict

First we will examine how major post-Cold War armed conflicts ended, together with the obstacles to conflict resolution in this period.

How major post-Cold War conflicts have ended

Peace agreements play a key role in the evaluation of contemporary conflict resolution. Given the complexity of transnational conflicts, this is now recognized to cover a spectrum of sometimes partial agreements at different levels, as elaborated below. Studies of war termination show that cases in which single all-inclusive peace agreements end the fighting are quite rare. More often, conflicts fizzle out, dropping below the thresholds that researchers use to classify them as armed conflicts. The underlying reasons for the conflict remain, and they are prone to break out again. This is consistent with the pattern of protracted social conflicts identified by Azar (see chapter 4). Between 1946 and 1989, Kreutz (2010) identifies 141 terminated conflicts, of which only 9 per cent ended in a peace agreement, 1 per cent ended with a ceasefire but no peace agreement, 58 per cent ended with victory for one side, and 32 per cent had other outcomes. In the post-Cold War period, from 1990 up to 2005, 147 conflicts terminated, with 18 per cent ending in a peace agreement, 20 per cent in a ceasefire but no peace agreement, 14 per cent in victory for one side, and 48 per cent in other outcomes. The post-Cold War period has thus seen a significant increase in the proportion of conflicts ending in peace agreements and a sharp reduction in the number ending in victory. But other endings, such as the end of violence with no agreement, form the largest category. Nevertheless the post-Cold War era has seen some significant peace agreements, as well as some less well-known ones. Conflicts continue to show a bewildering pattern of ceasefires, temporary agreements and occasionally permanent settlements. For a selection of recent agreements, see Box 7.1.

What constitutes a war 'ending' is itself a tricky question. Wallensteen and his colleagues use a miminal definition that fewer than twenty-five battle-related deaths occur in the following year; but peace settlements often break down, and repeated violence takes place. Cambodia, which produced a 'comprehensive political settlement' in 1990, again produced a high-intensity conflict in late 1996 (Schmid, 1997: 79). The Lomé peace agreement of July 1999 in Sierra Leone broke down in renewed fighting, which the intervention of UNAMSIL and the elections of May 2002 largely brought to an end. Guatemala experienced sixteen peace agreements, or partial agreements, between 1990 and 1996, and a pattern of multiple agreements, most of which fail, is the norm.[1] A war ending is not usually a precise moment in time, but a process. A violent conflict is over when a new political dispensation prevails, or the parties become reconciled, or a new conflict eclipses the first.[2] Perhaps for this reason, interstate peace agreements have been easier to conclude than intrastate agreements: only a quarter to a third of modern civil wars have been negotiated, whereas more than half of interstate wars have been (Pillar, 1983; Licklider, 1995).[3] However, if we take a long enough time period, armed conflicts *do* eventually end (Licklider, 1995).

Box 7.1 Selected peace agreements in armed conflicts, 2000–2014

Burundi	2000	Arusha Peace and Reconciliation Agreement
Sierra Leone	2000	Peace Agreement between government and RUF
Macedonia	2001	Framework Agreement
Bougainville	2001	Bougainville Peace Agreement
Angola	2002	Peace Agreement (Lusaka Protocol 1994)
Aceh	2002	Cessation of Hostilities Framework Agreement
Uganda	2002	Peace Agreement
Liberia	2003	Comprehensive Peace Agreement
Comoros	2003	Anjouan Agreement
Ivory Coast	2003	Linas-Marcousis Agreement
Senegal	2004	Casamance Agreement
Sudan	2004	Comprehensive Peace agreement
Cameroon/Nigeria	2006	Agreement on Bakassi Peninsula
Sudan	2006	Darfur Peace Agreement
Northern Ireland	2006	St Andrew's Agreement
Nepal	2006	Comprehensive Peace Agreement
Ivory Coast	2007	Ouagadougou Political Agreement
Sudan/Chad/CAR	2007	Cannes Declaration
Uganda	2007	Agreement on Accountability and Reconciliation
Kenya	2008	Power-sharing deal
Mauritania	2009	Dakar Accord
Chad	2009	Agreement with the Mouvement Nationale
Madagascar	2009	Charte des Valeurs
Sudan	2010	Framework Agreement on Darfur
Colombia	2012	General Agreement for Termination of Conflict
Sudan	2012	Sudan–South Sudan Cooperation Agreement
Philippines	2012	Government–MILF Decision Points on Principles
Philippines	2012	Framework Agreement on the Bangsomoro
Thailand	2013	General Consensus on Peace Dialogue Process
Colombia	2013	Democratic Opening to Construct Peace
Yemen	2014	Peace and National Partnership Agreement
South Sudan	2014	Agreement to Resolve Southern Sudan Crisis
Ukraine	2014	Minsk Agreement

For lists of peace agreements, see Wallensteen (2007), the UCDP Peace Agreement Dataset and the Peace Agreement Database on the UN Peacemaker site (http://peacemaker.un.org/document-search). For texts of agreements, see the Margarita S. Studemeister Digitial Collection of Peace Agreements, US Institute of Peace, the UN Peacemaker site and the INCORE Transitional Justice Peace Agreements Database at www.peaceagreements.ulster.ac.uk/. For analysis of peace processes and peace agreements, see Conciliation Resources' *ACCORD* series and Tonge (2014). For thematic analysis, see the Peace Accords Matrix at the Kroc Institute for International Peace Studies.

Licklider (1995) finds that civil wars ended by negotiated settlements are more likely to lead to the recurrence of armed conflicts than those ended by military victories; on the other hand, those ended by military victories are more likely to lead to genocide. Similarly, Toft (2010) argues that conflicts settled by negotiation are more vulnerable to recurrence and less likely to lead to a sustainable peace. This is often because negotiated agreements fail to resolve underlying issues and leave undefeated parties in contention. There may also be a selection effect, in that more intractable conflicts attract more negotiation efforts. In contrast, Wallensteen and Svensson (2014: 323) cite Kreutz's findings, which suggest that, in the 2000s, negotiated settlements led to recurrence less often than victories, reversing the trend of the 1990s. These findings point to the need for continuing efforts to resolve the underlying conflicts.

Peace agreements and international law

In her study of peace agreements and the law of peace, Christine Bell (2008) analyses 646 documents, 'which could lay claim to the name peace agreements', that were signed between 1990 and 2007, addressing 102 conflicts in 85 jurisdictions. Her definition of peace agreements is that they are 'documents produced after discussion with some or all of the conflict's protagonists that address militarily violent conflict with a view to ending it' (2008: 53). Of these, 91 per cent were 'intrastate', covering issues ranging from ceasefires to new constitutional arrangements for how power will be held and exercised (ibid.: 5–6). There has been a torrent of legally significant agreements since the end of the Cold War.

Christine Bell's thesis goes further than this, however. Her main argument is that this ongoing flood of agreements makes up a rapidly evolving 'law of peace' in which 'peace agreements assert their own legalization, and force changes in international law's core doctrines' (2008: 22). Drawing on the idea of 'Clausewitz in reverse' (Ramsbotham, 2000: 172), she sees the myriad aspects of 'hybrid self-determination' and 'constructive ambiguity' reflected in these documents as ultimately derived from the attempt to 'translate the conflict from violent to non-violent forms, rather than resolve it' (see chapter 8). In order to achieve this, competing ideologies, interests and identity groups have to be permanently accommodated by the adaptation of existing power structures in a wide variety of different ways. This forces innovatory forms of 'disaggregated' and 'dislocated' power arrangements that progressively redefine the nature of the state itself (Walker, 2003). Bell concludes that 'international law appears to be moving towards underwriting a more complex and ambiguous mix of representative and participative democracy linked to a more fluid concept of statehood with fuzzy sovereignty' (2008: 236) (see Kymlicka, 2007). Further discussion of this critical borderland where 'law and politics meet' can be found in chapter 11.

Peace agreements in complex, hybrid and mutating multi-party conflicts – Sudan

As mentioned above, an important aspect of the evolution of peace agreements over the past twenty-five years is the way they are now often now made up of a number of subsidiary agreements reached at different times, covering different issues and aspects as they arise, and where possible adapted to bring in new conflict parties as the opportunity emerges: 'Conflicts began to have layers of multiple agreements: renewing and revising agreements that had broken down (Algeria, Sierra Leone, Georgia/Abkhazia), extending agreements to new splinter groups or newly elected governments (Liberia), and addressing new issues or new mutations of violence (Sudan)' (Bell, 2008: 28). In other words, the art of peacemaking is constantly evolving to accommodate the new breed of complex, hybrid and mutating conflicts now prevalent, as discussed in chapter 4 above.

In box 7.2, for example, we show some of the agreements reached in three separate and overlapping conflicts in Sudan during this period. Since then, a fourth conflict site has been added in the form of armed clashes between different factions in South Sudan following independence. In each case, the list

---

Box 7.2 Peace agreements over Sudan

Sudan/Darfur

Darfur Peace Agreement, 5 May 2006

Declaration of Principles for the Resolution of the Sudanese Conflict in Darfur, 5 July 2005

Protocol on the Enhancement of the Security Situation in Darfur, 9 November 2004*

Protocol on the Improvement of the Humanitarian Situation in Darfur, 9 November 2004*

Agreement of the Modalities for the Establishment of the Ceasefire Commission and the Deployment of Observers, 28 May 2004*

Humanitarian Ceasefire Agreement on the Conflict in Darfur, April 2004

Protocol on the Establishment of Humanitarian Assistance in Darfur, 8 April 2004*

Sudan/Eastern Sudan

Eastern Sudan Peace Agreement, 14 October 2006

Declaration of Principles for the Resolution of the Conflict in Eastern Sudan, 19 June 2006*

Agreement on Providing a Conducive Atmosphere for Peace, 19 June 2006*

Implementation Agreement for the Provisions of the Tripoli Agreement, 25 December 2005*

Sudan/Southern Sudan

Comprehensive Peace Agreement, 9 January 2005

We do not list here all twenty-three contributory agreements made since 10 April 1995. These cover (a) agreements between the government of Sudan (GoS) and different rebel factions (e.g. the Sudan People's Liberation Movement (SPLM), United Democratic Salvation Front (Sudan) (UDSF)), (b) different sub-conflicts (e.g. Southern Kordofan/Nuba Mountains conflict and Abyei conflict), (c) different issues/aspects (e.g. humanitarian, security, structures of government, wealth-sharing, power-sharing), (d) different phases (e.g. cessation of hostilities, capacity-building and joint planning, interim arrangements during negotiations, implementation arrangements).

begins with the most comprehensive agreement and then moves back in time to give the different stepping stones of prior or subsidiary agreements that made this possible. Those prior agreements that are explicitly incorporated in the more comprehensive documents are marked with an asterisk.

Obstacles to conflict resolution

Chapter 4 has indicated some of the reasons why contemporary international-social conflicts are so hard to end. Sources of conflict, which usually persist in intensified form into the ensuing war, were identified at international, state and societal levels and were also located in the factional interests of elites and individuals. To these are added the destructive processes and vested interests engendered by the war itself, as described in chapter 6. The economic destruction wrought by war makes societies more likely to suffer war again (Collier et al., 2003). Violence spawns a host of groups who benefit directly from its continuation. Soldiers become dependent on warfare as a way of life, and warlords on the economic resources and revenue they can control (King, 1997: 37; Berdal and Keen, 1998). Even in a low-intensity conflict, protagonists may depend, economically or psychologically, on its continuation. Leaders who have become closely identified with pursuing the conflict may risk prosecution, overthrow or even death once the war is over, and so have strong incentives for intransigence (for example, Karadžić in Bosnia, Savimbi in Angola, Vellupillai Prabhakaran in Sri Lanka). Local and regional party officials or military officers who have made their careers in the conflict may develop a stake in its continuation (Sisk, 1997: 84). For such protagonists, peace may bring loss of role and status, and thus directly threaten their interests (King, 1997).

In most situations of conflict, intra-party disagreements add to the difficulty of resolving inter-party conflicts. In the Israeli–Palestinian case, for example, sharp disagreements between the PLO and Hamas, on the one side, and between Likud and the Labour Party, on the other, have made an inter-party agreement much more difficult. Cunningham (2014) explores the significance of intra-party disagreements on both the government side and on the side of their challengers in self-determination disputes. She finds that both unitary governments and highly divided governments are less likely to accommodate self-determination demands and more likely to get into civil wars than governments with a moderate number of veto players. She also finds that more divided self-determination groups are more difficult to accommodate and more likely to be involved in civil wars and engage in factional fights with each other. Accommodation tends to reduce the number of factions with self-determination claims, and thus lessens the likelihood of civil war.

Besides problems of spoilers who gain from continuing conflict and factions who resist accommodation, there are difficulties of bargaining and trust in reaching agreements. Parties may underestimate the costs and overestimate the benefits of continued fighting, and there is also the well-known problem of 'sunk costs' (as in the dollar auction), which induces parties to continue the fight in the hope of offsetting the losses incurred to date. In addition, since parties cannot readily give credible guarantees of agreement (Walter, 1997, 2002), other parties are unwilling to commit to a solution that they might prefer to continued fighting for fear that the other side will renege (Fearon, 1998: 107). We illustrate this dilemma in box 7.3 (p. 221). Discussions with third parties, external guarantees and using small steps to build confidence may help to overcome these difficulties.

Above all, there is the problem of the parties' own commitment to irreconcilable goals, a commitment that sometimes grows as the conflict brings harder-line leaders to power (see chapter 18). Here internal opposition and efforts by moderates to win support for peace policies may be needed, but in polarized conditions the positions of moderates are often as irreconcilable as those of hardliners, and pro-peace voices may have difficulty in being heard.

Conflict resolution is therefore very difficult, and many political groups, such as nations, will fight to the death to achieve their ends. However, we need to keep the obstacles in proportion. Violent conflicts impose massive costs on the societies concerned, and so there is usually a large segment of the population which will benefit from the conflict ending. This is a shared interest across the conflicting communities. Moderate politicians and constituencies, who may have been silenced or displaced by the climate of violence, will be keen to re-establish normal politics. Ordinary people will welcome a return to peace and wish to put the distress of war behind them. There is, therefore, a large reservoir of potential support that peacemakers should be able to tap.

We can point to many cases where conflicts have been settled by negotiation: examples include the ending of apartheid in South Africa, the ending of the internal conflicts in Nicaragua, El Salvador and Guatemala, the settlements in Mozambique and Namibia, the Ta'if Accord which brought the civil war in Lebanon to an end, and the still somewhat shaky settlement in Northern Ireland. In other cases, protagonists manage to pursue conflicts by non-violent or constructive means (Stephan and Chenoweth, 2008; Kriesberg, 1998a). Given political vision, engaged peacemakers, moderation and the right conditions, conflicts *can* be brought to a negotiated end. It is, therefore, worth trying to identify both the ingredients of an effective conflict resolution approach and the conditions under which attempts to end conflict are likely to succeed.

A Framework for Conflict Transformation

In looking at the scope for conflict resolution in ending violent conflict, we will follow Väyrynen in adopting a broad approach which recognizes the fluidity of the conflict process. Conflicts are inherently dynamic, and conflict resolution has to engage with a complex of shifting relations, often within a wider system that has become resistant to piecemeal change:

> The bulk of conflict theory regards the issues, actors and interests as given and on that basis makes efforts to find a solution to mitigate or eliminate contradictions between them. Yet the issues, actors and interests change over time as a consequence of the social, economic and political dynamics of societies. Even if we deal with non-structural aspects of conflicts, such as actor preferences, the assumption of stability, usually made in the game theoretic approach to conflict studies, is unwarranted. New situational factors, learning experiences, interaction with the adversary and other influences caution against taking actor preferences as given. (Väyrynen, 1991: 4)

The requirements are best seen as a series of necessary transformations in the elements which would otherwise sustain ongoing violence and war.

Väyrynen (1991) identifies a number of ways in which conflict transformation takes place. His ideas complement those of Galtung (1984, 1989, 1996, 2004), who has developed his views on the resolution of inter-party and intra-party conflicts, in their structural, attitudinal and behavioural aspects, into a full theory of non-violent conflict transformation. From these sources, and informed by Burton, Azar, Curle and the related theorists mentioned in chapter 2, we outline five generic transformers of protracted conflict which correspond to the outline framework for the analysis of contemporary conflict offered in chapter 4.

1 *Context transformation* Conflicts are embedded in a social, regional and international context, which is often critical to their continuation. Changes in the context may sometimes have more dramatic effects than changes within the parties or in their relationships. The end of the Cold War is the prime recent context transformation, which has unlocked protracted conflicts in Southern Africa, Central America and elsewhere. Local conflicts which are fuelled by global forces may not be resolvable at the local level without changing the structures or policies which have produced them.[4] This is central to systemic conflict resolution within a cosmopolitan framework as advocated in Part II of this book.

2 *Structural transformation* The conflict structure is the set of actors and incompatible goals or relationships which constitute the conflict. If the root causes of the conflict lie in the structure of relationships within which the parties operate, then a transformation of this structure is necessary to resolve the conflict. In asymmetric conflicts, for example, structural transformation entails a change in the relationship between the dominant and the weaker party. Empowerment of the weaker side (for instance, through international support or recognition or mediation) is one way this can be achieved. Another is dissociation – withdrawal from unbalanced relationships, as, for example, in the Kosovar Albanians' decision to boycott the elections in Serbia and set up a 'shadow state', or the similar approach adopted in 2009 by Palestinian Prime Minister Salam Fayyad.

3 *Actor transformation* Parties may have to redefine directions, abandon or modify cherished goals, and adopt radically different perspectives. This may come about through a change of actor, a change of leadership, a change in the constituency of the leader, or the adoption of new goals, values or beliefs. Transformation of intra-party conflicts may be crucial to the resolution of inter-party conflict (see chapter 18). Changes of leadership may precipitate change in protracted conflicts. Changes in the circumstances and interests of the constituency a party represents also transform conflicts, even if such changes in the constituency take place gradually and out of view. Splitting of parties and the formation of new parties are examples of actor transformations, though these can also make conflicts harder to resolve – for example, by creating more veto-players (Cunningham, 2006).

4 *Issue transformation* Conflicts are defined by the conflicting positions parties take on issues. When they change their positions, or when issues lose salience or new ones arise, the conflict is transformed. Changes of position are closely related to changes of interest and changes of goals, and hence to actor transformation and also to the context and structure of the conflict. Reframing the issues and linking issues in new ways may open the way to settlements (Aggestam, 1999; Starkey et al., 1999).

5 *Personal and group transformation* For Adam Curle, this is at the heart of change.[5] The former guerrilla leader, committed to victory through any means, becomes the unifying national leader, offering reconciliation; the leader of an oppressive government decides to accept his opponents into the government. Excruciating suffering leads in time, through mourning and healing, to new life (Montville, 1993).

Transformations of this kind do not necessarily move in a benign direction. It is characteristic of conflicts that they intensify and widen, power passes from moderate to more extreme leaders, violence intensifies, and restraint and moderation wither. These five types of transformation are useful, however, as a framework for analysing steps towards conflict resolution and for thinking about interventions in conflict.

The middle three transformers (structure, actor, issue) correspond to the conflict-level factors identified in our typology of conflict causes in chapter 4; context transformation corresponds to the global, regional and state levels, and individual and group transformation to the individual-elite level.

In many cultures conflicts are explained as 'tangles' of contradictory claims that must be unravelled. In Central America, the phrase 'we are all entangled', as in a fisherman's net, best describes the concept of conflict, and the experience of conflict is 'enredado' (to be tangled or caught in a net) (Duffey, 1998). At the root of conflict is a knot of problematic relationships, conflicting interests and differing worldviews. Undoing this knot is a painstaking process. Success depends on how the knot has been tied and the sequencing of the untying. The timing and coordination of the transformers is crucial (Fisher and Keashly, 1991; Reading 62). Sufficient energy and momentum need to be developed to overcome the conflict's resistance.

This broad view of conflict transformation is necessary to correct the mis-perception that conflict resolution rests on an assumption of harmony of interests between actors and that third-party mediators can settle conflicts by appealing to the reason or underlying humanity of the parties. On the contrary, conflict transformation requires real changes in parties' interests, goals or self-definitions. These may be forced by the conflict itself or may come about because of intra-party changes, shifts in the constituencies of the parties, or changes in the context in which the conflict is situated. Conflict resolution must therefore be concerned not only with the issues that divide the main parties but also with the social, psychological and political changes that are necessary to address root causes, the intra-party conflicts that may inhibit acceptance of a settlement, the global and regional context which structures the issues in conflict and the thinking of the parties, and the social and insti-tutional capacity that determines whether a settlement can be made accept-able and workable (Reading 39). The response must be 'conflict-sensitive' at a number of different levels.

Having outlined the main general requirements for ending violent conflicts in terms of conflict transformers, we now apply this in more detail – first, to the issue of the conditions under which conflicts do actually end; second, to the role of mediation and third-party intervention in war ending; and, third, to the nature of successful negotiations and peace settlements. We examine both the significance of turning points and sticking points in peace processes and the challenge of securing peace against the wishes of sceptics, who may reject the terms of a particular peace agreement, and spoilers, who may want to wreck any settlement.

De-escalation, Ripeness and Readiness: Conditions for Ending Violent Conflict

The end of the Cold War was a significant factor in transforming the context of many conflicts and contributed to the ending of a number of later conflicts. A notable factor was the reduction in the capacity or willingness of external powers to support fighting factions. In Central America, South Africa and South-East Asia, geopolitical changes, the end of ideological justifications for intervention and reductions in armed support for rebel groups contributed to conflict endings (for example, in El Salvador, Nicaragua, Mozambique and Cambodia). Even Northern Ireland's long conflict was positively influenced by the end of the Cold War, as the Republican belief that the UK had a strategic interest in Northern Ireland fell away.

The statistical basis for this section has been reviewed in chapter 3. As Hegre (2004: 244) shows, the global incidence of civil wars has fallen significantly since the end of the Cold War, reversing a forty-year increase to 1990. The rise before 1990 was due mainly to an increase in the duration of wars rather than to new starts; and the decline since 1990 has been the result of changes in duration. A central factor has been the capacity of rebel groups to finance their struggles. Rebel groups have increasingly turned from external state support to contraband and plunder of natural resources. There remain a group of insurgencies in the peripheries of weak states, in the 'global badlands', which remain very resistant to the ending of violent conflict (Fearon, 2004).

Although external interventions are usually important and sometimes decisive in conflict endings, a crucial factor is the willingness of the conflicting parties themselves to consider a negotiated agreement. A host of significant factors may bring about this willingness, and it is difficult to generalize across the heterogeneous group of post-Cold War conflicts (for discussions of de-escalation, conciliatory gestures and the factors influencing feasibility of settlement, see, for example, Mitchell, 1999, 2000; Downs and Stedman, 2002). In armed conflicts, parties become willing to consider negotiated outcomes when they lose hope of achieving their aims by force of arms. Even then, their ability to carry sceptical factions and constituencies is essential for a settlement. In Northern Ireland, for example, the decision of leading Republicans to pursue a political strategy as well as an armed strategy gradually led to involvement in political negotiations and a political outcome. But this alone did not bring about the ceasefire. Among other preconditions were the change in the position of the UK and Irish governments, from opposing protagonists to cooperating mediators, and the realization on the part of the Unionists that their preferred outcome, devolved government, also depended on multi-party negotiations.

Hurting stalemate

Zartman (1985; 1995b: 18; 2000) argues that conflicts are ripe for negotiated settlements only under certain conditions. The main condition is a 'hurting stalemate'. Both sides must realize that they cannot achieve their aims by further violence and that it is costly to go on. The concept of 'hurting stalemate' is widely accepted in policy-making circles, and some diplomats, such as Chester Crocker, have deliberately attempted to bring about a 'hurting stalemate' in order to foster a settlement. Others refer to the need for a 'ripening process' to foster 'ripe moments' (Druckman, 1986).

Zartman argues that, for negotiations to succeed, there must also be valid spokespersons for the parties, a deadline, and a vision of an acceptable compromise. Recognition and dialogue are preconditions, and for these to take place both parties have to be accepted as legitimate. In conflicts between a government and an insurgency, for example, the government must reach the point where it recognizes the insurgency as a negotiating partner. Similarly, a more equal power balance between the parties is held to favour negotiation: when the asymmetry is reduced, negotiations may become possible.

Druckman and Green (1995) suggest that changes in relative legitimacy as well as relative power between regimes and insurgents affect the propensity to negotiate.

The 'ripeness' idea has the attraction of simplicity, but a number of authors have suggested modifications or criticisms. Christopher Mitchell (1995) distinguishes four different models of the 'ripe moment': the original 'hurting stalemate' suggested by Zartman; the idea of 'imminent mutual catastrophe', also due to Zartman; the rival model suggested by games of entrapment such as the 'dollar auction' (Rapoport, 1989), where a hurting stalemate leads to even greater commitment by the parties; and the idea of an 'enticing opportunity' or conjunction of favourable circumstances (such as, for example, the conjunction of conditions which encouraged the first IRA ceasefire in Northern Ireland: a Fianna Fáil taoiseach, a Democratic president with strong American Irish support, and an understanding between the Northern Irish Nationalists and Republicans). Others argue that the concept is tautological, since we cannot know whether there is a hurting stalemate until the actions that it is supposed to trigger take place (Licklider, 1993: 309; Hampson, 1996: 210–14). If a stalemate that hurts the parties persists for a long time before negotiations, as it often does, the value of the concept as an explanation for negotiated settlements must be qualified.

It has been argued that the simple 'hurting stalemate' model gives too much weight to the power relationship between the parties and fails sufficiently to take account either of changes within the parties or changes in the context, which may also foster a propensity to negotiate (Stedman, 1991). Moreover, although it is possible to point to cases of successful negotiations which have followed hurting stalemates, it is also possible to point to hurting stalemates which do not lead to successful negotiations – for example, in Cyprus. It may be argued in these cases that the stalemate is not hurting enough; but then there is no clear evidence from case studies as to how long a stalemate has to last or how much it has to hurt before it triggers successful negotiations. And stalemates are likely to hurt the general population more than the leaders who in the end make the decisions. We should distinguish, too, between ripeness for negotiations to start and ripeness for negotiations to succeed; in Angola and Cambodia, for example, the conditions for settlement 'unripened' after negotiated agreements had been made because one or other of the parties was unwilling to accept the settlement terms, even though the condition of 'hurting stalemate' still obtained. A model that sees conflicts moving from 'unripeness' through a ripe moment to resolution is perhaps too coarse-grained to take account of the many changes that come together over time and result in a settlement: redefinitions of parties' goals, changes in the parties' constituencies, contextual changes, and shifts in perceptions, attitudes and behaviour patterns. 'Ripeness' is not sudden but, rather, a complex process of transformations in the situation, shifts in public attitudes, and new perceptions and visions among decision-makers.

Readiness theory

Dean Pruitt's readiness theory is a development of William Zartman's theory that conflicts are 'ripe' for settlement when parties mutually accept that the costs of continuing outweigh the benefits of a negotiated agreement. Pruitt (2007) describes the conditions in readiness theory that are conducive to entering negotiations and persisting in search of agreement in terms of two main 'psychological variables' that influence each conflict party separately but in linked ways: *motivation* to end the conflict and *optimism* that negotiations are likely to lead to an acceptable outcome (Reading 42). These two variables are mutually compensatory. Both need to be present if there is to be a readiness to negotiate, but not necessarily in equal measure at all times. Motivation is increased by the conclusion that the war is unwinnable or can be won only at unacceptable cost, as well as by pressure from powerful third parties. Leaders have four tactical choices here, the first three of which (persist, escalate, seek allies) are 'unilateral tactics' to defeat the enemy so that readiness to employ the fourth tactic (explore and enter negotiations) depends upon this seeming more advantageous than the other three. Optimism results from three states of mind: lowering expectations, developing trust that the adversary also wants a positive outcome, and perceiving 'light at the end of the tunnel'. Taking into account the spectrum of readiness within conflict parties (doves, moderates, hawks) and cases where there are more than two parties to a conflict leads to the addition of 'central coalition theory'. Given different levels of readiness across this spectrum, the crucial factor is that there must be a central coalition (for example, of doves and most moderates across respective conflict parties) at a sufficient level of readiness to negotiate and strong enough to withstand the counter-pull of spoilers. The better armed the hawks, the more powerful the central coalition needs to be. In general, the central coalition must include the bulk of the armed groups. Pruitt hopes both that readiness theory can offer explanatory power to explain the shifting evolution of conciliatory acts required for negotiations to succeed in intractable circumstances and that, as a result, it can also have some predictive value in guiding policy.

Amira Schiff (2014) has studied the eventual success of the Aceh negotiations between the Free Aceh Movement (Gerekan Aceh Mereka – GAM) and the government of Indonesia (GoI) up to 2005 and the eventual failure of the 2001–4 negotiations between the Liberation Tigers of Tamil Elam (LTTE) and the government of Sri Lanka (GoS) in order to test readiness theory. Her conclusion is that the theory does indeed give a useful framework for analysing the fluctuating, and increasingly divergent, paths that the two sets of negotiations took. But she finds that there are too many variables to offer predictive power and that, even in terms of explanatory power, because the variables are 'psychological' and therefore in large part inaccessible except through associated behaviour (e.g. acts of conciliation or rejection), the theory in application tends to be tautological. From behaviour we may infer psychological fluctuations in terms of 'motivation' and 'optimism', but we cannot then use these components of 'readiness' in turn to draw independent conclusions about behaviour. The theory also says little directly about asymmetry – although this is to some extent built into the differing psychological variables associated with the competing parties individually.

But perhaps the examples that Schiff takes differ from each other in too many respects to make clear comparison possible – for example, the gap between GAM field commanders and the exiled leadership in Sweden was in marked contrast to the ruthless control exercised by Vellupillai Prabhakaran over the LTTE; the decisive influence of mediator Martti Ahtisaari in persuading GAM to give up the uncompromising goal of independence and accept 'self-governance' was not matched in Sri Lanka; the role of the international community was different; relative military, political and economic strengths varied; and there was no equivalent in Sri Lanka of the offer of 70 per cent of oil and gas revenue for Aceh, or the eventual agreement of GoI to cede autonomy to local Acehnese political parties. Above all the impact of the December 2004 tsunami, devastating though it was in Sri Lanka, was overwhelming in Aceh. So it was that the peace processes in the two countries between 2001/2 and 2004/5 'moved in opposite directions'.

Readiness theory may be the best theory we have for tracing the various elements that influence leaders to enter negotiations, persist in the search for agreement, and (at the moment relatively neglected in the theory) move on to implement any agreement reached. If the theory in its present form is only partially explanatory and not yet robust enough to be predictive, it does clarify where the problems lie, and for this it will deserve credit for any future development that either readiness theory itself, or some other theory, may achieve.

Mediation and Third-Party Intervention

While the primary conflict parties have the most important role in determining outcomes, a feature of the globalization of conflict has been the increasing involvement of a range of external agencies in mediation efforts and third-party interventions of all kinds. Different kinds of mediators can bring helpful resources to the table, including access to the parties, access to civil society actors, knowledge of past peace processes and specialized knowledge of constitutions, power-sharing arrangements, and the like. Bercovitch (1996) found that about two-thirds of the post-Cold War conflicts he studied had been mediated, and, similarly, Wilkenfeld et al. (2005) found that this was the case with two-thirds of the post-Cold War international crises, compared with one-third of the crises between 1918 and 1996.

Track I, II and III interventions

Conflict resolution attempts involve different kinds of agency (international organizations, states, non-governmental organizations, individuals), address different groups (party leaders, elites, grassroots), and vary in form, duration and purpose. Chapters 1 and 2 referred to this developing practice, including Track I, Track II, Track III and multitrack diplomacy, employing a spectrum of 'soft' and 'hard' intervention approaches ranging from good offices, conciliation, quiet or 'pure' mediation at one end, through various modes of mediation and peacekeeping, to peace enforcement at the other. (We also have what is sometimes called 'Track One and a Half' mediation, involving informal representatives of the government parties.) There have been fierce debates over whether third-party intervention should be impartial or partial, coercive or non-coercive, state-based or non-state-based, and carried out by outsiders or insiders (Touval and Zartman, 1985; Curle, 1986; Mitchell and Webb, 1988; van der Merwe, 1989; Lederach, 1995; Bercovitch, 1996; Beardsley et al., 2006; Bercovitch and Gartner, 2006; Kydd, 2003, 2006; Svensson, 2007; Rauchhaus, 2006; Savun, 2008). Attempts to integrate different approaches, such as Fisher and Keashly's (1991) 'contingency model'[6] and life-cycle models of conflict (Creative Associates, 1997: 3–4), suggest appropriate responses at different phases of conflict, though such models resolve neither the ethical issues involved nor the practical issues of coordination (Webb et al., 1996). They do, however, point to the conclusion that third-party interventions usually need to be coordinated (Jones, 2002) and continued over an extended period, and that 'third parties need other third parties' (Hampson, 1996: 233; Reading 43; Crocker et al., 1999). Further to chapter 4, if conflicts are complex systems, then, given the interlocking and reinforcing nature of the syndrome, individual changes will often be insufficient to shift the overall pattern – it will fall back into its 'default' mode. On the other hand, if the situation changes to the point where the system becomes unstable, complexity-chaos theory predicts that small changes can push it suddenly into a new configuration (Coleman et al., 2005).

At the softer end of the spectrum, third parties are often essential in contributing to issue transformations. They typically help the conflicting parties by putting them in contact with one another, gaining their trust and confidence, setting agendas, clarifying issues and formulating agreements. They can facilitate meetings by arranging venues, reducing tensions, exploring the interests of the parties and sometimes guiding the parties to unrealized possibilities. These are tasks that are usually contentious and even dangerous for the protagonists to perform themselves. By allowing the parties to present their cases, exploring them in depth, framing and ordering the discussion, and questioning the advantages and disadvantages of different options, before the parties have to make a commitment to them, mediation can sometimes perform a valuable role in opening up new political space.

Mediation is especially important at a stage when at least some of the parties have come to accept that pursuing the conflict is unlikely to achieve their goals, but before they have reached the stage of accepting formal negotiations (Beardsley and Greig, 2009). At this point, face-to-face meetings may be very difficult to arrange, and mediation and back channels become important – they played a large role in the peace processes in Northern Ireland, South Africa and the Israel–Palestine conflict in the 1990s. In the Northern Ireland case, for example, the SDLP, Sinn Fein and the Irish government established communications by sending secret messages through representatives of the Clonard monastery, a religious community which ministers to Republican families living on the 'front line' in Belfast; this prepared the ground for the Hume–Adams proposals (Coogan, 1995; Cochrane, 2013; Powell, 2014; Reading 56). Community relations work and contacts between the divided communities were also vital (Reading 48). In the South African case, the contacts arranged between the ANC and the government by third parties enabled preliminary communication between the two sides before they were ready to negotiate openly.

Non-governmental mediation

International mediation has become an increasingly crowded field, with international organizations, governments and non-governmental organizations all involved. Although they usually have limited resources, NGOs, religious bodies, academics and individual mediators play an important role in mediation, though one that is often difficult to document. They are especially important in society-to-society contacts and in supporting peace efforts at an early stage. NGOs (such as the African Centre for the Constructive Resolution of Disputes (ACCORD), the Berghof Research Centre for Constructive Conflict Management, the Carter Center, the Community of Sant'Egidio, the Harvard Negotiation Institute, the Institute for Multi-Track Diplomacy, International Alert and Search for Common Ground) have gained experience of working in conflict (van Tongeren, 1996; Serbe et al., 1997). They use a variety of approaches, including facilitation and sustained mediation (Fisher and Ury, 1981) and problem-solving workshops (de Reuck, 1984; Burton, 1987; Kelman, 1992; Mitchell and Banks, 1996; Francis, 2002), and work with codes of conduct that usually stress impartiality and accountability to humanitarian principles (Reading 63).

It is possible to point to a number of cases where mediators from NGOs have contributed to transformation at key moments, usually in conjunction with governments and international organizations – the Community of Sant'Egidio in Mozambique (Hume, 1994; Msabaha, 1995: 221), Jimmy Carter in Ethiopia/Eritrea (Ottaway, 1995: 117), the Moravians and the Mennonites in Central America (Wehr and Lederach, 1996: 65, 69), the Norwegian organization Fafo in the Oslo talks between Israel and the PLO (Corbin, 1994) and the work of the University of Kent's Conflict Analysis Centre in Moldova. The first quantitative study of the interaction of Track I and Track II mediation suggests that Track I efforts supported by unofficial action at Track II is more effective than independent efforts at either track (Böhmelt, 2010).

It is difficult to establish the effects with certainty, but the evidence of careful studies supports the practitioners' views that Track II efforts have paved the way for Track I (Fisher, 2005). Analysing the impact of his workshops and other Israeli–Palestinian meetings on the pre-negotiations that led to the Oslo agreement, Kelman writes: 'the cumulative effect of this range of activities has helped to create a political atmosphere conducive to productive negotiations.' He continues, 'I am well aware that it is impossible to disentangle the impact of our own efforts from [the] array of unofficial activities at the elite and the grassroots levels.' He emphasizes that the impact of workshops is dependent on the political context. 'The parties' interests in the light of evolving realities were primarily responsible for persuading the leadership of the *necessity* of negotiating a historical compromise; and the interactions between the two sides were primarily responsible for persuading them of the *possibility* of such a compromise' (Kelman, 2005: 51, 55).

Track II mediators sometimes adapt their methods to the local culture, and can work usefully with one or several parties rather than with all. John-Paul Lederach, for example, found in his work in Central America that the parties look for *confianza* (trust) rather than neutrality in third parties, and that an 'insider-partial' would be more acceptable than impartial outsiders (Lederach, 1995; Wehr and Lederach, 1996).

The current trend in NGO interventions is away from entry into conflict situations by outsiders, towards training people inside the society in conflict in the skills of conflict resolution and combining these with indigenous traditions. We noted in chapter 2 how the constructions and reconstructions which took place in conflict resolution thinking in the direction of 'cosmopolitan conflict resolution' placed great stress on the need to bring into the discourse of conflict resolution the ideal of a global civic culture which was receptive and responsive to the voices often left out of the politics of international order. Thus Elise Boulding envisaged the evolution of a problem-solving *modus operandi* for civil society (Reading 12), and Curle (1971; Reading 40) and Lederach (1997, 2003, Reading 22) defined the priorities and modalities of indigenous empowerment and peacebuilding from below. Indeed, it is in the encounter with local traditions that important lessons about conflict resolution are being learned, particularly about the limitations of the dominant Euro-American model defined in chapter 2. In the study of the Arab Middle East, mentioned earlier, Paul Salem has noted a 'rich tradition of tribal conflict management [which] has thousands of years of experience and wisdom behind it' (1997: xi). Such perspectives are now beginning to emerge in contemporary understandings and practices of conflict resolution. Rupesinghe (1996) emphasizes the importance of building capacity to manage conflict within the affected society, a process which will necessarily involve the need for knowledge about the traditions of conflict management to which Salem referred. Kelman, Rothman and others draw on the wisdom of local cultures to stimulate creative dialogue and new thinking (Reading 47). Participants in their workshops have gone on to play significant decision-making roles in the Israeli–Palestinian peace process (Rothman, 1992; Kelman, 1997). Similarly, community relations organizations in Northern Ireland have built networks of people across the communities who are a long-term resource for peacebuilding, with the aim of influencing both the elites and grassroots opinion. The hope is that the encounter between conflict resolution ideas and social and political forces can subtly transform the context of conflict. Dugan's theory of nested conflict (1996; Reading 21) suggested how third parties can work at local and wider levels to make this happen. NGOs and civil society can also work towards structural transformation – for example, by helping to empower the weaker side (van der Merwe, 1989; Lederach, 1995; Curle, 1995).

Peacemakers develop their skills through working in such organizations and through experience on the ground. They can draw on the growing body of advice, training manuals, and accounts of mediation experiences. A number of simulation exercises are available for students to gain experience in negotiation (Rothman, 1992; Kumar, 2009). Training is also available for specific skills such as active listening and careful use of language by third parties (Readings 51 and 52).

UN mediation

Of course, international organizations and governments still play much the largest role in managing conflicts in the post-Cold War world. Martin (2006) provides an excellent account of recent high-profile mediation efforts. The UN secretary-general and his representatives exercise good offices in many parts of the world (Findlay, 1996) and made important contributions to the settlements in El Salvador, Cambodia, Mozambique and Namibia. Some remarkable people have taken up the baton on behalf of the UN, and their efforts are often very impressive: examples are Martti Ahtisaari for the EU and Jan Eliasson for the UN (Svensson and Wallensteen, 2010). States acting as the Group of Friends of the UN secretary-general also assist (Whitfield, 2007). The UN's legitimacy contributes to its special position, and its resolutions sometimes play a defining role in setting out principles for settlements (as in the case of Resolutions 242 and 338 in Palestine). It is true that the UN has also faced some dreadful failures in the post-Cold War world, including Bosnia, Rwanda and Somalia.[7] Nevertheless, as the instrument through which the international community arranges ceasefires, organizes peacekeeping, facilitates elections and monitors disengagement and demilitarization, the UN has an acknowledged corpus of knowledge and experience to bring to bear.[8] The UN has put some of this knowledge onto its 'UN Peacemaker' website, which is intended to assist both UN peacemakers and interested outsiders in the pursuit of peaceful settlements. To sharpen its effort, the UN established a Mediation Support Unit in 2006 and a mediation support standby team in 2008.

EU mediation

Regional organizations are playing an increasing role in mediation and are especially important in managing conflicts in their own region. We restrict ourselves here to a brief examination of the EU's role. The Lisbon Treaty stated the EU's aim of 'preserving peace, preventing conflicts from erupting into violence and strengthening international security', and its contribution over six decades 'to the advancement of peace and reconciliation, democracy and human rights in Europe' was recognized in 2012 by the award of the Nobel Prize for Peace. In the field of mediation, the 2009 'EU Concept on Strengthening Dialogue and Mediation Capacities' sets out the EU's definitions of mediation and dialogue.[9] It was followed in 2013 by the European Commission's 'Comprehensive Approach to External Conflicts and Crises'. This document urges early conflict prevention, a common conflict analysis, a common strategic vision, effective coordination of EU actors, and a long-term approach – perhaps points that have been difficult to achieve hitherto. The EU has a range of permanent officials who can take part in mediation efforts, from the High Representative and the European External Action Service (EEAS), which includes a specialist Mediation Support Team, to the EU Special Representatives and heads of EU delegation and missions. The EU also disposes of a wide range of funds and instruments for crisis management, conflict prevention and development cooperation. It funds not only its own actions but also those of the UN, other regional organizations and many NGOs. Among the peace agreements for which the EU can take credit are the Ohrid Agreement of 2001, between parties acting for the Albanian minority and the Macedonian government, and the Aceh Agreement of 2005. It is sometimes argued that the EU is more successful in distant parts of the world and that it tends to be more divided by different national interests in conflicts closer to home. Whitman and Wolff (2010, 2012) offer an assessment of its conflict management role.

Mediation by governments

Governments also play a prominent role as mediators. For example, Portugal (with the UN) facilitated the Bicesse Accord in Angola (Hampson, 1996: 87–127), the ASEAN countries took a leading role in Cambodia, and the United States mediated in Central America, Northern Ireland, India–Pakistan and elsewhere. The United States is often crucial, given its unique international position. But governments are not always willing to shoulder a mediating role when their national interests are not at stake, and, when they are, mediation readily blurs into traditional diplomacy and statecraft.

Any mediator changes the structure of a conflict. When governments bring coercion to bear, they become actors in the conflict. Forceful interventions clearly can bring forward war endings in some circumstances, as in the case of Bosnia. China, among others, helped equip the government of Sri Lanka in its ruthless crushing of Tamil armed resistance in 2009. The question is whether such interventions can lead to a stable ending of conflict, and whether imposed settlements stick.[10] We have discussed the dilemmas involved briefly both in the previous chapter and elsewhere (Ramsbotham and Woodhouse, 1996).

Multitrack diplomacy

We have discussed different levels and different tracks of mediation. Often different actors and tracks come together in complex ways as peace processes move backwards and forwards. The Northern Ireland case is a good example. It drew together a rich tapestry of public peace movements, private talks between political parties, and official and unofficial mediators. Mediation and back-channel negotiations were crucial at different times: the talks between the British and Irish governments that led to the Anglo-Irish Agreement, the back-channels through the Clonard monastery that led to the Hume–Adams talks, the secret contacts between the IRA and the British government over a ceasefire, the talks organized by US Senator George Mitchell over the peace agreement and those facilitated by the Canadian John de Chastelain over arms decommissioning. We can see examples of multitrack efforts in the case studies considered below, including the transition from majority rule in South Africa, the long and as yet unrewarded efforts to bring peace to Israel and Palestine, and recent efforts to deal with violence from criminal gangs in El Salvador.

The effectiveness of mediation

Mediation is an active and developing field of research. Wallensteen and Svensson (2014) offer a helpful summary of some of its findings. They claim that 'the overall body of literature that now exists on international mediation provides credible evidence of its effectiveness, although the particular conditions under which mediation is effective are still debated.' Definitions and measures of mediation success vary, and it is not yet entirely clear what kinds of strategies and styles are most likely to be effective in which circumstances. It is not easy to get a clear picture of the relationship between mediation attempts and peace agreements, either in an individual case or over a population of cases. Tracing a causal path from a particular effort to an outcome is difficult because of the complexity of conflicts, the multiplicity of mediation attempts, and the confidentiality that usually accompanies the attempts. There are endogenous effects to unravel: mediation attempts may influence the prospects of conflicts being settled, but conflicts in sight of settlement also attract mediation attempts, so mediation may be an effect as well as a cause of changes in the conflict. It is also difficult to reach clear criteria for effectiveness. There may be intermediate outcomes short of a peace agreement, such as a better understanding between the parties, which might suggest mediation has been effective even if it does not lead to a settlement. Conversely, if it is of only short duration, an agreement may be of little value. Three things need to happen for mediation to lead to a durable peace agreement. First of all, the parties have to accept the mediator. Second, they have to come to an agreement as a result of the mediation. Third, the agreement has to be durable. Achieving each of these stages is a measure of effectiveness. Different causal factors may be important at each stage. Even if all three are achieved, there is still the question of whether the agreement is fair and just and whether it leads to positive as well as negative peace. These are some of the complications with which mediation research has to wrestle.

We can give only some selective examples here of a burgeoning literature. One of the pioneers of research into international mediation was Jacob Bercovitch, who compiled the ICM dataset of international conflict mediation. Bercovitch and Gartner (2006) assessed the effectiveness of mediation attempts by individuals, states, and regional and international organizations by whether they resulted in failure, ceasefire, partial settlement or full settlement. They argue that international organizations (such as the UN) using directive strategies are more likely to achieve agreements in high-intensity conflicts, while regional organizations using procedural or facilitative strategies achieve better results in low-intensity conflicts. They also argue that mediation attempts build on one another and prepare the ground for subsequent efforts. Grieg and Diehl (2012: 147) show that 'the vast majority of conflicts remain unsettled after the first mediation, and require a string of multiple mediation attempts for settlement.' However, Beardsley (2011; Reading 44) argues that mediation tends to encourage short-term settlements that fail to resolve the underlying incompatibilities. Looking at the longer-term effects, there is some evidence that facilitative approaches are more likely to reduce post-crisis tensions and commitment problems, whereas coercive mediation is more likely to increase the probability of renewed fighting and manipulative strategies hinder long-term stability (Wallensteen and Svensson, 2014: 319).

In exploring the different incentives held by governments and insurgents for accepting invitation, Clayton (2013) found that stronger insurgent groups are more likely to force governments to accept mediation. Wilkenfeld et al. (2005) found that mediated international crises were twice as likely as crises without mediation to end in an agreed fashion, and Frazier and Dixon (2009) that negotiated settlements of militarized international disputes are six times more likely when third-party intermediaries are present than when the

disputants are left to themselves. Beber (2012) maintains that impartial mediators are more likely to forge settlements but less likely to be accepted as mediators. On the basis of his own dataset of post-Cold War mediation attempts in
intrastate wars, he argues, contrary to the view of Bercovitch and Gartner, that
unbiased mediators are likely to be more effective.

The statistical studies suggest that it is necessary to disaggregate conflicts
and look at different types and stages of mediation attempt. We still lack a
full picture of lower-profile Track II and Track III mediation efforts. The studies to date support the view that overall international mediation is beneficial
for reaching agreements but that a relationship with longer-term durable
resolutions of conflict is more difficult to establish. In general, it should not
be surprising that most mediation attempts in tough conflicts fail. What is
significant is that some of them succeed.

Peace Processes: Turning Points, Sticking Points and Spoilers

Conflict transformation may be gradual or abrupt; perhaps, more typically, a
series of rapid shifts are punctuated by longer periods of inertia and stalemate.
If this process is to go forward, the parties and third parties must identify an
acceptable formula for negotiation, commit themselves politically to a process of peaceful settlement, manage spoilers who seek to block the process,
and return after each setback to fresh mediation or negotiation.

This suggests that there is a range of appropriate actions and interventions
at different stages of the conflict, depending on the situation. If the parties are
not ready for mediation or negotiations, it may still be possible to support constituencies which favour peacemaking, to work for changes in actors' policies
and to influence the context that sustains the conflict. The international anti-
apartheid campaign, for example, gradually increased the pressure on international businesses involved in South Africa, to the point where sanctions and
disinvestment became a significant factor. External and internal parties can
contribute to the structural transformations which enable parties to break out
of asymmetrical relationships, by the process of raising awareness, gathering
external support and legitimacy, and creating more balanced relationships as
a prelude to negotiation and conflict resolution (see figure 1.12, p.31).

Once a peace process has begun, a dilemma arises as to whether the first
thing to do is to address the core issues in the conflict, which tend to be the
most difficult, or to concentrate on the peripheral issues in the hope of making
early agreements and establishing momentum. A step-by-step approach offers
the parties the opportunity to test each other's good faith and allows for
reciprocation (see box 7.3), in line with the finding from experimental studies of conflict and cooperation that small tension-reducing steps are easier to
sustain than one-off solutions in two-party conflicts (Osgood, 1962; Axelrod,
1984). Since durable and comprehensive agreements are difficult to establish

Box 7.3 Strategic dilemmas in peace processes

The obstacles to a peace process are almost always formidable. The parties to a violent conflict aim to win, and so they are locked in a process of strategic interaction which makes them acutely sensitive to prospects for gain and loss. Any concession that involves abandoning political ground, any withdrawal from a long-held position, is therefore resisted bitterly. This is reminiscent of aspects of Prisoner's Dilemma described in chapter 1.

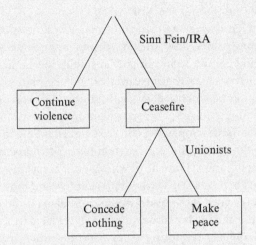

The strategic risks inherent in peacemaking can be illustrated in the tableau above, which is based on a simplified view of the Northern Ireland situation before the IRA ceasefire, but could apply to many other conflicts. Sinn Fein/IRA face a choice between declaring a ceasefire or continuing the violence. We assume they prefer a peace settlement to continuing the violence, but prefer to continue the violence than to stop if the Unionists hold out. The Unionists, too, we assume, prefer a settlement to a continuing conflict, but prefer holding out to settling. Sinn Fein/IRA have to choose first whether to cease fire, then the Northern Ireland Unionists choose between agreeing a settlement and holding out. Sinn Fein/IRA's dilemma is that if they declare a ceasefire the Unionists will continue to concede nothing; so the 'rational' strategy for the SF/IRA is to continue to fight.

The way out of this dilemma is for both parties to agree to move together to the option of peaceful settlement and so reach an option they each prefer to continued conflict. In order to do this, the parties have to create sufficient trust, or guarantees, that they will commit themselves to what they promise. For both sides, the risk that the other will renege is ever present. One way of making the commitment is for leaders on both sides to lock their personal political fortunes so strongly to one option that they could not go down the other path without resigning. (This is an equivalent of throwing away the steering wheel in the game of Chicken.) Another method is to divide the number of 'moves' available to the parties into many steps, so that both parties can have confidence that each is taking the agreed route. In real peace processes, confidence-building measures, agreement on procedures or a timetable for moving forward, and public commitments by leaders are among the methods of building and sustaining a peace process.

all at once, interim agreements are usually necessary in practice. They do need to address core issues, however, if the parties are to have confidence that the process can deliver an acceptable outcome. Interim agreements raise risks that, after obtaining concessions, parties may renege or refuse to reciprocate. Agreements that give the parties some incentive to stay in the process (for example, transitional power-sharing arrangements), that are supported by external guarantors and that mobilize domestic support are therefore more likely to succeed (Hampson, 1996; Sisk, 1997).

The fate of the Oslo agreement in the Israel–Palestine conflict illustrates that both 'turning points' and 'sticking points' are characteristic of peace processes. 'Turning points' occur not only at single ripe moments but at critical points when parties see a way forward through negotiations, by redefining their goals, opening new political space, finding a new basis for agreement, or because the conjunction of political leaders and circumstances are favourable. 'Sticking points' develop when elites are unfavourable to the process (as in Israel during the Netanyahu years), when parties to agreements defect (as in Angola, Cambodia and Sri Lanka), or when political space is closed or conditions are attached to negotiations which prevent forward movement. At turning points, the aim must be to find ways to capitalize on the momentum of agreement and the changed relationships that have led to it, building up the constituency of support, attempting to persuade the critics, and establishing a process with a clear goal and signposts to guide the way towards further agreements and to anticipate disputes. At sticking points, the aim is to find ways around the obstacles, drawing on internal and external support, establishing procedures and learning from the flaws of previous agreements.

As a negotiated agreement comes into sight, or after it has been negotiated, intra-party conflicts over the proposed settlement become very important. Lynch (2002) argues that 'sceptics', as well as 'spoilers', are crucially important. Sceptics are factions which reject the terms of the proposed settlement but are not against a settlement in principle. Spoilers are fundamentally opposed to any agreement and attempt to wreck it. Stedman (1997) suggests that sceptics may be managed by offering inducements and incentives to include them in the agreement or by being persuaded or socialized into acquiescing. Spoilers, he argues, have to be marginalized, rendered illegitimate or undermined. It may be necessary to accelerate a peace process – for example, by a 'departing train' strategy that sets a timetable on negotiations and hence limits the time for spoilers to work. In successful peace processes, the moderate parties come to defend the emerging agreement, and spoilers can even serve to consolidate a consensus in the middle ground.

Peace processes involve learning (and second-order learning), with the parties gradually discovering what they are prepared to accept and accommodate. Elements of an agreement may surface in early talks, but they may be insufficiently comprehensive, or sufficiently inclusive, to hold. They then fall apart; but the main principles and formulas of agreement remain, and can be refined or simplified, until a final agreement is devised. Negotiators and mediators learn from each other and from previous attempts and other peace processes.[11] Eventually they may reach fruition in a negotiated settlement; but even this is only a step, and not the last one, in the conflict resolution process.

Negotiations and Settlements

Negotiations have a fundamental importance in conflict resolution because they are the basic means by which parties search for peaceful settlements and aim to settle their differences. What types of negotiated outcome are likely to resolve protracted conflicts? It is difficult to generalize here, since different types of conflict are associated with different families of outcomes (Horowitz, 1985; Falkenmark, 1990; Montville, 1991; Miall, 1992: 131–63; McGarry and O'Leary, 1993; Sisk, 1997).

Negotiation processes are often slow and gradual. They start from pre-negotiations (Harris and Reilly, 1998: 59–68). Successive rounds of negotiations are typically punctuated by continuing conflict. Framing and reframing issues and changing parties' perceptions and understandings of the conflict and the potential outcomes are a crucial part of the process (Aggestam, 1999).

As regards outcomes of negotiations, we saw in chapter 1 how theorists distinguish *integrative* (or positive-sum) from *positional bargaining* (or zero-sum) approaches (Reading 46). Integrative approaches attempt to find ways, if not to reconcile the conflicting positions, then to meet the underlying interests, values or needs (Fisher and Ury, 1981; Galtung, 1984; Pruitt and Rubin, 1986; Burton, 1987). Examples of integrative approaches are setting the issue into a wider context or redefining the parties' interests in such a way that they can be made compatible, sharing sovereignty or access to the contested resource, increasing the size of the cake, offering compensation for concessions or trading concessions in other areas, and managing the contested resources on a functional rather than a territorial or sovereign basis. Positional bargaining divides a fixed cake, sometimes with compensations by linkage to other issues. In practice, negotiations combine both approaches. The aim is to find an outcome that neither will reject, but, even if there are outcomes that both prefer to the status quo, there is still room for a great deal of conflict over the outcomes.

Albin (1997) offers examples of several of these approaches in her study of options for settling the status of Jerusalem. Both Israelis and Palestinians agree that the city is indivisible, but the dispute over control remains at the core of their longstanding conflict. Both parties claim control over the holy places and the city as their capital. Proposals for settling the conflict have included suggestions for increasing the city boundaries of Jerusalem and dividing the enlarged area between the two states, each with a capital inside it (resource expansion), establishing decentralized boroughs within a Greater Jerusalem authority elected by proportional representation (no single authority: delegation of power to a lower level), Israeli sovereignty in return for Palestinian autonomy (compensation), dual capitals and shared access to the holy sites (joint sovereignty) or their internationalization, return to a federated one-state solution with Jerusalem as the joint capital (unification of actors), and transfer of control to a city authority representing both communities, but organized on functional rather than ethnic or national lines (functional division). In a later paper, Albin (2005; Reading 54) draws on these ideas in showing how Jerusalem became negotiable at the Camp David summit in 2000.

In ethnic conflicts, integrative solutions are especially elusive (Zartman, 1995b); nevertheless, consociationalism, federalism, autonomy, power-sharing, dispersal of power and electoral systems that give incentives to inter-ethnic coalitions all offer ways out of conflict in some circumstances (Lijphart, 1968; Horowitz, 1985: 597–600; Sisk, 1997; Tonge, 2014). When these are imposed, as in the Dayton Agreement, there may be an end to the violence but not to the underlying conflicts (Reading 55).

Good settlements should not only bridge the opposing interests but also represent norms and values that are public goods for the wider community in which the conflict is situated. Quite clearly, justice and fairness are crucial attributes for negotiations (Albin, 2001). At the same time, the criteria of justice are contested. In a more cosmopolitan world, outcomes are expected to meet wider criteria than those that might have been accepted in bargains between sovereign groups. For example, they should accord with international standards of human and minority rights (Bell, 2008).

Some negotiated settlements are more robust than others. Although generalization is treacherous, successful settlements are thought to have the following characteristics (Hampson, 1996: 217–21). First, they should include the affected parties, and the parties are more likely to accept them if they have been involved in the process that reaches them – this argues for inclusiveness and against imposed settlements. Second, they need to be well crafted and precise, especially as regards details over transitional arrangements – for example, demobilization assembly points, ceasefire details, voting rules. Third, they should offer a balance between clear commitments and flexibility. Fourth, they should offer incentives for parties to sustain the process and to participate in politics – for instance, through power-sharing rather than winner-take-all elections. Fifth, they should provide for dispute settlement, mediation and, if necessary, renegotiation in case of disagreement. And, sixth, they should deal with the core issues in the conflict and bring about a real transformation, incorporating norms and principles to which the parties subscribe, such as equity and democracy, and at the same time creating political space for further negotiations and political accommodation. To this cosmopolitan conflict resolution might add, seventh, that they should be consistent with cosmopolitan standards of human rights, justice and respect for individuals and groups.

Case Studies

We now turn to contrast two of the peace processes which have been central stories in post-Cold War conflict resolution. Their uneven progress and dramatic reversals offer insights into the difficulties encountered in ending protracted conflicts and the various kinds of transformations that shape their course.

First, South Africa: the transition from apartheid to multi-party elections there was one of the most remarkable cases of conflict resolution in the post-Cold War period. How did the white minority, which had been so determined to hold on to power, come to agree to majority rule? How was this extraordinary reversal in government achieved without a bloodbath?

Second, Israel–Palestine: when Israel's Prime Minister Yitzak Rabin shook the hand of PLO leader Yassir Arafat on 13 September 1993 to seal the signing of the Oslo Accords, it seemed that they were celebrating a historic breakthrough in the protracted conflict. The accords opened the way to a self-governing Palestinian authority, mutual recognition of Israel and the PLO, and final-status talks on other dividing issues. Yet the failure to implement the accords and Israel's continuing subordination of the Palestinians living in the occupied territories raise troubling questions about whether it was ever appropriate to attempt conflict resolution in the first place between such unequal parties.

South Africa: the transition to majority rule

The *structure* of the conflict lay in the incompatibility between the National Party (NP) government, which was determined to uphold white power and privileges through the apartheid system, and the black majority, which sought radical change and a non-racial, equal society based on one person, one vote. Transforming this conflict involved, first, the empowerment of the majority through political mobilization and the campaign of resistance against the apartheid laws. The revolt in the townships, political mobilization and movements such as Steve Biko's 'Black Consciousness' all expressed the refusal of the majority to acquiesce in a racially dominated society. Externally, the international pressure on the South African regime, through the anti-apartheid campaign, international isolation, sporting bans, partial sanctions and disinvestment, partly offset the internal imbalance of power.

Changes in the *context* cleared significant obstacles. While South Africa had been involved in wars in Southern Africa with Cuban-supported and Soviet-supplied regimes, it had been possible for white South Africans to believe that their regime was a bastion against international communist penetration and for the ANC to believe that a war of liberation based in the front-line states might eventually succeed. With the waning of the Cold War and changes in the region, these views became unsustainable. This separated the question of apartheid from ideological conflicts and concentrated the struggle in South Africa itself.

Another crucial contextual factor was economic change. It had been possible to run an agricultural and mining economy profitably with poorly paid black labour. But, as the economy diversified and modernized, a more educated and skilled labour force was necessary. The demands of the cities for labour created huge townships, such as Soweto, which became a focus for opposition to the regime. The more the government relied on repression to control the situation, the more exposed it became to international sanctions and disinvestment.

Significant changes of *actors* also made a crucial impact in the process of change. On the side of the National Party, the change in leadership from B. J. Vorster to P. W. Botha brought a shift from an unyielding defence of apartheid to a willingness to contemplate reform, so long as it preserved the power and privileges of the white minority. The change in leadership from Botha to F. W. de Klerk heralded a more radical reform policy and the willingness to abandon many aspects of apartheid. Changes at constituency level supported these shifts. For example, the businessmen in South Africa were among the first to see the need for a change in the policy of apartheid and took a leading role in maintaining contacts with the ANC at a time when the peace process seemed to have reached a sticking point – for example, in 1985–6. The bulk of the white population gradually came to accept the inevitability of a change, and this influenced the result of the 1988 elections and the referendum in favour of reform in March 1992. The split in the white majority in 1992 created an intra-party conflict between white extremists and the NP.

On the side of the black majority, the most important actor change was the split that developed between the ANC and Inkatha, starting in 1976 and growing gradually more serious, until it became a new source of internal armed conflict that threatened the peace process in 1992–4. It seemed that Inkatha and the white extremists might prevent a settlement, but in the end they helped to cement the alliance of the government and the ANC behind negotiated change. We return to this below.

With regard to the *issues*, both parties in the conflict made significant changes in their positions and goals (Zartman, 1995c). On the NP side, a series of shifts can be identified in the mid- and late 1980s. First there was Botha's shift from the defence of apartheid to the pursuit of limited reforms. He proposed a tricameral parliament which would include whites, Indian and coloured people, but exclude blacks. Botha also sought negotiations with Mandela, but Mandela refused to negotiate until he was released. The reforms failed in their intention to broaden the base of the government's support and led instead to intensified opposition in the townships. This resulted in the government's decision to declare the State of Emergency, which contributed in turn to further international pressure and disinvestment. By 1985 the process had reached a sticking point, with the government unwilling to make further reforms and the black population unwilling to accept the status quo.

It was at this point, with confrontation and no talks between the two sides, that third-party mediators made an important contribution.[12] A group of businessmen met with ANC leaders in Zambia and afterwards issued a call for political negotiations and the abandonment of apartheid. Botha made a new shift in September 1986, offering blacks resident outside the homelands a vote on township councils, but they were boycotted. Botha's reforms had stalled. By 1987–8 the situation had reached a second sticking point. The white electorate now showed that it was unhappy with the pace of change in the 1988 elections, and F. W. de Klerk's win in the election for the leadership of the NP brought a change of direction.

On the ANC side, too, there was change. Before 1985, the ANC saw itself as a national liberation movement and expected to establish a socialist government by seizing power after a successful armed struggle. By 1985 it had begun to accept that this goal was unrealistic and that a compromise was necessary.

A turning point came in 1989–90. De Klerk shifted decisively towards a policy of negotiations: he began to end segregation, lifted the ban on the ANC, and finally released Mandela on 11 February 1990. By the Groote Schuur Minute of May 1990, the government agreed to 'work toward lifting the state of emergency', while the ANC agreed to 'curb violence'. The ANC had now accepted that the NP would remain in power while negotiations were carried out, and the NP that it would have to give up its monopoly of power. The government's aim was now a power-sharing agreement, in which its future role in a multiracial government would be guaranteed. In February 1991 the parties took a further step towards each other's positions when the government agreed to tolerate the continued existence of an ANC militia force, and in return the ANC agreed not to activate it. The government released political prisoners in April 1991, and in September the parties signed the National Peace Accord, which set up a code of conduct for the security forces and mechanisms for dispute settlement during the course of negotiations. This was followed by the establishment of the Convention for a Democratic South Africa (CODESA), which agreed on a list of principles for a new constitution and set up working groups to formulate the details.

There was still a wide gulf between the parties' positions. The National Party sought to sustain white power by arriving at a federal constitution based on power-sharing, a bicameral parliament, proportional representation, protection of group rights and strong regional governments. The ANC, in contrast, wanted to see a short-lived interim government of national unity followed by elections based on one person, one vote, and a constitution based on individual rights and a centralized government. After further negotiations, the parties compromised on a Transitional Executive Council, which would oversee the government, and an elected constituent assembly, which would produce a new constitution. But they could not agree on the proportion of votes which would be required for a majority in the constituent assembly.

Meanwhile, the 'spoilers' were becoming active on both extremes. White extremists, who regarded the National Party's position as an unacceptable compromise, and the Inkatha Freedom Party, which feared that an ANC-dominated government would override the Zulu regional power base, found a shared interest in wrecking the negotiations. At first, their pressure caused a hardening of positions. After winning a referendum among the whites approving his conduct of the negotiations, de Klerk refused to make concessions on the voting issue. The ANC, facing escalating violence in the townships, which Inkatha was suspected of fomenting with the connivance of the police, decided to break off negotiations.

This was the third and most dangerous sticking point. Violence was rising and the threat of breakdown was clear. The ANC called a general strike and mass demonstrations. The police cracked down, and twenty-eight marchers were killed in Bisho, Ciskei, in September 1992. This disaster reminded both sides of the bloodbath that seemed likely if negotiations failed. Roelf Meyer, the minister of constitutional development, and Cyril Ramaphosa, the ANC's lead negotiator, continued to meet unofficially in hotel rooms as violence rose. In September 1992 the parties returned decisively to negotiations when de Klerk and Mandela agreed a 'Record of Understanding'. This spelt out the basis on which power would eventually be transferred: an interim, elected parliament to agree a new constitution and an interim power-sharing government of national unity, to be composed of parties winning more than 5 per cent of the vote, to last for five years. The ANC had shifted to accept power-sharing and a long transition; the National Party had shifted to accept that the continuation of white power would not be guaranteed. By now the NP was fearful of losing support to the right unless it acted quickly, and it stepped up progress, accepting a deadline for elections in April 1994. The Transitional Executive Council, set up in September 1993, gradually took on more and more of the key political functions of government, and the NP and the ANC found themselves jointly defending the settlement against Inkatha and the white extremists, who now supported a confederal alternative providing autonomy for the regions in which they lived.

The six months leading up to the elections were thus a struggle between the NP–ANC coalition and the spoilers, with the conduct of the elections as the prize. Inkatha left the Transitional Executive Council, and violence against ANC supporters in Natal intensified. Negotiations between the ANC and Chief Buthelezi, leader of the Inkatha Freedom Party, came to nothing, and Buthelezi prepared to exercise his threat of boycotting the elections. At the last moment the ANC offered King Goodwill of the Zulus a major concession over the trusteeship of land in Natal. Buthelezi's followers refused to follow him into the wilderness, and he was forced to accept a last-minute deal and participate in the elections. The elections thus proceeded legitimately and returned a parliament in which the ANC fell just below the two-thirds majority required to pass laws. Power-sharing would be a fact. Mandela became president of the government of national unity, with de Klerk and Buthelezi as ministers.

In the end, a process of negotiations and elections had replaced apartheid and white power (Waldmeier, 1998; R. Harvey, 2003). The legitimation of the black opposition had transformed the structure of the conflict, turning an asymmetrical relationship between minority and majority into a symmetrical relationship between parties and their followers. Though many tensions remained and real socio-economic transformation was slow to come, the elections conveyed 'participation, legitimation and allocation, the three elements necessary to the settlement of internal conflicts' (Zartman, 1995b: 339). The parties in South Africa had achieved an agreed and legitimate constitutional settlement in a situation so unfavourable that many observers had previously judged it to be impossible.

The Oslo Accords: the elusive search for peace in the Middle East

Of all the peace processes of the 1990s, the Israeli–Palestinian process has rightly gained the most attention. It is therefore important to review how the setbacks to the process reflect on the thinking and practice of conflict resolution. When the Oslo Accords were signed in 1993, it was widely believed that the Norwegian facilitation had brought about a breakthrough in the long conflict. But the provisions of the Oslo agreement were not put into effect, the key 'final status' issues of the conflict remained unresolved, the violent occupation of Gaza and the West Bank continued, and Palestinians retaliated with suicide bombs and rocket attacks. What had gone so wrong?

We will take two separate narratives of the peace process to illustrate the two views of the accords. According to the first, Oslo was indeed a breakthrough, but the prospects for conflict resolution were destroyed by spoilers on both sides and by the fundamental asymmetry of the parties. We shall rely here on accounts by Shlaim (2014) and Smith (2013) and analyses by Aggestam (1999), Galtung (2004) and Kriesberg (2001).

The second perspective is that, in the context of Israeli–Palestinian asymmetry, the attempt at conflict resolution was fundamentally flawed from the outset. As an example of this viewpoint we will quote Jones (1999: 130), who argues that the peace process became a means whereby 'a stronger party slowly and deliberately crushes the aspirations of the weaker party'. In Jones's view (ibid.: 160), the Oslo Accords, and the process that led to them, 'reproduce structures of inequality and domination', implying that conflict resolution in such contexts is fundamentally problematic.

In favour of the first perspective, it can be said that the back-channel approach made possible a breakthrough when the official diplomacy at Madrid was stalled. The Norwegian intervention was made in good faith, with the intention of reducing the suffering caused by the conflict. It opened the way to mutual recognition and a return of occupied territory to a Palestinian authority as a possible solution to the long conflict. The accords aimed to reconcile the needs of the two peoples to live side by side and to give autonomy in Gaza and Jericho as a first step towards what many Palestinians, Israelis and outsiders saw as the most realistic outcome, a two-state solution. Both parties agreed to resolve the major 'final status' issues in the conflict within three years. It was only through negotiation and exploration that the two sides could reframe their views of a conflict and create a new reality which opened the potential for a new relationship (Aggestam, 1999: 173).

In favour of the second perspective, the Oslo process was launched at a time when the PLO was weak and desperate and the Israeli government overwhelmingly strong. The outcome has been that the stronger party has crushed and humiliated the weaker, and the arrangements imposed by Israel have resulted in a dismembered and impoverished Palestinian entity, lacking not only statehood but even autonomy (Said, 2002). The denouement of this process was the construction of what the Arabs call 'the apartheid wall' and the criss-crossing of the West Bank by military roads and settlements.

Responsibility for the course that events took should not be laid at the door of the Norwegian facilitators. The 'spirit of Oslo' dissolved even before the accords were signed, as lawyers from the Israeli government hedged the agreement with restrictions and caveats (Corbin, 1994). Neither Rabin nor Peres was prepared at that time to accept a Palestinian state, and both lost opportunities to expedite the negotiations (Shlaim, 2014; Smith, 2013). Significant constituencies on both sides were opposed to the agreement. Violence on both sides followed the accords: the Hebron massacre, attacks by Hamas, and the assassination of Rabin. With the election of Netanyahu in 1996, the Israeli government turned decisively away from the Oslo process, stalling on implementation of the accords and accelerating the construction of settlements in the occupied territories.

It may be argued that an incremental process necessarily left the cards in the hands of the Israeli government and thereby exposed the weaker to the risk that the process would never proceed further. Nevertheless, subsequent developments suggested that a two-state solution was still a possibility. At the Camp David talks in 2000, Israeli Prime Minister Barak went further than any of his predecessors in appearing to accept Palestinian sovereignty over East Jerusalem and being willing to return some 90 to 95 per cent (a disputed figure) – but not all – of the West Bank to the Palestinians. There was a lively debate as to what had gone wrong (Agha and Mulley, 2001; Morris, 2002). The mainstream Israeli–US narrative blamed Yasser Arafat for failing to reach a settlement and for subsequently condoning the violent 'al-Aqsa Intifada' which the Israeli government had to repress (Ross, 2004). Needless to say, this view is in turn fiercely contested by Palestinians.

In October 2003, the unofficial Geneva Accords, between Beilin and other members of the Labour opposition and former Palestinian ministers, brought the Oslo process to an unofficial conclusion by agreeing a comprehensive settlement to the conflict. Under this peace plan, Israel would withdraw to the internationally recognized 1967 borders (save for a few territorial exchanges); Palestine would become a state. Jewish settlements, except those included in exchanges, would revert to Palestinian sovereignty; Jerusalem would be divided, with Palestinian sovereignty over Arab parts of East Jerusalem and the Temple Mount. In return, the Palestinian negotiators conceded the right of Palestinian refugees to return to their homes. It was a painful concession, abandoning a pillar of faith of the Palestinian struggle. Most Palestinians rejected the Geneva Accords on this account, while the Israeli government rejected the territorial proposals out of hand. Nevertheless, it was the closest that senior politicians on both sides have come to a full agreement.

In the following years, the conflict moved back to intractability. Between 2000 and 2008, the Bush administration viewed the conflict through the lens of the global war on terror, refusing to acknowledge Hamas's electoral success or Palestinian national unity, effectively freezing the status quo, despite the hesitant Road Map and Annapolis initiatives. Some progress was made in negotiations between the Olmert–Livni Kadima government in Israel and the new Palestinian leadership of President Mahmoud Abbas before the advent of a second Netanyahu government in Israel in 2010 rendered this once again impossible. Netanyahu did endorse the idea of a demilitarized Palestinian state in 2009 but, despite pressure from the Obama administration, refused to give up building new settlements. In 2013 Likud rejected a Palestinian state, and Netanyahu explicitly rejected the two-state solution in campaigning for the 2015 election. Meanwhile new settlement and new episodes of violence continued apace, the worst being the Gaza wars of 2008–9 and 2014. These brought about reconciliations between Hamas and Fatah and a wave of international sympathy for the Palestinians.

This chapter has indicated why a number of preconditions are required before a settlement is feasible. First, evidently, the Israeli government would have to agree it. External and internal changes are necessary for that to happen. A weakness of the conflict resolution attempts, arguably, has been their narrow basis. Only politicians from the Israeli Labour Party (and latterly Kadima) and the PLO have been able to come somewhere close to – but still some way from – a framework for an agreement. It will require changes of perspective and discourse for the Sephardic Jews and others who have supported Likud and the religious parties to accept a two-state solution, and also for Islamists on the Palestinian side to come to terms with a Jewish state.

This analysis highlights that conflict resolution often cannot be left to the conflict parties alone but must also address the wider regional and global context in which the conflict is situated. The two contrasting views we have discussed can only be reconciled if conflict resolution is seen to include conflict transformation. Following Etzioni's (1964) idea of encapsulated conflict, the conflict transformation process must reach out from the local level to the wider levels in which it is embedded. This is central to the whole idea of cosmopolitan conflict resolution, as developed in Part II of this book and advocated in Jones's idea of 'cosmopolitan mediation' (1999). To put the same thing in another way, the task of mediation is only a part of conflict resolution, broadly conceived. Overcoming the asymmetry of the conflict and changing its context is also essential. This may sometimes require advocacy and support for one side, as Curle and Francis suggest (see figures 1.9 and 1.12, pp. 28 and 31). People in the role of mediators should not be advocates, but mediation and advocacy are complementary. Peace and justice are indivisible and have to be pursued together (van der Merwe, 1989: 7).

Galtung (2004: 103–9) suggested that the conflict must be balanced by placing Israel and Palestine within a wider Middle Eastern community. Here the 2002 Arab Peace Initiative provided an initially promising regional context. Another way of balancing would be a change in the unconditional US economic, military and political support for Israel, which has been a lynchpin of the conflict. If the US came to believe that its wider position in the Middle East is threatened by Israeli policy, there could be a reduction in American support that might change Israeli calculations, perhaps opening the way to the type of agreement that has been under discussion in informal meetings for the last twenty years. This seems far off at present, and domestic US support for Israel remains strong, not only in the Jewish lobby but also in the religious right. But a change in international support for Israel, combined with a leadership change in the country, could transform the conflict. The precedent of disinvestment from South Africa is strong. The task of conflict resolution here goes beyond what facilitators and mediators can achieve and raises issues of how world society is to implement cosmopolitan standards of justice and human rights in a more even-handed way.

We will return to the question of the Israeli–Palestinian conflict in chapter 18. There we offer ideas on a new approach to the management of intractable conflict in the communicative sphere that works with, rather than against, the chief axes of radical disagreement and, thus, can keep open the possibility of communication across the conflict spectrum even during times of maximum intransigence, such as in the decade and a half that followed the collapse of the Oslo process in 2000–1. This suggests an alternative to most of the approaches described in this chapter and adds another string to the conflict resolution bow.

Peace agreements and organized crime – El Salvador and the gangland truce of 2012

Chapter 3 showed how it is only recently that attempts have been made to integrate statistics on organized crime into armed conflict statistics. What is less well appreciated is the extent to which there is also an overlap in terms of attempts to reduce and eventually eliminate violence in both cases. This can be seen by looking at efforts to bring about and then consolidate a 'gang truce' in El Salvador, despite major recent setbacks.

Social inequality, marginalization, violent political cultures, poor governance – familiar features from Edward Azar's analysis of protracted social conflict discussed in chapter 4 – have incubated an 'intractable' war between criminal gangs in El Salvador that in 2011 resulted in a homicide rate of 66 per 100,000 (with similar rates in neighbouring Honduras and Guatemala). The situation was exacerbated both by the failure to reintegrate a generation of fighters after the end of the civil war negotiated in the early 1990s and by repatriation to El Salvador of gang members who had been active in Los Angeles. It was also sustained by internationalized criminal networks. It is estimated that 10,000 members of the biggest gangs were in prison in appalling conditions (since 2004 segregated from each other), 60,000 were on the streets, and 400,000 were associated with the gangs as family members or friends – some 8 per cent of the national population of 6 million. In terms of Azar's 'process mechanics', gang violence had bred equally violent '*mano duro*' (firm hand) policies by the government (with majority popular support), leading to a self-reinforcing cycle of violence.

On 8 March 2012, with assistance from mediation by ex-guerrilla commander Raul Mijango, Roman Catholic clergy and some NGOs, the leaders of the two biggest gangs (*maras*), Mara Salvatrucha (MS-13) and Barrio 18, negotiated a truce while they were in prison. In April 156 homicides were registered, compared with the February total of 402. Over the next year the homicide rate was reduced to 59 per cent of what it had been previously.

The government could not admit to being party to these negotiations, but a Technical Coordinating Committee for the Reduction of Crime and Violence in El Salvador (CTC) was set up in September 2012 to coordinate efforts by mediators, representatives of the Ministry for Justice and Security, and internationals. Business leaders were associated with the process, and external bodies – the Organization of American States (OAS) (as a guarantor of the pacification process) and the Red Cross (which began monitoring prison conditions) – also became involved. An effort was made to convert a 'ceasefire' into a lasting settlement. This meant 'territorializing' the truce in the most violent municipalities – by January 2013, eleven of them had declared themselves 'violence free' – as well as backing this up with wider 'peacebuilding' measures in order to socialize the gang pacification effort, which implied the creation of collaborative local-level security and development policies negotiated in broader multi-stakeholder processes. This is reminiscent of the 'national dialogues' now being attempted in a number of countries wracked by intractable armed conflict, such as Burma/Myanmar (see chapter 10). In the words of Isabel Umana, Bernado de Leon and Ana Tager:

> Gang leaders' authority can only be sustained if their decisions deliver answers to the needs and aspirations of their brethren on the streets: freedom from aggression and

alternative livelihoods ... Stopping the killing would not transform the social and economic conditions that sustained the cycle of violence, but it created the political space in which alternatives to the failed securitized approach could be explored through a concerted effort with the participation of different stakeholders from state and society, including the gangs themselves. (2014: 98)

Unfortunately, in 2014 much of this seemed to be falling apart. After national elections in February 2014, the new president, Salvador Sanchez Ceren, declared that he would not 'make a truce with organized crime'. The attorney general began investigations into the role of some of the mediators. Above all, homicide rates rocketed upwards by 70 per cent, and by the middle of the year they seemed to be at much the same level as they had been before the 2012 truce. On the other hand, gang leaders called for the truce to be renewed, and the new security minister said that, so long as it is conducted transparently within the government's national security policy, there is no reason why gang leaders, including mediators such as Mijango, should not meet in penitentiaries for this purpose.

Whatever the outcome – and despite figures in 2015 suggesting that the death toll has risen to levels not seen since the end of the civil war in 1992 – the main point being made here is to confirm the conclusion of analysts such as Charles Tilly and Sydney Tarrow (2006) that the study of 'contentious politics' should include contestation between rival city gangs as well as more overtly politicized conflicts. Political conflicts often degenerate into organized crime, and organized crime often takes on political overtones.

Conclusion

We have identified the characteristics of a conflict resolution approach to ending conflicts, while acknowledging that in many contemporary conflicts such an approach is not applied. We argued that conflict resolution is more than a matter of mediating between parties and reaching an integrative agreement on the issues that divide them. It must also touch on the context of the conflict, the conflict structure, the intra-party as well as the inter-party divisions, and the broader system of society and governance within which the conflict is embedded. This is consonant with recent interest in analysing and responding to intractable conflicts as complex systems, as noted in chapters 2 and 4. It suggests that interventions should not be confined to the 'ripe moment'. Peace processes, we argued, are a complex succession of transformations punctuated by turning points and sticking points. At different stages, transformations in the context, the structure, the actors, the issues, and individual protagonists may be vital to move the conflict resolution process forward.

Even when settlements are reached, the best-engineered political arrangements can collapse again if the parties, their constituencies and external supporters do not breathe new life into them to make them work. For this reason, reconstruction and peacebuilding remain a constant priority, especially in the post-settlement phase. The next three chapters tackle the question of how settlements can be sustained without a return to fresh violence.

RECOMMENDED READING

Cochrane (2008), Crocker et al. (2015), Shlaim (2014), Stedman et al. (2002), Tonge (2014), Wallensteen (2011a).

RELEVANT EXTRACTS IN *THE CONTEMPORARY CONFLICT RESOLUTION READER*

Reading 12: E. Boulding, Building a Global Civic Culture: Education for an Interdependent World

Reading 21: M Dugan, A Nested Theory of Conflicts

Reading 22: J. P. Lederach, Building Peace: Sustainable Reconciliation in Divided Societies

Reading 39: P. Wallensteen, Understanding Conflict Resolution

Reading 40: A. Curle, Making Peace

Reading 42: D. Pruitt, Readiness Theory and the Northern Ireland Conflict

Reading 43: F. Hampson, Why Orphaned Peace Settlements are More Prone to Failure

Reading 44: K. Beardsley, The Mediation Dilemma

Reading 46: R. Fisher and W. Ury, Getting to Yes: Negotiating Agreement without Giving In

Reading 47: J. Rothman, From Identity-Based Conflict to Identity-Based Cooperation

Reading 48: M. Fitzduff, Approaches to Community Relations Work

Reading 49: A, Curle, Peacemaking Public and Private

Reading 51: Mediation UK, Training Manual in Community Mediation Skills

Reading 52: Use of Language by Mediators: Exercises

Reading 54: C. Albin, Explaining Conflict Transformation: How Jerusalem Became Negotiable

Reading 55: The Dayton Agreement

Reading 56: Northern Ireland Documents

Reading 62: R. Fisher and L. Keashly, The Potential Complementarity of Mediation and Consultation within a Contingency Model of Third-Party Mediation

Reading 63: International Alert, Code of Conduct for Conflict Transformation

CHAPTER EIGHT

Postwar Reconstruction

This chapter and the next consider the contribution that the conflict resolution field can make to postwar reconstruction and peacebuilding at the fragile stage when war ends but peace is not yet secure.

> When wars have ended, post-conflict peacebuilding is vital. The UN has often devoted too little attention and too few resources to this critical challenge. Successful peacebuilding requires the deployment of peacekeepers with the right mandates and sufficient capacity to deter would-be spoilers; funds for demobilization and disarmament built into peace-keeping budgets; a new trust fund to fill critical gaps in rehabilitation and reintegration of combatants, as well as other early reconstruction tasks; and a focus on building State institutions and capacity, especially in the rule of law sector. Doing this job successfully should be a core function of the United Nations. (UN High-Level Panel, 2004)

Astrid Suhrke and Ingrid Samset (2007) estimate from post-Cold War evidence that there is a 25 per cent likelihood of a 'recurrence of civil war' following negotiated agreements. Many argue that this figure would be considerably higher were it not for the efforts of postwar peace operations (Fortna, 2008). This chapter presents an account of the remarkable attempt by the international community in the post-Cold War era to underpin postwar peace processes globally by the wholesale institution of what is now usually known as the 'liberal peace' – sometimes identified with a political UN 'New York consensus' to set beside the 'Washington consensus' in the economic sphere. Liberal interventionism is made up of a set of assumptions well summarized by Roland Paris nearly twenty years ago:

> The central tenet of this paradigm is the assumption that the surest foundation for peace ... is market democracy, that is, a liberal domestic polity and a market-oriented economy ... Peacebuilding is in effect an enormous experiment that involves transplanting western models of social, political, and economic organization into war-shattered states in order to control civil conflict: in other words, pacification through political and economic liberalization. (1997: 56)

Since then these assumptions have been tested out in the field with mixed results, severely criticized, and to some extent adapted – but by no means abandoned. They still represent the core thinking behind most postwar peace operations in the middle of the second decade of the twenty-first century – although signs of resistance from the growing influence of China and Russia may call this into question in future, as discussed in chapters 11, 19 and 20. This chapter offers an overall analysis of this ongoing enterprise and of current controversy about it from a conflict resolution perspective. By the end of the chapter a general conflict resolution response should become clear, and this can then be carried through into chapter 9 to be developed further within a broader peacebuilding framework.

In view of current discussions it may be useful at the outset to distinguish between *peacebuilding*, *nationbuilding* and *statebuilding*, although these concepts are not clearly and consistently differentiated in the literature. Peacebuilding, as already defined earlier in this book, is the broadest of these terms and comes from the peace research and conflict resolution tradition. It is most succinctly characterized as the project of overcoming structural and cultural violence (conflict transformation), in conjunction with peacemaking between conflict parties (conflict settlement) and peacekeeping (conflict containment). This will be further developed and deepened in chapter 9. The term 'nationbuilding' has an intermediate range of reference, and it was widely used during the period of decolonization to refer mainly to the enterprise of forging national identity out of the diverse populations that made up many of the newer states so that citizenship would transcend subordinate loyalties. Statebuilding – a central concept for this chapter – has the narrowest range and refers to the attempt to (re)build self-sustaining institutions of governance capable of delivering the essential public goods required to underpin perceived legitimacy and what it is hoped will eventually become an enduring peace:

> One of the most important macro-level shifts in peacebuilding strategy occurred in the late 1990s and early 2000s, when major peacebuilding agencies began emphasizing the construction or strengthening of legitimate governmental institutions in countries emerging from civil war, or what we call 'statebuilding' in this book. Statebuilding is a particular approach to peacebuilding, premised on the recognition that achieving security and development in societies emerging from civil war partly depends on the existence of capable, autonomous and legitimate governmental institutions. (Paris and Sisk, 2009: 1–2)

Since then the concept has widened further in line with the 'merging of datasets' described in chapter 3, where 'fragile states and cities' in general, and the challenge from international terrorism and international crime in particular, are seen to require international support, not just cases where countries are emerging from civil war. The term sometimes used here is 'stabilization'. Stabilization missions were not specifically referred to in the UN Capstone Doctrine (UNDPKO, 2007; see also chapter 6) or in *A New Partnership Agenda: Charting a New Horizon for UN Peacekeeping* (UNDPKO and DFS, 2009). But, according to Robert Muggah, co-founder of the journal *Stability: International Journal of Security and Development*: 'Stabilization is catching on in security and development circles. It is the object of growing attention among military practitioners in particular, and US-led stability operations are currently going on in at least 50 fragile settings, especially in the Americas, Africa and the Middle East' (Muggah, 2014: 1). As yet, Muggah notes, 'although expanding in number and scale, the conceptual and operational parameters of these stabilization interventions are still opaque' and 'their actual record of success is still only dimly understood'. We return to the controversy about such missions later in this chapter.

All of this is contrasted with the earlier generation of peace operations (what in chapter 6 we called 'second-generation' peace operations), which 'tended to rely on quick fixes, such as rapid elections and bursts of economic privatization, while paying too little attention to constructing the institutional foundations for functioning post-war governments and markets' (Paris and Sisk, 2009: 2). One influential version of this change of strategy summed up the idea that constructing effective and legitimate governmental institutions should sometimes precede an otherwise premature introduction of market democracy in the phrase 'institutionalisation before liberalisation' (Paris, 2004). Paris and Sisk quote Lakhdar Brahimi in support:

> The concept of statebuilding is becoming more and more accepted within the international community and is actually far more apt as a description of exactly what it is that we should be trying to do in post-conflict countries – building effective systems and institutions of government. Indeed, acceptance of statebuilding as a generic term to describe our activities will help to concentrate international support on those very activities. (Brahimi, 2007:5)

From a conflict resolution perspective this is in itself a welcome development that in no way precludes a concomitant focus on wider aspects of peacebuilding as clarified in chapter 9. After all, as seen in chapter 4, in the 1980s John Burton and Edward Azar precisely located the focal point of their efforts to address deep-rooted conflict and protracted social conflict on the requirement to build effective and legitimate institutions and practices of governance that meet basic human needs. What is not welcome, however, is when the intervention is not driven primarily by the interests of the citizens of those countries but by the security interests of the interveners – for example, in pre-empting 'safe havens' for international crime and terrorism as part of a 'global war on terror'. We do not deny that this may be a separate consideration, but it cannot drive genuine peace operations. We will return to the question of vulnerable or fragile states and the question of response to terror in chapter 11, because these issues are more extensive than the specific challenge of postwar reconstruction looked at in this chapter.

Postwar statebuilding is considered from a conflict resolution perspective in this chapter, and the wider dimensions of postwar peacebuilding are discussed in chapter 9.

Postwar Peace Operations

Postwar reconstruction in the defeated Axis powers was carried out by the occupation forces following their outright victory at the end of the Second World War. Having disarmed their former enemies, the occupying forces installed new governments with democratic constitutions, supported physical and economic reconstruction, and gradually handed power to new indigenous governments. It is worth remembering this, because it represents the original prototype for the whole idea of liberal interventionism as a foundation for future peace and, in particular, was seen by planners in the US Department of Defense as the model for their postwar reconstruction of Iraq after 2003. According to this logic, after 1945 Germany and Japan were transformed from fomenters of war into bastions of peace – and principles of the liberal peace were given the credit (Reader 58).

In the first edition of this book, written at the end of the 1990s, the title of this chapter was 'post-settlement peacebuilding', and the dataset was made up of UN missions in Namibia (UNTAG), Angola (UNAVEM), El Salvador (ONUSAL), Cambodia (UNTAC) and Mozambique (ONUMOZ), all instituted between 1988 and 1992, together with the more complex division of labour in the management of the intervention in post-1995 Bosnia. In the second edition of the book, in response to the evolution of 'third-generation' missions in the wake of disillusionment in Somalia, Bosnia (UNPROFOR) and Rwanda (see chapter 6), and further complicated by the post-2001 'global war on terror', we changed the chapter title to 'postwar reconstruction' (despite what in some quarters are seen as the more directive and less transformational connotations of this term) and, equally controversially, widened the dataset to include interventions in countries where there had not been overt civil war (for example, Haiti) and in countries where intervention had been forcible (for example, Afghanistan, Iraq). The reason for doing this was to focus on the broad challenge of postwar reconstruction in general, no matter what the nature of the preceding war. What all these cases had in common was that they were major interventions (thus excluding operations with smaller numbers of military personnel) and that they were 'intervention–reconstruction–withdrawal' (IRW) operations. In each instance the declared aim was to *intervene*, in most cases in order to aid indigenous efforts to build an enduring postwar peace, to assist *(re)construction* efforts, and then to *withdraw*. We followed the same line of reasoning in the third edition of the book. Nearly all the missions listed in table 8.1 are still post-civil war peacebuilding operations. The inclusion of Iraq does not suggest that the invasion had anything to do with conflict resolution, nor does it say anything about whether the war was justified (in our view it was not). But lessons learned from the remarkable failure to understand or plan properly for postwar reconstruction in Iraq, and the subsequent belated attempts at adjustment, are important components in any comprehensive survey of the challenges of postwar peacebuilding.[1]

In this fourth edition of the book we have decided to leave table 8.1 as it was – running up to 2009 – because that accurately sets out the relatively distinct types of major intervention practised up to that time. Since then the situation has become more complicated in the wake of the Arab revolutions, the emergence of cross-border *jihadist* extremism in West and East Africa, the unravelling of what was meant to be the postwar withdrawal from Iraq, and continuing uncertainty in Afghanistan – as well as the merging of attempts to counter state fragility and combat international crime with postwar peacebuilding in some cases. In Libya, external intervention secured 'regime change' but was (rightly or wrongly) not accompanied by an IRW operation. In Latin America, site for a number of key IRW operations in the 1990s, external intervention on that scale is now rare. For example, the fitful peace process in Colombia, given a boost by the narrow re-election of President Santos in the June 2014 vote, is seen to have entered a critical phase (memories of the ultimately unsuccessful peace efforts in 1999–2002 are still fresh). The National Liberation Army (ELN) is undertaking separate talks to parallel those with the Revolutionary Armed Forces of Colombia's People's Army (FARC-EP). But, in answer to the question whether UN peacekeepers should now be deployed, Senator-Elect Claudia Lopez sums up why IRW missions, as used in the past, are no longer seen to be appropriate – even though the centrality of 'statebuilding' remains paramount:

> I hope that's not the path we are going to take. My message to the international community is: peace in Colombia is to build a state, civil society, and legal markets for people to work. That's what peacebuilding means in a country like Colombia. We have the problems we have because we don't have state presence and state ability to rule in at least half the territory of Colombia. And at least a third of the population of Colombia lives every day under the rule of no law or under the rule of criminal groups, whether the FARC, ELN or the BACRIMs [paramilitary criminal gangs]. Actually, the challenge for us in peacebuilding is to do statebuilding, and to do it properly, and to do it with the people, and with different localities at the regional level. Instead of United Nations Peacekeepers, what we need to strengthen is the Colombian national police and deploy it in rural areas so that they can offer rule of law with judges and attorneys-general, and all the things we don't have at this moment in half the country. It's a statebuilding perspective rather than any other perspective that should be supported in Colombia. (Lupel, 2014: 3)

So, because our focus in this chapter is primarily on external interventions, we do not want to suggest that external interveners are or should be the prime actors involved in determining outcomes. The internal actors and domestic constituencies are almost always the more important. But it is a feature of modern armed conflict that the devastation is often so great and the civil population's need for support is so pressing that external support for reconstruction is often badly needed (though this is not always the primary motive for outsiders to intervene). Whether interventions turn out to be in the interests of the civil population or not is a matter for investigation. In what follows we wish to assess what types of external intervention are helpful and what types are unhelpful from a conflict resolution perspective, recognizing that, as conflict persists in the postwar phase, so too must efforts at conflict resolution. We will conclude that the effectiveness of postwar reconstruction and peacebuilding in contributing to conflict resolution depends heavily on its legitimacy in the eyes of the domestic population.

Intervention–Reconstruction–Withdrawal Operations, 1989–2014

The 1978 Settlement Proposal in Namibia, devised by the Contact Group of western states, mandated the United Nations Transition Assistance Group (UNTAG) under Security Council Resolution 435 to assist a special representative appointed by the UN secretary-general 'to ensure the early independence of Namibia through free and fair elections under the supervision and control of the United Nations' (Ramsbotham and Woodhouse, 1999b: 167–72). The transition phase was to last a year. This unexceptional decolonization arrangement unexpectedly turned out to be the template for international postwar intervention and reconstruction programmes when it was revived ten years later, in 1988–9, in very different circumstances. The ending of the Cold War drew a line under what had been an almost automatic backing of rival sides and regimes by the superpowers and opened up the possibility of concerted external action to end debilitating wars or overthrow repressive and dangerous regimes, and subsequently help to create or rebuild domestic political capacity to the point where power could be safely handed back to a viable and internationally acceptable indigenous authority in the host country.

This remarkable era in world politics has unfolded in two main phases so far (see chapter 6). First came the period between the Namibia Accords and the Dayton Agreement in Bosnia (1995), in which it seemed to suit the major powers to encourage the United Nations to assume a lead coordinating role (this was the theme of the first edition of this book). This has been followed by a period in which, in different permutations, the norm has become one of multilateral coalitions under a lead nation or nations, supported by regional alliances or organizations, international financial institutions such as the G8, and a number of relief and development bodies, with the United Nations and its agencies playing a variety of more or less central or peripheral roles. What has been characteristic of both periods has been that the shape of intervention policy has been decided by the politically and militarily more powerful states. This is natural – strong states intervene in weak states, not vice versa – which is why some commentators are opposed to the entire enterprise, a point to be considered later.

In addition to changes over time, it is worth noting differences in the initial conditions and functions of IRW peace operations, particularly as articulated in mission mandates, because the context is often highly influential in setting the parameters for expected results – or should be. Initial declared functions often overlap, are the result of political compromise, and may subsequently alter as the operation proceeds. Nevertheless, they play a more significant role in determining the scope and outcome of peace operations than is often acknowledged.

Six different initial contextual functions for peace operations can usefully be distinguished during the twenty-year period 1989–2009 (see table 8.1).

Table 8.1 IRW operations, 1989–2009

	(a) Independence	(b) Democracy	(c) Peace support	(d) Humanitarian	(e) Defence/ regime change
1989	Namibia		Nicaragua[1]		
1991			Angola El Salvador[1]		
1992			Cambodia Mozambique	(Bosnia (UNPROFOR))[2] (Somalia (UNITAF))[2]	
1993			Rwanda		
1994		Haiti	Guatemala[1]		
1995			Bosnia (IFOR/ SFOR)		
1999	East Timor	Sierra Leone[3]		Kosovo	
2002					Afghanistan
2003			DRC (Zaire)[1] Liberia		Iraq
2004		Haiti	Burundi, Côte d'Ivoire	Sudan (Darfur)?	
2005			Sudan (South)		
2007				Sudan (Darfur)	

1　The mandate of the UN Observer Group in Central America (ONUCA) in Nicaragua and Honduras was initially to verify an interstate non-intervention agreement. It was subsequently expanded to take on something of an IRW role. The UN Observer Mission in El Salvador (ONUSAL) was established in 1991 to verify human rights agreements. It was expanded after the January 1992 peace agreement to take on a full IRW role. The UN Verification Mission in Guatemala (MINUGUA) was deployed for human rights verification and trust-building from 1994, then its mandate was expanded in 1997 to include verification of wider peace agreements. Initiated by the July 1999 Lusaka agreement, full-scale IRW operations did not effectively begin in the Democratic Republic of the Congo until 2003.

2　Neither Bosnia 1992–5 nor Somalia 1992–5 is an IRW operation, although they are included in parentheses here because they are often cited as such. Attempts to broker peace during the UN Protection Force (UNPROFOR) period in Bosnia proved abortive, while the UN Operation in Somalia (UNOSOM II) from May 1993 can be seen as a proto-IRW mission, but continued fighting precluded postwar reconstruction. The same applies to the interventions of the Military Observer Group of ECOWAS (ECOMOG) in Liberia from 1990 to 1996, much discussed in the humanitarian intervention literature, despite a UN presence after the abortive 1993 Cotonou agreement. The implementation of the 1996 Abuja II agreement through to the election of Charles Taylor in July 1997 is similarly not included, because it is better seen as an extension of Taylor's bid for power. Liberia truly enters IRW territory from 2003 after the negotiated abdication of Taylor under category (c).

3　Despite successful democratic elections in Sierra Leone in 1996, it was not until February 2000 that international efforts to restore elected President Kabbah evolved into a full IRW mission with the expansion of the October 1999 UN Mission in Sierra Leone (UNAMSIL). The 1994 IRW restoration of elected President Aristide in Haiti was initially seen as successful, with further elections following in 1995. The subsequent unravelling of the IRW effort, particularly in the wake of disputed elections in 2000, eventually triggered a new IRW attempt in 2004.

- *Interposition and monitoring operations* are traditional 'first-generation' functions, some of which, such as UNDOF (Israel–Syria), survive from the Cold War period. A more recent example was UNMEE (2000–8), tasked with monitoring cessation of hostilities in the Ethiopia–Eritrea conflict. UNIFIL (Lebanon) changed character after the 2006 Israel–Hezbollah war and was seen by some as a prototype for possible future interposition and monitoring missions in the region. These missions are not included in table 8.1 because they do not encompass postwar reconstruction and are not therefore IRW operations.
- *Decolonization operations* are mounted to assist the transition to self-rule after wars of national liberation (Namibia, East Timor (Timor Leste)). Here the fact that the 'colonial' power (South Africa, Indonesia) had already agreed withdrawal evidently made the task of the interveners easier.
- *Democracy restoration operations* are tasked to defend an already existing democracy or restore an ousted democratically elected leader (Haiti, Sierra Leone). Although resistance from the usurper is likely to be strong, the existence of an already elected alternative again makes prospects better so long as this is generally seen to have been legitimate ('free and fair elections').
- *Peace support operations* are interventions to help manage the transition from war to peace after a ceasefire or some form of already agreed peace arrangement (Cambodia, El Salvador, Mozambique, Burundi). This is the *locus classicus* for peace operations – indeed, sometimes conflated with peace operations in general. A prior peace agreement again greatly increases chances of success; however, since making peace between undefeated conflict parties in civil wars does not end the conflict but merely transmutes it into intense political rivalry, the post-agreement period is often the most dangerous. The collapse of agreements in Angola and Rwanda in the 1990s subsequently engulfed the peace operations intended to support them (UNAVEM II, UNAMIR). This is where lessons about postwar international intervention did indeed need to be learned – and to a considerable extent have been.
- *Humanitarian intervention operations*, unlike during the Cold War period, when they were directed mainly against over-powerful tyrants (for example, Idi Amin's Uganda), were usually interventions in ongoing internal conflicts or civil wars, initially driven principally by concern for the welfare of civilian populations (Bosnia, 1992–5; Somalia, 1992–5) – although tyrannous abuse is often still associated with them, as in Kosovo (1999) and Darfur (2007). (There are also humanitarian interventions that are not peace operations, such as Operation Provide Comfort in Iraq after 1991.) This contextual function should be clearly distinguished from peace support operations commented on above. Failure to make this distinction led to the 'wrong lessons' being learned from debacles in Bosnia (the massacre in Srebrenica) and Somalia (the deaths of eighteen US rangers). UN peace

support operations in general were wrongly implicated in the failure of what were not peace support operations. Conversely, when as a result no action was subsequently taken by the most powerful members of the Security Council in the first weeks of the Rwanda genocide (1994), it was again UN peace operations in general that were mistakenly discredited.

- *Regime change operations* are explicit attempts to topple existing governments seen to threaten international peace and security, and in particular the national interests of the most powerful interveners (Afghanistan, 2001; Iraq, 2003). Here came another major shift in contextual functions as international peace operations were co-opted into the war against terror. Weak or failed states were also seen as actual or potential havens for terrorism (US Office of the President, 2002), and US defence and foreign policy requirements expanded to encompass forcible democratization and 'nationbuilding' as a national security priority: 'stability, security, transition and reconstruction (SSTR) operations' became a 'core US military mission' (USDOD, 2005).

There is no suggestion that these are watertight distinctions. But it is helpful to bear them in mind when it comes to the question of assessing the success and effectiveness of peace operations, as indicated below.

For the period 2010–14, we have commented above on the way in which former distinctions between IRW operations have now been blurred. For example, the as yet unclarified designation 'UN stabilization mission' covers a number of hybrid operations, such as the UN Organization Stabilization Mission in the Democratic Republic of Congo (MONUSCO) of 2010, strengthened by an 'intervention brigade' in 2013; the UN Multidimensional Integrated Stabilization Mission in Mali (MINUSMA) in 2013 (see chapter 6); and the Multidimensional Integrated Stabilization Mission in the Central African Republic (MINUSCA) in 2014. Earlier missions, such as the Stabilization Mission in Haiti (MINUSTAH) of 2004 have also been renewed. The composite nature of some of these mandates can be indicated by that of MINUSCA, which has been tasked to protect civilians, support implementation of the transition process in extending state authority and preserving territorial integrity, facilitate delivery of humanitarian assistance, protect UN personnel, promote human rights, support international justice and the rule of law, disarm, demobilize and reintegrate forces, repatriate refugees, support security-sector reform and police, etc. (UNDPKO, 2015b). Stabilization missions are regularly tasked to manage or remove an aggressor and are sometimes described as 'late peacekeeping' or 'early peacebuilding' (Muggah, 2014: 2).

With reference to table 8.1, it is highly significant from a conflict resolution perspective that the perceived legitimacy of interventions among host populations can be seen to decrease concomitantly in general terms as we move progressively from decolonization operations to regime change operations, and that this has a major effect on both the scale of the challenge and the prospects for success. This is surprisingly rarely taken into account in evaluations of postwar peace operations.

Finally, we can also now see that none of these cases approximates to the post-1945 context of total defeat and unconditional surrender after a classic interstate war as in Germany and Japan, despite initial US delusions to the contrary. In 1945 the political conflicts were decided on the battlefield and were emphatically over before reconstruction began. This is not the situation in most of the cases considered here. Despite common parlance, these are precisely not 'post-conflict' contexts, as will be elaborated below. Nor is this an accidental feature, but is part of the transformation in the nature of major armed conflict in the latter part of the twentieth and the first part of the twenty-first century. It is also the difference between, say, the Northern Ireland peace process, involving the accommodation of undefeated conflictants, and the peace process in South Africa, where the outcome of the main conflict had already been decided by the irrevocable defeat of apartheid. This does much to explain why, despite the much greater long-term difficulties facing the reconstruction process in South Africa, it was the Northern Ireland peace process that seemed to encounter the greater initial problems.

Filling the Postwar Planning Gap

Another important point about the 1989–2014 postwar reconstruction experience from a conflict resolution perspective is the fact that no one operating model can fit the needs and complexities of each country's situation. The crucial negotiations are ultimately those between domestic parties, their constituencies and the affected populations, but these are not always well supported by conflict-sensitive external policies – as noted in the Somalia case study in chapter 6. The United Nations has lacked adequate capacity in this area, and nationally organized interventions tend to be strongly influenced by the national priorities and short-term political interests of the intervening states. There are extensive institutional bases and planning structures for relief and disaster work at one end of the spectrum and for longer-term international development at the other end of the spectrum, both within national administrations and within international organizations, including the United Nations. But when the international community first plunged into large-scale postwar intervention, reconstruction and withdrawal missions, there was at first nothing much in between, which is exactly where the requirements for support for reconstruction and peacebuilding were located. Previous European imperial colonial offices had been closed down, and the UN Trusteeship Council had been effectively mothballed (the General Assembly agreed to formalize this at the 2005 World Summit). In the UN secretary-general's words, this left 'a gaping hole in the United Nations institutional machinery' with respect to 'the challenge of helping countries with the transition from war to lasting peace' (Annan, 2005, § 114; see also Chesterman, 2004).

At national level, one of the main catalysts for filling this gap was the catastrophic failure of postwar reconstruction efforts in Iraq from 2003. Most responses were ad hoc, such as the UK Post-Conflict Reconstruction Unit (PCRU) set up to coordinate the efforts of the Foreign and Commonwealth Office (FCO), Ministry of Defence (MOD) and Department for International Development (DFID) (it was indicative that before the Iraq invasion this had been attempted only in the area of conflict prevention – see chapter 5). In 2010, a 1,000-strong Civilian Stabilization Group of experts (800 civilians, 200 civil servants) funded from the FCO, MOD and DFID was announced to respond to the demands both of conflict zones and of natural disasters. In the US at first, the incoming Bush administration had torn up the Clinton Presidential Decision Directive (PDD) 56 on Interagency Planning for Complex Contingencies, and there was a reluctance to think that anything could be learned from previous UN experience in postwar reconstruction – hence the startling inadequacy of the original Office for Reconstruction and Humanitarian Assistance (ORHA) in Iraq in 2003, run from the Pentagon and almost immediately abandoned. Thereafter at first a Joint Interagency Cooperation Group (JIACG) attempted coordination, although the vast discrepancy in planning capacity between the military planning resources of the Department of Defense (USDOD), with a total personnel of nearly 1.3 million, and those of the Agency for International Development (USAID), with a personnel of 1,000, made this difficult. A new Office of the Coordinator for Reconstruction and Stabilization was subsequently set up in August 2004, with a brief to draw up 'post-conflict' plans for up to twenty-five countries seen to be at risk and a capacity to coordinate three reconstruction operations 'at the same time', each lasting 'five to seven years'. This was linked to control of the World Bank, whose investment in 'post-conflict' countries rose from 16 per cent of its lending in 1998 to between 20 and 25 per cent ten years later. From a conflict resolution perspective, many were alarmed at the prospect of such grandiose national plans to reshape 'the very social fabric' of target countries, associated as they were with great power interests, including huge potential contracts for western (and in particular US) businesses (Klein, 2005).

At international level, strenuous efforts have also been made to fill the 'peacebuilding gap', reaching from efforts within the UN Department for Peacekeeping Operations (DPKO) to integrate field operations and to clarify the role of peacekeeping during the stabilization phase in peace operations via the new capstone doctrine, as discussed in chapter 6, through to the setting up of a new UN Peace Building Commission (PBC), recommended in the High Level Panel report on Threats, Challenges and Change (UN High-Level Panel, 2004) and endorsed at the 2005 World Summit (UNGA, 2005: § 97), to be discussed further in chapter 9.

For Alex Bellamy and Paul Williams, it was 'too early to make definitive judgements about the extent to which the PBC ... [has] improved the UN's capacity for assisting the transition to self-sustaining stable peace', but it is seen to have the potential to increase support for existing long-term missions, which are at the moment 'woefully under-resourced', and to bridge the gap between the security focus of the UN Security Council and the economic focus of the World Bank (Bellamy and Williams, 2010: 253–4). Roland Paris (2009) sees value in country-specific meetings sponsored by the PBC, which include host country representatives, because it may help to increase understanding of and adaptation to country-specific requirements: the commission is encouraged 'to consult with civil society, non-governmental organizations, including women's organizations, and the private sector engaged in peacebuilding activities as appropriate' (UNPBC, 2007: § 21, cited in Paris, 2009: 72). This is a vital dimension from a conflict resolution perspective, as will be stressed further in chapter 9. But Paris is not sanguine about prospects in general. The PBC is financed from existing budgets with no extra funding. Institutional jealousies between DPKO and PBC may bedevil the relation between immediate postwar stabilization and longer-term peacebuilding. And the PBC lacks authority within the UN Secretariat beyond convening meetings and agreeing somewhat amorphous 'priorities' that are described only as 'normally' having 'implications' for participators. Above all, because it proceeds by consensus, Paris fears that difficult choices will be avoided, bland 'lowest-common-denominator' priorities will be listed, and actors will generally carry on doing what they were doing anyway. In short, the PBC is as yet 'largely a discussion forum with no executive functions':

> The challenge … is to strike a balance between preserving the flexibility of the existing networked structure of the international peacebuilding system on one hand, and the requirement for some measure of hierarchy on the other … The Peacebuilding Commission, as it is currently designed, does not strike that balance. It errs on the side of preserving the self-directed qualities of the existing peacebuilding network without introducing a capacity to make difficult choices between competing approaches and objectives. (Ibid.: 74–5)

This discussion will be taken up again in chapter 9.

The Internatonal Postwar Reconstruction Blueprint: Dilemmas and Trade-Offs

At this point we offer what may at first appear an over-rigid schema that combines reconstructive *sectors* (security, law and order, political, economic, social/cultural) and temporal *phases* (intervention, stabilization, normalization) in IRW operations in order to clarify the enormity of the task undertaken by the interveners and the difficult and constantly varied tensions and trade-offs involved. It has recently become popular to interpret postwar peace interventions in terms of *dilemmas* of peacebuilding (Jarstad and Sisk, 2008) or of statebuilding (Rothchild and Roeder, 2005; Paris and Sisk, 2009; Reading 57). This is very helpful – although these are not strictly dilemmas, because the choices are rarely mutually exclusive, and in nearly every case the authors in question end by recommending 'a bit of each', as Anna Jarstad does here, for example: 'In the long run, the central issue is not choosing between peace or democracy, but rather what steps toward peace *and* democracy should be taken when, and how are they best timed, sequenced and combined' (Jarstad and Sisk, 2008: 35; original emphasis).

It would be better to describe these as apparent contradictions, unavoidable tensions and uncomfortable trade-offs – often resulting in paradoxical outcomes. Nevertheless, the suggestion that explicit 'dilemma analysis' be undertaken both before and during IRW statebuilding and peacebuilding operations (Paris and Sisk, 2009: 310) is a good one. It introduces a sober appreciation of the scale of the challenge from the outset, lowers unrealistic expectations and induces humility. This ties in exactly with conflict resolution analysis, which, as in the first edition of this book (1999: 188–94), emphasizes that, because of the nature of conflict at these levels, these are complex and contested relations. What is distinctive of the conflict resolution approach is the insight that many of these tensions are not so much dilemmas (two incompatible alternatives, neither of which is desirable) as combinations of options that are at the same time both mutually dependent (there cannot be one without the other) and mutually in tension (each has a tendency to undermine the other). This is characteristic of difficult choices in intense conflict fields in general. For example, it applies to the central element in IRW operations – the intervention itself – because only the strong intervene in the weak, and the requirement of outside assistance is both needed but also in tension with the aim of building independent and sustainable indigenous capacity. And it extends to the central relation between the shorter-term negative goal of ending direct violence and preventing a relapse into war and the longer-term positive goal of building sustainable peace.

Postwar reconstruction is made up of the 'negative' task of ending continuing violence and preventing a relapse into war, on the one hand, and the 'positive' task of constructing a self-sustaining peace, on the other. In the words of the 2000 Brahimi Report: 'History has taught that peacekeepers and peacebuilders are inseparable partners in complex operations: while peacebuilders may not be able to function without the peacekeepers' support, the peacekeepers have no exit without the peacebuilders' work' (Brahimi, 2000, § 28). In other words, the negative and positive tasks are mutually interdependent. Yet they are at the same time in mutual tension. The logic inherent in the negative goal is at odds with important elements in the positive goal, while key assumptions behind the positive goal are often at cross-purposes with the more pressing short-term priorities of the negative goal. The task of mopping up a continuing war or preventing an early relapse back into war is likely to demand uncomfortable trade-offs that might jeopardize the longer-term goal of sustainable peace – for example, deals with unscrupulous power-brokers, or the early incorporation of largely unreconstructed local militia to shore up a critical security gap. Conversely, measures adopted on the assumption that it is market democracy that best sustains peaceful reconstruction long-term may *en route* increase the risk of reversion to war. On the governance front, conflictual electoral processes may exacerbate political differences and favour the 'wrong' politicians. On the economic front, the competitive nature of free-market capitalism may engender turmoil, while externally imposed 'conditionalities' may also be disruptive. On the social front, there are the well-known tensions between stability and justice. Both democracy and the market economy are inherently conflictual processes which may offer a greater measure of political stability in the long run but, as is often noted, are likely to increase political instability during the transition phase, particularly where there is little or no prior experience of them.

In short, the task for those undertaking major IRW operations, whether with broader peacebuilding aims or with more focused statebuilding priorities, is daunting. Indeed, returning to our main theme, the two concepts of statebuilding and peacebuilding are themselves both in mutual tension in the unruly conditions of postwar recovery – as seen in the Somalia case study in chapter 6. But they are also mutually dependent. Without effective governmental institutions, deeper peacebuilding is not sustainable, while the fact that governmental institutions must at the same time be perceived as legitimate and accountable in order to be effective reintroduces considerations of wider peacebuilding – and reconciliation.

Figure 8.1 and box 8.2 encapsulate the daunting nature of the task for postwar statebuilding and peacebuilding IRW operations that result from these dynamics. In figure 8.1 the phases are not sequential, but 'nested'. In other words, unlike the situation in pre-war prevention (see chapter 5), in postwar peace support the key tasks must be initiated at the same time (longer-term peacebuilding and middle-term statebuilding must from the start accompany what it is hoped will thereby be shorter-term peacekeeping). And box 8.2 is intended not to represent a rigid template but to sum up much of IRW practice over the past two decades that continues to this day. As Roland and Sisk say, in recommending ongoing 'dilemma analysis':

> The more typical approach to mission planning involves identifying a number of steps to be completed at particular moments by particular actors, with the moments defined either according to a timetable or on the basis of having achieved specific preconditions; current instruments designed to aid decision-making tend to be based on this essential premise. By contrast, dilemma analysis begins from the assumption that many of the elements of statebuilding will not fit easily together. Rather, they will often work at cross-purposes. If fact, some of these elements are likely to interact in ways that have the potential to undercut, not advance, the goal of establishing legitimate, effective state institutions in war-torn countries. (2009: 310)

We agree. But a phased sectoral approach has been widely evident since the original list of tasks for postwar peacebuilding was outlined by the UN secretary-general in 1992: 'disarming the previously warring parties and the restoration of order, the custody and possible destruction of weapons, repatriating

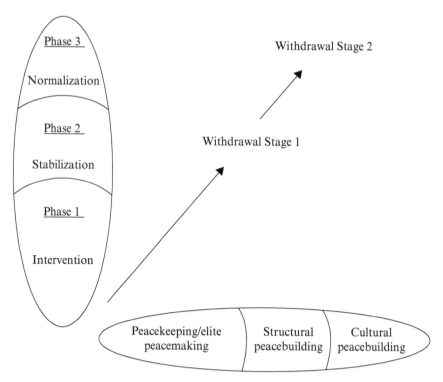

Source: Ramsbotham 2000, 2004; for nested paradigms, see Dugan, 1996, pp. 9–20; and Lederach, 1997, pp. 73–85

Figure 8.1 *IRW operations: nested phases, nested tasks and withdrawals*

refugees, advisory and training support for security personnel, monitoring elections, advancing efforts to protect human rights, reforming or strengthening governmental institutions and promoting formal and informal processes of political participation' (Boutros-Ghali, 1992: 32).

In 1997 these were seen to involve 'the creation or strengthening of national institutions, the monitoring of elections, the promotion of human rights, the provision of reintegration and rehabilitation programmes and the creation of conditions for resumed development' (Annan, 1997). This was reflected in the make-up of associated UN missions. In the heroic days of the early 1990s, for example, with breathtaking compression, UNTAC in Cambodia was expected to achieve all these sectoral tasks, in a country where conflict parties were as yet unreconciled – the Khmer Rouge broke out of the peacebuilding process before the elections – in four phases between its planned initial intervention in March 1992 and its final withdrawal in September 1993 (see box 8.1). Although 'third-generation' peace operations have since evolved in many complex ways beyond this original template, a phased sectoral approach in one form or another still represents 'the more typical approach to mission planning', as noted by Paris and Sisk.

> ### Box 8.1   Components of the UN Transition Authority in Cambodia
>
> 1 *Military component*: verify withdrawal of foreign forces; monitor ceasefire violations; organize cantonment and disarming of factions; assist mine-clearance.
> 2 *Civilian police component*: supervise local civilian police; training.
> 3 *Human rights component*: secure signing of human rights conventions by Supreme National Council; oversee human rights record of administration; initiate education and training programmes.
> 4 *Civil administration component*: supervise administration to ensure neutral environment for election in five areas – foreign affairs, national defence, finance, public security, information.
> 5 *Electoral component*: conduct demographic survey; register and educate voters; draft electoral law; supervise and verify election process.
> 6 *Repatriation component*: repatriate 360,000 refugees.
> 7 *Rehabilitation component*: see to immediate food, health and housing needs; begin essential restoration work on infrastructure; development work in villages with returnees.
>
> In addition, there was an information division.
>
> *Source:* United Nations, 1996: 447–84

Reading across phases and sectors in box 8.2 enables us to comment on some of the key tasks to be undertaken. Under *phase 1* (intervention) we focus on the immediate trade-offs between the negative and positive priorities commented on above and note that this is where the security and law and order sectors are at their most significant. Under *phase 2* (stabilization), which has to begin at the same time, we offer a brief analysis of the interlocking requirements for political stability and note the critical significance of the government sector at this point. This is the core of the statebuilding enterprise. Under *phase 3* (normalization) we note the increased relative importance of the economic and socio-cultural sectors within the longer-term peacebuilding enterprise and discuss what 'normalization' means. The difficult trade-offs and dilemmas uncovered in this way show why many conflict resolvers have deep misgivings about many of the assumptions behind interventions of this kind – and why in some cases they disagree among themselves.

Phase 1: Intervention

Putting together the phase 1 tasks from across all five sectors of the matrix in box 8.2, we can see at a glance what a daunting prospect the initial phase of the intervention is:

> Control armed factions; supervise DDR (disarmament, demobilization, rehabilitation); help restructure and integrate new national armed forces; begin de-mining; reconstitute courts and prisons; break grip of organized crime; train police; promote human rights and punish abuse; in many cases oversee new constitution, elections and restructuring of civil administration subject to local conditions; prevent intimidation; provide humanitarian relief; restore essential services; limit exploitation of movable primary resources by spoilers; overcome initial distrust between groups; monitor and use media to support peace process; protect vulnerable populations; supervise initial return of refugees.

Box 8.2 Postwar reconstruction/withdrawal matrix

Phases in host country postwar reconstruction

Sector A	_Security_
Phase 1	International forces needed to control armed factions; supervise DDR; help reconstitute national army; begin de-mining.
Phase 2	National armed forces under home government control stronger than challengers.
Phase 3	Demilitarized politics; societal security; transformed cultures of violence.
Sector B	_Law and order_
Phase 1	International control of courts, etc.; break grip of organized crime on government; train civilian police; promote human rights/punish abuse.
Phase 2	Indigenous capacity to maintain basic order impartially under the law.
Phase 3	Non-politicized judiciary and police; respect for individual and minority rights; reduction in organized crime.
Sector C	_Government_
Phase 1	In most cases international supervision of new constitution, elections, etc., subject to local conditions; prevent intimidation; ...
Phase 2	Ability to collect sufficient taxes and formulate national budget; reasonable representative governments; ...
Phase 3	Manage peaceful transfer of power via democratic elections; development of civil society within genuine political community; integrate local into national politics.
Sector D	_Economy_
Phase 1	International provision of humanitarian relief; restore essential services; limit exploitation of movable resources by spoilers.
Phase 2	Formal economy yields sufficient revenue for government to provide essential services; capacity to re-employ many former combatants; perceived prospects for future improvement (especially employment).
Phase 3	Development in long-term interest of citizens from all backgrounds.
Sector E	_Society_
Phase 1	Overcome initial distrust/monitor media; international protection of vulnerable populations; return of refugees under way.
Phase 2	Manage conflicting priorities of peace and justice; responsible media.
Phase 3	Depoliticize social divisions; heal psychological wounds; progress towards gender equality; education towards long-term reconciliation.

International intervention transitions

Phase 1	Direct, culturally sensitive support for the peace process.
Phase 2	Phased transference to local/civilian control avoiding undue interference/neglect.
Phase 3	Integration into cooperative and equitable regional/global structures.

In this immediate post-intervention phase it can be seen that security (peace-keeping) and elite bargaining (peacemaking) predominate in ensuring the negative task of preventing a relapse into war. At the same time, a transition has to be achieved from the outset from emergency relief towards the phase 2 political stability requirements. Three features determine the core challenges in phase 1.

First, there is the fundamental *fact of continuing conflict*. Short of total prior military victory for one of the contending parties, the surviving undefeated conflictants are still intent upon achieving their pre-existing political goals. In the first edition of this book we called this 'Clausewitz in reverse', because in this sense the peace is best seen as a continuation of the war 'with the addition of other means'.[2] This is an insight that comes directly from the conflict resolution tradition. Where the war has been brought to an end by a peace process, its essence lies precisely in the effort to persuade undefeated conflict parties that their persisting and no doubt undiminished political aims can best be served by non-violent politics rather than by a perpetuation or a resumption of violence. Where the main power struggle has initially been decided by military means (as in Kosovo, Afghanistan and Iraq) the same still applies, inasmuch as surviving conflict parties continue to vie for postwar influence, and additional actors and sub-actors emerge as the reconstruction process unfurls to complicate the situation further. What Grenier and Daudelin, drawing on experience in El Salvador, have called the peacemaking or postwar reconstruction 'marketplace' is focused around a series of trade-offs in which cessation of violence is traded for other commodities, such as political opportunity and economic advantage (Grenier and Daudelin, 1995: 350). In phase 1 of the post-intervention process, it is the interveners who usually play the key role in ensuring that there are incentives to discontinue violence by creating what the UN secretary-general has termed negative and positive inducements (under the latter, distinguishing the two conflict resolution approaches of 'civic action' and 'peace initiatives') (Annan, 1997). This pattern can be seen across the range of IRW cases, from international pressure to corral the South African administration and South-West Africa People's Organization (SWAPO) leaders into the Namibian elections in November 1989, through to the complex manoeuvring in Afghanistan from the time of the Bonn negotiations in November 2001, and on to the effort to keep all legitimate parties involved in the post-November 2003 preparations for a phased transfer of sovereignty in Iraq. In the words of the Brahimi Report (Brahimi, 2000) with reference to the earlier period, 'United Nations operations did not *deploy into* post-conflict situations but tried to *create them*.' Even when armed conflict comes to an end, political conflict continues, which is why we should refer strictly to 'postwar' reconstruction rather than employ the usual 'post-conflict' misnomer. In Afghanistan and Iraq, postwar reconstruction attempts began while the war was still continuing.

The second key feature is *the fact of the cost of war*, the fact that, in the course of the preceding war (or under the preceding regime), the instruments of governance in all five thematic dimensions are likely to have been much debilitated if not destroyed (see chapter 3). It is difficult to convey the scale of devastation: from huge loss of life (in the millions in countries such as Cambodia and Afghanistan); hundreds of thousands of refugees and internally displaced people (a quarter of the population in Mozambique); ruined economies even in naturally rich countries (Angola's budget deficit of 23 per cent of GDP; El

Salvador's per capita income at 38 per cent of pre-war figures); the destruction of pre-existing political structures even in quite developed systems (in Kosovo with the collapse of Serb-dominated Yugoslav institutions; in Iraq with the instantaneous flight of public employees at all levels); and the substitution for all this of predatory warlords, criminalized economies and institutionalized 'kleptocracies' (Cranna, 1994). In the Democratic Republic of Congo (DRC) in the four and a half years to autumn 2003, out of a population of 53 million, up to 3.5 million are estimated to have died as a result of the violence (International Rescue Committee, 2003), 3.4 million were internally displaced and 17 million were left without food security (Swing, 2003: 25). In the first phase, intervening military forces are often the only large-scale organization with the capacity to respond, as in Basra (Iraq) from April 2003, when British troops found themselves having to run emergency services and begin rebuilding the whole of the local infrastructure. Bernard Kouchner, head of UNMIK in Kosovo, describes how the UN was initially dependent on NATO for much of its logistics and personnel (Kouchner, 2001). This raises critical questions about civil–military relations at many levels, including the staged handover to host-country civilian authorities that defines phase 2 (Williams, 1998). Faced with the task of disarming militias and beginning to reconstruct a national army, of training police and rebuilding courts and prisons, of producing electoral rolls and overseeing the creation of a new constitution followed by 'free and fair elections', of repatriating and resettling refugees and internally displaced persons (IDPs), of restoring emergency services and beginning to revive the economy, of introducing human rights training and safeguards for threatened minorities – all in the face of severe time constraints – it is little wonder that Gareth Evans, Australian foreign minister and one of the architects of the 1991 Paris Peace Accords in Cambodia, described the UNTAC mandate as 'overly ambitious and in some respects clearly not achievable' (Evans, 1994: 27). Similar verdicts have been passed on the comparable efforts in Afghanistan and Iraq.

The third key feature is *the fact that there are enemies of the reconstruction process – especially where wars are ongoing and parties see the interveners as combatants.* In peace processes, the spoilers range from ideologically implacable enemies, through disappointed political interests, to unscrupulous exploiters who profited from the previous dispensation and are reluctant to accept its demise (Stedman, 1997; Kydd and Walter, 2002). Here there has been an evolution of experience since 1989, when the military component of IRW operations was still conceived as a variant on traditional peacekeeping, since the early cases were seen as the implementation of agreed settlements in which all the main players concurred. Bitter experience in Angola, Bosnia, Somalia and Rwanda taught that provision had to be made for the Savimbis, Karadžićs, Aideeds and Interahamwe militias. As a result, intervening forces have been asked to combine what had hitherto often been seen to be incompatible combat/enforcement and peacekeeping/consent-creating roles. As we have seen in chapter 6, combat troops are likely to find themselves in peacekeeping situations, while peacekeepers have been compelled to evolve also into peace-enforcers: 'neutrality' has been reinterpreted as robust 'impartial' support for the peace or reconstruction process. But one of the main conflict resolution insights applies here – in intense conflict zones no intervener will be seen as impartial. This has been a steep learning curve exacerbated by problems of coordinating best practice across what are often widely divergent national contingents, the lack of experience of such roles in some forces (including those of the United States), and the rapid turnover of troops just when such experience has been gained. Depending upon the type of spoilers involved, it is now generally recognized that it is essential to make provision in advance for transforming spoilers into stakeholders in a peace process (as has happened, for example, in Northern Ireland) or, failing that, by accommodating those who are biddable without serious damage to the reconstruction process (a difficult question of judgement); for reducing the scale and significance of their support constituencies (a demanding exercise in 'winning hearts and minds') (Avant, 2009); and for defeating or marginalizing those who remain irreconcilable (a challenge for robust enforcement). This may be easier said than done. Spoilers have become increasingly sophisticated at deliberately exploiting the tensions and contradictions between the negative and positive tasks pinpointed above – for example, squaring the discrepant priorities of assuring the security of interveners and 'winning the hearts and minds' of the host population, or attempting to reduce initial expectations while at the same time being seen to be 'making a difference'. In Cambodia, the Khmer Rouge succeeded in forcing the abandonment of the cantonment and demobilization plan in November 2002, but, surprisingly, not the 23 May 2003 national elections. In Afghanistan and Iraq, opponents of the postwar outcome targeted UN and international aid workers with devastating effect, as well as those engaged in economic reconstruction and the nascent reconstituted police, armed forces and administration, using violence to frustrate the objectives of what they see as occupying forces.

In short, the main problem for conflict resolution in phase 1 is the fact that these are unavoidably militarized environments in which longer-term conflict resolution goals may be sacrificed to shorter-term security and emergency requirements. They also tend to be 'top-down' and 'external-actor-driven' processes in contradiction to the conflict resolution principles of 'bottom-up' and 'local-empowerment' peacebuilding (see chapter 9).

Phase 2: Stability

We have commented above on how the label 'stabilization' is now – misleadingly – sometimes used for the whole IRW enterprise rather than for just one phase of it, as here.

Phase 2 is defined as the point at which enough progress has been made in stabilizing the domestic political situation to enable a safe handover of power to a host government and to undertake the first stage of international withdrawal. Reading across the sectoral phase 2 stipulations from the matrix in box 8.2, we can summarize the requirements as:

> *National armed forces under home government control stronger than challengers; adequate indigenous capacity to maintain basic order impartially under the law; sufficient governmental legitimacy, which may include democratic credentials of elected government with system seen to remain open to those dissatisfied with the initial result; a reasonably stable relationship between centre and regions; a formal economy and taxation system yielding sufficient revenue for government to provide essential services (with continuing international assistance); economic capacity to absorb many former combatants and progress in encouraging general belief in better future employment prospects; adequate success in managing conflicting priorities of peace and justice, protecting minority rights and fostering a reasonably independent yet responsible media.*

What are the core state functions that are required from a 'statebuilding' perspective if the aim is to help (re)construct governmental institutions that are legitimate enough and capable enough to underpin the wider peacebuilding process?

> most definitions of core functions include some or all of the following: the provision of security, the rule of law (including a codified and promulgated body of laws with a reasonably effective police and justice system), basic services (including emergency relief, support for the poorest, and essential healthcare), and at least a rudimentary ability to formulate and implement budget plans and to collect revenue through taxation. None of these functions requires Western-style democracy or 'neo-liberal' market ideologies. Although democratization and marketization have been routine features of peacebuilding to date, they are analytically distinct from the concept of statebuilding used in this volume. (Paris and Sisk, 2009: 15)

Given the non-sequential and nested nature of postwar reconstruction phases, the attainment of these demanding phase 2 requirements is initially a task for phase 1. Their consolidation, accompanied by further progress towards phase 3 goals, is the proper task for phase 2. Here it is the 'structural peacebuilding' aspect of postwar reconstruction that predominates in general and the 'government' sector around which the other sectors can be seen to hinge in particular. This phase evidently poses particular problems for conflict resolution, because of the severe compromises that have to be made on conflict resolution principles in the name of stability. In order to clarify this, we will outline the phase 2 stability requirements here without criticism and then summarize these difficult issues when we come on to consider phase 3.

The literature on the *security sector* tasks is large, covering as it does the ponderously termed 'disarmament, demobilization, repatriation, resettlement and reintegration' (DDRRR) operations and the (re)construction of national armed forces under the control of the government (Collier, 1994; Cillers, 1995; Berdal, 1996; Ball, 1997; Kingma, 1997, 2001; Edelstein, 2009). This can be seen to cover a wide range of more specific issues, from control of small arms and light weapons (UNIDR, 1996) to the reintegration of child soldiers (Goodwin-Gill and Cohn, 1994; McCalin, 1995) and de-mining (USDOD, 2005). In 1992–3 in Angola, some 350 UNAVEM II military observers were expected to supervise the process for more than 150,000 combatants – and unsurprisingly failed (Anstee, 1996). Since then, the international community has acquired a better understanding of what is required in these more challenging cases. For rebel forces or warlords to disarm is to give up their trump card, so there are huge incentives to cheat, and the interveners need clear vision, steady will and skill in applying the right combination of pressure, independent verification and positive political and economic inducements. The key point is reached when reconstituted national forces are, first, under secure host government control and, second, decisively stronger than remaining undemobilized forces or private armies. Until this stage is reached, the situation is too volatile to contemplate withdrawal by intervening military forces (short of effective abandonment of the whole project). At the time of writing (2015) it remains to be seen, for example, whether this will be the case in Afghanistan after the withdrawal of US-led forces.

The *law and order sector* is equally well covered in the literature, with particular focus on the related topics of civilian policing (Call and Barnett, 1999), transitional justice (Kritz, 1995; Mani, 2002; Albin, 2009, Fischer, 2011) and human rights (O'Flaherty and Gisvold, 1998). Once courts and prisons have been rebuilt and the judiciary and police reconstituted and trained, the phase 2 requirement is that politically volatile elements should not be tempted to gain significant advantage through incitement to violence, and that criminal elements should not be able to operate with impunity. The 'impartiality' requirement is crucial, since otherwise the judicial and policing systems lose legitimacy, but this cannot be expected to go unchallenged, because disappointed interests will interpret the maintenance of order as suppression. As most of the 1989–2009 IRW cases in table 8.1 suggest – as also subsequent 'stabilization missions' – law and order issues tend to get worse before they get better. The crime rate soars, as the peacetime economy is unable to absorb large numbers of unemployed ex-soldiers and their families as well as hundreds of thousands of returning refugees, while a continuing wartime black economy, a ready availability of weaponry, and the destabilizing effects of what has usually been an abrupt introduction of free market conditionalities further destabilize the situation. In El Salvador, for example, there were more killings per year in 1998 than there had been during the war. The lesson is that this must be expected and planned for. Negotiating acceptable conditions for justice and policing may involve issues that go to the heart of divided societies, as in post-conflict Rwanda, South Africa and Northern Ireland.

It is with the phase 2 *government sector* requirements that the heart of the postwar reconstruction challenge is reached. The literature on constitutional arrangements and elections is extensive and controversial (Kumar, 1998; Sisk and Reynolds, 1998; Reading 65). Unfortunately, this also tends to be the most testing and intransigent of the challenges because it concerns the fundamental question over which all major political conflicts are in the end waged – who rules? Agreements have to be made on constitutional frameworks and electoral processes where domestic political interests want to secure advantages for themselves, and a process is needed to establish a structure that is in the interests of the population as a whole. The interveners have to tread warily, therefore, and this is where the international legitimacy provided in cases where the main domestic players have already agreed to the process in outline, and where it has been endorsed by regional organizations and the United Nations, is so beneficial. Evidently there are numerous possible constitutional arrangements that work in different circumstances, and there is no space to discuss the permutations here (Shain and Linz, 1995). But the phase 2 requirements are clear: first, sufficient perceived (democratic) legitimacy for the government of the day and, second, enough general confidence in the continuing openness of the system to encourage losers to continue their struggle non-violently within the constitution. This is absolutely critical to success in consolidating phase 2 and moving on to phase 3, as we note in the next two paragraphs on the economy and the social sectors. In cases where there is little or no previous experience of such practices, or where there is a new state, or where central government has had little control over the provinces or has imposed itself only by authoritarian or tyrannical means, these requirements become very daunting indeed. For this reason, as seen above, some have questioned the wisdom of a 'rush to elections' in intense and volatile political environments of this kind. Further discussion would include questions about the legitimacy of international democratic norms in relation to the power and interest of those promoting them and to the different cultures into which they are to be transplanted, about the role that external actors can or should be expected to play, and about the relative effectiveness of top-down government assistance programmes or those that work more from the bottom-up with civil society and non-government groups (see chapter 9).

In the *economy sector* the phase 2 benchmarks are determined by three main linked factors (Ball and Halevy, 1996; Kreimer et al., 1998; Pugh, 2000; Ball, 2001; Berdal and Wennmann, 2010; Wennmann, 2011). The first is that the official economy should yield sufficient revenue for the government to be able to provide essential services (with continuing support from international donors where needed). This is a major requirement that is closely dependent upon success in the 'government' sector because it presupposes progress in taming or pegging back the unofficial economy and, in many cases, in overcoming the continuing reluctance of regional authorities to hand over revenues to the central government. The second requirement is to have understood and made strenuous provision to begin dismantling the entrenched war economy (or authoritarian kleptocracy) that allows exploiters to continue to resist reconstruction. We have seen that is likely to include an international regime to control exploitation of movable assets such as diamonds, drugs or oil. The third requirement is harder to measure because it involves the broad development of the economy as a whole. The phase 2 need is, first, to absorb enough of those previously employed in disbanded militia as will reduce disaffection to containable levels and, second, more generally, for there to be a sense that, however difficult and indeed miserable material conditions may be now, there is sufficient evidence of likely future improvement – particularly in employment prospects. Fortunately, the withdrawal of most or all of the intervening armed forces at this stage does not preclude longer-term engagement and commitment from external development agencies. Experience teaches that it is the management of future expectation that is, if anything, even more important than the delivery of present gain. Several commentators advise that market conditionalities should not be imposed too precipitately – as was, by common agreement, the case to begin with in Mozambique. Paris is one who recommends a shift to 'peace-oriented adjustment policies' that both recognize the priority of stimulating economic growth, even at the risk of inflation, and target resources at those hardest hit during the transition period (1997: 85–6). The central phase 2 aim in this sector is to persuade as many as possible that things will improve so long as they continue to participate in the reconstruction process.

Finally, in the *social sector*, the phase 2 benchmarks are not so clear-cut, beyond the aim of containing intergroup antagonism below levels that might threaten the reconstruction process and preventing its exploitation by unscrupulous political interests (UNRISD, 1995). This means adequate reassurances for threatened minorities (Gurr, 2000), the settlement of refugees (Stein et al., 1995; Black and Coser, 1999) and the management of conflicting priorities of peace and justice (Boraine et al., 1997; Schuett, 1997; Skaar, 1999; Baker, 2001). Measurements of social divisions are very difficult to make, but most of the deeper recourses for overcoming them, including the healing of trauma and reconciliation, can only be expected to come to fruition over the longer term (see chapter 10). One key dimension now widely recognized as vital is what Luc Reychler calls 'the education, information and communication system' (to be elaborated in chapter 9):

> Here we look at the degree of schooling, the level of discrimination, the relevance of the subjects and the attitudes held, the control of the media, the professional level of the journalist, the extent to which the media play a positive role in the transformation of the conflicts, and the control of destructive rumours. (Reychler and Paffenholz, 2001: 13)

Turning to the sixth part of the matrix in box 8.2, 'International intervention transitions', it should now be evident that the sectoral developments listed above, taken together, make up the demanding requirements for an ordered stage 1 *military withdrawal*. This should not be seen as an 'exit strategy' so much as a 'safe handover strategy' to indigenous civilian control. Interveners who are not prepared to see it in these terms should not intervene in the first place. As it is, the familiar tension between short-term 'negative' and long-term 'positive' goals now plays right through to the withdrawal process itself. On the one hand, the message to the wider population of the host country (as also no doubt to domestic constituencies in the intervening countries) is: 'We are not permanently occupying forces; we will be leaving very soon and handing over to you.' But at the same time the message to would-be spoilers has to be: 'It is no good waiting for us to go so that you can resume your old ways; we are here for the duration and will only pull out when the situation is secure. You had better realize this and join in the peace process on the best terms available to you while there is still time.' This was a central dilemma, for example, for the Obama 2010 'surge' in Afghanistan. It is clearly easier to resolve the tension between these positions when the forces involved have international and domestic legitimacy.

As to the length of time that the stage 1 military–civilian transition takes, there are evidently no fixed rules. It depends upon the depth and complexity of the challenge in each case. In the heroic days of the early 1990s, for example, swift transitions were envisaged – for example, UNTAG in Namibia from April 1989 to March 1990; ONUSAL in El Salvador from July 1991 to April 1995; UNTAC in Cambodia from March 1992 to September 1993, etc. In some cases there was a handover to follow-on missions (UNAVEM II to UNAVEM III in Angola), in some there was a handover to a beefed-up intervention force (UNPROFOR to IFOR in Bosnia), and in some there was almost unconditional withdrawal (UNOSOM II in Somalia and UNAMIR in Rwanda). In the post-1995 period there has been a greater readiness to stay longer in Bosnia and Kosovo, since these were new political entities under effective international trusteeship (and in Kosovo with the added continuing uncertainty about future status). The operation in East Timor (now Timor Leste) lasted from 1999 to 2002, but then required renewed support after 2006. With Afghanistan and Iraq, initial plans for swift withdrawal (the original planning framework for the UK's Post-Conflict Reconstruction Unit in 2004 was for eighteen months) soon unravelled. More than ten years later the whole issue of withdrawal remains highly problematic. Once again we suggest that this is linked to the relative lack of legitimacy of 'regime change' interventions compared with the other types of interventions distinguished in the 'intervention, reconstruction, withdrawal' section earlier in this chapter.

Phase 3: Normalization – and beyond

A cross-sectoral conspectus from the matrix in box 8.2 shows that many of the longer-term phase 3 requirements, often listed among the initial rhetorical aims of the intervention, constitute desiderata beyond the present capacity of many postwar countries (though they are very relevant to the current stage in Northern Ireland, for example):

> Demilitarized politics; societal security; transformed cultures of violence; non-politicized judiciary and police; respect for individual and minority rights; reduction in organized crime; peaceful transition of power via democratic elections; development of civil society within genuine political community; equitable integration of local and national politics; development in the long-term interest of citizens from all backgrounds; depoliticization of social divisions; the healing of psychological

wounds; progress towards gender equality; education towards long-term reconciliation; integration into cooperative and equitable regional/global structures.

Here we reach a major difference of opinion among conflict resolution commentators between those, on the one hand, who suggest that goals such as local empowerment, gender equality or long-term reconciliation are better postponed in the interest either of stability or of conceptual and operational clarity and those, on the other, who insist that they are what justify the intervention in the first place and must therefore be forefronted from the start. This issue cuts across the conflict resolution community. For example, Michael Lund argues in the first direction: 'It is laudable to wish to improve society by eliminating as many of its deficiencies as possible ... but such an approach risks making peacebuilding into a grab bag of unfulfilled human wants' (2003: 26; see also Cousens and Kumar, 2000: 4). But others argue the opposite way (Lederach, 1997; Reychler and Paffenholz, 2001).

In general, from a conflict resolution perspective it can be seen that, whereas in phases 1 and 2 it is peacekeeping, elite peacemaking and structural peacebuilding that predominate, in order to secure the more far-reaching and deeply rooted declared sectoral goals of phase 3 normalization, it is social and cultural peacebuilding that becomes more important. In other words, over time 'software' becomes relatively more significant than 'hardware'. Until this socio-cultural transformation happens, therefore, much of the formality of, say, an apparently independent judiciary or an electoral democracy or declaratory instruments on minority rights remains just that – a formality, behind which authoritarianism and partisan discrimination will continue to prevail.

As to the next stage of withdrawal of intervention personnel associated with phase 3 normalization, this is also less clear-cut than stage 1 withdrawal. It varies widely from case to case and merges into what might be termed 'normal' international presence and intrusion in developing countries, where it has been said, for example, that 'UNDP never leaves'. The sixth section of the matrix in box 8.2 describes the aim as 'integration into cooperative and equitable regional and global structures'. This emphasizes the importance of regional stability in IRW operations, as noted in chapters 4 and 5. It also evidently begs the big questions about global equity and the global distribution of power that form an important sub-theme of this book and will be addressed more directly in Part II.

Current Controversies

So far in this chapter we have aimed to convey something of the comprehensive and extraordinarily ambitious nature of postwar statebuilding and peacebuilding operations as they have evolved over the past twenty years. But what is the overall status of the 'liberal peace' enterprise at the end of this period? A review of the literature suggests that opinion is polarized and also complicated by the way the agenda has been swamped by the travails of reconstruction efforts in Iraq and Afghanistan. The liberal peace has been hijacked by neo-liberalism, and neo-liberalism in turn by neo-conservatism. The main declaratory justification for the Bush administration's military actions between 2000 and 2008, in addition to protecting US interests, was to 'spread freedom'. The result has been a complicated set of reactions in which strange bedfellows find themselves opposed to liberal interventionism, while those who want to rescue the liberal peace offer differing, and sometimes con-flicting, counsel. This is now merged into growing current controversy about 'stabilization' missions, as noted above.

Some *object* to liberal interventionism from a 'conservative' perspective. Jeffrey Herbst (2003) advises against fixing 'failed states' when this artificially keeps unviable political entities on a life-support system that simply preserves insecurity. It is better to let them fail. Jeremy Weinstein (2005) sees interna-tional intervention freezing unstable power struggles, when they should be left to settle the issue via 'autonomous recovery'. Others, in contrast, reject lib-eral interventionism from a 'critical' perspective. David Chandler (2006, 2008) opposes interventionary statebuilding because, within the general 'political economy of the liberal peace', it is a thinly veiled form of neo-colonial coercion enforced by international institutions. Michael Pugh, Neil Cooper and Mandy Turner endorse Mark Duffield's argument (2007) that what is needed is:

> a fundamental change in the approach to the analyses of war economies and the politi-cal economy of peace. The political economy of post-conflict peace and statebuilding in a liberal peace framework has involved a simulacr[um] of empowerment where peacebuild-ers transfer responsibility to societies without transferring power. Moreover, populations have been subjected to calculated techniques of discipline under liberal agendas requir-ing individual self-reliance, a loss of public goods and unequal integration into the world economy. (Pugh et al., 2008b: 391)

Those who want to *rescue* liberal interventionism are also divided. Roland Paris and Timothy Sisk, although critical of liberal interventionism as it has been carried out in individual cases, argue strongly that, in general terms, the main lesson is not to abandon the liberal peace but to do it better: 'although most experts hold that these operations have, on the whole, done considerably more good than harm, serious doubts persist about the ability of international agencies to create the conditions for sustainable peace' (2009: 11).

Apart from the security danger that results from 'spillovers, contagions, instabilities, and vitiation of international norms that occurs when authority and order disappear', to retreat from the postwar statebuilding project alto-gether would from this perspective be the height of irresponsibility and would 'be tantamount to abandoning tens of millions of people to lawlessness, preda-tion, disease and fear'. But here agreement ends, and there is a parting of the ways as the statebuilding project itself is variously interpreted. James Fearon and David Laitin, for example, look at the situation from a mainly realist per-spective and, in the case of 'weak states', advocate a transfer of power 'not to full sovereignty' but, rather, to a form of 'neo-trusteeship' where the state in question is 'embedded in and monitored by international institutions' (2004: 42). Stephen Krasner (2004) goes further, recommending 'shared sovereignty' arrangements for 'collapsed and failing states', where external bodies assume responsibility for aspects of governance in the most vulnerable states on a permanent basis – they are no longer seen in international law as sovereign states. This is much more radical than middle-ground discussions about 'transitional administration' as in the cases of East Timor (Timor Leste) and Kosovo (Chesterman, 2004; Caplan, 2005). But these are complex relations. Even when the recommendation is for a more nuanced, disaggregated or 'lighter touch' in statebuilding, the result may well be that, as a result, there will be more lengthy and extensive outside involvement overall – for example, when compared with the 'short sharp shock' approach of the early 1990s.

Since the third edition of this book there have been substantial critiques of wider UN peacekeeping, for example by Philip Cunliffe (2013), as noted in chapter 6. Roger Mac Ginty (2012) has mounted a fierce polemic against the doctrine and practice of 'stabilization' as exercised and controlled by 'the leading states from the global north'. And Ian Spears (2012) has fired a broadside against the whole 'false promise of peacebuilding' itself. The examples chosen by Spears are Afghanistan, Iraq, Somalia and Rwanda. Although many points are valid, we do not think that selective and sweeping condemnation which does not discriminate or compare with cases where there was no intervention prove the case. It could well be that, like democracy in Churchill's famous remark, peacebuilding is the worst response to conflict 'except for all the others'. Afghanistan and Iraq were not peace operations. The first (Afghanistan) assumed the form of taking sides in a civil war. The second (Iraq) overthrew a previous dominance by the Sunni minority. It is not surprising that these operations ran into difficulties. Somalia was also not a fair example of the failure of peacebuilding, since it was a brief intervention in a civil war (originally for humanitarian reasons) followed by the absence of peacebuilding – rapid withdrawal (see the case study at the end of chapter 6). As for Rwanda, this was an example of a failure of peacemaking (the Arusha Accords), of peacekeeping (UNAMIR did not stop a massacre) and of humanitarian intervention (the French Operation Turquoise gave an escape route for the *genocidaires*). It was not at that time a failure of peacebuilding.

Conclusion

At this point we will postpone further current controversy about postwar reconstruction in general – as well as the vital question of 'measuring peacebuilding performance' (Mack, 2014: 109) – to the next chapter. Here we will conclude with a summary of issues raised in this chapter. Setting aside intense disagreement about specific interventions, the argument has been that the success of post-settlement and postwar reconstruction efforts must be judged according to conflict resolution and conflict transformation principles. We have stressed the importance of domestic opinion within the host countries as the true arbiter, however hard it may be to ascertain and however internally controversial this may be, and have suggested that the perceived legitimacy of interventions appears to decrease as we move across the spectrum of intervention types in table 8.1. We have argued that the shift from UN-led post-settlement peacebuilding to mixed or non-UN interventions where there is no settlement or the settlement is imposed has compounded the problems of legitimacy. This has been further compromised by the hybrid nature of a number of as yet loosely defined 'stabilization missions'. We have drawn attention to the reconstruction 'planning gap', which dictates that IRW enterprises have to be international. Whatever the initial war-fighting requirements may be in some cases, the overall postwar reconstruction effort requires coordinated endeavours across national agencies, across civil–military operational divides, and across domestic–multinational/multilateral partnerships. Winning the peace makes even greater demands than winning the war. We have produced a matrix of the phased sectoral tasks that constitute the postwar reconstruction programme according to the principles of complementarity and contingency (box 8.2) and noted how, from a conflict resolution perspective, both phases and sectors are 'nested' (figure 8.1). The sectors interconnect, and the admittedly ambitious goals of phase 3 must imbue the entire undertaking from the start. This places a huge onus on effective cooperation between domestic parties and the interveners. In phase 1 (immediate post-intervention), when there is a situation of ongoing conflict, we have seen how the peacekeeping and elite peacemaking components tend to predominate. But, as elaborated in chapter 6, in a postwar reconstruction context, military forces are there to support the peace process within an overall conflict resolution scenario. In phase 2 (stabilization) we noted how there is an unavoidable tension between the political stability requirements that enable a safe withdrawal of intervening armed forces and the longer-term normalization and transformation norms that legitimized the intervention in the first place. It is the government sector and the political and economic tasks of structural peacebuilding that predominate in this phase (statebuilding). The key requirement of the intervening military at this point is that their withdrawal should be seen as a function of political stability in the host country orientated towards the construction of a sustainable peace. At all these stages it is important to draw parties into negotiations, hold open political space, and continuously develop and reframe the grounds for agreement. Finally, it is in phase 3 (normalization) and beyond that the full conflict resolution and conflict transformation goals can be attained. Cultural peacebuilding and the social-psychological sector come into their own here. We elaborate on this in the next chapter.

RECOMMENDED READING

Berdal and Wennmann (2010); Cousens and Kumar (2000); Ghani and Lockhart (2008); Hampson (1996); Jarstad and Sisk (2008); *Stability: International Journal of Security and Development*, 4(1) (2015); Lund (2003); Mac Ginty (2012); Muggah (2013); Paris (2004); Paris and Sisk (2009); Reychler and Paffenholz (2001); Spears (2012); Stedman et al. (2002); Wennmann (2011).

RELEVANT EXTRACTS IN *THE CONTEMPORARY CONFLICT RESOLUTION READER*

Reading 57: R. Paris and T. Sisk, Understanding the Contradictions of Postwar Peacebuilding
Reading 58: J. Dobbins et al., The US and UN Roles in Nation-Building
Reading 65: S. Wolff, Governing (in) Kirkuk: Resolving the Status of a Disputed Territory in Post-American Iraq

CHAPTER NINE

Peacebuilding

We have seen how the concept of peacebuilding is wider than the idea of state-building and reconstruction, as discussed in chapter 8. We have also seen from earlier chapters how, from the outset, peacebuilding has been at the core of the conflict resolution field, originally through the pioneering work of Johan Galtung (1975). The importance of this today is that it provides the basis for a sustained conflict resolution critique of many aspects of postwar reconstruction practice since the end of the Cold War. This chapter aims to sketch out the main contemporary contributions that this is making – for example, through the way peacebuilding norms have been built into international institutions, how criteria for evaluating peacebuilding efforts from a genuinely emancipatory perspective are now being developed, and how the topic has progressed beyond its original preoccupation with 'peacebuilding from below', as described in the first edition of this book. It is now well understood that peacebuilding from below is not a panacea or magic wand, and can itself conceal vested interests and the influence of possibly corrupt and self-seeking actors. Recognizing this, we argue that peacebuilding from below cannot be seen in isolation from the broader processes of conflict resolution, acting as they do to confront the global and higher-level forces that impact on local communities. Local or particular values and interests need to be negotiated and legitimized via what are appealed to as universal human values – for example, the justice component of peace which seeks the satisfaction of human rights and needs. Ample recognition has been given earlier in this book to the dangers that lie in uncritical appeals to 'universal values'. Nevertheless, conflict resolution does not abandon the no doubt endless struggle to determine how best publicly to redeem such claims when they are made. Here we suggest a powerful role for peace education as a component of postwar peacebuilding, which privileges peace (non-violence) and which enables a space and a process for Oliver Richmond's *via media* (see below) through which the values and interests of the local-particular and the universal may be negotiated.

Summing up a conflict resolution response to international postwar reconstruction efforts since the end of the Cold War from this perspective, Mark Hoffman asks 'what is left of the liberal peace?' and answers that genuine peacebuilding means an abandonment of uniform and bureaucratically imposed structures, a far greater sensitivity and nuanced understanding of local conditions, and a readiness to encompass the variety of voices, often

Box 9.1 A transformationist critique of IRW practice

At least eight components can be discerned in transformationist critiques over the 1989–2015 period:

1 an insistence on greater emphasis on 'bottom-up' rather than 'top-down' initiatives and the empowerment of indigenous grassroots participation;
2 criticism of the relative neglect of the social-psychological dimension;
3 unhappiness about sequenced and foreshortened time frames that fail to dovetail short-, medium- and long-term priorities properly;
4 a questioning of the motives of powerful interveners and an insistence that they be made accountable to host peoples and the international community;
5 a demand for more emphasis on gender equality;
6 an insistence on greater cultural sensitivity;
7 unease about, if not opposition to, military involvement in and often control of what should be non-military tasks;
8 disquiet at the way what were UN-led operations in the early 1990s have now come to be controlled by the militarily more powerful countries, with the UN increasingly sidelined and used as little more than a rubber stamp.

conflicting, that must participate if there is to be inclusive 'collective reasoning' about the peacebuilding project:

> As a first step it would mean a move away from the paternalistic, technocratic one-size-fits-all approach to peacebuilding. Shifting to a more bottom up, society building approach, there is a need to engage creatively and dynamically with local dynamics without falling into the trap of 'romanticising the local' or entrenching existing structures of violence and/or inequality. A peace that is built on the ground needs to reflect the interests, needs and aspirations of local populations rather than those of the international peacebuilding community. If we start by asking what 'we' want to achieve then we are starting with the wrong question. (2009: 11)

This would, we think, be endorsed by most others in the conflict resolution field (Lederach and Moomaw Jenner, 2002; Keating and Knight, 2004; Richmond, 2008). Here box 9.1 is reproduced from earlier editions of this book, not because it is exhaustive, but to give an idea of the consistency of the conflict resolution critique of statebuilding and peacebuilding intervention operations as carried out since the 1990s. From a conflict resolution perspective the primary aim in postwar peace operations is not to secure western norms but to empower indigenous capacity. This certainly requires state functions adequate to the needs of the population (effective governance) but also consultation and participation with all stakeholders (legitimate governance). So the concept of statebuilding, as conceptualized in chapter 8, turns out after all to be inseparable from wider issues of peacebuilding, despite the tensions between them.

The Mainstreaming of Peacebuilding Models in International Policy

In much the same way that both conflict prevention policy and gender-sensitive approaches became 'mainstreamed' in the agendas of international organizations in the 1990s, as noted in chapters 5 and 13, so postwar peace-building also emerged as an explicit policy objective of a wide variety of key actors concerned to define their role in the resolution of international conflict. Chapters 6 and 8 have outlined the evolution of the idea of post-conflict peacebuilding as far as the UN was concerned from its inception in *An Agenda for Peace* in 1992, through the *Supplement to the Agenda for Peace* in 1995, to current attempts to develop a UN Peace Building Commission (PBC). The World Bank has also emerged as a leading player in post-conflict peacebuilding. It has administered a Post-Conflict Fund (PCF) since 1997, set up through its Conflict Prevention and Reconstruction Unit (CPRU). Recognizing that, on average, a country coming out of civil war has a 50 per cent chance of relapsing into conflict in the first five years of peace, and that it can take a generation to return to pre-war living standards, the World Bank devotes a significant proportion of its total funding to projects that address the effects of war. Its support for peacebuilding in fragile states and states in conflict is managed by its Fragile and Conflict-Affected Countries Group, which in 2008 created a new State and Peacebuilding Fund (SPF), replacing two earlier funds for supporting its peacebuilding work: the Post-Conflict Fund and the LICUS (Low Income Countries Under Stress) Fund. The World Bank organizes its peacebuilding programmes around the three thematic areas of gender-based violence, youth empowerment and employment, and community-led development. However, within these thematic definitions, there are wider connections with peace-building objectives that are concerned with deeper transformation related to root causes of the conflicts in question. In Thailand, for example, where since 2004 there has been a violent separatist insurgency of Malay Muslims in the three southern provinces of Pattani, Yala and Narathaiwat, the World Bank funds a peacebuilding programme to promote trust within and among local communities and civil society organizations and between the institutions of the Thai state. The project was categorized under their community-driven development theme, but phase 1 of the project concluded that this had to be underpinned by a better understanding of the causes of the conflict among the communities in southern Thailand, by the use of peace education to enhance the prospect for peace through dialogue on aspects of non-violence, and through the sharing of knowledge from other conflict areas (Ropers and Anuvatudom, 2014; and see the World Bank Database – Fragility, Conflict and Violence, 2015)

The range and quality of information on specific peacebuilding projects and organizations has grown enormously over the past ten years and indicates a myriad of organizations, from the World Bank and the UN to thousands of grassroots civil society groups, engaged in peacebuilding activities. The World Bank has its own publicly accessible State and Peace-building Grant Database, launched in 2008 with nearly 300 projects in forty-three countries, as well as forty-four multi-country profiles (World Bank Database – Fragility, Conflict and Violence, 2015). The Global Partnership for the Prevention of

Armed Conflict based in the Netherlands also has an open platform to support communication and collaboration of people and organizations involved in conflict prevention and peacebuilding that currently has over 2,300 members registered (Peace Portal at www.peaceportal.org), while the Peacebuilding Portal (developed by the UN Department of Social and Economic Affairs, the UNDP, the German Foreign Ministry and the African Union) lists 577 non-governmental, academic, governmental and international organizations dedicated to peacebuilding worldwide.

Within this framework, a particularly important role in the institutionalization of peacebuilding capacity has come with the entry of the UN into the peacebuilding field. Its failure to implement the prescriptions of the 1992 *Agenda for Peace*, especially in the most challenging tests faced in Somalia, Rwanda and former Yugoslavia, as noted in chapter 6, led to a series of reports, investigations and proposals for reform that would eventually result in policies to institutionalize peacebuilding in the UN system. Two influential reports in December 2004 (the UN High-Level Panel on Threats, Challenges and Change) and in March 2005 (Kofi Annan's *In Larger Freedom*) called for the formation of a dedicated body to advance peacebuilding. The political will to strengthen postwar peacebuilding capacity also gained momentum from an increasing recognition of the proneness of peace agreements to collapse. The World Summit, held in the UN headquarters in New York in September 2005, agreed to establish a Peacebuilding Commission (PBC) as an intergovernmental advisory body within the UN system, a decision formalized in the UN General Assembly's World Summit Outcome of September 2005.[1]

We have discussed the work of the Peacebuilding Commission – and offered a brief evaluation – in chapter 8 from a statebuilding and reconstruction perspective. Here we return to this theme, but now within the wider conceptual setting of peacebuilding itself. The PBC was mandated to operate strategically in three areas: first, to advise on integrated strategies for post-conflict peacebuilding and recovery; second, to marshal finance for early recovery and sustained resources in the medium and long term; and, third, to develop peacebuilding best practices in collaboration with political, security, humanitarian and development actors. The PBC is composed of an Organizational Committee of thirty-one members, assisted by a Peacebuilding Support Office (PBSO), based in the UN Secretariat in New York, and a Peacebuilding Fund (PBF). The commission began to operate in October 2006 by evaluating peacebuilding needs in Sierra Leone and Burundi. By late 2009 the PBF also had active projects supporting peace processes in the Central African Republic, Côte d'Ivoire, Guinea, Haiti, Liberia, Kenya, the Comoros Islands, the Democratic Republic of Congo, Sierra Leone, Somalia, Timor Leste and Nepal. Despite the challenging mandate of the PBF, the budget for peacebuilding was relatively low, with a target allocation of $165 million in over 100 projects in twelve countries. At late 2009 the bulk of this had been spent on the two

> **Box 9.2 Countries funded by the UN Peacebuilding Fund and nature of projects funded, 2014**
>
> | | | |
> |---|---|---|
> | Burundi | Haiti | Sierra Leone |
> | Central African Republic | Kenya | Somalia |
> | Chad | Kyrgyzstan | South Sudan |
> | Comoros | Lebanon | Sri Lanka |
> | Congo, Democratic Republic | Liberia | Sudan |
> | Côte d'Ivoire | Libya | Timor-Leste |
> | Guatemala | Nepal | Uganda |
> | Guinea | Niger | Yemen |
> | Guinea-Bissau | Papua New Guinea | |
>
> *Priority Area 1* supports projects that attempt to address peace-sustaining processes, such as disarmament, demobilization and reintegration, as well as strengthening prisons, police forces and peacetime militaries. Projects totalling approximately $114.6 million approved by 2012.
>
> *Priority Area 2* supports projects that bolster good governance and promote national dialogue and reconciliation, including those that promote human rights, aim to end impunity and stamp out corruption. There is also a strong focus on programmes that strengthen the participation of women in the peacebuilding process. Projects totalling approximately $66.8 million approved by 2012.
>
> *Priority Area 3* supports projects that stimulate economic revitalization to general peace dividends. Activities include strengthening economic governance through the promotion of partnerships with the private sector, the development of micro-enterprises, youth employment schemes and the management of natural resources. Projects totalling approximately $51.3 million approved by 2012.
>
> *Priority Area 4* supports projects that rebuild basic infrastructure, such as energy, transportation, safe drinking water and proper sanitation. Projects totalling approximately $35.1 million approved by 2012.
>
> *Source:* www.unpbf.org/countries/

initial priority countries, Sierra Leone ($35 million) and Burundi ($35 million) (UNPBF, at www.unpbf.org).

By 2014, eight years after its formation, the Peacebuilding Fund was supporting 290 projects in twenty-seven countries, with a total of $456 million allocated since its inception to the end of 2013 (see box 9.2).

A somewhat lukewarm assessment of the effectiveness so far of the PBC has been given in chapter 8. But these are early days, and it is evident from the survey above that there has been a significant maturing of peacebuilding policy and institutionalization, which has survived the impact of the 'global war on terror' that seemed likely at one point to divert and dilute it at the time we were writing the second and third editions of this book, and seems now set to continue. Indeed, the catastrophic failures to set military action within robust peacebuilding frameworks in Afghanistan, Iraq and Libya have graphically demonstrated why this is a major international priority, in tandem with the recently much enhanced focus on the priority of 'saving failed states'. The World Bank initiated efforts to collaborate with the UN Peacebuilding Fund to improve the methodology for evaluation of the effectiveness of peacebuilding projects and programmes (World Bank, 2009) (see below). Lessons are also being learned from specific projects and case studies in order to improve the general effectiveness of peacebuilding (for example, for a case study of Sierra Leone, see Curran and Woodhouse, 2007).

Peacebuilding Debates and Discourses: Beyond Blueprints and Towards an Emancipatory Conflict Resolution Ethic

In parallel with the institutionalization of support for peacebuilding marked by the formation of the UN PBC and the range of activities indicated in the various databases noted above, the literature on post-conflict peacebuilding has also burgeoned, and this literature has now matured to the point where the strategic purpose and ideological content of the discourse on peacebuilding has been questioned and reassessed. This section reviews these debates and discourses and provides a case for reasserting the values of the conflict resolution field to the definition of peacebuilding, including the idea that there must be an ethical dimension which is responsive to the needs of those communities who are the targets of peacebuilding projects (Murithi and Dower, 2008; Mac Ginty, 2013).

The debate about peacebuilding and what it means inevitably raises wider questions, which we pursue further in Part II of this book, on peace and conflict theory and on future developments of the field. Defining what peacebuilding is, what peacebuilders seek to achieve, and how they pursue peacebuilding raises fundamental questions about the nature of conflict resolution and its relationship to the peace that it wants to build. Oliver Richmond has suggested that the ontologies, epistemologies, theories and methods used to study and to negotiate what peace is requires an engagement with multiple issues, with a complex interdisciplinary research agenda, and with an openness to hybridity and difference. We agree with him in the view that, in order to satisfy the emancipatory norm, based on a fusion of negative peace (security, freedom from fear) and positive peace (the development of human potential) that has defined the field since its inception, conflict resolution needs to be open to multiple conceptions of peacebuilding, to avoid technically or ideologically defined blueprints and, in Richmond's words, to allow 'for the negotiation of a discursive practice of peace in which hegemony, domination and oppression are identified and resolved' (Richmond, 2008: 163). In other words, peacebuilding should reflect and be a product of a negotiated discursive practice and not the outcome of a technically defined and externally imposed blueprint. Current debates in the conflict resolution field reflect this challenge to evolve a negotiated and discursive praxis of peacebuilding, and these debates are reviewed below.

Contending Concepts of Peacebuilding

Initially, peacebuilding was seen as a self-evidently benevolent pursuit, motivated by a desire to realize an internationalist agenda that was inclusive and concerned to act on behalf of those harmed and traumatized in conflict. This was very much how it was presented in the formative documents and discourses from *An Agenda for Peace* through to the reports that led to the formation of the Peacebuilding Commission in 2004–5. However, as it became established as the term used to describe the main driver for postwar reconstruction, researchers and commentators began to question aspects of the peacebuilding programme as it was presented and increasingly mainstreamed in the policies of leading international organizations. For Roger Mac Ginty, for example, there is a danger that peacebuilding can be reduced to a functional and technocratic exercise of 'ticking boxes, counting heads and weapons, amending constitutions, and reconstructing housing units' (Mac Ginty, 2006: 3–4; 2013). Used in this sense, what is being constructed is not an emancipatory peace but a liberal peace led by hegemonic powers, who may be more concerned to stabilize a world order dominated by the rich and powerful than to enable a liberating transformation out of violence (Reading 59). Recent research has built on Richmond's call to develop a research agenda which unpacks or deconstructs the liberal peace idea to reveal variants within it and opposed to it. Heathershaw (2008), for one, has argued for the need to talk, not about peacebuilding, but about 'peacebuildings'. In an attempt both to define and to categorize different peacebuilding discourses, he goes back to three of the original four conceptions of peace set out by Michael Banks (1987) in one of the seminal papers in the conflict resolution field. Banks defined conceptions of peace with three variants of the liberal peace. The three variants are: (i) a conservative order-stability-based variant equated with the statebuilding end of the peacebuilding spectrum; (ii) an orthodox liberal peacebuilding model equated with pluralism and democratic reform (democratic peacebuilding); and (iii) a justice-emancipatory variant equated with a civil society dominated mode of peacebuilding (Heathershaw, 2008). This is a useful categorization and can be seen to correspond to comparable peacekeeping categories as suggested in chapter 6. Boege and his colleagues (2009) relate the third, emancipatory, mode to the idea that sites for building peace should not be classified as 'failed states' but as 'hybrid political orders', and that peacebuilding should then draw on 'the resilience embedded in the communal life of societies within the so-called fragile regions of the global South'. They suggest that Somaliland (see the case study in chapter 8) and Bougainville provide examples of situations where this model has worked, balancing customary practices and institutions with the institutions of the modern state (ibid.: 599). Each of these 'discourses' has its advocates and a surrounding literature, helpfully evaluated by Heathershaw.[2]

While civil society, people to people, or peacebuilding-from-below variants of the peacebuilding model gained influence through the 1990s, the events of 11 September 2001 and the subsequent war on terror tended to reassert the stability–order–statebuilding discourse and policy especially within the US administration and those allied to it and its policies in Iraq and Afghanistan. In the middle of the second decade of the twenty-first century, however, and especially within the conflict resolution community, as noted in chapter 8, there is increasing concern about calling statebuilding and regime change interventions 'peacebuilding'. This concern is especially acute in view of the over-reliance on military force to generate regime change in Afghanistan and Iraq, for example, together with erroneous claims that this is peacebuilding (Rogers, 2007).

There is now a concern to reassert and develop the relevance of the original concept of peacebuilding based on people to people, peacebuilding from below, and civil society-led discourses (for an example of bottom-up peacebuilding in Kenya led by women, see Reading 64). The concluding part of this chapter, therefore, first locates this concept within the conflict resolution field and, second, suggests a development of the original concept to take account of peacebuilding experience in the 1990s, 2000s and beyond. We conclude by proposing a reconstructed variant of peacebuilding, which we describe as a transformative and cosmopolitan model, consistent with the model sketched out for peacekeeping in chapter 6. This model seeks to privilege local capacity-building, while recognizing the necessity of negotiating between local/communal and international/global perspectives. Oliver Richmond has expressed the challenge as follows:

> Bottom-up, social ontologies developing an empathetic account ... based on mutual ontologies and methods of peace should shape institutions. This does not preclude peace being legitimate and formalised in governmental, institutional or constitutional structures and legal frameworks, ... but these must rest on consent and an engagement with difference and hybridity. ... Any viable concept of peace ... must not displace indigenous legitimacy with preponderant institutions that are inflexible and actually obscure the indigenous. (Richmond, 2008: 163)

Richmond calls for a *via media* (middle way) between such hybrid discourses of peacebuilding, and much current research on peacebuilding centres on this preoccupation with a focus on moving beyond 'northern epistemologies of peace' (Lidén et al., 2009). Notable here has been the work of Severine Autesserre (2014), whose book *Peaceland: Conflict Resolution and the Everyday Politics of International Intervention* offers new insight into reasons why outsider attempts at peacebuilding so often fail at the local level. She uses extensive ethnographic fieldwork research in conflict zones in different parts of the world, such as South Sudan, Palestine, Nicaragua and Cambodia, to show how the everyday aspects of the social practices and habitual understandings of the conflict environment by expatriate interveners deeply influence peacebuilding effectiveness – sometimes for the good but far more often deleteriously.

We return to this idea in the concluding section of this chapter and pick it up again in chapter 19.

Hybrid Peace and Peacebuilding from Below in the Discourse of Conflict Resolution

Phase 1: Origins of the idea of peacebuilding from below

Scholar-practitioners within the conflict resolution field played a pioneering role in the revision of thinking about the complex dynamics and processes of post-conflict peacebuilding, including the idea that effective and sustainable peacemaking processes must be based not merely on the manipulation of peace agreements made by elites but, more importantly, on the empowerment of communities torn apart by war to build peace from below, marked by a recognition of the significance of local actors and of the non-governmental sector and the links with local knowledge and wisdom. This approach also set out to enhance sustainable citizen-based peacebuilding initiatives and to open up participatory public political spaces in order to allow institutions of civil society to flourish. The framework within which peacebuilding from below might operate, and the peacebuilding constituencies involved, are shown in figure 9.1.

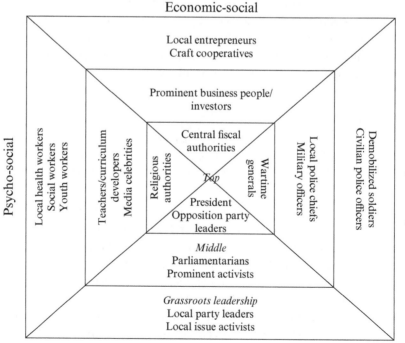

Source: Reynolds Levy 2004, developed from Lederach, 1995, 1997

Figure 9.1 *Framework for peacebuilding from below*

Much of the development of thinking about peacebuilding came during the course of experience gained in supporting local groups trying to preserve or cultivate cultures of peace in areas of armed conflict in the 1990s. The wars in former Yugoslavia, for example, provided challenging situations for local peacemakers, and approaches were developed representing what Fetherston (1998) called anti-hegemonic, counter-hegemonic and post-hegemonic peace-building projects, and what Nordstrom (1992: 270) referred to as 'counter-lifeworld constructs' that challenge the cultures of violence. The idea of peacebuilding from below also echoes Elise Boulding's insight, to be noted in chapter 13, that cultures of peace can survive in small pockets and spaces even in the most violent of conflicts. These shifts in thinking moved the emphasis in conflict resolution work from an 'outsider neutral' approach towards a partnership with local actors, and it is this relationship which is one of the key characteristics of peacebuilding from below. The emergence of the approach is best illustrated in the work of two scholar-practitioners, Adam Curle (see chapter 2) and John Paul Lederach. Throughout his academic career (which ended formally in 1978, when he retired from the chair of peace studies at the University of Bradford), and also through the period of his 'retirement', Curle, a Quaker, was deeply involved in the practice of peace-making. In the 1990s much of this involvement took the form of supporting the activity of the Osijek Centre for Peace, Nonviolence and Human Rights, the site of the most violent fighting of the Serb–Croat War from 1992. Curle realized through his involvement with the Osijek project that the range of conflict traumas and problems was so vast that the model of mediation based on the intervention of outsider-neutrals was simply not powerful or relevant enough to promote peace: 'Since conflict resolution by outside bodies and individuals has so far proved ineffective [in the chaotic conditions of con-temporary ethnic conflict – particularly, but not exclusively, in Somalia, Eastern Europe and the former USSR], it is essential to consider the peacemak-ing potential within the conflicting communities themselves' (Curle, 1994: 96). He now saw the role of conflict resolution in post-Cold War conflicts as providing a variety of support to local peacemakers through an advisory, consultative-facilitative role via workshops and training in a wide variety of potential fields which the local groups might identify as necessary. The task is to empower people of goodwill in conflict-affected communities, and the starting point for this is to help in 'the development of the local peacemakers' inner resources of wisdom, courage and compassionate non-violence' (ibid.: 104). This in turn was linked in Curle's thinking to a deeper transformative quest to 'tame the hydra' of violence by understanding not only the politics of conflict but the deeper spiritual and philosophical sources of wisdom which would favour peace (Curle, 1999).

John Paul Lederach, working as a scholar-practitioner within a Mennonite tradition, which shares many of the values and ideas of the Quakers, and with practical experience in Central America, has also stressed the importance of this approach, which he calls indigenous empowerment. For Lederach, cognate ideas were explored and advanced in a series of highly influential publications from the mid-1990s (1995, 1997, 1999, 2001, 2003).

Within the conflict resolution field, then, peacebuilding from below became linked with the idea of liberating communities from the oppression and misery of violence in a project whose main goal was the cultivation of cultures and structures of peace (in Galtung's terms, positive peace). The pedagogy appropriate for this was defined as elicitive and transformative rather than prescriptive and directive. Thus, for Lederach:

> The principle of indigenous empowerment suggests that conflict transformation must actively envision, include, respect, and promote the human and cultural resources from within a given setting. This involves a new set of lenses through which we do not primarily 'see' the setting and the people in it as the 'problem' and the outsider as the 'answer'. Rather, we understand the long-term goal of transformation as validating and building on people and resources within the setting. (1995: 212)

The approach also suggests that it is important to identify the 'cultural modalities and resources' within the setting of the conflict in order to evolve a comprehensive framework which embodies both short-term and long-term perspectives for conflict transformation. The importance of cultural relevance and sensitivity within conflict resolution theory has emerged, partly in response to learning from case experience, and partly as an explicit critique of earlier forms of conflict resolution theory where local culture was given marginal significance (see chapter 15).

Phase 2: From peacebuilding from below to negotiated peacebuilding: towards a transformative cosmopolitan model

The prioritization of the local and the indigenous in the peacebuilding model developed through the 1990s remains a defining characteristic of the conflict resolution approach, but recent research has also led to the realization that indigenous empowerment and the role of civil society and local cultural values in peacebuilding is not a straightforward and unproblematic issue. Just as top-down institutionally driven peacebuilding can, and frequently does, marginalize local interests and the disempowered, so too local cultures and communities are sites of power asymmetry, patriarchy and privilege in which customs and civil society actors and organizations may replicate what external actors are sometimes accused of in the international arena (see Autesserre (2014) and box 9.3).

Similar findings are reported in many other areas. In Sri Lanka, for example, Goodhand found that politics at the central government level is dominated by personalities and patronage, and that this is 'mirrored also in the centralised and clientalistic nature of civil society' (Goodhand and Klem, 2005: 24). Chopra (2009) argues along similar lines in relation to peacebuilding in Kenya,

Box 9.3 Local barriers to effective peacebuilding in Sierra Leone

Attempts at 'peacebuilding from below' in Sierra Leone reflected some of the structural barriers confronting post-conflict peacebuilding, many of which are the result of severe economic underdevelopment and poverty. However, some of that poverty at least is sustained and entrenched by local tradition and power structures. A significant part of the recovery strategy in Sierra Leone is to resource community-driven development projects, one of the thematic drivers of the World Bank peacebuilding strategy. In a study of the impact of one such project in Sierra Leone, and in an attempt to understand the sources of poverty and vulnerability, it was found that, in the traditional rural areas, there is a ruling lineage whose elders exercise control over marriage and over the labour of young men who are in dependent lineages. The effect of this is to push many of the young men to leave the rural areas to find work in the diamond mining areas, where they become vulnerable to recruitment by militias or where they become more marginalized and disaffected. The same study also found that 'there was a lack of true social cohesion in rural communities to support community driven development'. Village development committees, set up to administer development and humanitarian aid as part of post-conflict recovery, were often dominated and controlled by local ruling elites, and undemocratic practices and fraud also undermined the peacebuilding objectives of community-driven development. In a situation where local institutions had failed, the report suggested that problems of poverty and underdevelopment could only be tackled by both international and local implementing partners developing new roles and skills.

Source: Richards et al., 2004: 6–7

as does Donais in the case of approaches to peacebuilding from below in Sri Lanka, which

> have been hampered not only by the fact that the country's civil society is itself ethnically divided but also by the reality that grassroots mobilization in Sri Lanka has traditionally been aggressively nationalist in orientation. In other words, activist civil society organizations may not necessarily be pro-peace, but might just as easily engage in the type of factionalized, zero-sum politics that stand in the way of sustainable peacebuilding. (2009: 14)

There are, therefore, potential contradictions between international norms and values and the role of the state, on the one hand, and the 'authenticity' of peacebuilding from below, on the other, and this is reflected in many other post-conflict peacebuilding environments.[3] This strengthens the case for a cosmopolitan model and ethic which mediates between these levels. Much of the leading research on the next stage of peacebuilding, advocating a move beyond both the institutional constraints and orthodoxy of the liberal peace, on the one hand, and the controlling and stabilization-oriented approach of statebuilding, on the other, is tending in a direction which is cosmopolitan, in that it 'exemplifies a model of global governance where a cosmopolitan human rights agenda is consistent with the communitarian defence of political autonomy and cultural diversity' (Lidén, 2009: 616; see also Heathershaw,

2008; Richmond, 2005, 2008; Donais, 2009; Pearce, 2005; Pouligny, 2005; Ropers and Anuvatudom, 2014).

We see this transformative cosmopolitan model as the best way to advance the quest for the negotiation of a discursive practice of peace and peacebuilding, with peace education as a key component. Similar work to uncover multiple options for peace within the framework of systemic conflict theory (recognizing that conflict is a complex and holistic system, not a simple linear process) has also been conducted by Norbert Ropers and his colleagues at the Berghof Foundation for Peace Support, as noted earlier in this book. Reflecting on their experience of programmed peacebuilding in Sri Lanka, Ropers has argued both for the need to continue generating multiple options and spaces for peacebuilding and to be aware of the need to utilize feedback loops in order constantly to review, in a critical and reflective practice of peace research, the multiple causes and realities of conflict and similarly the multiple meanings of and pathways to peace (Ropers, 2008a; Smith, 2008; Fisher and Zimina, 2009; Mac Ginty, 2013).

Peace Education and Peacebuilding in Conflict Resolution

It is instructive at this point to reflect on where we began – that is, to reflect on the original norms and ethics which guided the work of those who evolved the concept of peacebuilding. Galtung, as we have seen, defined peacebuilding as systemically connected with peacekeeping and peacemaking, providing three grand strategies through which the three main manifestations of violence (structural, behavioural and cultural) could be addressed. The core guiding principle of Galtung and others was to reject violence as a means of resolving conflicts. The inspiration for this approach came from histories and philosophies of pacifism, non-violence and resistance to militarism, to counter oppression, and to connect this aspiration with an optimistic view of human potential which was emancipatory and non-violent.

Curle and Lederach acknowledge the influence in the development of their ideas of the radical Brazilian educator Paolo Freire, whose *Pedagogy of the Oppressed* was published in 1970. Freire, working with the poor in Brazil and Chile from the 1960s, argued against the 'banking' or teacher-directed nature of education as a form of oppression and in favour of 'education as liberation'. Freire was a visiting professor at Harvard in 1969, during the period when Adam Curle was director of the Harvard Center for Studies in Education and Development and beginning his own journey towards peace education. Curle's *Education for Liberation* was published in 1973, showing strong influences from Freire, and his *Making Peace* (1971) represented his attempt to integrate his ideas on education and peacemaking in the broader project of liberating human potential and transcending violence. More recently, reflections by some theorists and activists have suggested that the field has lost touch with its radical core values and has become implicated in the technocratic and blueprint-dominated version of the liberal peace outlined above. Diana Francis, for example, in a call to re-examine the basic values and objectives of conflict transformation and peacebuilding, has pointed out that

> the language of 'basic human needs', so central to conflict resolution, [has left] little place for the discourse of liberation, justice and human rights. Correspondingly, the theory and practice of nonviolent resistance and engagement in conflict have remained marginal to the conflict transformation field. If armed conflict is ever to be displaced as the recourse of oppressed groups (as 'conflict prevention' would seem to require) this is a serious limitation. (Francis, 2010; see also Fisher and Zimina, 2009)

Her proposed agenda is indeed a reminder that the field of peacebuilding, despite its successes, will not achieve the radical goals of liberation from oppression and violence which lie at the core of its original value system unless peacebuilders also take on the challenge, not only of resolving particular conflicts but of opposing the global phenomenon of war with non-violence.[4]

We conclude the main argument in this chapter with the suggestion that the development of peace education as a central component of peacebuilding provides an opportunity both to embed the core values of conflict resolution around non-violence and emancipation and to define a transformative cosmopolitan model which seeks to apply these values in peacebuilding. The literature on the effect of civil war on education and the importance of education in postwar peacebuilding is now conclusive. The World Education Forum held in Dakar in Senegal in April 2000 highlighted the problems of the impact of war and humanitarian emergencies on children's education and called for support for educational programmes that both addressed the need to promote mutual understanding, peace and tolerance and helped to prevent violence (World Education Forum, 2000). 'Education for All' goals were agreed at the Dakar Forum, but a study by Marc Sommers showed that the majority of primary-school children in war-affected areas have no realistic hope of attending school, and that, even in those situations where some schooling exists, girls are much more likely to be excluded than boys. Beyond primary-level education, programmes for youth are poorly supported, and the pressure or coercion to join aggressive militias is powerful. Sommers's conclusion makes a persuasive case for a major investment in education as a necessary component of post-conflict peacebuilding: 'Lack of investment in creative, participatory work on education for children and youth at risk makes a return to peace extremely difficult if not impossible' (Sommers, 2002: 1; see also Davies, 2005; Baxter and Ikowba, 2005).

It is also the case that a provision for the development of education and educational resources is increasingly a component of peace agreements. Dupuy has shown that, out of a total of 105 peace agreements signed between 1989 and 2005, fifty-seven had some provision for education as a component of postwar reconstruction. Four main themes emerge in these agreements:

'respecting and implementing the right to education; resuming education services; responding to conflict-created issues within the education sector; and actively reforming the education system as a way to address the issues at the heart of the incompatibility between the warring parties' (Dupuy, 2008: 155).

In this context, investment in education for peace provides a strategically effective driver for the transformative cosmopolitan model. Ian Harris has identified five key postulates that characterize contemporary peace education as follows: (i) it explains the roots of violence; (ii) it teaches alternatives to violence; (iii) it adjusts to cover different forms of violence; (iv) peace itself is a process that varies according to context; and (v) conflict is omnipresent (Harris, 2004). Developing this definition, Audra Degesys, citing recent research, has shown the potential of new pedagogies of peace education to address the goals of education as liberation:

> As education systems can sustain conflict within schools, they can also liberate it. Just as racism, sexism, and xenophobia were mentioned earlier as embedded and learned through the curriculum, these same power structures can be 'unlearned' and replaced with humanism, tolerance, diversity, democracy, and critical thinking. Schools can play an important role in promoting alternative understandings of racism, xenophobia, and what it means to be tolerant or democratic. To participate in this world as conscientious citizens or peacemakers, students need to be educated so that they might bring with them their own worldviews to respond to conflict. ... The pedagogy which engages students as participatory learners and envisioners of alternate possibilities of social reality is called transformative learning. Reflections, active learning, and transformative methods are necessary for the content of peace education to change attitudes towards conflict. (Degesys, 2008; see also Nagda et al. 2003; Fetherston and Kelly, 2007; Bush and Saltarelli, 2000; Nells, 2006)

Nick Lewer, working in partnership with the University of Bradford in the UK, has pioneered this pedagogy in Sri Lanka, advocating the advantages for peacebuilding for an education-based as opposed to a training-based approach, where education is associated with deeper acquisition of knowledge and critical capacity and training is limited to the learning of technique. Lewer and his colleagues engaged in the design and implementation of a peace education postgraduate diploma in Sri Lanka, a country which has been affected by a protracted social conflict over the last twenty-five years. The programme was designed in the context of a developing culture and capacity for conflict transformation that had evolved in Sri Lanka and was intended to utilize and develop high-level academic capacity to support 'peace preparedness' in the country. Despite the escalation of the conflict and its apparent termination following the military victory of the Sri Lankan government over the LTTE in 2009, the programme continues to have relevance and value in the context of the need to rebuild the country postwar in a manner that requires a peacebuilding orientation so as not to alienate and radicalize a new generation of Tamils (Harris and Lewer, 2005).

Peace education, defined in this way, provides a space for exploring the *via media* called for by Richmond in the negotiation of context-sensitive and hybrid values of peace and peacemaking. It also carries within it the core values of resistance to war and violence. Peacebuilding, as has been seen, is a complex and multi-level process involving a diversity of actors, a wide range of essential professional expertise, and a multiplicity of civil society actors. Within this range of expertise, conflict resolution serves as an enabling resource and a networking and connecting community of theorists and practitioners.

The Question of Evaluation

It can be seen from chapter 8 and from this chapter – indeed, from the whole of Part 1 of this book – that a great deal of emphasis in the conflict resolution field is placed on the principle that, for reconstruction and peacebuilding interventions to be justified, they must be seen to be in the best interests of those in whose name they are carried out. But how is this to be determined or evaluated? This is the main challenge in the arena of what is sometimes called peace and conflict impact assessment (PCIA). It is bedevilled both by methodological problems and by the fact that the conflict environment is highly politicized, so that statistics are themselves often found to be part of what is contested. The rest of this section should be seen as a continuation of the analysis of 'statistics of deadly quarrels' in chapter 3 and subject to many of the strictures considered there.

The literature on individual postwar reconstruction cases is too large and diverse to summarize usefully here, although many of the general accounts already referenced also include specific cases (see works listed in chapter 8, note 1). The key questions are: what are the *criteria* for measuring success, what are the appropriate *indicators*, and how can they be *measured*? For example, Doyle and Sambanis (2006) use a dataset of 145 civil wars running from 1945 to 1999 to determine criteria for measuring success in postwar peace processes. Here there is clear statistical evidence that, in difficult cases, a peace treaty combined with a 'transformative' UN intervention 'are crucial in maintaining the probability of success' and that, without them, the likelihood is 'very low' (see also the similar conclusion in Fortna, 2008; see also Diehl, 2008). There have been attempts to compare the relative success of different types of peace operation – for example, the RAND Corporation's studies of the 'use of armed force in the aftermath of a conflict to promote a transition to democracy' in UN-led and US-led 'nationbuilding' efforts (Dobbins et al., 2004; Reading 58), although see criticism of this by Durch (2007: 26–7).

Within this the discrepancy of evaluations is wide. Given the variety of approaches adopted, it is not surprising that overall statistical assessments sometimes produce wildly discordant results (Gartner and Melin, 2009). In the case of individual interventions, for example, Michael Lund notes that Cambodia 1992–3 has been variously classed as a 'success' (Doyle and Sambanis, 2000), a 'partial success' (Hampson, 1996) and a 'failure' (Durch et al., 2003; Roberts, 2009). The two most common criteria used are subsequent levels of violence, because these can be relatively easily measured, and whether post-intervention 'free and fair' elections have been held, because this is also easily verified (Downs and Stedman, 2002). But, as Lund notes, while there are many studies 'that take an interest in the restoration of minimum physical security, it is much harder to find rigorous, data-based analyses of the other desired outcomes of macro-level peacebuilding, especially using comparative data across several countries' (Lund, 2003: 31). If the criteria are widened, the perceived success rate falls. This is where more detailed analysis of the kind undertaken in chapter 8, which clearly distinguishes *phases* and *sectors* when assessing success, is useful. For example, whereas intervention in Haiti was widely classified as a success right through to the end of 2003 on the basis of intermediate levels of violence and initial elections (ibid.: 30), consideration of other sectors and phases painted a very different – and more informative – picture. With reference to box 8.2 (p. 252), taking each sector in turn: the arming of President Aristide's own *Chimères* militia instead of reliance on national armed forces and civilian police; the failure to prosecute political murders; the fiasco of an opposition boycott and 5 per cent turnout for the 2000 presidential election; the failure of the government to begin to provide essential services (exacerbated by the blocking of foreign aid); and the deepening social rift between Aristide's populism and business and professional interests – all clearly showed that, far from consolidation and progress towards normalization, even the phase 1 achievements of the 1994–6 intervention were unravelling.

As for evaluation and impact assessment of wider peacebuilding projects and enterprises, there has been an explosion of increasingly sophisticated methodologies since the pioneering work of Kenneth Bush and others, who noted at the end of the 1990s that: 'peace and conflict impact assessments now form established methodological elements of policy-making, and are used to minimize the likelihood of negative impacts of policy and to capitalize on positive impacts' (Bush, 1998). See box 9.4 for developments in the following ten years.

Since then, these efforts have gathered pace (Paffenholz and Reychler, 2007). In the third edition of this book, guided by Christine Hirst (2009), we noted the excellent analyses (also available online) from the OECD (Anderson et al., 2007); from the Berghof Research Centre of Constructive Conflict Management (Paffenholz, 2005; Schmelzle, 2005); from INCORE (Church and Shouldice, 2003); from the donor government 'Utstein' programme (Smith, 2004; Reading 61); from the European Centre for Conflict Prevention (Galama and van Tongeren, 2002); and from the Reflecting on Peace Practice Project (Woodrow, 2006). Studies such as these attempt to relate conflict-sensitive initiatives to stakeholder concepts of desirable peaceful change and to measurable criteria of effectiveness (Lederach et al., 2007; Davidson, 2007). This gives a good indication of the wealth of material now available. The task still is to put all of this together into a readily usable form that can be more widely disseminated and applied by the remarkable range of agents now engaged in reconstruction and peacebuilding activities.

Box 9.4 Peace and conflict impact assessment

An important element in assessing 'peacebuilding from below' is evaluating the effects of particular projects on the overall conflict dynamics. This raises methodological issues similar to those discussed in chapter 5 in relation to conflict prevention. How can we determine whether a particular intervention has positive or negative effects? There are two issues here: first, how to trace the chain of effects of a particular intervention in conflict; second, how to attribute any changes in the situation (such as a reduction in violent incidents) to a particular intervention.

Attempts to develop a methodology for peace and conflict impact assessment (PCIA) have developed rapidly in recent years. The main impetus for this tool has been the need of development agencies and donors to assess projects, and in particular to screen the positive or negative impacts on conflict of proposed projects. One approach, for example, is to develop indicators of the conflict, indicators of the project's effectiveness, and then to map the factors or variables that lie between the project and the conflict in an effort to trace connections. Impacts can be checked by interviews, questionnaires or focus groups with stakeholders. This micro-appraisal approach tends to relate a project to its immediate effects (for example, a workshop project might strengthen a particular constituency for peace; a cross-community training project might improve inter-ethnic relations in a particular locality). The next, demanding stage is then to assess how these low-level effects influence the overall conflict.

Another approach is pitched at analysing the overall impact of external interventions on a conflict's parties, dynamics and structure. Conflict analysis and conflict mapping are the main tools. DFID's Conflict Assessment approach, for example, combines conflict analysis, assessment of responses to the conflict by different departments of donor governments and analysis of strategic opportunities:

> The impacts of development policy and programmes at the macro- and micro-levels should be mapped. The approach is to make connections with the conflict analysis and consider whether development interventions have affected sources of tensions identified in the structural analysis; or affected incentives, capacities and relationships between warring groups identified in the actor analysis; or whether they have affected factors likely to accelerate or slow conflict identified in analysis of conflict dynamics. This draws on an analysis of the strategic context of the conflict and includes the preparation of conflict scenarios and identification of possible triggers for violence. (DFID, 2002)

As Hoffman (2004) warns, humility is important with regard to claims made for the impact of peacebuilding measures. The evidence to assess such claims may not always be available and the complexity of processes in conflicts will always make attribution difficult. Nevertheless, developing careful, well-evidenced evaluations of interventions by actors at different levels in conflict is a critical part of peacebuilding.

In this fourth edition of the book we follow Andrew Mack in concluding that what is now most required is a 'data revolution for measuring peacebuilding performance':

> Research and policymaking on peacebuilding in war-affected states are severely hampered by the lack of the most basic data on the most relevant issues. States emerging from what are often long periods of warfare tend to have grossly inadequate administrative data, very weak statistical capacity and long outdated census data. For both donors and 'fragile' state governments this means that creating peacebuilding policies and monitoring their impact based on evidence is currently extraordinarily difficult, if not impossible. (Mack, 2014: 109)

Mack usefully relates this to the evaluation of the Millennium Development Goals, where 'reliable survey-derived quantitative data on health, education and some other development goals were already being collected in many countries' (2014: 110). The 2008 launch of the International Dialogue on Peacebuilding and Statebuilding (IDPS) took this further. Fragile state members are now (in intention at any rate) given the lead role in shaping the dialogue, and issues of security, governance and justice – deemed too politically sensitive in the MDG process – are now central. In 2011, a New Deal for Engagement in Fragile States was supported by forty-one countries and international organizations committed to pursuing five Peacebuilding and Statebuilding Goals (PSGs): enhancing political legitimacy; improving security; increasing access to justice; promoting good economic governance; and managing taxation and service delivery capacity.

International meetings through 2012 and 2013 sought agreed *indicators* for the five PSG goals and how appropriate *sources of data* could be gathered. Mack explains how strenuous attempts were made to overcome tensions between the group of fragile and conflict-affected states and their northern partners. *Country-level indicators* capable of differentiating between different situations suffer from the lack of national statistics in many countries – as noted in chapter 3. Here 'nationwide household surveys' are often the only available sources. The alternative *common indicators* as used to assess MDG progress – for example, the 5-level measurement between 'fragility' to 'resilience' – are quite widely seen to reflect northern donor concerns rather than recipient choices, to ignore developmental successes that fall outside the radar, to imply stigmas of failure, and to be subject to mistrust after years of failure to measure the efficacy of aid in reducing poverty, let alone measures supposed to enhance peacebuilding (Mack, 2014: 110–11).

Mack ends with a powerful argument that what is now required is a 'data revolution', which he sees 'not, of course, [as] a sufficient condition for overcoming poverty or preventing war', but 'it *is* a necessary condition for evidence-based policies that pursue such goals' (original emphasis). In short:

> A data revolution would enhance peacebuilding activism, it would provide the evidence base needed to track progress, determine the impact of policy, and challenge governments – donors as well as agile states – that renege on their commitments. Such a revolution could also play a crucial role in providing the hard evidence that peacebuilding and post-conflict development policies are succeeding – or not. In fragile states, successes in these areas are key determinants of state legitimacy, and hence of reduced risks of conflict recurrence. (Mack, 2014: 112)

Conclusion

It is now generally established that a sustainable peace process must be embedded in the grassroots or communal levels of Lederach's conflict pyramid. However, what constitutes the authentic grassroots or the local community is frequently difficult to discern, and peacebuilding from below is subject to many of the same constraints, dilemmas and instabilities as elite-level peacebuilding. While respect for the cultural traditions and social mores of the local population is important, and while peacebuilding interventions should be conducted in partnership with community elders and leaders and in harmony with traditional conflict management practices, it should not be assumed that civil society operating at the local level is inevitably a quintessentially pure locus for peaceful activity and values. As a result of the impact of the conflict, of population displacement and of other factors, traditional communal relations may have become submerged under new militaristic hierarchies. Local groups may not be benignly autonomous actors, and they are susceptible to the effects of structural global forces, structural pressures, and national and regional power plays that characterize most violent conflicts. Indeed, local groups operating at the grassroots may well be either highly disempowered and fragmented and lacking any capacity for peace activity; they may be local agents of stronger external groups, including militias or criminal groups or clan-based politics; or they may be genuine peacebuilding organizations with authentic roots in the community, but compelled to speak the language of peacebuilding as defined by powerful donors and patrons.

For these reasons, peacebuilding from below is not a panacea that avoids the complex challenges of conflict resolution and peacebuilding at all levels and dimensions of conflict. But this chapter has shown how genuine peacebuilding has from the start been at the heart of conflict resolution. It embodies the deepest level of response in the hourglass model as presented in chapter 1. Postwar peacebuilding enshrines the norm of non-violence in all its aspects through the creation and enhancement of institutions and practices that permanently transform what has been cruel destruction into new spaces where the lives and life hopes of future generations can flourish. In this task it joins hands with 'deep peacemaking', which, in the shape of reconciliation, forms the topic of the next chapter.

RECOMMENDED READING

Autesserre (2014); Dayton and Kriesberg (2009); Francis (2010); Galama and van Tongeren (2002); Lederach (2005); Mac Ginty (2013); Mack (2014); Reychler and Paffenholz (2001); Woodhouse (1999a).

RELEVANT EXTRACTS IN *THE CONTEMPORARY CONFLICT RESOLUTION READER*

Reading 58: J. Dobbins et al., The US and UN Roles in Nation-Building
Reading 59: R. Mac Ginty, Hybrid Peace: The Interaction Between Top-Down and Bottom-Up Peace
Reading 61: D. Smith, Towards a Strategic Framework for Peacebuilding: Getting their Act Together
Reading 64: P. van Tongeren et al., Women Take the Peace Lead in Pastoral Kenya

CHAPTER TEN

Reconciliation

Reconciliation – restoring broken relationships and learning to live non-violently with radical differences – can be seen as the ultimate goal of conflict resolution. As suggested in chapter 8, the ending of direct violence makes conflict resolution possible, negotiation between overlapping interests opens the door to settlement, and the overcoming of structural injustice creates an enduring space within which further transformations can occur. But it is the long-term process of reconciliation that constitutes the essence of the lasting transformation that conflict resolution seeks – the hallmark of the integrative power that alone binds disparate groups together into genuine societies. In the terminology of chapter 1 (figure 1.3, p. 16), reconciliation constitutes the heart of deep peacemaking and cultural peacebuilding. Indeed, sometimes reconciliation is equated with peacebuilding in general, and thereby with conflict resolution (Reading 22: Lederach, 1997), and is contrasted as such with approaches that focus mainly on power brokerage and institutional statebuilding – as, for example, in this criticism of international involvement:

> statebuilding and peacebuilding are not synonymous and are potentially contradictory: the former involves the consolidation of government authority and the latter compromise and consensus-building. The establishment of government institutions cannot be the sole measure of successful reconciliation. In a culture where reparations are at the heart of peacemaking, reconciliation cannot simply be reduced to power-sharing arrangements. (Bradbury and Healy, 2010: 107)

Among Palestinians, similarly, there is much debate about the extent to which national reconciliation (for example, between Hamas and Fatah) must precede, or at any rate accompany, Palestinian statebuilding, on the one hand, and political settlement with the Israelis, on the other. From a different angle, in *The Politics of Reconciliation in Multicultural Societies* (Kymlicka and Bashir, 2008) two approaches to overcoming the problem of political exclusion are seen to be both mutually dependent and mutually competing in a manner familiar from chapter 8: the *politics of difference*, which concerns the 'recognition and empowerment of minorities in multicultural societies', and the *politics of reconciliation*, which is seen to involve 'reparations, truth-telling and healing among former adversaries'.

These views echo another theme in recent writing on reconciliation. Political theorists such as Mouffe argue that political conflict is unavoidable, but that the aim should be to move from antagonistic to agonistic relations – from fighting to adversarial relations contained in a political system. In this view, it is accepted that societies must live with enduring differences and complete reconciliation may be unrealistic. Some argue that reconciliation may even suppress conflicts that need to be pursued (Little, 2014). In the agonist's view, the aim should be to recognize the legitimacy of the opponent, to accept adversary relations, but to avoid enmity. Reconciliation is seen not as a means of eliminating differences but as providing a framework for the contending parties to work through and live with their differences (Schaap, 2005).

We see both of these as part of the wider process of transforming violent relations into peaceful relations after war. All of this is further compounded by the fact that the scope for reconciliation – and the different ways by which it can be achieved – varies greatly from culture to culture. The question of what we understand reconciliation to mean and at what point it is expected to take place has divided scholars (Reading 45; Assefa, 1999; Bar-Siman-Tov, 2004; Rosoux, 2009). Although the question of reconciliation is central at other points on the conflict scale, in this chapter our main focus is on long-term reconciliation between former enemies after violent conflict.

Four Meanings of Reconciliation

Reconciliation in this broad sense is a complex process made up of several components that all play their part. There is reconciliation in the sense of acquiescence in what already exists ('I am reconciled to my fate'). Although this seems negative, it captures the idea of voluntary acceptance of what is as yet not an ideal outcome – a necessary element in peaceful politics. Then there is reconciliation in the sense of 'reconciling financial or other accounts'. This again may seem limited, but it encapsulates the notion of comparison and correlation of stories to the point where they are at least not fatally incompatible or irreconcilable. Third, and more creative, is the idea of 'reconciling opposites' or bridging diversity. Here we begin to encounter the possibility of mutual change in the interest of opening up otherwise inaccessible opportunities. And, finally, we reach the culminating sense of 'reconciliation between former enemies' in which past enmity is set aside and emotional space is created for reforging new relationships (Pankhurst, 1998). This last stage happens more usually between individuals in small groups, such as families or villages, where personal contacts have been strong – particularly in more traditional pastoral societies. But reconciliation between larger groups – even nations – is also possible, reaching from a reopening of diplomatic relations, through to symbolic gestures such as the laying of wreaths or formal expressions of regret, and on to elaborate efforts to create common institutions or foster cultural exchanges, as in Franco-German relations after the Second World War. Table 10.1 sets out these four senses of reconciliation and relates them to the stages of conflict escalation and de-escalation first introduced in

Table 10.1 Four dimensions of reconciliation

	Aspects of reconciliation	Stages of conflict de-escalation
1	Accepting the status quo	Ending violence
2	Correlating accounts	Overcoming polarization
3	Bridging opposites	Managing contradiction
4	Reconstituting relations	Celebrating difference

figure 1.2. This shows how the first three meanings, although falling short of full reconciliation, are necessary constituent moments in the passage from violence and polarization to the peaceful management of contradiction and on to a final normalization of relations under a new dispensation.

Some processes of reconciliation encompass more of these meanings and embrace them more fully than others. We can distinguish shallow reconciliation, where elites agree a political settlement, from deeper reconciliation, in which not only elites but also institutions and the societies are fully involved.

Between Separation and a Fusion of Identities

Needless to say, the road to deep reconciliation is often long and tortuous. In cases involving states, it may be necessary first to win sufficient domestic support to launch a reconciliation initiative. Successfully carrying it through then depends on sustaining domestic support in each country and on successful negotiations between countries leading to reciprocated actions. Non-governmental initiatives are often important in the early phases of such processes and in implementing reconciliation at the societal level. The successful cases of Germany's postwar reconciliation with its neighbours indicate what a long period of time this can take (Feldman, 2012).

We ended chapter 8 by noting how, in postwar reconstruction, many insist that there is no point in attempting reconciliation in the early stages and, indeed, that it might be counter-productive. Deeply traumatized individuals and groups are not ready for such an undertaking. This relates to controversy about the 'contact hypothesis' in conflict resolution – the argument that the more contact there is between conflict parties, the more scope there is for resolution (Hewstone and Brown, 1986). A number of commentators deny this and advocate, on the contrary, a separation of conflictants wherever possible – good fences make good neighbours: '[T]he data supports the argument that separation of groups is the key to ending ethnic civil wars. ... There is not a single case where non-ethnic civil politics were created or restored by reconstruction of ethnic identities, power-sharing coalitions, or state-building' (Kaufmann, 1996: 161).

At the other end of the spectrum are those who argue that what is required is nothing less than an eventual redefinition of 'self/other' identity constructs themselves, so that a sense of 'we' replaces the 'us/them' split (Northrup, 1989: 80) – or at least identities based on a view of 'them' as the enemy and 'us' as embattled victims begin to dissolve (Kelman, 2004).

Given the mismatch between state borders and the geographical distribution of peoples, we do not see physical separation as a feasible general strategy. And increasing interdependence in a globalized world dictates that, whatever conclusion is reached about the contact hypothesis, individuals and groups, including former enemies, will in most cases have to learn to accommodate difference and live together. On the other hand, we think that most of the problems of mutual accommodation lie on this side of a final transformation in basic identities.

Dealing with the Past: Trauma and Atrocity

Although there is a continuing general need for reconciliation within and between all societies in order to sustain social cohesion, the greatest difficulty from a conflict resolution perspective comes when conflict has escalated through the stages of difference, contradiction, polarization and violence to the point where atrocities have been perpetrated and deep injuries received. It is reconciliation after violent conflict that poses the most acute challenge. In these circumstances it is rarely a case of 'putting Humpty Dumpty together again' in any simple sense. Too much has happened, too many relations have been severed, too many norms violated, too many identities distorted, too many traumas endured. To reach the transformative levels of bridging differences and restoring trust requires a capacity for innovation and creative renewal likely to be beyond the capacity of many societies in the immediate aftermath of violence:

> People know if they are from a war-torn country how difficult it is to sit down across the table in the same room with an adversary. ... It is likely that adversaries will say: 'We cannot negotiate because we despise the other side too much. They have killed our children, they have raped our women, they have devastated our villages.' (Carter, 1992: 24)

Before reaching the point where it is possible to climb down the escalation ladder, it is necessary for individuals and groups to recover from trauma, and for the time-bomb of remembered injustice to be defused. In other words, we have to deal with the past in order to clear the ground in the present for the building of a shared future (Lederach, 1997: 27). We will, therefore, look at the challenge of overcoming psychological trauma and at the contentious debate about restoring justice before returning at the end of the chapter to a reconsideration of the wider role of reconciliation in conflict de-escalation and the reconstruction of a shared future.

Acknowledging trauma

There is space here to deal only briefly with the complex and still controversial subject of psycho-social healing (Herman, 1992). The 'invisible effects' of war are often harder to treat than the physical effects:

> The first victims of war are often women and children. Even though they do not lose life or limbs, they are often deeply traumatised in ways not visible to the naked eye. Victims of violence and rape cannot just walk back into everyday life as if nothing happened. As we all know, in the former Yugoslavia, peace has yet to break out for many of the victims. That is why psycho-social work deserves to be a high priority in our emergency aid programmes. (Emma Bonino, European commissioner with responsibility for humanitarian aid, quoted in Agger, 1995: foreword)

Whether western post-traumatic stress disorder (PTSD) approaches are appropriate in non-western cultural settings or not (Summerfield, 1996), the important point from the perspective of conflict resolution and reconciliation is, as Patrick Bracken explains, that psychological transformation has to accompany the relational tasks of reconciliation if the deeper processes of conflict resolution are to be achieved (Bracken and Petty, 1998). These are evidently culturally sensitive and long-term undertakings, and many can never recover from such terrible injuries and losses. Even when reconciliation is not possible at the individual level, however, acknowledgement of trauma at the level of the group or the nation may be a precondition of moving forward towards a shared future – as in the South African case.

Amnesia, justice or revenge?

A great deal has been written from a conflict resolution perspective on the relationship between justice and peace in attempting to rebuild social relations after large-scale violence and war (see the recommended reading at the end of this chapter). Here we will take Andrew Rigby's *Justice and Reconciliation: After the Violence* (2001) and Rama Mani's *Beyond Retribution: Seeking Justice in the Shadows of War* (2002) as our initial guides.

Rigby frames his book by contrasting 'amnesia', or a forgive-and-forget approach, as one way of 'moving on' for societies emerging out of 'division, bloodshed, and collective nightmare' with the alternative of 'trials, purges and the pursuit of justice', which he sees as at the opposite pole (2001: 2–3). He suggests that truth commissions and compensatory reparations lie somewhere between the two.

Mani distinguishes between three interdependent dimensions of public justice, all of which, in our view, have a role to play in opening the way to eventual reconciliation by providing an alternative to private vengeance. There is, first, what she calls legal justice or the rule of law, the 'entire apparatus of the justice system', which has usually been delegitimized if not effectively destroyed during the violence and needs to be rebuilt. Then there

Table 10.2 Justice: between amnesia and vengeance

Amnesia	Public justice	Vengeance
Forgive and forget	Dealing with the past publicly and collectively	I will repay

is 'rectificatory justice' to deal with past abuses in response to gross human rights violations, war crimes and crimes against humanity. Third comes 'distributive justice' to address 'the structural and systemic injustices such as political and economic discrimination and inequalities of distribution that are frequently underlying causes of conflict' (Mani, 2002: 3–11).

Adapting these distinctions, we can usefully define the broad terrain of public justice that concerns us here by contrasting it with amnesia on one side (let us forget about the past) and private revenge on the other (let us avenge the past by taking the law into our own hands) (see table 10.2). Some societies seem able to 'forgive and forget' much more easily than others and to achieve full reconstitution of relations between former enemies without having to go through the travails of justice, perhaps for cultural reasons. Others appear to be unable to do so no matter what efforts are made by internal and external peacemakers – only private vengeance, it seems, can requite the burning sense of injustice. We return to these two alternatives below. But first we will try to clarify the resources that have been used by those societies that have chosen to deal with past atrocity through our broad definition of public justice.

Peace or Justice? Not Exclusive Alternatives

It has often been said that there is a contradiction between peace and justice. Pauline Baker, for example, poses the question like this:

> Should peace be sought at any price to end the bloodshed, even if power-sharing arrangements fail to uphold basic human rights and democratic principles? Or should the objective be a democratic peace that respects human rights, a goal that might prolong the fighting and risk more atrocities in the time that it takes to reach a negotiated solution? (Baker, 1996: 564)

She contrasts 'conflict managers' for whom the goal is peace (as in Angola, Cambodia and Mozambique) with 'democratizers' whose goal is justice (as in Namibia, El Salvador and Bosnia).[1]

The field of 'transitional justice', which deals with such dilemmas, has now emerged as an important area of research (Reading 60; Fischer, 2011). Although in chapter 8 we acknowledged a tension along these lines between the negative and positive tasks of postwar peacebuilding, we do not see the alternatives in such stark terms. The concepts of peace and justice are not as monolithic as is often made out. Although the negative peace of order and the cessation of direct violence may in some situations appear to be incompatible with the requirements of justice, the positive peace of reconciliation and psycho-social healing largely presupposes it. In other words, the passage from

Table 10.3 From negative to positive peace via justice

Negative peace	Justice	Positive peace
Absence of violence	Rule of law	Long-term reconciliation
	Truth commissions/trials	
	Reparation/distributive justice	

negative to positive peace runs through justice (see table 10.3). And, following Mani, we see justice itself as multidimensional, opening space for reconciliation via a range of combinations of truth commissions, trials, or reparation and rehabilitation measures, depending upon the legal capacity and the nature of the social divisions in the country in question. In other words, for reconciliation to be possible there usually needs to be sufficient *acceptance* by former enemies of the legitimacy of postwar rule of law, sufficient *correlation of accounts* to allow truth commissions and trials to defuse issues of rectificatory justice, and sufficient *bridging of differences* through compensation, reparation or structural adjustments to deliver adequate prospects of improved distributive justice in future. We will look at each of these in turn before exploring in the final section the possibilities for reconciliation in the full sense of a *reconstitution of relationships*.

Alternative Paths to Reconciliation

Having established our conceptual framework, let us briefly review the range of experiments undertaken by different societies in navigating the difficult journey from war to social reintegration in recent years. Good case studies can be found in Rothstein (1999), Whittaker (1999) and Rotberg and Thompson (2000), as well as in Rigby (2001) and Mani (2002). We look first at amnesia as a deliberate policy choice, then at three linked approaches within the broad ambit of justice (truth commissions, trials and compensations). We conclude with what seem to be the culturally conditioned opposites of traditional peacemaking, sometimes in the form of ritual healing, that are possible in some societies and with an apparently never-ending retaliatory settling of accounts that seems to prevail in others.

Official amnesia – letting go of the past

As Rigby reminds us (2001: 2–3), despite the previous vindictiveness of Franco's regime in Spain, in the transition to democracy after his death in 1975 'there was no purge, but rather an exercise in collective amnesia'. Here the suggested explanation is that this was a 'pact of oblivion' made by two elites for fear of counter-coups by the Spanish military. Similarly, in Cambodia, the initial renunciation of the 'spirit of revenge' was a consequence of agreements between 'the Cambodian political elite' and the surviving Khmer Rouge leadership. At the time of the first edition of this book, many Cambodian school textbooks still devoted fewer than ten lines to the Pol Pot years, although this has now changed. In both cases Rigby notes that apparent general acquiescence in this approach may have been a result of the widespread complicity of grassroots membership on either side of the previous divide, often splitting families. Even so, in both countries a younger generation, born after the violent period and therefore not implicated, is demanding more information and a public reckoning on the previous traumas, if for no other reason than to ensure that there can never be a repetition: 'lest we forget'. So perhaps there are some things best forgotten, such as 'ancient hatreds' (here we need the waters of Lethe), but others we want to remember, such as the memory of the victims and reasons why violence is best prevented (here we need the waters of Acheron). Ultimately, when all significant links with current politics are broken, we are no doubt left with pure historical enquiry – who can now really understand why Guelphs and Ghibellines were so passionately opposed to each other in medieval Europe?

Truth commissions – honouring the past

In contrast to this is the risky path of 'truth commissions' – what Desmond Tutu, chair of the South African Truth and Reconcilation Commission, calls the 'third way' between 'Nuremberg and national amnesia' (Tutu, 1999: 10–36). Truth commissions have been set up in more than twenty countries, including abortive or half-hearted efforts in Sri Lanka and Haiti and rather more substantial attempts in El Salvador, Chile and Guatemala. Each reflects the nature of the situation in that country (see box 10.1). A searching discussion of dilemmas and controversies can be found in Rotberg and Thompson (2000).

More elaborate still has been the most famous example: the Truth and Reconciliation Commission (TRC) in South Africa. The 1995 Promotion of National Unity and Reconciliation Act required the TRC to contribute to the building of 'a historic bridge between the past of a deeply divided society characterised by strife, conflict, untold suffering and injustice, and a future founded on the recognition of human rights, democracy and peaceful coexistence and development opportunities for all South Africans, irrespective of colour, race, belief or sex' (quoted in Villa-Vincencio and Verwoerd, 2000: 280). The plan was for societal reconciliation to be effected through as wide a sample as possible of individual testimonies and responses. Avoiding vindictiveness, on the one hand, and a disregard for wrongs and suffering, on the other, the hope was that full public disclosure of human rights violations since 1960 and an attempt to harmonize competing versions of the past within what Lyn Graybill calls 'a single universe of comprehensibility' (1998: 49), together with some acknowledgement of responsibility, if not expression of regret (Committee on Human Rights Violations), and some measure of reparation for

Box 10.1 Truth commissions in the 1990s
Secretary-General

In El Salvador, the Commission on the Truth set up on 5 May 1992 reported back to the UN Secretary-General and President Cristiani on 22 September with a 200-page assessment of 22,000 complaints received of violations perpetrated since 1980. Direct evidence was confirmed in 7,312 cases and indirect evidence in a further 13,562, with 97 per cent of the human rights violations attributed to the 'rightist military, paramilitary, security forces, and death squads' and 3 per cent to the opposition rebels (UN Doc. S/25500). Perpetrators were named, despite protests from the ruling ARENA party, and 103 army officers were dismissed, but a blanket amnesty was granted by the ARENA-controlled National Assembly and recommendations for a purge of the Supreme Court of Justice were obstructed (Hampson, 1996: 156–7).

In Chile, the National Commission on Truth and Reconciliation set up in 1990, as a result of a deal with General Pinochet, had to complete its work in only eighteen months, met behind closed doors and could name none of the perpetrators – although the report was handed to President Aylwin on television and a public apology was made. It was greatly aided by the thousands of transcripts on disappearances that had been collected during the seventeen-year Pinochet dictatorship by the Roman Catholic Church's Vicaria de la Solidaridad.

In Guatemala, the official Commission on Historical Clarification, despite a limited mandate and scant resources that frustrated some, used provisions in the National Reconciliation Law to recommend trials in a number of cases (Guatemalan Commission for Historical Clarification, 1999). This was supplemented by civil society initiatives, notably the Roman Catholic Church's unofficial Project for the Recovery of Historical Memory, recorded 6,000 testimonies in local Indian languages and disseminated its report via theatre, radio, workshops and ceremonies. The army and civilian self-defence patrols were blamed for most of the 150,000 deaths and 50,000 disappearances. Two days after the presentation of the report, its coordinator was beaten to death in Guatemala City (Crocker, 2000: 111).

---

the victims (Committee on Reparations and Rehabilitation), would open up an emotional space sufficient for accommodation, if not forgiveness, with the question of punishment or amnesty abstracted or postponed (Committee on Amnesty) (Asmal et al., 1996; Boraine et al., 1997; Boraine, 2000).

Needless to say, as a middle way, the TRC has been severely criticized from opposite directions, by those arguing that the country should not look back and risk causing new wounds and by others (for example, Steve Biko's family) arguing that human rights violations should be tried and punished in courts of law (Gutmann and Thompson, 2000). From the point of view of the ANC, the main purpose of the TRC was to be a truth commission: reconciliation was something of an afterthought (and one for which Archbishop Desmond Tutu had the main responsibility). There is little evidence that the TRC made much impact on reconciliation at the individual level, and this was not its original purpose. For the ANC, the overwhelming political purpose was to force proponets of apartheid to acknowledge the evils of the apartheid regime. Along similar lines, parallel to the International Criminal Tribunal for Rwanda (ICTR), the 1998 National Unity and Reconciliation Commission in Rwanda employed some 11,000 local community courts (the *Gacaca* system) to deal with lower-level crimes through processes of confession, apology and repara-tion (fines and community service). This can agan be interpreted as a contribu-tion to peaceful community-building and reconcilation, but it has also been seen in some quarters as a means whereby the victorious Rwandan Patriotic Front government aimed to assign collective guilt to the defeated Hutus.

Defenders of the TRC maintain that justice is broader than retributivists make out – involving procedural justice as well as the wider healing and therapeutic qualities of restorative justice, which are what is needed in a raw politicized atmosphere where legitimacy is still in question (Kiss, 2000). A punitive approach would be interpreted as partisan 'victor's justice'. These compromises are unavoidable aspects of 'transitional justice' in societies coming out of violence and attempting to rebuild the foundations of social consensus (Kritz, 1995). Rotberg describes the TRC experiment as an 'enriched form of justice' in which 'truth for amnesty is said to achieve justice through reconciliation' (2000: 14). We comment briefly on each of these components.

Many agree that, in an environment where 'truth' is still bitterly contested, a commission of this nature can uncover 'truths' inaccessible to courts of law.[2] Unlike most other truth commissions, proceedings in the TRC were held in public and communicated as widely as possible. The outcome was not a single 'official' version of the truth but painfully and emotionally elicited insights and understandings, as the heart-rending stories of victims were listened to with the deepest respect in the Committee on Human Rights Abuses and sometimes explicitly acknowledged by perpetrators. The commissioners' *Final Report*, containing the evidence given by 20,000 victims, is an extraordinary and very moving record. Although it fell far short of a full measure of atonement and forgiveness, many attest to the healing power of the process, as past sufferings were acknowledged and honoured (Minow, 2000), and to the narrowing of the opportunities to continue to circulate unchallenged lies about apartheid.

As far as punishment or immunity was concerned, unlike what was done in many other countries, no blanket amnesty was given. Amnesty was awarded or withheld on an individual basis for more than 7,000 applicants, according to whether the Committee on Amnesty was satisfied that full disclosure had been made and whether the motives had been 'political' rather than merely criminal – an admittedly difficult and loosely defined distinction. The judge-ments were often highly controversial and on occasion overturned by South Africa's High Court (Slye, 2000).

Such in outline was the compromise attempted in South Africa in condi-tions where the defeat of apartheid had been decisive, where there were suf-ficient resources to mount the TRC, where Christian and indigenous African *ubuntu* traditions could be drawn upon and, above all, where outstanding leadership was providentially displayed. Even then, a public opinion survey published in July 1998 suggested that two-thirds of South Africans at that time thought that the TRC had led to a deterioration in race relations rather than societal reconciliation (Rotberg, 2000: 19). Nevertheless, in our view this experiment, no doubt in its details unique to conditions in South Africa at that time, offers a magnificent and hopeful example of a creative attempt to handle the past in a way that furthers societal reconciliation in the present and promotes conflict resolution into the future.

Trials – bringing the past before the tribunal of the present

This is a large subject, but we will confine ourselves to one main point (for the wider debate about war crimes tribunals, compare Mak (1995) and Meron (1993)). Although often presented as an alternative to truth commissions, we suggest that national or international criminal tribunals are better regarded in most cases as complementary. We can see this through the example of Richard Goldstone, head of the 1992 commission to investigate criminal conduct in South Africa and subsequently appointed as the first chief prosecutor of the United Nations International Criminal Tribunals for the former Yugoslavia and Rwanda. Goldstone acknowledges that the relationship between peace and justice is a complicated one, inasmuch as without a cessation of violence there is usually no hope of bringing perpetrators of atrocities to justice. Nevertheless, he insists that: 'Without establishing a culture of law and order, and without satisfying the very deep need of victims for acknowledgement and retribution, there is little hope of escaping future cyclical outbreaks of violence' (1997: 107).

The mention of retribution makes it appear that the non-retributory mechanism of truth commissions would not be deemed adequate. But in a chapter entitled 'The South African Solution: Is Truth Sufficient?' (2000: 59–73), Goldstone concludes that the TRC achieved results that 'made South Africa a better country' and could not have been achieved 'through normal criminal processes', which would have been long and costly and rejected as politically motivated by the majority of white South Africans: 'Suffice it for me to state here my great admiration for the awesome task it performed during its thirty-month existence. I have no doubt that South Africans will live to appreciate its work and legacy' (ibid.: 71–2).

There are many critics of international tribunals, not least supporters of those indicted, who are usually convinced that the tribunal is a political tool of their enemies. But for the authors of this book they are an essential ingredient in the struggle to assert internationally endorsed humane standards, even in the crucible of intense conflict.

Apologies – regretting the past

State apologies are an increasing phenomenon in modern politics. In cases where they are made by leaders of state in their official capacity and repeated, reinforced by appropriate gestures and clearly shared by the society, state apologies appear to be helpful for reconciliation, especially as they are supported by restitutive actions (Cohen, 2004). However, when these conditions are not met, apologies can create a domestic backlash, as Lind (2010) argues, which can make matters worse. The evidence of deep reconciliation cases, such as in postwar Germany, suggests that apologies need to be complemented by further measures such as joint commemorations, people-to-people contacts, and restitution and reparations.

Reparation – future compensation for the past

We will say little about compensation and reparation except to remind ourselves that this is often recognized to be a key element in the wider ambit of justice enabling greater scope for reconciliation. In Chile, efforts were made to compensate survivors and the families of victims, while the Reparation and Rehabilitation Committee of the South African TRC recommended to parliament who should be compensated and by how much (Rotberg, 2000: 11). In the event, victims rarely receive much, and the spread of compensation is inevitably seen as arbitrary and controversial. Martha Minow (2000) includes not just money payments, but monuments, parks and renamed buildings as part of the compensation and sees this as essential to the long-term vision of social transformation. This merges into issues of reconstruction and improvements in distributive justice that become part of the wider peacebuilding effort. On the other hand, in some cases – for example, reparations for Palestinian refugees as part of a final settlement with Israel – the cost of reparations may run into billions of dollars (even then this may not match the costs borne by the 5 million Palestinian refugees), and the issue may be decisive for the success of the peace process as a whole.

We end this section by noting two contrasting cultural responses to past violence in order to underline the particularity of different cultures and traditions.

Ritual healing and indigenous peace initiatives – exorcizing and redeeming the past

Here we draw attention to resources found within many indigenous societies that have impressed conflict resolvers, such as the role of traditional healers in Mozambique (Nordstrom, 1995) or the work of lineage leaders, women's initiatives and local community peace processes in Somalia (Farah, 1993; Bradbury and Healy, 2010).

In some cultures, where misfortune and violence is often attributed to possession by bad spirits, there is scope for remarkably swift reconciliation through public cleansing ceremonies. In these cases, the war is seen as a calamity imposed from outside which was the fault of no individual or group. One of the criticisms of the Regional and Local Dispute Resolution Committees set up in South Africa after the 14 September 1991 National Peace Convention was that this was elitist and dominated predominantly by white business and legal, political and church leaders out of touch with grassroots cultures, which is where the deepest sufferings have been felt (Gastrow, 1995: 70-1). On the other hand, there are pertinent warnings against indiscriminately resourcing 'indigenous processes' which may turn out to represent transparent mechanisms for perpetuating local systems of oppression, exclusion and exploitation (Pankhurst, 1998).

The remarkable story of indigenous reconciliation and peacemaking in Somalia has been outlined briefly in chapter 6. Because the situation was made possible by a mixture of unwritten customary law, Somali shari'a law within the Islamic Sunni Shafi'i school, traditional values, and local codes of social conduct by clan elders, Muslim *ulema* and women's groups demonstrates the complexity and variety of the resources available. The reality that 'making reparations' lies at the heart of Somali peacemaking shows how many western assumptions about reconciliation need to be revised. And the fact that all of this was achieved in the middle of ongoing conflict, often of ongoing war, makes it all the more remarkable and impressive. Here are examples of the rich resources for reconcilation available in most societies, often wrongly neglected by the international community and, despite much inspiring work, as suggested in chapter 9, still not adequately understood by many within the conflict resolution community.

Retaliation – *cleaning the slate by avenging the past*

A very different response comes in societies where traditions of clan-based reprisal and vendetta are endemic, as exemplified in the Balkans. Although retaliation is usually – and rightly – condemned from a conflict resolution perspective as the antithesis of reconciliation, we must acknowledge that, in the eyes of many in these traditions, it is only after reprisal and redress that the balance of justice is restored and relations can be re-formed. Needless to say, the trouble with this is that what to one party is restoration of balance to another is usually a sharp disequilibrium. This can even be seen in the aftermath of the 11 September 2001 attacks, where an initial wave of sympathy for the United States was enhanced by a widespread sense that the suffering there had somehow restored a measure of equivalence that opened space for reconciliation if used creatively. That was not how it was viewed in the United States, however, where the clamour for reprisal was loud.

Reconciliation and Conflict Resolution: Going Down the Escalation Ladder

In conclusion, having noted the political and cultural differences from case to case, we return to our main theme of the essential ingredients in the general process of what Mervyn Love (1995) calls 'peacebuilding through reconciliation'. Conflict resolvers have made important contributions here over the years, notably Joseph Montville, whose work on reconciliation and healing in political conflict resolution comprises a three-stage 'conflict resolution strategy' for reconciliation through a process of 'transactional contrition and forgiveness' based on the problem-solving approach (1993: 122–8). Kelman (1999) offers a comparable method for 'transforming the relationship between former enemies'. Lederach (1997, 1999, 2001) looks to Psalm 85, verse 10, for his inspiration that reconciliation is the place where 'truth and mercy have met together, justice and peace have kissed', while Kriesberg (1998b) also sees the components as truth (revelation, transparency, acknowledgement), justice (restitution) and mercy (acceptance, forgiveness, compassion, healing) leading to peace (security, respect, harmony, well-being). Using a psychodynamic approach, Volkan et al. (1990) argue that the fundamental need is for public acknowledgement of past hurts, which lets the protagonists and victims begin to move on from rage and hatred to acceptance of loss and ultimately acceptance of each other.

It is important to recognize, however, that forgiveness of enemies is not necessary for some of the most remarkable examples of the trasformation of the deepest levels of hurt imaginable into highly impressive initatives in reconcilation and non-violent peacemaking (see box 10.2).

We end the chapter by retracing the four stages of reconciliation in relation to the de-escalation stages introduced in chapter 1: ending violence, overcoming polarization, managing contradiction and celebrating difference.

Political closure and acceptance: preconditions for reconciliation

The first requirement is for some measure of political closure, at least to the point where a return to violence has become unlikely. It is much harder to

---

Box 10.2 The Tim Parry Johnathan Ball Foundation for Peace

On 20 March 1993, a bomb exploded in the centre of Warrington, a town in the north of England. It was planted by a paramilitary group opposed to the British presence in Northern Ireland, but its only victims were two young boys who happened to be near the site of the explosion. The boys were twelve-year-old Tim Parry and three-year-old Johnathan Ball. The response of Tim's parents, Colin and Wendy Parry, was not to seek revenge, but to transform their loss, and honour Tim's and Johnathan's lives, by working to break the cycle of violence. Their motive had nothing to do with forgiving the perpetrators, whose identity they still do not know. They decided to establish a peace foundation in Warrington to support all victims of political violence in Northern Ireland and elsewhere, and to foster an understanding of conflict and how to manage it nonviolently, particularly among young people. They set up the Tim Parry Johnathan Ball Foundation for Peace in 1995, with the simple purpose of inspiring people, through various programmes of peace education, to resolve their differences non-violently. In 2004 Colin Parry won Rotary International's 'World Understanding and Peace' Award. The Warrington Peace Centre has now worked for over twenty years to develop values and skills related to peacemaking among young people (see Parry and Parry, 1994, and www.foundation4peace.org/).

Box 10.3 Magnanimity in victory: winning the peace after winning the war

At the time of the conquest of Britain, the Roman poet Claudian boasted how Rome:

> Took the conquered to her bosom,
> Made mankind a single family,
> Mother not mistress of the nations,
> Turning her subjects into citizens,
> Conquering far-off lands a second time,
> By the bonds of affection.

The conquered aristocracies were made Roman citizens – every five years all male citizens had to register for the census in Rome. From this all the privileges of citizenship followed. While an empire had been forged through the force of 'threat power', enduring consolidation could only be achieved by converting this into the legitimacy of 'integrative power'.

Readers will have their own responses to this imperial boast – echoed by comparable claims by some British and French imperialists in more recent history.

But within the context of national politics it is also possible to see attempts to use victory to reconcile past defeated enemies, as in the treatment of Biafrans by the victorious General Gowan after the 1967–70 Biafran war in Nigeria, or in Nelson Mandela's efforts to create a 'rainbow nation' in South Africa after the overthrow of apartheid in 1994. Some may think that Israel lost a chance to do the same in relation to the Palestinians after its 1967 victories – although it succeeded with Egypt and Jordan. And the Sri Lankan government has an opportunity to make a historic settlement with Tamil (as well as Muslim and other) citizens after the 2009 military crushing of the LTTE.

Why should victors give up anything? Because this is the way to maximize gains permanently at least cost. It may seem more natural after winning a hard-fought war at great sacrifice to further crush and punish a defeated opponent – as in the case of Germany after 1918. But this may be to store up future trouble. It may be best to display higher reaches of statesmanship by treating the conquered party as the US treated both Germany and Japan after 1945. In admittedly very different contexts, both the Israeli and Sri Lankan governments might do well to take note. It is always possible to win a war but then to lose the subsequent peace.

move forward with the deeper processes of reconciliation if the divisive political issues are still active and threatening. That is why reconciliation is often easier after decisive defeat and victory, as in Germany and Japan after 1945 or Biafra after the Nigerian civil war. The losers may feel that they must 'reconcile' themselves to the outcome because it is unavoidable, while the winners may find it possible to be magnanimous (see box 10.3). This goes a long way towards explaining the greater space for reconciliation in post-apartheid South Africa than in post-Dayton Bosnia, or in Kosovo while the issue of final status was still undecided.

If it is hard to forgive a defeated enemy, and harder to forgive a finally victorious enemy, it is harder still to forgive an enemy who is still seen to be an immediate and potent threat. When an unreconciled past conflict is mixed with current political tensions, a dangerous cocktail can result. We illustrate this with the case of relations between China and Japan, where differences over the past have combined with territorial conflict and competing geopolitical interests.

Case Study: China and Japan – Tensions and Reconciliation

In 2013–14, the tense relationship between China and Japan seemed to be on the verge of hostilities. Ships and planes had engaged in near-miss confrontations around the disputed Diaoyu/Senkaku islands. Opinion polls recorded the highest level of reciprocal distrust between the two peoples. Contacts between societies and governments were much reduced and Japanese investment in China fell by half. The Japanese decision to nationalize three of the islands in 2012, to stop them falling into the hands of private right-wing individuals, outraged the Chinese. Anti-Japanese demonstrations took place in a hundred Chinese cities. General Xu Caihou, chair of the Chinese Central Military Commission, said that the Chinese were 'prepared for any possible military combat'. In December 2013, China declared an Air Defence Identification Zone over the East China Sea. Japanese and US fighter planes immediately challenged it.

Three issues lay behind these worrying moves. First, there was the long-standing territorial conflict over the Diaoyu/Senkaku islands, claimed by China, Japan and Taiwan. They were small and uninhabited, but strategically significant for demarcating rights over the continental shelf under the East China Sea. Second, China was resentful of US and Japanese support for Taiwan and regarded the US–Japanese alliance as a security threat. This was heightened in 2014 when the US announced that it regarded the mutual defence provisions of the alliance as applying to the territorial integrity of the Diaoyu/Senkaku islands. Third, both countries were worried about the military build-up in the other, and both were engaged in a broader competition in regional and international affairs. China had blocked Japan's bid for Security Council membership. For both countries, the troubled triangle of relations between China, Japan and the US are crucial for the future and connect East Asian politics with wider international relations.

Against this background, the significance of the past is that, without a process of reconciliation, historical memories may poison prospects for mutual understanding and better relations. China's losses at Japan's hands in the 1930s and 1940s were enormous. Up to 20 million people lost their lives and about three-quarters of Chinese territory was occupied. Nanjing suffered exceptionally devastating treatment. Both peoples came out of the war feeling a sense of victimhood, which has subsequently fuelled a sense of grievance and nationalism.

Yinan He (2007) divides the history of postwar reconciliation efforts into four phases. Between 1945 and 1972, no reconciliation took place. In the immediate postwar years, China's civil war was raging. Japan was occupied by the United States. When Mao won power, he declared that, as victor, China would not demand reparations. But, in the context of the Cold War and China's isolation, there was no prospect of reconciliation. Japan, along with the US, recognized the nationalist government in Taiwan, not the communist government in Beijing. Conservative governments in Japan published textbooks which said little about the behaviour of Japanese troops during the occupation.

It was not until 1972, following the Sino-Soviet split and Nixon's opening to China, that the first steps towards normalization were taken. Japan and China established diplomatic relations, and the Japanese prime minister offered an ambiguous apology for the 'unfortunate period' of the war, which merited 'deep reflection'. China agreed to forego reparations for the sake of improved relations, and Zhou En Lai avoided raising the Diaoyu/Senkuku issue, even when the US transferred control of the islands from American forces to the Japanese. In 1974 Deng Xioaping offered to set the sovereignty dispute on one side and suggested joint exploration of the continental shelf. These moves were accompanied by youth exchange programmes and a programme of 'friendship cities', linking fifteen pairs of cities in the two countries. Polls showed that the majority of Japanese people said that they felt 'close to China' in this period. A gift of two pandas by China created 'panda fever' in Japan. But there was no dialogue of historians and no effort to develop a deeper public engagement with the past. The degree of reconciliation between the two peoples remained limited.

Relations worsened in the 1980s in the context of the Second Cold War, Sino-Soviet rapprochement and Reagan's pro-Taiwan policy. In Japan, a split developed between progressives and conservatives over how much to acknowledge Japan's wartime role. The ruling Liberal Democratic Party (LDP) demanded that textbooks should 'foster national pride' and play down Japan's wartime excesses. In China, the Communist Party was divided between reformers who wanted more opening up and conservatives who wanted to block reforms. Deng Xiaoping chose to open up economically and pursue a hard line on political reform. To bolster his position, he asserted China's interests against Japan. He intervened in the Japanese textbook issue and objected to Prime Minister Nakasone's visit to the Yasukini shrine (which commemorates Japanese war dead, including several Class A war criminals). China established a museum to commemorate the Nanjing Massacre which bears a wall inscription in Deng Xiaoping's handwriting: 'Never forget national humiliation'.

In the early 1990s, Sino-Japanese relations improved. Tomiichi Murayama, a rare socialist prime minister, issued the fullest apology yet made on the fiftieth anniversary of the end of the war. Murayama said Japan had caused 'tremendous damage and suffering' to the people of Asia and other countries through its colonial rule and aggression, and he expressed 'feelings of deep remorse' and 'heartfelt apology'. Unfortunately the apology led to a backlash among conservative nationalists in Japan. Some LDP conservatives denied the veracity of Chinese claims about wartime events, infuriating the Chinese, and new textbooks were issued that deleted previous references to wartime atrocities. Under prime ministers Koizumi and Abe, Japan began to adopt a more assertive foreign policy. The government considered reforms to Japan's postwar constitution, including changes to Article 9, which renounces war and prohibits the development of 'war potential'.

From the late 1990s to 2010, nationalism became an increasingly significant force in both China and Japan. In China, the spread of the internet and the partial opening up of society that followed Deng Xiaoping's reforms enabled more expression of public opinion. One of its manifestations was in anti-Japanese sentiment. Chinese leaders courted public opinion by condoning anti-Japanese demonstrations. The government launched a 'patriotic education' programme to teach the Chinese people about the atrocities Japan had committed in the past, with predictable effects on anti-Japanese sentiments. A Chinese historian accused the government of feeding its children 'wolf's milk'.

At the same time a strong current of nationalist feeling was running in Japan. Successive prime ministers played to the nationalist sentiments by visiting the shrines of the Japanese war dead at Yasukuni. School textbooks were published which minimized or ignored the depredations of the Japanese armed forces in China. In the context of rising nationalism and negative public attitudes on both sides, the recriminations over historical memory fanned mutual suspicion. Although Japan has been a remarkably peaceful country since 1945, people in China feared that it might once more become an aggressive and dangerous power, while on the Japanese side there were fears that China's 'peaceful rise' would end in a return to Chinese hegemony in Eastern Asia, at Japan's expense.

In order to avert a further deterioration in the situation, it is necessary to find a way to deal better with the past, manage the tensions of the present and agree on a negotiated future course. A step in this direction was taken at the end of 2014. Following exploratory feelers from the Japanese side, Premier Xi Jinping met Japanese Prime Minister Abe in the course of an APEC meeting in Beijing in November 2014, and the two leaders exchanged an awkward handshake. Officials discussed the possibility of crisis reduction mechanisms and an agreement to disagree on the disputed islands. It was reported that Abe did not intend to make further visits to the Yasukuni shrine during his period of office.

The seventieth anniversary of the end of the Second World War offers a fresh opportunity for another move forward towards reconciliation. It is clear that success will depend on sincere communications between the two sides and a negotiated and well-prepared sequence of steps to defuse current tensions and address the historical issues, as well as a proactive approach to institutionalizing a better relationship in the future. If the two Asian countries were to follow the German precedent, this might suggest not only an official apology but also some measures of restitution, joint commemoration of the war, and bilateral discussions on history teaching. No doubt the different cultural and regional context will suggest different measures from those that were taken in Western Europe. What is clear is that both sides need to act energetically to prevent the fires of nationalism from getting out of control.

Overcoming polarization and reconciling accounts

At the second stage of overcoming polarization, it is a question of combating what have often been irreconcilable accounts of the conflict entertained by rival parties (see box 10.4). The deeper processes of reconciliation cannot be

---

Box 10.4 Reconciling Israeli and Palestinian narratives of conflict

As an example of an attempt to reconcile deeply disparate accounts along the lines indicated here, this is how the editor of *Israeli and Palestinian Narratives of Conflict* (2006), Robert Rotberg, sums up the 'lessons from the book':

> The Israeli–Palestinian conflict for primacy, power, and control encompasses two bitterly contested, competing narratives. Both need to be understood, reckoned with, and analysed side by side in order to help abate violence and possibly propel both protagonists toward peace. This is an immensely tall order. But the first step is to know the narratives, the second to reconcile them to the extent that they can be reconciled or bridged, and the third to help each side to accept, and conceivably to respect, the validity of the competing narrative. (Rotberg, 2006: vii)

In the body of the text, four strategies are variously suggested by Israeli and Palestinian participants for doing this.

1 Ilan Pappe advocates 'bridging the narrative concept' along the lines already initiated by the new 'post-Zionist' revisionist Israeli historians, among whom he is a prominent figure, in order to narrow differences and, if possible, produce shared historiographical reconstructions.
2 Daniel Bar-Tal and Gavriel Salomon do not think that it is possible to overcome the way rival narratives oppose each other's fundamental truths and, as psychologists, hope to promote reconciliation by 'building legitimacy through narrative' – fostering mutual acknowledgement of sincerity and therefore validity by recognizing 'that there are two (legitimate) narratives of the conflict'.
3 Mordechai Bar-On recommends acceptance of the fact that the Zionist and Palestinian narratives 'negate the very existence of the foe as a collectivity' and suggests that the focus should, rather, be on a critical re-examination of the historical record by each side separately. He sees this as a particular task for the Palestinians.
4 Finally, Dan Bar-On and Sami Adwan aim to promote 'better dialogue between two separate but interdependent narratives' that 'are intertwined like a double helix' through their work on the production of parallel texts on the Balfour Declaration, the 1948 war and the 1987 Intifada, including the idea of getting Israeli and Palestinian schoolchildren to fill in intermediate commentaries.

For an appreciative but critical assessment of these approaches in periods of intense and ongoing political conflict, see chapter 18.

reached while dehumanized images of the enemy are still current and mutual convictions of victimization are widely believed. We enter the territory of reconciling stories, at any rate to the point where those with a political interest in demonizing the other lose influence, and it may become possible for each party to comprehend that all feel that they are victims and have suffered tragic losses. The key point is reached when the other is 'rehumanized'. Here the link is between reconciliation in its second sense and peacemaking – particularly among political elites and opinion-formers.

Managing contradiction and reconciling conflicting demands

With the third stage, the reconciliation process definitively enters the realm of transformation, as efforts are made to bridge continuing deep differences by structural political and economic rearrangements and, despite persisting conflicts, by strengthening the psychological possibilities of living together peacefully. These are often highly complex, but the chief requirement is that, even though there may not be a possibility of reparation in most individual cases, a general belief is strengthened that basic needs will be increasingly met through measures of more inclusive political representation and more equitable economic opportunity. The space for deeper reconciliation is much widened if parents feel that things are likely to get better for their children. The link is between the third sense of reconciliation and structural peacebuilding.

Reconciliation remains an elusive goal in Bosnia, where unsolved constitutional issues remain, the nationalist parties who were present at the start of the war are still in power, and bitter memories live on in hundreds of villages and towns. In all of the three formerly warring communities, people regarded as war criminals by one side are seen as heroes by another, and there is a culture of denial and selective memory about the past. Nevertheless, numerous local NGOs are involved in efforts to encourage mutual acknowledgement of the suffering imposed by all sides and to create new institutions for transitional justice. In Sarajevo, a Research and Documentation Centre laboured to collect reliable statistics about the number who had been killed. The aim was to counter propaganda on all sides. After initial controversy and scorn, the Bosnian 'Book of the Dead' project has earned wide respect. The authors hope that, by recognizing every victim, a basis for reconciliation will be laid. The Sarajevo Centre has gone on to cooperate with the Centre for Peace, Nonviolence and Human Rights in Osijek, Croatia, the Dokumenta Centre in Zagreb, and the Humanitarian Law Centre in Belgrade to share information and discuss ways to improve transitional justice and the rule of law.

In Rwanda, reconciliation and the rebuilding of society depend heavily on diasporas, which provide large capital inflows in the form of remittances. Here reconciliation is highly polticized, since the government side is seen to insist on reconciliation on its own terms, and the unequal status between

Rwanda's ethnic and social groups remains. Nevertheless, there is evidence that attitudes to reconciliation are more positive when 'bridging social capital' links different groups than when 'bonding social capital' preserves exclusive groups with little interdependence. There are indications that efforts at dialogue, such as the Rwandan Intra-Party Dialogue launched from the diaspora with support from the Spanish parliament, may offer space for progress that is difficult within a still polarized country.

Celebrating difference and reconciling former enemies

Only when the fourth and final stage is reached has true reconciliation been achieved. For example, this is Archbishop Desmond Tutu's vision of the central role of reconciliation in conflict resolution as expressed to an audience in Northern Ireland in 1998:

> I told those dedicated workers for peace and reconciliation that they should not be tempted to give up on their crucial work because of the frustrations of seemingly not making any significant progress, that in our experience nothing was wasted, for when the time was right it would all come together and, looking back, people would realise what a critical contribution they had made. They were part of the cosmic movement towards unity, towards reconciliation, that has existed from the beginning of time. (Tutu, 1999)

Central here is repairing violations of human dignity, which Donna Hicks (2011) sees as the psychological root of deep conflict, and therefore essential to resoving it.[3] In his comment on the jacket of Hicks's book, Tutu agrees: 'Without an understanding of dignity, there is no hope for such change. If you want to find the weak links in a democracy, look for where people are suffering. You will most likely see a variety of violations. If you want peace, be sure everyone's dignity is intact.' And so does Willam Ury in a parallel comment: 'no single factor is more critical, yet more neglected, in the successful resolution of conflicts than basic human dignity.'

Here we may enter the realm of atonement and forgiveness (although Hicks sees the 'dignity model' as 'an alternative to forgiveness'). Former enemies may be reconciled to the point where differences are not only tolerated but even appreciated. Many never reach this stage, which often includes formal acts of acknowledgement and apology on behalf of previous generations and general acceptance that a shared future is now more important than a divided past. This involves deeper levels of peacemaking and cultural peacebuilding that stretch from revisions of formerly polarized official accounts and media representations, as noted in the last section, through pluralization of education and stories told in school textbooks, and eventually on to leavening everyday experiences that affect localized transmissions of memory within communities and families (Kelly, 2002). Identities themselves may become softened and transformed, as a broadening of self-understanding combines

Box 10.5 Deliberating the Holocaust and the Nakba

We offer as an example this outline of the courageous attempt by Bashir Bashir and Amos Goldberg, and their Palestinian and Israeli colleagues, to address the portentous issue of the Holocaust and the Nakba – the traumatic roots of the Israel–Palestine conflict. In this outline of their work, they refer to Dominick LaCapra's notion of 'empathic unsettlement', a theme to which we will return in chapter 15 with reference to the work of Hans-Georg Gadamer.

> This article develops a theoretical framework for shared and inclusive Jewish and Palestinian deliberation on the memories of the Holocaust and the Nakba. It argues that a joint Arab–Jewish public deliberation on the traumatic memories of these two events is not only possible, however challenging and disruptive it may be, but also fundamental for producing an egalitarian and inclusive ethics of bi-nationalism in Israel/Palestine. In order to develop this conceptual framework, we first present some examples, most notably Elias Khoury's epic novel *Gate of the Sun* (Bab al-Shams), which bring the memories of the Holocaust and the Nakba together in a fashion that disrupts the dominant, antagonistic and exclusionary Israeli and Palestinian national narratives. We then interpret Dominick LaCapra's notion of 'empathic unsettlement', which transforms 'otherness' from a problem to be disposed of into a moral and emotional challenge, as a political concept that best captures and explains the disruptive potential of a joint deliberation on these traumatic events. The figure of the refugee, constitutive of Palestinian and Jewish histories and identities, we suggest, serves as a herald of this bi-national and disruptive ethics. We conclude that 'empathic unsettlement' also has a productive and transformative potential, which gives further (however partial and initial) meaning, shape and content to the ethics and democratic politics of bi-nationalism heralded by the refugee. (Bashir and Goldberg, 2014: 77)

with a reperception of others as fellow human beings. Deep levels of trauma may at last engage each other (see box 10.5). Confidence-building may turn into trust (Booth and Wheeler, 2007).

Transformation of this kind may be the exception. Perhaps only remarkable individuals can achieve it at a single leap. The argument here has been that earlier stages on the path to reconciliation are more likely to offer the space required for overcoming violent conflict. Nevertheless, it is this full measure of transformative reconciliation that in the end underpins the cosmopolitan vision to which we turn in Part II.

Case Study: National Dialogue in Burma

We end Part I and introduce Part II with a brief case study of the unexpected attempt to promote national dialogue in Burma. We choose this case study because it links the theme of national reconciliation, looked at here, to the wider institutional and procedural prerequisites for 'cosmopolitan conflict resolution' introduced in chapter 11. Although highly precarious at the time of writing, and subject to the criticism that it is more a case of 'top-down management' than genuine reconciliation, it gives an example of what may be possible even in the most apparently complex and intractable conflicts.

National dialogues are 'inclusive extra-constitutional decision-making mechanisms' that aim to embrace all national stakeholders in an effort (a) to address 'the root causes of constitutional failures' and (b) to 'provide space and instruments for reconciliation' (Siebert, 2014: 37). National dialogues are usually seen to be formally mandated, as in the cases of South Africa (the National Peace Accord structures), Nepal (the Ministry for Peace and Reconstruction and the initiative Nepal Transition to Peace), Lebanon (the Common Space initiative) and Yemen (the National Dialogue Conference). Sometimes they can be informally initiated – as in the case of the 2013 Social Forum in the Basque Country, which aimed to make up for deficiences in the formal 2006 peace process. For national dialogue in general, see Collen (2014).

The postcolonial history of Burma has been plagued by unresolved issues of identity and constitutional accommodation of ethnic nationalities since the 1947 Panglong Conference, at which General Aung San persuaded the non-Myanmar (non-Burman) peoples from the frontier states to join the Union of Burma on expectation of a later federal constitution, which in the end did not materialize. The Burma Army (*Tatmadaw*) seized power in a coup in 1962 to prevent what the right wing saw as a break-up of the great pre-British Myanmar nation. Instead of federalism, a strongly centralized structure was imposed on the ethnic nationalities which made up over 40 per cent of the population and inhabited some 60 per cent of the territory. Fifty years of army rule followed, spawning resistance from what became a multiplicity of ethnic armed groups fighting separately and negotiating ceasefires with the government. After elections in 1990 – and again in 2012 – ethnic political parties among more than fifty opposition parties challenged the ruling Union Solidarity and Development Party (USDP). Prominent here for many years has been Aung San's daughter, Daw Aung San Suu Kyi, leader of the party with the biggest national majority, the National League for Democracy (NLD), which in 1990 won 59 per cent of the votes and 81 per cent of the parliamentary seats. She spent fifteen of the next twenty years under house arrest, building an international reputation that rivals that of Nelson Mandela. One main difference is that, whereas, when Mandela came out of prison in 1990, apartheid had already effectively been defeated, when Aung San Suu Kyi emerged from house arrest in 2010, the army was still in control. In 2012 the NLD won forty-three of the forty-five vacant seats. Aung San Suu Kyi has announced that she will run for the presidency in the 2015 elections.

In 2011, President Thein Sein surprised many by declaring at his inauguration that his main aim was to rebuild national unity. He initiated ceasefire talks with the armed groups. But this was reminiscent of similar attempts in the 1990s, which amounted to little more than bargaining with militia leaders to renounce violence in exchange for economic and other privileges – such as trade in drugs (some had degenerated into 'opium armies'). Ethnic political organizations protested that this was a 'sell-out' which ignored the deep core issues of self-determination, legitimacy, and betrayal of the original federal aspirations for a genuinely democratic union of Burma. This could not be achieved within a unitary constitution and parliament controlled by the Burman majority. Remarkably, the government responded in 2012 by setting up the Union Peacemaking Committee chaired by the president, and in 2014 an Ethnic Peace Plan eventually emerged in the shape of an elaborate 'extra-parliamentary dialogue ... to seek a political solution in the form of a federal union' (Yawnghwe, 2014: 49). An idea of the ambition of the enterprise can be gauged from the elaborate 'Panglong II Roadmap' signed in April 2013 by seventeen armed ethnic groups, which proposed the Panglong Union Conference with an envisaged 900 participants – 300 each from government/army, democratic forces, and opposition – an impressive effort to include all major stakeholders. The process would proceed from a comprehensive national ceasefire, via a joint military code of conduct and a monitoring mechanism to impose discipline on armed militia and the sometimes semi-autonomous units of the *Tatmadaw*.

In a further move to support the process of reconciliation, in October 2012 the government of Myanmar established the Myanmar Peace Centre (MPC) to provide an active agency for negotiating with ethnic insurgent groups. The MPC made some tangible progress, notably the evolution of a more liberal political environment in which the government freed many political prisoners, provided an amnesty to political exiles living abroad, and accommodated leading members of the 88 Generation Group, who were involved in anti-government demonstrations. It is also a positive quality of the MPC that its mandate includes 'deep engagement in the process of political dialogue with the insurgent groups as well as peace building activies to consolidate on-going efforts' (Ganesan, 2014: 131). One consequence of this is that the insurgent groups who have agreed to a ceasefire have called for the inclusion of Aung San Suu Kyi's NLD in dialogue with the government. However, it is also recognized that the MPC faces serious obstacles. Despite a number of extended deadlines and a series of bilateral agreements for a ceasefire with fourteen of the sixteen armed ethnic groups, as of February 2015 a general ceasefire agreement had not been signed. Ganesan points out that, following sixty years of ethnic civil wars, Myanmar has neither a culture of peace nor robust infrastructures supporting peace and reconciliation below the level of the MPC. At the stage it had reached by March 2015, with important elections planned for the following October, the process of national dialogue still lacked the levels of inclusion which characterized successful peace processes seen elsewhere (for example, as in the case of Mindanao profiled in chapter 13).

In economic terms, resource extraction (tin, tungsten, antimony, teak, gems, gold, coal) and infrastructural projects such as hydro-electical power have been exploited by military groups and elites in a process of what has been termed 'militarized development', leaving the majority of people and local communities in Myanmar bearing the costs of development (displacement from homes and livelihoods) with little of the benefits. If the Panglong process is successfully to address the long history of violent conflict in Myanmar, it will need to tackle severe economic inequalities and to continue the process of political reform to make it inclusive and representative. Land reform is especially important, with 70 per cent of Myanmar's population living and working in rural areas, the majority of them smallholder farmers whose land rights are under threat. Women play a crucial role as food producers throughout this rural economy, but their rights to land access are recognized even less than those of men, and ethnic minority women are even more marginalized (Transnational Institute, 2015).

Reconciliation will also need to be based on a system of justice to address both past abuses and continuing violations of human rights. The importance of human rights awareness and education in peacebuilding is well recognized, but in Myanmar there is a strong perception that awareness of rights as well as access to systems protecting them are sorely inadequate. In a survey of communities in south-eastern Myanmar about local priorities for stopping abuse, conducted by the Border Consortium in 2014, the highest priority was given to the need for human rights education for villagers (41 per cent), followed by the withdrawal of the *Tatmadaw* from their areas (26 per cent) (Border Consortium, 2014; Holland and Martin, 2014). There are some positive signs. The MDC has plans to launch an Office of Public Diplomacy and a Public Outreach Programme, as well as a Land Centre to investigate the illegal seizure of farmland. The outcome of the elections, due in 2015, will have a decisive influence on the continued development of dialogue and reconciliation, with the prospect of Aung San Suu Kyi, a reconciling leader whose status is equal to that of Mandela, gaining more power in the process.

RECOMMENDED READING

Bar-Siman-Tov (2004); Bracken and Petty (1998); Clark and Kaufman (2009); Collen (2014); Fischer (2011); Hicks (2011); Kriesberg (1998a); Lederach (1997, 2001); Mani (2002); Minow (1998); Rigby (2001); Rosoux (2009); Rotberg and Thompson (2000); Schaap (2005); Tutu (1999); Whittaker (1999)

RELEVANT EXTRACTS IN *THE CONTEMPORARY CONFLICT RESOLUTION READER*

Reading 22: J. P. Lederach, Building Peace: Sustainable Reconciliation in Divided Societies
Reading 45: H. Assefa, The Meaning of Reconciliation
Reading 60: M. Fischer, Transitional Justice and Reconciliation: Theory and Practice

PART II

Cosmopolitan Conflict Resolution

CHAPTER ELEVEN

Towards Cosmopolitan Conflict Resolution

In the second part of the book we begin by summing up where the enterprise of conflict resolution, as outlined in Part I, has reached by the middle of the second decade of the twenty-first century. At the beginning of the new millennium the attacks of 11 September 2001 on the World Trade Center and the Pentagon dramatically illustrated the rapid and deep changes in international relations brought about by globalization. This has been further underlined by the complexity and violence of patterns of conflict generated in the aftermath of the Arab revolutions a decade later (looked at in chapter 4) and by the unexpected crisis posed by Russia's response to events and challenge to the post-Cold War settlement in Ukraine, in what is seen as a deliberate blurring of boundaries between acknowledged and unacknowledged actions amid a fog of subterfuge and deniable disinformation, now sometimes referred to as 'hybrid warfare' (see chapter 5). Both the bipolar Cold War world and the brief unipolar moment are now over. The emerging multipolar world is more turbulent and unpredictable. It has been accompanied by an explosion of transnational human, material and information flows associated with the communications revolution. As Part I of this book has shown, local conflicts are manifesting themselves globally and global conflicts locally, and the effects of conflicts can be felt far from their sites. As states and societies become open more than ever to events outside their borders, and images, belief systems, communications and ideas flow rapidly across societies divided by different ways of life and cultures, it is not surprising that conflicts of interest and perceived conflicts are experienced not only at the intrastate and interstate levels, but also globally. A hybrid mixture of local, regional and global conflicts has emerged, which in chapter 4 we called *transnational conflict*. Accompanying this change are uncertainties over how and where this form of conflict should be addressed. New doctrines of intervention and new understandings of 'peace and security' imply a redefinition of jurisdiction. If interests cut across states and communities, where does appropriate jurisdiction lie? How is democratic accountability to be effective in a world of interdependent decisions? How are conflicts to be resolved when they cross borders and levels of analysis? In this new post-Clausewitzean order, conflict resolution is challenged to redefine its scope and its praxis.

In figure 3.1 (p. 71) we indicated the proliferation and merging of datasets that now embed conflict statistics within wider categories of international terrorism and international crime statistics, and then further embed these in turn within even broader assessments of state fragility and indicators for positive peace. We have seen how a new interpretative framework for transnational conflict is generated as a result, set out in table 4.2 (p. 123). This defines the main contemporary challenge to conflict resolution. In response, in chapters 5 to 10 we described how conflict resolution is now working to prevent, contain and end violent transnational conflict, and ultimately to transform it so that it does not recur.

In Part II we sum all of this up by introducing the term *cosmopolitan conflict resolution* (CCR) – the counterpart to transnational conflict (TNC) – as the name of the whole enterprise. CCR has to match the dimensions of TNC across its full range of application if it is to succeed in transforming violent into non-violent contestation and change. This means that it must address the *global-level* drivers of TNC, together with their transnational connectors, the *regional-level* conflict complexes where TNC is primarily manifested, the *state-level* determinants of TNC, the *identity-group-level* emergence of the conflict parties, and the *elite/individual-level* actions and strategies that stoke up or dampen down the virulence and ferocity of TNC.

But cosmopolitan conflict resolution is not just *reactive*. It is also *proactive*. It actively promotes a global agenda based on certain values. It has an overarching strategy, which is to further this transformation. It has *allies* who are not specifically engaged in conflict resolution but are essential to it – for example, those who work for human development, democratic participation, human welfare and rights, including, more controversially, as discussed in chapter 14, the military engaged in humanitarian protection, peacekeeping, and preventing or redressing violations of international peace and security. Cosmopolitan conflict resolution also has *enemies*. Its enemies are violence in all its forms – direct violence, structural violence and cultural violence (see chapter 1). That is why, in order to promote its values and defeat its enemies, cosmopolitan conflict resolution must think *strategically*. Where is it now, where does it want to go, how can it get there? It must think short term, medium term and long term. It must have a clear view of what it is up against. It must understand its own strengths and weaknesses. And it must learn how to coordinate aspects and levels as appropriate in a rapidly changing conflict environment. The aim of the rest of Part II is to fill out this proactive programme.

We use the term 'cosmopolitan conflict resolution' to indicate the need for an approach that is not situated within any particular state, society or established site of power but, rather, promotes constructive means of handling conflict at local through to global levels in the interests of humanity. We emphasize that this is not a covert name for imposing hegemonic interests under a subterfuge of unexamined 'universal values', but a genuine and inclusive local–global effort to determine what contributes to human welfare in general and to human emancipation worldwide. Fundamental to the whole cosmopolitan conflict resolution effort is the perception that, whatever particular forms it may take, it is always at *local level* that the most damaging aspects of transnational conflict impact and that those who suffer are overwhelmingly the most vulnerable. Cosmopolitan conflict resolution is normatively devoted to the task of preventing, alleviating and ending this, however difficult it may be and however long it may take.

This agenda is, therefore, related to wider debates about transitions in international order and the emergence of possible future cosmopolitan forms of economic and political governance sufficient to address the deep roots of violent conflict, as well as their more overt manifestations. In recent years David Held has developed his analysis of cosmopolitan governance from foundations both in the democratic peace ideals of Immanuel Kant in the political field (1995) and in the idea of a 'social-democratic alternative to the Washington Consensus' (2004) in the economic field. Mary Kaldor (2003) has promoted the idea of a global civil society. Andrew Linklater (1998) has called for a 'transformation of political community'. All of this has been influential in the evolution of the conflict resolution field.

The cosmopolitan conflict resolution project has been further enriched by several powerful contributions that converge on the idea that unacceptable levels of present and prospective human conflict can only be addressed within a cosmopolitan framework. Paul Collier (2008) argues that the 'conflict trap' that ruins so many lives in the poorest countries can only be overcome by concerted international action within a 'framework of international charters' coordinated by multiple financial and political agencies tasked to deliver 'global public goods'. Daniele Archibugi (2008) calls for a deepening of the instruments of 'cosmopolitan democracy' as a way to transform the most destructive conflicts, so that principles of inclusion, responsibility and impartiality progressively come to define the idea of a 'global commonwealth of citizens'. Amartya Sen identifies the 'idea of justice' with an evolving cosmopolitan order that does not presuppose a non-existent global state but builds progressively on 'assessments of social realizations' (what actually happens) and 'comparative issues of enhancement of justice' (progressive reduction of injustice) in order to address the roots of conflict associated with 'the deprivation and suppression suffered [by] so many people across the world [despite] the substantial material progress of others' (2009: 410–12). At theoretical level, Ken Booth (2007: 124–33) offers a conceptual framework for all of this by linking pragmatic 'emancipatory realism' both to Habermasian critical theory and, beyond this, to a trans-Kantian vision of a future institutionalized world community.

For Kant, 'the greatest evils which affect civilised nations are brought about by war, and not so much by actual wars in the past or the present, as by never ending and indeed continually increasing preparations for war' (cited in Held, 1995: 226). One of Kant's remedies was his idea of an association of citizens who would form a moral community, a pacific federation in which war would be renounced as a means of politics (Reading 1). Similarly, cosmopolitan conflict resolution seeks to open new political spaces in which citizens from different parts of the world can tackle the transnational sources of violent conflict. But, as we hope Part I has shown, in rapidly changing circumstances it is now forced to go beyond traditional Kantian liberalism by, on the one hand, engaging with actualities of traditional power and security issues, so that the enterprise is rooted in existing structures, while, on the other hand, opening itself up to critical ideas about the reform of international institutions along emancipatory lines derived ultimately from Marx but now shaped by post-structural concerns for local participation and human diversity.

Above all, this is driven by the deep logic within cosmopolitan conflict resolution itself that only full engagement with emerging non-western and non-northern practices and norms can deliver what is needed and fulfil the original aspirations of the founders of the field. This, centrally, includes Islamic and other non-western teachings. In other words, Part II takes the form of a protracted conversation with realist, critical theoretic, post-structural, feminist – and especially non-western – critics, in which the authors hope to link discussion about existing capacity to an open future in which diverse contributions at different levels from all parts of the world can come together to promote non-violent change in the broad direction sketched out by the founders in the 1950s and 1960s.

But has any progress been made at all from a conflict resolution perspective in the evolution of something approximating to a true international community over the past sixty years, as the first generation of founders hoped? Can tangible changes be discerned in the realities of global politics, not just in the hopes or aspirations of theorists? It has long been fashionable in critical circles to scorn the eighteenth-century Enlightenment idea of social and political progress, particularly on a world scale (Bury, 1932). But we do not take this view. Conflict resolution rejects determinism, whether in realist or in Marxist guise. Instead, conflict resolution and conflict transformation insist that, although human conflict is inevitable, the path to violence is not. Part I has summarized current attempts to build the understanding, policy framework and capacity needed to contain violence when it breaks out, to settle conflicts that threaten to turn violent, and to transform conditions likely to foster violent conflict so that continuing political struggles can be conducted non-violently.

In the rest of the chapter we first locate the enterprise of conflict resolution within what we suggest is a slowly and fitfully emerging cosmopolitan order and then illustrate this in relation to three aspects of particular relevance to the conflict resolution field: *international institutions*, *international law* and ideas of *cosmopolitan democracy*. The chapter ends by applying this to the question of conflict resolution responses to the challenge of *international terrorism*.

The Nature of the International Collectivity

In orientating the conflict resolution enterprise within the current phase of world politics, our starting point is the observation that the international collectivity is not a homogeneous entity. It is made up of successive layers of economic, political and cultural deposits, in which later accretions rarely replace earlier strata entirely but come to predominate or are themselves absorbed in unpredictable patterns. The continuing debate about the nature, significance, novelty and impact of globalization tells us that we should not expect unambiguous answers here (Held et al., 1999; Held and McGrew, 2007). In table 11.1 we offer a schematized model of five coexisting aspects of the international collectivity, none of which can be finally reduced to the others. This is intended to sum up similar categorizations offered in chapter 6 (in relation to conflict resolution and peacekeeping) and chapter 9 (in relation to conflict resolution and peacebuilding) in Part I. It will also be carried through into chapter 19 (conflict resolution theory and its critics).

The first aspect is the continuing survival of pre-state structures in various parts of the world (albeit continually transformed by rapid changes in communications and technology) interspersed with newer urban sprawls – or a collapse back into them in the case of 'fragile states' that subsequently implode. Here, local resilience and the capacity of traditional conflict resolution and economic self-help to build coping structures in the absence of formal state institutions are often remarkable (see the Somalia case study in chapter 6), but a genuine Hobbesian anarchy may also prevail when older traditional forms of authority succumb to the worst features of marginalization and an often criminalized modernity (which is why the terms 'charisma' and 'traditionalist' are bracketed in table 11.1) (Jackson, 1990; Kaplan, 1994; van Crefeld, 2000).

The second aspect is the unregenerate state system in which state interest remains the political currency and militarized power the main organizing principle. This can be recognized as still dominant in regions such as the Middle East and South and East Asia and at geopolitical level manifest in neo-conservative US circles and the revivalist ambitions of the Russian Federation (Mearsheimer, 1990; Gray, 2002; Waltz, 2002).

Third, there is the international society of states, distinguished by a

Table 11.1 The international collectivity: five aspects

	Aspect	Organizing principle	Theory
1	Pre-state alternatives	(Charisma)	(Traditionalist)
2	International system of states	Power	Realist
3	International society of states	Order	Pluralist
4	International community	Legitimacy	Solidarist
5	World community	Justice	Cosmopolitan

sufficient reciprocity and mutuality of interest to underpin a reasonably ordered and predictable intercourse of nations. Here, relative power is acknowledged, but even the most powerful share an interest in mutual restraint. Non-intervention and cultural pluralism are the presiding values and international order the organizing principle (Bull, 1977; Wight, 1977; Bull and Watson, 1984; Jackson, 2000).

Fourth comes the international community – an informal term not defined by specialists, but widely used by non-specialists (in more formal terms we define 'international community' as at the Grotian end of the broad spectrum of international society). Here, for the first time, non-state actors move into prominence, as well as states. The presiding values are solidarist, and the chief organizing principle is international legitimacy as determined through relevant international institutions, international organizations and international law (Doyle, 1999; Wheeler, 2000).

Finally, we can discern the still faint outline of a possible future world community in which particularities have been overcome to the extent that genuine cosmopolitan values prevail. Here suitable instruments of global governance have evolved, and international justice is widely accepted as the overarching organizing principle (Falk, 1995; Held, 1995; Linklater, 1998; Kaldor, 2003).

There is also the external challenge to all this mounted by attempts to revive even older dispensations such as an Islamic caliphate. But, despite the unexpected success of IS in Syria and Iraq, to be discussed below, this has very little support even in predominantly Muslim countries. The further question of whether the whole of the conflict resolution enterprise is a feature of western dominance and will wane in a new multipolar world will also be discussed in Part II and summed up in chapter 20.

These five aspects coexist, and none is yet finally reducible to the others. Our question about progress within the world collectivity from a conflict resolution perspective can now be made a little more precise. Can we discern a relative overall shift of emphasis over, say, the past 500 years – but particularly over the past seventy years – in a general direction from aspect 1 towards aspect 5? To the extent that this is the case, is it to be welcomed? Is it likely to continue? If so, what are the tasks for conflict resolution? If not, what are the implications?

The Arrow of the Future: Conflict Resolution and World Politics

The response from the field of conflict resolution would, we think, take the form of a decided 'yes' to the first two questions. Despite manifold setbacks and disappointments, there appears so far to be an overall direction to world politics, in which the development of a global international society of states, and the partial development of an international community, have finally brought conflict resolution principles and practices to prominence within world politics. This is seen as a benign development. Looking to the future, despite all the dangers and challenges, conflict resolution sees every prospect of further evolution in the same direction – so long as strenuous international efforts continue to be made to ensure that this takes place, and, at a time of rapid shifts in global demographic, economic, political and cultural influence and power, the trap of allowing conflict resolution to be identified with western or northern interests is avoided.

As can be seen in table 11.2, in line with conflict resolution principles, we can now replace the one-dimensional realist understanding of power, as represented in table 11.1, with Kenneth Boulding's more sophisticated tripartite analysis, as outlined in table 1.3 (p. 26; see also Nye, 2004). Here 'threat power' is seen to predominate under the realist definition of international system, 'exchange power' under the pluralist conception of international society, and 'integrative power' under the solidarist and cosmopolitan understandings of international community. We noted earlier how Boulding saw these as 'fuzzy sets', inasmuch as each aspect also contains elements of the other two. In chapter 1 we identified three complementary conflict resolution responses to escalation and de-escalation conflict phases (figure 1.3). Here we suggest the appropriateness of extending this analysis more widely by aligning the three main conflict resolution responses – conflict containment, conflict settlement, conflict transformation – to the three aspects of the international scene where they most aptly apply. The interpenetration of aspects, together with the principle of complementarity, determines that, in practice, all three conflict resolution responses will need to be applied at the same time in most cases (for example, in regions of 'pre-state anarchy' the violence has to be *contained* if possible and malign external influences curtailed, but at the same time local *settlements* may be reached between biddable and legitimate parties, while attempts at long-term *transformation* into sustainable peace may need to be negotiated among a range of disparate indigenous stakeholders. The job of external parties is to support and facilitate this, not pre-determine it). In short, conflict resolution wants to replace threat power by exchange power and integrative power in human transactions at all the different levels.

We illustrate this with reference to a possible future evolution of world politics in three key areas from a conflict resolution perspective: international institutions (political and economic), international law, and forms of democratic governance.

Table 11.2 Three forms of power and three associated conflict resolution responses

Aspect	Predominant form of power	Conflict resolution response
System	Threat power	Conflict containment (also applies to pre-state anarchy)
Society	Exchange power	Conflict settlement
Community	Integrative power	Conflict transformation

Conflict Resolution and International Institutions

The United Nations, like all other international institutions, including the modern state, reflects both its own history and the present balance between the different coexistent, often competing, aspects of the international collectivity within which it operates (see table 11.3). This provides the context both for reviewing current controversies about the United Nations in relation to conflict resolution and for consideration of the role of regional and subregional organizations. It also allows brief discussion about the 'long history' of the state system itself from a conflict resolution perspective.

Part I of this book has given many examples of UN procedures for settling international disputes as guided by Article 2(1) of the UN Charter:

> All members shall settle their international disputes by peaceful means in such a manner that international peace and security, and justice, are not endangered.

Article 33(1) specifies the mechanisms available:

> The parties to any dispute, the continuance of which is likely to endanger the maintenance of international peace and security, shall, first of all, seek a solution by negotiation, enquiry, mediation, conciliation, arbitration, judicial settlement, resort to regional agencies or arrangements, or other peaceful means of their choice.

As Part I has clarified, most of these (except negotiation) involve third parties, and the first four are political rather than judicial (Ziring et al., 2000: 211). 'Enquiry' involves establishing points of fact. 'Arbitration' and 'judicial settlement' will be considered briefly below. In addition, there is the use of 'good offices' – for example, by the UN secretary-general, to bring disputing parties together, backed up since 2006 by a Mediation Support Unit in the UN Department of Political Affairs to aid special envoys and special representatives in this endeavour. The General Assembly, but more usually since the early years the Security Council, can initiate and pursue attempts to prevent, halt and reverse outbreaks of hostility. There are many excellent accounts

Table 11.3 The United Nations, international law and international intervention

Aspect	United Nations	International law	Intervention
System	International organization as tool of great power politics	Great power diktat	Intervention (A) (realist)
Society	United Nations as forum for interstate accommodation	International law as limited mutual adjustment of state interests	Non-intervention (pluralist)
Community	United Nations as repository for genuine cosmopolitan norms; legitimizer for international action	International law as instrument of progressive change	Intervention (B) (solidarist; internationalist)

of such UN activities (Weiss and Daws, 2007). Inevitably, as seen in Part I, outcomes vary, with success depending on the levels of internal unity and fluctuating political will of those operating within the UN system, the conflict context, the relative strength and nature of the disputing parties, the perceived importance of the national interests involved, the skill and timing of the peacemakers, and the adroitness of antagonistic conflict parties in using – or delaying – the often cumbersome UN system itself to derive maximum bargaining advantage (Peck, 2009).

But the peacemaking role of the UN as a whole has been, and is, denigrated, if not dismissed, by critics both from the realist and from the Marxist camp.

From a realist perspective, Bobbitt (2002), for example, gives the UN short shrift, with very few mentions and those mainly derogatory. He sees the UN as one of the 'discredited multinational institutions of the nation-state', incapable of responding effectively to the new challenges of the era of the market-state and, if anything, more likely to be used 'as a way of frustrating action in order to control the acts of its strongest member, the United States' (2002: 821). Instead, he looks to coalition-building and cooperation among allies to deliver the collective goods (shared intelligence, surveillance information, missile and cyber defences) needed to 'forestall peer competition and defeat international terrorism'. This is as far as the scope for conflict resolution goes. It is dwarfed by the fight against international terrorism, which Bobbitt sees as a struggle with a non-territorial 'virtual state' (indeed, a form of market-state) (ibid.: 820). In this way, as with Huntington and his substitution of clashing civilizations for competing states, quasi-realists project traditional realist understandings into the future, albeit no longer posited on the persistence of the traditional nation-state. Conflict resolution, together with the UN, is drastically sidelined in these scenarios.

From a traditional Marxist perspective, the UN is also often denigrated. It is seen to be hopelessly enmeshed in – indeed, to be an expression of – the late capitalist power structures that have produced it. Together with attendant international financial institutions (IFIs), such as the International Monetary Fund and the World Bank, with which it is seen to be complicit, the entire paraphernalia of UN conflict resolution work is regarded from this perspective as an attempt to rescue a fundamentally flawed system, when it should not be rescued but replaced (D. Harvey, 2003).

Nearly all those who work in the conflict resolution field take a very different view. While well aware of its shortcomings and its hybrid nature, they nevertheless see the UN both as a manifestation of clear progress having been made over the last seventy years from a conflict resolution perspective and as central to aspirations for further progress in future. We saw in chapter 2 how, after each convulsion in global politics over the past five hundred years, a new system has emerged. The UN system is the first to have evolved into a truly global society of states, as the central process of decolonization quadrupled its membership from some fifty to some two hundred members. Despite valid criticism of what has from one perspective been a western imposition, the global triumph of the principle of *self-determination* has nevertheless been an epoch-making event and a major step in the direction of emancipation. It is an example of the transformative potential in the legitimization of global norms of a kind hardly suspected by some of the UN's founders.

It is possible to see the conflict containment, conflict settlement and conflict transformation dimensions of conflict resolution as all previsaged in the overlapping UN systems.

Conflict containment principles are clearly recognizable in the development of UN peacekeeping and the way in which this is linked via UN Charter Chapter VII enforcement provisions authorized by the UN Security Council to wider processes of positive peacebuilding (see chapters 6 and 8).

Conflict settlement principles are central to UN Charter Chapter VI provisions on the peaceful settlement of disputes, as noted above. There is also Chapter VIII, where regional arrangements are encouraged to play active roles in furthering these aims (Peck, 1998). Here again it is possible to see substantial progress made – if unevenly – from a conflict resolution perspective. The EU – as prophetically foreseen in David Mitrany's book *A Working Peace System* (1943) – has proved to be a powerful force for conflict resolution, as witnessed by its progressive absorption of the new Balkan states and their acceptance in the process of the *acquis communautaires*. The Organization for Security and Cooperation in Europe (OSCE) has moved on decisively from its origins as an ad hoc conference between Warsaw Pact and NATO countries, albeit now severely tested in the Ukraine crisis. The African Union has reconstituted itself and begun to take on a more active conflict resolution role (as have sub-regional organizations in Africa). The Association of South-East Asian Nations (ASEAN) has developed significantly from its beginnings in the 1960s as an arrangement whereby governments in the region agreed not to support each other's rebels. The Organization of American States (OAS) has perhaps the longest continuous history of conflict resolution of them all. It is true that in many cases regions that need such organizations most (the Middle East, South Asia) have them least. But this can be argued both ways.

Conflict transformation principles on structural and cultural peacebuilding do not have a section to themselves in the UN Charter but are foreshadowed in clauses on equal development and human rights; they are strongly present in the work of many of the sixteen associated UN specialized agencies, in the work of the International Court of Justice, in the emphasis on conflict prevention that culminated in the 1990s and has recently been revived (as set out in chapter 5), and in the focus on the UN's role in postwar reconstruction and peacebuilding (as discussed in chapters 8 and 9). At this point we must acknowledge that, in the economic sphere, it is international institutions such as the Organization for Economic Cooperation and Development (OECD) and the Group of Eight countries (G8) that play the key roles, together with the International Monetary Fund (IMF) and the World Bank. This carries us beyond the main remit of this book, although we have seen in Part I how, as the complex interconnections that link conflict to issues of aid, trade, governance and security are recognized and traced through in enough detail to begin to influence policy (Collier, 2008), these organizations have been coming to play an increasingly prominent and explicit role in conflict management.

Perhaps the main conceptual development here since the publication of the third edition of this book has been Thomas Piketty's surprise best-seller *Capital in the Twenty-First Century* (2014). In revised Marxist mode, Piketty argues that, because of the general law of capitalism that return on capital (r) exceeds growth in the economy (g), inequality is bound to increase despite the temporary decrease caused by the two world wars and the great recession in the twentieth century. This will lead to a point where the current political order becomes unsustainable. The only remedy, as Piketty sees it, is a tax on inequality-causing capital worldwide – or an equivalent achieved country by country. This has been challenged, among others, by Deirdre McCloskey (2010, 2015), who argues that the 'bourgeois' virtues of liberty and dignity have provided the space for innovation, resulting in the consistent rise in productivity since 1800 that has led to – and continues to drive – the 'great enrichment': over the past forty-five years the percentage of the world's population living on less than $1 per day (adjusted for purchasing power in relation to the US dollar in 2000) has gone down from 26 per cent in 1970 to 5.4 per cent in 2006. This key debate about the relationship between levels of poverty and levels of inequality, and about how this bears differentially on political stability and prospects for human conflict, has been touched on in chapter 4 and is discussed further in chapter 20. The theme of sustainable development is clearly fundamental in conflict resolution. This resonates with the main thrust of Edward Azar's analysis of protracted social conflict, as described in chapter 4, and is key to a conflict resolution response to terrorism, as outlined below.

Those who work in the conflict resolution field are well aware that the UN remains a hybrid organization, reflecting its coexisting aspects – at the same time an *instrument of great power interest*, a *forum for the mutual accommodation of state interests*, and a *repository of cosmopolitan values* (see table 11.3). They understand that in the key relationship between the military/economic power of the United States and the legitimacy power of the UN lie the twin dangers of the US either sidelining the UN or integrating it into its own global strategy. They know that the UN food-for-oil programme in Iraq, for example, was scandalously subject to abuse, and that UN operations such as those in Cambodia, Somalia, Bosnia and Liberia were marred by 'sex, drugs and corruption' (Cain et al., 2004). They recognize the scorn in some quarters for such bodies as the UN Human Rights Council, presided over as it regularly is by some of the worst human rights abusers. They understand why, like all statespersons, the UN secretary-general has to adapt to the existing dispositions of political power, while at the same time trying to preserve and promote the cosmopolitan values inherent in the organization (some see the activities of the current

UNSG as disappointingly deferential to state interests). In short, the project of cosmopolitan conflict resolution clearly includes the idea of continual reform of the United Nations in the cosmopolitan direction – although efforts so far show that there is more agreement abut the need to reform existing arrangements (notably the UN Security Council) than about what should replace them. But many in the conflict resolution field are encouraged that, despite all this, and without its own military threat power or independent economic exchange power, the UN still retains its unique reservoir of legitimacy or integrative power. The United States could overthrow the Saddam Hussein regime in Iraq with its military power. But it was not able to win the subsequent peace because it had no legitimacy power. These are precisely the resources in the end most valued in conflict transformation – like those long-range gravitational forces that are easily overwhelmed over short distances but eventually prevail over greater ones. That is why most of those engaged in conflict resolution still see the United Nations as the essential institutional global framework for the realization of conflict resolution goals.

At this point a brief thought may also be interjected on an even larger subject from a conflict resolution perspective – the 'long history' of the most important global institution of all – the state system itself. Robert Cooper (2003) distinguishes three phases in the evolution of the state that still coexist in the world: the *pre-modern world* ('the pre-state, post-imperial chaos'), the *modern world* ('here the classical state system remains intact') and the *post-modern world* ('here the state system is collapsing, but unlike the pre-modern it is collapsing into greater order rather than disorder'). Cooper sees the EU as the pre-eminent harbinger of the post-modern world. Developing a theme introduced in chapter 4, we offer the following alternative in which the historical evolution of the modern state system is aligned to conflict resolution analysis of negative and positive peace, as outlined in Part I (see table 11.4). Table 11.4 is clearly only schematic, and in particular does not do justice in its fourth column to the fuller requirements for a genuine 'transnational positive peace', such as addressing the impact of the global economy, remedying historic injustices, and opening politics to wider participation, international accountability or protection of the vulnerable. Nor does it reflect the current systemic crisis of the postcolonial state system in a number of regions – notably the Middle East and North Africa (MENA).

Table 11.4 The long history of the modern state system

Intrastate negative peace	Intrastate positive peace	Interstate negative peace	Transnational positive peace
C16–C18 dynastic state: internal order	C19–C20 nation-state: internal welfare	Post-1945 postcolonial state: UN Charter article 2(4)	A possible cosmopolitan future

Highly schematized though table 11.4 is, it might suggest the outline of an admittedly over-optimistic 'long history of the state' in terms of the development of international norms from a cosmopolitan perspective.

The internal order imposed by the dynastic state in Europe in the sixteenth to eighteenth centuries was brutal and bloody, expelling pope and emperor, monopolizing internal violence, destroying subordinate sources of authority (the nobility, the church), crushing internal provincial independence, and eliminating non-conforming cultures.

The internal welfare reforms that followed mass mobilization and industrialization in the late nineteenth and twentieth centuries are also easily criticized – for example, as a mainly palliative buying-off of internal opposition using wealth plundered from the colonies. But, based on an ability to tax and therefore a need to justify taxation, the principle that states are also responsible for satisfying the internal basic needs of all their citizens, and that there must be some accountability to them, became – and remains – a rhetorically unchallengeable international norm.

The principle of interstate negative peace since 1945 is equally open to criticism (masking the export of violence to the peripheries of the power blocs). But, once again, the very fact that every UN member state has, at any rate in principle, accepted that 'All members shall refrain in their international relations from the threat or use of force against the territorial integrity or political independence of any state' (Article 2(4)) is an astonishing normative landmark, a rejection not only of the use of force but of its threat, a categorical contradiction of a fundamental tenet of unbridled realism.

Needless to say, as emphasized in Part I, many of the 150 new 'postcolonial' states that emerged in the second half of the twentieth century have not been able to move through these stages. They have been unable to crush internal opposition (some of them are disintegrating), they are not wealthy or stable enough to provide internal welfare (some of them are governed by predatory and corrupt regimes), they are porous to malign regional and global economic and political forces (often criminal), and 'new wars' have overwhelmed the simple 'negative peace' provisions in the UN Charter. Nevertheless the middle-term aim remains to 'rescue' them and to (re)build capacity to fulfil the functions outlined above. This is widely seen to be integral to prospects for positive conflict containment, management and transformation. Since the third edition of this book, the collapse of order in Syria and Iraq in the wake of the Arab revolutions and US withdrawal have led to a direct challenge to the international state system, represented by the IS declaration of a caliphate, the seizure of control of swathes of territory in both states, and the elimination of the borders between them in those areas. It remains to be seen whether this is a temporary aberration or whether it presages a break-up of the 'Sykes–Picot' structure. These permutations are too complex to factor in here in detail. But we do not expect them to affect the overall nature of the current state system – i.e., if permanent radical change does come, it is more likely to take the form of a new constellation of states than a replacement of the state system itself.

So we are left with the final – and most difficult – task: namely, to define what it means for the state system as a whole, set in a late capitalist global economy, to evolve within the context of an emergent cosmopolitan order in such a way that 'interstate positive peace' genuinely overcomes existing gross imbalances, deprivations and insecurities and delivers some form of protection, insurance and chances of betterment for all world citizens. This may at the moment seem entirely utopian – delivering global public goods is not in the interest of politicians in a statist system and presupposes the existence of 'republics that in fact have never been known or seen', as Machiavelli puts it in chapter 15 of *The Prince*. But adumbrations of a possible cosmopolitan future already exist – such as the whole paraphernalia of international humanitarian law, international humanitarian assistance and international human rights. And a central argument in Part II of this book is that, unless further progress is made in this direction, what has already been achieved in terms of the *acquis cosmopolitain* is likely to begin to unravel – with highly unstable, dangerous and perhaps catastrophic consequences for the human experiment. Revived polarization between Russia and the West and between China and Japan, as well as the challenge to the postcolonial state system in the Middle East, indicates the imminence of the threat and the scale of the challenge.

Conflict Resolution and International Law

For similar reasons, those in the conflict resolution field also see further development in the evolution of international law as essential for the cosmopolitan enterprise.

At the 'heart of the UN mission' is 'promoting the rule of law at the national and international levels'. In the words of the UN secretary-general's *Report on the Rule of Law and Transitional Justice in Conflict and Post-Conflict Societies*:

> For the United Nations, the rule of law refers to a principle of governance in which all persons, institutions and entities, public and private, including the State itself, are accountable to laws that are publicly promulgated, equally enforced and independently adjudicated, and which are consistent with international human rights norms and standards. (United Nations, 2004)

The Rule of Law Coordination and Resource Group, chaired by Deputy Secretary-General Jan Eliasson, includes the UN Department of Political Affairs (DPA) and the Department of Peacekeeping Operations (DPKO), etc., and has produced a joint strategic plan (2009–11), which is now being implemented.

But what does this mean in relation to the turbulent nature of the international scene of competing and overlapping jurisdictions, and in the absence of the sinews of effective cosmopolitan governance? Given its problematic nature in comparison with positive state law, debates about applications of international law usually end up as disagreements about what international law is (see table 11.3). For example, Adam Roberts asks:

> Is international law to be seen as a progressive instrument of change, as a means of furthering the interests of peoples rather than governments, as something antithetical to the Hobbesian world of brute force? Or is it to be seen as a practical means of devising modest and limited adjustments between conflicting interests of the great powers, who are the principle agents of its creation? (1990: 84)

We think that international law is both of these – as suggested, for example, in Article 38 of the Statute of the International Court of Justice, which gives the sources of international law as:

(a) international conventions, whether general or particular, establishing rules expressly recognised by the contesting states;
(b) international custom, as evidence of general practice accepted as law;
(c) the general principles of law recognised by civilised nations;
(d) judicial decisions ... of qualified publicists [are] subsidiary means for the determination of rules of law.

In terms of the second of Adam Roberts's alternatives, where international law is seen as a 'practical means of devising modest and limited adjustments between conflicting interests', from a conflict resolution perspective this is located within the sphere of *conflict settlement* and *exchange power*. Here is found a whole complex of overlapping international regimes, conventions and customary practices accepted as having the form of law, thickening in some areas into reasonably consistent norms and procedures capable of surviving substantial disputes – for example, the law of the sea. This is always reversible in individual instances and can be overridden in cases of 'supreme national emergency'. Nevertheless the costs of doing so are often high. Here, too, are the conflict resolution instruments of 'arbitration' and 'judicial settlement' referred to in UN Charter Article 33(1) cited above – as yet admittedly scarcely used, but nevertheless retaining considerable potential for a cosmopolitan future (Merrills, 2005).

In *arbitration*, the disputing state parties voluntarily agree to a free choice of arbitrators (typically each party chooses two, who then together choose a fifth), jointly determine the legal or other rules that apply (the initial *compromis*), and undertake a voluntary obligation to abide by the outcome. Since 1945, arbitration 'has been used extensively in resolving trade and investment disputes but less frequently to resolve political disputes between states' (Ziring et al., 2000: 212). Well-known exceptions were arbitration between India and Pakistan in the Rann of Kutch dispute in 1965–6 and the setting up of the US–Iran Claims Tribunal after the release of the American hostages in 1981.

In *judicial settlement* by international courts, the judges making the adjudication are not chosen by the parties to the dispute but are already members of an existing international tribunal or court. The International Court of Justice

(ICJ), for example, was established as one of the six principal organs of the UN in the UN Charter and began work in 1946. It has fifteen judges chosen by the UN General Assembly and the UN Security Council. Its caseload has not been heavy – only sixty-nine contentious cases (actions by one state against another) by 1998 (with further 'advisory opinions'). The ICJ has limited jurisdiction – only states can be parties – and all parties have to consent, not only the applicant but also the respondent. States can give conditional preliminary consent but attach reservations to limit this. The procedure is expensive, lengthy and public. Unsurprisingly, states tend to apply when it is seen to be to their advantage, but not otherwise. In the early years, for instance, many new states were reluctant to have recourse to the ICJ because they saw the system as biased towards the West. From the 1970s, when the number of new states had reached a critical majority, this was reversed. In April 1999, the government in Belgrade brought ten cases to the ICJ against the attacking NATO countries (Butler, 2009: 215–28). Regional courts – in the EU, OAS, AU and elsewhere – also form part of the system.

Turning to Adam Roberts's other pole, where international law is seen as a 'progressive instrument of change, as a means of furthering the interests of peoples rather than governments, as something antithetical to the Hobbesian world of brute force', this can be seen to be located within the sphere of *conflict transformation* and *integrative power*. This is where international humanitarian and human rights law is located, as already mentioned. Previsaged in the 1993 International Criminal Tribunal for the Former Yugoslavia (ICTY) and the 1994 International Criminal Tribunal for Rwanda (ICTR), this now includes the new International Criminal Court (ICC), which was founded by the 1998 Rome Statute and came into effect in 2002. By June 2014, 122 states were parties to the ICC. Unlike the ICJ, where only cases involving states can be settled and only states are allowed to petition, the ICC can try individuals. It has a competence to prosecute for war crimes, crimes against humanity and genocide (but not for crimes against peace or of aggression). The deep ambivalence in international law about questions of legitimate interest, responsibility and enforcement in the humanitarian field will be discussed further in chapter 14 with reference to what used to be called 'humanitarian intervention' (Ramsbotham and Woodhouse, 1996) but is now usually referred to under the broader concept of a 'responsibility to protect' (R2P) (ICISS, 2001). A landmark here was the first indictment issued against an existing head of state – Sudanese President Omar Al-Bashir – in July 2008, albeit tempered by the latter's ability in May 2015 to escape arrest in South Africa.

Summing up the scope and effectiveness of international adjudication, Michael Butler comments:

> Not surprisingly, much of the current discourse surrounding the use of adjudication as a tool for the management of international conflicts is framed by the diametrically opposed views of idealistic proponents and realist skeptics. Somewhere between the position of those who consider arbitration and judicial decision as the means for transforming

the nature of the international system through the promotion of transnational norms and those who cite the enduring influence of power, force and interests as prima facie evidence of adjudication's epiphenomenal appeal lies a muted reality, in which adjudication serves as one vehicle available to overcome the obstacles to the management of international conflicts and settlement of their underlying disputes. (2009: 225)

With reference to a 'responsibility to protect', the third column of table 11.3 serves to clarify this issue from a conflict resolution perspective. What we label 'Intervention (A)' – the intervention of more powerful states in less powerful states in pursuit of national interest – is precisely characteristic of the realist world of international anarchy. This is extended by quasi-realists into the use of intervention by 'coalitions of the willing' to forestall emerging threats along the lines envisaged in the September 2002 US *National Security Strategy* report. This contrasts dramatically with the fundamental international society norm of non-intervention, seen to be constitutive because without it such a society could not exist. And this contrasts again with 'Intervention (B)' – intervention sanctioned by the international community to uphold the solidarist norms of international law (including humanitarian law as well as collective security).

The conflict resolution community is torn between these last two positions. There is wide recognition of the force of the pluralist argument that the non-intervention norm is an essential bulwark against hegemonic intervention, and that to breach it in favour of Intervention (B) may open the floodgate to Intervention (A). But there is also appreciation of the moral power of the solidarist argument that to insist on non-intervention and stand back in the face of tyranny, barbarity and state collapse is to hand control to the unscrupulous and abdicate those very values that constitute a humane international community in the first place. We can readily understand why conflict resolution is pulled in both directions. This represents the as yet unresolved clash between settlement and transformation principles within the international society/ international community heartland where conflict resolution approaches are chiefly found (see chapter 19). But there is agreement in rejecting quasi-realist arguments that envisage 'public goods' essential to the society of states being upheld by its most powerful members unconstrained by questions of international law and legitimacy.

Summing up this section, table 11.3 suggests that, on these issues, international law can be said to be pulled in one direction by *international politics* and in another by *international ethics*.

Uncompromising realists, who continue to interpret world affairs solely in terms of an international system of states, dismiss international law as irrelevant at best and follow George Kennan (1984) in his scorn for 'the legalistic-moralistic approach to international relations'. Others, following Hans Morgenthau (1973), may acknowledge state compliance in practice with most of the rules of international law but think that this is no more than a 'self-enforcement' of what in any case simply reflects complementary state interests. Neo-realists do not even discuss international law, and a quasi-realist such as Bobbitt (2002) does not include it as a topic in the index of his 900-page book.

Those writing in the peace research and conflict resolution field generally take a radically different view. They turn either to 'institutionalist' theorists of the international society of states or to 'liberal' theorists of the international community for an understanding of international law within which conflict resolution can operate (Barker, 2000: 76–82).[1]

Here, at the intersection of international relations and international law, Robert Jackson defines international society as 'still predominantly pluralist in its normative framework' (2000: 122–9), so that international law protects the integrity of community within state boundaries but does not yet extend to determining how international society as a whole should 'act collectively in regard to common goals' (ibid.: 127). This is consonant with the conflict containment and conflict settlement dimensions of conflict resolution.

For Richard Falk (1995), on the other hand, the imagined reality of world community presupposes that state sovereignty would provide 'no exemption from the obligations of international law', drawn as these obligations would be 'as impartially as possible' from the procedures of international institutions such as the UN or guided by quasi-democratic transnational bodies such as citizen's associations (ibid.: 101–3). Here it is conflict transformation that moves centre stage.

One of the most fruitful recent developments in this area comes from the constructivist idea that, although international rules and regimes may initially arise from a convergence of state interest, once these international legal rules are normalized and internalized, they subsequently alter the nature of state interest and even of state identity (Koh, 1997; Byers, 1999; Barker, 2000: 82–94, quoting Arend, 1998): '[A] legal system such as the international legal system does more than simply create expectations and promote stability. It also fulfils the essentially social function of transforming applications of power into legal obligation, of turning "is" into "ought"' (Byers, 1999: 6). This is an admirable encapsulation of the kind of structural and cultural metamorphosis that cosmopolitan conflict transformation aims to achieve. Michael Butler, referring to the 'settlement' dimension of international adjudication, puts it like this:

> Despite its roots in the state-centric realm of international law, the concept of employing adjudicatory bodies to render binding decisions as a method of managing international conflict has always been at least mildly subversive of that paradigm. This subversion stems from the fact that international adjudication is steeped in a form of legal and political theorizing that seeks to draw an analogy between the legal systems and rules governing most domestic societies and polities and the nascent and much weaker body of international law. (2009: 212)

And all of this is consonant with Armatya Sen's account (2009) of the 'idea of justice', which does not attempt a 'transcendental institutional' once-and-for-all definition of universally ideal justice but sees commonalities of sympathy, understanding and appeal to reason within pluralistic and compet-ing approaches to comparative justice that are sufficient to underpin a shared notion of what it is to be human, thus identifying the direction in which the reduction of injustice (poverty and tyranny) and the progressive practical realization of justice in the world now lies. To which nearly all those working in the conflict resolution field would simply say, 'amen'.

Conflict Resolution and Cosmopolitan Democracy

Ever since Kant's identification of 'perpetual peace' with a voluntary confed-eration of republican states (1795) (not forgetting Thomas Paine's rather more radical version ([1776] 1986; Walker 2008)), the link between conflict resolu-tion and democracy has been seen to be a close one (Rousseau, 2005). This has recently taken two main forms. What follows should be seen to be a develop-ment of the discussion of democratization and prevention in chapter 5.

First, there is the less well-substantiated version of the 'democratic peace' theory – the claim that mature democracies have the best record for handling *internal* conflict non-violently. In this view, democracies are associated with attempts to protect human rights under the rule of law, to inhibit abuse of power through internal checks and balances (including an independent judi-ciary and a free press), to hold governments to account through universal suf-frage and secret ballots, to replace 'winner takes all' politics with guarantees that defeated parties can regain power non-violently, to accommodate ethnic diversity through various forms of regional and local autonomy, and to pro-vide protection and insurance for the basic needs of citizens through universal taxation. We can recognize the lineaments of the 'liberal peace' that became the norm for UN-led interventions to prevent and end civil wars after the Cold War and that has since been both severely tested in practice and criticized in principal (as discussed in chapters 5, 8 and 9). One often cited problem here is the argument of Mansfield and Snyder (1995, 2005) that *transitions to democ-racy* are often associated with increased levels of conflict and turbulence – as demonstrated dramatically after the Arab revolutions (see chapter 4). And whether democracy is capable of accommodating either ethno-secessionist conflicts that challenge the very definition of the electorate in the first place, or ideological conflicts that challenge the western secular assumptions on which the idea of liberal democracy is itself built, remain deeply testing and as yet unanswered questions in the conflict resolution field, to which we return in chapter 20. For example, in his book *Islam and Liberal Citizenship: The Search for an Overlapping Consensus* (2009), Andrew March offers a highly detailed and nuanced investigation into the possible terms on which Muslims can accept the principles of pluralist liberal democracy. Even in Turkey the ques-tion remains open as to whether an elected Islamist government can coexist with the Kemalist tradition of secular institutions and state authority. In the view of Khaled El Fadl, 'the issue of whether Islam can support and bolster a democratic order that respects individual human rights is by far the most important challenge confronting Muslims today' (2005: 180).

Second, there is the much better substantiated argument that links democracy to peace *between* states. This is associated with parallel arguments that also identify democratic interstate peace with economic interdependence (Gartzke, 2007) and international institutions (Hasenclever and Weiffen, 2006), as noted in chapter 5. The modern version of this argument was introduced by Michael Doyle in his articles 'Kant, liberal legacies, and foreign affairs' (1983) and 'Liberalism and world politics' (1986), where he compared lists of liberal states and interstate wars between the eighteenth and twentieth centuries and concluded that democratic states do not fight each other (the *dyadic* version of the democratic peace theory). Discussion has focused on whether this statistical correlation holds up, and, if so, why. In his 2005 book *Democracy and War*, David Rousseau concludes that the dyadic theory is now very strong. The *monadic* version of the theory, which claims that democracies fight fewer wars generally than autocracies, is seen to be weaker. We may call to mind UK Prime Minister Tony Blair, who involved British forces in five foreign military operations between 1997 and 2007.

Behind all of this lie deep discussions about what counts as democracy in the first place – a close look at the situation in countries listed as 'democracies' (for example, the democracy/autocracy indices in Marshall and Cole, 2009) shows a bewildering variety of practice merging into various forms of 'semi-democratic' or 'quasi-democratic' polities. As noted in chapter 5, semi-democratic states have, if anything, a worse record in fighting wars than both democratic and non-democratic states. A key aspect in many new states, for example, is how apparently recognizable party-political democratic structures at the top relate to what are in practice usually entirely different regionally and locally varied social and political formations in the middle and at the bottom. This is also where the problem of defining 'corruption' lies in cases where what is viewed in one part of the world as 'nepotism' is regarded in another as a binding ethical-social duty to 'fulfil family obligation'.

But beyond these more familiar versions of the democratic peace, consonant as they are with the pluralist 'conflict settlement' end of the conflict resolution spectrum, stretches the more visionary outline of the idea of 'cosmopolitan democracy' itself, located at the 'conflict transformation' end of the spectrum. To some extent this can be seen to be bridged by the emerging *systemic* version of the democratic peace theory, which compares the overall proportion of democratic states to the evolving perceived international legitimacy of democratic institutions in general and their relation to the international use of force. Some see the idea of cosmopolitan democracy as a key to evolving new forms of transnational solidarity and community to help overcome present current gross global imbalances that are seen to be unsustainable and a potent source of future human conflict. From this perspective, cosmopolitan democracy is seen as an essential underpinning of the 'interstate positive peace' that is needed if there is to be a cosmopolitan future at all. What David Held soon after the end of the Cold War called 'the cosmopolitan model of democracy' aims to encourage 'a new international democratic culture and spirit – one set off from the partisan claims of the nation-state' (1995: 44; Reading 73). Territorial boundaries of 'systems of accountability' need to be 'recast so that those issues which escape the control of a nation-state – aspects of monetary management, environmental questions, elements of security, new forms of communication – can be brought under democratic control.' New forms of political association linked to regional parliaments and eventually a democratized international assembly ('a re-formed UN, or a complement to it') would be the main 'standard-setting institutions'.

Daniele Archibugi's book *The Global Commonwealth of Citizens: Toward Cosmopolitan Democracy* (2008) has carried this further. Archibugi offers the cosmopolitan democracy project as the main way to overcome what he calls the 'schizophrenia' between the benefits delivered to their own citizens by the leading democratic states and the opposite outcome for the citizens of other states, delivered by the global system that the leading democracies have largely created and still sustain. He attributes a dangerous halting, and possible reversal, of the post-Cold War trend towards greater numbers of democracies to this fact: the 'wars of aggression' of the Bush era 'have had the effect of blocking any authentic mass movement in support of democratization' (2008: 278). Certainly the idea that democracy can be imposed from outside by force of arms is now thoroughly discredited. Rather than looking in what he sees as the 'old-fashioned' pluralist direction by appealing to principles of non-interference and state sovereignty in opposing such interventions, Archibugi looks in the opposite direction, towards the transformative project of cosmopolitan governance. What is needed, in his view, is to extend the 'values of democracy' to the global scene, based on principles of inclusion, impartiality and responsibility: 'it is preferable to look ahead and propose a world political system in which self-determination establishes internal democracy, impartial institutions intervene to people's advantage, and global constitutionalism replaces sovereignty' (ibid.: 278–9).

Testing Conflict Resolution: Responding to Terrorism

In conclusion we can now return to the major challenge of outlining an appropriate conflict resolution response to international terrorism in light of the above. This is one of the greatest tests of conflict resolution principles and approaches today. For realist critics, conflict resolution is identified with 'talking to terrorists' and is ruled out accordingly. Conflict resolution is seen to have nothing significant to offer in an area where deadly security threats from fanatical ideologues can be countered only through technical surveillance methods, denial of sanctuary, the shutting down of financial sources of supply, public protection, the strengthening of front-line allies and, where necessary, direct military action. 'Talking to terrorists' is seen to be part of a strategy that, on the contrary, merely rewards violence, and thereby encourages and legitimizes it.

Needless to say, this is not how the matter is viewed from a conflict resolution perspective. John Burton was discussing the subject as long ago as his 1979 book *Deviance, Terrorism and War*, which is why, drawing on decades of analysis of the relationship between frustrated human needs and terrorism, he was one of the few who can be said to have predicted a dramatic increase in terrorism before the events of 9/11 (Burton, 2001). We also applaud the refreshing frankness and courage of a theorist-practitioner such as John-Paul Lederach (2001), who, within days of 9/11, offered his fellow Americans an imaginative conflict transformationist alternative at a time when calls for punitive revenge were understandably loud.

In this final section of the chapter we use the challenge of terrorism to illustrate the cosmopolitan conflict resolution response to transnational conflict in general.

A good way to begin is to recall the 2014 Global Terrorism Index (GTI) analysis discussed in chapter 3. The GTI covers 162 countries and is the most comprehensive and up-to-date statistical analysis available at the time of writing. As seen in chapter 3, the index shows an upswing in deaths from terrorism of 61 per cent since 2012, to a level five times what it was in 2000. But, as figure 3.4 (p. 96) also shows, 80 per cent of these have come in five countries – Afghanistan/Pakistan, Syria/Iraq and Nigeria – with over one-third of the deaths in Iraq. If these figures are abstracted, the graphs suggest that overall global levels of deaths from terrorism between 2000 and 2013 have remained the same or even gone down (although this calculation is in turn distorted in the other direction by including zero for these five countries).

It seems no coincidence that the predominantly military response to the 9/11 attacks in 2001 was focused in Aghanistan and Iraq. Lederach's essay, written before the attack on the Taliban in late 2001, had presciently warned that a mainly punitive response would be like hitting a seeding dandelion with a golf club. In Afghanistan, the US-led coalition plunged into the middle of a civil war by using the Northern Alliance of mainly non-Pashtun Tajik and Uzbek Afghans to oust the mainly Pashtun Taliban. The US then took its eye off the ball by invading Iraq less than two years later. Here it made four widely anticipated mistakes: first, greatly enhancing the power of Iran by knocking out the balancing power of a strong Iraq; second, overthrowing the previous dominance of the Sunni minority and assuring permanent democratic preponderance to the politically inexperienced majority Shia (exacerbating sectarianism and further enhancing Iranian influence); third, as seen in chapter 8, wrongly assuming that Iraq in 2003 was like Germany in 1945 and disbanding the Iraqi military and Baath party adminstrative structure as if this were equivalent to de-Nazification; and, fourth, beginning by thinking a small coterie of administraters could be flown in to administer postwar peacebuilding run almost entirely from the Pentagon (the Office for Reconstruction and Humanitarian Assistance). George Bush senior had deliberately not moved on to take Baghdad after driving Iraqi forces out of Kuwait in 1991, as he easily could have done, for precisely these reasons. So it is that, despite the final bill of some $4 trillion to $6 trillion (in recent estimates) for the 'war on terror' in Afghanistan and Iraq since 2001 (Bilmes, 2013; Watson Institute, 2014), Afghanistan/Pakistan and Iraq/Syria have remained the focal points for global terrorism. Box 11.1 gves a brief resume of the emergence of IS (Islamic State) to illustrate this.

It may be noted that the Taliban had earlier emerged via a comparable sequence of mutations from its source in the *madrasas* of Afghanistan and Pakistan, encouraged and armed by the West via the CIA as *mujahideen* fighters against the Soviet occupation of Afghanistan. These forces were not demobilized or reintegrated in the late 1980s, even though they were known to be practising terrorist tactics against Soviet forces and civilians. This helped to sabotage the 1988 Geneva Accord and greatly increased the subsequent task of denial and suppression when many of those ignored at this time refocused their efforts against the United States. Despite ample warning signals, the greatest world power was blind to the dynamics that its own policies were playing during the crucial years when most could have been done at least cost. Such are the perils of intervening in the multi-level complexities of transnational conflict without full understanding of its nature – a theme we will pick up again in chapter 14.

Box 11.1 The emergence of Islamic State, 2003–2014

Some 66 per cent of deaths from terrorism in 2013 were perpetrated by four groups – al-Qaeda, the Taliban, Islamic State and Boko Haram. Islamic State and Boko Haram both emerged post-2001.

The immediate origin of Islamic State (IS) was in its predecessor, al-Qaeda in Iraq (AQI), set up in the wake of the invasion of Iraq in 2003. Taking advantage of the power vacuum in the country following the defeat and dismantling of Saddam Hussein's military and security apparatus, and using the fears of the hitherto dominant Sunni minority at the sudden access to power of the Shia majority via the process of democratization, AQI, under the vicious leadership of Abu Musab al-Zarqawi, was seen to constitute the main threat to US and allied plans for post-Saddam Iraq. AQI was subsequently defeated by a combination of fierce military assault from the US 'Task Force 145' in Operation Arcadia (reinforced by the 2007 'surge' in US forces in Iraq) and, crucially, the success of the 'Anbar Awakening', when Sunni tribal leaders were persuaded to shift support to the new Iraqi government. Al-Zarqawi was killed in 2006.

Two major factors shaped the (re-)emergence of what eventually became Islamic State and its subsequent success – the chaos of the civil war in Syria and the sectarian policies of the post-occupation Shia-dominated government in Iraq of Nouri al-Maliki. Resistance continued after the defeat of AQI from what was then called the Islamic State of Iraq (ISI), whose leader was killed in 2010, to be succeeded by Abu Bakr al-Baghdadi. In 2004 Al-Baghdadi had been held in the main US prison at Camp Bucca (which at one

Box 11.1 (continued)

time or another held four of the six future chief leaders of IS). Taking advantage of the stalemate in the civil war, ISI subsequently expanded into Syria in 2013, changed its name to the Islamic State of Iraq and the Levant/Syria (ISIL/ISIS) and immediately challenged for pre-eminence among *jihadist* groups. Instead of fighting the al-Assad government, it concentrated mainly on carving out its own area of control. In particular, it attempted to absorb the already established Syrian al-Qaeda offshoot the al-Nusra Front, but was rebuffed by the al-Qaeda leader Ayman al-Zawahiri. In January 2014, ISIL expelled the Nusra Front from ar-Raqqah in Syria and took control of Fallujah in Iraq. In June 2014 there was the unexpected overrunning of Mosul and the seizure of a huge swathe of territory in Iraq. In the process ISIL acquired large numbers of heavy weapons and vehicles, which greatly increased its relative military strength compared with other opposition forces in Syria. On 29 June came the announcement of the establishment of a caliphate. ISIL was renamed the Islamic State (IS) – although this was widely challenged – and al-Baghdadi restyled himself Caliph Ibrahim. IS now controlled a third of Syria and a quarter of Iraq – a territory the size of the UK and with a population of 7 million.

The brutal terror tactics of IS succeeded in scattering Iraqi government forces, most of whom were Shia and feared reprisals from the alienated Sunni population in Western Iraq, whose tribal leaders now saw IS as a way of throwing off the hated tyranny of the al-Maliki government and its Iranian sponsors.

IS went on to challenge al-Qaeda for global leadership of the neo-*jihadi* movement as a whole, using its economic resources (see below) to poach recruits from other *jihadist* groups, including in Afghanistan, via propaganda translated into Pashto and Dari, and received acknowledgement from groups across India, Pakistan, Libya, Uzbekistan, Indonesia and elsewhere – for example, Ansar Beit al-Maqdis in Egypt. The reality is far more complicated than this, however, as innumerable splinter groups emerge, mutate, rename themselves, compete, break up and and coalesce. For instance, characteristic of IS under al-Baghdadi has been its espousal of *takfiri* extremism, in which fellow Muslims – including Sunni Muslims – are accused of apostasy (*takfir*) and attempts are made to eliminate them accordingly. According to al Jazeera, the 150,000 strong Sunni Sheitat tribal group in Iraq was denounced as apostate for fighting against IS, and in one progrom 700 were killed, crucified and beheaded (among whom were an estimated 600 civilians). A number of foreign fighters who had joined IS were alienated by these actions. This is reminiscent of the vicious fragmentation and in-fighting in previous periods of sectarian warfare, together with similar apocalyptic millenarianism, such as the 'wars of religion' in Europe in the sixteenth and seventeenth centuries (Cohn, [1957] 1970).

There is no intention in all this of suggesting that US policy has been solely, or even mainly, to blame for the level of deaths from terrorism since 2001. Prime responsibility rests with those who perpetrate such atrocities. In conflict resolution, condemnation of these strategies and actions is clear and unequivocal, no matter who carries them out and whatever the claimed justice of the cause.

But what the previous discussion does demonstrate – and box 11.1 illustrates – is how international terrorism is embedded within the wider dimensions of transnational conflict in general, as described in chapter 4, and needs to be addressed within this framework. The central thrust of a cosmopolitan conflict resolution response, therefore, is the argument that, in combating terrorism, *denial* must from the outset be clearly embedded within much broader strategies of *prevention, persuasion,* and *international cooperation and legitimacy* (see box 11.2), and that these must in turn be comprehensively related to the dimensions of transnational conflict within which the phenomenon of international terrorism is incubated and through which it spreads. This in no way tempers uncompromising denunciation and outrage at the egregious inhumanity and brutality of acts of terror that violate all civilized ethical and religious principles. The analysis in the 2014 Global Terrorism Index has reached a similar conclusion: according to the index, 80 per cent of terrorist organizations over the period reviewed have been stopped by a combination of confrontation by security forces and a political process to address grievances. In only 7 per cent of cases has a military campaign to smash a terrorist organization succeeded by itself. In the words of Steve Killelea, executive chairman of the Institute for Economics and Peace, which produces the GTI: 'We need to have a rational discussion of terrorism based on the statistics and figures. The best way to beat terrorism is to get it under control globally' (*The Independent*, 18 November 2014).

Audrey Cronin (2015) developed a further perspective on this analysis which, combined with the policy framework outlined below in box 11.2, enables us to define a strategic conflict resolution response to terrorism that is both global in reach and cosmopolitan in content. She argues that, while IS uses terrorism (and a particularly brutal and abhorrent form of it), it is better understood not as a terrorist organization but as what she terms a pseudo-state, which is theocratic and revisionist and based on a perversion of Islam. By 'pseudo-state', she means it has control of territory, finance, resources, weapons and military capability way beyond that of terrorist organizations such as al-Qaeda, as we have seen. If this is so, then it cannot be defeated solely by counter-terrorist strategies such as were used against al-Qaeda. Cronin suggests instead that, since IS has managed to make an enemy of every state not only in the region but also in the world, a global coalition combining military, diplomatic and economic elements should be built, including, as well as the US, Iran, Saudi Arabia, France, Germany, the United Kingdom, Russia and China, as well as Iraq's and Syria's neighbours. The diplomatic/political and economic response would involve a stronger international arms embargo and sanctions, joint border patrols, more aid for displaced persons and refugees, and, interestingly, the proposal to deploy UN peacekeeping missions in countries that border Iraq and Syria.

This proposal and analysis may seem remote in present conditions. But, given the collapse of existing structures, particularly in Iraq and Syria, nothing less than the construction of a new regional peace order based on a reconstituted Arab League acting in cooperation with Iran and Turkey, and supported by the wider international community, can resolve all the levels and sectors that constitute the current transnational conflict. For example, answers have to be found for the future of the Alawite (Shia) minority in

Box 11.2 A cosmopolitan conflict resolution framework for addressing terrorism

1 Prevention   **Reduce proneness to terrorism**

Address global-level drivers
Address regional systems
Address state legitimacy and capacity

2 Persuasion   **Reduce motivation and support**

Contest ideological rationales
Separate extremists of ends and extremists of means
Influence identity-group and government strategic choices
Address recruitment, especially in diasporas

3 Denial   **Reduce vulnerability and defeat hardliners**

Limit target vulnerability to terrorism
Address transnational connectors that sustain terrorism
Strengthen international policing capabilities
Break up terrorist networks and arrest activists
End military occupation of cities and land

4 Coordination   **Promote international cooperation and legitimacy**

Coordinate regional and local initiatives within as wide a coalition
of international actors as possible
Apply principles of contingency, complementarity and
comparative avantage
Ensure that action is sanctioned internationally so far as is
possible and that it is seen to comply with international law

Syria if the regime of Bashar Al-Assad falls, and for the Sunni minority in Iraq, in order to deny IS the fault lines onto which it has thus far been able to batten.

The first dimension: prevention – reducing proneness to terrorism

Reducing proneness to terrorism lies at the heart of a conflict resolution anti-terrorism strategy for the same reason that addressing the preconditions for protracted social conflict lies at the basis of Edward Azar's PSC strategy, as outlined in chapter 4. This is consonant with the initial response of the Policy Working Group on the UN and Terrorism (UNPWG) to the aftermath of the September 2001 attacks:

> If such efforts assist societies to resolve conflict peacefully within the rule of law, grievances that might have been expressed through terrorist acts are more likely to be addressed through political, legal and social means ... In addition, effective structural prevention measures would strengthen the capacities of States to avoid the type of pro-tracted armed conflict that weakened Afghanistan and enabled the rise within its terri-tory of transnational terrorist networks. (United Nations, 2002a)

Although directions of causation are complex, there seems little doubt that international terrorism is rooted in similar drivers to transnational conflict in general. For example, in addition to ideology (see *The second dimension: persuasion* below), the 2014 Global Terrorism Index found that three main factors 'correlate globally with terrorism': high levels of violent crime, often associated with economic frustration; high levels of social hostility between 'different ethnic, religious and linguistic groups' linked to discrepancies between the distribution of peoples and postcolonial state borders; and high levels of 'state-sponsored violence such as extra-judicial killings and human rights abuses'. In the Middle East and North Africa (MENA) region, the first factor is stressed by Gilbert Achcar, in his study *The People Want* (2013), while the other two are emphasized by Marwan Muasher, in his analysis of *The Second Arab Awakening and the Battle for Pluralism* (2014).

Broad policy recommendations follow from this, such as the importance of prevailing upon 'rentier states' and patriarchal cultures in the region to reinvest income domestically. For example, Achcar (2013) calculates that, at the moment, some nine-tenths of the money spent by Gulf Cooperation Council governments is invested overseas, half in sovereign wealth funds. Another priority is to build institutional capacity for pluralistic democracy throughout the region in order to avoid the trap of 'winner takes all'. In Tunisia, for example, the post-revolution electoral law now means that it is hard for one party to get an overall majority. The catastrophic consequences of governments choosing discrimination and repression over inclusion and pluralism have been shown in the cases of the partisan regimes of Bashar al-Assad in Syria and Nouri al-Maliki in Iraq. It is well understood that, in general, acts of terror perpetrated by governments have killed many times more people in recent history than those of insurgent groups (see chapter 3). And such actions can alienate target populations, which is why insurgent groups often seek to provoke them. For example, it remains to be seen whether repressive policies in Egypt (including more than 400 condemned to execution at the time of writing) will drive the Muslim Brotherhood to move further away from democracy and towards *jihad*. The Muslim Brotherhood in Egypt, together with salafist allies, had themselves missed a vital chance to do the opposite when the Morsi government was in power.

Over the years, western governments have been seen as hypocritical because they 'espouse democracy and human rights worldwide, yet support elitist and non-democratic governments in these states' (Laqueur, 1999: 145; see also von Hippel, 2002: 36). This is compounded by western-led interventions into predominantly Muslim countries and by unresolved conflicts such as those in Kashmir, Chechnya and, above all, Israel/Palestine. For most Muslims, no satisfactory answer has yet been given to the simple question: Why does the West oppose nuclear programmes in predominately Muslim countries so fiercely, when for decades it has condoned, if not encouraged, Israel's acquisition of more than 200 nuclear weapons, together with the means of delivery to Muslim countries?

In addition to the long-term role of general 'preconditions' in reducing the chance that terrorist violence will gain a niche, there is the equivalent of Azar's 'process dynamics' (see chapter 4) – the perhaps fifteen- to twenty-year processes of particular party formation, alienation, radicalization and militarization to the point where organized insurgent violence actually does break out and terrorist tactics may be adopted (see chapter 5). This is often a critical period when such dynamics need to be noticed, taken seriously and acted upon within an overarching 'prevention' strategy. Unfortunately it is still what is rarely done, because the international community only notices escalation at the point when it finally erupts into major violence that registers on the international radar screen. For example, the process of Tamil alienation and radicalization in Sri Lanka leading to the formation of the LTTE, the creation of its highly authoritarian command structure, and its adoption of a suicide terrorist strategy gave ample warning signs over a twenty-year period. It was the Tamil LTTE, not radical Islamist groups, who first demonstrated the devastating effectiveness of suicide bombing in asymmetric conflicts. Something similar occurred in the radicalization and militarization of the Taliban in Pakistan and Afghanistan, as noted earlier. Halliday (2002) brilliantly dissected the general and particular causes of this crisis. The original aim of the Islamists was to create a society and a state based on Islamic principles. This drew them into resistance to the secular, modernizing trends in Islamic states as well as to the sources of those trends. The movement bound together political movements in disparate conflicts, from Palestine to Afghanistan to Kashmir and beyond. Combined with the crisis of the state in the region, this led to what Halliday calls a general 'west Asian crisis'. As noted above, it was the Islamists' seizure of power in Afghanistan, helped by Pakistani intelligence, Saudi finance and US support for what were at the time anti-Soviet *mujahideen*, that created the conditions for a new, militaristic and large-scale training ground for terrorism to be established.

The second dimension: persuasion – reducing motivation and support

Equally important to preventive measures from a conflict resolution perspective is persuasion. There are three main elements in a conflict resolution persuasion/dissuasion strategy: to challenge ideologies of terror; to persuade conflict parties to use non-terrorist means; and to reduce the appeal of terrorism within wider actual or potential support constituencies (including the diaspora).

Challenging ideologies of terror   Since all four of the groups responsible for most terrorist attacks in 2013 use religious ideologies based on extreme interpretations of Wahhabi Islam, the 2014 Gobal Terrorism Index advises that, to counteract the rise of religious extremism, moderate Sunni theologies need to be cultivated by credible forces within Islam. It is important – indeed inevitable – that 'moderate Sunni countries and not outside influences' lead such a response.

Challenging ideologies of terror is a large topic that can only be touched upon here. To understand the conflict means taking the relevant belief systems seriously (for example, Sunni and Shia *jihadist* ideologies that draw on the past legacies of Maududi in the Indian subcontinent, Qutb in the Sunni Middle East, and Khomeini in Shia Iran (Armstrong, 2001)) and supporting the efforts of those culturally best placed to counter them. Although some are relatively optimistic about the prospects for centrists to win the battle to define political Islam (for instance, Shadid (2002) and Feldman (2003)), others are less sanguine. Khaled El Fadl, for example, sees a continuing 'state of war' between a 'humanist' understanding of Islam that embraces modernity and an increasingly 'aggressive, zealous, vocal, and well funded' 'puritan' version that rejects it – 'two main groups wrestling for the soul of Islam', as he describes it (2005: 25). As a strong supporter of the former, he is not hopeful about the eventual outcome: 'it is not an exaggeration to say that there is a real danger that the puritans will be able to redefine the nature of the Islamic religion' (ibid.: 280). Central here is a dispute about the meaning of *jihad* itself, which for most Muslims means 'struggle to further the will of Allah on earth'. It does not mean war (*harb*) or battle (*qital*) but refers mainly to the struggle to overcome our own frailties and sins (the greater *jihad*) and to bring about justice on earth (the lesser *jihad*). Islam is a religion of peace. For example, in Egypt, the Grand Mufti, using the Arabic term for IS, *Daesh*, wants the media to adopt the acronym 'al-Qaeda separatists in Iraq and Syria' (QSIS), because such extremists violate all Islamic principles and are a danger to Islam (*The Times*, 26 August 2014). Similarly, in dramatic contrast to the grotesque violence of the *jihadism* pursued by Boko Haram in Nigeria is the Islamic programme promoted by Mohammad Sanusi II, Emir of Kano, in the Muslim north of Nigeria, who supports women's education, ending child marriage, and investing heavily in development, including a 'Marshall Plan' to make a decisive difference in enhancing agricultural livelihoods.

In short, the strategy here is to strengthen and support the goals and ideals of pro-reform networks that in their own quiet way have obtained the support of the great majority of Sunni Muslims worldwide and represent the best hope for the future. It is important to remember that this does not mean opposing salafist Islamic movements. It does mean opposing ideologies of violence.

Separating extremists of ends from extremists of means   As shown in chapter 3, in most cases, acts and strategies of terror are not part of the identification or aims of a government or insurgent group, but are taken up or set aside according to strategic advantage. This can even be discerned in the case of Boko Haram, which began in North-East Nigeria in the years of transition from military rule after 1999 as a relatively peaceful salafist movement that focused on preaching. But the violent attempt to crush the movement in 2009, when its founder, Mohammed Yusuf, was arrested and killed in custody, led to its re-emergence in 2010 under the fanatical and ferocious leadership of Abubakar Shekau. Since then, thousands have been abducted, tortured and killed, and a caliphate has been declared in territory around Borno state the size of Scotland.

Here we reach the vital distinction from a conflict resolution perspective between what Oliver Ramsbotham calls 'extremists of ends' and 'extremists of means' (2010: 194–5). Extremists of ends are those who are uncompromising in their pursuit of strategic goals. Extremists of means are those who espouse violent methods. Mahatma Gandhi and Martin Luther King were extremists of ends. They were implacable in their determination to confront and eliminate British imperialism and racial discrimination. They maximized conflict rather than trying to reduce it. But they were moderates of means. They did so non-violently. In the case of political Islam, for example, there are key distinctions between violent and exclusionary movements such as al-Qaeda that appear to be ideologically and organizationally wedded to violence, political 'national-ist' movements such as Hamas in Gaza and Hezbollah in Lebanon that aim to liberate their countries from foreign occupation and might be weaned from violence, and those many salafists who espouse what they see as a pure form of Islam but accept obedience to the ruler. The key conflict resolution strategy is to separate what may be the majority who embrace uncompromising political or ideological goals from the minority who want to employ terrorist means.

This is where the question of 'talking to terrorists' comes in. There is a considerable literature on the technical aspect of 'negotiating with terrorists' (Zartman, 2006). William Donahue (2009), for one, lucidly sums up many years' work on the link between the immediate 'crisis bargaining' phase, where a series of paradoxical 'relational issues' predominate, and the longer-term 'nor-mative bargaining', where 'substantive issues' come to the fore. This relates in turn to the hotly debated public issue of whether governments should do deals for the release of hostages. But the more central point is one made by commentators such as Jonathan Powell (Tony Blair's chief of staff, 1995–2007) in his book *Talking to Terrorists: How to End Armed Conflics* (2014): 'experience over 30 years shows that in the end, if such groups enjoy substantial political support, we will need to talk to them.' For example, channels were opened to the IRA from 1972 without which 'the negotiations between John Major and Martin McGuinness in 1993 would not have been possible'. The US has negoti-ated with the Taliban; Israel has negotiated a ceasefire with Hamas. Above all, if the aim is to detach IS fanatics from the Sunni tribal leaders in Iraq who see them as liberators from Shia/Iranian persecution, this can only be done via negotiations, which, among other things, convince them that, this time (unlike last time), promises of power-sharing and security will be honoured. This includes former Baathist and Iraqi military commanders who lead the IS military wing. The same applies in a case such as Mali, in order to separate the *jihadist* ideologues from the underlying grievances and aspirations of the Tuareg people onto which they batten, as also to the deprivations and resentments of Muslims in Borno, Adamawa and Yobe provinces in North-East Nigeria, which Boko Haram is trying to commandeer, and the similar socio-political and economic discrimination claimed by Kenya's Muslim minority (11 per cent of the population) against the Christian-dominated government, used by al-Shabaab to fuel a potential religious war in the country in revenge for Kenya's earlier intervention in Somalia to overthrow the Islamic Court regime (see case study in chapter 6).

Reducing incentives for recruitment   Linked to this is the challenge of reducing the scope for recruitment and support from potentially sympathetic outside constituencies. These are always much larger than the core intransigent group and defined by the general appeal of the political programme at issue. This is well understood by those who espouse terrorism and often aim to provoke repressive government response in order to activate this wider support. The same applies to the diaspora, which in may cases plays a key role in sustaining terrorist capabilities. Here another factor comes into play – how governments in the diaspora countries react. For example, a great deal of research has been done over the past decade and a half on motives that induce so many international *jihadis* to take part in insurgencies in other parts of the world. There are many theories here, mostly psychological, to explain the alienation and radicalization of young Muslims in other countries (including Tunisia, despite the fact that its own main Islamic party, Ennahda, is participating in the democratic process there). In his interviews with *jihadists* in Indonesia and Morocco, for example, Scott Atran (2010) concluded that the key attraction was a group dynamic. Membership of the group gives a new identity and meaning, and the duty of group loyalty acts if anything more powerfully than religious conviction. Recruitment itself is a kind of conversion. This is familiar from studies of religious extremism and terror in general, such as Mark Juergensmeyer's *Terror in the Mind of God: The Global Rise of Religious Violence*, published in 2000, not long before the 9/11 attacks. Often the families and siblings of these *jihadis* also find such radicalization hard to explain, particularly because recruitment is kept deliberately secret by *jihadist* groups for security reasons. This is in turn reminiscent of analyses of why so many young Europeans from other countries joined the Spanish civil war in the 1930s on the side of the republicans or became Maoist revolutionaries in the 1950s, 1960s and 1970s.

All of this requires a sophisticated and detailed understanding of insurgent support – for example, in the make-up of the estimated 35,000 Taliban fighters in Afghanistan/Pakistan:

> Some are ideological full-time *jihadis*, some are linked to the insurgency because of local grievances, some because it's a way to make a living, some because they like to fight, some because their communities are hedging their bets between the government and the insurgency. (Major-General R. Barrons, *The Times*, 4 March 2010)

In box 17.2 (p. 428), we give further detail of the way in which IS, through 'its globalist and apocalyptic ambitions ... its heady millenarianism ... and its powerful social media campaign', had by early 2015 attracted over 18,000 foreign fighters from more than ninety countries (Schori Liang, 2015: 2). We also expand on how, in the past few years, there has been a response to this propaganda by developing greater knowledge and capacity for countering violent extremism (CVE) online, following the call in UN Security Council Resolution 2178 (September 2014) for greater cooperation on such issues, including measures to prevent terrorists from exploiting the rapidly growing number of 'anti-violent extremist' websites.

The third dimension: denial – reducing vulnerability and defeating hardliners

We will deal briefly with this dimension of the anti-terrorist policy framework, including the use of military force, not because it is not of central importance, but because there is less that conflict resolution can contribute when faced with those implacably set on murderous policies. It involves all the measures being taken in the name of 'homeland security' in countries threatened by reprisal attacks – increasingly from returning *jihadis*.

Confining attention to the immediate response to 9/11, under UNSCR 1373 (2001) the purpose of the UNCTC of the Security Council was to 'improve the flow of information with and among international, regional and sub-regional organizations on counterterrorism' with a view to helping member states to coordinate their duty to deny financial support, suppress safe havens, and share information about 'any groups practising or planning terrorist acts'. In monitoring implementation of UNSCR 1373, a good idea of the range of activity involved was offered in the February 2003 report, where relevant bodies provided summaries of their 'activities, experiences and plans, including best practices, codes or standards they have developed' (S/AC.40/2003/SM.1/2; 26/2/03). This covered legislation and implementation machinery such as police and intelligence structures, customs, immigration and border controls, weapons access controls, cooperation and information exchange, and judicial cooperation between states on extradition and early warning, as well as links to other threats such as arms trafficking, drugs, organized crime, money laundering, and the illegal movement of chemical, biological and nuclear weapons. Among relevant associated bodies were the International Atomic Energy Authority, the UN Global Programme on Money Laundering, and the Office for Drug Control and Crime Prevention, which launched a Global Programme Against Terrorism in October 2002, identifying countries needing assistance and coordinating the combating of transnational organized crime. The greatest single concern, dwarfing all the others, has been to prevent the nightmare scenario in which terrorist groups gain access to weapons of mass destruction.

Prominent here is reducing the financial resources that support those practising terrorism – crucially, the large sums flowing from anonymous funders in Saudi Arabia, Qatar, Kuwait, Bahrain, etc., that underwrite the spread of hardline Islamic globalism. The IS holding of territory has greatly expanded the resources available because of access to oil revenues via the black market, confiscations, taxation, etc. – on some estimates IS had a war chest of about $2 billion by the end of 2014, although this may have been exaggerated. On the other hand, the responsibility of providing for millions of people on whose continuing goodwill IS depends places huge burdens on the rudimentary governing structures put in place.

In many eyes, the central dimension in all this in the wake of the increased capacity of extremist groups to seize and hold cities and territory is the physical military task of removing them. In a city such as Mosul in Iraq, for example, this is a daunting prospect, given severe restrictions on air attack capabilities in crowded urban space, the reluctance of outside powers such as Turkey as well as the West to be drawn in with ground troops, the fanaticism of the occupiers, and the sectarian divisions plaguing national forces within those countries themselves. At the time of writing, the forces being gathered and trained to undertake this task are forming. For many in the conflict resolution field this is the most difficult question of all, as discussed further in chapter 14.

In short, whatever denial policies may be adopted, these must be contained within and guided by broader conflict resolution measures. For example, persuasion strategies can be linked to denial strategies when policies of greater inclusiveness, protection of minorities, and social accommodation deny terrorists the capacity to recruit. We return to this in chapter 17 when we address the rapidly evolving power of social media in what is now termed cyber-conflict resolution and cyberpeacemaking.

The fourth dimension: promoting international cooperation and legitimacy

The overarching necessity from a conflict resolution perspective is, so far as is possible, to ensure that the response to the transnational threat of terrorism is both coordinated and legitimized internationally – globally and regionally. This is a fundamental premise for cosmopolitan conflict resolution – as also emphasized in chapter 14.

A coordinated framework of this kind reflects the original recommendations of the UN's Policy Working Group on the UN and Terrorism (UNPWG), set up by the UN secretary-general to complement the work of the Counter-Terrorism Committee of the Security Council (UNCTC) (established under Security Council Resolution 1373 in September 2001):

> Terrorism is, and is intended to be, an assault on the principles of law, order, human rights and peaceful settlement of disputes on which the world body is founded. ... So it is through a determined effort to bolster and reassert these guiding principles and

purposes that the world body can best contribute to the struggle against terrorism. (A57/273 S/2002/875)

Fundamental to all of this is the stipulation that 'this is a genuinely international enterprise that upholds the values being defended'. Here again we note the recommendations of the UN Policy Working Group: 'States should be encouraged to view the implementation of UNSCR 1373 as an instrument of democratic governance and statecraft ... All counter-terrorism measures must be consonant with international human rights law.' One suggestion at the time was for the UNDPI, with the Office of the UN High Commissioner for Human Rights, to publish a digest of core jurisprudence of international and regional human rights bodies on the protection of human rights in the struggle against terrorism, and to convene a consultation with international, regional and sub-regional organizations and NGOs. Needless to say, this is where it is fundamentally imperative that counter-terrorism does not fall into the trap of itself employing instruments of terror – for example, the use of torture, as confirmed in the US Senate 'dark prisons' report of December 2014. Statements such as those by CIA chief John Brennan, that 'enhanced interrogation techniques' had elicited critical intelligence that had saved lives (although he said that whether this information could have been obtained in some other way was 'unknowable'), are entirely inadequate – and ethically and legally repugnant. Meeting terrorism with due process of law is the most powerful – even sacred – strength of those insisting that all acts of terror, whoever commits them and whatever the cause – are violations of the deepest values that underpin the cosmopolitan enterprise.

Swamped by the gathering momentum of the 'global war on terror', the initial response through the UN set out at the beginning of this section was often drowned out. But it is worth reasserting. For the UN's Policy Working Group, the key role for the United Nations in the coordination of international anti-terrorism activity was to provide a framework for cooperation in which regional organizations would be encouraged to develop strategies appropriate to their own regions and which worked on the benefits of the comparative advantages each of them possessed. The UNPWG proposed that meetings between the secretary-general and representatives of regional organizations should develop an international action plan in which the United Nations would cooperate with regional organizations in identifying best practice in the field of counter-terrorism and promote its adoption: 'The potential role of the United Nations in working with regional multilateral efforts fits within the Organization's roles of norm-setting, coordination, cooperation and capacity-building.'

Since then, of course, the situation has changed dramatically. But, as suggested above, the approach proposed by Audrey Cronin (2015) points exactly to the way in which the counter-thrust of cosmopolitan conflict resolution is what is needed to overcome the grave challenges posed by the use of terror in all its shifting forms. Views will differ on the ability of global institutions, regional organizations, and major states under current leaderships to undertake these coordinated roles. Much depends on the capacity of those affected by terrorism to work together. This brings together 'strange bedfellows', as, for example, in Syria and Iraq, where the situation would be transformed at *global level* if the United States and Russia could work together – as at one moment seemed possible after the Syrian regime's chemical weapons atrocities – and at *regional level* if Saudi Arabia and Iran were able to coordinate where required. Legitimization through the Arab League would also seem essential. The fact that events in Ukraine have had such dire repercussions on any prospects of coordination in the Middle East demonstrates again the interconnected systemic nature of transnational conflict.

Seen in this way, the response to terrorism is one part of a response to a much larger set of global issues, which have to do not only with violence but also with human rights, opportunities for livelihood and free expression, and the life chances of ordinary people. An opportunity is available to be seized here, since there is a genuine international consensus that terrorist methods are entirely abhorrent and unacceptable but also that, where associated political aspirations are legitimate, they must be seen to be addressed with the utmost seriousness. Global injustices and the failure of existing institutions to recognize and respect political aspirations need remedying for their own sake. But, in the process, there is hope of addressing the sources of humiliation, rage and despair that are the fuel of terrorism.

RECOMMENDED READING

Achcar (2013); Archibugi (2008); Atran, S. (2010); Booth and Dunne (2002); Brachman (2009); Cronin (2015); Forrest (2006); Held (2004); Held and McGrew (2007); Kaldor (2003); Lacqueur (2004); Muasher (2014); Powell (2014); Wilkinson (2006).

RELEVANT EXTRACTS IN *THE CONTEMPORARY CONFLICT RESOLUTION READER*

Reading 1: I. Kant, On Perpetual Peace: A Philosophical Sketch
Reading 73: D. Held, Cosmpolitanism after 9/11

CHAPTER TWELVE

Environmental Conflict Resolution

By the start of the second decade of the twenty-first century, it was clear that environmental and resource issues would be central to prospects for global conflict and cooperation. The outcome of the Copenhagen Conference on Climate Change in December 2009 suggested that cooperation to prevent dangerous climate change would be hard to achieve. With no legally binding limits in place, there seemed little to stop the onward rise of global temperatures and the corresponding impacts on vulnerable populations. Time is short, since an effective response in the next ten or at most twenty years is required to avert dangerous climate change. But so far our capacity to respond appears alarmingly limited.

It is easy to forecast an apocalyptic picture of interconnected global emergencies. Gwynne Dyer (2010: back cover), for example, argues that 'an increase of as little as two degrees Celsius in average global temperatures – which is almost inevitable – would heat global politics to boiling point', while James Lovelock (2006: 60) is even more pessimistic: 'although the earth has recovered from fevers like this in the past, if these huge changes do occur, it seems likely that few of the teeming billions [of human beings] now alive will survive.' Drying out of the continental interiors, prolonged droughts, melting of the ice in the Himalayas on which the river valleys of China and India depend, ocean acidification, harsher conditions for agriculture, melting ice caps, rising sea levels – all these present an alarming picture. Moreover, climate change is only one of a range of environmental challenges. We face a devastating crisis of biodiversity and unprecedented pressure on the renewable and non-renewable resources on which the world at present depends. Will societies be able to feed their populations and provide the energy and material basis of life to all? Will the poor and vulnerable be able to survive?

There are many who challenge these pessimistic views. But if we picture the world as a single country, it would surely be a Third World country. It would have great inequalities, widespread denial of basic needs, weak or non-existent governance, human insecurity, and a mass of religious, ideological, ethnic and cultural divisions.[1] Would such a country be capable of responding to these overwhelming challenges? It surely has all the conditions for transnational conflict.

What can conflict resolution offer to conflicts on this scale? What is the relationship between environmental damage, conflict between societies and potential conflict resolution? In this chapter we argue that conflict resolution can make a positive and creative contribution in response to environmental challenges.

We begin our discussion by looking at local, small-scale environmental conflicts and the responses which characterize the new field of 'environmental conflict resolution'. We then move up a scale to look at conflicts of interest over climate change within a single country and then between and within countries. We sketch a role for conflict resolution in the negotiation and evolution of cooperative agreements and look at the conditions for cooperation to evolve. We allude to the social transformations that may be needed to make the transition from the carbon era and suggest that, insofar as we are dealing with an asymmetric conflict, confrontation as well as conflict resolution may be required. Finally, we discuss the potential for armed conflicts over climate change, concluding that we cannot speculate on whether climate change will become an important factor in the causation of wars but that we would be well advised to adopt policies of prevention and conflict transformation to avoid this risk.

Tragedies of the Commons

Garret Hardin (1968) pointed out the fundamental dilemma of collective action problems that lead to environmental conflicts of interest. If interdependent actors pursue only their own interests, with no concern for the collective good, they risk collective ruin. Thus, for example, over-exploitation of North Sea fish led to the collapse of the Hull fishing industry, where most of the trawlers have been driven out of business. As Hardin put it, 'freedom in a commons brings ruin to all.'

The Tragedy of the Commons is an extension of the Prisoner's Dilemma to many players. Each farmer (or fisher) can cooperate, by limiting withdrawal of common resources, or defect, by withdrawing resources without restraint. If the renewal of resources depends on collective restraint, a policy of restraint is collectively rational. But if the farmers cannot trust one another, it is individually rational to defect, whatever strategy others play. Rapoport (1988) demonstrated in a series of experimental games that sustained cooperation is difficult to achieve in an n-person Prisoner's Dilemma even when the social trap is explained, although cooperation increases when players are allowed to communicate.

Nevertheless, in real commons, people often do cooperate. Historians have shown that, in the medieval and modern period, peasant farmers generally did not ruin the commons. Instead they developed institutions to regulate access.

Ingleborough is one of the 'three peaks' in Western Yorkshire in the UK, a mountain whose long, flat summit and steep sides form a familiar landmark for miles around. In 1652, the rights of the tenants of the neighbouring manor of Twistleton to common lands at Ingleborough were defined:

> so much common of pasture on and throughout all the commons on Ingleborough within the Lordship of Ingleton formerly agreed upon and to be occupied and enjoyed by the said Tenants and thacke and stone thereunto belonging with egress and regress at all times, as doth or ought to belong unto three oxgange and a-half to any of the tenants of Ingleton aforesaid without any rent paying for the same. (Balderston and Balderston, 1888: 272)

The implication was that access was regulated by the size of the peasant's holding in the manor (an 'oxgang' was about 15 acres). In other words, Hardin's assumption that peasants had unrestricted freedom in the commons was wrong.[2] Although at times unregulated competition does take place, in general people are aware of the consequences of the competition and use rules specific to the particular social setting to regulate collective use.

A Californian water conflict

Elinor Ostrom, in her book *Governing the Commons* (1990), has studied how traditional and modern communities cooperate to manage scarce resources. Here we summarize her example of water abstraction conflicts in California to give a sense of what can be done. She shows that, even when large numbers of parties are involved (in one case as many as 500 parties, more than the number of states in the world), people were able to overcome a potential tragedy of the commons by negotiating, adopting common rules and creating new institutions.

In the 1930s, landowners, cities and water supply companies were pumping water from groundwater basins in southern California. These basins were fed by runoff from the surrounding hills, but the amount of groundwater that could be taken without damaging the groundwater basins was limited. Up to the 1930s, the legal regime gave incentives to water users to pump as much water as they could use. As a result, too much water was extracted, the water table began to sink, and intrusion of seawater threatened the groundwater basins. The communities and producers had different interests and were vulnerable to different extents. Communities closest to the coast were most affected. Those communities who were higher up could extract water longer without suffering from seawater intrusion. Since different producers operated in different areas, the course of negotiations was distinctive in each basin. In the first basin to reach an agreement, the largest water user, the city of Pasadena, attempted to secure a voluntary agreement that all the users should restrict the amount they extracted. When the other users would not agree, Pasadena took legal action against the city of Alhambra and thirty other producers. A long legal case ensued. As part of this case, scientists undertook detailed hydrological studies. With the legal case outstanding and the results of the science clearly favouring restraint, the parties eventually agreed to reduce their abstraction under a new legal regime, which clarified the mutual obligations of the producers and created a new authority to monitor the agreement. This agreement then became a model for other basins. Elsewhere, though, the legal battles were more prolonged. Negotiations reached impasses. In one basin, an adjudicating committee finally arrived at an agreement after two years of negotiations. Even after the agreement was reached, one of the cities refused to sign up and continued to abstract more than its share of water. It was only brought into line by successful legal action by the other cities. Recognizing that agreements could not be policed by continuous resort to the courts, and also acknowledging the interdependence of the coastal and interior basins, the producers eventually negotiated an agreement to create a new authority in charge of water management across the whole of southern California. This authority built freshwater reserves along the coast that could be used to prevent seawater intrusion and protect the interior basins. It was no longer in the interests of the producers to withhold cooperation. The improved regulatory regime gradually put an end to over-extraction and the water tables in the basins recovered to a sustainable level. Although the negotiation process was protracted and uneven, a satisfactory outcome was eventually reached. The key ingredients were the ability of the parties to negotiate, the presence of a legal system that could resolve legal conflicts, and the multiplicity of basins, which allowed the evolution of cooperation in one basin to become a model for another. Having resolved the main conflicts, an institution evolved with the capacity to act as a dispute settlement regime. The producers were able to monitor each other's impacts, and they eventually came to accept an individual and collective interest in the rules that regulated access to the water basins.

This outcome was reached as a result of negotiation, adjudication, legal settlement and cooperation on rules and institutions. In more recent environmental conflicts in the United States, a new breed of environmental conflict resolution professionals is applying third-party methods to manage local environmental conflicts (Blackburn and Bruce, 1995; O'Leary and Bingham, 2003). The idea is to identify the key stakeholders, map their conflicts, bring them together, and set up a facilitated process which allows the key issues to be identified and collective approaches negotiated, ideally without the costs of legal action. In 1998, the US Environmental Policy and Conflict Resolution Act set up the US Institute of Environmental Conflict Resolution to assist parties in conflicts involving federal agencies.

Can such an approach be applied to the more global environmental challenges we face, in an international environment where agreed norms and legal enforcement are harder to achieve? We will approach this question by focusing on climate change – perhaps the most dramatic of the linked environmental crises that we face.

Conflicts of Interest over Climate Change

Climate change is a collective action problem because the individual and collective incentives to reduce carbon emissions are different. There is a strong collective benefit in reducing greenhouse gas emissions, as the Stern report (Stern, 2007) demonstrated. The social cost of mitigation and adaptation is far lower than the cost of unrestricted climate change. The problem is that different individuals, interest groups and states perceive very different costs and benefits, and institutions capable of balancing global costs and benefits do not yet exist. For example, the Association of Low Lying Island States would like more radical mitigation policies than OPEC.

Consider first the conflicts of interest within a single country over the response to climate change. Let us take as an example a country with different stakeholder groups, some representing fossil fuel industries, who perceive high costs in a programme of mitigation, others representing cities and householders, who perceive higher costs from failure to act. We can represent the actors' preferences for a collective policy on climate change as lying along an axis representing a more or less ambitious carbon mitigation policy for that country. The conflict of interest between any two actors can be taken as a function of their perceived costs and benefits over the range of possible collective policies. In general, the further they are apart, the greater the conflict of interest. Each actor will have a range of acceptable outcomes on the axis. Following Putnam (1988), let us call this range its 'win-set'. Now, if there are joint outcomes that lie within the win-sets of the actors, an agreement on a collective policy is possible – otherwise, not.

There are a number of ways in which the conflict can be overcome. Either or both parties can move their position to adjust to the other. They might accept a compromise in between their positions, even though the compromise is not the highest preference of either. They might reward or coerce each other to move position. Or they might rely on an arbitrator, such as a government, to make a decision for them.

If the government is perfectly responsive to the wishes of the stakeholders and represents their interests equally, it will choose the policy that maximizes joint benefits. In practice, however, governments respond to influence from the stakeholders, so the stakeholders compete to move the government closer to their own position. In countries where the government has a large stake in the fossil fuel industry, which is usually the case in countries with large fossil fuel industries, governments are more likely to favour industry. In countries which import fuel and are vulnerable to climate change, the government is more likely to favour the cities. Both the governments and the stakeholders seek to influence one another's positions.

Of course, positions are not fixed, and they move in response to changing conditions. Stakeholders may reassess their preferred positions in the light of new information. We know that one way to achieve conflict resolution is for the parties to find new positions that meet their underlying interests and needs. For example, if the government were to set up a market in reducing carbon emissions, the fossil fuel producers might be able to offset a potential loss of demand for fuels by higher-value operations in energy efficiency. They might then move towards supporting a more active climate mitigation policy, which might in turn bring both the government and the cities to adopt still more active proposals. Such a shift in positions could become self-sustaining.

A process like this took place in California in the 1980s and has now spread to energy companies elsewhere. Facing both rising marginal costs of supplying electricity and regulatory constraints on investment in new supply capacity, utilities such as Pacific Gas and Electric invested in energy efficiency and renewable energy in consumers' dwellings. They gave substantial incentives to consumers to invest in solar panels and energy efficiency, offering to install these measures themselves and creating financing packages that were competitive with new energy supply. In effect, the electricity company became an energy services company, providing the end user with energy services through an appropriate mixture of energy efficiency and energy supply. Because the electricity company had the expertise and access to finance to invest in energy efficiency and renewable energy, and many householders did not, this innovation removed one of the barriers to change.

Such cooperation could make householders and fossil fuel companies more willing to accept policies aimed at reducing carbon emissions. If fossil fuel companies realign themselves as energy service companies and find new markets in providing energy efficiency and renewable energy services, or if new companies emerge to provide these services in competition with the fossil fuel companies, a more favourable environment for further steps to mitigate climate change would develop.

This process is an example of changing preferences, which is an important element of conflict resolution. Of course, such a change is unlikely to take place all at once. Many actors will wait to see what others do. There are likely to be unconditional cooperators who will pursue mitigation strategies irrespective of what others do, and unconditional non-cooperators who will resist mitigation policies irrespective of what others do. But many will be conditional cooperators, who will move towards pursuing mitigation if others do, and if the economic and institutional context changes to make mitigation a strategy with higher payoffs to inaction (as in the case of the Californian groundwater basins). There are social learning effects here, which may produce a tipping point and a change in system behaviour over time.

Such changes do not depend entirely on cooperation and goodwill. If there is sufficient demand for mitigation, governments will require stakeholders to accept different policies, and they have sufficient legal, fiscal and regulatory powers to enforce a change. Conflict, as well as conflict resolution, may be a necessary part of the transition from carbon. While the major governments remain heavily under the influence of the fossil fuel industries, such changes may require both political mobilization and a general swing away from the carbon economy. There is already a movement gathering pace for disinvestment from exploring new fossil fuel resources. It is possible to imagine that measures such as this, and the more positive outlook for energy efficiency and renewable energy, will gradually swing public policy away from subsidies for fossil fuels towards mitigation and more sustainable policies. But the stakes involved in the transition are enormous, and the timescale is crucial. There are likely to be feedbacks between public policy and the behaviour of energy users, which will make some countries 'leaders' and others 'laggards' in the transition from fossil fuels.

Multi-Level Negotiations

How will the interaction between individuals, interest groups, public opinion and government behaviour play out across multiple states? Here the processes can become more complex. The political scientist Robert Putnam (1988) suggested that, in environmental, trade and similar negotiations, states and interest groups bargain together in a two-level game. In order to conclude an agreement, states must agree at the international level, but they also have to carry domestic coalitions, who may be able to block the legislation necessary to ratify an agreement and the policy measures needed to put it into force. Domestic coalitions can therefore be seen as veto-players who have an important stake in the negotiations at the interstate level. Any successful outcome must therefore lie within the win-sets of all the key veto-players, including governments and domestic interest groups. As Putnam puts it:

> At the national level, domestic groups pursue their interests by pressuring the government to adopt favorable policies, and politicians seek power by constructing coalitions among those groups. At the international level, national governments seek to maximize their own ability to satisfy domestic pressures, while minimizing the adverse consequences of foreign developments. Neither of the two games can be ignored by central decision-makers, so long as their countries remain interdependent, yet sovereign. (1988: 434)

Ward, Grundig and Zorick (2001) draw on Putnam's approach to analyse two-level bargaining in international climate change negotiations. For the sake of simplicity, they consider a situation with two governments, one a 'leader' in international climate negotiations favouring strong mitigation, the other a 'lagger' who favours an outcome close to the status quo. They suggest that both the leader and the lagger can use political capital to move the positions of the interest groups. But they intimate that the lagger will always have an advantage, since it can concentrate political capital on just one vested interest that can be used to block political change. Thus, they argue, 'climate change negotiations proceed at the pace of the slowest.'

This is a strong argument, and it seems to capture what has actually happened in the international climate change negotiations to date. But note that the model of Ward and his colleagues assumes that the governments' and interest groups' preferences stay the same, except insofar as the latter are 'bribed' to move by political capital. If we allow for the possibility that interest groups might evolve towards a cooperative policy through mutual interactions along the lines of the Californian energy services model, one could see different dynamics. Indeed, over a larger number of countries, the possibilities for cooperation (and for conflict) are increased. Energy companies in one country may benefit from investing in energy efficiency or renewable energy in another, and this may not only yield returns in terms of carbon credits and tax breaks or under Kyoto-style joint implementation, it may also offer real economic opportunities. Demand for end-use energy services will grow strongly across the world, but this could be met by different combinations of energy supply and energy efficiency. There is a large market opportunity in assisting developing countries to leapfrog over the 'dirty' industrial mode of development. Energy service companies in one state may therefore be able to make alliances with cities and householders in another, setting up networks of cooperation, assisted by favourable states. In such a way, cooperation could evolve in different 'basins', even while other states and stakeholders remain laggards. Once such patterns of cooperation are set up, the benefits of sustaining them may be considerable and may not depend only on environmental benefits. Indeed, as Giddens (2009) has argued, action on mitigation is most likely to take place when it meets other needs besides collective environmental benefit, such as economic advantage and reduction of air pollution. Already we can see examples of significant cross-national cooperation, such as European investment in Chinese carbon capture and sequestration and plans for trading solar electricity from the North African deserts to Europe.

Experiments with the evolution of cooperation (see chapter 1) have shown that players can do better if the chance of bumping into another cooperator is not random (Bowles, 2004). That is, if they can reliably recognize a cooperator and predict who will be a cooperator through some marker, such as group identity, cooperation becomes easier to establish. If the population is not homogeneous but is broken up into groups, cooperation may get established more quickly in some groups than others. Cooperative practices can then spread from one group to another. A group that is cooperating can share the benefits of cooperation and do better than other groups.

Applying this logic to climate change, even if major vested interests remain intransigent, if there is a way of cooperators recognizing each other and sharing the benefits of cooperation, then the cooperative strategy may spread.

This can be expected to lead to a process of polarization, with 'leaders' (governments and interest groups) pulling away from 'laggards' and creating mutual benefits from cooperation, from which laggers are excluded. If a point is reached where these benefits are clearly seen to outweigh the disbenefits of cooperation, the incentive structure for the laggards will change and the whole system tips towards mutual cooperation.

International Negotiations

In practice, the actual course of events and negotiations in arranging agreements on climate change has proven challenging (Depledge, 2006). While there is growing consensus on the need for international action, states disagree on the terms for cooperation. Considerations of development, sovereignty, equity, trade, and protection of national economies and national industries have come into play. The disappointing outcome at the Copenhagen Conference in December 2009 made cooperation to prevent dangerous climate change look harder to achieve and brought the conflicts of interest between states into a sharper focus.

In the lead-up to the crucial Paris talks in 2015, a number of states and the EU made important unilateral commitments which the UN is now attempting to marry to an international framework agreement in order to keep the rise in global temperatures within 2 degrees Centigrade of the pre-industrial average. President Obama committed the US to reducing carbon emissions by 26 to 28 per cent below 2005 levels within a decade. Premier Xi Jinping of China set a goal for the first time that Chinese emissions should fall after 2030. The EU has committed to a 40 per cent reduction below 1990 levels by 2030. The G7 has committed to cut greenhouse gas emissions by between 40 and 70 per cent by 2050 compared with 2010 levels and to limit global warming to 2 degrees Centigrade.

International agreement remains of vital importance, and it is unlikely that a fully effective climate regime can come into play until a stronger basis for international agreements has been achieved. Climate change has proven more difficult to negotiate than other environmental agreements, since it involves issues of equity and national development and is closely related to the patterns of asymmetric conflict and hegemony which divide the world. It may be that progress between willing cooperators will have to develop alongside resistance on the part of non-cooperators before the context for the transition from carbon is clear.

Climate change and armed conflict

At present, then, the situation is at the stage of conflict of interest and political conflict, but there are as yet no armed conflicts over climate change. If we count climate change as a factor in conflict and violence, it is indirect, through the structural violence which puts vulnerable populations at risk from natural disasters, droughts and storms or through the indirect impact of climate on drought-related conflicts such as Darfur. Migration from areas at risk from sea and storms has certainly contributed to ethnic conflict – for example in north-east India. But predictions that climate change will be associated with armed conflict in a major way remain speculative at present, since we do not know how climate change or future conflict will unfold.

Droughts and falling rainfall seem likely to affect agriculture, significantly lowering the incomes of poorer farmers while possibly raising those of richer farmers. Lower runoff to rivers may trigger disputes between riparian states. Parching continental interiors and loss of low-lying land to the sea may intensify disputes over land and other agricultural resources – for example, destabilizing relations between pastoralist and agrarian communities. There will certainly be increased migration, both internally and internationally, though whether this triggers or mitigates conflict depends on circumstances. Over the longer term, the melting of the Himalayan glaciers will have a devastating impact on the river valleys of India and China. Rising sea levels and storms will affect the large deltas, which are densely settled and economically important. The melting of the Arctic is already contributing to a race for the hydrocarbon resources thought to lie beneath the ice. So an impact on armed conflicts is quite possible, though international cooperation has so far proved to be a viable option (Reading 36).

Thomas Homer-Dixon (2001) has triggered an as yet unresolved debate with his argument that pressure on resources and environmental degradation leads to scarcity and violence. He carefully assembles evidence of the causal pathways through which scarcity may be linked to social responses and may lead to ethnic conflicts, coups or insurgencies. He illustrates the argument with the case of Haiti, suggesting that deforestation and erosion contributed to migration to the towns, continuing poverty, strife between the urban elite and poor slum-dwellers, and protracted conflict.

Homer-Dixon's thesis is challenged, on the one hand, by those who argue that the evidence to date does not support a link between scarcity and conflict (Gleditsch, 1997; Nordås and Gleditsch, 2007; Buhaug et al., 2014) and, on the other, by those who suggest the causation works in reverse – unequal social structures generate both environmental scarcity and conflict (Suliman, 1999). Theisen, Gleditsch and Buhaug (2013) review the evidence that climate change is a driver of conflict and find it inconclusive, with a striking lack of consensus and little support for a relationship between rainfall, short-term warming and civil conflict. Saleyhan (2014) offers a useful review of the research to date in a special issue of *Political Geography*.

There may well be an impact on structural violence and on the continuing exclusion of the poor and disadvantaged. Rogers (2010) argues that the West is adopting a 'fortress' approach to the problems of the global South, constructing barriers at the borders to keep out migrants fleeing from environmental and other disasters. This is likely to be unsuccessful, however, and merely contributes to insecurity as the disadvantaged and repressed strike back with unconventional means. Barnett and Adger (2007) makes a similar argument, that climate change is most likely to affect the poorest – the 'bottom billion', who already live in weak economies and weak governance. It will weaken economic prospects, result in loss of income and horizontal inequalities, and contribute to human insecurity and to the fragility of governments. Poor countries will be least able to adapt to the challenges of climate change. It is no accident that a large proportion of countries in the bottom billion fall into conflict and find it difficult to escape what Collier et al. (2003) call 'the conflict trap'. Likewise, Smith and Vivekananda (2007) present a list of countries which have experienced recent armed conflict and are on the DFID list of fragile states; all of them face additional challenges from climate change.

The Intergovernmental Panel for Climate Change for the first time suggested a link between climate change and conflict in 2014, in its *Fifth Assessment Report* (IPCC, 2014). It stated (with medium confidence): 'Climate change can indirectly increase risks of violent conflicts in the form of civil war and inter-group violence by amplifying well-documented drivers of these conflicts such as poverty and economic shocks. Multiple lines of evidence relate climate variability to these forms of conflict.' However, the *Fifth Assessment Report* also observed that 'collectively the research does not conclude that there is a strong positive relationship between warming and armed conflict' (Adger et al., 2014: 16).

Climate change is best seen as a potential background or proximate cause of conflict rather than as a direct cause on its own. It will always be mediated by other social, political and international relationships. Other causes of conflict may be more immediate sources of violence. Competition over hydrocarbons and 'lootable' resources, which become scarce for political as much as environmental reasons, may well be a more immediate cause of wars. The way in which these issues are 'securitized' is itself an essential aspect of the transition from conflict of interest to armed conflict, as the Copenhagen School suggests (Buzan et al., 1997). Energy is already more 'securitized' than climate change, but both are rising rapidly up the list of 'new security challenges' with which states are concerned. Similar policies of transition are required to deal with the potential conflicts over both energy and climate change, so, whether we regard environmental conflict resolution in this case as a form of conflict prevention or as an approach to transforming existing political conflicts, the need for imaginative collective response is similar.

Despite the speculative nature of the relationship between patterns of climate change and armed conflict and the lack of a strong relationship between climate variables and conflict over the last fifty years, we cannot anticipate what changes may develop as climatic change becomes more intense. Lee (2009; Reading 67) argues persuasively that climate change may become a direct driver of armed conflict in the future as well as exacerbating structural or indirect violence as a secondary consequence. He maintains that conflict research and conflict analysis need to be adapted and developed in order to provide problem-solving and conflict prevention methodologies for anticipating climate-generated conflicts and to provide space and time to avoid these emerging and becoming violent. He outlines six future scenarios of climate change and conflict, based on the end of the Ice Age (the melting of polar ice); raised temperatures in the tropics; water wars related to desertification; livelihood wars in Africa; the heating up of Central Asia and the prospect of resource wars between nation-states; and rising sea levels in South Asia and the islands of the Indian and Pacific oceans. Each of these scenarios contains latent and, in some cases, manifest patterns of conflict in response to climate changes. One of them will suffice to illustrate Lee's thesis and its relevance for environmental conflict resolution.

In Lee's scenario, Central Asia will see increasing desertification and the heating of the interior of the landmass will affect the river systems and the large downstream populations in many countries in the region. Control of the headwaters provides control of the rivers and water resources. Of the ten great rivers in the region, eight originate in China. In Lee's assessment, China's control of water resources will put it on a collision course with downstream users, intensifying water scarcity in South and South-East Asia and potentially leading Russia, India, Pakistan and Vietnam, if threatened in this way, to consider violent means to ensure their water supplies.

Lee's conclusion about the choices that need to be made to increase the chances of managing climate-generated conflict in non-violent ways echoes what has been found in research about other modes of conflict. Climate change and conflict needs to be understood in a long-term time frame; second, good analysis and scientific understanding are necessary preconditions for effective policy response; and climate-driven conflict needs to be taken seriously as a driver within the conflict resolution field.

James Lovelock and Gwynne Dwyer, quoted at the beginning of this chapter, argue that it is already too late to prevent the devastating effects of global warming, including associated political struggles and 'climate wars'. Lovelock thinks that a catastrophic reduction in the size of the human population is now inevitable. These apocalyptic scenarios, together with the proposed causal connections that underlie them, are in turn contested. The cosmopolitan conflict resolution response to this controversy is to refuse to accept either the resignation characteristic of the former or the complacency that can accompany the latter. The supreme test for the human species is to learn collectively how to understand and anticipate these 'unintended' systemic effects of human action and, even at this late hour, to succeed in adapting conflict resolution approaches for overcoming local 'tragedies of the commons', as described in this chapter, to a global setting.

RECOMMENDED READING

Gleditsch (1997); Homer-Dixon (2001); Lee (2009); O'Leary and Bingham (2003); Ostrom (1990); Theisen et al. (2013).

RELEVANT EXTRACTS IN *THE CONTEMPORARY CONFLICT RESOLUTION READER*

Reading 36: A. Hart, B. Jones and D. Steven, Chill Out: Why Cooperation is Balancing Conflict among Major States in the New Arctic
Reading 67: J. Lee, Climate Change and Armed Conflict

CHAPTER THIRTEEN

Gender and Conflict Resolution

For Jane Addams, American pacifist and founder member of the Women's International League for Peace and Freedom:

> It took the human race thousands of years to rid itself of human sacrifices; during many centuries it relapsed again and again ... So have we fallen back into warfare, and perhaps will fall back again and again, until in self-pity, in self-defence, in self-assertion of the right of life, not as hitherto a few, but the whole people of the world will brook this thing no longer ... We, [the Womens' International League for Peace and Freedom] wish to loosen within our own members and in all people those natural and ethical human impulses which, once having their way in the world, will make war impossible.

It has been pointed out by a number of observers that conflict resolution, in its development, conceptualization and methods, has been 'gender blind' (Reimann, 1999, 2002). Gender, which is taken to mean the historical and social construction of role differences between men and women, implies a relationship of power, which has a pervasive effect on all areas of behaviour and in all social institutions and practices. Since the conflict–war continuum is also a constructed social practice embedded in a set of linked institutions, the field of conflict resolution, which attempts to engage non-violently with that continuum, if it is to be effective, cannot afford to be as gender blind as its critics have implied.

Although much of it emanates from fields of enquiry outside the peace and conflict research field, there is an extensive literature on war, women, and gender relationships (Perrigo, 1991; Mazurana et al., 2013; Gizelis and Olsson, 2015). In the international relations literature, for example, the work of Cynthia Enloe (1988, 1993, 2000) has been a major influence in subverting the gender-blind assumptions of realist and neo-realist theory and has insisted on the importance of gendered analysis in the international system. Enloe has provided a potent analysis of what she sees as pervasive militarization, defined as 'the step-by-step process by which something becomes *controlled by, dependent on*, or *derives its value from* the military as an institution or militaristic criteria' (2000, 281; original emphasis), and argues that women globally are being incorporated and co-opted 'to the threshold of all those social institutions that promote militarization' (ibid.: 33). Other analysts stress the commonalities in the discourses implicated in the exercise of hegemonic power in the international system and in those of patriarchy in the family. Evidently, different schools of feminism and gender studies approach the topic of conflict

Box 13.1 Four stages in engendering conflict resolution

Stage 1	Making women visible as agents of change in conflict resolution
Stage 2	Removing male bias in conflict resolution data-collection and empirical research
Stage 3	Rethinking conflict resolution theory to take gender into account
Stage 4	Incorporating gender into conflict resolution policy-making and practice

and conflict resolution from different perspectives, from the original 'liberal' feminism that wants women to occupy positions of political influence and authority in the same proportion as men, through to the much more radical versions of 'difference feminism' that trace oppositional thought itself to the idea of language as a symbolic (thetic) system that is already gendered through its exclusion of the pre-symbolic (semiotic) other. This goes beyond the scope of the chapter.[1]

In this section we examine the progress made in developing a gender-sensitive approach in conflict resolution and in correcting the gender blindness that has concerned critics. Pankhurst and Pearce (1997) suggest that, although different disciplines follow different paths, there seem generally to be four steps involved in the process of engendering a discipline or area study. First, making women visible as change agents; second, the removal of male bias in the collection of data and the conduct of empirical studies; third, through the rethinking of theoretical constructs, to take gender into account; and, finally, the stage where gender becomes part of the mainstream in terms of institutional policy-making and practice (see box 13.1).

Stage 1: Making Women Visible as Agents of Change

Significant progress in the first of these steps, making women visible as agents of change in peacemaking and conflict resolution, was made through the lifelong contribution of Elise Boulding, whose work in establishing the foundations of conflict research and conflict resolution was noted in chapter 2. As a young sociologist concerned, as were all of the pioneers of the new field of conflict research in the 1950s, to avoid the mistakes which led to the Second World War and which might lead again to a catastrophic nuclear third world war, she was influenced by *The Image of the Future* (1961), a study of 1,500 years of European history by Dutch historian-sociologist Fred Polak. In the efforts to rebuild a peaceful European and global society after 1945, Polak offered the idea of 'imaging' a better future as a way of empowering people to bring it about. The idea attracted Boulding, and her major contribution to both the foundation of conflict research and its gender sensitization was to open up a discourse and practice in contemporary conflict resolution, where women and children were included as radical change agents and empowered peacemakers. Taking Polak as her guide, as we saw in chapter 2, she placed the idea of imaging the future within the context of what she called the '200-year present' – that is, the idea that we must understand that we live in a social space which reaches into the past and into the future: 'it is our space, one that we can move around directly in our own lives and indirectly by touching the lives of the young and old around us' (Boulding, 1990: 4). Boulding was a member of the Women's International League for Peace and Freedom (WILPF, formed in 1915, the oldest women's peace organization in the world) and was its international president from 1968 to 1971. This important organization provided a vehicle within which the voices of women in Boulding's 200-year present could be activated and heard.

Boulding's study of women in history, *The Underside of History* (1976), presented the case for a feminist project to abolish structural and behavioural aggression against women and to establish gender equity. However, she also insisted that 'equity feminism', while representing an important phase of feminist aspirations, was a limited mode of action. It needed to be augmented by a social and transformational feminism which focuses on the broader malformations that produce violence and oppression for both sexes, while also identifying women's culture historically as a resource for development and peacebuilding.

During the 1980s Boulding organized a series of 'Imaging a World without Weapons' workshops, an extension of the idea of problem-solving workshops and influenced by Polak's thinking on future imaging. Initially western-oriented, the workshops were subsequently reformulated in an effort to incorporate perceptions and values globally. In *Cultures of Peace: The Hidden Side of History* (2000), Boulding surveyed over fifty years of research on human culture and society and on the activity of peace movements working within a culture of war, arguing that the resources and energies for peace cultures are deep and persistent and are nourished by collective and communal visions of how things might be. In a manner not often displayed by the value-neutral exponents of problem-solving-based conflict resolution, Boulding was explicit about the norms and objectives that characterized her transformative agenda. In 2001, at the age of eighty-one, she imagined herself looking back at the way the world had changed in the 100-year future – that is, looking back from 2101:

> By 2050 the population had, through both disaster and design, fallen below five billion: human life on earth became viable again. School-based peace education joined with health and social education, leading to mutual solving of problems in and across communities and faiths. Industrialisation slowed down, older technologies and skills were revitalised, steady-state economies were achieved. Dismantling the military and its institutions began. People's organizations (NGOs) now provided vital communication networks round the world, linking the growing thousands of locally-run communities, sharing information, skills, problems, solutions.
>
> By 2100, the biosphere was beginning to recover from the destruction of the twentieth century, though used-up resources were gone for ever. National boundaries still existed for administrative convenience, but regional intergovernmental bodies skilled in conflict management handled disputes peacefully ... Humans had learned to listen to one another and the planet. (2001: 1)

Many women have followed and built on the pioneering work of Elise Boulding and have projected women's voices and gender-sensitive perspectives into the academic, policy and activist discourse of conflict resolution (Reading 21), and many also are voices from the global South (McKay and Mazurana, 2004; Ashe, 2010). One influential example has been the work in the Philippines of Irene Santiago, who is a peace activist and peace scholar from Mindanao. She is chair and CEO of the Mindanao Commission on Women and convenor of Mothers for Peace, and between 2001 and 2004 she was a member of the peace panel of the Philippine government negotiating with the Moro Islamic Liberation Front. She has worked with Muslim communities in Mindanao, especially women, and is a leading voice calling for the recognition and involvement of women in peace processes. Box 13.2 gives an account of her work in Mindanao, in which she adapts the ungendered conflict analysis framework of Edward Azar (described in chapter 4 of this book)

Box 13.2 Case study of conflict in the Southern Philippines: Irene Santiago and the Mindanao Commission on Women

Gender is usually not central to an armed conflict and therefore is not seen as central to its resolution. However, with Azar's conclusion that long-term development is essential to address the issues around protracted social conflict, it becomes evident that gender is in fact central to its resolution. Men and women are involved in war differently. Although more women are now involved as combatants, war is largely male in both its leaders and its participants. Because of the gender roles assigned to them by society, men and women also suffer differently in times of war. Women are usually left to care not only for their children but also for their extended family. Destruction of infrastructure and loss of property burden women, who have to cook, clean, wash, look for food and generally care for the young and elderly. On top of this environment of economic insecurity, women suffer physical insecurity, as rape is used as an instrument of war.

In my work with women in Mindanao, women have consequently defined the four fundamental human needs that form the basis of Azar's analysis differently:

Security needs
Gender-based violence is a concern during the war and also the post-peace agreement period when men, who have become used to a life of violence, return home. Having taken full responsibility for children and extended family in wartime, women have become more independent. This independence may not sit well with the returning combatant who still believes that everything is what it was before the war. That is why I have recommended training in non-violence for ex-combatants in post-peace agreement programs. Women also view the security problem in the aftermath of war differently. The Mindanao Women's Peace Summit (entitled 'If Women Negotiated the Peace Agreement') organized by the Mindanao Commission on Women in February 2006 recommended that, instead of the traditional DDR, there should be a 'de-militarized Mindanao'. They believed that no armed groups – whether government or rebels – should be allowed to operate in the areas once wracked by violent conflict if their communities are to feel secure.

Development needs
Because of their role as primary providers of basic family needs in times of war and in its aftermath, women give much importance to food security. Only when food is secure will they have time to attend to other things. The ability to provide basic sustenance gives women status. It is important to bear this in mind in designing reconstruction and rehabilitation programs. For example, the way houses are designed has a bearing

Box 13.2 (continued)

on whether women are able to continue to play the food-provider role effectively. In Cotabato, a row of government-constructed housing for internally displaced families was built with very little space in between the houses. Such a design meant that there would be no space for a woman to plant her vegetable gardens and rear her small animals. This meant she would have no contribution to the family's basic need for food. Her status in the family – as a major contributor to the family's food security – would be diminished. With a diminished status, she would have less voice in family decisions. Women's development needs and priorities being different from those of men, it is important for women to be trained as program officers and community organizers. In Mindanao, a foreign-funded training program excluded women, because the local partner agency believed only men should be trained for reconstruction and rehabilitation projects. The training facilitators convinced the agency that women were needed, not only to approach other women but also to provide a different perspective on how to assist families and communities who have suffered from war.

Fair access to decision-making

Women's role in decision-making in conflict situations depends on the role they are made to play. In the armed conflict between the Philippine government and the Moro National Liberation Front (MNLF), the women's committee chair held an important position as a member of the central committee. However, after the peace agreement was signed in 1996, women's role in decision-making reverted to what it was status quo ante. So, even where women played a significant role in the liberation struggle, rarely does it happen that they are put in decision-making bodies that are created for reconstruction and recovery. After the peace agreement was signed in 1996 by the Philippine government and the MNLF, most of the positions in the newly created structures were held by men. Resources were directed to state commanders, who were all men. Women had a difficult time trying to access those resources. In the end, the MNLF women calculated that they were able to access less than 10 per cent of the resources, and only after much negotiation. Learning from this lesson, the Mindanao Women's Peace Summit recommended that a Special Fund for Women be established in the Mindanao Trust Fund. In this manner, women will not only get immediate access to funds but also have decision-making authority over these funds (access and control). Women have expressed the desire to use the funds to develop an economic development model that will not lead to the impoverishment of others.

Acceptance of identity

Because Moro women are readily identified because of their headscarves, they are more easily the objects of discrimination. Whether in public transportation or in employment, they suffer in ways that Moro men do not. The demand of the Moro struggle for their right to self-determination includes the right of Moro women to be proud of and secure in their identity. This involves also recognition of the identity and proactive role of women as peacemakers. Many of the projects initiated by the Mindanao Commission on Women recognize, support and project this positive role. For example, the Women Healing Communities project harnesses women's experiences in managing violent clan feuds or *rido*, a blood feud or a chain of killings provoked by an affront to family honour. A *rido* may erupt any time this honor or *maratabat* is besmirched. Taking the form of tribal conflict or clan warfare, the killings are often carried on for generations. The goal of the project is to prevent or reduce *rido* by involving women who are respected in their communities as effective mediators.

In conclusion, if long-term development is indeed essential to addressing the grievances arising from the deprivation of fundamental human needs, it is critical that we recognize that gender issues must be integral to our analysis.

Source: text provided by Irene Santiago

to show how much richer and more relevant it becomes when women's needs are factored into the PSC model.

Stage 2: Data Collection and Case Studies

In view of this consideration of the feminist and gendered analysis of Elise Boulding, it is perhaps fair to comment that conflict resolution has not been quite as gender blind as has been alleged. Nevertheless, following Boulding, a generation of women writers and activists have been highly effective in the field at the theoretical, policy and applied levels and often committed to the radical and transformative agenda associated with her. It is women such as these who have engendered conflict resolution by making women visible and active, and also by effecting the second and third steps in the process of raising gender awareness mentioned at the beginning of this section – that is, the removal of male bias in the collection of data and the formation of case studies and the re-examination of theoretical constructs. We start with an example of the former.

The process of making women visible as agents of change has produced a wider array of case studies where women have taken leading roles in peacebuilding and recent studies which correct male bias in data gathering and analysis, especially in relation to the participation of women and girls in armed militias and fighting forces (McKay and Mazurana, 2004). During the wars in former Yugoslavia, women and women's organizations sustained and developed local cultures of peace against considerable opposition in highly militarized and sharply polarized communities. One of the most influential of these initiatives was the Centre for Peace, Nonviolence and Human Rights (Centar za Mir for short) in the Croatian town of Osijek, as noted in chapter 9.

The proximity of Osijek to the border with Serbia rendered it vulnerable to attack, and the city was heavily shelled for almost a year, from August 1991 until June 1992. Most of the population fled, leaving some ten thousand people in the city. Around eight hundred people were killed, and many more were wounded (Jegen, 1996: 14). The city, surrounded on three sides by Serb forces, continued to experience sporadic shooting and other war-related incidents until 1995, but was never overrun.

The Centar za Mir (CZM) came into being in 1992 in order to address both the psychological and the social and human rights issues of the war, and has generated new projects to meet local needs. While not a feminist organization in any explicit sense, women held leading positions in the organization and the needs of women and children were firmly addressed in its projects and agenda. Its director was Katerina Kruhonja, a doctor at the University Hospital of Osijek. A member of the Catholic Church from the beginning of the war, she sought to create an influence for peace in public prayer meetings outside the army headquarters in Osijek and by broadcasting prayers on the local radio network. She was supported by a teacher, Krunoslav Sukić. Kruhonja and

Sukić affiliated the CZM with the anti-war organization Anti-Ratna Kampanja (ARK) in Zagreb. The Centar za mir has now grown into an organization well known throughout Europe, attracting visitors from across the world and providing a strong example to many small groups of peaceworkers who are attempting to sustain cultures of peace in zones of conflict and violence (Mitchels, 2003, ch. 4; 2006).

By the end of the 1990s it was recognized that many of the activities to sustain peace in countries beset by violence were conducted by a wide range of community-based organizations. Many of these were formed and run by women, who were involved across the spectrum of peacemaking, from activity in conflict areas through to supporting peace agreements in post-conflict peacebuilding. The way in which their voices have emerged in peacemaking in recent years has still to be fully and properly chronicled, but, because of their relative exclusion from the formal political structures of war-torn societies, grassroots organizations provide an outlet for women, who are trying to respond to the various needs of their beleaguered communities (see box 13.3).

Since the third edition of this book was published, the capacity and methodology for data collection and analysis on women's experience in conflict and their roles in peace processes has improved significantly, in the same way that general conflict and peace-measuring databases and indictors have improved, as noted in chapter 3. Two widely used systems are the GEM (Gender Empowerment Measure) and the GDI (Gender Development Index), the former providing a measure of the relative power and participation of women and men in political and economic life, the latter a gender-sensitive enhancement of the Human Development Index, related to basic standards of living, literacy rates and longevity. In an attempt to overcome weaknesses in both systems, the WomanStats Database has been developed to collect data from 174 countries around nine 'conceptual clusters', namely

1 women's physical security
2 women's economic security
3 women's legal security
4 women's security in the community
5 women's security in the family
6 security for maternity
7 women's security through voice
8 security through societal investment in women
9 women's security in the state.

Preliminary analysis by the authors of the database shows promising results, indicating, for example, levels of physical security for women globally (Caprioli et al., 2009).

Other analyses based on the GDI have indicated a correlation between high levels of gender inequality and proneness to armed conflict. Escola de Cultura

Box 13.3 Engendering conflict resolution: case studies of women responding to conflict

Case study research into the role of women and conflict resolution has increased dramatically in recent years. Among a number of examples, we can cite work done by International Alert and by Peace Direct, whose *Unarmed Heroes* (2004) offers excellent case studies. Research sponsored by the United States Institute of Peace (2000) provides examples from the following war-torn countries.

- **Somalia** (see chapter 6), where women have met in a variety of venues since 1993 to develop a long-term vision for Somali society and there has been a proliferation of women's NGOs addressing issues of migration and displacement and creating avenues for peace. Women have taken the initiative to restore destroyed schools, to establish clean water sources and to open an inter-clan dialogue on peace. An alliance of seventeen NGOs, formed and led by Somali women, emerged to coordinate peacebuilding activity, to exchange information between their different clan groupings and to establish opportunities for dialogue.
- **Colombia**, where grassroots organizations led by women have been active in protesting about the prolonged civil war. Indigenous women have begun to speak out against the damage to their communities, caught in the cross-fire between Marxist guerrilla organizations, drug traffickers, right-wing death squads, and the forces of the Colombian government.
- **The Middle East**, especially in relation to the Israeli–Palestinian conflict, where there are a number of cross-community efforts led by women to create opportunities for grassroots conflict resolution activities. One such project is the Jerusalem Link, which connects the Palestinian Jerusalem Centre for Women with the Israeli Bat Shalom. The Jerusalem Link has worked to develop an International Women's Commission, a tripartite and independent body of women of Palestine, Israel and the international community to provide a gender perspective on peacemaking and human security issues and to have a more specific mandate to take an advisory role in any formal negotiation processes related to Middle East peacemaking.
- **Northern Ireland**, where the Northern Ireland Women's Coalition (NIWC) provided an example of a political movement to enhance women's power and influence in an official peace agreement and the ensuing peace process. NIWC had representatives in the talks process, and the outcome was that provisions of the Good Friday Agreement included clauses that related to human rights and equality issues, care for victims of the conflict and provisions for a Civic Forum.

Source: Marshall, 2000

de Pau (ECP) in Barcelona estimated that 77 per cent of the countries listed in their active armed conflict data for 2008 were also characterized by serious levels of gender inequality, and alarming levels of sexual violence against women and children were reported in these conflicts (ECP, 2009: 147–9). More positively, data is also being collected systematically on the roles and impact of women in peacebuilding. Gizelis has shown a positive link between gender empowerment and successful UN peacekeeping and peacebuilding, a finding supported by Caprioli and her colleagues, who, in a survey of peace agreements which had positive provision for the involvement of women in post-conflict reconstruction, found that peace was much more likely to be sustained where this was the case, while the likelihood of conflict recurring was high in cases where there was no recognition of women's roles in the peace agreement (Gizelis, 2009; Caprioli et al., 2010: 25).

Stage 3: Rethinking Conflict Resolution Theory

In parallel with an accumulating body of empirical evidence about the experiences, roles, and transformative influence of women in challenging cultures of violence and constituencies of war has come an increasingly powerful conceptual assault on ungendered assumptions in conflict resolution. Considering these two steps together – that is, the research methods used in peace and conflict research, on the one hand, and the dominant theoretical constructs, on the other – a younger generation of women in conflict research has now opened up areas of enquiry around categories of power and participation in their concentration on transformation as the deepest level of conflict resolution (Francis, 2002). For example, in terms of methodology, some women in the field of conflict research have argued strongly in favour of qualitative methods, where the experiences of people are heard and recorded, rather than relying on the aggregation of conflict-related statistics – as we noted with regard to 'war zone ethnography' in chapter 6 (Nordstrom, 1994; Fetherston, 1994). This point is not only technical and methodological but also has fundamental implications for theory. In particular, Vivian Jabri has identified the importance of embedding these perspectives in a more searching critical theoretic approach: 'Violent conflict generates a hegemonic discourse, which seeks to subsume subjectivity and its multiple forms of representation into a singular entity involved in a confrontational interaction with another assumed/constructed monolithic entity' (1996: 180–1; see also Reading 68; Jabri, 2007).

These monolithic entities are also reproduced 'through the representation of observers, conflict researchers and third parties attempting mediation', especially if such third parties interpret the conflict through the definitions of its leading actors, in which case conflict resolution may merely 'reproduce the exclusionist, violent discourses and practices which perpetuate it' (Jabri, 1996: 180–1). In order to subvert these ways of thinking, Jabri introduces the idea of an emancipatory politics as the most relevant discourse for conflict resolution and peace, in which the main stress is on the interrelated elements of public space, participation and individuality, thereby at the same time transforming institutional and discursive gender distortions. The production of new meanings in the encounter between the 'self' and the 'other' is seen to be at the core of these hoped for transformations, and, as we noted at the end of chapter 2, theorists have looked to the work of Habermas on discursive ethics and the theory of communicative action to provide the required critical theoretic framework. See also Reading 69 and Francis, 2010, for a different argument that addresses the same issue.

If theoretical reformulations of this kind are sustained and developed, this might go some way towards meeting Reimann's complaint that conflict resolution has always been a 'gendered discourse' based on unexamined ontological and epistemological assumptions and methods which obscure its own gender blindness. The way the causes, courses and endings of violent conflicts are examined has strong implications for the lived experience of men and women in society, so that 'to ignore gender as both constituting and being constituted by conflict in general, and conflict management in particular, is to valorize and leave unexamined the existing power structures' (1999: 18).

It is no longer possible for the conflict resolution field to ignore this theoretical challenge. Recent analyses, again from feminist-oriented versions of critical theory, have pointed to the limitations inherent in an unchallenged acceptance of binary categories (including femininity and masculinity), which excludes 'the variety of ambivalent and unsecured femininities and masculinities'. Gender-aware analysis of this kind has impacted on the field of conflict research by insisting on diversity: 'Allowing dissident, and not always affirming, voices to be heard can offer an element that celebrates uncertainty and multiplicity' (Väyrynen, 2004: 140).

Stage 4: Mainstreaming Gender in Policy-Making and the Empowerment of Women

The fourth stage in the engendering of an area of study is the mainstreaming of gender perspectives in the policy implications of research. A historically significant move in this mainstreaming was the passing of UN Security Council Resolution 1325 on 31 October 2000, described by Kofi Annan as 'a landmark step in raising awareness of the impact of armed conflict on women and girls, and of the vital role of women in conflict resolution and peacebuilding' (United Nations, 2002b). Resolution 1325 called both for fuller representation of women in peace negotiations and in the highest offices of the UN and for the incorporation of gender perspectives in peacebuilding, peacekeeping and conflict-prevention activities. Although there are dangers in the process of formal mainstreaming, as noted by Diana Francis (2010; see Reading 69), we regard this as a landmark in the engendering of peace and conflict resolution policy as originally envisioned in the field by Elise Boulding. It was wonderful that, having suggested developments along these lines from the 1950s, she witnessed this moment of fruition half a century later when in her eighties.

We noted in chapter 2 that the UN, despite all its recognized limitations, has become a forum for and generator of seminal ideas of central importance in conflict resolution, and UNSCR 1325 was built upon a series of treaties and conventions relating to women's rights and human rights since the inception of the UN in 1945 (Weiss, 2015) (see box 13.4).

It was because of disappointment with the lack of recognition of women's roles in peacekeeping and peacemaking in the Brahimi Report that women's organizations intensified their lobbying of the Security Council. Their goal was to press for a resolution that would mainstream the role of women in peace and security issues and confer the status of recognition in international law on that role. The immediate factor which influenced the passing of UN Security Council Resolution 1325 was, therefore, linked to the

Box 13.4 Engendering peacebuilding and conflict resolution: the evolution of UN policy

1948 (Dec)   The *Universal Declaration of Human Rights* (General Assembly Resolution 217A) recognized the equal rights of men and women.

1966 (Dec)   Resolution 2200A on the Protection of Women and Children in Emergency and Armed Conflict recognized that women suffered as civilians in armed conflict. Member states should make all efforts to spare women from the ravages of war and ensure they are not deprived from shelter, food and medical aid (Articles 4 & 6).

1975 (June)   The First UN World Conference on Women, which led to the *Declaration of Mexico on the Equality of Women and their Contribution to Development and World Peace*. This recognized the multiple roles as peacemakers played by women at the level of the family and community, as well as at national and international levels, and called for fuller representation of women in international fora concerned with peace and security. The declaration had the status of a recommendation and was not binding on states.

1979 (Dec)   General Assembly Resolution 34/180 on the *Convention on the Elimination of All Forms of Discrimination Against Women* (CEDAW) recognized that global peace and welfare were linked to the equal participation of women in all areas.

1985 (July)   The Nairobi Conference to Review and Appraise the Achievements of the United Nations Decade for Women produced the *Nairobi Forward-Looking Strategies for the Advancement of Women*, a collective plan of action for women and their advocates.

1989 (Nov)   The UN secretary-general reported to the Commission on the Status of Women to review the implementation of the Nairobi Strategies and concluded both that women remained victims of violence disproportionately and that they had not progressed significantly in decision-making roles since 1985.

1993 (July)   The World Conference on Human Rights issued a *Programme of Action* to integrate women's needs into human rights activities. The programme identified a variety of forms of discrimination against women, including rape in situations of armed conflict.

1995 (Sept)   The Fourth World Conference on Women, in Beijing, held during the fiftieth anniversary of the formation of the UN, issued the *Beijing Declaration*, which identified six strategic objectives related to promoting the role of women in peacemaking, including commitments to increase their participation in decision-making, to reduce military expenditures, and to promote non-violent conflict resolution and the contribution of women to fostering a culture of peace.

2000   Women in the Balkans and Rwanda claim that systematic rape is a form of genocide. Influenced by the Women's Caucus for Gender Justice, the Rome Statute of the International Criminal Court recognized these issues for the first time as crimes against humanity and war crimes. The Rome Statute also demanded the equal participation of female judges in trials and on gender-sensitive processes in the conduct of trials.

2000 (Aug)   The UN conducted a comprehensive review of peacekeeping operations under the direction of Lakhdar Brahimi. The Brahimi Report produced a wide range of recommendations for the reform of peacekeeping, which, although it did make some proposals to increase the role of women in leadership positions in peacekeeping operations, did not fully recognize the significance of gender perspectives.

2008 (June)   UNSCR 1820, together with UNSCR 1888 (September 2009) and UNSCR 1889 (October 2009), strengthened calls to take effective action against sexual violence in armed conflicts and post-conflict situations and to support the interagency initiative 'United Nations Action against Sexual Violence in Conflict'.

2010 (Feb)   Margot Wallstrom appointed as first SRSG on Sexual Violence in Conflict.

2012 (Sept)   Zainab Hawa Bangura of Sierra Leone took over as SRSG on Sexual Violence in Conflict.

Source: adapted and updated from Poehlman-Doumbouy and Hill (2001), WILPF and Global Network of Women Peacebuilders (www.gnwp.org)

lobbying conducted by the Coalition on Women and International Peace and Security, which consisted of Amnesty International, the Hague Appeal for Peace, International Alert, the International Peace Research Association, the Women's Commission for Refugee Women and Children, and the Women's International League for Peace and Freedom. The original project to review peacekeeping operations was declared in May 2000 in the form of the Windhoek Declaration from Namibia, a country which had itself experienced years of conflict and which had also provided a successful model for UN-led post-conflict peacebuilding. The Coalition on Women and International Peace and Security persuaded Namibia to hold an open session on women, peace and security during their month of Security Council presidency in October 2000, which ended with the passing of resolution 1325. One of the key campaigning groups in the coalition which secured the resolution was the Women's International League for Peace and Freedom; another was the International Peace Research Association. We have noted that Elise Boulding served as secretary-general of both of these organizations.

Empowerment of Women in Peace Processes

Despite the passing of UNSCR 1325 in 2000 calling for the fuller representation of women in peace negotiations, peacekeeping and peacebuilding and the appointment of the first SRSG on Sexual Violence in Conflict, reviews of progress towards these goals and objectives suggest that it has lagged behind claims and declarations. Gizelis and Olsson (2015) have pointed to the need not only to assert the normative claims of 1325 in speeches and policy documents but also to develop evidence-based evaluations of the degree to which there has been concrete action and results. On the fifteenth anniversary of the adoption of UNSCR 1325, work has already begun on developing quantitative and evidence-based testing of its impact. The Transitional Justice Institute at the University of Ulster has developed a Peace Agreements database providing details of 640 agreements signed since 1990 (Bell and O'Rourke 2010) and have supplemented this with a Women and Peace Agreements 1325 dataset, containing agreements signed between 1990 and 2010. Bell and O'Rourke listed a total of 585 peace agreements in 102 peace processes, 399 of which were signed before and 186 after Resolution 1325. The dataset was designed to enable analysis of the impact of 1325 on peace agreements and peace processes and to provide information on explicit references to women and gender in peace agreements between 1990 and 2010.[2] In essence, the data shows that, pre-1325, forty-two peace agreements made reference to women (11 per cent of the total) and, post-1325, fifty did so (27 per cent of the total), showing an overall increase of 16 per cent. Significantly, the data also showed that peace agreements were more likely to involve women in processes where the UN had a third-party role. Bell and O'Rourke further interpreted the data with a qualitative analysis of the substantive ways in which women's roles were defined and found that these remained patchy, insubstantial and unsystematic across peace agreements. Women were also frequently defined more as victims to be protected than as proactive agents for change.

The conclusions of Bell and O'Rourke are instructive, particularly in questioning the default architectures of many peace agreements, where the elite (male) military and political powers who fought the conflict are also the main actors in negotiating the terms and structures of the peace process:

> in the struggle to survive conflicts and peace processes there is an abiding need to carve out a literal and conceptual 'space in-between' an apparently fixed analysis of the conflict as military fighting between men, and the fixed prescriptions for its resolution that flow from this analysis, in which women can question the parameters of the process as currently set. This plea for a space to be left to women to fundamentally reconceive the job of peacemaking might seem curiously abstract, luxurious and irrelevant when compared to day-to-day battles of inclusion and survival. Yet, a more general skepticism as to what current peace processes and agreements are capable of achieving is increasing, as is concern over their use as a vehicle for old imperial projects in new guises. It is important that we use the task of influencing particular processes to reinforce, rather than obliterate, the question of whether and for whom these processes deliver and whether there might be a better way. (Bell and O'Rourke, 2010: 980)

This conclusion makes the case study of the work of Irene Santiago and the role of women in the Mindanao peace process (as noted in box 13.2 earlier in this chapter) even more salient. Largely because of the work of feminists and peace activists in Mindanao, the peace process there, although it still has some way to go, has been remarkably successful in opening up spaces for women at the peace table and in mainstreaming gender in the dialogue and in the institutions and practices of peacebuilding which have been implemented in the peace agreement. On 27 March 2014, women leaders in the Philippines negotiated and signed an agreement with the Moro Islamic Liberation Front (MILF), the Comprehensive Agreement on the Bangsamoro, bringing peace to the predominantly Muslim region of Mindanao, where a conflict has been raging for over forty years. The chief negotiator for the Philippine government was Miriam Coronel-Ferrer, the first woman chief negotiator in Philippine history to sign a major peace agreement between two negotiating parties. The way in which the peace agreement evolved is outlined in box 13.5.

Conclusion

It is fitting to end this chapter, first, with the voice of Elise Boulding, who expresses more eloquently than we can the underlying centrality of gender to all aspects of conflict resolution, and then with another example of how this call is being heard and acted upon.

> We are a long way from our pre-industrial village sisters who understood very well the structures and resource systems within which they operated. One of the greatest dangers of our time is despair, and feelings of helplessness in the face of macro-level social forces. The possibility is there that the human race will self-destruct. It is precisely at

Box 13.5 Women, gender and peace processes: the Mindanao case study revisited, 1968– 2015

1968 Violent conflict erupted in the predominantly Muslim areas of Central and Western Mindanao in the southern Philippines between the government and an armed separatist movement.

1996 The government and the Moro National Liberation Front (MNLF) reached an agreement on regional autonomy. A splinter group, the MILF, dissatisfied with the terms of the agreement, continued fighting.

2001 The parties agreed to negotiate outside the country. The government of the Philippines invited Malaysia to facilitate.

2004 The parties invited an unarmed International Monitoring Team (IMT) to observe the ceasefire.

2009 The parties agreed to include a civilian protection component and a humanitarian, rehabilitation and development component in the IMT and to establish an International Contact Group to observe the peace negotiations.

2010 The Philippines became the eighteenth country, and the first in Asia, to develop a National Action Plan in response to United Nations Security Council resolutions 1325 and 1820, the landmark resolutions calling for women's full participation in peacebuilding activities and the protection of women during armed conflict.

2012 A Framework Agreement approved a Muslim self-governing, political and geographical entity, the Bangsamoro, and established a three-year roadmap to peace, with provisions for additional hybrid bodies to ensure and monitor implementation.

2014 A Comprehensive Agreement on the Bangsamoro (CAB) was reached. Miriam Coronel-Ferrer said that the CAB 'would be unique in that it would be the first such agreement to be signed by a woman, not only as one of two chief signatories to a comprehensive agreement, but also because a total of three women – one half of the 6-person negotiating team of the GPH and about one-fourth of the total number of signatories – would be signing it.'

2014/2015 (and beyond) To emphasize that the CAB represented not merely participation but, more importantly, that women's influence was necessary to make peace achievable and sustainable, a global campaign entitled 'Women, Seriously!' was launched in 2014. Lead convener Irene Santiago described the aim of the campaign as the creation of political will so that women's indispensable role in peace processes would be recognized and acted upon. Santiago stressed that peace was not a technical but a political issue and that the Women, Seriously! campaign was designed to power a social movement advocating strongly and consistently for women to be taken seriously. The campaign used the symbol of Women's Peace Tables to create a broad constituency around the world. Physical peace tables were formed in highly conflicted areas to bring out the issues women cared about and their recommendations for conflict resolution. Virtual peace tables were formed through social media platforms such as Facebook and Twitter. Inputs from various Women's Peace Tables around the world were consolidated to form the Women's Global Peace Agenda – a showcase of what a peace agreement would look like when women are taken seriously in peace processes.

Sources: Dwyer and Cagoco-Guiam (2011); Herbolzheimer and Leslie (2013); Office of the President of the Philippines: Office of the Presidential Adviser on the Peace Process, at www.opapp.gov.ph/milf/news/women-make-history-signing-gph-milf-comprehensive-peace-deal#sthash.uHVE36CT.dpuf; Womens Nobel Initiative at http://nobelwomensinitiative.org/2014/04/women-lead-philippines-in-historic-peace-accord/#sthash.8koPfAo2.dpuf; Women's Peace Table and Women, Seriously!, at www.womenseriously.org/; and discussions with Irene Santiago

this historical moment that it can be useful to reflect on the accumulated experience of women's cultures over the centuries in the work of feeding, rearing and healing humans, building their social and physical environments, and then rebuilding them after destruction. It was the need for that kind of reflection that led me to take a year of solitude in 1974 and begin the mental journey that led to the writing of *The Underside of History*.

Today, 20 years later, this process of feminist reflection on the social order and its workings is more urgent that ever. Also, more of us are doing it. That development should be celebrated by exploring how women think about the future and the action models they generate to bring these futures into being. (Boulding, 1994)

In an exact demonstration of the power of this idea, in the face of drought and mounting conflict in North-Eastern Kenya, from informal beginnings at a wedding which brought clans together, the remarkable Wajir Peace Group was formed by many of the women present:

Discussions began, first at the workplace, and in the homes of other women and men. When they encountered more police indifference, the women went to see the District Commissioner. They asked for his cooperation. The District Commissioner approved their plan to intervene and asked for feedback as to the outcome. Meetings were held with professional women from all the clans. They were informed about the problems and of the group's intention to bring the key women's leaders together. Contact was made with other women from different strata. Sixty people attended one of the meetings arising out of this overture. After a freeflowing discussion, they agreed to form a Joint Committee of the clans. This group would act as a kind of vigilante body, defusing tension and reporting incidents to the police ... Extensive research into ways of achieving permanent peace in the district led to another initiative. When elections approached, the peace group organized discussions involving elders, chiefs, parliamentarians and candidates, so as to reduce the tension normally associated with campaigning ... In essence, the Wajir peace initiative has taken the region back to the future, by reviving basic methods of conflict resolution used in pre-colonial times to encourage the equitable sharing of the region's limited resources. Within five years, the Peace Group has touched almost everyone in this remote region: its basic approach – community involvement, and the use of dialogue as a counterpoint to conflict. (Abdi, 2010: 243–9, extracts from the original reordered; for a fuller version, see Reading 64).

RECOMMENDED READING

Ashe (2010); Mazurana et al. (2005, 2013); Nordstrom (1997); Gizelis and Olsson (2015); Pankhurst and Pearce (1997); Skjelsboek and Smith (2001); Steans (1998); Weiss (2015).

RELEVANT EXTRACTS IN *THE CONTEMPORARY CONFLICT RESOLUTION READER*

Reading 21: M. Dugan, A Nested Theory of Conflict
Reading 64: P. van Tongeren et al., Women Take the Peace Lead in Pastoral Kenya
Reading 68: V. Jabri, Revisiting Change and Conflict: On Underlying Assumptions and the De-Politicisation of Conflict Resolution
Reading 69: D. Francis, From Pacification to Peacebuilding: A Call to Global Transformation

CHAPTER FOURTEEN

Conflict Resolution and the Ethics of Intervention

There has always been a sense of unease about third-party intervention in the conflict resolution field. It is an unease shared by aid workers and others, as summed up in Mary Anderson's famous plea for interveners to 'do no harm':

> Who do we think we are? Is it justified for outsiders to choose among people or institutions, to make judgments about who or what is 'truly' a local capacity for peace? To what extent might our attempts to do so constitute dangerous and inappropriate social engineering? ... The fact that aid inevitably does have an impact on warfare means aid workers cannot avoid the responsibility of trying to shape that impact. The fact that choices about how to shape that impact represent outsider interference means that aid workers can always be accused of inappropriate action. There is no way out of this dilemma. (Anderson, 1999)

Third parties have an effect on conflict dynamics, and their good intentions do not guarantee good outcomes (Anderson, 2004). Even if they are invited in, there are legitimate questions to be asked about who invited them and why, what constituencies they represent, how well they understand their own motives and roles, and whether their actions are likely to have beneficial or deleterious consequences. These questions become more acute as the interventions become more coercive or even forcible.

Not intervening also makes a difference, however, and must be assessed as one of the policy options. We may recall British Prime Minister Neville Chamberlain's refusal to intervene in Czechoslovakia in September 1938, because it was a conflict 'in a faraway country between people of whom we know nothing', or the refusal of the UN Security Council (UNSC) to intervene in Rwanda in April 1994. This brings to mind Edmund Burke's ringing imperative: 'All that is required for evil to triumph is that good men do nothing.'

This chapter wrestles with the challenge of the implications both of 'doing something' and of 'doing nothing' from a conflict resolution perspective.

In the conflict resolution field, questions about the ethics of intervention have been seen to be important from the start – as exemplified in contributions to classic texts such as the *Ethics of Social Intervention* (Bermant et al., 1978). Continuing in this tradition, we begin by looking at the nature of social intervention in general in order to define the main intervention relations, and from this we elucidate framework principles for conflict resolution and comparable kinds of international intervention (including intervention by aid and development workers and peacekeepers). Within this conceptual framework

---

Box 14.1 A hierarchy of intervention relations, principles and criteria

A General intervention relations

B Framework principles for international   *See figure 14.1*
      intervention

C Criteria for forcible international intervention   *See box 14.4*

---

we can then consider guidelines for coercive and forcible intervention, insofar as this is seen to be ethically permissible or needed to protect the international values being promoted and defended (see box 14.1).

Conflict Resolution Roles and General Intervention Relations

We can begin with James Laue's thoughtful analysis of the ethics of conflict intervention, first offered in the 1970s (Laue and Cormick, 1978; Laue, 1981, 1990). Drawing on experience in 'labor–management relations, international and intercultural conflict, racial and community disputes, court diversion and other arenas', Laue based his analysis on the nature of conflict intervention roles:

> The major point of the typology presented here is that there are definable, analytically distinct intervention roles that cut across all the other variables of personality, skills, type of issue, system level of the dispute, etc. These roles are based ... predominantly on an intervenor's base and credibility – for whom does the intervenor work, who pays for the intervenor to be there, and consequently what are the structured expectations for behaviour of the intervenor in that role? (1990: 268)

Laue identifies five main conflict intervention roles: the *activist*, 'who is in, and almost of, one of the parties', such as one of the tenants in a tenant–landlord dispute; the *advocate*, who works on behalf of one of the parties but is likely to play a less 'hard game' than the activist, perhaps in a formal consultative capacity or like a diplomat 'working on behalf of the interests of one party in international relations'; then comes the *mediator*, whose ultimate advocacy 'is for the process rather than for any of the parties *per se*'; followed by the *researcher*, such as a journalist or crisis observer, who might see the intervention as 'objective' or 'neutral', but, 'once he or she engages in a conflict situation, the configuration of power in that situation is altered' and the intervener 'is likely to be used by the parties for their ends'; and, finally, the *enforcer*, including arbitrators, judges and police, who have 'formal powers to sanction either or all the parties' – funding agencies may have such leverage, and 'superior physical force' will often characterize enforcers in international conflicts (Laue and Cormick, 1978).

In comparable vein, William Ury (2000) distinguishes ten 'Third Side' conflict resolution roles, both from within and from outside the conflict parties (see figure 1.14, p. 32):

- To *prevent* conflict there is *the provider* (enabling people to meet their needs), *the teacher* (giving people skills to handle conflict), and *the bridge builder* (forging relationships across lines of conflict);
- To *resolve* conflict if prevention fails there is *the mediator* (reconciling conflicting interests), *the arbiter* (determining disputed rights), *the equalizer* (democratizing power to level the playing field), and *the healer* (repairing injured relationships);
- To *contain* conflict if resolution fails there is *the witness* (paying attention to escalation), *the referee* (setting limits to fighting), and *the peacekeeper* (providing protection).

Important questions are raised here about shifting intervention roles (see the discussion about figure 1.13 in chapter 1) and about the different expectations of powerful in-parties and powerless out-parties, where the former want classic 'neutral' conflict resolution from the third parties in order to preserve the status quo, while the latter seek assistance in their quest for 'power, justice and change'. These are issues with which we are now familiar.

Conflict Resolution Intervention Principles

Figure 14.1 sets out the main relations that in our view characterize all social conflict interventions of the kinds described by Laue and Ury and the associated framework principles for ethical international intervention (Ramsbotham and Woodhouse, 1996; Ramsbotham, 2006). If we consider large-scale international interventions, such as those described in chapter 8, the first three principles can be seen to concern relations with target populations, the fourth and fifth to concern relations among interveners, and the last three to concern relations with the wider international community.

These principles are confirmed by a survey of two overlapping literatures: the rapidly expanding sets of principles and guidelines for ethical intervention produced by aid, development and conflict resolution organizations, on the one hand (see, for example, Reading 63), and the criteria recommended for principled and effective international peacekeeping, on the other. As an example of this, we may note the way in which the May 2004 publication on the British military contribution to peace operations, mentioned in chapter 6 (UK MOD, 2004), stressed the importance of the liaison with non-military peacebuilders and reproduced in an appendix extracts from the *Principles of Conduct for the International Red Cross and Red Crescent Movements and NGOs in Disaster Relief* as an overall guide. The latter, in addition to the overriding universal humanitarian imperative, covered:

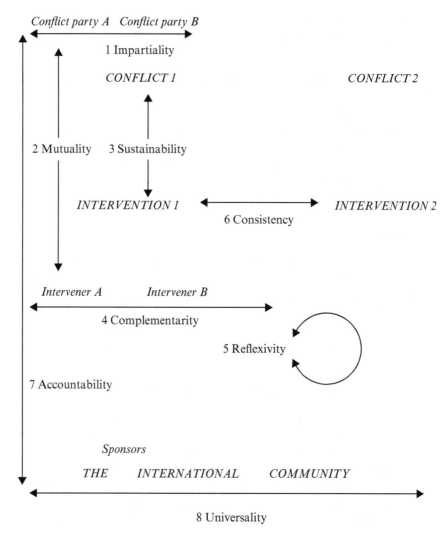

Figure 14.1 *General intervention relations and framework principles*

- impartiality and non-partisanship in response to crises (including proper support for the role of women);
- respect for local cultures, and mutuality in the involvement of beneficiaries and the empowering of indigenous capacity;
- the importance of sustainability and reduction of future vulnerability;
- cooperation with other disaster relief agencies so that there is no damaging mutual competition;
- the integrity of the interveners in genuine commitment to their stated aims;
- accountability both to those assisted and to sponsors so that effectiveness can be transparently assessed. (ICRC, 1996)

The principle of impartiality

From a conflict resolution perspective, the principle of impartiality implies that, whatever role an intervener plays, conflict resolution is incomplete unless the interests of all those affected are properly taken into account. Behind this lies the whole idea of win–win outcomes and the importance of responding to human needs that we have seen have played a central role in the evolution of the field.

This parallels the International Committee of the Red Cross (ICRC) idea of impartiality as non-discrimination in responding to need: 'The Red Cross makes no discrimination as to nationality, race, religious belief, class or political opinions. It endeavours to relieve the suffering of individuals, being guided solely by their needs, and to give priority to the most urgent cases of distress.' This is a core value, enshrined in Article 3, common to the four 1949 Geneva Conventions, and in Article 75 of the 1977 Additional Protocol I.

We should distinguish this from the related ICRC principle of neutrality, which means non-political engagement: 'In order to continue to enjoy the confidence of all, the Red Cross may not take sides in hostilities or engage at any time in controversies of a political, racial, religious or ideological nature.' Increasing involvement in intense internal conflicts (in contrast to the interstate wars that formed the usual original ICRC environment), since at least the time of the 1967–70 Biafran war, has put the principle of neutrality under growing strain. What Forsythe has called 'humanitarian politics' forces interveners to choose between the ICRC tradition, based on consent from public authorities with little or no overt criticism of their behaviour, and more uncompromising approaches, such as that of Médecins sans Frontières, which is not afraid to disregard the wishes and legal claims of public authorities, both in condemning atrocities and in intervening without permission (Forsythe, 1977: 227). This remains highly controversial.

In the evolution of peacekeeping doctrine, we saw in chapter 6 how the original idea of neutrality, in the sense of operating only with the consent of all parties, gave way in the 1990s to that of impartiality, in fulfilling an international mandate as the key criterion that distinguishes principled peacekeeping from traditional interstate war (see table 6.3, p. 189). Peacekeepers could not be neutral if one party, perhaps the government, was seen to be responsible for atrocities (although we noted how, in response to attempts through the UNDPKO to adapt traditional peacekeeping doctrine in this direction via the 'capstone' doctrine, given resistance from some UN member states, 'consent' was nevertheless in the end rhetorically reaffirmed).

The conflict resolution field tends to confirm this logic but is particularly aware of the fact that, in intense conflict fields, everything is politicized, so that the impartiality of interveners will be contested, no matter how elaborate their international mandates. In these circumstances, as noted in chapter 11, the UN Security Council, International Criminal Tribunals, the International

Criminal Court, the UN Human Rights Council, and so on, are regarded as political tools by those whose interests they are seen to be damaging. This does not render the principle of impartiality otiose, but it does suggest that it is a value that has to be struggled for.

The principle of mutuality

The principle of mutuality is the fundamental intervention relation between interveners and those they purport to be assisting. It determines that interveners take care to ascertain that the intervention is seen to be likely to do more good than harm from the conflict parties' perspective. If there is little or no mutuality – if the arrow is not double-headed – then the outsiders are likely to be imposing their own concepts and values without due regard for the needs and wishes of the protagonists. Experience suggests that they will more often than not be oblivious of this. We noted in chapters 8 and 9 that there are problems in determining the views of target populations, and the situation will be complicated to the extent that the primary conflict parties have conflicting interests and perceptions and are internally divided. The principle of mutuality demands that indigenous initiatives and capabilities be forefronted and empowered, and that interventions are carried out without damage to local economies and with respect for local cultures. As we note in chapters 13 and 15, there may be tensions here, for example, between the priorities of recognizing and supporting the role of women as understood in international instruments and the possibly conflicting patriarchal and authoritarian nature of local tradition.

The principle of sustainability

The principle of sustainability is central to humanitarian, development and conflict resolution interventions. Interveners who are not prepared to 'stay the course' or commit the resources required should not undertake the intervention in the first place. We saw in chapter 8 that this is also a key principle for military forces in intervention, reconstruction and withdrawal (IRW) operations. The principle requires careful estimates of the appropriateness and viability of entry strategies, given contingent conditions in the target states, and rules that exit strategies should be determined by the needs of those on whose behalf the intervention has been undertaken, not by domestic opinion in the intervening countries or the interests of intervening governments. Once again, there may be tensions in target countries between those wanting interveners to leave as soon as possible and those wanting them to stay. The longer interveners stay in ongoing conflicts, the more likely they are cumulatively to offend interests and to be seen to be unwelcome intruders.

The principle of complementarity

With the principle of complementarity we reach the important issue of relations between different interveners. Here the overarching requirement must be that the efforts of interveners should, where appropriate, complement each other for the greater good of those for whom the intervention is undertaken. The word 'appropriate' is a reminder that complementarity does not mean limiting diversity, which can often be beneficial. But the aim of the principle is to overcome the all too familiar dangers of 'competitive altruism' by prohibiting damaging rivalries, unnecessary duplications and avoidable failures of communication. We saw in chapter 8 how, in IRW operations, the early preponderance of military tasks in assuring 'negative peace' progressively gives way, it is hoped, to the essentially non-military tasks of building 'positive peace', however difficult military–civilian relations may be from time to time.

The principle of reflexivity

The principle of reflexivity asks interveners to look at themselves. What are their motives, aims and interests? What constituencies do they represent? What kinds of advocacy do they pursue and why? On what authority do they act? What resources of power and influence do they bring? As in the equivalent just war principle of intentionality, motives and subjective purposes are notoriously difficult to self-determine or externally impute, but the underlying principle is clear – that interveners' purposes must at any rate not be incompatible with the declared aim of the intervention. For example, the unedifying spectacle of outsiders battening onto other peoples' disasters in order to raise their own profiles or to pull in extra funding is clearly ruled out by the principle of reflexivity.

The principle of consistency

With the principle of consistency, we move from relations that concern interventions within a particular conflict arena to relations between interventions in different conflict arenas – although it may at times not be clear where one arena ends and another begins. The requirement is that, in similar circumstances, equal provocation or challenge should elicit equal response. The aim here is to meet often voiced accusations of hypocrisy and double standards. In the context of IRW operations, this is subject to unavoidable dispute about what counts as 'similarity'. Apart from anything else, different states have different geographic and historic ties, which often determine who takes a lead, who is prepared to provide resources and who is acceptable in the target country.

The principle of accountability

The principle of accountability governs relations between interveners and those in whose name they claim to act. In individual cases these may in the first instance be sponsors such as governments or international organizations. But sponsors are themselves part of the intervention they are sponsoring, so they too should be prepared to answer for their own motives and actions. Behind this may lie wider claims to be acting in the name of the conflict parties (which links this principle to the principle of mutuality) or of the international community as a whole (which links with the principle of universality below). The double-headed arrow represents the conferral of legitimacy in one direction (answering the question *quo warranto?* – by what authority do you intervene?) and transparency and accountability in the other (answering the question *quis custodiet ipsos custodes?* – who judges the judges?). Unlike equivalent traditional just war criteria, which concern prior estimations of likely future benefit and harm, the principle of accountability forefronts the importance of ongoing comparative assessments of the effectiveness of present and past operations. Here we enter the important and burgeoning field of 'impact assessments', as discussed in chapters 8 and 9, essential for learning lessons and improving performance, albeit beset by difficulties such as those referred to at the beginning of chapter 5.

The principle of universality

Finally, we reach the principle of universality, which can be said to sum up the other principles within an overall transformative cosmopolitan framework. When it comes to cross-border intervention conducted in the name of the international collectivity, either because it is authorized by a regional or global international organization or because it purports to be undertaken according to internationally endorsed values, the principle of universality rules that such enterprises must be cross-culturally endorsed. This, too, is an ICRC principle, and the renaming of the League of Red Cross Societies as the League of Red Cross and Red Crescent Societies in 1983 was a significant move in this direction: 'The Red Cross is a world-wide institution in which all Societies have equal status and share equal responsibilities and duties in helping each other. Our movement's universality stems from the attachment of each of its members to common values.'

We have seen how claims to be acting in accordance with international law and in defence of international norms have been made by almost all interveners in IRW operations since the end of the Cold War. Similarly, one of the main themes of this book has been that the conflict resolution field has to reflect universal values if it is to qualify as a truly cosmopolitan enterprise. The question whether there are such universal values is a fundamental and deep question, which is considered again in chapters 15 and 19. And chapter

20 asks the further question: How may what some see as a passing of western hegemony affect this?

The Responsibility to Protect

In the second part of this chapter we address one of the most testing questions for the conflict resolution field: What role, if any, do various forms of coercion and, in particular, the use of armed force have in conflict resolution interventions? It is the issue of forcible intervention above all that divides those in the conflict resolution field. Some are pacifists, who do not condone the use of military force under any circumstances and would restrict conflict resolution to the attempt to make *peace by peaceful means*. For them, there is no place for an appeal to just war criteria in conflict resolution. They would argue instead for the principles of non-violence: conflict is to be seen as a search for truth in which no party has final or valid answers; and the intervener must take actions that are self-limiting and consistent in all respects with the ends sought, must seek to persuade and never to destroy other parties, and must trust to the potential for transformation which is always present, however difficult to find (Wehr, 1979: 55–68). But others think that, when faced with murderous opponents of peace processes or egregious assaults on human rights, there is a legitimate role for armed forces as neutralizers and protectors (see chapter 6). For them, the further question cannot be avoided: In that case, what are the circumstances in which such uses of force would be justified? They find it unavoidable to enter the territory of what has traditionally been termed 'just war' – albeit, as we will argue below, only if there is a fundamental reappraisal to bring this into line with the cosmopolitan conflict resolution principles outlined above. Two of the authors of this book, for example, think that, if traditional just war criteria are adapted in this way, military force can serve to protect cosmopolitan values – indeed, that it would in the circumstances be wrong not to do so. One of us, however, believes that these principles are as likely to be distorted to justify the wars of the powerful and doubts whether, in the end, they are consistent with the framework principles for justified conflict resolution intervention at all.

Galvanized by UN Secretary-General Annan's call for international consensus on 'developing international norms' against violent repression and the 'wholesale slaughter of civilians' in the wake of failures to protect civilians in Srebrenica and Rwanda and in the context of the Kosovo intervention (1999: 39), attempts have been made to suggest criteria for just forcible international intervention in these cases (for a good account, see Stromseth, 2003: 261–7). This followed similar efforts to find guiding criteria for legitimate 'unilateral' intervention ('self-help by states') during the Cold War in response to excessive humanitarian threats in other countries (Lillich, 1967; Ramsbotham and Woodhouse, 1996: 33–66). The Cold War criteria have been well summarized by Chesterman (2001: 228–9): that the threats of abuse must be egregious; that there must be no realistic non-military alternatives; that collective action through the UN Security Council must have failed; that military action must be limited to what is necessary, must be proportionate, and must have a reasonable chance of success; and that the intervening state must act 'disinterestedly' so that the humanitarian objective is paramount. These are, in effect, traditional just war criteria. After the end of the Cold War it became easier for the UN Security Council to act, and Annan himself listed a number of factors it should consider when deciding whether to intervene forcibly on humanitarian grounds – for example, the nature of the breaches of international law and numbers affected; the inability or unwillingness of the governments responsible to remedy the situation; the exhaustion of peaceful or consent-based efforts; the UNSC's ability to monitor the intervention; and the limited and proportionate use of force, mindful of effects on civilian populations and the environment (Stromseth, 2003). This again was broadly in line with traditional just war criteria for 'war decision' (*jus ad bellum* – whether to go to war) and 'war conduct' (*jus in bello* – how to fight the war).

As noted in chapter 6, Canadian Prime Minister Jean Chretien set up an International Commission on Intervention and State Sovereignty (ICISS) in response which included discussion at eleven regional round tables and national consultations. The Commission reported in August 2001, just before the 9/11 attacks in the United States. Although in many ways eclipsed by the latter, the central thrust of the report survived subsequent dilution, led by China, Russia, India and a number of G77 and Non-Aligned Movement (NAM) countries, to emerge in the final adoption of a Responsibility to Protect (R2P) agreement at the World Summit in September 2005. This is encapsulated in paragraphs 138 and 139 of the Summit Outcome Document (see box 14.2).

As can be seen, UN member states accept the fundamental principle of the 'responsibility to protect' and the legitimate interest of the international community in general in 'encouraging' this. Measures to be taken involve the use of UN Charter Chapter VI 'peaceful means' but go further by accepting the possibility of coercive collective action under Chapter VII should this prove inadequate. Chapter VII includes the use of sanctions and non-military coercion (Article 41) and forcible military action if this is not deemed to be sufficient (Article 42). The 'responsibility to protect', therefore, offers a gradient of international action within which forcible action is a 'last resort'. There are, therefore, two main differences between this and the earlier 'humanitarian intervention' debate during the Cold War. First, R2P is broader than traditional humanitarian intervention because it envisages a wider spectrum of responses, not just forcible intervention (Ramsbotham (1997) had been arguing for a 'reconceptualization' along these lines since the mid-1990s). Second, R2P focused mainly on the response of the UN Security Council, whereas the

Box 14.2 2005 World Summit Outcome Document: the Responsibility to Protect

138. Each individual state has the responsibility to protect its population from genocide, war crimes, ethnic cleansing and crimes against humanity. The responsibility entails the prevention of such crimes, including their incitement, through appropriate and necessary means. We accept that responsibility and will act in accordance with it. The international community should, as appropriate, encourage and help States to exercise this responsibility and support the United Nations in establishing an early warning capability.

139. The international community, through the United Nations, also has the responsibility to use appropriate diplomatic, humanitarian and other peaceful means, in accordance with Chapters VI and VIII of the Charter of the United Nations, to help protect populations from genocide, war crimes, ethnic cleansing and crimes against humanity. In this context we are prepared to take collective action, in a timely and decisive manner, through the Security Council, in accordance with the Charter, including Chapter VII on a case-by-case basis and in cooperation with relevant regional organizations as appropriate, should peaceful means be inadequate and national authorities are manifestly failing to protect their populations from genocide, war crimes, ethnic cleansing and crimes against humanity …

Source: UNGA, 2005

Cold War debate was almost exclusively about unilateral action by states in the absence of UN sanction, because the polarized UNSC at the time was unable to act in concert. This leaves a gaping hole in R2P provision about what can or should be done when – as, for example, in the cases of Kosovo in 1999 and Darfur in 2003 (see box 14.3) – there is no UNSC consensus. In these circumstances, the ICISS had, somewhat lamely, resorted to repeating traditional just war criteria, and even this was omitted from the 2005 World Summit Outcome Document. In the absence of explicit authorization by the UNSC to maintain or restore international peace and security, legal opinion is divided. At one end of the spectrum are restrictionists, who rule out the legality of all such interventions and argue that to allow them would be 'inimical to the emergence of an international rule of law' (Chesterman, 2001: 217). From this perspective, international ethics offers spurious justification for what is legally inadmissible, thus opening the door to 'vigilantes and opportunists to resort to hegemonial intervention' (Brownlie, 1973). At the other end of the spectrum are those who hold that such nominally illegal actions – for example, in Kosovo in 1999 – may produce results 'more in keeping with the intent of the law [i.e. more 'legitimate'] – and more moral – than would have ensued had no action been taken', thus saving international law from being strangled by its own formalism or collapsing into a rubber stamp for political *force majeure* (Franck, 2003: 226).

Box 14.3 The responsibility to protect in Darfur?

Many saw Darfur as a 'litmus test' for the new R2P regime – and one that it failed: 'until this first ethnic cleansing campaign of the twenty-first century is reversed, R2P will remain aspirational, not operational, and "never again" will be "yet again" once again' (Nick Grono, 2006, quoted Bellamy, 2009: 149). Rooted in historic tensions between mainly nomadic Arab cattle grazers and sedentary Fur, Massalit and Zaghawa farmers in Western Sudan, the crisis was triggered by an agreement among some of the latter in July 2001 to defend themselves against government-backed assaults. In April 2003 the SLM/A (Sudan Liberation Movement/Army) and JEM (Justice and Equality Movement) rebel groups attacked a military outpost at al-Fashir. This prompted a ferocious response as the Khartoum government supported Arab Janjaweed militia (including air support) in a savage campaign of pillage and ethnic cleansing. By the time of the World Summit adoption of R2P, some 200,000 had been killed and 2 million displaced, with conflict spilling over into neighbouring Chad.

With their hands full in Afghanistan and Iraq, western leaders were disinclined to act decisively. One reason given was not to jeopardize the precarious ongoing separate north–south peace process in Sudan that culminated in the January 2005 Comprehensive Peace Agreement. Other leading members of the UN Security Council were even more strongly opposed. The African Union, despite its new-found aspiration to shift from 'non-intervention' to 'non-indifference' (see chapter 5), did not speak with one voice, and the stipulation of 'African solutions to African problems' could be used – and was used – as much to delay or prevent wider international intervention as to galvanize an active response. This was a highly complex debate, in which, despite passionate and widespread calls for action (Mepham and Ramsbotham, 2006), experienced voices cautioned against forcible intervention. The former Australian foreign minister Gareth Evans, for example, one of the prime sponsors of the R2P project itself and a prominent member of the UN High-Level Panel, supported the October 2006 recommendation of the International Crisis Group (ICG), of which he is chair, which advised against such action. This recommendation was reached after reviewing traditional just war criteria as used by ICISS. Despite manifest 'just cause', on the two just war criteria of 'last resort' (non-forcible avenues had not yet been exhausted) and 'balance of consequences' (it would be likely to do more harm than good), forcible intervention was ruled out.

But Alex Bellamy, for one, has countered by using the same just war criteria to argue the opposite way:

> if the Security Council had authorised intervention to protect civilians [in Darfur], this would have satisfied the [just war] criteria set out by ICISS. It is hard to envision the ICG opposing an intervention in such circumstances, especially one that has succeeded. My main point here, though, is not to argue the case one way or the other, but to show that even among supporters of the R2P there remains the possibility of profound disagreements on the best way to act in particular crises. Thus, despite the headline-grabbing qualities of [just war] criteria for intervention decisions, they are of limited utility in practice. (2009: 155)

In the end efforts were made to apply targeted sanctions on the Khartoum regime under UN Charter Article 41. For the first time an acting head of state, President Oman al-Bashir, was indicted by the new International Criminal Court; and strong pressure was exerted to forge a political understanding that eventually allowed the deployment under UN Charter Chapter VII of the hybrid UN/African Union peace operation UNAMID (UNSCR Resolution 1769, July 2007).

From Just War to Just Intervention: Bringing Just War Criteria under Conflict Resolution Intervention Principles

But the main argument in this part of the chapter is that, if military force is to be used, not for national security purposes but to uphold cosmopolitan values, then traditional just war criteria on their own are not enough. Just war criteria must be brought under the wider ambit of the conflict resolution intervention principles if just war is to become just intervention. This requires two major revisions (Ramsbotham, 2006): first, the just war criteria themselves need to be adapted and, second, additional criteria must be added to them – including the entirely new category of *jus post bellum* ('justice after war'). What happens after the use of military force is integral to overall judgements about whether such force was justified in the first place. This can no longer depend only on the prior 'good intentions' of the interveners, as in traditional *jus ad bellum* criteria. We comment briefly on each in turn.

Box 14.4 indicates what happens to traditional just war criteria when they are brought under the wider conflict resolution principles. It can be seen that all the traditional criteria are transformed in fundamental ways.

But this is still not enough. In addition to a widening reinterpretation of traditional just war criteria, entirely new criteria must be added. These are derived from the framework principles for just conflict resolution intervention, listed earlier in this chapter (figure 14.1), that are not already covered by traditional just war criteria – for example, criteria of mutuality, sustainability, consistency, accountability and universality. And there must also be further *jus post bellum* criteria to govern outcome, aftermath and final result – as discussed in relation to evaluation and impact assessment in chapter 9. In other words, critical evaluation does not stop with the question *whether*, at the moment of initial decision and in the intentions of interveners, the actions were reasonable or sincere. It has to extend to the *effects* of the intervention on the target populations in whose name the intervention has been carried out. This may well deliver a different retrospective judgement, and one that may fluctuate over time.

To put this into perspective, and to link it to chapter 15, it is worth relating the ethical discussion in the second half of this chapter briefly to non-western traditions. In the case of Islam, for example, Hashmi (1993) has argued that Muslim theorists have fewer problems than western thinkers with the question of humanitarian intervention, since state sovereignty is not a Qur'anic concept, and that there is widespread support for the idea of forcible intervention to defend threatened people. This was confirmed by a joint Muslim–Christian study-group meeting in 1997–8 (Ramsbotham, 1998). But we should note the strong caveat enunciated at the time by Chandra Muzaffar:

> For justified humanitarian intervention to be viable, there will have to be fundamental changes in international politics and in international authority structures. International

Box 14.4 Western just war criteria transmuted into criteria for just intervention

For Thomas Aquinas, writing in the fourteenth century, 'three things are required for any war to be just': 'the first is the authority of the sovereign on whose command war is waged', 'secondly a just cause is required' and 'thirdly the right intention of those waging war is required, that is they must intend to promote the good and avoid evil'. Just war criteria today are usually divided into those that determine when it is right to wage war (*jus ad bellum*) and those that determine how the war should rightly be fought (*jus in bello*). There is no generally agreed list, weighting between criteria, or ruling on whether a war has to satisfy all criteria to count as just.

War decision criteria

Just cause: The difference from traditional just war is that military force is to be used to defend a range of international norms, including decolonization norms (East Timor), democratic norms (Sierra Leone), conflict settlement norms (DRC), humanitarian norms (Kosovo) and anti-terrorism norms (Afghanistan).

Legitimate authority: The difference is the idea that such interventions should be multilateral, and that UNSC authorization or at any rate subsequent cooperation should be sought.

Right intention: Here the loftiness and disinterestedness of the professed motive makes it harder to convince sceptics that the intervention is not conducted with a view to domestic politics, oil, or a quest for hegemony.

Prospect of success at acceptable cost: This, too, becomes more problematic – likely success and anticipated balance of benefit and loss are harder to assess when the aim is not just military victory, but reconstruction and nationbuilding.

Last resort: The difference here is, first, that every effort is made to induce target governments to act responsibly, and, second, that interveners climb the ladder of UN response: Chapter VI peaceful settlement, Article 41 sanctions (UNSC sanctions have been imposed on half the IRW target states in table 8.1 in chapter 8), and only when these are seen not to be viable, Article 42 all necessary means.

War conduct criteria

The aim of *in bello* criteria is to limit the use of force to the *minimum necessary*, and to ensure in each case that such use is *proportionate* and *discriminate* (non-combatants must not be deliberately targeted). In international interventions these criteria become even harder to determine, particularly in terms of targeting when conflict zones are chaotic and civilians are caught up in the fighting. Training for such interventions requires additional skills to those of normal combat, and the importance of transparent mechanisms for determining and punishing breaches of international law by the interveners becomes even more evident (see, for example, UK MOD, 2004).

politics should cease to be the domain of the powerful. As long as global political decisions are shaped primarily by the interests of a handful of powerful elites in powerful states, intervention will almost certainly reflect their dominant foreign policy preoccupations and have little to do with justice for the powerless. For intervention to be viable, the institution that is given the task of intervening must also reflect the interests and aspirations of the human family as a whole. Without these changes in international politics and within the international system as a whole, it will not be possible to apply Islamic principles of humanitarian intervention. (Ibid.: 102)

Once again, as with the question of conflict resolution and the ethics of intervention in general, only a genuinely cosmopolitan framework can in the end underpin the perceived legitimacy of international action of this kind.

Conclusion

The framework intervention principles in figure 14.1 are derived from the conjunction of basic intervention relations and the guidelines suggested in the growing IGO, NGO and peacekeeping literatures on good practice. We think that they are clear and well-grounded principles to guide conflict resolution interventions in both domestic and international conflicts. On the question of forcible intervention, we have admitted that the conflict resolution field is torn. Problems here have been compounded by the seizure of territory by groups prepared to commit the utmost barbarity, such as Islamic State and Boko Haram in 2014. Does cosmopolitan conflict resolution utterly oppose such ideologies and practices of violence? Yes. So how can they be defeated except through the use of military force to end their depredations (see the case study of Mali in chapter 6) and expel them from territory seized – for example, from Mosul in Iraq (see chapter 11)? The authors of this book do not agree about whether forcible intervention is ethically legitimate at all in conflict resolution work. But what the framework principles indicate for all three of us, and what the more restricted criteria for just forcible intervention spell out for two of us, are widely endorsed international requirements that must be fulfilled *if* those operations are to count in the way that political leaders claim. What we all agree on is that firm and carefully applied ethical criteria form an essential consideration for those who intervene in conflict, at any level. As the quotations at the beginning of this chapter indicate, difficult ethical choices cannot be avoided. Both acts of omission and acts of commission carry moral dilemmas and risks. The search for a worldwide set of principles that can command adherence and respect is a central task for cosmopolitan conflict resolution. We hope that the discussion in this chapter contributes to this task.

RECOMMENDED READING

Bellamy (2009); Chandler (2004); Elshtain (1992); Holzgrefe and Keohane (2003); ICISS (2001); Ramsbotham (2006); Ramsbotham and Woodhouse (1996).

RELEVANT EXTRACTS IN *THE CONTEMPORARY CONFLICT RESOLUTION READER*

Reading 63: International Alert, Code of Conduct for Conflict Transformation

CHAPTER FIFTEEN

Culture, Religion and Conflict Resolution

In his 1998 book *Culture and Conflict Resolution*, Kevin Avruch argues that:

> Much of the field of conflict resolution ... is based ... on the fundamental belief that resort to physical violence in the processing of social conflict ... is a prime example of wrongheaded problem solving. And the fact that most cultures at some point ... sanction this solution is proof to these conflict resolutionists that culture needs to be not only analysed and understood for purposes of activist conflict resolution, but rethought and re-imagined – *re-engineered* – as well. (Avruch, 1998: 20–1)

With the topic of culture and conflict resolution we reach an underlying motif that has resonated throughout this book. Indeed, for us, it is in the end the most important issue of all. Most of the definitions and models offered in chapter 1 were seen by the founders of the field as generic – they applied across cultures and societies. Cultural variations were emphasized – less by those who defined conflict 'objectively' in terms of structure, behaviour and power struggle over scarce resources, more by those who defined it 'subjectively' in terms of perceived incompatibility of interest, interpretation and belief. However, even the latter did not usually regard cultural variation as particularly problematic, since they tended to come from a background in individual and social psychology rather than in cultural studies. It was above all the influx of anthropological ideas into the field that first sharpened awareness of the culture question, then leavened most aspects of conflict resolution thinking, and then challenged the validity of many of its basic assumptions.

The fundamental question is this: *How far down does cultural variation reach?* We will suggest in this chapter that conflict resolvers have given three different answers to this question – not at all, a little way down, and a long way down – but that they agree in rejecting a fourth possibility – the whole way down – or there would not be a coherent field of conflict resolution at all.

Let us remind ourselves of the recurrence of the culture theme in this book. In chapter 2 we saw how, although the inspiration from precursors came from many religious traditions, the founders of the formal field in the 1950s were mainly from Northern Europe and North America. Latterly there has been a proliferation of conflict resolution centres throughout the world, raising questions about many of these assumptions. Chapters 3 and 4 raised similar questions about conflict analysis and chapters 5 to 10 about conflict resolution responses – for example, about the appropriateness of intrusive prevention strategies across cultural boundaries, about the problems of multinational peacekeeping in third countries, about how radically negotiation and mediation are affected by cultural difference, about the suitability of universal democratic market economy models in postwar reconstruction in non-western settings, or about cultural variations in approaches to reconciliation. Part II of the book has also been drawn to this theme, whether the topic was the refusal to see ideologies that condone or encourage terrorism as legitimate cultural alternatives, the tension between the principle of gender equality and patriarchal cultures, or the universality of conflict resolution intervention principles. In chapter 16 we will link this to the more popular aspects of worldwide cultural expression in relation to conflict resolution – a theme carried further in chapter 17 when we look at the enormous energies released through rapidly widening access to the internet. But, at the same time, as argued in chapter 20, all of this is now coming under mounting pressure as the centre of gravity in world politics shifts away from the West and North to parts of the world where entirely different traditions hold sway. How much of the cosmopolitan conflict resolution approach is likely to survive this transformation?

How Far Down Does Cultural Variation Reach?

Edward Hall (1976: 91) distinguished high-context communication cultures, in which most of the information is transmitted implicitly through context and comparatively little is conveyed directly through verbal messages, from low-context communication cultures, in which most of the information is transmitted through explicit linguistic codes. He identified the former with languages like Arabic and Chinese and the latter with languages like German, English and French. Perhaps synaptic pathways in the brain are programmed differently as these languages and their associated cultural mores are learned. For example, the subject–predicate grammar of English creates a fixed world of objects and attributes and encourages stark logical dichotomies (true/false, right/wrong), exclusive categories and adversarial relationships.

There is limited space to indicate the wider debates about cultural variation that have informed conflict resolution. But paramount here was the influence of the anthropologist Franz Boas, and particularly of his students, such as Ruth Benedict and Margaret Mead, with their emphasis on the uniqueness of different cultures and critique of earlier value judgements about evolution from primitive to civilized cultures (Benedict, 1934). This came to be associated with refutation of the idea of biologically determined human instincts for rapacity, violence and war and with promotion of the idea of what Sponsel (1996) called 'the anthropology of peace', which saw cooperation and coexistence as natural, war as an 'invention',[1] and the causes of violence lying in the organizational structures and psycho-cultural dispositions of particular societies. Ross's *The Culture of Conflict* (1993) adopts this approach, comparing ethnographic data from ninety pre-industrial societies in an attempt to answer the question 'Why are some societies more conflictual than others?' He accepted the thesis that, among the Yanomami of southern Venezuela, a 'militant ideology and the warfare associated with it are the central reality of daily existence' (Chagnon, 1983) (now strongly refuted by many anthropologists),[2] whereas the Mbuti pygmies of the Zaire rain forest are 'at peace with themselves and with their environment' (Turnbull, 1978). His explanation for this was that, 'In the most general terms, the psychocultural dispositions rooted in a society's early socialization experiences shape the overall level of conflict, while its specific pattern of social organization determines whether the targets of conflict and aggression are located within a society, outside it, or both' (Ross, 1993: 9). He then generalizes this 'culture of conflict theory' to post-industrial societies and – surprisingly – finds it precisely confirmed in explaining the protracted conflict in Ireland and the 'relatively low levels of conflict in Norway' (ibid.: ch. 9). Animal ethologists have taken the predisposition to peace and war even further back: for example, de Waal (1989, 1998) shows that primate societies practise reconciliation – a different emphasis from that of Jane Goodall (1986), in her observation of the murderous propensities of our genetically nearest cousins, the chimpanzees.

Similar conclusions have been drawn in attempts to explain human aggression, where the 'determinism' of Freud (the innate self-destructiveness of his death drive *thanatos*) and Lorenz (his 'hydraulic' model, in which the drive to aggression builds and seeks outlet) are partially challenged in the 'frustration/aggression' theory of Dollard and his associates (1939) and refuted in the 'social learning theory' of Bandura (1973), with the idea that aggression is neither an innate drive nor an automatic reaction to frustration, but a learned response. Via this route, psychologists could join anthropologists and ethologists in denying the evolutionary functionality of competition and war and in emphasizing the cultural malleability of individuals and societies with a view to fostering conditions for the non-violent resolution of conflict. So it is that, having looked at 'cultural influences on conflict resolution' and offered examples of varying practice from culture to culture, the editorial 'final words' of Fry and Bjorkqvist's *Cultural Variation in Conflict Resolution* are:

> We conclude that the source of conflict lies in the minds of people. External, social conflict is a reflection of intrapsychic conflict. External control does not solve the roots of the problem. If we wish a conflict really to disappear, then a change in attitude is needed. Only when people learn to understand and respect each other can peaceful coexistence begin. (1997: 252)

It is interesting at this point to consider the implications for conflict resolution of the wider current battle between anti-evolutionism of this kind and a new generation of evolutionists. On the surface it might seem portentous, since each accuses the other of professional unreliability, political bias and dire consequences for understanding and responding to conflict. We will argue that it turns out to be less serious than might at first appear.

The new evolutionists attack what Tooby and Cosmides (1992) call 'the standard social science model', currently dominant in sociology, anthropology and social-psychology, and attempt to reassert the primacy of biology (Dawkins, 1998; Wilson, 1998; Pinker, 2002). This is said to represent a confluence of ideas from 'four frontiers of knowledge' – mind, the brain, genes and evolution – that, it is claimed, are at last bridging the gap between biology and culture and finally providing a secure basis for the understanding of human nature (Pinker, 2002: ch. 3). The 'politically correct' assumption that human nature is a benign 'blank slate' on which different cultures can 'construct' variation uninhibited by innate characteristics is rejected, including the idea that: 'violence has nothing to do with human nature but is a pathology inflicted by malign elements outside us. Violence is a behavior taught by the culture, or an infectious disease endemic to certain environments' (ibid.: 307). Pinker rejects this as 'the central dogma of a secular faith'. He points to human bodies and minds for 'direct signs of design for aggression' (male body size, the effects of testosterone, anger and teeth-baring, fight-or-flight response of the autonomic nervous system, aggressive acts initiated by circuits in the limbic system), to the transculturally rough-and-tumble behaviour of boys, 'which is obviously practice for fighting', to evidence that the 'most violent age is not adolescence but toddlerhood', to the 'shockingly high homicide rates of pre-state societies, with 10 to 60 per cent of the men dying at the hands of other men', and so on. Pinker espouses Hobbes's analysis that morality has been a late invention, only 'discovered by our ancestors after billions of years of the morally indifferent process known as natural selection', in which violence paid off in certain circumstances for rational and self-interested agents – in response to competition for the scarce resources required for survival and self-reproduction; in response to fear of others similarly motivated; and in response to the male cultures of 'honour' that resulted (ibid.: ch. 17).

Anti-evolutionists have in turn fought back, identifying the political agenda of evolutionary psychology as 'transparently part of a right-wing libertarian attack on collectivity, above all the welfare state', and rejecting its claims as 'not merely mistaken, but culturally pernicious', legitimizing male 'philandering', the favouring of our genetic kin and human aggression, as if a propensity to violence was biologically imprinted in human nature between 100,000 and 600,000 years ago on the Pleistocene savannahs where *Homo sapiens* originated (Rose and Rose, 2001: 8, 3, 2).

We do not think that debate at this level of abstraction has portentous implications for conflict resolution. The arguments of psycho-cultural theorists such as Ross or Fry and Bjorkqvist point to the significance of manipulating structural and psychological aspects of culture in order to produce non-violent societies. But the implications suggested by the evolutionary theorists for conflict resolution turn out to be not too different. We saw in chapter 1 how, in the light of iterated game theory, Dawkins's 'selfish gene' hypothesis suggests that, over a sufficient time span and under non-apocalyptic conditions, 'nice guys come first'. Similarly, the two main conflict resolution conclusions from Pinker's chapter on violence are, first, that democratic state structures are the best political antidote to the three Hobbesian 'reasons for quarrel', because 'by inflicting penalties on aggressors the governing body eliminates the profitability of invading for gain', which in turn 'defuses the Hobbesian trap in which mutually distrustive people are each tempted to inflict a pre-emptive strike', while a system of laws disinterestedly applied 'can obviate the need for a hair trigger for retaliation and the accompanying culture of honour' (2002: 330). The fact that the state is democratic is seen to be the best way to neutralize the danger that the state authorities themselves may turn violent. The second main conflict resolution conclusion that Pinker derives from his evolutionary theory is that the central psychological aim should be to bring potential enemies 'into each other's moral circles by facilitating trade, cultural exchanges, and people-to-people activities' (ibid.: 335). Since, for Pinker, mind is a 'combinatorial, recursive system', we not only have thoughts, but thoughts about thoughts, etc., so, in a passage reminiscent of Burton's second-order learning argument, he sees the 'advances in human conflict resolution' as 'dependent on this ability'. For Pinker, the mindsets predisposed to violence 'evolved to deal with hostilities in the ancestral past, and we must bring them into the open if we are to work around them in the present.' Anti-evolutionists avert their gaze from 'the evolutionary logic of violence', because they fear that 'acknowledging it is tantamount to accepting it or even to approving it':

> Instead they have pursued the comforting delusion of the Noble Savage, in which violence is an arbitrary product of learning or a pathogen that bores into us from outside. But denying the logic of violence makes it easy to forget how readily violence can flare up, and ignoring the parts of the mind that ignite violence makes it easy to overlook the parts that can extinguish it. With violence, as with so many other concerns, human nature is the problem, but human nature is also the solution. (Ibid.: 336)

In short, both evolutionists and anti-evolutionist culturalists in the conflict resolution field turn out in the end to be deriving remarkably similar policy recommendations from their apparently incompatible theories.

Culture and Conflict Resolution: Three Responses

In reply to the question 'How far down does cultural variation reach?', conflict resolvers give three different levels of response (see table 15.1). We will comment briefly on each in turn.

We have already noted how the central conflict resolution approach of Burton is based on the claim that deep-rooted conflict is caused by the failure of social and political institutions to satisfy non-negotiable ontological human needs for recognition, security, development, and so on (chapter 2). In the Burtonian model, culture operates at the shallower level of values and

Table 15.1 Three conflict resolution answers to the culture question

	Response	Responder
1	Cultural variation is not relevant to conflict resolution	Burton, Zartman
2	Cultural variation should be taken into account in conflict resolution, but only as a variable	Bercovitch, Cohen, Gulliver
3	Cultural variation is fundamentally significant in conflict resolution	Avruch, Black, Lederach, Galtung
4	Cultural variation reaches right to the bottom, precluding cross-cultural generalization	

therefore does not affect the conflict resolution imperative of mining down to the underlying level of universal or generic human needs. As Avruch puts it, Burton's theory of conflict 'marginalizes the role of culture to the extreme, silencing it as effectively as does the power-based realist paradigm, which Burton so clearly opposes in most other ways' (1998: 89–90).

In the second category, we find conflict resolution specialists who recognize the significance of cultural variation but regard it as one variable among others, important to take account of but not serious enough to transform generic approaches. Perhaps the best examples come from the negotiation literature. Prominent here have been studies such as Gulliver's pioneering analysis of cross-cultural negotiations in quasi-Gadamerian terms, as interlocutions in which both parties have to try to educate each other (Gulliver, 1979), and Cohen's analysis of Israeli–Egyptian culturally based misunderstandings and miscommunication leading to damaging 'dialogues of the deaf' (Cohen, 1990, 1991). This work relates to that of Jervis (1976) on 'perception and misperception' in international politics and that of Janis (1973) on 'groupthink'. In sharp contrast to this has been the scorn poured by Zartman on the significance of culture for international negotiation: 'Culture is indeed relevant to the understanding of the negotiation process ... every bit as relevant as [the] breakfast [the negotiators ate], and to much the same extent' (quoted in Avruch, 1998: 42). Zartman gives three reasons for this, each challenged by Avruch (that negotiation is a universal process and 'cultural differences are simply differences in style and language', that in any case there is now a universal culture of diplomacy, and that cultural difference is trumped by considerations of power) (ibid.: 42–55). In general, conflict resolvers vary in the weight they accord cultural variation in this area. In the view of Avruch, neither those who approach the study of negotiations from an analytical social-psychological perspective (such as Pruitt and Carnevale, 1993) nor those who adopt the more popular and prescriptive 'how-to' approach (Fisher and Ury, 1981) take much note of cultural factors. Others do pay more attention, such as Bercovitch (1996), as also many of those whose main focus is on cross-cultural mediation (Augsburger, 1992).

In the third category come those conflict resolvers for whom cultural variation is of fundamental significance. We may point here to three contributions in particular: to the comprehensive and highly effective critique of culture-blind 'generic' conflict resolution mounted by Avruch and Black (1987, 1991; Avruch et al., 1991; Avruch 2012; Reading 70); to Lederach's definition of conflict transformation in terms of a culture-sensitive 'elicitive' approach rather than an externally imported 'prescriptive' approach drawn originally from his experience of the different assumptions about mediation in Latin America (Lederach and Wehr, 1991; Lederach, 1994, 1995); and to Galtung's comparison of Occidental ways of thinking with Oriental and Hindu cosmologies and traditions, usually to the disadvantage of the former (1990, 1996: 196–264).[3] In this category also come numerous individual and comparative ethnographic studies of differing ways of handling conflict across diverse cultures. Gulliver, for example, examined how disputes and negotiations over land in Tanzania reflected the local context, beliefs and power structures (Reading 53). A section in Fry and Bjorkqvist's *Cultural Variation in Conflict Resolution* (1997: 51–231) compares conflict resolution practices among the Semai of Malaysia (community resolution through the *becharaa'* process), the Toraja of Indonesia (avoidance strategies), the Margariteno of Venezuela (formal and informal resolution, 'non-violent but often cruel') and the kingdom of Tonga (the *kava* drinking circle), and then sets this in turn beside conflict resolution initiatives in contemporary major armed conflicts, as in Sri Lanka, Mozambique or Latin America, and beside smaller-scale conflict in inner cities and schools. In our view, the wealth and diversity of this kind of material at the moment swamps most attempts at detailed cross-cultural analysis on this scale. So there is still much work to be done here.

We will leave the last word with Avruch, whose careful overall assessment we are happy to endorse. In defining conflict, Avruch warns us to guard against six 'inadequate ideas' which oversimplify and 'fail to reflect the 'thickness' or complexity of the phenomenological world [they seek] to represent' (1998: 12). The six conceptual inadequacies are: to assume that culture is homogeneous; to reify culture as if it were a 'thing' that could act independently of human agents; to ignore intercultural variation by assuming that it is uniformly distributed among members of a group; to assume that an individual possesses only one culture; to identify culture superficially with custom or etiquette; and to assume that culture is timeless (ibid.: 12–16). Avoiding these pitfalls leads to an understanding of culture as inherited experience in responding to life's problems (possibly genetically rooted) that is at the same time continually being locally transformed: 'This means (contrary to the reified or stable or homogenous view of culture) that culture is to some extent always situational, flexible, and responsive to the exigencies of the worlds that individuals confront' (ibid.: 20). In terms of the scope for cross-cultural understanding, Avruch frames the debate in terms of two approaches drawn from anthropology: 'One strategy is based on an actor-centred, thickly described, and context-rich – an emic – way of looking at culture. The other strategy is based on an analyst-centred, "objective," and transcultural – an etic – way of looking at culture' (ibid.: 57).

The emic approach 'brings with it all the strengths of ethnography: the attention to context and detail and nuanced translation' (Avruch, 1998: 62). On the other hand, there are criticisms that this can end up being 'merely descriptive', may prevent comparisons and cross-cultural insights, and might suggest unhelpful ideas that reify cultures and see them as timeless and uniform: 'this is how the such-and-such people think'. In contrast, etic schemes identify 'underlying, structurally deep, and transcultural forms' that 'enable efficient, retrievable handling of large amounts of cultural data' and allow comparison across cases (ibid.: 70).[4] The weakness of etic approaches is that they tend to oversimplify: 'When the continuums are turned into dichotomies (as they usually are, despite the cautions of their authors), these schemes become very crude instruments for measuring rather fine aspects of culture' (ibid.: 68). In short, Avruch rejects theories that see cultural variation going all the way down to the bottom, as in some forms of cultural relativism, because in that case no cross-cultural conclusions could be drawn at all, and this would preclude the prescriptive principles on which conflict resolution is based (for a classic discussion on 'rationality and relativism', see Hollis and Lukes, 1982; on 'universalism vs. communitarianism', see Rasmussen, 1990). But, within these constraints, Avruch lays his greatest stress on the importance of an understanding of and sensitivity towards what he and Black have called ethnoconflict theory and ethnoconflict praxis in conflict resolution – the indigenous conflict understandings and resolution practices among the principal parties in the conflict in question (Avruch and Black, 1991; Avruch et al., 1991). This is precisely Lederach's 'elicitive' approach described in chapter 9.

Religion and the Dialogue of Civilizations

Are we in the middle of a 'clash of civilizations', as predicted in the 1990s by Samuel Huntington (1996) and affirmed today by a number of *jihadist* apologists? Or is this attempt to construct a global ideological struggle a distortion of a much more complex interplay? Can current secular-religious, inter-religious and sectarian political turmoil in many parts of the world be overcome by a 'dialogue of civilizations'? Most western academics were taken by surprise when religion erupted again as a major ideological challenge to both East and West in the last decade of the Cold War. It is worth retracing the story.

Douglas Johnston and Cynthia Sampson called their edited 1994 volume *Religion, the Missing Dimension of Statecraft*. They argued that, while 'religion may not be the primary catalyst' for many post-Cold War conflicts, 'it is clearly a complicating factor'. They strongly advised that religion should be taken seriously in international diplomacy and suggested that 'the use of a religious rationale to justify a conflict creates opportunities for spiritually motivated peacemakers' (1994: 332). It may seem surprising that this call came so late. Religious differences within and between faith communities had been associated for some time – sometimes centrally – with longstanding political conflicts such as those in Sri Lanka, Northern Ireland and Kashmir. And an explicit challenge to the prevailing universalist secular value system, which included the ideologies identified with both the superpowers, had been mounted from post-1979 Iran – and was widely evident much earlier.

Within this context the twin enterprises of comparative religious ethics (Twiss, 1993) and inter-religious dialogue (Kung and Kuschel, 1993) came to focus either on the search for 'normative appropriation' between religions, along Gadamerian lines, or on the search for common values supposed to be already shared by all the great religions (see chapter 2). This was an ethical-spiritual counter to the politico-military thesis that there would be an inevitable 'clash of civilizations' (Huntington, 1996). The organizers of the 1993 Parliament of World Religions, for example, claimed that 'there is already a consensus among the religions which can be the basis for a global ethic – a minimum fundamental consensus concerning binding values, irrevocable standards, and fundamental moral attitudes' (Kung and Kuschel, 1993: 18). By 2000, the idea that the world's religions had a major role to play in conflict resolution, peacemaking and peacebuilding had inspired a meeting of the United Nations Millennium Summit of World Religious Leaders, attended by more than 1,000 representatives. 2001 was designated the Year of the Dialogue of Civilizations.

Further to the theme of Hans-Georg Gadamer's hermeneutic (interpretative) approach discussed in chapter 2 (Ramsbotham, 2015), Fred Dallmayr's 'Dialogue of civilizations: a hermeneutical perspective' (2002) and Richard Shapcott's *Justice, Community and Dialogue in International Relations* (2001) are cited in Fabio Petito's thought-provoking and persuasive argument that 'the Gadamerian-hermeneutical model of "fusion of horizons" can help us to understand what the process of inter-civilisational dialogue might look like' (Petito, 2011: 14). Gadamer himself – by now in his nineties – seemed to concur:

> And if we then have to become part of a new world civilization, if this is our task, then we shall need a philosophy which is similar to my hermeneutics; a philosophy which teaches us to see the justification for the other's point of view and which thus makes us doubt our own. (Misgeld and Nicholson, 1992: 152)
>
> The human solidarity that I envisage is not a global uniformity but unity in diversity ... Such unity-in-diversity has to be extended to the whole world – to include Japan, China, India, and also Muslim cultures. Every culture, every people has something distinctive to offer for the solidarity and welfare of humanity. (Pantham, 1992: 132)

For Pinar Bilgin, writing on the interface between dialogue of civilizations and critical security studies, 'Civilizational dialogue initiatives are currently considered our best chance to prevent a potential clash between states belonging to different civilizations' (2014: 9).

But, in the middle of all this, the dramatic events of 11 September 2001 gave a savage reminder, if one were needed, that religion can also play a more sinister role. Juergensmeyer's *Terror in the Mind of God: The Global Rise of Religious Violence* (2000) was one of several books tracing connections between all the major religions and political violence. Hugo Slim explained why this was something that secular analysts now needed to take seriously:

> The flurry of new books on charismatic Christianity in Africa, on Islamist theology and the increasingly routine monitoring of cults shows that it is both possible and important for secular political and military analysts to engage with and understand religious ideology and the political and military programmes that flow from them. Faced with the texts and creeds of certain groups, secular analysts and policy-makers may still react by saying 'Do people really believe this stuff?' But confronted with repeated suicide attacks in the Middle East and child abductions in northern Uganda, the answer is obvious to many ordinary people on the front line: 'Yes, they do'. The burden of credulity is now on the side of the secular analysts. It makes sense to believe that religious movements do believe this stuff and to examine why they do, where such belief might lead and how best it may be challenged. (Slim, 2005: 23)

For Marc Gopin this also works the other way:

> It seems clear from what I have studied and uncovered that there will continue to be a significant radicalization of many religions on the part of some believers for the foreseeable future. This dynamic is likely to continue as long as the range of human needs, physically and especially spiritual, continue to be unmet by the evolving global civilization, whose principal offering to human beings is the promise of a materialist civilization in which a few become wealthy, some are reasonably comfortable, but very insecure, and most are poor. This materialist, exclusivist vision of the future has turned out to be attractive on one level, motivating a great deal of economic ingenuity among some in every civilization and yielding impressive material benefits. But this global civilization, as it is currently conceived, is also turning out to be repulsive to many others. (Gopin, 2000: 223)

Gopin's remedy, reminding us that it is not only religion but also secular materialism that needs to adapt, is a call to respiritualize prevailing world culture.

In summary, what has been called the 'ambivalence of the sacred' emphasizes the widely recognized point that within all the great world religions are traditions that can be co-opted to legitimize violence and war but also deep resources for promoting non-violent conflict resolution and peace (Appleby, 2000). This is a function of the way in which these religions emerged from certain social and political backgrounds and subsequently, as a result of their success, came to permeate every aspect of culture, society and politics in those parts of the world where they prevailed. This enmeshed the deep spiritual teachings in the changing political institutions, social arrangements and cultural practices within which they were reflected, variously understood and transmitted. So it was, for example, that the theme of warfare, endemic in the Jewish scriptures and often enjoined by God at a time when the Jewish people first achieved political self-consciousness as a distinct people in a hostile environment, is not developed further during the long period after 70 CE when there was no longer a Jewish state, but became prominent again from 1948. Early Christians were predominantly pacifist (to become a soldier meant swearing allegiance to non-Christian gods), but ever since the conversion of Constantine in the fourth century CE, just war doctrines have prevailed. The Meccan suras of the Koran are notably eirenic compared with the post-Medina suras, when Muhammad was administering the first Islamic *umma* and fighting wars – followed by one of the most remarkable phases of military expansion after his death. The Hindu *Mahabharat* is full of battles, notably the setting for Gandhi's favourite text, the *Bhagavad Gita*, which he interpreted as a spiritual allegory. Even Buddhism, usually seen as a peace-loving religion, can become a rallying point for militant chauvinism, as witnessed in Sri Lanka (see below). Religion can be used to sharpen exclusive identities and lend conviction and passion (including a promise of future reward) to destructive political programmes. But, of course, it also offers a deep source for understanding, reconciliation and human fellowship that transcends secular divisions.

In short, from a conflict resolution perspective, perhaps the key struggles lie not so much *between* as *within* religions, to determine which of the two faces – constructive or destructive – prevails in different settings and from different points of view. This is a theme that has been introduced in chapter 11 and identified as a key site in the struggle against extremist violence and terror. Harold Coward and Gordon Smith's edited book *Religion and Peacebuilding* (2004) analyses this in relation to Hinduism, Buddhism and Confucianism. In Sri Lanka, for example, Eva Neumaier sees the critical question as follows:

> Working toward peace in Sri Lanka will depend on whether the various ethno-religious communities are prepared to engage in critical self-reflection to demystify their own mytho-historic narratives that gave rise to fundamentalist movements not only among Sinhala-Buddhists but also among the Tamils and Muslims of the island. So far nothing indicates such moves toward self-reflection have begun. (2004: 80)

In chapter 11, we saw how Khaled Abou El Fadl describes the key struggle within an Islam 'torn between extremism and moderation' in similar vein: 'Between the puritans and the moderates, which of the two groups is more likely to define the meaning and role of the word's second largest religion in future?' (2005: 25). He himself strongly supports the 'humanist' moderate reading of Islam, sees the extremist or puritan assault as a 'heresy', and calls for a 'counter-*jihad*' 'to reclaim the truth about the Islamic faith and win the hearts and minds of Muslims and non-Muslims all around the world' (ibid.: 286).

A practical example of attempts to bridge cultural differences and build consensus in problem-solving and conflict resolution on issues of common concern along these lines can be seen in the formal ongoing dialogue between the League of Arab States (LAS), the Organization of the Islamic Conference (OIC) and the European Union. And, more broadly, in the enterprise of creating the

Box 15.1 The UN Alliance of Civilizations

The United Nations Alliance of Civilizations (UNAoC) was established in 2005 to counter extremism and in 2015 had 142 member states. Its purpose is 'to improve understanding and cooperative relations among nations and peoples across cultures and religions' in order to 'counter the forces that fuel polarization and extremism' (UNAoC, 2012). The alliance is 'an intergovernmental organization which aims to foster cooperation between and within nations, across cultures, and to reduce conflict and tension at all levels – locally, nationally, and globally. It incorporates a firm commitment to include civil society, philanthropic and business organizations to achieve these objectives.' Mindful of the deep global and regional inequalities that still fuel intercultural resentment, suspicion and conflict, the UN High-Level Group that established UNAoC identified 'the deep structural drivers of extremism and polarisation – presenting a picture of local populations pushed towards violence by inequality and lack of democratic expression, subject to cultural domination through pervasive economic globalisation, and denied outlets of reform given a UN system frozen by the existing patterns of wealth and power' (Camilleri and Martin, 2014: 9).

At the Beijing Annual Forum (2013), the UN high representative emphasized the four priorities of youth, education, media and migration/integration and added engagement with the arts, entertainment and sport as a deep level of civil society involvement (see chapter 16). He also commented on the remarkable rise of China and drew attention to the importance of its Confucian legacy, together with the enormous contribution that it could make to the 'harmony of civiliziatons and prosperity for all'.

Within this global enterprise there are regional initiatives – for example, in the Asia–South Pacific area (Camilleri and Martin, 2014).

United Nations Alliance of Civilizations (see box 15.1). These initiatives clearly fit centrally within the framework of the conflict resolution response to terrorism set out at the end of chapter 11.

Buddhism and conflict resolution

The idea that conflict resolution is not a western inheritance but a universal human skill that different cultures practise and understand in different ways has gained further strength with the realization that conflict resolution practices can be found embedded at the heart of Buddhism. Guatama Siddhartha, the Buddha, himself personally practised mediation, as well as meditation, in Northern India in the fifth century BC. He intervened in a dispute over water between neighbouring Indian states and brought them back from the brink of war (McConnell, 1995: 315–29). He also mediated between his own monks when they split into factions, meeting no success until he withdrew from the monks and induced them to reconsider (ibid.: 284–314).

John McConnell has shown how closely a contemporary view of conflict fits with a Buddhist view. He reads conflict into the Four Noble Truths as follows.

1 Conflict (suffering) is part of the human condition.
2 Understanding the deep roots of conflict is the first step to transforming it.

3 By engaging with and transforming the roots of conflict, peace can emerge from conflict.
4 Peace is a way of life, a process, not something that lies in the future but something to be engaged in now.

A basic idea in a Buddhist understanding of conflict is that 'the causes of the situation are not in the past, where they would be inaccessible, but in the present, where they can be tackled if we have the tools' (McConnell, 1995: 185). The causes lie in the minds of the conflictants and especially in how they 'concoct' wants, desires and illusory projections of the self, to which the self clings.

Conflict arises from *loba* (greed, craving for fixed goals, striving for mastery), *dosa* (hatred or generalized suspicion) and *moha* (self-distorted perceptions). The self attaches itself to the goals one adopts, misperceives the self as the self-and-the-objects-desired, and suspects others of thwarting its desires. 'Greed, hate and delusion interact within and between the minds of conflictants, manifesting themselves in perceptions and behaviour.' Using these categories, and the precise understanding of successions of mental changes incorporated in the *paticca-samupadda*, the practitioner can 'trace the origins and history of a conflict and observe the psychological interactions that perpetuate it in the present' (McConnell, 1995: 7). The mediator, like the meditator, uses awareness as the key tool to transform the seeds of anger, craving, and so on, into seeds of compassion and understanding.

One of the best-known – and most inspiring – exponents of a Buddhist approach to conflict resolution and peacemaking is the Vietnamese Buddhist master Thich Nhat Hanh (1987). As a champion of the Buddhist 'third way' in the Vietnam War, Nhat Hanh developed a non-violent approach to the conflict that rejected both communist and capitalist doctrines, and he took an active part in the anti-war movement. Since those days he has practised and taught in the West, expounding 'engaged Buddhism' as a response to conflict and injustice. He speaks to audiences in both the East and the West in an approach that achieves a remarkable synthesis of different cultures.

Islam and conflict resolution

We noted in chapter 1 Salem's argument that the 'western' assumptions on which conflict resolution rests are not applicable universally (1993, 1997). In particular, he suggested that concepts and values related to peace and conflict were not necessarily understood in the same way in the Arab–Muslim Middle East as they might be in Europe and North America.

Mohammed Abu-Nimer (2003, 2010) has pointed out that attempts to develop peacebuilding strategies in the Middle East and in other Muslim countries have been constrained because of a dominant stereotype of a bellicose and intolerant Islamic worldview, which brands Islamic and Arab culture and religion as inherently violent. There are also internal characteristics which have inhibited the development of democratic pluralist and peacebuilding activities. This has been linked to a crisis within Islamic thought, where the traditional practice of *ijtihad*, which means the continuous and evolving interpretation of the Qur'an, has declined and been replaced by dogmatic and narrow interpretations. Muslim scholars are now engaged in a process of critical re-examination of Islamic belief systems and are identifying a rich tradition of non-violent conflict management ideas and practices which are vital in the quest for appropriate responses to the political and developmental challenges of the region.

In a partial challenge to Salem, Abu-Nimer insists that Islamic tradition encompasses a whole galaxy of ideas, principles and practices which are entirely consonant with a conflict resolution approach – and of course long pre-date it. In the light of this, he identifies guidelines for non-Muslim activists to take into consideration when engaging in predominantly Muslim societies. Initiatives properly set within well-informed cultural and religious frameworks might entirely transform the possibilities for cross-cultural cooperation.

There is an abundance of cultural and religious indigenous practices and values in Muslim communities that can be drawn upon in designing models of intervention to promote social and political change and development; there is no need mechanically to import western-based models, which may at best produce a short-term impact but in the long term typically do not take root in the life of the community. They also eventually run up against certain problematic core values in the socio-cultural structures of many Muslim communities (especially in the Muslim Arab context), such as hierarchy, authoritarianism, patriarchy, and so on. These structures are threatened by the democratic participatory elements of community peacebuilding. This is an inevitable confrontation that ought to be anticipated by both interveners and community members. Utilizing the community's local forces for change in such projects is an important step in overcoming some of those structural challenges.

There are, therefore, significant differences between western modes of conflict resolution and the assumptions, rituals and practices of the Arab-Islamic world. Cosmopolitan conflict resolution in the context of Middle East peacemaking means that peacemakers have to be aware of specific indigenous methods of conflict resolution and reconciliation.

George Irani (1999), for example, has identified *wasta*, which is patronage-based mediation, and the rituals of *sulh* (settlement) and *musalaha* (reconciliation) as key elements of traditional practices widely used at the village level throughout the Middle East. This offers a good example of cultural variation in reconciliation mentioned in chapter 10. Through *sulh* and *musalaha*, conflict management takes place within a communal, not an individualized, framework. Kinship and patriarchy are important aspects of the process, and elements of the conventional western model are reversed. Mediators are respected not for their neutrality but for their authority and their ability both to determine and to apply a solution. Reactions to being wronged in a conflict range across a spectrum from revenge to reconciliation, and there are strong customs and rituals, justified in the Qur'an, which work in favour of reconciliation. Thus, while the Qur'an provides for equity in cases of revenge, it also favours forgiveness in cases of apology and 'remission'.

There is some tension here between the strong injunction to overcome quarrels *within* the Islamic *umma* – sometimes extended to the 'people of the book' (Jews and Christians) and subject peoples within *dar al-Islam* (the 'realm of peace') who accept Muslim rule (the *dhimmis*) – and the question of relations with those who live *outside* Islam in *dar al-harb* (the realm of war). Different Quranic *suras* are quoted – together with appeal to the *Sunna* (the example of the Prophet's life) and the *hadith* (the sayings of the Prophet) – to support such contending interpretations. The fundamental idea here – that at its deepest the Islamic *umma* is identical with the community of humanity as a whole – offers huge potential for enlisting the great power of Islam on the side of superordinate values of cosmopolitan human solidarity. The overriding Islamic injunction, though, is that this must be firmly based on the principles of equity and justice taught by the Prophet. It is the failure of western conflict resolution approaches to recognize and remedy historic injustices and current inequalities that, above all, is seen to block the path to genuine global cooperation in the view of most Muslims worldwide. For example, here is a passage from the Qur'an that may be seen to previsage the charter of the United Nations:

> And if two parties or groups among believers fall to fighting, then make peace between them both, but if one of them rebels against the other, then [all of] you fight against the one that rebels until it complies with the Command of Allah; then, if it complies, make reconciliation between them justly, and be equitable. Verily! Allah loves those who are equitable. (Qur'an: 49: 9)

The process of *musalaha* which follows from this injunction is one based on transformation and empowerment. Therefore, in order to increase the efficacy of conflict resolution and peacebuilding initiatives in Muslim communities, there is a necessity to emphasize justice, empowerment of the weak, social solidarity and public support.

Both Abu-Nimer and Irani conclude that such a use of non-violent peacebuilding strategies and activities in Muslim communities has potentially far-reaching consequences in terms of political and religious leadership, non-governmental organizations and third-party interveners. Similar conclusions are reached in a number of other studies of Arab approaches to conflict resolution (Yassine-Hamdan and Pearson, 2014) and conflict management in the Middle East (Youssef, 2009).

Conclusion

Let us end by reminding ourselves how Avruch noted that, contrary to conflict resolution beliefs, most cultures 'at some point' sanction resort to violence in processing social conflict. We have seen how both the Buddhist and the Islamic tradition contain deep resources for non-violent conflict resolution. But we are aware that, like other religions, notably Christianity, they can also be used to justify violence and repression. For this reason Avruch concludes that culture needs not only to be understood but also to be 're-engineered'. He sees this as possible, because he rejects the 'reified or stable or homogenous view of culture' and favours the idea that 'culture is to some extent always situational, flexible, and responsive to the exigencies of the worlds that individuals confront' (1998: 20). We agree with him, but we are also painfully aware that conflict parties, as often as not, have a very reified and homogeneous view of culture, and that this represents their accepted discourse on culture and identity and the pragmatic interest of those who seek to use it to further political goals.[5] Indeed, a naturalized view of culture can be seen as more universal than the fashionable western social science view that claims to be able to recognize its contingency and fluidity (see chapter 19). Irony tends to be in short supply in intense conflict – including that between western constructivists and non-western fundamentalists. This, in our view, is the most testing challenge to conflict resolution in the culture debate today.

Recommended reading

Abu-Nimer (2003, 2010); Appleby (2000); Avruch (1998, 2012); Cohen (1991); Coward and Smith (2004); Fry and Bjorkqvist (1997); Gopin (2000); Gulliver (1979); Irani (1999); McConnell (1995); Ross (1993); Yassine-Hamdan and Pearson (2014).

Relevant extracts in *The Contemporary Conflict Resolution Reader*

Reading 53: P. Gulliver, Disputes and Negotiations
Reading 70: K. Avruch, Culture and Conflict Resolution

CHAPTER SIXTEEN

Conflict Resolution in Art and Popular Culture

This chapter explores the cultural and artistic dimensions of conflict resolution, expressed in art, theatre and music, and also in sport. These creative and expressive areas of human activity provide a powerful source of peacebuilding energy and passion that is not always apparent in the formalized processes of political conflict resolution. At the same time creative conflict resolution both nourishes and defines the emergence of a culture of peace, which has been defined by the UN as 'a set of values, attitudes, modes of behaviour and ways of life that reject violence and prevent conflicts by tackling their root causes, to solve problems through dialogue and negotiation among individuals, groups and nations' (United Nations, 1998).

We begin our exploration by referring once again to the work of Elise Boulding. As a sociologist and peace researcher, she acknowledged the importance of institution-building in peacemaking, but she also stressed the importance of imagination, creativity and human desire in creating what she called a global civic culture. Boulding identified three 'modes of knowing' – the cognitive/analytic, the emotional/affective and the intuitive. In a world increasingly governed by science and technology, the cognitive/analytic mode has come to dominate and the emotional/affective and intuitive modes have become relatively less used. For Boulding, it was important to find ways of 'freeing the other modes for action by developing the skills of the imagination' (Boulding, 1990: 95).

Creative Networks: Museums, Visual Arts, Music and Theatre in Conflict Resolution

Peter van den Dungen has recorded the history of one of the most dynamic areas of growth of the values and practices of peace culture and conflict resolution in the form of the development and internationalization of peace museums. The Sixth International Conference of Museums for Peace was held in Kyoto, Japan, in October 2008. Its theme was 'building peace literacy for global problem-solving', indicating the commitment of the peace museums network not just to preserve the artefacts of peace but to engage actively in the promotion of peace culture and peace education. Peace museums define themselves as unique spaces for learning 'situated within a series of contexts that includes the personal, sociocultural and physical'. At these levels peace museums are educational centres which may have different emphases according to location and context, from 'sites for historic narratives and survivor stories, to centres for conflict resolution and transformative imagining, to memorial and reconciliation sites'. Most importantly, they have a common value in forming 'an alternative voice or resistance to the dominant and dominating voices of violence' (van den Dungen, 2008: 17)

The peace museum movement has grown remarkably since its first international conference, held at the University of Bradford, UK, in 1992. It is estimated that there are now more than a hundred centres recognized as peace museums worldwide, and since 2008 the International Network of Museums for Peace has established itself with a permanent secretariat in The Hague, in the Netherlands. Looking forward to the next stage in the development of the peace museums network, van den Dungen has outlined a set of objectives and activities that it might prioritize in the years ahead, among which are the continued development of new museums; further coordination between them; study tours; the development of courses at university and college level; and the endowment of a peace fund and peace prizes to recognize creativity and achievement in promoting peace education (van den Dungen, 2008 : 23).[1]

Peace museums provide spaces in which use is made of art and other media to present and project the values of peace and conflict resolution. Carol Rank has described in more concrete terms what peace museums worldwide actually do, particularly where they preserve and present the material of peace culture (art and artefacts) in programmes where art and history are utilized to advance peace and conflict resolution education. She points to the range of visual and performing arts – 'drama, literature, poetry, film and the visual arts such as paintings, prints, posters, sculpture and photography' – and reiterates the idea that 'the power of the arts lies in their emotive nature: the arts can help people feel the pathos and waste of war and help instil a desire and commitment to end war and work for peace' (Anzai et al., 2008: 15). In the visual arts she observes that paintings have been used as both witness and resistance to war and as imagery to express peace vision and transformation. In the former category, Spanish examples are powerful and instructive. Goya's series *The Disasters of War* provides dramatic and disturbing images of Spanish resistance against the invasion of the French during the Napoleonic Wars of the early nineteenth century. This was the first example in the modern era of what was to be termed guerrilla war, in which no distinction was made between civilians and regular military forces. Goya's *The Third of May 1808* depicts the execution of Spanish civilians by French troops. The painting was described by Kenneth Clark as 'the first great picture which can be called revolutionary in every sense of the word, in style, in subject, and in intention', and it directly influenced Picasso's depiction of the bombing of Guernica over one hundred years later (Clark, 1968: 130).

The Spanish Civil War provided a frightening foretaste of the rise of fascism and the violence which was to spread worldwide. It was also the first war in which photography, film and photojournalism was used to record intimately and comprehensively the events that took place. Gerda Taro, the partner of Robert Capa (whose photograph *The Fallen Soldier*, taken at the Cordoba Front in 1936, provided another iconic image that was distributed worldwide), was the first female war photographer to die in action – in the Battle of Bunuette in July 1937, when she was covering the retreat of Republican forces. Her photographs, still little known, are among the most moving and powerful depictions of civilians as victims of modern indiscriminate war (see the web-site of the International Center of Photography, at www.icp.org). In April 1937, when Guernica was bombed, Picasso responded by producing a painting that represented complex and unsettling images of war, including one of a woman grieving over a dead child, that represented an enduring condemnation of both war and repression. The work was first exhibited in Paris in 1937 and is now in the Museo Reina Sofia in Madrid. For Picasso, the painting was clearly a political piece, an angry declaration against the militarism that was engulf-ing Spain and was soon to engulf Europe: 'in the picture I am now working on and that I will call Guernica, and in all my recent work, I clearly express my loathing for the military caste that has plunged Spain into a sea of suffering and death.' A tapestry copy of the painting was placed in the United Nations in New York, displayed symbolically at the entrance to the Security Council (Smith, 2002: 3; Patterson, 2007).

Dimensions of feeling, emotion, imagery and imagination, which are stimu-lated when peace and conflict are the subjects of the visual and other arts, are clearly important but under-utilized reservoirs and motivators for conflict resolution. They exist just as powerfully in the arts in general, but here we refer to the roles of music and drama in conflict resolution. Music can stimu-late a whole range of emotions and perceptions, some forms of it uplifting and likely to work in favour of peace and harmony, other forms quite the oppo-site. Urbain, in one of the few studies that has comprehensively explored the conflict transformation potential of music, provides many examples where it has been used to promote peace, including the concert organized by Daniel Barenboim and Edward Said in 1999 which united Israeli and Palestinian musicians (Urbain, 2008: 2). This event developed into a permanent pro-gramme, the West-Eastern Divan Orchestra, where Israeli musicians play and study with musicians from other countries in the Middle East and combine this with 'the sharing of knowledge and comprehension between people from cultures that traditionally have been rivals' (www.barenboim-said.org/). In this case, music provides the opportunity for contact, and therefore the potential for better understanding. Music in general is neither inherently good nor bad, neither positive nor negative, in its impact on conflict resolution. Yet there are many examples where music unites peoples, to 'promote our self aware-ness and self esteem, mutual tolerance, sense of spirituality, intercultural understanding, ability to cooperate, healing ...' (Lawrence, 2008: 14), and there are many studies that illustrate how music can have these effects in certain places and contexts. In South Africa, for example, the national anthem of the post-apartheid state, 'Nkosi Sikelel' iAfrica', was sung as song of liberation in the era of apartheid and inspired many in the struggle for freedom (Gray, 2008: 63–77). In the US, 'We Shall Overcome' became the anthem of the civil rights movement, evolving from a spiritual-religious into a social protest song first used in 1945. It later crossed over from the black community, inspiring a new generation of white protest singers such as Joan Baez and Bob Dylan (Whitehead, 2008). In Israel, and in the context of Israelis' relationship with the Palestinians, Karen Abi-Ezzi has shown how the jazz music of Gilad Atzmon challenges Israel to rethink its treatment of Palestinians and their political claims by reinterpreting traditional Jewish/Israeli music and musical themes through a fusion with Arab-Palestinian styles and Israeli-Palestinian musicians (Abi-Ezzi, 2008). More generally, the emergence of the highly popular world musical genre epitomized by Peter Gabriel's WOMAD (World of Music, Arts and Dance), which started with its first festival in 1982 with the aim of bringing together the musicians of the world 'to excite, to inform, and to create an awareness of the worth and potential of a multicultural community', demonstrates the power of music to unite and inspire in a way that both acknowledges and transcends national and ethnic divides and traditions (Boyce-Tilman, 2008) (see box 16.1).

Box 16.1 Music as a force for peace in Mali, 2012–2014

In chapter 6 we explored the role of peacekeeping in the conflict in Mali, which had its roots in Tuareg demands for independence in the north, but which also became seen as a front line in Africa against extreme *jihadi* groups, who attacked not only the political and military centres of the Mali state but also the cultural institutions and traditions of the people. Music in Mali was a powerful political social and cultural force. Mali is on the fault line between the African and Arab worlds and the country's musicians found themselves on the front line of the conflict. As Ian Birrell expressed it, 'at root this is now a cultural war – between modernity and the past, between tolerance and brutality, between unity and division. And this is why the music of Mali remains such a vital force in the fight for all our futures' (*The Guardian*, 18 January 2013). The culture and music of Mali were both targeted in the conflict and also formed rallying points for resistance and opposition to the destructive impact of extreme Islamic groups. When the Islamic *jihadi* groups took control of large areas in northern Mali, including Timbuktu, regarded as the spiritual, cultural and intellectual centre of Malian society, it was clear that their puritanical values and their brutal imposition of shari'a law was a danger not only to the people of Mali but also to the music, musicians and the cultural life of the country. Traditional Malian music had become a force in world music, where the traditional and the modern are fused in a cosmopolitan music style. According to one report, culture, and music in particular, was Mali's greatest ambassador. However, in August 2012, the self-styled Islamic groups set about the systematic destruction of Malian culture. Ould Abdel Kader, a spokesperson for MUJAO (Movement for Oneness and *Jihad* in Mali) declared:

> We, the mujahedeen of Gao, of Timbuktu and Kidal, henceforward forbid the broadcasting of any western music on all radios in this Islamic territory. This ban

Box 16.1 (continued)

takes effect from today, Wednesday. We do not want Satan's music. In its place, there will be Quranic verses. Shari'a demands this. What God commands must be done. (Morgan, 2013: 13)

In a remarkable, and perhaps unprecedented, example of cultural resistance, the musicians of Mali reacted to this pronouncement with a series of concerts, media events, declarations and festivals. The cultural resistance peaked with the release in February 2013 of a stirring anthem for peacemaking in Mali, *Mali-ko* (Peace), recorded by all the country's top musicians, headed by the most iconic of all, Fatoumata Diawara, achieving what Morgan calls 'the widest global reach of all the Mali crisis initiatives' (2013: 44). Using Facebook and other social media platforms, Mali's younger generation of rappers, such as Sidike Diabete and Iba One, who recorded *On veut la paix* (We Want Peace), added to the power of the cultural response. The whole experience reflected what Morgan terms 'an immense musical wealth', without which 'the global reaction to Mali's crisis would no doubt have been equally sympathetic and widespread but possibly not as enchanted and empathetic as it has been' (for a fuller account, see ibid.: 47–52).[2]

Significantly, after the military defeat of the insurgent groups and their retreat to the mountains in the north, the restoration of cultural artefacts and institutions formed a very important part of the work of peacekeepers and peacebuilders, both local and international. Two of the World Heritage mausoleums and libraries housing 300,000 rare documents destroyed by insurgents in Timbuktu were rebuilt in 2014 by UNESCO, working in partnership with local communities, and MINUSMA was mandated, in addition to its political and security roles, to support the government in the preservation of cultural artefacts.

The case study of Mali demonstrates clearly that the destruction of cultural artefacts and assaults on cultural heritage and practices are fundamentally directed against the identity and values of the people and communities being attacked. Cultural heritage has been defined as a reservoir of identity and meaning for communities, and it is protected in three legally binding international treaties – the 1954 Hague Convention for the Protection of Cultural Property in the Event of Armed Conflict; the 1970 UNESCO Convention on the Means of Prohibiting and Preventing the Illicit Import, Export and Transfer of Ownership of Cultural Property; and the 1972 World Heritage Convention. UNESCO has called for the recognition of cultural heritage as an international security issue, and in post-conflict situations the restoration of symbols of cultural heritage forms an important part of the reconciliation process. The restoration of the Mostar Bridge, the image which forms the cover of this book, is another example of this.

Source: Morgan, 2013, and Stanca Mustea, 2013

Perhaps the most established use of music for peace is in the field of music therapy, which also, according to Maria Elena Lopez Vinader, has the potential to be used not only to alleviate illness in individual and group therapy, where it has been highly successful, but also as 'social music' therapy. Music therapy has matured as an acknowledged and effective form of psycho-therapeutic intervention since its emergence in 1945. There are a variety of recognized and tested methods, but Lopez Vinader points to the emerging work of a new network, Music Therapists for Peace, whose members are working on combining a specific therapeutic method (Logotherapy) with the peacebuilding training methodology of Galtung (the TRANSCEND Method) (Lopez Vinader, 2008). An example of a more case-tested approach is the GIM model (Guided Imagery in Music), which has been used to put clients into 'a deep state of relaxation, which gives the possibility of entering into another state of consciousness, [allowing] the person to heal wounds from the past', under the guidance of the therapist. The method has been used by Vegar Jordanger as part of a reconciliation workshop between Chechen, North Ossetian and Russian participants. Jordanger described how music was used in the workshop to create a response of 'collective vulnerability' among the participants, which creates the space in which 'negative emotions, particularly unacknowledged shame and anxiety, may be transformed into positive emotions and possibly a state of flow in the group' (Jordanger, 2008: 137).

The theatre, too, has for long been a powerful force for the exploration and transformation of perception, understanding and feeling. Perhaps more than any other art form, it has been used, especially in Africa, South America and Asia, as an explicit tool for empowerment and peacemaking. As Richard Boon and Jane Plastow have argued, 'theatre, in a variety of forms and contexts, can make, and indeed has made, positive political and social interventions in a range of developing cultures across the world' (Boon and Plastow, 2004: 1). In a series of case studies, their book describes how theatre has in various forms confronted and explored issues from genocide, poverty, AIDS, violence, human rights, racial, sexual, and political intolerance, divided communities and the power of the state (ibid.: 1–12). Sometimes this movement for empowerment through theatre is guided by the theories, methods and philosophies of writers such as Augusto Boal and Paolo Freire, whose Theatre of the Oppressed and Pedagogy of the Oppressed, respectively, have inspired activists in radical theatre. However, Boon and Plastow have shown that the most vital forms of theatre for development, or theatre for peace and political engagement, are those which represent real lives, or theatre 'from below', as they describe it, echoing the values of peacebuilding from below, familiar in the literature of conflict resolution (see chapter 9). While they acknowledge that theory is important in analysing the uses, forms and impacts of theatre, avoidance of dogma is also crucial when the main aim is to produce learning and insight that genuinely comes from the communities, cultures and contexts which the theatres serve. Perhaps appropriately for advocates of transformation through theatre, Boon and Plastow link their analysis to the positive power of human action and creativity. Summarizing the various case studies in their book, taking in community theatre in cultures as diverse as Northern Ireland, the UK, the US, South Africa, Ethiopia, South Asia and India, they say 'we were repeatedly struck by the power of joy as an agent of transformation'. Theatre in this form shares something that it has in common with the arts in general, with the visual arts and music surveyed in this chapter and, as developed below, also with sport. Boon and Plastow express this well: 'Creativity is joyous ... [and] ... the pursuit of happiness is likely to be a human right, which, once glimpsed, will not be lightly discarded' (ibid.: 12). This captures the sense of invigoration that the political dimension of conflict resolution can gain by widening its horizons to engage with the creativity that is permanently available in the arts and popular culture. This links in turn to a different connection between drama, conflict and conflict resolution in the context of game theory, where Jim Bryant has shown how drama theory can be used as a model to explore and simulate options for individuals engaged in collaborative decision-making even in a context of potential or actual conflict (Bryant, 2003).

Sport and Conflict Resolution

While sport is not in itself an obvious primary vehicle for conflict resolution, there are many examples where different sports and sportspeople have explicitly worked in a conflict resolving manner, and where sport has been seen as a bridge-building activity and an alternative to violence and destructive conflict. In presenting the potential conflict resolving potential of sport, it is once again recognized that there are aspects of sport in general as a global commercial enterprise that do not fit comfortably with the values of conflict resolution. In the first place, in its most heavily commercialized aspects, it is a male-dominated activity. Second, it is often sustained by and associated with the marketing and advertising strategies of powerful multinational companies. Third, it can breed nationalistic and competitive sentiment and behaviour. On big sporting events and their impacts on political economy, see Grix and Lee (2013). Despite these concerns, however, sport also has the potential to unite and to inspire cooperation. For example, within the UN it is seen as being consistent with the objectives of the UN Charter:

> [F]rom indigenous sport to global sporting events, sport has 'convening power' ... Sport can contribute to economic and social development, improving health and personal growth in people of all ages – particularly those of young people. Sport-related activities can generate employment and economic activity at many levels. Sport can also be used for conflict resolution by bringing people together on common ground, crossing national and other boundaries to promote understanding and mutual respect. (UN Sport for Development and Peace, www.un.org/wcm/content/site/sport/)

The right to participate in sport is enshrined in the Convention on the Rights of the Child (1989) and the Convention on the Elimination of All Forms of Discrimination Against Women (1979), and the International Olympic Committee (IOC) has agreements with a range of UN agencies (UNICEF, UNHCR, UNDP, UNESCO) to use sport in support of refugees and others suffering in areas of conflict. The impact of sport and its potential to promote conflict resolution goals are illustrated here by reference to the Olympic Games and to football, the 'world game'.

The Olympic movement

The most famous and most universal sporting event in the world, the Olympic Games, began in ancient Greece with an Olympic Truce or '*Ekecheiria*'. According to some interpretations, the purpose of the original games was primarily to stop war between the Peloponnesian city-states, when a formal agreement was signed declaring that all wars should cease, arms should be laid down, and competitors and spectators be allowed to travel safely to and from the games. The modern games were revived by the French humanist and educational reformer Pierre de Coubertin, who founded the modern Olympic movement with the formation of the International Olympic Committee and the first games of the modern era, held in Athens in 1896.

The potential of the Olympic movement for peacemaking was described in October 2007 by the president of the International Olympic Committee, Jacques Rogge, as follows: 'Sport alone cannot enforce or maintain peace. But it has a vital role to play in building a better and more peaceful world' (www.olympic.org/). Although the Olympic Games are more popularly associated with heightened national passions as countries compete to outdo each other in the medals tables, the peace ethic in the Olympic Charter and Olympic history is often underestimated and undervalued. Yet its potential to motivate conflict resolution in the way indicated by Rogge is prominent in the Olympic Charter, which explicitly recognizes peace as a cardinal principle and objective of 'Olympism', and the second of six fundamental principles from the Charter states that 'the goal of Olympism is to place sport at the service of the harmonious development of man, with a view to promoting a peaceful society concerned with the preservation of human dignity.'

While these statements signify noble aspirations, they have been given more substance in the past ten years by a commitment of the International Olympic Committee to revive the idea of the Olympic Truce, and to support and stimulate initiatives in support of peace, conflict resolution and reconciliation. For example, in July 2000, the IOC launched the Olympic Truce Foundation and the Olympic Truce Centre 'to promote its peaceful principles into concrete action' (www.olympictruce.org).

For the conflict resolution community, there are significant opportunities for engagement and partnership in support of the programmes launched by the Olympic Truce Centre which to date have not yet been fully realized. They offer refreshingly new and exciting prospects for conflict resolution by linking sport and peacemaking. Advocates of the extension of the Olympic Truce are not naive and do not see the idea as a panacea, but they do argue that it can use the power of sport both to be a 'peace-inspiring tool for our age' and to exploit opportunities afforded by the Olympic movement and its resources. The Olympic Truce movement has invited partnership arrangements with civil society organizations and NGOs to pursue the practical objectives as expressed in box 16.2.

Box 16.2 Conflict resolution through the Olympic Truce

The Olympic Truce Foundation (OTF) and the Olympic Truce Centre (OTC) build up educational programmes that seek to activate a culture of peace through sport and the Olympic ideal, motivating the development of grassroots initiatives in favour of the Olympic Truce and serving the fundamental educational mission of Olympism. Through their educational programme:

- they formulate a 'knowledge bank' on the Olympic Truce, by developing educational and research programmes in cooperation with academic institutions worldwide;
- they disseminate the values of Olympism and the Truce in schools and universities;
- they organize cultural activities in favour of peace;
- they bring academic contributions together through the organization of conferences and seminars;
- the Foundation and the Centre seek to foster the support of the civil society through the creation of 'Truce Action Kits' that educate and involve the general public in the objectives and projects of the Olympic Truce.

Through their truce building activities, they:

- provide support, through sport and the Olympic ideal, in cooperation with relevant national and international organizations, in areas facing armed conflict;
- provide, together with their partners, humanitarian support to countries in conflict;
- activate the support of international and national organizations for the observance of the Olympic Truce;
- organize sport and symbolic Truce events in areas of tension;
- organize sporting events, youth camps and round tables on sport and a culture of peace.

Source: www.olympictruce.org

The commitments embedded in the charter and policies of the IOC, linking the ideals of the movement with the values of peace and conflict resolution, are also widely reflected in the policies of key UN agencies (IOC, 2007), particularly since the adoption of UN General Assembly resolution 48/11 of 25 October 1993. These commitments have had some practical impact, beginning, for example, with an effective ceasefire that allowed ten thousand children to be inoculated in Bosnia in 1994 (Lambrinidis, 2002).[3]

Football and conflict resolution

In the same way that the Olympic Games are perhaps more often associated with nationalism than with peace, football is seen as a global business with grossly and even obscenely overpaid celebrity star players. At the top level of the game this may well be true, and we must exercise caution about claims that football or any other sport can resolve conflict or build peace. Andrew Rigby provides a good critical overview of the ways in which sport is claimed to help the process of conflict resolution (as character building, as displacement for aggression, as bridge-building between divided societies, as resistance to oppression and occupation) and concludes that it is inherently a force neither for good nor for evil, but that conflict resolvers may find ways and situations where sport can *help* the process of peacebuilding (Rigby, 2008).

This is certainly the case in relation to football, and there are many and, for some perhaps, surprising ways and places where football has been used potently to support peace, conflict resolution and internationalism. The Open University of Catalunya, for example, has signed a partnership agreement with the city's world-famous football club, FC Barcelona, whereby the club would make its support network available to promote the peace and development education programmes of the university. FC Barcelona, which itself served as a symbol of resistance to the oppression of the people of Catalunya under the rule of Franco, has made substantial and tangible contributions to campaigns for peace, solidarity, justice and social inclusion (Burns, 2000).

In 2006, the president of FC Barcelona, Joan Laporta, announced that the club would wear the logo of UNICEF on its team shirt, thus foregoing the practice normal for top football clubs to carry the logo of commercial sponsors. The FC Barcelona Foundation would pay 1.5 million euros annually to UNICEF to support its programmes.[4]

Very little research has been conducted about the effect and impact of this kind of involvement by football clubs on affected communties and on the process of conflict resolution and peacebuilding, but there is a developing literature which traces and analyses the growing extent of the use of sport for peace work. For football, recent literature and programmes have been described and analysed by Lea-Howarth within a framework of evaluation based on familiar concepts of peacebuilding as defined by Galtung, Lederach and others. Using case studies of grassroots football for peace projects based in Sierra Leone (World Vision International Youth Reintegration Training and Education for Peace), Israel (Football4Peace), Liberia (Bosco United Sports Association) and Bosnia Hercegovina (Open Fun Football Schools, Balkans and the Middle East), he concludes that, while much of the literature on peacebuilding agrees with the desirability of peacebuilding from below, practical ways of engaging in this process are often lacking. Sport and football provide one important and still under-used practical entry point for conflict resolvers and a dimension of activity that is transcultural and universal in its appeal (Lea-Howarth, 2006; Sugden, 2008; Gannett et al., 2014).

Specifically in relation to peace and conflict resolution promotion, FFCB (Foundation of Football Club Barcelona) has recently launched its 'FutbolNet' programme to teach the skills of dialogue and conflict resolution. FutbolNet is a project that attempts to educate children and young people via the promotion of the positive values that come from playing sport, in this particular case, football. During the 2011/12 season, the FC Barcelona Foundation developed this programme of social action in five areas of Catalonia: Banyoles, Olot, Salt, Santa Coloma de Gramanet and the neighbourhood of Carmel in Barcelona. At an international level, the project has also been developed in Rio de Janeiro (Brazil). In each area FutbolNet has worked with sixty young people identified by local social services as being socially vulnerable. The foundation has discovered the effectiveness of the programme of methodology with regard to social development through sport. The programme is based on a series of rules that produce social interaction between those taking part – it obliges them to understand one another and use the tools available to resolve conflicts and to get along. One of the main features is the absence of a referee, who is replaced by a 'teamer', a figure who accompanies the participants in the game without intervening. FutbolNet was inspired and developed from experiences in Colombia (in the context of the long conflict there and following the murder of the footballer Andes Escobar) and also via the organization streetfootballworld, which developed the original methodology of dialogue and mediation applied through football (Gannett et al., 2014). There are now many examples and case studies where football is used in peacebuilding and as a tool for strengthening social cohesion and social inclusion, including the Goals for Peace in Bucaramanga, Colombia, and in the flourishing football foundation and football in the community projects run, for example, by most professional clubs in the English football leagues (Woodhouse, 2014).[5]

Building a Global Peace Culture

We return here to the theme announced at the beginning of this chapter, namely the potential for cultural activities to reinforce the effectiveness of conflict resolution programmes. This potential can be realized at two levels: first at the macro-level, by nourishing the more long-term evolution of peace values embedded in the idea of a global peace culture (Reading 12), and, second at the micro-level, by the inclusion of cultural projects in the strategies of conflict prevention and peacebuilding.

Turning first to the macro-level, the idea of a culture of peace was founded on a number of important events and initiatives during the 1980s, which attempted to provide a unifying philosophy for the disparate strands of the work of the UN around promoting human rights and development, justice and solidarity, and gender equality, where peace was the unifying core value. Thus an International Congress on Peace in the Minds of Men, held in Yamoussoukro, Côte d'Ivoire, in July 1989, called for the construction of 'a new vision of peace culture', and in May 1986 an international group of natural and social scientists working in fields as diverse as evolutionary theory, genetics, ethology, neurophysiology and social psychology was convened in Seville in by the Spanish National Commission for UNESCO. Their findings were published as the Seville Statement on Violence, which declared that war was a cultural and not a biological construction (although see the controversy about this outlined in chapter 6). The Seville Statement provided a theoretically persuasive basis for the idea of promoting a global peace culture and was subsequently adopted by UNESCO (www.culture-of-peace.info/history/page2.html; Adams, 1989)

The empowering nature of peace culture became increasingly recognized during the 1990s. In 1997 the General Assembly of the United

Nations, anticipating the new millennium, declared the year 2000 to be the International Year of the Culture of Peace and followed this in 1998 by declaring a manifesto for an International Decade for a Culture of Peace and Non-Violence for the Children of the World. This was the result of the convergence of three initiatives, all of which had strong support in Latin American countries and in Africa: the proposal for the International Year of the Culture of Peace, the proposal for a UN Declaration and Programme of Action on a Culture of Peace, and an initiative of Nobel Peace Laureates called the Campaign for the Children of the World (United Nations, 1998).

The main impact of the commitment to a global peace culture by UNESCO was twofold: first, to emphasize the value of peace as a positive experience and value in everyday life, not only as a negative definition of the absence of violence; and, second, to accelerate and promote interest in the cultural dimensions of peacebuilding generally.

This brings us to the micro-level options for engaging cultural action in conflict resolution programming. There are many cultural programmes and arts-based initiatives, often sponsored by international organizations, to promote recovery at grassroots level after conflict. The Japan Foundation has provided one of the few research programmes to date which has attempted to classify and locate the work of these projects within a broad spectrum of peacebuilding and conflict resolution activity, both in preventative and in postwar interventions. Box 16.3 summarizes this work.[6]

Box 16.3 The role of cultural initiatives in peacebuilding

Conflict prevention

Confidence building by mutual understanding, tolerance and trust-building, and awareness-raising – through publishing picture books, concerts, library support, literacy classes, early childhood education, peace education

In conflict

Support for cultural activities designed to assuage feelings of loneliness and hopelessness, giving hope, putting pressure on conflict parties, demonstrating inhumane aspects of the conflict region – through exhibitions, photography, plays and performances

Post-conflict first stage: humanitarian aid

Culture as catalyst for care of trauma – through psychological and drama workshops, support for refugee and community sports, library and learning resource support

Post-conflict second stage: reconstruction

Support for reconciliation through cooperative drama workshops and performance, multi-ethnic orchestras and music, IT education, emotional aid through art therapy workshops, music therapy workshops, theatre workshops, confidence-building for people coming out of conflict trauma though vocational training, restoration of cultural heritage sites, landmine avoidance education, activities to 'sense' peace, peace museums, peace prizes, peace education

Source: Gakuin, 2009: 1; see also Japan Foundation, 2008

While this classification provides an example of a preliminary attempt to systematize understanding of the role of the arts in conflict resolution, Michael Shank and Lisa Schirch have called for more work to be done to strategize the potentials of arts-based peacebuilding. Drawing on Lederach's *Moral Imagination* (2005), which places the creative process at the centre of conflict resolution, they argue for the need to understand the strategic 'what, when and how' questions: that is, what the arts contribute to peacebuilding, when in the conflict cycle different art forms can make a contribution, and how they make that contribution. They point out that communications theorists calculate that anything up to 93 per cent of all communicated meaning is non-verbal, yet the dominant mode of action adopted by conflict resolution is to encourage people to talk. If much of what is important in human interaction is communicated non-verbally, then arts-based peacebuilding, drawing on the creative arts commented on in this chapter, is clearly at present underutilized within the field of conflict resolution and provides exciting opportunities for engagement in the future (Shank and Schirch, 2008).

Conclusion

This chapter has argued for a place for the arts, sport and popular culture in conflict resolution as a means of energizing the field by liberating the imagination and the emotions in pursuit of creativity in peacemaking. Conflict resolution would be diminished as a field of academic and practical endeavour if this were ignored. It has been possible to give only a limited number of examples here, and many more could have been offered from the visual arts, from music, theatre and sport, as well as from the richness of literature, cinema, photography, dance, sculpture, and so on, not touched on in this chapter (Rowe, 2008; Knight, 2014; Grau, 2013; Gesser-Edelsburg, 2011). Johan Galtung has expressed, with his usual imaginative insight, what is important about all these creative arts in their relationship to peace:

> Art and peace are both located in the tension between emotions and intellect ... Life unites what concepts and dualisms keep apart. And art, like peace, has to overcome such false dichotomies by speaking both to the heart and to the brain, to the compassion of the heart and the constructions of the brain. (Galtung, 2008: 60; see also Readings 49, 71)

RECOMMENDED READING

Boon and Plastow (2004); Gannett et al. (2014); Grix and Lee (2013); Lederach (2005); Shank and Schirch (2008); Sugden (2008); Urbain (2008).

VIDEO

Goals for Peace Bucaramanga, Colombia, at www.goalsforpeace.com/video/ [Spanish with English subtitles].

WEBSITES

The International Network of Peace Museums, at www.museumsforpeace.org/, contains links to visit the websites of many of world's leading peace museums.

The United Nations International Decade for a Culture of Peace 2001–2010, www3.unesco.org/iycp/

Theatre, peace and conflict at Theatre without Borders, www.theatrewithoutborders.com/peacebuilding

Global Peace Film Festival, www.peacefilmfest.org/

International Olympic Truce Centre, www.olympictruce.org/

Football 4 Peace International, www.football4peace.eu/contact.html

RELEVANT EXTRACTS IN *THE CONTEMPORARY CONFLICT RESOLUTION READER*

Reading 12: E. Boulding, Building a Global Civic Culture: Education for an Interdependent World

Reading 49: A. Curle, Peacemaking Public and Private

Reading 71: W. Dietrich, Peace Studies: A Cultural Perspective

CHAPTER SEVENTEEN

Conflict Resolution, the Media and the Communications Revolution

Communications are a central part of how societies constitute themselves. Whether there are no communications or universal communications, they shape the ways conflicts are conducted and the potential for conflict resolution. The modern communications revolution, affecting existing media such as journalism, television and radio and creating new decentralized networks of instant and cheap knowledge and information transmission globally, is having a transformative effect, both on the nature of conflict and on that of conflict resolution. This chapter examines the role of the media in conflict resolution and, in the second part, explores the potential of the World Wide Web to become a technology for conflict resolution. In their excellent edited survey *Communication and Peace: Mapping an Emerging Field*, Julia Hoffmann and Virgil Hawkins describe how, although there has been considerable emphasis on the 'contribution of the media to processes of conflict escalation', the topics of 'de-escalation, conflict transformation, reconciliation and processes of pecebuilding and peace formation' still remain a cinderella subject:

> [T]he crucial function of the mass media for positive change, social cohesion, the development of democratic politics, and even reconciliation and peace, is increasingly being recognized. It remains, however, lamentably under-theorized. Popular culture; new technologies that enable and conduct data flows that increasingly connect (parts of) us; legacy news media formats; radio soap operas; public information and social marketing campaigns; SMS; satellite imaging – all of these dynamics are relevant for the study of peace, yet they have largely been left out of the mainstream peace and conflict studies literature. (2015: 8)

Jack Lynch points to the distorted image of reality in media reports constructed by 'the operation of conventions' such as 'frequency' (media deadlines dictate what counts as a 'story'), 'threshold' (numbers of deaths in Africa have to reach a much higher threshold to count as news than numbers of deaths in Europe or the US) and 'negativity' (bad news crowds out good news) (2015: 17). This overall neglect applies particularly to the role of 'local media' within what Roger Mac Ginty and Oliver Richmond call 'the local turn in peacebuilding' (2013: 763; see also chapter 9).

The Mass Media and Conflict Resolution

In Burundi, not long ago, there were two villages with no communications between them. Guards from one of the villages looked out upon the other across the valley and saw a helicopter landing there. They were alarmed. What did the helicopter signify? They warned their neighbours. The villagers prepared to defend themselves. In the other village, people observed these preparations and began to fear an attack. They too made preparations to defend themselves. The guards in the first village observed these. Deciding the other village was about to attack, they launched a pre-emptive attack. Several people died in the resulting fighting. When all the villagers were finally able to speak to one another, they learned that the helicopter had come to take away a pregnant woman to hospital.

Mobile phones are now sweeping through Africa, as will be noted later in this chapter, and mobile phones might have prevented this incident. A conflict resolution initiative in Burundi has managed to train as many as 8,000 local leaders in conflict resolution, in workshops and retreats.[1] Mobile phones are used to communicate to the local leaders who, in turn, use phones to communicate to their constituencies. In this way, one in a thousand of the Burundi population has been involved in conflict resolution workshops – such a high proportion that the re-entry problem virtually disappears. In this way, modern communications have transformed the scope for conflict resolution.

But, in the Congo, the same mobile phones are used to sell minerals and purchase arms on global markets. They enable militia leaders to participate directly in global markets, and so transform the scope for financing armed conflicts.

Mass communications have always been a two-edged sword. On the one hand, they inform and educate, and this can empower and unite; on the other hand, they also divide people and turn them against each other. Newspapers created the mass society, helped to educate and inform its citizens, and established a literate public opinion. But, by fostering nationalism, projecting an image of the world seen from a national point of view, and creating a means of national mobilization, they played their part in the events which led to the great wars of the twentieth century. Modern television can bring different elements of a global conflict with unprecedented immediacy and range, explaining the perspectives of the decision-makers in conflict and bringing together the separate elements of a crisis with extraordinary speed, vividness and detail. But at the same time TV images can mobilize communities, serve as tools of propaganda, and propagate assumptions or simplifications that ignite wars.

In conflicts, people view others through the prism of pre-formed perceptions, stereotypes and 'enemy images', as Chris Mitchell (1981a) explains. In modern societies, the mass media filter the news people receive and influence our perceptions of ourselves and others. They can readily reinforce the

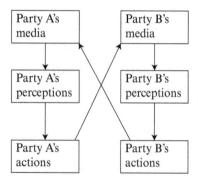

Figure 17.1 *The role of the media in conflict*

psychological processes which characterize group conflict: selective perception, the quest for cognitive consistency, and rejection of information that does not fit an existing picture. We can thus modify Mitchell's diagram of perceptions in conflict (ibid.: 124) to include the media, as in figure 17.1.

It is easy to see from figure 17.1 how crucial the role of the media is in shaping either a constructive or a destructive response to conflict. Good journalists are well aware of this. They stress the importance of reporting all sides of a story, pursuing an independent, critical and objective approach, exploring the context and background, and using multiple sources of evidence.

Even so, it is difficult for journalists to avoid the influence of their own societies' collective outlook. They operate within a media environment in which the relevance of a particular news item is determined by a social and political process. Ultimately, what counts as news depends on its relevance to a home audience, those who pay to receive the media's output. While well-run media insist on the principle of editorial independence, it is difficult for the media to ignore the agendas of the corporations to which they are accountable. Even if the media are able to be critical towards their governments, they remain highly sensitive to the prevailing political culture, which they help to constitute. In an age when the media are global, the political communities they serve remain divided. We speak of the global media, but few truly global media exist.

The media therefore shape the information environment in which conflicts develop, are fought and are settled (Carruthers, 2000; Thussu and Freedman, 2003). The tendency for the media to see conflict from one side is well known, especially when national media are reporting on a war in which their own country is engaged. Analysts have documented this in the case of the British media's reporting of the Falklands War and western reporting of the Gulf War (Allan and Zelizer, 2004). More insidious, perhaps, are the ways in which the modern media industry influences the reporting of all conflicts. Owing in part to a herd effect and in part to current news values, the media tend to focus on a limited group of conflicts at any one time and, even then, mainly on new or dramatic episodes of violence that count as breaking news. The preference for visual, moving images adds to the preference for the violent and the photogenic over longer-term and deliberative explanations. Armed conflict is more likely to produce sensational images than peacemaking and peacebuilding, which tend to be carried on confidentially, away from the limelight. There is, therefore, a bias in reporting of violence over the measures to end or mitigate violence. In turn, the 'CNN effect' makes politicians, publics, NGOs and funders focus on the particular conflicts that are most in the news. The glaring, but fast-moving and ultimately superficial spotlight of world media attention, combined with 24/7 coverage and the preference for television over printed media, has intensified the trends for the international community to concentrate on the 'hot' crises on which everybody else's attention is also engaged.

Meanwhile, the global media have formed such an important arena for influencing publics that war itself is adapted to influencing that audience. As Ignatieff (2000) suggests, this leads to a kind of 'virtual war', in which decisive events are not those which turn the battlefield but those which sway the domestic audience.

Alongside the global media industry, recent technological trends are enabling a much wider participation in media creation. Cheap mobile phones with inbuilt cameras enable virtually instantaneous reporting from scenes of conflict anywhere around the world. This creates wider awareness of conflict but also allows for much faster mobilization and spread of involvement. The internet enables a new virulence of propaganda and the dissemination of news with little editorial control. The cheapness and accessibility of media also enable more media outlets to flourish, to supply a more fragmented market, and this creates the potential for extremist views to reach wide audiences. Radio Mille Collines in Rwanda was a warning of the dangers of an unregulated, open media market.

Yet, despite their overwhelming focus on violent conflict, there is also a growing potential for peacemaking through the modern media. They can not only serve an informed public by reporting the news responsibly and objectively but also play an active role in promoting a constructive approach to conflicts.

Some even argue that journalists are in a position to play a conflict resolving role, using their unique access to bring parties together, to foster talks, and to promote exploration of positions (Baumann and Siebert, 2001). Certainly journalists are able, sometimes, to set the agenda and frame the way issues are discussed. They can tone down language, clarify positions and underlying interests and needs, and explore potential ways forward that might be agreeable. In many ways they can act like mediators, but they do so in public and in a forum in which decision-makers from different sides are accustomed to being heard together. Just after 9/11, for example, a British television programme brought together audiences in Pakistan, Britain and the US to discuss the events – a type of 'workshop' that, if handled sensitively, can span continents and add to mutual understanding (see box 17.1).

Box 17.1 Principles for responsible journalism in conflicts

The following principles for responsible journalism in conflicts are drawn from the work of Lynch and Galtung (2010) and others.

- Avoid simplifying conflicts by presenting them as two sided when many sides are involved; cover the differences within the parties. Show that there are multiple goals involved, thus opening the scope for a range of outcomes.
- Avoid presenting conflict as a contest between good and evil.
- Give full coverage to peace initiatives; explore how conflict can be transcended.
- Use precise language, avoiding emotive words and demonizing labels ('terrorist', 'extremist', etc.).
- Explore common ground and shared goals.
- Counter misperceptions; provide accurate information.

It is not surprising, then, that supporting constructive journalism has become one of the major forms of responding to conflict. Practising journalists 'have a tremendous potential to contribute to understanding and bridge-building', argues the International Federation of Journalists (Rejic, 2004: 324–5).

An example of such journalism is the work of the multi-ethnic radio station Ijambo in Burundi, supported by the conflict resolution NGO Search for Common Ground. The Ijambo project was launched as a counter-example to Radio Milles Collines in neighbouring Rwanda. Hutus and Tutsis staff the radio station and report on events together. The journalists are careful to check stories and question rumours and have gained a national reputation for their balanced approach to news and commentary and their even-handed reporting (Austin et al., 2004: 308).

External donors are still happy to support such initiatives. Workshops for journalists are still taking place in Burundi and other African countries with support from the EU and major national development agencies. George Soros has poured resources into supporting independent news media in Central and Eastern Europe.

What has been the long-term impact? As always with conflict resolution initiatives, it is difficult to trace the outcomes. In Bosnia, for example, the support of Soros did not prevent politics from continuing to be dominated by the nationalist parties. The media themselves criticize the West for policies which encourage the nationalists and cut across support for media and human rights. There is little doubt, though, that the presence of serious, independent and critical media, even if not a politically dominant voice, makes an important change in many transitional and post-conflict societies. The key challenge for such organs is to ensure they are sustainable when external funding is withdrawn.

Some recent reviews rightly warn of the dangers of uncritical reliance on the principle of 'press freedom' in conflict situations (parallel to the concerns about assumptions about the 'modernizing paradigm of development' and possible 'imperial' overtones of 'peace education' discussed elsewhere): 'However, there is also forcible criticism of an overly simplistic reliance on liberal media theories and the strength of the "marketplace of ideas" – especially when it comes to fragile states emerging from crisis and conflict' (Hoffmann and Hawkins, 2015: 8). Vladimir Bratic (2015: 159) extends this to the 'non-journalistic' media effort in general, where the main theoretical criticism is of 'over-reliance on individual change theories, which presuppose that change is a matter of individual choice for people who are of equal status and in command of their cultural environment. This is rarely the case; and, therefore, culturally contextual theories of change must be brought into consideration to improve practice in the future' (see also Betz, 2015).

More generally, Virgil Hawkins sums up the challenge:

> This highly selective nature of news production raises several important questions pertaining to conflict and peace in the world. To what extent is coverage of the violence phase of conflict selected over the non-violence phase? And when peace is covered, which regions are being covered and which are being marginalized by the media? What are the gatekeepers letting slip and why? (2015: 52)

An example is international media coverage in Kenya, where Ross Howard notes how the 'critical evaluation came in March 2013, in the month of the Kenyan national election. The event went exceptionally calmly, with media coverage being some of the most restrained in Kenyan history – despite the political parties' attempts to appeal to tribalism during their campaigns' (2015: 71). Nevertheless, 'many had a sense that foreign journalists were interested in bearing witness to bloodshed and not a peaceful election process; that they had come to cover the elections because they were *expecting* violence to break out, as it had in the wake of the 2007 elections' (Hawkins, 2015: 57).

Nevertheless, it is also possible to find many examples of constructive journalism in areas of conflict. The journalistic profession upholds the values of independent, critical and questioning approaches and aims to instil them in trainee journalists, however challenging the industrial environment may be. The second part of this chapter explores the latest transformation in global communications, the rapid spread of the internet and the World Wide Web, which we see as an exciting new technology for conflict resolution.

Conflict Resolution in the Age of Cybertechnology

In the third edition of this book, we acknowledged that the work of our fifth generation of conflict resolvers would take place in a world that is changing rapidly, most especially under the impact of global information communications technology (ICT). The field of peace and conflict studies has been radically affected by the impact of ICT in such a way that traditional distinctions between national, international and local levels of activity are being eroded and the basis for a global partnership for peacebuilding is being constructed.

The internet opens up a uniquely global or cosmopolitan space, which peace-makers can use as a potent tool and environment within which to educate, advocate and problem-solve (Levy, 2004). The communications revolution provides a technology for peace unparalleled in history, and the main developments in this ICT-driven revolution, as they affect conflict resolution, are outlined below.

It has been a constant concern of peace researchers and peace activists throughout the modern era that new scientific and technological knowledge has frequently been appropriated to advance the military power of states and also the lethality and efficiency of military systems in general. In the early years of the twenty-first century, the same phenomenon seems to be about to repeat itself as the massive processing capacity of new information and communication technologies is applied to the revolution in military affairs (RMA), where precision-guided and automated weapons systems threaten a new era of automated war. The impetus for this shift in the concept of warfare came in part from the dramatic military superiority of US forces in the first Gulf War against Iraq in 1991, the war in Kosovo in March 1999 and the 2003 invasion of Iraq, where what were regarded as conventionally strong enemies were defeated by a twenty-first-century American military with overwhelming superiority in satellite, communications and weapons technology, with zero or very limited battle losses of soldiers or equipment to their own or allied forces. What Michael Ignatieff (2000) termed 'virtual war' had become a reality. Warfare and conflict have entered the domain of what is now labelled cybernetics and cyberspace, a global virtual interactive space linked in an electronic network of rapid communication technologies. The mathematician Norbert Wiener developed the concept of cybernetics in the late 1940s, drawing on game theory and general systems theory and concerned to research the science of the human and electronic interface. Wiener's work on this was published in 1948 as *Cybernetics: Control and Communication in the Animal and the Machine*, which suggested a concern with feedback loops and second-order learning systems that would later enter the conflict research domain – for example, through the work of John Burton, who also saw conflict resolution in the world system of international relations as a process of controlled communication (as we have seen in chapters 2 and 4).

Wiener's concept of cyberspace served to inspire those pioneers who later went on to develop the concepts of cybernetics into the virtual electronic world of the internet when it was invented as the ARPANET in 1969. In what is now a well-known story, the pioneers of the internet were funded through the US Defense Advanced Research Project Agency (DARPA) in a strategic response by the Eisenhower administration to the threat of Soviet leadership of the space race and the perceived danger posed from their nuclear weapons systems. The remit of the DARPA researchers was to ensure that the communications infrastructure of the US would survive any nuclear or space-launched attack. The resulting decentralized 'survivable' computer network became the internet and, in a later phase of evolution, which we consider below in relation to its potential as a medium for peace, the World Wide Web (Wiener, 1948; Naughton, 1999; Nayar, 2004).

Perhaps predictably, from its origins, the internet is now a global site where conflict is conducted, but, as we will argue below, it is also a massively but presently under-utilized yet powerful tool for conflict resolution. Initially seen as an information 'superhighway', the internet now, through the ease of access and the interactivity and creativity enabled by the World Wide Web, is a global space not only for information sharing and email communication but also for new media, social networking sites, user-centred and collaborative resources such as wikis and blogs, e-commerce, globally accessible e-learning and so-called e-cademies, fourth-party dispute resolution (the use of the internet to mediate disputes online), and more (Hörnle, 2009; Katsch and Rifkin, 2001). In the past ten years new terminologies for conflict conducted through the internet, such as netwars and cyberwars, have been used to describe the impact of the revolution on conflict and conflict dynamics (Healey, 2013; Singer and Friedman, 2014). From a conflict research perspective, for example, Athina Karatzogianni (2006) has defined and analysed these new forms of conflict generically as cyber conflicts, and there is a whole sub-set of associated terms, such as cyber-attacks, cyberwar, cyberterrorism, cyberwarriors, cyber-security, and so on. Cyber conflicts have already been fought on the internet in disputes between Russia and Georgia and between Russia and Estonia, using cyber-attacks to compromise their opponent's computer and communications network. Analysts and experts are so concerned about the militarization of cyberspace that they now talk of it as the next 'warzone'. Rex Hughes has shown how the US, the UK, India, China, Russia and South Korea have begun to form command and control (C2) systems for military action in cyberspace, while a range of non-state actors, from al-Qaeda to the Zapatistas, are well established there. In recognition of the potential level of threat, Hughes has argued for a Treaty for Cyberspace to control and regulate interstate cyber conflict (Hughes, 2010; Parker, 2009). Since 2004 there has also been a Cyber Conflict Studies Association, which has research programmes focused on, for example, the impact and use of cyber-conflict methods by transnational actors – including the question 'How will the variety of trans-state actors (*jihadists*, anarchists, political activists, criminal organizations, etc.) differ in their approaches to the possibilities for cyberwar?' and 'How might cyberwarfare influence approaches to peacekeeping and peacemaking?' (www.cyberconflict.org). As noted in chapter 11, by 2015, 'cyber-*jihad*' and 'electronic-*jihad*' had entered the lexicon as analysts began to explain the rise of Islamic State and its use of the internet and social media to recruit supporters for its caliphate (see box 17.2).

Conflict resolution has clearly come a long way since Lewis Fry Richardson's research data was rediscovered in the early 1960s stored on microfiche film – the early inspiration for the 'founders' of the field, as described in chapter 2.

Box 17.2 Cyber-*jihad* and countering violent extremism (CVE)

Bin Laden had realized the power of the internet to promote al-Qaeda as early as 1997, and the organization's current leader claimed in 2005: 'we are in a battle and more than half of this battle is in the media. In this media battle we are in the race for the hearts and minds of our Umma.' Islamic State has now surpassed al-Qaeda in its appeal to disaffected Muslims and has taken its use of social media to new levels. Christina Shori Liang explains their success as follows:

> Today, IS has brought cyber jihad to a whole new level, evolving from static websites, chat forums, and online magazines to making efficient use of today's interactive and fast-paced social media platforms. While Al Qaeda and its affiliates see the internet as a place to disseminate information and meet anonymously, IS followers are loud and noisy, tweeting, streaming and Instagramming their exploits. Terror is now being transmitted across the globe in real time. IS is an active user of blogs, instant messaging, video sharing sites, Twitter, Facebook, Instagram, WhatsApp, Tumblr and Ask FM. Their media campaign underscores that terror can be streamed and sold with graphic images, audio messages, and music. This highly successful campaign is an effective tool for psychological operations and for recruitment. Social media is the most popular medium for young people to communicate today. It is trendy, interactive, and is populated by a very young and sometimes naïve demographic. The IS crisis has become one of the most documented and socially-mediated conflicts in history.

Through the sophisticated use of social media (YouTube, Facebook, Twitter), IS has been able to create a 'wireless caliphate' to convince young men and women that it is the 'winning brand' and that they are joining the 'winning team'. It has also created a new media wing, the Zora Foundation, designed to attract younger women through projecting the idea of supporting their 'brother fighter' and having 'jihadist children'.

In the past few years there has been a response to this propaganda by developing greater knowledge and capacity for countering violent extremism (CVE) online. UNSCR 2178, passed in September 2014, called for greater cooperation on CVE issues, including measures to prevent terrorists from exploiting social media. A number of public- and private-sector initiatives have been mounted to enhance CVE, some of which are listed below. One group, calling itself Anonymous, is a global 'hacktivist' project that has declared 'war' on IS in cyberspace, declaring the intention to counter and shut down IS social media websites, in a move that Christina Shori Liang has described as 'the first recorded wars by non-state actors battling it out in cyberspace'. What follows is a selection of 'anti-extremist' websites.

- Against Violent Extremism (AVE) – Google Ideas and the Institute for Strategic Dialogue connect former extremists, survivors and projects to exchange and disseminate information to tackle violent extremism.
- Al-Sakina – Online repository of information and intervention programmes to answer questions on Islamic belief and to bring radicalized individuals back into the mainstream.
- The Clarion Project – An independently funded, non-profit organization dedicated to exposing the dangers of Islamic extremism while providing a platform for the voices of moderation and promoting grassroots activism.
- Global Center on Cooperative Security – Works with national, regional and international stakeholders to promote holistic and integrated responses to violent extremism that underscore the critical importance of human rights, the rule of law and community engagement.

Box 17.2 (continued)

- Global Survivors Network – Provides a platform for survivors of terrorism to share their experiences in their own words, working to spread their messages in vulnerable communities.
- MyJihad – Promotes a moderate understanding of the term *'jihad'* and derives a new user-generated, centre-ground narrative on matters of religion and faith.

Source: Schori Liang, 2015: 2; also available at www.gcsp.ch/Emerging-Security-Challenges/Publications/GCSP-Publications/Policy-Papers/Cyber-Jihad-Understanding-and-Countering-Islamic-State-Propaganda

But the opportunity to engage with and utilize the full power of the web for the resolution of conflict still lags behind the efforts of those who are using it rather to conduct and intensify conflict. The rest of this chapter provides an overview and some examples of how the web can be conflict resolution 'friendly', and also how better understanding and uses of cyberpeace can advance the real-world cause of non-violent conflict transformation (Karatzogianni, 2006; Halpin et al., 2006).

From Cyberwar to Cyberpeace

The internet is inherently neither a weapon of war nor a weapon of peace. Although its origins as an operational electronic communications system lay, as we have seen, in military R & D programmes and needs, the ideals and values of some of its key innovators were centred around human needs and aspirations and international, global and cosmopolitan values. Norbert Wiener's mathematical genius, for example, was initially applied to solving problems that would enable the military to guide a weapon to a target, but he became increasingly disaffected with the appropriation of scientific research for military purposes and refused to join the Manhattan Project, which between 1942 and 1945 developed the knowledge that led to the atomic bomb. Following a period of association with the philosopher, mathematician and pacifist Bertrand Russell, Wiener became increasingly concerned with the ethics of scientific research and the potential of cybernetics to advance the human uses of scientific discovery (Wiener, 1988). The power of the internet as a force for enabling human progress and social change was also an explicit concern of the inventor of the World Wide Web, Tim Berners-Lee. As a physicist working in the CERN laboratory in Switzerland at the end of the 1980s, Berners-Lee developed the World Wide Web as a massive enhancement of the ease of use and the interactive power and creativity of internet computing. His ability and knowledge as a scientist combined with his decision not to exploit his revolutionary innovation for commercial gain, but to make it freely available as a public good, placed Berners-Lee firmly in the tradition of those who saw the positive transformative and emancipatory power of the internet and the web. He described his aspirations for what he hoped the web would provide in a manner that reflects the cosmopolitan ethics and values that permeate this book:

> Suppose all the information stored on computers everywhere were linked, I thought. Suppose I could programme my computer to create a space in which anything could be linked to anything. All the bits of information in every computer at CERN, and on the planet, would be available to me and anyone else. There would be a single global information space. (Berners-Lee, 2000: 4)

In November 2009, Berners-Lee, who sees the web not as mere technology but, in the spirit of early cybernetics, as 'humanity connected by technology', launched the World Wide Web Foundation in order to 'advance the Web to empower humanity by launching transformative programs that build local capacity to leverage the Web as a medium for positive change' (www.web-foundation.org). Once again, the cosmopolitan conflict resolution sentiments are evident.

We are not able to provide a comprehensive survey of how the web might serve the real-world goals of global peacemaking through the kind of transformative programmes and local capacity-building called for by Berners-Lee, but we can indicate how projects and programmes are evolving in ways which suggest that cyberpeacemaking, and what we term cyberconflictresolution, are emerging to form one of the most exciting new areas for conflict resolution praxis. At the global level, the UN has become a norm-setter, keen to follow the transformative potential of cyberpeacemaking, as indicated in box 17.3.

There is an explosion of activity and innovation around cyberpeace projects. The social networking site Facebook has a 'Peace on Facebook' area, still in the early stages of development, that measures friendships and connections made by members across national, religious and ethnic divides and polls members daily on attitudes to achieve peace. Other sites such as openDemocracy.net

---

Box 17.3 The UN as cyberpeacemaker

On 10 December 2003, using the original computer on which the Internet was created, United Nations Secretary-General Kofi Annan sent an electronic message to young people around the world urging them to keep communicating with each other and to build bridges of understanding between cultures and societies. At the World Summit on the Information Society (WSIS), the secretary-general sent his message to students participating in the World Summit Event for Schools, a three-month-long initiative, co-organized by the UN CyberSchoolBus and European Schoolnet, offering online activities to students in order to look at the effect of communication technologies on education and human rights. Tim Berners-Lee said he hoped that everyone could use the web to realize that 'other people are just like ourselves, even if they speak different languages or have different abilities'. 'I believe it is important to preserve our local cultures and languages', he added. 'We must also share enough understanding planet-wide to bring peace.'

Source: UN News Centre, at www.un.org/apps/news/story.asp?NewsID=9157&Cr=wsis&Cr1

provide intensive coverage of global issues around security, peacebuilding and democracy. The Conflict Information Consortium at the University of Colorado has an extensive web-based resource with gateways to eight key programme specialized areas: Beyond Intractability on complex conflicts; CRInfo on tractable conflicts; CETR on conflict education and training systems; Conflict Frontiers; How to Stop the Fighting; Online Courses; Cultures of Peace; and a Civil Rights Mediation Oral History Project. The consortium has 'pioneered efforts to use rapidly advancing information technologies to provide people from all walks of life with the information that they need in order to deal with conflicts more constructively' (http://conflict.colorado.edu/).

Similar resources exist for peacebuilding (such as the Peacebuilding Portal at ww3.peacebuildingportal.org), while online dispute resolution and e-mediation services are also expanding rapidly, usually in the form of alternatives to court-based processes in commercial disputes, especially in the US but increasingly also in Europe (Katsch and Rifkin, 2001; Hörnle, 2009).

With this level of activity and excitement about the potential of the World Wide Web to facilitate peacemaking in various ways, there is a sense of optimism and confidence that the transformative impact of the web is only in its early stages and presents an unparalleled opportunity and challenge for conflict resolution globally, especially among younger people who are growing up to be web-literate and who are aware of its power. The cosmopolitan political theorist Daniele Archibugi sees ICT as key to the prospects for cosmopolitan democracy (see chapter 11), while, ten years into the development of a worldwide networked society and approaching the new millennium, Jon Katz wrote optimistically about the revolutionary political transformation taking place, led by the emergence of what he termed the 'digital nation' and its 'digital citizens', or 'netizens', acting outside the US political mainstream:

> The people rushing toward the millennium with their fingers on the keyboard of the Information Age could become one of the most powerful political forces in history. Technology is power. Education is power. Communication is power. The digital young have all three. No other social group is as poised to dominate culture and politics in the twenty-first century. (Quoted in Nayar, 2004: 175)

At that time Katz's 'digital young' were, as he recognized, largely young Americans and, we could argue, more generally young people from the global North. The web provides the potential for the kind of transformation its idealists hope for, but the world of cyberspace also replicates and in some senses may accentuate the power disparities and exclusions of the non-cyber world of politics and economics. The 'digital divide' is well recognized and acknowledged as a solid barrier to the participation in knowledge sharing and knowledge creation that forms the core of the transformation project aspired to by Berners-Lee and the web idealists. Indeed some critics go further than complaints about exclusion and interpret the expansion of the information revolution via ICT as a new form of colonialism. For example, Castells has written about a Fourth World composed not only of regions such as sub-Saharan Africa and parts of South America and Asia but also of the ghettos of many of the cities of the developed North, where 'information capitalism' has 'oppressed, stigmatised, criminalised, sick and illiterate persons' excluded from the knowledge and benefits of the digital revolution (quoted ibid.: 183). In an extension of this view, and echoing the discourse of older forms of colonialism, the language of the promoters of the information revolution 'is about "frontiers" and "new territories" and "worlds"' – reminiscent of the era of colonial expansion at the expense of indigenous peoples (Sardar and Ravetz, 1996).

The virtual world of cyberspace is, therefore, contested and conflictual in much the same way as the 'real' world is, but the challenges are the same in the sense that the emancipatory agendas of conflict resolution apply as much to cyberpeacemaking as to 'conventional' peacemaking. Berners-Lee has been conscious of this from the earliest years of connecting the web. His World Wide Web Foundation works to open access to the net and to democratize it. In the following section we explore the recent expansion of ICT, the transforming impact it is having on conflict resolution, conflict analysis and peacebuilding, and the challenges and opportunities presented.

In the rest of this chapter these questions are addressed further by examining six themes in particular – the global digital divide; developing ICT for peace; the mobilization of peace constituencies; big data analytics; peace drones; and ICT for conflict and peace education – each of which will define the degree to which ICT may be successfully utilized to promote the values and processes of cosmopolitan conflict resolution.

Pacifying Cyberspace in the Age of the Zettabyte: Challenges and Opportunities

Addressing the global digital divide

When the third edition of this book was published, in 2011, we presented figures based on a 2009 survey which showed that only 25 per cent of the world's population accessed the web and that 35 per cent of the world's population lived in regions with low internet penetration, regions which not surprisingly correspond closely to the zones of conflict we noted in chapter 2. By January 2014, world usage had grown by 10 per cent, to 35 per cent (see figure 17.2). While South Asia, Africa, South-East Asia, Central Asia and Central America lagged behind, when all forms of digital connectivity (internet, social media and mobile phone connectivity) are included, the picture points to an increasingly interconnected world. In 2014, 93 per cent of the population of the world were connected via mobile phone network and 26 per cent via social networking platforms; 67 per cent of the population in Africa, 72 per cent in South Asia, 90 per cent in Central Asia used mobile phones, and in South-East Asia there were more mobile phones than people. With 2.5 billion people

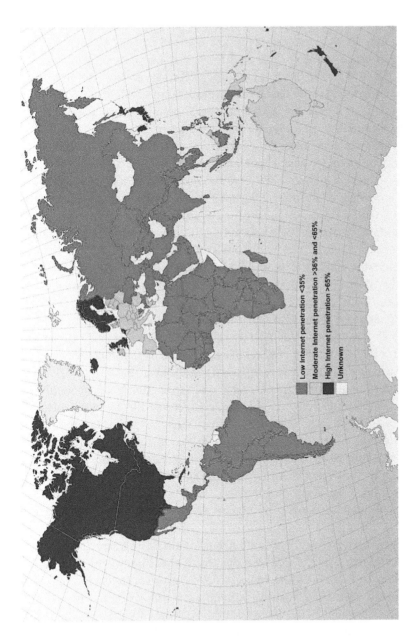

Map 17.1 *Internet usage worldwide, by region, 2014*

connected on the web, 1.9 billion on social media platforms, and 6.5 billion of the world's 7.1 billion people using mobile phones, the single global information space envisaged by Tim Berners-Lee is now very much in evidence.

The capacity of global digital technology to store and disseminate information has grown at a corresponding rate. Cisco Systems, the California-based corporation that designs and manufactures web-based networking technologies, has estimated that data carried across the web globally by the end of the twentieth century, merely one decade after the invention of the web, was about 12 exabytes of human-produced information and communications media. Expressed more concretely, 1 exabyte can hold 36,000 years of HD video. In the projection of Cisco and other monitors of web growth, the web will pass another huge marker of expansion when, by 2015–16, it will be measured not in exabytes but in zettabytes. A zettabyte is some 1,000 exabytes, and we are about to enter what Cisco analysts have termed 'the dawn of the Zettabyte era'. In 2009 the whole of the web was estimated to have reached 500 exabytes, or one half of a zettabyte. By 2013 it had grown again to contain 4 zettabytes of data (Arthur, 2011). These figures provide a measure of the capacity to store data, or information, technologically and electronically. To put this into perspective, the UNDP has pointed out that, in the year 2012 alone, humans generated more data than had been the case over the course of their entire history (Mancini, 2013: iii). In addition to the capacity to store data, there has been a corresponding, though somewhat slower, revolution in the power to disseminate or broadcast it. The capacity to broadcast information stood at nearly 2 zettabytes in 2009. If we compare 'old' print media with new electronic media, this is the equivalent of every person on the planet receiving 174 newspapers every day of the year (Hilbert and López, 2011).

This rate of growth and the processing and dissemination capacity of information and communications technologies (characterized by laptops, tablets, mobile phones, social media, crowdsourcing, crisis mapping, blogging, big data analytics, web-based open access data, web-learning platforms, and so on) is truly an epic shift or revolution equivalent to or greater than the industrial revolution of the nineteenth century, and the agricultural revolution before that, in its speed, range and global impact.

In the league table of numbers of internet users by country, by 2014 China had the largest number (642 million), with 22 per cent of the total and more than the next three largest users combined (US, India and Japan). In the top twenty-five countries, in addition to India, Brazil and Turkey (which are difficult perhaps to classify as developing), Nigeria, Mexico, Indonesia, Egypt, the Philippines, Vietnam, Colombia, Argentina, South Africa and Iran also feature. Of course, many of the countries in the bottom fifty are in Africa, but Africa also has the faster growth rate. Between 2011 and 2014 all regions of the world showed a double-digit growth rate of internet usage, but over the same period Africa stands out, with a growth rate of over 40 per cent – twice as high as the global average. By the end of 2014, mobile-broadband penetration in

Africa had reached almost 20 per cent, up from less than 2 per cent four years earlier (Livingston, 2011).[2] The gender gap is also narrowing. In 2004, Nayar cited research showing that 69 per cent of internet users were young males.[3] By 2013, 41 per cent of all men were online worldwide, compared to 37 per cent of all women.[4]

Nevertheless, despite clear trends of widening access globally, a digital divide remains. The rapid expansion of digital connectivity in Africa masks real differences regionally and by country. Eritrea, for example, only has 5 per cent mobile phone penetration, and poor and marginalized people and communities continue to be excluded from digital communications. To balance this, however, there is also an increasing number of inspiring examples of ICT-driven initiatives to bridge the divide and make knowledge and information available to excluded groups. Worldreader is a project established in 2009 to tackle the problem of global illiteracy – there are 750 million illiterate people in the world and 250 million primary school children who lack basic reading and writing skills. Worldreader supports literacy particularly in Africa. The project exploits the relatively low costs of digital technology and mobile phone networks, using a specially designed mobile app to promote literacy and to disseminate knowledge via e-readers and e-book libraries, which would otherwise be inaccessible to African communities. By 2015 Worldreader had reached readers in thirty-nine countries, providing them with more than 11,000 titles in forty-four languages (www.worldreader.org/).

New frontiers: developing ICT for peace and conflict resolution

Within the context of the expansion of the unparalled power, storage capacity, dissemination speed and data-analytic qualities of the internet at the 'dawn of the zettabyte era' referred to above, a key challenge is to ensure that as much as possible of this virtual digital space is placed in the service of conflict research and peacemaking by continued development of digital peace technologies. The literature on this and the emergence of supporting websites is also developing. The World Summit on the Information Society in Geneva in December 2003 (referred to as the Tunis Commitment) declared a commitment

> to build a people-centred, inclusive and development-oriented Information Society, premised on the purposes and principles of the Charter of the United Nations, international law and multilateralism, and respecting fully and upholding the Universal Declaration of Human Rights, so that people everywhere can create, access, utilize and share information and knowledge, to achieve their full potential and to attain the internationally agreed development goals and objectives, including the Millennium Development Goals. (World Summit on the Information Society, wsis-05/tunis/doc/7-e, 18 November 2005, at www.itu.int/wsis/docs2/tunis/off/7.html)

The ICT4Peace Foundation was established in 2006 to raise awareness of the Tunis Commitment and specifically 'to enhance and facilitate improved, effective and sustained communication between peoples, communities and stakeholders involved in conflict prevention, mediation and peace building through better understanding of and enhanced application of Information Communications Technology (ICT) including Media' (http://ict4peace.org/; see also Diamond, 2010). The ICT4Peace Foundation provides one of the most comprehensive resources for understanding how peace technologies will transform the field of conflict resolution in ways that will make it unrecognizable to the founders and those who have worked in the field as academics and practitioners over the past fifty years. In this section we review some of the initiatives and developments that are already driving this transformation, but it is important to recognize both that those covered below represent only a small range of examples and that ICT impacts on conflict resolution are likely to accelerate rapidly, quantitatively and qualitatively in the coming years.

Mobilizing peacebuilding constituencies

Larry Diamond mentions one of the first dramatic demonstrations of the power of digital mobilization (text messaging, Twitter, Facebook, YouTube, WhatsApp) by:

> vast networks of individuals who communicate rapidly and with little hierarchy or central direction in order to gather (or 'swarm') at a certain location for the sake of protest. In January 2001, Philippine president Joseph Estrada 'became the first head of state in history to lose power to a smart mob,' when tens of thousands and then, within four days, more than a million digitally mobilized Filipinos assembled at a historic protest site in Manila. Since then, liberation technology has been instrumental in virtually all of the instances where people have turned out en masse for democracy or political reform. (Diamond, 2010: 78)

Examples of this are now well known: the Orange Revolution in Ukraine (2004); the Cedar Revolution in Lebanon (2005); protest for women's political rights in Kuwait (2005); the Saffron Revolution in Burma (2008); the Green movement in Iran (2009); and the Umbrella movement in Hong Kong (2014) (ibid.: 79–80).

In Africa, where, as we have seen, 67 per cent of the population use mobile phones, open source software such as FrontlineSMS enabled large-scale, two-way text messaging purely via mobile phones. We have seen in chapter 3 how this led to the breakthrough innovation in the case of the Ushahidi system, using crowdsourcing to track real-time events to provide crisis or conflict maps to help prevent conflict (Reading 72). However, younger researchers in particular, who are engaging in this work at the front end of systems design and implementation, are cautioning against uncritical acceptance of the positive impacts of web-based and social media technologies on people in conflict areas. Gwyneth Sutherlin, for example, has identified the problem of cultural misfit 'in the technological union of humans and software, known as *crowdsourcing*, to manage the flood of information produced during recent crises'. She analysed four crises – in Haiti (2010), Egypt and Libya (2011), and Somalia (2011–12) – where design flaws resulting from linguistic and cultural differences resulted in poor decision-making by international actors (Sutherlin, 2012). Her concern is that, in the pursuit of quantifiable aggregate data to produce conflict maps, for instance, international agencies involved in conflict resolution and humanitarian work strip out local context and narrative, a problem compounded by cultural misunderstanding and failure to translate communications from the ground (the source) to the data source managers. The problem encountered in traditional or non-digital conflict resolution is replicated by conflict managers in the digital crowdsourced world. As a result there is a major barrier to democratic participation inherent in much of the cognitive design of ICT software and in data gathering and analysis. This is a salutary warning not to take the 'transformative power of technology' for granted.[5]

There are nevertheless increasing examples of locally sourced and culturally contextually rooted uses of ICT for violence prevention. In Latin America, now one of the most digitally connected regions of the world, a variety of grassroots networks across the continent have emerged that report and share information on various types of violence.

> In Brazil there are blogs that actively reflect on violence prevention measures in recently pacified slums, or favelas, of Rio de Janeiro. Community residents, many of whom are now purchasing tablet computers and smartphones and actively using Facebook, are tracking trends. Other ICT tools designed to prevent sexual violence and developed outside of Latin America, including Hollaback!, are establishing chapters in the region. Two other prominent examples are Say No to Violence, a social-mobilization platform established in 2009 and connected to UNiTE and Bem Querer Mulher (Cherish Women), supported by UN Women ... new ICTs are routinely emerging that explore ways of enhancing the protection of women and girls from violence in Brazil, Colombia, and Mexico. (Mancini, 2013: 37–8)

Big data analytics and peace and conflict datasets

We noted in chapter 2 the aspiration of conflict researchers to develop large datasets focused on conflicts in order to provide some capacity to observe patterns and regularities in conflict over time. This would make it possible to predict the outbreak of conflict and so to fashion conflict prevention and early warning. In chapter 3 we saw how, by the end of the twentieth century and into the present, there was a proliferation of these datasets, ranging from those such as UCDP Uppsala (which provides sophisticated cumulative datasets on conflict occurrence, intensity and location) to those such as the *Global Peace Index* (which provides data on the variables and qualities that sustain peaceful communities). In recent years, because of the huge increase in the storage and processing power of electronic/digital technology, another transformation is occurring, referred to as *big data analytics*, which has been applied in a number of areas – though little to date has been developed in relation to peace and conflict research. The promise of big data analytics is the potential to provide predictive capacity much more accurately and powerfully than is possible from the datasets currently in use. Put simply, big data means the aggregation and analysis of information from a large range of relational databases into a single source which may be applied across all fields – science, climate and environment policy, healthcare, natural disasters, astronomy, simulation scenarios, and so on.

In March 2014 the UK government announced the formation of the Alan Turing Institute to enable commercial organizations and academics to advance methodologies and technologies for big data analytics. The United Nations Global Pulse programme is using big data analytics to support research and policy formation in the areas of development and climate change. As for peace and conflict research, we noted in chapter 3 that, despite the impressive advances made in development, there are limitations to existing databases. We also suggested ways in which these might be overcome – principally in the merging of datasets to provide richer information across the spectrum from positive to negative peace, from measuring direct violence to providing indicators of structural and cultural violence, and from measuring and understanding the positive correlations between these measures and variables that sustain peaceful societies (see figures 3.1 and 3.2 pp. 71, 83). Big data analytics promises one way of approaching this, and readers may follow developments in the use of big data in conflict resolution on the Big Data and Crisis Mapping area of ICT4Peace, at http://ict4peace.org/ict4peace-big-data-and-crisismapping-magazines-on-flipboard/.

Peace drones and unmanned aerial vehicles (UAVs)

The use of drones and remote control warfare has stimulated a strong debate and an understandably adverse reaction in a wide spectrum of world opinion in recent years, with human rights groups, humanitarian agencies, peace organizations and think tanks expressing concern about their use.[6] However, an intriguing alternative to their use in warfare has also been explored in the idea that drones might be – and indeed are – employed for a variety of non-military purposes, in the form of conflict and crisis mapping, human rights surveillance, conservation monitoring, and even specifically as a peace multiplier in UN peacekeeping operations (Dorn, 2011). The first application of drones within a UN peacekeeping mission occurred in 2006 in the Democratic Republic of Congo and to monitor the movement of armed groups along the borders of Sudan, Chad and the Central African Republic. The next significant extension of the use of 'peacekeeping drones' occurred in 2013, when the UN Security Council agreed that the mission in the DRC (MONUSCO) should be allowed to employ them, not only for surveillance but also in support of an intervention brigade mandated to neutralize and disarm groups which posed a threat to state authority and civilian security. In a pioneering study of peacekeeping drones, based on an examination of their use within MONUSCO, Karlsrud and Rosen (2013) listed a range of advantages that drones could deliver within peacekeeping: surveillance to protect civilians; improved access to vulnerable populations in high-risk conflict areas; monitoring and responding to human rights violations; stealth surveillance of spoilers and militias; and monitoring obligations under international law. Put in this way, the prevalent image of 'killer drones', associated especially with American military uses in the 'war on terror', might be countered by a more positive image of drones operating for humanitarian and conflict resolution/peacekeeping objectives. Karlsrud and Rosen point to the dilemmas of drones being employed in peacekeeping and the need for accountability and clarity about the ownership and use of data collected; they also mention the necessity of recognizing that remote surveillance by drones is not a substitute for political solutions and that their deployment must be strictly under UN control. Despite their call for caution, they conclude that, on balance and properly managed within the mission, drones can enhance the effectiveness of peacekeepers and that it may not be long before human rights groups demand that they be part of the standard package of peacekeeping – indeed, that *not* to have them may come to constitute a breach of international humanitarian law. Similarly, decisions not to use weaponized drones may be ethically questioned where mandates require peacekeepers to protect civilians physically threatened by armed violence.

However these debates and applications work out in peacekeeping, unmanned aerial vehicles (UAVs) are now being used widely in aspects of humanitarian work in conflict areas and in response to natural disasters. This has progressed to the degree that there is now a humanitarian UAV network, called UAV*iators*, which describes itself as 'global network of civilian and hobbyist UAV pilots who safely and responsibly fly UAVs to support peaceful, humanitarian efforts'. According to their foundation document, UAV*iators* would not fly in conflict zones. However, the ICT4Peace Foundation is also supporting research into the use of UAVs, and in November 2014 it organized a meeting with the Office for the Coordination of Humanitarian Affairs on their serviceability in conflict zones as well as the ethics of their suitability in delivering humanitarian aid (see http://uaviators.org and http://ict4peace. org/?p=3547#sthash.FhQ7ej7W.dpuf).

Technologies for education in peace and conflict resolution

We conclude this section with a comment on the power of the web to transform peace education through e-learning programmes, which can deepen and distribute knowledge about peace values and peacemaking, and which can serve to generate cosmopolitan open clouds[7] – open, that is, to new voices as well as to new knowledge. Ruth Firer (2008) is one who has argued strongly in favour of virtual peace education (VPE), suggesting that it has special advantages in locations of active conflict, where direct communication between learners in divided communities would be difficult – as is the case, for example, in the context of her case study, the Israeli–Palestinian conflict. In her overview of the advantages of web-based learning and VPE from her experience, four points in particular resonate with the argument of this chapter and contribute to an understanding of the evolution of an international peace education 'cloud' (see box 17.4).

Since Ruth Firer defined the set of goals and objectives for web-based education in conflict resolution and peace studies (in 2008), the field has been affected by a further wave of change which is digitally driven and challenging traditional territorially based institutions. On the one hand there are projects such as Worldreader, established in 2009 and noted above, which uses e-book technology to promote literacy, especially across Africa. Worldreader itself is part of a wider manifestation of the emergence of global open access learning in the explosion of what are termed MOOCs – massive open online courses. The term was coined in 2008 when the first course ('Connectivism and Connected Knowledge'), offered by the University of Prince Edward Island in Canada, went online. MOOCs proliferated in North America, with professors at Stanford offering their courses online. These were then developed commercially through MOOCs such as Udacity and Corsera. In response, noting the popularity of these courses, other universities, led by MIT, offered versions of their own courses via open online access. Within six years, most of the top US Ivy League universities offered MOOCs, and by 2014 over 5 million students were signed up for courses, with an average of 33,000 students per course. EDEX, for example, was started by Harvard and MIT and in 2014 offered 125

Box 17.4 Promoting virtual peace education

1 Face-to-face computer conversations and videoconference plenary meetings should come after the team or classroom establishes collaboration and experiences joint learning. Such a gradual process that is carried out in stages gives the learners enough time to exercise methods of discourse among parties who differ deeply in interests and opinions (all the more so with enemies; see the unsatisfactory impacts of the traditional models). It is an effective way to teach and to exercise skills of conflict mediation and negotiation.

2 Learning from an international experience. Very often people who are fenced in their local conflicts are isolated from the world by their grievance and pain. VPE opens windows to other conflict zones where aggressive fighting has been successfully resolved, thereby giving hope to the participants. Learning from the experience of different people and being encouraged by others from different situations is very important for peace education learners and activists in the midst of bloodshed.

3 Preventive peace education. Individuals from non-violent societies have the chance to learn about the price of conflicts and the difficulties of practising peace education during open conflicts. It gives them a chance to enhance preventive peace education methods in order to avoid such hostile situations. It is especially relevant for societies facing difficulties of co-existence within democracies.

4 Global presence: all the models of peace education should be translated into VPE, creating a new community of peace activists, educators, researchers and learners. Such a virtual international peace school will eventually promote the global culture of peace.

Source: Firer, 2008

courses to 1.65 million students in more than 225 countries and territories. MOOCs still have some way to go to convince educators that they will ever provide the quality and depth of knowledge provided by conventional institutions and methods, but they are another indicator of the profound changes occurring in ICT, and conflict resolution and peace studies courses, although still underrepresented, are beginning to be offered.[8]

Conclusion

Ruth Firer's call for developing networks to evolve a virtual global peace education centre, the emergence of MOOCs and other open learning sites and platforms, the narrowing digital divide, the potential of big data applications in fashioning new datasets, and a variety of digital technologies for peace are all significant pointers to exciting new opportunities for conflict resolution. Such networks already exist and are being rapidly developed and extended. They will undoubtedly contribute greatly to the globalization of the field in the years ahead. Indeed, the nature, shape and future of all learning institutions are set to change under the forces of the ICT revolution. The World Wide Web is transforming not only technologies and knowledge but, as Davidson and her colleagues have argued, the process of learning itself:

> the single most important characteristic of the internet is its capacity to allow for a worldwide community ... to exchange ideas, to learn from each other in a way not previously available. ... [T]he future of learning institutions demands a deep, epistemological appreciation of the profundity of what the internet offers humanity as a model of a learning institution. (Davidson and Goldberg, 2009)

Learning institutions such as universities, where conflict resolution was conceived and evolved as an academic enterprise in the 1950s, will have to respond to and embrace the knowledge revolution driven by the internet and its cognate technologies if they are to remain relevant to the challenges of the twenty-first century. This is as true for conflict resolution as it is for learning (education and knowledge acquisition). So perhaps the biggest challenge for the media in general in a globalizing world is how and whether it can find a constructive, cosmopolitan and creative response to the global conflicts with which we are now faced. The media remain one of the institutions with the greatest potential for rising to the challenge of global conflict formations, but also one with great potential for fuelling global conflicts. How this tension plays out will be one of the litmus tests for the feasibility of cosmopolitan conflict resolution.

RECOMMENDED READING

Berners-Lee (2000); Diamond (2010); Healey (2013); Hoffmann and Hawkins (2015); Karatzogianni (2006); Livingston (2011); Naughton (1999); Nayar (2004); Rejic (2004); Singer and Friedman (2014).

WEBSITES

ICT4Peace Foundation, http://ict4peace.org/

Reports of the Global internet Society, www.internetsociety.org/doc/global-internet-report

Gwyneth Sutherlin, 'Open access or silent culture: ICT user experience in conflict', TEDxBradford, at https://www.youtube.com/watch?v=Fe421sryaVQ. We are grateful to Gwyneth Sutherlin for her guidance and advice on ICT issues and debates on peace and conflict and also her work on linguistics and culture as neglected components.

RELEVANT EXTRACTS IN *THE CONTEMPORARY CONFLICT RESOLUTION READER*

Reading 72: Ushahidi, From Crisis Mapping in Kenya to Mapping the Globe

Linguistic Intractability: Engaging Radical Disagreement When Conflict Resolution Fails

One does not make peace with one's friends. One makes peace with one's enemies.

(Rabin, 1996)

This chapter is about intractable conflicts and what can be done about them. Its focus is on the communicative dimension. It is drawn from Oliver Ramsbotham's book *When Conflict Resolution Fails: Engaging Radical Disagreement* (forthcoming, 2017). Intractable conflicts are those in which attempts at peaceful containment, settlement and transformation have so far failed (in 'frozen' conflicts there is a semblance of peaceful management, but this is superficial and is liable to break down again). We say 'so far' because it is always possible that such attempts will succeed in future, as systemic conflict transformation wants, and as has happened in many other cases. But 'so far' can go on for years, if not decades, during which time unimaginable destruction and damage to human lives and life hopes may be inflicted. What, if anything, can be done in these circumstances? Intractable conflicts have long preoccupied conflict resolution specialists (Kriesberg et al., 1989) and have now become a locus of renewed interest, as noted in chapter 2 (Burgess and Burgess,1996, 1997, www.beyondintractability.org; Mayer, 2009; Ramsbotham, 2010; Coleman, 2011; Little, 2014; Mitchell, 2014). The focus here is on how best to manage what Ramsbotham calls *linguistic intractability* and its chief verbal manifestation *radical disagreement*.

In light of the analysis in Part I, given the depth and complexity of contemporary transnational conflict, it is not surprising that conflict resolution recurrently fails. When this happens, as argued in chapter 1, the principle from the outset has been to invoke 'second-order social learning' and to change approach accordingly. This implies three main responses to the impasse:

- acknowledge it;
- understand it;
- adapt existing practice.

The case study used here to illustrate the argument is the Israeli–Palestinian conflict, fiercely resistant as it has been in recent years to all conventional

Table 18.1 Negotiation, problem-solving and dialogue

Conflict resolution approach	Negotiation for political accommodation	Interactive problem-solving	Dialogue for mutual understanding
Example	Principled negotiation	Problem-solving workshops	Hermeneutic dialogue
Third-party role	Mediation	Training	Facilitation
Aim	Getting to yes	Transform win–lose (= lose–lose) into win–win	Fusion of horizons
Radical disagreement seen as	Positional debate	Competitive debate	Adversarial debate

Source: Ramsbotham, forthcoming, 2017

conflict resolution efforts, particularly during the phase of maximum intransigence between the breakdown of the Camp David/Taba talks in 2000–1 and the aftermath of the breakdown of the Kerry talks in April 2014.

In conflict resolution in the communicative sphere, as noted in chapter 1, there are three main overlapping approaches – negotiation for political accommodation, interactive problem-solving, and dialogue for mutual understanding (see table 18.1). Negotiation for political accommodation is associated with conflict settlement, dialogue for mutual understanding is associated with conflict transformation, and interactive problem-solving – historically the core conflict resolution approach – bridges the two. So we begin by asking why the three approaches indicated in table 18.1 so far have not worked in intractable conflicts.

Linguistic Intractability and the Challenge of Radical Disagreement

The best way to see why conflict resolution fails in the communicative sphere is to look at what each of the three main approaches is trying to do.

Here is a famous account of what *principled negotiation* seeks to achieve, taken from the original edition of *Getting to Yes* (Fisher and Ury, 1981), still by far the best-selling book in the field (over 2 million copies sold in more than twenty languages) (Reading 46):

> The answer to the question of whether to use soft positional bargaining or hard is 'neither'. Change the game. At the Harvard Negotiation Project we have been developing an alternative to positional bargaining: a method of negotiation explicitly designed to produce wise outcomes efficiently and amicably. This method, called *principled negotiation* or *negotiation on the merits*, can be boiled down to four basic points. These four points define a straightforward method of negotiation that can be used under almost any circumstances. Each point deals with a basic element of negotiation, and suggests what you should do about it.

- People: separate the people from the problem
- Interests: focus on interests, not positions
- Options: invent multiple options looking for mutual gains before deciding what to do
- Criteria: insist that the result is based on some objective standard

... Each side should come to understand the interests of the other. Both can then jointly generate options that are mutually advantageous and seek agreement on objective standards for resolving opposed interests ... To sum up, in contrast to positional bargaining, the principled negotiation method of focusing on basic interests, mutually satisfying options, and fair standards typically results in a *wise* agreement. The method permits you to reach a gradual consensus on a joint decision *efficiently* without all the transactional costs of digging into positions only to have to dig yourself out of them. And separating the people from the problem allows you to deal directly and empathetically with the other negotiator as a human being regardless of any substantive differences, thus making possible an *amicable* outcome. (Fisher and Ury, 1981, original emphasis; see Reading 46)

The nature and aim of *interactive problem-solving* is succinctly summed up here by one of the pioneers in the field – Morton Deutsch:

In brief, the theory equates a constructive process of conflict resolution with an effective cooperative problem-solving process in which the conflict is the mutual problem to be resolved cooperatively. It also equates a destructive process of conflict resolution with a competitive process in which the conflict parties are involved in competition or struggle to determine who wins and who loses; often the outcome of a struggle is a loss for both parties ... At the heart of this process is reframing the conflict as a mutual problem to be resolved (or solved) through joint cooperative efforts. (Deutsch, 2000: 31)

And this is how the editors of a well-regarded review of *dialogic approaches* describe their purpose:

The most common dictionary definition of dialogue is simply as a conversation between two or more people. In the field of dialogue practitioners, however, it is given a much deeper and more distinct meaning. David Bohm went back to the source of the word, deriving from the Greek root of 'dia', which means 'through', and 'logos', which is 'the word' or 'meaning', and therefore saw dialogue as meaning flowing through us. Elements of this deeper understanding of the word include an emphasis on questions, inquiry, co-creation, and listening, the uncovering of one's own assumptions and those of others, a suspension of judgment and a collective search for truth ... [In contrast] a debate is a discussion, usually focused around two opposing sides, and held with the object of one side winning. The winner is the one with the best articulations, ideas and arguments. (Bojer et al., 2006: 10)

Why do these approaches not work in intractable conflicts? Let us consider each in turn in relation to three key examples from 2014: the situations in Gaza, Ukraine and Afghanistan.

In *principled negotiation*, 'each side should come to understand the interests of the other. Both can then jointly generate options that are mutually advantageous and seek agreement on objective standards for resolving opposed interests.' The key starting point is that conflict parties should set aside 'positional debate' or radical disagreement (what they say they want) and focus instead on their 'interests' (why they want what they say they want), which the conflict parties themselves may not realize, but which third parties can see to be the 'underlying reasons for those positions' (Fisher et al., 1994: 39). In relation to Gaza, however, the conflict parties are not ready to make this move. The Israeli position is that indiscriminate violence against Israeli citizens must cease. The Palestinian position is that the siege of Gaza and the occupation of the West Bank must end. The conflict parties are a long way from being prepared to 'jointly generate options that are mutually advantageous'. And what the 'objective standards' are by which the outcome is to be judged is also part of the ongoing battle. All of this is what makes it an intractable conflict. Principled negotiation may succeed in future. But at the moment it is premature, because its underlying assumptions do not yet apply.

Turning to Ukraine, how does *interactive problem-solving* relate? The idea here is to 'reframe the conflict as a mutual problem to be resolved through joint cooperative efforts'. The aim is also to begin by setting aside 'competitive debate' or radical disagreement in order to be able to do this. But, once again, this is not yet possible. The radical disagreement is the chief verbal expression of the ferocious struggle to determine the whole future orientation of Ukraine, torn as it is internally between different cultures in the East and West and externally between Russia and the EU/US (see case study in chapter 5). The radical disagreement cannot be set aside so easily. In these circumstances, whatever may become possible in the future, the ambition to move straight on to 'an effective cooperative problem-solving process in which the conflict is the mutual problem to be solved' is precipitate. The conditions are not yet in place.

Finally, there is *dialogue for mutual understanding*. How does this apply to the as yet intractable conflict in Afghanistan? Yet again, according to dialogic principles, 'adversarial debate' or radical disagreement is to be ignored. Indeed, in this case radical disagreement is seen to be the antithesis of dialogue itself. What is wanted instead, we are told, is 'an emphasis on questions, inquiry, co-creation, and listening, the uncovering of one's own assumptions and those of others, a suspension of judgment and a collective search for truth'. This is 'hermeneutic' (interpretative) dialogue along lines suggested in the philosophy of Hans-Georg Gadamer (see chapter 2 and Ramsbotham, 2015). The ultimate goal is a 'fusion of horizons' or the 'co-creation' of a new and expanded understanding. Here the Canadian philosopher Charles Taylor invokes hermeneutic dialogue in order to overcome cultural differences and to accommodate radically different ways of 'holding things true':

> For instance, we become aware that there are different ways of believing things, one of which is holding them as a 'personal opinion'. This was all that we allowed for before, but now we have space for other ways and can therefore accommodate the beliefs of a quite different culture. Our horizon is extended to take in this possibility, which was beyond its limit before. But this is better seen as a fusion rather than just an extension of horizons, because at the same time we are introducing a language to talk about their beliefs that

represents an extension in relation to their language. Presumably, they had no idea of what we speak of as 'personal opinions', at least in such areas as religion, for instance. They would have had to see these as rejection, rebellion, heresy. So the new language used here, which places 'opinions' alongside other modes of believing as possible alternative ways of holding things true, opens a broader horizon, extending beyond both the original ones and in a sense combining them. (Taylor, 2002: 287)

But how does this apply to the struggle between western-style democracy and the determination of the Taliban to resist this and impose shari'a in Afghanistan? Can we overcome this radical disagreement by setting it aside in favour of a premature 'fusion of horizons' in the way Taylor suggests? In the first place, does 'our' realization that there are 'other ways of holding things true' than as 'personal opinions' mean that we are therefore prepared for the imposition of shari'a that is based on these 'other ways'? If not, will 'they' not see this dialogic approach as a subterfuge in which 'our' horizon has not been expanded at all? Conversely, what does it mean to suggest that 'they' now realize that putting human 'opinions' on the same footing as the revealed word of God means that western secular and Islamic horizons are now 'combined'? It can be seen that the idea of a fusion of horizons is premature in those cases where its own underlying assumptions are at odds with what is in contention in the as yet continuing radical disagreement:

> Democracy means sovereignty for man. Islam means sovereignty for the *sharia*. In the American form of democracy any issue is allowed to be put to a vote of the people, and the majority decision prevails upon all. Can we Muslims put an issue that has already been decided for us by Allah up for a vote and accept the will of the majority if they vote against the will of Allah? Of course we cannot, so we can never accept democracy as defined, practiced and promoted by America. (www.Islamic-world.net/war/Islamic-world_position.htm, 2003)

This example shows how dialogue for mutual understanding can itself be seen to be based on assumptions that are part of what is in dispute. Is this not, for example, why many Muslims – and Christians – are opposed to ecumenicism? Dialogue for mutual understanding *depoliticizes* the conflict.

The phenomenon of radical disagreement is also discounted in other forms of discursive conflict transformation (see box 18.1).

So it is that, by underestimating and ignoring radical disagreement, the nature of linguistic intractability is itself often misinterpreted in conflict resolution – and, we will suggest, in the social, psychological and political sciences in general. The result is the recurrent failure of those conflict resolution approaches that are based on such as yet inadequate readings.

But, if that is the case, what is the alternative? We must invoke the principles of second-order social learning and turn from conflict resolution to conflict engagement.

> ## Box 18.1   How radical disagreement is discounted in transformative discursive approaches
>
> The same applies in most of the transformative discursive attempts to address systemic complexity, on the one hand, and asymmetric conflict, on the other (see chapter 2) – as, for example, in:
>
> *   *dilemmatic conflict transformation*, where John Paul Lederach advocates ignoring the false simplifications of radical disagreement in order to develop dilemmatic thinking:
>
>   We are not able to handle complexity well if we understand our choices in rigid either/or or contradictory terms. Complexity requires that we develop the capacity to identify the key energies in a situation and hold them up together as *interdependent goals* ... The capacity to live with apparent contradictions and paradoxes lies at the heart of conflict transformation. (Lederach, 2005: 53)
>
> *   *systemic complexity modelling*, where the verbal dimension is incorporated in the form of 'mental models' (see chapter 4). Ramsbotham (2010: 45–51) shows how, in systems perspective mapping, the phenomenon of radical disagreement does not appear, among other reasons because the aim is to dispel the verbal antagonisms associated with 'linear' thinking.
> *   *critical discursive conflict transformation*, where Vivienne Jabri, following Jürgen Habermas, wants to lift the entire realm of argumentation out of the sphere of radical disagreement, where the terrain is irrevocably saturated in power imbalances that favour the hegemon, and to reconstitute it on a terrain where rules dictated by the pure formal-pragmatic requirements of the theory of argumentation in relation to communicative action prevail (Jabri, 1996; Ramsbotham, 2010: 86–91, 149–56).

The Turn to Conflict Engagement

At this point we should make clear that, in looking at cases where so far conflict resolution approaches do not work, we are in no way disparaging those approaches. On the contrary, dialogue for mutual understanding, interactive problem-solving and principled negotiation achieve remarkable results. These are, indeed, the communicative foundations upon which conceptual and cultural peacebuilding are constructed. What follows is an outline of another approach – conflict engagement rather than conflict resolution – that can work when conflict resolution is premature and can help to prepare the ground for its appearance or return. This should be seen, therefore, not as a replacement but as another string to the bow – the promotion of conflict engagement is an extension of conflict resolution (see table 18.2).

A second disclaimer concerns the Israeli–Palestinian example used in this chapter. Evidently this quintessentially intractable conflict is made up of many elements at many levels and is a prime instance of the systemic complexity of transnational conflict. If it is eventually to be transformed, therefore, this will require change across sectors (economic, political, security, social, psychological) and levels (domestic, regional, global) that cannot be analysed here. An analyst such as Stefano Casertano (2015), for example, discounts the significance of the 'local' relation between Israelis and Palestinians entirely and traces the key determinants to Russian and Iranian regional machinations. Nevertheless, in the linguistic sphere we still think that the core task is to meet the challenge of the radical disagreement that lies at its heart. It can be argued that all the other dimensions in the end come down to this – including questions of relative balance of power.

In the turn from conflict resolution to conflict engagement, we will invoke the three stages of second-order social learning in turn: first, *acknowledging* what blocks the way, second, *understanding* it (heuristic engagement) and, third, *adapting practice* accordingly (strategic engagement).

Acknowledgement: Recognizing Agonistic Dialogue

We have seen how in communicative conflict resolution the radical disagreement at the core of linguistic intractability is dismissed as an 'all too familiar' and unproductive dead end, a terminus to dialogue that must from the outset be overcome, not learned from. Conflict resolution seeks to unravel the knot of intractable conflict. Radical disagreement is seen to tie the knot tighter.[1]

In acknowledging the challenge of radical disagreement, therefore, we have to look in the opposite direction. Instead of dismissing radical disagreement from the beginning as mere superficial 'adversarial debate', 'competitive debate' or 'positional debate', we should take it seriously as the main impediment to the whole conflict resolution effort in the linguistic sphere. We should recognize that, in intractable conflicts, despite the remarkable transformations achieved in individual dialogue groups and problem-solving workshops, these have not so far fed back into substantial change at the core. Most Israelis and most Palestinians, for example, have lost faith in these approaches after so many years of setbacks. Palestinians identify problem-solving and dialogue for mutual understanding with a normalization of oppression that ignores asymmetry of power. Many Israelis regard them as pointless in view of past Palestinian unreliability as they see it – and the greater urgency of other issues both domestic and foreign. Indeed, at the time of writing, in the run-up to 17 March 2015 Israeli election, the Palestinian issue as a whole seems to be marginal.

When confronted by radical disagreement, Morton Deutsch advises conflict parties to eschew 'competitive debate':

> Place the disagreements in perspective by identifying common ground and common interests. When there is disagreement, address the issues and refrain from making personal attacks. When there is disagreement, seek to understand the other's views from his or her perspective; try to feel what it would be like if you were on the other side ... Reasonable people understand that their own judgment as well as the judgment of others may be fallible. (Deutsch, 2000: 32, 35)

But what can be done when reasonable people do not do this, as in the case of most Israelis and Palestinians? What when conflict parties refuse to distinguish positions from interests and needs, resist reframing competition into shared problem-solving, and will not convert adversarial debate into constructive controversy? What when, instead, they directly challenge the very assumptions on which third-party conflict resolution approaches of this kind are constructed? This is not a rare event. It is the norm in the intractable conflicts that are most resistant to conflict containment, conflict settlement and conflict transformation. Acknowledging this is the first step towards finding alternatives.

To anticipate the next section, taking radical disagreement seriously shows that it is not 'all too familiar' but, perhaps, the least familiar feature of intense political conflict. Nor is it a terminus to dialogue but, on the contrary, the main characteristic of dialogue in intractable confrontations. Ramsbotham calls this 'agonistic dialogue', or dialogue between enemies: 'agonistic dialogue is that part of radical disagreement in which conflict parties directly engage each other's utterances' (2010: 254). Agonistic dialogue is nothing other than the war of words itself at its deepest level. The word 'agonistic' comes from the Greek word for struggle: 'agon'. It is not to be confused with 'antagonistic'. It has been made academically popular through Chantal Mouffe's 'agonistic' model of democracy (agonistic pluralism), although 'agonistic dialogue' means something somewhat different.[2] Agonistic dialogue is the dialogue of struggle.

As we move on to the second and third stages of second-order learning – understanding radical disagreement (heuristic engagement) and doing something about it (strategic engagement) – it is worth repeating that the aim of doing this is to *extend* conflict resolution, not abandon it (see table 18.2).

Understanding: Exploring Agonistic Dialogue (Heuristic Engagement)

What happens if agonistic dialogue – direct radical disagreement between conflict parties – is made the subject of enquiry according to the programme of heuristic engagement? The process is called *heuristic* because it involves *exploring* agonistic dialogue with the conflict parties as far as is possible (the word 'heuristic' refers to a methodology for discovery). After several years of investigating this, it has become clear that, despite the infinite variety of types of verbal exchange between individuals and across classes, cultures and genders, in radical disagreement conflict parties are nearly always found to be much further apart than had been supposed. This is a separate finding from all the work done on negotiation and dialogue across cultures and genders (Gulliver, 1979; Cohen, 1991; Augsburger, 1992; see also chapters 7 and 15). Indeed, the distance between conflict parties is often shown to be greater, not less, to the extent that cultural misunderstandings are cleared up – insofar as they can be. Radical disagreement *within* cultures can be more virulent than radical disagreement *between* them. In radical disagreement, conflict parties do not agree what the conflict is about. The disagreement

Table 18.2 Extended conflict resolution

How conflict engagement informs conflict resolution in intractable conflicts			
CONFLICT ENGAGEMENT →		**CONFLICT RESOLUTION**	
Starts where conflict parties are		Starts where third parties want conflict parties to be	
Heuristic engagement			
Takes radical Disagreement seriously		Sets radical disagreement aside	
Explores agonistic dialogue			
	strategic dialogue (SD)	→ **dialogue for mutual understanding (DMU)**	
Strategic engagement	↓		
Promotes strategic thinking within and across conflict parties, and by third parties	**strategic problem-solving (SPS)** →	**interactive problem-solving (IPS)**	Promotes cooperative thinking
		↓	
Shares the aim of conflict resolution, but links to strategic studies and engages reality, including threat power	**strategic negotiation (SN)** →	**principled negotiation (PN)**	Does not link to strategic studies and wants from the outset to transform existing political reality and reject threat power
Intractability	→		*Tractability*

Note: **The elements of conflict engagement in extended conflict resolution:**

Strategic dialogue explores agonistic dialogue in order to identify what blocks dialogue for mutual understanding.

Strategic problem solving, using the information from strategic dialogue, promotes strategic thinking within and across conflict parties, and by third parties, with a view to learning what is required for there to be interactive problem-solving in the first place. Strategic problem-solving clarifies what the problem is.

Strategic negotiation, in the light of strategic dialogue and strategic problem-solving, is focused on the preconditions for principled negotiation to be possible. It links strategic thinking within conflict parties to the strategic context that structures the scope for negotiations and informs third parties accordingly. It helps to clarify what is needed to promote 'ripeness'.

All three, taken together, make up a site where conflict resolution and strategic studies can mutually reinforce each other in addressing the most intractable conflicts. Conflict resolution takes on some of the methodology of strategic studies. Strategic studies takes on the normative goal of conflict resolution – how to reduce violence in international politics.

extends as far as the eye can see – issues and principles appealed to are themselves found to be already part of what is disputed. It reaches as deep as the distinctions invoked in the process of disagreeing – distinctions such as those between fact and value, opinion and reality, form and content, subject and object. These are implicated through contestation about such distinctions and what they do or do not distinguish (Ramsbotham, 2010: 109–32). Radical disagreement moves at lightning speed. From the outset, fact, value, emotion and action are fused into one – for Palestinians, for example, the *fact* of the Nakba (what happened in 1948), its *injustice*, the *emotion* of indignation, and *action* against it form a complex that cannot be disassembled and that erupts into the radical disagreement as a single entity. Such pre-existing fused complexes are what confront those wanting to resolve the conflict and are the chief linguistic barriers to the transformation sought by dialogue for mutual understanding.

All of this is related to the second discovery that comes from pursuing heuristic engagement by exploring agonistic dialogue – this time by comparing it with third-party descriptions and explanations. Surprising though it may seem, there is no adequate third-party theory or philosophy of radical disagreement (Ramsbotham, 2013). This can be illustrated by the following example.

Here is the editor's summary of the outcome of the impressive survey of *Israeli and Palestinian Narratives of Conflict* (as already illustrated in box 10.4, p. 304) (Rotberg, 2006):

> The Israeli–Palestinian conflict for primacy, power and control encompasses two bitterly contested, competing narratives. Juxtaposing the two justifying/rationalizing narratives helps us to understand the roots of the conflict and the differentially distorted prisms that fuel it. At the core of such narratives lie symbolic constructions of shared identity or collective memories, which do not usually so much reflect truth as portray a truth that is functional for a group's ongoing existence. Narratives are motivational tools.
>
> Both [narratives] need to be understood, reckoned with, and analysed side by side in order to help abate violence and possibly propel both protagonists toward peace. This is an immensely tall order. But the first step is to know the narratives, the second is to reconcile them to the extent that they can be reconciled or bridged, and the third is to help each side to accept, and conceivably respect, the validity of the competing narrative. What is required is a greater appreciation of two separate truths that drive Palestinians and Israelis, because this could plausibly contribute to conflict reduction. The lessons of this book are that the fundamental task of the present is to expose each side to the narratives of the other in order, gradually, to foster an understanding, if not an acceptance, of their deeply felt importance to each side. (Rotberg, 2006)

But neither Israelis nor Palestinians are saying that they refer to mere subjective 'symbolic constructions' that do not so much 'reflect truth' as portray a truth that is 'functional' for their ongoing survival. In radical disagreement this is categorically denied by all the conflict parties.

For Palestinians:

> Above all it is important to combat a central idea in the peacemaking discourse that what is at issue is two equivalent 'Israeli' and 'Palestinian' 'narratives'. No doubt there are Israeli and Palestinian narratives. But what is centrally at issue is not a mere Palestinian narrative, but a series of incontrovertible facts – facts of expulsion,

exclusion, dominance and occupation bitterly lived out by Palestinians day by day over the past 60 years and still being endured at the present time. This is not a narrative. It is a lived reality. Finding the best strategy for ending this lived reality is the main purpose of this Report. Transforming the discourse within which it is discussed is a major part of that effort. (PSG, 2008: 14)

The discursive battle is to make the Palestinian discourse the primary language within which the Palestinian issue is discussed, not because it is a narrative, but because it is *true*.

Nor do Israelis refer to a mere narrative; they point to a traumatic lived experience in which, since before 1948, Arabs have repeatedly refused a state of their own and have instead repeatedly assaulted Israel with a view to destroying it. References to rocket attacks on civilians from Gaza and the likelihood that this would be multiplied several times over if Israel also withrew from Judea and Samaria (the West Bank) silence most Israeli critics of current policy. As does the following extract from the Hamas Charter:

[Pro-Zionist forces] were behind the French revolution, the Communist revolution, and most of the revolutions throughout the world ... Concerning local and international wars ... they were behind the First World War in which they destroyed the Islamic Caliphate, picked the material profit, monopolized the raw wealth, and got the Balfour Declaration. They created the League of Nations through which they could rule the world. They were behind the Second World War, in which they became fabulously wealthy through the arms trade. They prepared for the establishment of their state; they ordered that the United Nations be formed, along with the Security Council, so that they could rule the world through them. There was no war that broke out anywhere without their hands behind it ... Today it is Palestine and tomorrow it may be other countries, because the Zionist scheme has no bounds; after Palestine they want to expand from the Nile River to the Euphrates. When they have occupied the area completely, they look toward another. Such is their plan in the *Protocols of the Elders of Zion*. That present is the best proof of what is said. (Hamas Charter, 1988: Articles 22 and 32)

Rocket attacks and the Hamas Charter are cited as *facts*. They are not just an Israeli *narrative* that serves a merely subjective function and does not 'reflect truth'.

More widely, the political, social and psychological sciences in general share similar reductionist assumptions about linguistic intractability – for example, by describing and explaining radical disagreements as:

- rationalizations of political interest
- social constructions
- psychological projections
- historico-cultural posits

and so on. There is nothing wrong with such descriptions and explanations within their own fields. They are no doubt true. But, in intense political conflicts, reductionist readings of this kind miss what is characteristic of radical disagreement. They explain radical disagreement *away* – as if radical disagreement were no more than a coexistence of equivalent pluralities within some supposed innocuous third space. But in intense political conflict there is no room for this. Radical disagreement is not a mere juxtaposition of subjectified attributions 'explained' by contextual conditioning. It is a fight to the death to occupy the whole of discursive space – and act accordingly. Box 18.2 contains an example of a radical disagreement between two contributors to *Israeli and Palestinian Narratives of Conflict*. This example does not conform to the editor's description. The speakers are not saying that their discourses coexist as equivalent 'separate truths' or that they are merely 'functional for group identity'. These are not just narratives *of* conflict. They are narratives *in* conflict. Both speakers are 'moderates'. Their verbal clash gives deep insight into the heart of the struggle. Before moving on to conflict resolution, therefore, the prior linguistic task is to understand this. What is required is a further development and exploration of the agonistic dialogue so that both parties genuinely engage each other and thereby uncover the otherwise hidden dimensions of their linguistic battle. This is what is blocking dialogue for mutual understanding (Ramsbotham, 2013: 58–60).

Box 18.2 An example of radical disagreement from *Israeli and Palestinian Narratives of Conflict*

The first speaker is Nadim Rouhana, a professor at the Fletcher School, Tufts University, and formerly the Henry Hart Rice Professor of Conflict Analysis and Resolution at George Mason University. The second is Mordechai Bar-On, a historian and former Israel Defense Forces chief education officer who was for many years a leader of the Peace Now movement.

> Israel will have to face at least part of the truth that the country that they settled belonged to another people, that their project was the direct cause of the displacement and dismantling of Palestinian society, and that it could not have been achieved without this displacement. Israel will also have to confront the realities of the occupation and the atrocities it is committing, and will have to accept that Palestinian citizens in Israel are indigenous to the land and entitled to seek the democratic transformation of the state so that they have equal access to power, resources and decision making, and are entitled to rectification of past and present injustices. (Rouhana, in Rotberg, 2006: 133)
>
> There are many historiographical faults in the way Rouhana tells the story … The main problem with Rouhana's thesis … lies in his sweeping conclusion that 'from the moment Zionism was conceived, force has been a central component of its relationship with the Palestinians' … Is it not possible for a Palestinian such as Rouhana to understand that, in 1948, the Jews of Palestine, to their chagrin, could not but use force to defend themselves and impose a solution that was legitimated by a majority of nations? … [T]here is no chance that I shall ever consider that my father and mother, who immigrated to Palestine as Zionists in 1924, were criminals. Nor do I consider my actions illegitimate when I gave the order 'Fire!' and perhaps killed or wounded assailants in response to an ambush on the troop that I commanded on the way to Tel Aviv in December 1947 … There is hardly any question that, in December 1947, the fire that later spread throughout the country was ignited at that time by the Palestinians. (Bar-On, in Rotberg 2006: 147–8, 167–8)

Action: Promoting Strategic Thinking within and across Conflict Parties, including Third Parties (Strategic Engagement)

Exploring agonistic dialogue has shown why conflict parties are not nearer, but much further apart than had been supposed. It has also shown why third-party descriptions and explanations that treat radical disagreements as a mere coexistence of equivalent subjectivities are inadequate. This uncovers the main reason why, so far, linguistic conflict resolution does not work.

So what can be done about this? How can practice be adapted accordingly? We move from heuristic engagement (understanding) to strategic engagement (practice). Instead of beginning *between* conflict parties, we begin *within* them. And instead of starting where third parties want conflict parties to be, we start with strategic thinking in which conflict parties ask where they are, where they want to go, and how they get there (see table 18.3).

This can be illustrated by the work of the Israeli Strategic Forum (ISF), the Palestine Strategy Group (PSG) and, more recently, the Palestinian Citizens of Israel Group (PCIG).[3]

Two main questions arise here. Why should conflict parties want to participate in such work at a time of intractability when conflict resolution gains no purchase? And how can this nevertheless help to maximize chances of a possible future revival of conflict resolution?

> *Why should conflict parties want to engage in strategic thinking when they are not ready for conflict resolution?*

The best answer to the first question is given by those involved in setting up the strategy networks. On the Palestinian side, for example, one participant described the process like this:

> Over the past several months, I participated together with a group of sixty Palestinians from all walks of life, men and women, on the political right and left, secular and religious, politicians, academics, civil society, business actors, from occupied Palestine, inside Israel, and in the diaspora. We were a group that is a microcosm that reflects the dynamics of Palestinian society. We could not all meet in one room anywhere in the world because of the travel restrictions that Israel has created. Nevertheless we continue to plan and to act. Our mission is to open a discussion on where we go from here: What are the Palestinians' strategic options, if any? After several workshops in Palestine and abroad and a continuous online debate, we have produced the first iteration of *Regaining the Initiative: Palestinian Strategic Options to End Israeli Occupation*, published in Arabic

Table 18.3 Promoting strategic engagement in intractable conflicts

Level 1	Promote strategic thinking within conflict parties
Level 2	Promote strategic engagement across conflict parties
Level 3	Clarify the roles of third parties

and English. The document is posted at www.palestinestrategygroup.ps and reflects an alternative to an official but impotent Palestinian discourse that will very shortly, in the judgement of most Palestinians, run head-on into a brick (cement) wall. (Sam Bahour, 30 August 2008)

Here is an assessment of the project by another participant:

> The overwhelming majority of the members of the project *Regaining the Initiative* are still in touch and extremely eager to further develop and continue the initial ideas they have agreed on and reached in their meetings and discussions. I have had the opportunity to speak with participants who are members of Fatah, Hamas, or women, student, academic, and human rights and democracy organizations. They all passionately agree about the desperate need to develop and sustain long term Palestinian strategic thinking. Indeed, this approach has already had a real major impact. A few months ago I received a phone call from a senior member of the Negotiation Support Unit (NSU) of the Palestine Authority informing me that the unit has discussed thoroughly the Palestinian strategy document and adopted several parts of it. (Bashir, 2009)

A major shift in Palestinian strategic thinking followed over the next five years in response to the challenge of prevailing predominantly right-wing governments in Israel, as outlined briefly below.

On the Israeli side a comparable inclusive network – albeit only of Jewish Israelis – undertook an exploration of options for the future of Israel, as described here by an Israeli participator:

> The main criteria for selecting the participants was that together they represent the major currents of thought in Jewish-Israeli society ... The group thus included several members of the Knesset with diverse political views, former heads of the security services (GSS, IDF), leading business people, key religious and spiritual leaders (ultra-orthodox, national-religious, [secular] Jewish renewal), prominent social activists, well-respected journalists, senior academics and various celebrities and publicly known figures ... To a large extent the group's thinking was led by the assumption that internal cohesion is the key to resolving the problems of Israel's Jewish population ... This is as a result both of social cleavages (religious–secular, socio-economic left–right, Ashkenaz–Sepharad, immigrants–natives) and of the pressures caused by the Israeli–Palestinian conflict ... As a result the national conversation about the conflict has become a cacophony. To a large extent as time passes the discussion becomes increasingly polarised, filled with taboos and thus simplistic. This leaves Israeli Jews with no real capacity to agree on a common strategy ... After so many decades of violence, and with Israel facing a truly complex rapidly changing reality, a mapping of alternative scenarios should be used to broaden the discursive space, alleviate some taboos, and legitimise a conversation on certain futures that are so far unspoken. This is a requirement if Israeli Jews are to take a well-informed decision about their future – one that takes seriously into account the domestic, regional and international constraints, costs and benefits. (Zalzberg, 2009)

In this case, four possible scenarios were formulated and discussed (Ramsbotham, 2010: 183–5). There was a particular focus on Judaism (religious identity), Zionism (political identity) and Jewishness (national identity). A second phase concentrated in addition on linking strategic thinking to *complexity*. The aim was to overcome the short-term unreflective responses characteristic of political decision-making under pressure in order to base strategy on deeper analysis of alternative medium-term and long-term alternatives and feed this into the public debate. A third phase – still ongoing at the time of writing – has discussed requirements for making Israel a more 'equal' country.

This links to parallel strategic thinking undertaken by the Palestinian Citizens of Israel Group. This, the most recent of the strategy networks to be set up, aims to add strategic thinking to the 'vision' documents of 2007 and 2008, which represented the political 'coming of age' of the 1.5 million Arab/Palestinian citizens of Israel who make up, on some estimates, 20 per cent of the Israeli population. Equally as in need of bridging internal differences as the Israeli Strategic Forum and the Palestine Strategy Group, the members of the Palestinian Citizens of Israel Group could have been members both of an Israeli and of a Palestinian group. This encapsulates the deep 'identity divide' that separates them both from Jewish Israelis and from non-Israeli Palestinians. This makes it difficult for them to participate in plans for a separate Palestinian state, but at the same time they are potential catalysts for creative change. It is they who would be most affected by any 'land swaps' associated with the creation of a Palestinian state. And it is they who live at the epicentre of current controversy in Israel about a (re)definition of Israel as the nation-state of the Jewish people and demands that this must be recognized by the Palestinian leadership outside Israel as a prerequisite for the bilateral negotiations from which Palestinians in Israel are excluded. At the time of writing, just before the 17 March 2015 election in Israel, the creation of a new coalition of Israeli Arab parties – the Joint Arab List – might secure enough Knesset seats to make it one of the largest three or four parties. This demonstrates the importance of promoting collective strategic thinking *within* conflict parties – in this case among Palestinians in Israel – in order to overcome internal divisions, clarify strategic options ahead, and enable effective action to alter the status quo.

It can be seen that the main motive for conflict parties to engage in this work is not to do with attempts to understand the other or to solve a shared problem. It is to overcome internal divisions in order to attain national goals – in this sense, it is to *win*. Both Israelis and Palestinians are deeply concerned about such internal divisions. In the case of Palestinians, these are multiplied by physical separation – in Israel, Gaza, Jerusalem, the West Bank, and the near and far diaspora. Without sufficient internal cohesion there can be no coherent and effective national strategy.

But is the aim of 'winning' not the antithesis of conflict resolution? Is it not just what principled negotiation, problem-solving and dialogue for mutual understanding want to transcend? In that case, how can it help to create conditions for their future revival?

How can strategic thinking be a placeholder for a revival of conflict resolution?

It is always possible that inclusive strategic thinking within conflict parties may deepen anatagonisms and make things worse. Conflict parties may come to realize more clearly why they hate each other. But there are also a number of reasons why, nevertheless, such thinking may be able to act as a 'placeholder' when conflict resolution is not yet possible.

- Strategic thinking can 'mimic' conflict resolution.
- Overcoming internal divisions can often be a prerequisite for conflict resolution.
- The gap between elite decision-making and societal levels can be bridged.
- Channels of communication can be kept open that are otherwise closed.
- Issues can be raised that are otherwise not on the radar screen.
- The question of conflict asymmetry can be addressed.
- The role of third parties – especially would-be third-party peacemakers – can be clarified.

We briefly consider each of these in turn. The first three operate mainly *within conflict parties*, the next three operate mainly *across conflict parties*, and the last operates mainly in relation to *third parties* (see table 18.3).

How strategic thinking can mimic conflict resolution   Box 18.3 gives an idea of ten possible ways in which, by its very nature, strategic thinking has characteristics that can help to give possible future conflict resolution initiatives more traction even in intense phases of conflict.

There is much that can be said about these ten features. Commenting briefly on them in pairs: numbers 1 and 2 can help to avoid the 'capture' of

---

Box 18.3 Ten ways in which strategic thinking can mimic conflict resolution

1 Strategic thinking is inclusive.
2 Strategic thinking looks to the future.
3 Strategic thinking analyses the status quo as a complex system.
4 Strategic thinking evaluates scenarios (future possibilities) not just in terms of desirability but also in terms of attainability and likelihood.
5 Strategic thinking, on this basis, determines short-term, medium-term and long-term goals.
6 Strategic thinking prepares alternative routes (plan A, plan B, etc).
7 Strategic thinking distinguishes between different forms of power (threat, exchange, integrative).
8 Strategic thinking assesses strategic means in terms of relative effectiveness under different conditions.
9 Strategic thinking looks at the chessboard from the perspective of the opponent.
10 Strategic thinking takes care that strategic messages are expressed appropriately for different audiences.

Source: Ramsbotham, forthcoming 2017

strategic thinking by any one faction and preoccupation with past resentments; numbers 3 and 4 can go some way towards ensuring that analysis is sophisticated and realistic – not just wishful thinking; numbers 5 and 6 can add flexibility and an understanding that there are often many possible routes; numbers 7 and 8 can encourage evaluation of alternatives to violence; number 9 can open the way for consideration of enemy perspectives even though the aim is not to 'understand' but to 'win'; and number 10 can add greater critical awareness of how communications are likely to be received.

How overcoming internal divisions can be a prerequisite for conflict resolution   One of the main prerequisites for inclusive internal strategic thinking is 'strategic unity'. Strategic unity does not mean political unity between constituencies, parties or factions. But it does mean that internal differences must not make effective collective strategic thinking and strategic action impossible. Palestinians often say that their enemies aim to 'divide and rule' – in which case the strategic response is not to be divided and not to be ruled. Without strategic unity there can be no effective collective strategy.

But this can also contribute to increasing opportunities for future conflict resolution, because it is often internal divisions within conflict parties that are the main obstacles to peace processes between them. This is a well-known dynamic. Leaders who move towards political accommodation with opponents, for example, often thereby open dangerous space behind their backs that can be filled by more radical internal rivals. Innumerable peace processes have been derailed in this way.

How strategic engagement can help to bridge the gap between elite decision-making and societal levels   One of the most debilitating impediments to conflict resolution is the gap between decision-making elites and popular societal levels. Again and again agreements made behind closed doors at elite level founder on 're-entry' into an unprepared public arena. Conversely, insights, possibilities and breakthroughs at societal or grassroots level do not penetrate politicized party-political hierarchies or official political and security institutions. This was one of the main reasons why the Oslo process began to lose momentum in the mid-1990s and why, even if there had been a breakthrough in the 2013–14 Kerry talks, most commentators doubted that either government could have carried this successfully through what would inevitably have been a prolonged implementation phase.

Inclusive internal strategic thinking that is continually fed into the national debate at all levels can go some way towards remedying this. By its very structure, as many internal constituencies as possible participate in the strategic thinking. Strategic thinking is something that can be promoted in all parts of society. Here is the key difference between what Ramsbotham calls *strategic planning/manipulation* and genuine *strategic thinking*. Strategic planning is done secretly or in private, accompanied by a controlled exercise in public persuasion. It is characteristic of ideological, party-political and commercial versions of 'strategy'. The difference between this and the genuine inclusive public strategic thinking that is the subject of this chapter can easily be tested. A comparison between possible scenarios that lists all the advantages on one side and all the disadvantages on the other is clearly a hallmark of strategic manipulation. It is bad strategic thinking, because situations are almost never as clear-cut as this. Strategic thinking, in contrast, weighs up strategic options and compares pros and cons. If anything, it deliberately encourages a 'devil's advocate' critique of favoured strategies in order to test them for weaknesses, to encourage creative inventiveness, and to retain strategic flexibility.

How strategic engagement can help to keep channels of communication open that are otherwise closed   Figure 18.1 illustrates how inclusive strategic thinking within conflict parties (axes 2 and 3) can also keep channels of communication open across them.

In this model there are two conflict parties (A and B), each of which is internally composite (both contain extremists and moderates). This generates six *axes of radical disagreement.* Evidently this is a highly simplified model. There may be more than two conflict parties. There are many cross-cutting internal divisions. The terms 'extremist' and 'moderate' will vary across different issues and are themselves contested. Third parties have not yet been included. And so on. Nevertheless, the model is useful for illustrating the main dynamics involved. Above all, it clearly demonstrates one of the main reasons why it is best to begin not with radical disagreement *across* conflict parties (axes 1, 4, 5, 6) but with inclusive strategic engagement of discourses *within* them (axes 2, 3).

Radical disagreement is popularly identified with *Axis 1* – the disagreement between extremists (as normally defined). But this is, if anything, the least significant axis. As repeatedly demonstrated in the exploration of agonistic

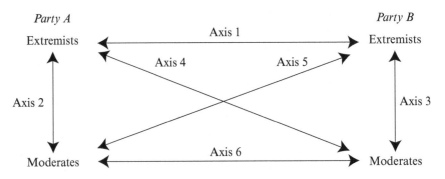

Figure 18.1 *The hexagon of radical disagreement*

dialogue, it is radical disagreement between moderates (as normally defined) that is much the most important element. Extremists often feed off each other and are mutually dependent.

Axes 2 and 3 are the key axes that constitute level 1 of the strategic engagement process. They form the basis for the possibility of maintaining inclusive strategic engagement between a majority on either side, even in times of maximum intractability. It is via axes 2 and 3 that the other axes remain operational.

Axes 4 and 5 are exchanges (often indirect) that are made possible only so long as axes 2 and 3 remain inclusive and Axis 6 remains active. Extremists (as normally defined) do not want to participate directly in, or to encourage, these axes of communication. Extremists are more at home in the stark standoff of Axis 1. These are axes of radical disagreement that strategic engagement makes possible – and, if the aim is to dilute extremism, promotes.

Axis 6 is the most crucial – and underrated – axis of radical disagreement. It is easy to assume that there is bound to be agreement across this axis among 'moderates' (for example, being opposed to violence) about most of the main issues. But that is not the case in intractable conflicts, as shown in the quarrel between Rouhana and Bar-On in box 18.2. On the contrary, this is where the central lines of radical disagreement lie and where agonistic dialogue to explore this is most urgently needed. With reference to the radical disagreement in box 18.2, for example, Rouhana says that most Palestinans would agree with him. Most Israelis would be likely to agree with Bar-On. So far the arguments in box 18.2 mainly miss each other. The protagonists are not yet arguing about the same things. This is very common in radical disagreement. It is what needs to be overcome by onging engagement and continuous alignment. And this can be done only by promoting and exploring the agonistic dialogue.

As noted in chapter 11, one key element to be emphasized here is that the main strategic aim for conflict resolution in actually or potentially violent conflicts is to separate what Ramsbotham calls *extremists of ends*, who may be a majority – as in this case – from *extremists of means*, who, it is hoped, remain a minority (Ramsbotham, 2010: 210–13). In Northern Ireland, this distinction was fundamental to the peace process. The Republicans, for example, remained extremists of ends – they still struggle for a united Ireland. But in the 1990s the Sinn Fein leadership decided that, in the present circumstances, they were now more likely to attain their strategic goal via power-sharing than via the armed struggle. This paved the way for what eventually became the Good Friday Agreement in 1998.

How strategic engagement can help to raise issues that are otherwise not on the public radar screen   For reasons given in the previous sub-section, it is only through alignment and exploration of radical disagreement via strategic engagement that the full lineaments of the struggle are made plain. Issues otherwise not debated appear for the first time on the radar screen. Hitherto taboo subjects are brought into the sphere of public debate. These often turn out to be the critical points, both in perpetuating the conflict and defeating attempts at resolution and in suggesting possible new configurations ahead. 'Everybody knows what a final settlement will look like' is the common refrain in the Israeli–Palestinian conflict. But the strategic engagement of discourses shows that everyone does not know what a final settlement will look like. That is the problem. Even in relation to the familiar dossier of issues over which repeated attempts to resolve the conflict have foundered, as in 2000, 2001, 2004, 2007 and 2014 – such as the determination of future borders, the law of return (Jewish diaspora) and right of return (Palestinian diaspora), the status of Jerusalem, security arrangements, economic resource management – clashing conceptions do not properly engage. There is no agreement about what a 'Palestinian state' means (Reading 54).

So it is that the crucial question of possible *alternatives* to the existing status quo – essential in negotiations, as noted below – is not argued out. One example is the possibility that the existing 'one-state' reality, if perpetuated, might eventually transmute into some form of 'two states', albeit by violent means. Another is that a possible 'two-state' outcome might eventually evolve into some approximation to 'one state' if future forms of federation became feasible between Israel, Palestine and perhaps Jordan. Without a strategic engagement of discourses, possible futures such as these – however remote they may appear at the moment – do not enter the debate, even though they might prove to be critical catalysts in shifting perceptions of relative comparative risk and benefit and in opening up new strategic vistas. To put it another way, it is only by strategic engagement of this kind that the 'Plan Bs' of conflict parties and third parties can engage each other. And it is this – otherwise absent – strategic engagement that is often the key to opening space for a peace process.

How strategic engagement can help to address conflict asymmetry   Similarly, a strategic engagement of discourses can reach deeply into the issue of asymmetry, which, as seen in earlier chapters, often lies at the heart of intractability. *Quantitative asymmetry* (one conflict party is larger than the other) poses problems, but this is greatly compounded when there is also *qualitative asymmetry* (for instance, one conflict party is a government and the other is not). This means that conflict parties are seeking entirely different strategic goals. For example, the primary strategic question for 'the possessor' in the Israeli–Palestinian conflict is 'Why should Israel give up anything at all?' Whereas the primary strategic question for the 'challenger' is 'How can Palestinians transform the status quo?'

At the heart of strategic thinking is the issue of the 'balance of power'. How can challengers prevail upon possessors to share power? How can possessors prevail upon challengers to give up violence? Who minds most? In this struggle we are already familiar from the work of Kenneth Boulding and Joseph Nye (see chapter 1) that there are different types of power to be weighed up against each other. In the Israeli–Palestinian conflict, for example, Israel, as possessor, has overwhelming military and economic power as well as the support of the greatest world power in 'guarding its back'. But Palestinians also have power – the power of international legitimacy, much enhanced over the past decade, to the point where an overwhelmimg number of countries support the principle of a State of Palestine on the 22 per cent of historic Palestine endorsed in UN General Assembly resolutions, most recently in November 2012. As a result, Palestine is already a non-member observer state and can be a contracting party to international organizations and international treaties accordingly, including the International Criminal Court. This has been a triumph of Palestinian strategy. The main strategic question for Palestinians here, therefore, is how *de jure* legitimacy can be converted into *de facto* reality.

How strategic engagement can clarify the role of third parties   Peacemaking analysis repeatedly shows that, given the strategic impasse, it is often only a third party that can break the deadlock. In the Israeli–Palestinian conflict, for example, it is the Quartet of the US, Russia, the EU and the UN that officially represents the international community. All are deeply implicated historically. Russia, in its former embodiment in the Soviet Union, was among the earliest to encourage the creation of the State of Israel and played a highly intrusive role thereafter. Russian immigrants to Israel have had a profound demographic and political impact. The US was at first more ambivalent, at one point in 1948 advising against the setting up of an Israeli state and forcing Israel to withdraw from lands taken in 1956, but it is now the main guarantor of Israeli survival. The EU contains Germany, France (provider of Israel's first nuclear reactor in 1957) and the UK, prime actors in the events in question. The UN set up the commission which advised that Palestine be partitioned, and the General Assembly voted in support.

Two things are worth noting about the role of third parties in general in the light of strategic engagement in intractable conflicts.

No matter how they may interpret their own motives, intentions and roles, it can now be seen why, from the perspective of strategic negotiation, third parties are not neutral, impartial or disinterested. Whatever their own self-understandings and self-descriptions, such judgements are not up to them. Third-party peacemakers – including 'elicitive' or 'transformative' peacemakers such as Norway or various NGOs – want to change the discourses of the conflict parties so that they are different to what they were before. They, too, want to 'win'. That is why third-party interveners, even if initially welcomed, so often end by quarrelling with all the conflict parties. Conflict parties expect third parties to support them. When they do not, conflict parties may turn against them and then may agree with each other that the third parties do not understand the situation at all.

In light of this, peacemakers – including 'internal' peacemakers – are wise to acknowledge the situation. Recognizing that they are not neutral, impartial or disinterested, they are as much in need of strategic thinking as the conflict parties. How can they bring about the desired terminus of ending the confrontation? In this struggle they, too, need to analyse the existing complex system, to assess strengths and weaknesses, to compare possible scenarios, to determine shorter- and longer-term goals, to prepare alternative routes, to find strategic allies, to evaluate and adapt strategic means, and so on. What is their preferred outcome? How can they best get there? In these calculations, third-party peacemakers at level 3 of strategic engagement are greatly assisted if they are able to draw on the information about internal constituencies and cross-cutting issues made available at levels 1 and 2. This carries us through to the final section of this chapter.

Principled Negotiation, Strategic Negotiation and Extended Conflict Resolution

We can now end this account of the turn to strategic engagement by relating all of this to the conflict resolution aim of promoting *negotiation for political accommodation*. Again we take principled negotiation – getting to yes – as an example. And we may illustrate this in turn by the efforts of US Secretary of State John Kerry to bring the two sides in the Israeli–Palestinian conflict together between July 2013 and April 2014 (Ramsbotham and Schiff, forthcoming).

The aim of what Ramsbotham and Schiff call a *strategic negotiation approach* is to 'focus on the prerequisites that make principled negotiation possible' (see table 18.3). In this task it simplifies and clarifies what is required for success in complex negotiations – a useful supplement to ripeness and readiness theory (see chapter 7):

- all parties must conclude that entering negotiations is better for them than not entering negotiations;
- all parties must conclude that reaching agreement is better for them than not reaching agreement;
- all parties must conclude that implementing agreements is better for them than not implementing agreements.

These are tough conditions. A strategic negotiation approach is not pre-negotiation, or even pre-pre-negotiation. It is a wider process that runs throughout the operation and at any one stage has to be able at the same time to engage the others.

The best way to clarify this is to look at three strategic scenarios in the Israeli–Palestinian conflict and then relate these to the strategic calculations

The Green Line ⌐ ⌐ ⌐ ⌐ ⌐ ⌐

Map 18.1 *Israel, Gaza and the West Bank*

of conflict parties and third parties. These scenarios are of course greatly simplified and should be taken as expository only.

Scenario (A)	A genuinely independent Palestinian state as internationally agreed
Scenario (B)	Permanent effective Israeli control over the whole of historic Palestine
Scenario (C)	Indefinite continuation of the status quo – incremental Israeli settlement in the West Bank and international life support for an otherwise unviable Palestinian Authority

Let us now briefly consider the incentives for conflict parties to enter negotiations, reach agreement and implement agreement – and for third parties to help bring this about – within this strategic framework.

In terms of strategy, why should Israel enter negotiations? Let us say: in

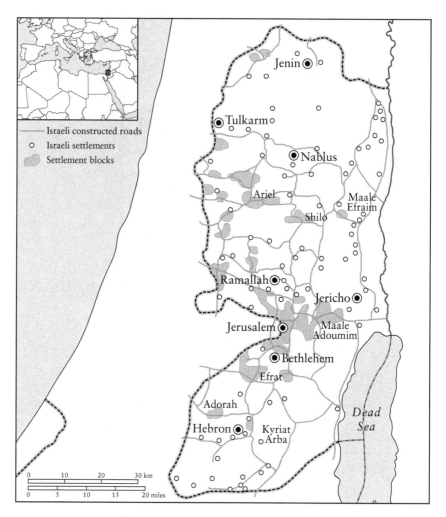

Map 18.2 *Israeli settlements in the West Bank 2015*

order to satisfy international opinion, especially in the United States, and in order to ensure that bilateral negotiations as conducted over the past twenty-two years (since the 1993 Oslo Agreement) continue to be the only route to a peace deal. What are the inducements for reaching actual agreement in the negotiations? There are few, because scenario (C) is seen to be always available to the possessor and carries fewer risks than both the other two scenarios. Scenario (B) may carry greater risks than scenario (A), but these are long term and indeterminate, whereas the risks in pulling out of the West Bank are immediate and palpable. Israeli withdrawal from Gaza in 2005 was followed in 2007 by Hamas' seizure of power and rocket attacks on Israeli citizens. How could a weak Palestinian government prevent this from happening again? In the meantime, scenario (C) has the added advantage of masking parallel incremental implementation in the directon of scenario (B) – for example, this could be varied to encompass a Palestinian 'pseudo-state', unilateral with-drawal and partition of the West Bank (to prevent a Palestinian majority in Israel), and the possibility that Egypt and Jordan might absorb the rest (Israel already has treaties with both). So Israel is ready to enter negotiations, but it is far from ready to reach agreement on scenario (A) and probably unable to implement agreement even if one were reached.

Why should Palestinians enter negotiations? Whereas Israel is happy with the *process* of bilateral negotiation but does not want the internationally pre-ferred *outcome*, Palestinians would welcome the *outcome* (having agreed to it since the 1988 decision to that effect by the Palestinian National Council) but are now almost unanimously opposed to the *process*, which is seen to mask and reinforce scenario (B). Together with the other two elements that make up the 'Oslo process' – division of the West Bank into areas A, B and C, which allows piecemeal absorption, and the function of the Palestinian Authority in 'collaborating' with occupation by ensuring security for Israel and removing the financial burden – bilateral negotiation brokered by the United States is regarded as an instrument of continuing oppression, not a liberation from it. So the most popular Palestinian strategy now is to attain scenario (A) by an international rather than a bilateral route – for example, via an interna-tional conference or via the UN. In this case, negotiation would cease to be an unequal contest between occupier and occupied and would simply be a means of implementing an already internationally agreed outcome. As far as scenario (B) is concerned (seen as the current 'one-state' reality), the strategy is of course to resist it by a concerted domestic/international campaign against what is regarded as an already existing apartheid. So long as a Palestinian state continues to remain a distant prospect, Palestinian strategy is meanwhile to demand equal individual and collective rights throughout Palestine as it exists now – without prejudice to a possible future Palestinian state. That is why the 'one state/two state' alternative, as regularly cited in the past, no longer applies in that form. Palestinians have to pursue both tracks at the same time, however difficult – even dangerous – that strategy may be.

As far as scenario (C) is concerned, Palestinian strategy is to dismantle it as soon as possible (albeit incrementally, given attendant risks) so that it is removed from the strategic chessboard and scenarios (A) and (B) offer a stark choice both to Israel and to the international community. Only when convinced that scenario (B) means never-ending conflict, international de-legitimization, and eventual equal rights for Palestinians throughout Palestine is Israel likely to opt for scenario (A). The fundamental Palestinian strategic appeal here is to the ethical and legal discrepancy between scenario (B), which is based on rights for the Jewish people that are thereby denied to the Palestinian people, and both scenario (A) and the alternative of equal rights for Palestinians throughout historic Palestine, which are based on the principle of equity for all peoples. That is why Palestinians are reluctant to re-enter bilateral negotiation, as in the past, would accept (but do not expect) agreement on scenario (A) and, given current divisions among Palestinians and the weakness of the leadership, might find it very hard to implement scenario (A) if it were to be agreed in watered-down form.

Such are some of the formidable strategic impediments to prospects for successful principled negotiation that any would-be third-party peacemaker – in this case, the US secretary of state – might have to contend with. Box 18.4 sums up some differences between principled negotiation and the strategic negotiation approach. The contrast drawn in box 18.4 is no doubt somewhat stark, and readers are reminded that the overall aim is to extend and enrich principled negotiation, not to reject it.

The tenth difference in box 18.4 is that, whereas in principled negotiation third parties should be impartial, in the strategic negotiation approach they 'should think and act strategically in order to win'. For example, what was the preferred outcome for the US secretary of state in the talks from July 2013 to April 2014? Was it scenario (A)? If so, what was his strategy for attaining this? What strategic prerequisites were needed? How could these be brought about? Did he begin from an understanding that the process of negotiation was itself part of the struggle? Did he see asymmetry as a major factor to be

---

Box 18.4 Principled negotiation and a strategic negotiation approach

1   In principled negotiation, the negotiation is seen as an end to the conflict; in strategic negotiation, the negotiation is seen to be part of the conflict.

2   Principled negotiation assumes symmetry between conflict parties; strategic negotiation sees asymmetry as a major factor to be engaged with.

3   Principled negotiation wants to separate the people from the problem; strategic negotiation sees people (the fusion of facts, values, emotions, actions) as part of the problem to be addressed.

4   Principled negotiation wants to focus on interests, not positions; strategic negotiation begins from where conflict parties are and takes positions (what conflict parties say, including strategic planning) seriously.

5   Principled negotiation wants conflict parties to look for mutual gains; strategic negotiation wants conflict parties to think strategically.

6   Principled negotiation wants agreed outcomes to be based on objective standards; strategic negotiation sees the definition of objective standards as part of the disagreement to be overcome.

7   Principled negotiation wants to avoid the 'blame game'; strategic negotiation sees the blame game as integral to the negotiations – for example, a possible weapon for third-party peacemakers.

8   In principled negotiation, final agreements end the conflict; in strategic negotiation, 'final agreements' in hitherto intractable conflicts usually lead to a 'continuation of the conflict by other means' (see chapter 7).

9   Principled negotiation sees the removal of extremism as a precondition; in strategic negotiation the precondition is to separate extremists of ends from extremists of means.

10 In principled negotiation, third-party peacemakers should be neutral, impartial and disinterested; in strategic negotiation, peacemakers should think and act strategically in order to win (transform conflict-party calculations as required for success).

Source: Ramsbotham and Schiff, forthcoming; Ramsbotham, forthcoming, 2017

overcome? How did he propose to surmount the built-in Israeli preference for scenario (C) and perception that, although the risks of scenario (B) may have been greater, the risks of scenario (A) were more immediate and probably fatal for the incumbent government? How did he propose to overcome the Palestinian identification of the negotiation process and the US role in it with the continuing occupation that the talks were meant to end? What negative and positive inducements was he able to deploy? Was he prepared to use the 'blame game' as a means of putting pressure on the conflict parties? Was he prepared to bring in other third parties to increase pressure – for example, from the Quartet or the Arab League? What did he think could be done about the Christian Zionist espousal of the Israeli cause and its dominance in the US Congress (leading to the 400–1 vote in support of Israel during the June 2014 Gaza war)? And, as in all good strategy, did the US secretary of state have a Plan B in case the negotiations failed? If so, what was Plan B? Was it something he was prepared to use as an added inducement to the conflict parties to settle by persuading them that it would not be a 'better alternative to a negotiated agreement' but worse from their perspectives? And did he have plans to help overcome anticipated difficulties over implementation in case agreement was, after all, reached? In short, did he have a short-term, medium-term and long-term strategy for shifting perceptions in the required direction in Israel and among Palestinians about the balance of risks and benefits at both governmental and societal levels?

Anything is possible in the swirl of events that surround complex and intractable conflicts within the wider dimensions of transnational conflict. Perhaps the US initiative may bear fruit during the remaining year or so of the Obama presidency. Whatever the outcome, this is likely to be followed by concerted international efforts finally to drive a genuine peace process through. In case of initial success, what is, say, the US and EU strategy for maintaining momentum through the long implementation phase? In case of failure, what is Plan B? At the moment it is hard to discern any serious strategic thinking by the US or the EU, or any other international actor, about what Plan B – an alternative to the 22-year-old 'Oslo process' – might be and how it could be used now both as a genuine alternative and as a lever to help finally expedite Plan A.

Conclusion

Whatever the outcome, a sustained strategic engagement of discourses as described in this chapter is needed when, so far, conflict resolution fails. In the Israeli–Palestinian conflict, it was missing in the 1990s in support of an apparent breakthrough. And it was missing after 2000 to help fill the dangerous vacuum after the collapse of the Camp David talks. It will be needed in the case of future peace efforts, both if they succeed (the immediate post-settlement period is often the most dangerous) and if they fail.

When negotiation for political accommodation, interactive problem-solving, and dialogue for mutual understanding do not yet work in intractable conflicts, it is best to look in the opposite direction and to promote a strategic engagement of discourses within, across and between conflict parties, and including third parties. Strategic engagement may not lead to a revival of conflict resolution. But at least it helps to keep sails up to catch any winds of opportunity that may be blowing. The sails may not catch enough wind to propel the ship forward in a particular preferred direction. But one thing is certain: if the sails are not raised, there will be no motion, however many winds are blowing. Without sails permanently hoisted in this way, it will be much more likely to be a continuing story of mistiming and missed opportunities.

RECOMMENDED READING

The items by Chilton, Dédaic and Nelson, and Schaffner and Wenden are about language and conflict in general. The others relate to dialogue, negotiation and intractability.

Bojer et al. (2006); Chilton (2004); Coleman (2011); Dédaic and Nelson (2003); Hayward and O'Donnell (2010); Mitchell (2014); Ramsbotham (2010; forthcoming, 2017); Ramsbotham and Schiff (forthcoming); Schäffner and Wenden (1995).

RELEVANT EXTRACTS IN *THE CONTEMPORARY CONFLICT RESOLUTION READER*

Reading 46: R. Fisher and W. Ury, Getting to Yes: Negotiating Agreement without Giving In

Reading 54: C. Albin, Explaining Conflict Transformation: How Jerusalem Became Negotiable

CHAPTER NINETEEN

Conflict Resolution: Theories and Critiques

We have now completed our account of the challenges and promises of cosmopolitan conflict resolution – bar our final summing up in chapter 20 – as a complement to the more structured and systematic survey of the conflict resolution field offered in Part I. So it is time to reflect on the theoretical underpinnings of the conflict resolution enterprise in relation to its critics, along the lines suggested in chapter 1. In this chapter we are looking not at theories of conflict, as in chapter 4, but at the theoretical status of conflict resolution itself. The theorization of conflict resolution is best conceived in terms of an 'internal' conversation among analysts within its own pluralist/cosmopolitan heartland, as outlined in chapter 11, and an 'external' conversation with realist critics, on the one hand, and critical theoretic and post-structural critics, on the other. A reminder of this theoretical spectrum is given in figure 19.1. In addition, the most important dialogue of all in our view, and one not represented in figure 19.1, is the conversation with non-western, non-northern cultural traditions that lie entirely outside these largely western/northern academic discussions. This chapter attempts to chart some of this complex terrain.

The Pluralist/Cosmopolitan Heartland of Conflict Resolution

In chapter 11 we identified the mainstream conflict resolution tradition since the 1950s, both with the idea of an *international society of states*, where the organizing principle is international order protected by the non-intervention norm which thereby preserves plural values from outside domination, and with the idea of an emergent *world community*, where the organizing principle is cosmopolitan justice delivered through reformed structures of global governance progressively more capable of delivering locally defined welfare, particularly to the poorest and most marginalized. The former is identified with *conflict settlement*, the latter with *conflict transformation*. We also noted the tension between the two, as reflected in continuing quarrels between communitarianism and universalism in international ethics (Rasmussen, 1990), heated debate about humanitarian intervention and the responsibility to protect in international law (see chapter 14), and impassioned dispute about peacebuilding and the 'liberal peace' in international politics (see chapters

Realist   Pluralist   Cosmopolitan   Critical   Post-structural

Figure 19.1 *Theoretical perspectives on conflict resolution*

8 and 9). Conflict resolution analysts and practitioners are divided on these issues – and have been almost from the outset, as illustrated in Kenneth Boulding's 'Twelve friendly quarrels with Johan Galtung' (1977) and Galtung's 'Only one friendly quarrel with Kenneth Boulding' (1987) (see chapter 2).

In chapter 11 we suggested that, to some extent, the tension between the norms of an international society of states and the ideals of a world community can be mediated through the 'solidarist' concept of an evolving 'international community' that contains elements of both (see table 11.1, p. 317). We further noted how these and other aspects are perhaps best seen to coexist unevenly in the global collectivity – which is why no overall descriptive term is available that is not already caught up in these debates. But in this chapter we will focus rather on the theoretic bipolarity around which the conflict resolution field has traditionally revolved by comparing Robert Jackson's analysis of the future of international society, in his book *The Global Covenant: Human Conduct in a World of States* (2000), with Richard Falk's vision of a future world community, in *On Humane Governance: Toward a New Global Politics* (1995).

Jackson defends the virtues of the present international society of states and predicts that it will continue to predominate in future. He sees it as the best practical response to irreducible human diversity, reflecting the realities of human nature and protecting pluralist values under international law:

> If I had to place a bet on the shape of world politics at the start of the twenty-first century, my money would still be on the prognosis that our great-great-grandchildren will live in a political world that would still be familiar to us, that would still be shaped politically by state sovereignty. Peoples around the world will still be organized and recognized as independent states. They will still coexist and communicate and transact their political business to a significant extent via the *societas* of states. ... Notwithstanding its very real limitations and imperfections, to date the *societas* of sovereign states has proved to be the only generally acceptable and practical normative basis of world politics. (2000: 424–5)

This is a world in which the *conflict settlement* dimension of conflict resolution is forefronted. The concepts, methodologies and practices of conflict settlement, ranging from diplomacy through negotiation and mediation to various forms of institutional accommodation, can be seen to be integral to the whole enterprise of preserving order and allowing space for communities to develop in their own way within the overarching framework of the international society of states. Within this framework, the conflict settlement approach provides the essential capacity for managing unavoidable deep conflicts non-violently.

This pluralist agenda is in tension with the transformative cosmopolitan agenda, inasmuch as the latter is seen to have an innate tendency to ride roughshod over non-intervention norms, thus opening the way for what are likely in the event to be hegemonic intrusions. Whatever the no doubt sincere intentions of transformative cosmopolitan conflict resolution, from a pluralist perspective it is seen to be a dangerous breach of state sovereignty, in which, given the discrepancy in power between interveners and those subject to intervention, it will inevitably be the interests of the former which prevail and the local cultures, traditions, economies and autonomies of the latter that will suffer. David Chandler (2008) is one who has consistently opposed cosmopolitan programmes that breach non-intervention norms on these grounds, no matter how lofty the principles in whose name the interventions are carried out, such as humanitarianism, democracy, economic development, self-determination – and conflict resolution.

From the cosmopolitan pole of the conflict resolution spectrum, however, the situation looks different. Richard Falk, for example, is more visionary in this respect than Robert Jackson, as befits a leading contributor to the World Order Models Project (WOMP), which for many years has conducted its research in terms of individuals, vulnerable groups and the wider environment within a global analytic framework, rather than in terms of the state system. Falk's idea of 'humane governance' is a normative project that 'posits an imagined community for the whole of humanity, which overcomes the most problematic aspects of the present world scene' (1995: 243). The ambitious undertaking is summed up under ten dimensions, which range from the abolition of war, through the protection of individual and collective human rights, including the economic and social concerns of the poor, and on to a proper stewardship of nature and cosmopolitan democracy. Falk describes this programme as 'attainable', while acknowledging that it will be 'incredibly difficult' to achieve given the strength of the top-down forces of militarist, market-driven, materialist globalization. In the end it is driven by the imperative of the survival of whatever is humane in humanity:

> At the same time, such a shift in fundamental prospects for governance is a sufficiently plausible outcome as to make the struggle to achieve it the only responsible basis for positive citizenship at this stage of history. Whether ours is an axial moment of normative restructuring of collective and individual life cannot yet be determined, but such possibilities inherent in the present situation provide us with the best and most realistic basis of hope about how to work toward human betterment, as understood and applied in many separate ways around the world. (Ibid.: 254–5)

This is a framework within which the *conflict transformation* dimension of conflict resolution becomes prominent. The challenge centres on a non-violent transformation of present deep asymmetries and unequal relations at global and regional levels, linked to a multiplicity of 'bottom-up' initiatives which define the meaning of the 'human betterment' thus delivered and ensure that it satisfies genuine human needs as variously 'understood and applied in many separate ways around the world'. The pluralist critique is noted, but then set aside on the grounds that non-intervention, as a statist principle, merely serves to protect the interests of existing states and elites, not the genuine interests and needs of peoples – and is therefore not genuine pluralism after all. Instead, the cosmopolitan vision aims to address and transform the discursive and institutional continuities that perpetuate direct, structural and cultural violence at all levels – including reform of the state system itself – in harmony with the logic inherent in conflict resolution values and principles as set out and exemplified in Part I of this book.

Mindful of the force of the pluralist caveat about the dangers of abuse by unreconstructed interveners, however, the cosmopolitan enterprise is predicated on a radical transformation of the global order along the lines sketched out in chapter 11. Here we can recognize the kinds of cosmopolitan transformation envisaged in different ways many years ago by founders of the conflict resolution field. In chapters 2 and 4, for example, we noted Johan Galtung's prescriptions for overcoming structural and cultural violence; John Burton's 'paradigm shift' in transforming oppressive global/local institutions of economic and political governance so that they satisfy basic individual human needs rather than the interests of the powerful; Edward Azar's aim to anticipate 'protracted social conflict' by overcoming the injustices of the postcolonial state in relation not just to individual needs but to the collective needs of heterogeneous 'identity groups'; or Elise Boulding's idea of reaching across generations, genders and cultures by 'imaging the future' within the context of a '200-year present' in order to build a peaceful global civic society and avoid 'Armageddon'.

The Realist Critique

The realist critique dismisses all this as 'utopian' and 'idealistic'. In announcing the early modern state, Machiavelli, Bodin and Hobbes were writing in times of civil war and looked, respectively, to the emergence of a powerful Prince, to the Magna Persona of the sovereign state, or to Leviathan in order to overcome it. Gentili recognized the corollary in interstate relations: 'Where the sovereign has no earthly judge it is inevitable that the decision between sovereigns should be made by arms' ([1598] 1964: 15). This has broadly delineated realist discourse in relation to civil wars and interstate wars ever since.

In *civil wars*, as discussed in chapter 4, a number of analysts point to the impact of globalization on the weakening of vulnerable states, the provision of cheap weaponry suitable for 'asymmetric war', and the generation of shadow economies that make 'new wars' self-perpetuating and profitable. Conflict resolution is seen to be incapable of addressing this nexus. In the 1990s, for example, critics such as David Shearer (1997), in his analysis of 'conflict resolution in Sierra Leone', questioned whether a conflict resolution consensus-promoting strategy, based on impartial mediation and negotiation by the international community, is appropriate in cases where war is fuelled by 'greed' rather than 'grievance'. 'Warlord insurgencies' or clan-based criminal mafias driven by economic motives are unlikely to be amenable to resolution by consent and negotiation. Indeed, pursuit of mediated settlements and the bringing in of humanitarian aid can have the unintended effect of prolonging the conflict and feeding the warring factions, with civilian populations suffering most. Targeted military action, on the other hand, is said to be much more likely to have the effect of foreshortening the conflict by persuading those losing ground to accept a settlement – as demonstrated in Bosnia in 1995. Or it may be better to let civil wars burn themselves out, including allowing one side to win, as eventually happened in Rwanda and more recently in Sri Lanka – in Edward Luttwak's phrase, 'give war a chance' (1999). This is a variant of the traditional realist criticism of conflict resolution, in which international politics is seen as a struggle between antagonistic and irreconcilable groups with power and coercion as the only ultimate currency, and 'soft power' approaches of conflict resolution dismissed as ineffective and dangerous.

Tom Woodhouse's response to this criticism (1999b) is that, in the kinds of conflict prevalent since the end of the Cold War, a 'quick military fix' is rarely possible. Moreover, as exemplified particularly in chapters 6 and 8, where we describe how military force has been used by international interveners in response to conflicts of this kind, its function has been to create political space for a postwar reconstruction process defined, at any rate rhetorically, largely in terms of conflict resolution principles. Civil wars do not 'burn out' quickly. In Sri Lanka, eventual government victory came only after fifteen years of fighting – nor is there much indication that military victory on its own will end that conflict. This applies *a fortiori* to realist reaction to the destruction of the World Trade Center and the attack on the Pentagon on 11 September 2001, together with the 'war on terror' that followed. The realist asks: What possible answer can conflict resolution have to the lethal combination of 'rogue states', globalized crime, the proliferation of weapons of mass destruction, and the fanatical ideologues of international terrorism? (Gray, 2002; Waltz, 2002). The conflict resolution response, as outlined in chapter 11, is to ask in turn what has been learned from the subsequent military interventions in Afghanistan and Iraq other than lessons about the limits of military coercion on its own. Even the undisputed global military hegemon discovered with remarkable speed where the limits of 'hard power' lie. Similarly, in the military struggle to reverse *jihadist* seizures of territory in Syria, Iraq and Nigeria in 2014, again as stressed in chapter 11, this is only possible when such force is deployed as part of wider conflict resolution strategies to conciliate the legitimate dissatisfactions and remedy the failures of governance that created the niche for violent extremism in the first place.

Turning to *interstate* relations, neo-realists such as Kenneth Waltz dismiss the whole language of conflict resolution as inappropriate at system level. The evolution of international diplomacy in the sixteenth century is seen to have had everything to do with hard-headed appreciation of individual state interest and nothing to do with vague 'win–win' notions. This remains the context for realist conceptions of negotiation and mediation, notwithstanding the slow evolution of the non-intervention norm and its eventual enshrinement in international law through the highly non-realist Article 2(4) in the UN Charter. The determinants of interstate peace from a realist point of view are seen to be deterrence (*si vis pacem para bellum* – if you want peace prepare for war) and balance of power, not conflict resolution. Here the conflict resolution response is to remain highly aware of the possibility of a revival of major inter-state war over scarce resources, or of its heightened likelihood during a period of unstable power transition as the hegemonic order imposed by the United States passes with extraordinary rapidity into a more uncertain multipolar future with the rise of China. The unexpected eruption of the crisis in Ukraine in 2014 can be seen as a salutary warning here. A conflict resolution analysis of this highly dangerous revival of the idea of settling interstate power struggles by force has been given in chapter 5. Either way, the conflict resolution critique of the danger of over-reliance on threat and coercion power alone remains unchanged. And the importance of sustaining the epochal move away from the very idea of settling interstate confrontation through war and towards improving the capacity and expectation of handling future conflicts of interest between major states non-violently as envisaged in the UN Charter is seen to be not misplaced but, on the contrary, ever more urgent. The world can no longer afford future classic great power resource or sphere-of-influence wars – for example, between China and India – or a future Thucydidean geo-political power transition war caused, for instance, by 'the growth in Chinese power and the fear this causes in America'.

The Critical Theory Critique

Tom Woodhouse (1999b) sees the second set of critics of cosmopolitan conflict resolution exemplified in Mark Duffield's paper 'Evaluating conflict resolution' (1997). Duffield argued that, far from contemporary internal wars being aberrant, irrational and non-productive phenomena, they represent 'the emergence of entirely new types of social formation adapted for survival on the margins of the global economy' (1997: 100). Instead of recognizing this, however, the most powerful economies and governments treat these wars as local symptoms of local failures, and therefore expect 'behavioural and atti-tudinal change' in those countries (Duffield, 2001). The disciplinary norms of 'liberal governance' are imposed from outside. Conflict resolution, described by Duffield as a 'socio-psychological model', together with aid and human development programmes, is seen to have been co-opted into this enterprise – used as an instrument of pacification in unruly border territories so that existing power structures can continue to control the global system. This is a variant of the traditional Marxist criticism, which sees 'liberal' conflict resolution as naive and theoretically uncritical, since it attempts to reconcile interests that should not be reconciled, fails to take sides in unequal and unjust struggles, and lacks an analysis within a properly global perspective of the forces of exploitation and oppression.

As an initial response to this analysis, in earlier editions of this book, following Woodhouse, we argued that what is criticized is a caricature of conflict resolution, not conflict resolution itself, and that, from the beginning, the field incorporated the imperative of structural change in asymmetric conflict situations – albeit not in a classic Marxist manner. Since then the debate has moved on and has focused in particular on the question of liberal peacebuilding as discussed in chapters 8 and 9 (Reading 59; Reading 68; Duffield, 2007; Jabri, 2007; Richmond, 2008; Pugh et al., 2008a; Hoffman, 2009; Mac Ginty, 2012; Spears, 2012; Cunliffe, 2013). The main target of attack on conflict resolution here is its identification in the eyes of some critical theorists with a 'problem-solving' approach that merely adjusts and shores up the liberal (read illiberal) peace programme without subjecting it to critical scrutiny. As a result, the transformative cosmopolitan agenda is seen to have been absorbed into the neo-liberal (read neo-conservative) global project, together with all the external aid, development, and human rights initiatives and agencies (states, international institutions, NGOs) that have been co-opted in the process. The requirement from a critical perspective, therefore, is not to 'save' the liberal peace but to jettison it – not reform but revolution. There should be no further truck with peacebuilding in the guise of securitizing the 'other' as problematic for those who are most secure, or with development as pursuit of the myth of local 'self-reliance' when, in a predatory capitalist system, this merely guarantees further dependency on those who are richest. Instead, the new dispensation should be a 'paradigmatic shift' onto an entirely new foundation. What is needed is an emancipatory transformation of global economic and political power structures themselves so that 'political economies of life welfare' finally deliver genuine protection and betterment for the least fortunate through firm control of the rampant trans-border depredations of 'casino capitalism', protection of public goods from unbridled capitalist accumulation, social insurance for the as yet uninsured, and whatever social contracts and material redistributions are required to effect all of this (Pugh et al., 2008b: 290–7; Duffield, 2007: 227–32).

The immediate conflict resolution response to this attack, as noted in chapters 8 and 9, is to acknowledge the power of the critical critique of the liberal peace. External interventions in the name of liberty, democracy and human rights led by the US Bush administration between 2000 and 2008, for example, particularly in Afghanistan and Iraq, did indeed discredit the cosmopolitan values inappropriately invoked. This certainly removes any hint of complacency on the part of transformative cosmopolitan conflict resolution. We may point out *en passant* that 'problem-solving' in conflict resolution does not mean what Robert Cox meant in his since often repeated (perhaps too often repeated) 1981 article. In Part I, we saw how, for Morton Deutsch and others, problem-solving is usually applied to symmetric relations between conflict parties, and means reconceptualizing 'either–or' antagonism into recognition that there is a systemic problem that can only be solved jointly. For John Burton, on the other hand, problem-solving was a broader term and meant analysis of deep-rooted conflict to uncover the structural/institutional failures of governance to meet basic human needs that underlie it and can only be resolved when these deficits are transformed accordingly. Problem-solving in the Burtonian sense is nearer to the critical perspective than is often realized. Nevertheless, there is clearly force in the critical observation that, given the vast imbalances, inequalities, unfairnesses, dominations and exclusions that make up the current global system, attempts at cosmopolitan amelioration that turn a blind eye to this and lack reflexive awareness are conceptually inadequate and that, even when this is recognized, such attempts are bound to be contaminated by existing power relations – indeed, to be seen to reinforce them – before such time as the system itself changes.

But two counter-critiques can be mounted before concluding by acknowledging the much greater shared agenda that cosmopolitan conflict resolution and critical international political economy theory have in common.

First, cosmopolitan conflict resolution does not conclude that pluralist, solidarist and cosmopolitan ideals, principles and aspirations as outlined in chapter 11 have themselves been discredited, or that the enterprise of progressively transforming existing unjust structures, institutions and discourses of power must be indefinitely postponed until they are somehow superseded at a stroke by an entirely different dispensation, as critical theory sometimes seems to demand. Pluralist values of non-violent conflict settlement, solidarist humanitarian values, and cosmopolitical values of self-determination and human rights (individual and collective, political, economic and cultural) are clearly enshrined in international law as recognized by all members of the United Nations (despite the well-known tension between them, as already acknowledged). These are the foundational values on which the conflict resolution enterprise rests. They represent a painfully accumulated international *acquis* that should not be lightly cast away. Whatever their historical origins or current distortions, they are seen to represent the best hope for the continuing evolution of an increasingly cosmopolitan human future in the long-term interest of the whole human family. If there is hypocrisy among those who pay lip service to them rhetorically while abusing them in practice, even this itself has some value – as La Rochefoucault put it: 'hypocrisy is the tribute vice pays to virtue'. While as to the question whether these are truly cosmopolitan values in the first place, this, too, is something to be argued out – and struggled over – in future within the transcultural ethico-political global arena that has now come to characterize late modernity. There is no complacency in the transformative cosmopolitan agenda. But the original vision of the founders of the field remains valid and has not yet been replaced by an obviously better one.

Second, cosmopolitan conflict resolution notes that many, if not most, critical approaches devote much of their energy to exposing present hegemonic abuse and relatively little to suggesting practical future alternatives. It is easier to bundle most current efforts into the 'liberal' (read illiberal) catchall, and to dismiss them as new forms of exclusion and domination, than it is to try to discriminate between those efforts that may and those that may not have emancipatory potential. But of course there is no incentive to do the latter if all forms of gradualism or piecemeal amelioration are seen as a sell-out to unreconstructed capital domination. This is a major difference compared to the transformative cosmopolitan approach. The very idea of 'lessons learned' is scorned from a critical perspective as mere problem-solving. So those currently grappling with in-field struggles to sustain and enhance cosmopolitan humanitarian values in the most heart-breaking conditions (for example, many NGOs) are more likely to find themselves criticized as 'petty sovereigns' by critical theoretic analysts than guided by practical suggestions as to how to improve their practice. If the critical alternative were already in place, this would not matter. But, since it is not, there is a yawning policy gap where, despite the potency of its critical analysis, the practical pay-off from a critical perspective as yet remains unclear.

But we would rather end this section on the ground where cosmopolitan conflict resolution and critical approaches meet, because on the key issues we see both theoretical stances as allies.

The conflict resolution field has learned a great deal from critical approaches over the past twenty years, as outlined in chapter 2. There we noted, for example, the influence in the 1990s of critical thinkers such as Andrew Linklater and the widespread introduction of Habermasian discourse ethics by theorists such as Mark Hoffman and Vivienne Jabri. In this fourth edition we can acknowledge a further conversational and dialogic turn in the writing of critical analysts such as Ken Booth (2007), Mark Duffield (2007), Michael Pugh, Neil Cooper and Mandy Turner (2008a) and Roger Mac Ginty (2012). This is partly a result of their reluctance to rely on more traditional arguments for a stronger statist interventionary framework for delivering the required controls on capital and redistribution of resources that a critical perspective demands – for example, as argued by David Harvey (2003) or, from a different perspective, Thomas Piketty (2014) (see chapter 11). This is seen to be in tension with the paramount value placed in this version of critical thinking on diversity and on the empowerment of local communities in defining their own welfare goals. So the emphasis has shifted to safeguarding principles of accountability and local ownership through Foucault's idea of global solidarity among 'the governed' – those, in all their diversity, who find themselves on the receiving end of biopolitics and associated practices of governmentality:

> In contrast, global solidarity emphasizes mutuality and reciprocity between provider and beneficiary while blurring the differences between them. It involves a 'more extensive global consciousness that constructs the grievances of physically, socially and culturally

distant people as deeply intertwined' (Foucault, 1984: 259). While difference is acknowledged, *it is similarities that are important*. Global solidarity is also political: distant struggles are common points of departure that collectively problematize the overarching, anti-democratic and marginalizing effects of global neoliberalism, whether as struggles against hospital closures in mass consumer society or the ruination of pastoralist livelihoods beyond its borders ... Today the fear of radical interconnection, with its ability to threaten the stability of mass consumer society, dominates Western political imagination. For an international citizenship, however, it offers possibilities for new encounters, mutual recognition, reciprocity and hope: it represents the magic of life itself. (Duffield, 2007: 233; original emphasis)

This is very close to the transformative cosmopolitan vision of global citizenship. How is this solidarity of the governed to be effected? Here again the suggested means is recognizable within the family of elicitive conversational conflict resolution approaches looked at in chapter 2:

In a reversal of the Schumachian paradigm of knowledge, instead of educating the poor and marginalized, it is more a question of learning from their struggles for existence, identity and dignity and together challenging the world we live in. As a precondition, the liberal inclination to prejudge those who are culturally different as somehow incomplete and requiring external betterment has to be abandoned. It requires a willingness to engage in unscripted conversations and accept the risks involved, including the inability to predict or control outcomes – a situation that a security mentality continually tries to avoid. (ibid.: 234)

Pugh, Cooper and Turner (2008b) endorse this conversational turn, calling for a paradigm shift away from 'universalist panaceas' and towards an engagement with 'heterogeneity' in optimizing life potential in all its variety, to be achieved through 'dialogue between heterodoxies' in the determination of ends and 'serial negotiation' in agreement about means:

A life welfare paradigm would encompass alternative notions of life (the individual, community, the biosphere and planetary environment) and alternative understandings of the political economy of peacebuilding in war-torn societies. This is not, however, a prescription for resigned relativism but rather a prescription for a politics of emancipation in which the need for dialogue between heterodoxies is a core component ... While [such a politics of emancipation] would not be about abstract individuals, or about the imposition of liberal values on non-Western societies that do not subscribe to these, it would incorporate the goal of optimizing the life potential of both individuals and diverse forms of community, recognizing that the means to reach such a goal would be the object of serial negotiation. (Ibid.: 395).

Here is a highly promising terrain for future exploration. But it is not yet clear what this proposed programme implies. What is meant by 'unscripted conversations among the governed' or 'dialogue between heterodoxies' or 'serial negotiation' among diverse lifestyles? Who participates and how? What kinds of conversation, dialogue or negotiation are envisaged? Is this likely to contain internal power struggles to determine who speaks for the protesters? If so, how will these be handled? Are all anti-liberal grassroots movements to be included? Or all globalized reactions against US/western hegemony? How do similarities that underpin global solidarity relate to differences that constitute diversity? Are the kinds of outcome hoped for indeed entirely unpredictable? In which case, what is the incentive to continue the conversations and dialogues? Is joint action envisaged, including coordination of strategy? If so, by whom and to what end? And how does all of this impact on the huge inertia of inherited structures of power that have hitherto found so little difficulty, according to critical analysis, in diverting, suppressing, co-opting or dispersing the protests and disruptions that continually emerge from and play around the margins?

These are crucial emancipatory questions in an irredeemably agonistic (conflictual) world. And it is here that Ramsbotham's (2010) exploration of managing *linguistic intractability*, the chief verbal manifestation of these struggles, may prove a useful supplement – as it were, another string to the emancipatory bow – in addition to those offered by critical theory. The politics of emancipation is the politics of conflict and is therefore itself inherently agonistic. This is overlooked in unproblematic critical references to 'recognizing alterity' or 'negotiating heterodoxies'. To acknowledge this serves to remove any lingering condescension in talk of 'a willingness to engage in unscripted conversations', as if such independent unpoliticized conceptual space were available and it is up to some of the actors to decide whether or not to occupy it.

The Post-Structural Critique

The blanket term 'post-structural critique' brings together a group of stances that variously define their topic in terms of anti-essentialism, anti-foundationalism and anti-representationalism (Richmond, 2008: 134–48). They embrace a variety of non-positivist, constructionist and deconstructionist discursive approaches. Language is generally taken to be a signifying system through which material objects and social formations are given meaning. And human discourse is seen as a site of contestation in which competing versions of 'reality' are constructed in the service of interest and power. There are no unalloyed truths, only various constructions of the world that may be endorsed as 'truth' within different historico-cultural settings.

The post-structural and critical theoretic fields overlap to the extent that the former is prepared to be critical of universalizing, totalizing and reifying systems that are unaware of their own contingency. These are then associated with tyranny, and the emancipatory aim may emerge of dissolving the binary and discriminatory categories that underpin perceptions of difference on which such exclusions and dominations depend. Here some post-structural approaches join hands with critical approaches.

But other post-structural approaches are more radical still and shy away from explicitly endorsing political emancipation in this way, preferring to 'outflank' critical theory by accusing it in turn of harbouring residual elements of Enlightenment rationalism (didacticism) that consigns it to the ever capacious 'liberal' limbo. Some critical theorists accuse post-structuralism in reverse because it provides no basis from which unjust or unequal systems of power can be challenged (relativism). Within this nexus, Michel Foucault and Jürgen Habermas, for example, compete for the prize of maximizing the emancipation of difference. For Foucault:

> The freeing of difference requires thought without contradiction, without dialectics, without negation; thought that accepts divergence; affirmative thought whose instrument is disjunction; thought of the multiple – of the nomadic and dispersed multiplicity that is not limited or confined by the constraints of similarity ... What is the answer to the question? The problem. How is the problem resolved? By displacing the question ... We must think problematically rather than question and answer dialectically. (Foucault, 1977: 185–6)

Habermas, for his part, strongly rebutted accusations that his theory implies a hegemony of social coordination that stifles dissent and smothers what it purports to emancipate: 'Nothing makes me more nervous' than the imputation that the theory of communicative action 'proposes, or at least suggests, a rationalist utopian society' (Habermas, 1982: 235). He claimed, on the contrary, that only the idealizations presupposed in 'the intersubjectivity of linguistically achieved understanding' can open up the space for divergent voices to be heard: 'linguistically attained consensus does not eradicate from the accord the differences in speaker perspectives but rather presupposes them as ineliminable ... More discourse means more contradiction and difference. The more abstract the agreements become, the more diverse the disagreements with which we can non-violently live' (Habermas, 1992: 140).

As far as the conversation between post-structuralism and cosmopolitan conflict resolution is concerned, the main post-structural critique is of the 'universalizing' assumptions about truth and reality that are seen to permeate cosmopolitan discourse. These criticisms have hit home, and the peace and conflict field has drawn from them accordingly in a significant redefinition of terms, as described in chapter 9. Oliver Richmond, for example, with reference to Homi Bhabha's (1994) concept of hybridity, suggests adopting the language of 'diversified and fragmented peaces' in recognizing alterity and abandoning ideas about 'universal peace':

> This means that peace itself is radically reconceptualised, not necessarily as an objective but as a method and process, and never a final end state. In this context difference is accepted, others are acknowledged, but not at their own expense or that of hybridity. Uncovering hybridity – the fluid and intersecting identities shared by all – forms a *via media* between difference. This requires the acceptance of difference as a method of peace, rather than an emphasis on sameness or universality. The process of handing agency to critical social movements, for example, and providing ways in which they are empowered to develop their voices, identities and ideas, moves towards indicating a post-structural methodology for achieving a more inclusive and less predatory form of peace. (Richmond, 2008: 147)

Mark Hoffman (2009) similarly invokes Amartya Sen's reconceptualization of the idea of justice (see chapter 11) in a comparable nuancing and hybridization of the post-structural idea of peace:

> This leads to a rethinking of the nature of peace itself. Rather than assuming that peace is a coherent project which can be readily transplanted from one society to another, there needs to be a recognition that the nature and meaning of peace should be heavily debated and constantly evolving ... Paralleling Sen's move away from 'transcendental institutional' accounts of justice, it would recognise that peace is multi-faceted, pluralistic and that when the competing conceptions of peace circulating within a society run up against each other, there is no absolutist account that provides a privileged perspective from which to judge one being better than the other. Instead there needs to be an ongoing, continuous process of collective reasoning that injects more perspectives, more voices that can actually be heard, into an understanding of how peace might best be conceived and enacted in a given context. (2009: 11)

But once again there is a tendency here for post-structural thinking to ignore the fierce disruption and disconinuity of radical disagreement – the chief linguistic manifestation of intense political conflict. With reference to this section and the previous section, therefore, taking the phenomenon of radical disagreement seriously, as advocated by Ramsbotham (2010; forthcoming, 2017), may in some measure help to temper what is at times a somewhat didactic tendency in critical theory and a relativist tendency in post-structuralism, while politically grounding what can be a predilection for abstraction in both.

Non-Western/Non-Northern Critiques

Here, finally, is what should be the most important conversation in this chapter. We first acknowledge the embarrassing – indeed, shaming – compartmentalizations that still segregate differing epistemic communities within western/northern academia, much of it stemming from the singular achievement of many in the English-speaking world to resist successfully any temptation to read other languages. We also note how calls to move 'beyond northern epistemologies', for example, are often made by northerners (as in Lidén et al., 2009), including 'honorary northerners' from Australia and New Zealand. And how many of the other 'voices from the East and South' that are now increasingly being raised are still only heard widely in the West and North to the extent that they come from those who have first been programmed through the western and northern academies and can therefore use the appropriate concepts and language. For example, outside the self-referential western/northern academies lie whole universes of entirely different epistemological approaches, vast libraries of complex and specialist commentary and exegesis as extensive as the western/northern corpus, including internal controversies and hierarchies of acknowledged authority, of which western/northern academia, beyond a very small number of scholars, is still almost entirely ignorant. The various schools of Islamic scholarship, for instance, continue to draw on centuries of living textual analysis that reaches back unbroken to the time when, before the advent of the humanist revolution, western scholasticism was still the prevailing academic language in European universities. None of this is recognized in western/northern academia today, where students hitherto trained in these other traditions have to jettison their methodologies and conceptual frameworks altogether and adopt an entirely different intellectual disposition.

In previous editions of this book we noted criticisms of the conflict resolution field such as Paul Salem's 'critique of western conflict resolution from a non-western perspective' (1993, 1997). Salem argued that the 'western' principles on which conflict resolution rests are not applicable universally. He questioned some of the 'hidden assumptions in the Western approach to conflict resolution' from an Arab Muslim perspective and suggests that they are not shared in other parts of the world. These are examples of the wider 'culture critique' that has already been discussed and commented upon in chapter 15. Tom Woodhouse (1999b) argued in response that, although many of the recent theories and practices of conflict resolution may have been articulated more vociferously in the West, their deep roots reach into far older world traditions from which they draw their inspiration. Indeed, every culture and society has its own version of what is, after all, a general social and political need (Reading 71). This lies at the heart of the cosmopolitan conflict resolution programme.

But what about the most difficult cases of all, where the very idea of cosmopolitan conflict resolution is rejected in its entirety? This is the most serious challenge of all, and we think that the conflict resolution field has hardly begun to address it. To illustrate this, we can give the example of Vivienne Jabri's heroic attempt to apply a Habermasian framework in these cases. In the following passage she considers the problem of religious belief that rejects the whole basis of Habermasian discourse ethics. This includes western as well as non-western religious belief. She correctly identifies this as characteristic of 'some of the most pervasive conflicts of late modernity':

> Discourse ethics as process is a locale of emancipation from the constraints of tradition, prejudice and myth. However, some of the most pervasive conflicts of late modernity concern issues of religious belief which preclude a questioning of norms, where the text and image considered sacred are not allowed into an intersubjective space of equal interpretation and contestation. This defines a situation where it is not merely inter-subjective consent as an outcome of discourse that is the problem. This is, in fact, a condition, which does not allow the occurrence of discourse and precludes any possibility of an emergent dialogic relationship. (Jabri, 1996: 166–7)

In response, Jabri follows Seyla Benhabib (1992) in expanding Habermas's framework to include 'moral substance' as well as 'process' in the discursive ethical realm:

To incorporate concrete issues of lived experience into the framework of communicative ethics renders it more responsive to the challenges of contextualised social relations. While the process contains universal constitutive rules framing communicative action, it concedes that it must take place within conditions of value differentiation and heterogeneity. A peace located in discourse ethics must therefore recognise difference as a formative component of subjectivity. (Jabri, 1996: 167)

The trouble here is that the radical challenge is now not so much overcome as swept under the carpet. Portentous issues of religious belief are reinterpreted as mere 'concrete issues of lived experience' against the will of those who profess them, and are thereby reincorporated into the universal constitutive secular rules that they reject. The protests that fuel intractable conflicts of this kind are consequently absorbed back into 'a discursive ethics, which not only incorporates difference but celebrates such agency' (ibid.: 185). The appeal once again is to the background assumptions that define the constitutive framework of 'dialogue for mutual understanding'. But the religious beliefs in question explicitly refute the idea that they can be 'celebrated' as mere 'formative components of subjectivity' within a wider field of onotologically equivalent 'difference' that includes other beliefs that are incompatible with them. That is what they are rebelling against. So it is that the whole Habermasian conceptual framework is now itself found to be radically implicated in what is being contested in these cases (Ramsbotham, 2010: 86–91 149–56). More generally, Ramsbotham argues that the same is true of other attempts to encompass radical disagreement within an overarching conflict resolution framework – including, for example, that of Hans-Georg Gadamer, as discussed in chapter 15 (Ramsbotham, 2015).

In the final analysis, therefore, cosmopolitan conflict resolution is not neutral or 'above the fray'. Conflict resolution takes sides. It has allies and enemies. As is made clear in chapter 11, atrocities such as those associated with Islamic State and Boko Haram – together with their justifying ideologies – are utterly repudiated in cosmopolitan conflict resolution. But beyond this there remain very difficult issues where illiberal western and non-western approaches and practices confront what conflict resolution insists are truly cosmopolitan standards. We do not have easy answers in these cases. In this chapter – and more generally in Part II as a whole – the theoretic and normative assumptions behind the transformative cosmopolitan conflict resolution tradition, shared by the authors, have been made explicit and defended against dismissive realist and critical/post-structural critiques and against both western and non-western 'cultural' rejection. Conflict resolution is resolutely opposed to all forms of direct, structural and cultural violence. This is where it makes its stand. Readers are thereby invited to join the debate and reach their own conclusions.

RECOMMENDED READING

Miall (2007); Ramsbotham (2010; forthcoming, 2017); Richmond (2008); Woodhouse (1999b).

RELEVANT EXTRACTS IN *THE CONTEMPORARY CONFLICT RESOLUTION READER*

Reading 59: R. Mac Ginty, Hybrid Peace: The Interaction Between Top-Down and Bottom-Up Peace

Reading 68: V. Jabri, Revisiting Change and Conflict: On Underlying Assumptions and the De-Politicisation of Conflict Resolution

Reading 71: W. Dietriech et al., Peace Studies: A Cultural Perspective

CHAPTER TWENTY

Conflict Resolution and the Future

In his book *Emergent Conflict and Peaceful Change* (2007), Hugh Miall offers a comparative study of emergent conflict formations of all kinds associated with political, economic, cultural and environmental change. As has been argued throughout this book, social change is itself conflictual. Shifting contexts generate varying focal points for competing interests, and the balance of perceived advantage and disadvantage ebbs and flows accordingly. So what dictates whether change turns out to be peaceful or violent, and can lessons be derived for increasing the likelihood of the former and decreasing the likelihood of the latter in particular cases? Is it possible, not just for individuals, but for societies, to learn how to manage internal and external conflict non-violently? And what are the penalties likely to be for failing to do this? These have been, and remain, key questions for the conflict resolution enterprise.

This final chapter, therefore, begins by taking a hard look at emergent conflict formations that seem to be appearing over the horizon and, in the light of this, and of what has been shown earlier in the book, considers the prospects for increasing future capacity for managing conflictual change and political struggle non-violently. This builds on the analysis of prevailing patterns of contemporary conflict in chapter 4 – particularly the interpretatative framework for transnational conflict offered in table 4.2 (p. 123) and the preliminary outline of a cosmopolitan conflict resolution response as set out in chapter 11. What is the overall picture that this book presents?

The gathering clouds of future conflict may at first appear overwhelming – and there are plenty of alarmist analyses that make them seem so, as noted below. In 2014, the seizure of territory by *jihadist* groups in areas where government weakness, civil war and international paralysis left a power vacuum, as in Syria, Iraq, Nigeria and elsewhere, was seen to presage a breakdown of the state system, widescale disorder and an upsurge in violence. The crisis in Ukraine was interpreted in some quarters as a return to the Cold War, if not to the hot wars that preceded it. The latest attempt to secure a settlement in Israel/Palestine collapsed back into war in Gaza. These – and other setbacks – could be regarded as part of a systemic reversal of the reduction in levels of violent conflict recorded since the early 1990s and a refutation of Steven Pinker's claim that 'we may be living in the most peaceable era in our species' existence' (2011: xxi). Other examples are the return to autocracy in Egypt, civil war in Libya and Yemen, internecine violence in South Sudan, and the dangerous drift in the Democratic Republic of the Congo.

But what in chapter 3 we called the 'merging of datasets' and the caveats discussed there about methodologies for gathering and assessing data for conflict, violence and peace should make us wary of basing assessment on instinctive responses to media headlines. In other chapters we have noted a more varied picture – for example, the remarkable upsurge in peace settlements and peace agreements even in chaotic multi-conflictual environments discussed in chapter 7. Here there are indications of a deepening international capacity to accommodate conflicting ethno-national aspirations non-violently by incremental adjustments in international law. The benign development in the longstanding conflicts in Mindanao in the Philippines noted in chapter 13 offers another example. The situations in Colombia and El Salvador at the time of writing still hold out prospects for reducing levels of violence, in the case of Colombia including hopes of ending decades of war. The same may also be true in Burma (Myanmar), despite recent setbacks and the underlying continung gross exploitation of local resources by both indigenous and extraneous forces, particularly in border regions. Sri Lanka – to the surprise of many – has so far achieved a peaceful change of government through the ballot box, which may increase opportunities for transforming what has been a forcible and brutal end to civil war into a deeper process of long-term political accommodation and even eventual reconciliation. Tunisia is still setting an example of transition from autocracy to the rudiments of democratic constitutional rule. The current round of nuclear talks with Iran and cooperation against Islamic State in Iraq, though precarious, still suggest possibilities for accommodation that may ease tension in an area of enduring instability in recent decades – *pace* understandable Israeli alarmism. The election of a new government in Afghanistan (albeit contested) may offer similar opportunities, despite the ongoing civil war (Loyn, 2015). And so on. By the time this book is published no doubt the picture will have changed in further unexpected ways.

Although life on earth began about 3,500 million years ago, the human species has only existed for fewer than 200,000 years (the era dominated by the dinosaurs lasted 160 million years). Short of a catastrophic cosmic collision, the earth should remain habitable for another 4,000 million years, until the sun, having consumed its inner hydrogen, expands into a red giant and incinerates the earth in the process. How long can the human species survive? Let us begin modestly with the next fifty to a hundred years. What needs to happen to prolong human existence that long? Setting aside the ongoing medical battle with mutating generations of viruses such as Ebola (Davies, 2013), what 'man-made' threats loom?

Emergent Conflicts

It is notoriously difficult to predict the future in the social sciences. Few can guess what will happen even ten years ahead when there are sudden major discontinuities. Which experts in 1919 foresaw the Wall Street crash of 1929? Or in 1929 predicted the outbreak of the Second World War in 1939? Or in 1969 anticipated the Iranian revolution of 1979? Or in 1979 (at the height of the 'second Cold War') expected the collapse of the Soviet system in 1989? Or in 1998 previsaged the onset of the 2008 economic collapse? Even one year before the 2011 Arab revolutions, when we were completing the third edition of this book, we had no inkling of what would follow in a few months' time. Perhaps the only thing that can be safely predicted is that commentators will later read back into their accounts of the past the *post hoc* knowledge that was so conspicuously absent before.

Nevertheless, all four of the main types of large-scale conflict looked at in chapter 3 seem likely to recur in the foreseeable future – interstate conflict, identity/secession conflict, revolution/ideology conflict, and economic/resource conflict (see table 3.2, p. 91). We have acknowledged in chapter 4 that neat categorizations of this kind break down and that complex and protracted large-scale conflicts are hybrid, multi-level and multi-factorial, sometimes transmuting rapidly as circumstances change. Categorization is also controversial and, as often as not, part of what is being fought over. Nevertheless, for the sake of clarity, as in chapter 3, we will accept these working analytic distinctions, reflected as they are in most statistical attempts to categorize large-scale conflicts.

In an essay in *Foreign Policy*, former UN Under-Secretary for Peacekeeping Operations Jean-Marie Guéhenno (2015) anticipates 'ten wars to watch' in 2015. Readers will be able to assess this prediction by the time the fourth edition of the book is published. Attributing the turmoil to a mixture of increasing geopolitical competition, regional instability, and the 'worrying tendency toward violence in countries attempting to transition to democracy', together with a spread of extremist ideology that 'comes late to the party' and battens onto 'other sources of violence' (2015: 1–3), Guéhenno lists the following wars expected in 2015: (1) Syria, Iraq and the Islamic State, (2) Ukraine, (3) South Sudan, (4) Nigeria, (5) Somalia, (6) Democratic Republic of Congo (DRC), (7) Afghanistan, (8) Yemen, (9) Libya and the Sahel, and (10) Venezuela.

Interstate conflict

It can be seen that none of the ten wars is a classic interstate war – although the fighting in Ukraine comes closest and is by far the most threatening in general terms (although still relatively low in casualties compared with others). For that reason we will postpone further comment until we come to consider 'drivers of future conflict' below – particularly the driver of 'geopolitical transition'. The key question is whether Russia and China are 'revisionist' powers that are now prepared to challenge western hegemony and, in the case of Russia, to attempt to redraw international borders by force. This would reverse at a stroke the foundation of international political order established since the Helsinki Accords in 1975 between the thirty-five countries of the communist bloc and the West, consolidated by the 1990 Charter of Paris for a New Europe, which set out for the OSCE area what, instead of confrontation and division, was intended to be an irreversible path ahead of military, political, economic and human rights cooperation (see the case study in chapter 5).

Identity/secession conflict

Given the global mismatch between state borders and the distribution of peoples described in chapter 4, it will be no surprise if ethno-national and other forms of identity conflict persist. A number of the predicted wars on Guéhenno's list are rooted here, posing severe tests for what are in nearly every case the postcolonial state entities that are struggling to contain them. Once again, the fundamental question can be postponed to a consideration of 'drivers of future conflict' below, in this case the current 'crisis of the state system' represented by the long (and possibly lengthening) list of 'fragile states' now merged with traditional 'conflict' data, as described in chapter 3.

Revolution/ideology conflict

It is much harder to predict future ideological contests to determine the nature of government – communist versus capitalist, authoritarian versus democratic, religious versus secular, including vicious intra-religious sectarian struggles to define and impose orthodoxy. We must not forget the revolutionary potential for authoritarian regimes of democratic ideology now irreversibly implanted in most regions, or the communist-inspired insurgencies in countries such as Nepal, Colombia and India, or the disruptive potential of non-Islamic Jewish, Christan, Hindu and Buddhist political radicalism, as noted in chapter 15. But centre stage at the time of writing is the unexpected and chaotic upsurge of neo-*jihadist* extremism and its extraordinary capacity to impose its categories on existing political and economic struggles, including a majority of those on Guéhenno's list: Syria/Iraq, Nigeria, Somalia, Afghanistan, Yemen, Libya – as illustrated in several case studies earlier in this book. It is the rapid mutations and permutations characteristic of contemporary patterns of transnational conflict, lubricated as they are by the 'transnational connectors' described in chapter 4, that make these challenges so hard to predict and prevent, and so difficult to respond to once they are established – as discussed in chapter 11.

Economic/resource conflict

Under this category are included resource struggles between states familiar to classic realist readings of international relations – for example, 'water wars' or efforts to compete for control of Arctic and Antarctic resources, undersea oil – even extending to the moon – for instance, the £480 million plan led by the Russian Academy of Sciences to colonize the moon by 2030 in anticipation of 'geopolitical competition for natural lunar resources in the near future' (*Izvestia*, as reported in *The Times*, 10 May 2014). But perhaps of more relevance to Guéhenno's list are those conflicts driven mainly not so much by secessionist or ideological ambitions as by factional in-fighting to control resources of the state – 'greed' rather than 'grievance'. This is quite widely seen to be the case in South Sudan and DRC, but, as noted in chapter 3, it is also widely characteristic of other types of conflict, particularly when they degenerate into the rapacious free-for-all of chaotic war zones (see chapter 6).

Future Drivers of Conflict

Beneath these overt manifestations of large-scale conflict lie the more subterranean global drivers of conflict that generate them, as noted in chapter 4. These were identified early on within the conflict resolution field both as the systemic 'preconditions' for deep-rooted or protracted social conflict and as the ultimate targets of the long-term enterprise of conflict prevention through strategies to overcome structural and cultural violence. Cosmopolitan conflict resolution has to recognize them and learn how to anticipate and respond to them. In each case the very testing question must be asked: How can conflict resolution approaches hope to engage and transform such large-scale global trends?

This is where the most dire predictions of a 'return of geopolitics and the revenge of the revisionist powers' (Mead, 2014), or even a 'collapse of global civilization' (Ehrlich and Ehrlich, 2013), are made. But this is also where the prophets of doom are vigorously challenged by those who argue, on the contrary, that the idea of a return of geopolitics of a revisionist kind is an 'illusion' and point instead to the 'enduring power of the liberal order' (Ikenberry, 2014). Let us weigh up some of the evidence.

Geopolitical transition

We noted in chapter 1 how, while we have been producing the four editions of this book, successive transformations of the world scene have taken place. At the risk of oversimplification, the first edition marked the transition from a *bipolar world* to what US President George Bush senior reluctantly called a *New World Order*. By the time of the second edition we were faced with the *unipolar moment*, when the US hyperpower saw itself – and was widely seen – as the main shaper of world history. By the time of the third edition we had moved with remarkable rapidity into a much more *multipolar* world. And now, contemplating the situation towards the end of the second decade of the twenty-first century, we are confronted by a highly complex and shifting balance of forces that has once again made analysis both difficut and controversial. From a realist perspective, shifts in global and regional balance of power of this kind are usually accompanied by interstate war.

The pessimistic school has certainly increased its forebodings since the third edition of this book. In July 2014, a UK Ministry of Defence think tank envisaged the possibility of a future war between the rising power of China and the previous hegemon, the US – along classic Thucydidean lines.[1] The Chinese leader, Xi Jinping, is seen to be moving away from the former caution of Deng Xiaoping and to be challenging US global hegemony. Others are more optimistic (*Foreign Affairs*, 2015). However, this was seen to be tempered by the strong economic link between Beijing and Washington, which should reduce the chances of war between the two powers (UK MOD, 2014). In January 2015, the World Economic Forum (WEF) warned that the danger of a big global conflict is greater today than at any point since the fall of the Berlin Wall. The most likely threat to stability was seen as 'interstate conflict with regional consequences' that could roll back the benefits of twenty-five years of globalization. The study pointed to Russia's annexation in Ukraine and tensions over the Diaoyu/Senkaku islands between China and Japan. There was also increased risk of 'water wars' in view of the fact that, by 2025, 1.8 billion people will be living with absolute water scarcity (WEF, as reported in *The Times*, 16 January 2015). It is in this vein that Walter Russell Mead has argued:

> So far, the year 2014 has been a tumultuous one, as geopolitical rivalries have stormed back to the center stage. Whether it is Russian forces seizing Crimea, China making aggressive claims in its coastal waters, Japan responding with an increasingly assertive strategy of its own, or Iran trying to use its alliances with Syria and Hezbollah to dominate the Middle East, old-fashioned power plays are back in international relations. The United States and the EU, at least, find such trends disturbing. Both would rather move past geopolitical questions of territory and military power and focus instead on ones of world order and global governance: trade liberalization, nuclear nonproliferation, human rights, the rule of law, climate change, and so on ...
>
> All these happy convictions are about to be tested. Twenty-five years after the fall of the Berlin Wall, whether one focuses on the rivalry between the EU and Russia over Ukraine ...; the intensifying competition between China and Japan in East Asia; or the subsuming of sectarian conflict into international rivalries and civil wars in the Middle East, the world is looking less post-historical by the day. In very different ways, with very different objectives, China, Iran and Russia are all pushing back against the political settlement of the Cold War ... What binds these powers together ... is their agreement that the status quo must be revised. (Mead, 2014: 1,3)

This is reminiscent of Samuel Huntington's argument in the heyday of the 'clash of civilizations' dispute, predicting a global confrontation between 'the West and the Rest' (Huntington, 1996).

But this updated version of Huntington has been strongly refuted by others, notably John Ikenberry:

> Walter Russell Mead paints a disturbing portrait of the United States' geopolitical predicament ... But Mead's alarmism is based on a colossal misreading of modern power realities. It is a misreading of the logic and character of the existing world order, which is more stable and expansive than Mead depicts ... [I]t is a misreading of China and Russia, which are not full-scale revisionist powers but part-time spoilers at best, as suspicious of each other as they are of the outside world. True, they look for opportunities to resist the United States' global leadership, and recently, as in the past, they have pushed against it, particularly when confronted in their own neighbourhoods. But even these conflicts are fuelled more by [the] weakness [of] their leaders and regimes than by strength. They have no appealing brand. And when it comes to their overriding interests, Russia and, especially, China are deeply integrated into the world economy and its governing institutions ... Alliances, partnerships, multilateralism, democracy – these are the tools of U.S. leadership, and they are winning, not losing, the twenty-first century struggles over geopolitics and the world order. (Ikenberry, 2014: 80–1)

Ikenberry goes on to argue that, although 'many liberal democracies are struggling at the moment with slow economic growth, social inequality, and political instability', 60 per cent of all countries were democracies by the late 1990s, a number that has continued to grow despite disappointment in Egypt and slippage in Turkey. Quoting Larry Diamond, Ikenberry notes that, if Argentina, Brazil, India, Indonesia, South Africa and Turkey 'regain their economic footing and strengthen their democratic rule', then the G20 will have become 'a strong club of democracies', with only Russia, China and Saudi Arabia holding out. Russia is acting not out of strength, but out of weakness, 'experiencing one of the greatest geopolitical contractions of any major power in the modern era'. Russia may have made small gains near its borders but has in the process lost Ukraine as a whole to the West. As for China, as a permanent member of the UN Security Council and a nuclear power, it is not trying to break the systems of global and regional cooperation in which it is a powerful 'insider' (for example, the Association of South-East Asian Nations and the East Asia Summit) or the world trade system of which it is a signal beneficiary – although it does seek (and should be accorded) greater say in global economic fora such as the IMF and the World Bank. It is also – to the alarm of the US – seeking to build a complementary Asian Infrastructure Investment Bank. The idea that China is seeking to replace these institutions is therefore seen as a misreading.

Behind this dispute, from a conflict resolution perspective, the biggest fear is that a shift in the global balance of power in which the long western hegemony comes to an end may prove to be the harbinger of a 'revaluation of all values' (to quote Nietzsche) in which conflict resolution itself may come to be seen as no more than one aspect of a fading *imperium*, to be replaced by entirely different value systems. That is why we define the main task for the new (fifth) generation of those engaged in the conflict resolution field to be to push forward decisively with the central mission of ensuring that conflict resolution is seen to be a truly cosmopolitan venture, derived from and owned by all civilizations and parts of the world. We return to this theme at the end of the chapter.

The North–South economic divide

In his article 'Cosmopolitanism after 9/11' (2010; Reading 73), David Held clearly identifies global inequality as a main driver of future conflict and therefore a central site for cosmopolitan conflict resolution concern:

> [F]inally, there must be a head-on acknowledgement that the global polarization of wealth, income and power, and with them the huge asymmetries of life chances, cannot be left to markets to resolve alone. Those who are poorest and most vulnerable, linked into geo-political situations where their economic and political claims have been neglected for generations, may provide fertile ground for terrorist recruiters. The project of economic globalization has to be connected to manifest principles of social justice; the latter need to frame global market activity. (Held, 2010: 55)

As stressed throughout this book, economic and welfare inadequacies and inequalities remain a huge source of weakness at global, regional and national levels, generating instability and providing a breeding ground for antagonism, extremism and war. The powerful global political economy critique of late capitalism along these lines has been a constant theme and reference point in earlier chapters.

In terms of absolute levels of deprivation and poverty, we have noted the emphasis by Paul Collier (2008) on the plight of the 'bottom billion' and the dangers for future turbulence if these paramount needs are not met. Others place even more emphasis on 'horizontal inequalities': 'It is my hypothesis that an important factor that differentiates the violent from the peaceful is *the existence of severe inequalities between culturally defined groups*, which I shall define as *horizontal inequalities*' (Stewart, 2002: 1–7; and see Reading 19).

In other words, it is not so much absolute levels of deprivation as 'unequal access to political, economic and social elements', even when these are improving, that may lead to revolution (what used to be called revolutions of 'rising expectations'). It may be true that overall global 'well-being', in terms of life expectancy, income and educational attainment, continues to rise faster than has been supposed – as argued, for example, in a 2014 OECD report *How Was Life?* – but the plight of Paul Collier's 'bottom billion' and pockets of deep deprivation even in relatively more affluent regions continue to fuel instability. In chapter 11 we have discussed the dispute between Thomas Piketty (2014) and Deirdre McCloskey (2015) about economic inequality in this regard.

Much greater relative population growth in poorer parts of the world concentrates increasing numbers of unemployed young people – particularly young men – in politically fragile, often autocratic and repressive, states without hope of betterment. Kept on the margins of global capitalism and largely excluded from rapid development in the richer areas, a huge pool of recruits for revolutionary movements and, often violent, black market operations is continually being replenished and deepened. These populations are increasingly concentrated in cities. In 1975, one-third of the world's population lived in cities; by 2025, it is likely to be two-thirds. In many poorer countries half the population is under sixteen. By 2050, Nigeria is projected to overtake the US as the third most populous country in the world, with nearly 500 million people. By 2100, Africa's population is estimated to reach more than 4 billion (the current world population is 7.2 billion), with Nigeria having over 1 billion. Some countries (for example, in Europe, Japan, Russia – even China) face a crisis of rapid aging due to population decline; others are challenged in the opposite direction – for example, with 60 per cent of the Arab world aged under twenty-five, it is estimated that 100 million jobs will need to be created across the region to absorb the increase (United Nations, 2014).

The crisis of the postcolonial state

Turning to the political dimension, another central driver of future conflict is widely identified as what we call the current crisis of the postcolonial state – a main focus for conflict resolution analysis as exemplified in the account of Edward Azar's theory of protracted social conflict given in chapter 4. As noted there, given the continuing mismatch between state borders (some 200 states) and the geographical distribution of peoples (on some estimates, perhaps as many as 5,000 groups that could harbour ambitions for independence), there is no prospect of the two coinciding.

The reason for this concern is that, whatever other levels of analysis may be prominent or even paramount, it is at state level that the crisis is in the end usually still played out. As argued in chapter 4, states remain the chief actors on the international stage and the chief satisfiers of human needs in the domestic arena. So a systemic crisis of the modern state is a crisis for the whole of world politics.

Chapter 3 showed how concern about the apparently still growing number of 'fragile states' is now merged centrally into statistics of large-scale violence and war. In the Middle East and North Africa region (MENA) there is a widespread view that Iraq is now irrevocably split into its three components of Sunni, Shia and Kurds, that the Alawite region in Syria might break away, and that Libya and Yemen may also break up – not to mention the post-Sykes–Picot pretensions of Islamic State. Elsewhere this book has been full of instances where the international community has been struggling to accommodate particularist and secessionist forces within the existing state system through a combination of overlapping processes of internal power-sharing (minority rights within democratic constitutions), sometimes combined with cross-border 'territorial self-governance' (TSG) arrangements (see Whitman and Wolff, 2010, and Reading 65). In chapter 7 we noted Christine Bell's account of ways in which a flexible 'law of peace' has been evolving via end-of-conflict agreements in the direction of hybrid self-determination and creative ambiguity, engineered through different forms of 'internal disaggregation' and 'external dislocation' (Bell, 2008).

And this is why the Russian flouting of the OSCE and UN principle that international borders – however apparently arbitrary – will not be changed by force is seen as such a serious blow to conflict resolution hopes for a non-violent international future at great power level.

What are the prospects for international conflict resolution capacity being able to contain these fissiparous and disintegrative forces?

Gender oppression

From a different angle of analysis, the continuing plight of a high proportion of one half of the human family, oppressed by structures and traditions of patriarchy, is highlighted both as a deep source of future conflict and as a site for emancipatory struggles that will challenge most of the dominant power structures, attitudes and behaviours that are in one way or another based on it. Here the very idea of conflict resolution is challenged by some forms of difference feminism, as discussed in chapter 13. Countering this is the real progress made in recognizing the role of women in peace processes and conflict resolution and the emergence of the Women's Global Peace Agenda, enhanced by physical and virtual global networks facilitated by the Women, Seriously! and Women's Peace Tables initiatives, also outlined in chapter 13.

Weapons development

Into this complex systemic set of actual and potential conflict formations flow ever evolving military technologies and supply. This ranges from what are numerically by far the largest killers – knives and small arms – up to the potentially catastrophic weapons of mass destruction. Looking a hundred years ahead, the odds on biological, chemical or nuclear weapons technology at some point falling into the hands of governments or groups willing to use them are impossible to calculate but frighteningly easy to imagine. Linked to this are the extraordinary prospects for enhanced governmental control via new generations of surveillance technologies, 'non-lethal' crowd control weapons and methods of persuasion.

From a conflict resolution perspective, how can the huge global enterprise of weapons development, manufacture and dissemination be stemmed, implanted as it is in the very heart of the most vital and closely guarded economic and security interests of the most powerful states? What can constrain the irresistible urge towards dispersal driven by weakness of central control in some cases and temptations to offset development costs by arms sales in most cases, together with the gains of profiteers and the opportunities for domination and plunder that beckon for local end users? Despite these dangers, innovative research aiming at effective regime-building and policy-making for arms control continues to be developed. Malcolm Dando has led a research team working on bioethics and biosecurity, aiming to understand and to provide controls on and alternatives to the development of lethal chemical and biological weapons systems (Dando, Dual Use Bioethics Project, at www.brad.ac.uk/bioethics/). At the other end of the scale, Greene and Marsh (2012) have analysed the connections between small arms/light weapons (SALW) and their impact as causes of violence, injury and insecurity in communities across the world. They carefully examine the steps necessary to bring these weapons under control in a regime of global governance, reminding us that failure to deal with SALW as part of the peacemaking process will derail efforts at conflict resolution and peacebuilding.

The environment

Finally, and in some eyes even dwarfing other drivers of future conflict, the linked effects of material scarcity, climate change and natural resource depletion are widely projected to have major political impacts, as described in chapter 12. Thomas Homer-Dixon (1991, 1994) predicted some time ago a looming concatenation of severe environmental constraints and human conflict, with 'simple scarcity' conflicts over oil, water, forests, fishing and agricultural land, 'group-identity conflicts' triggered by large-scale population movements (climate change will disproportionately affect tropical and sub-tropical landmasses where most of the world's population lives) and 'deprivation' conflicts caused by relative depletion of natural resources. However, given the weak evidence for a link between changing rainfall and temperatures and armed conflict over the last fifty years, the conflict research community is sceptical of 'climate war' determinism, as noted in chapter 12. In addition to the effects of global warming, there are any number of major issues which could lead, on the one hand, to enhanced cooperation or, on the other, to greater conflict, including the management of the resources of the Arctic, the fate of the great rivers fed by the Himalayas, and the control of trans-border water resources.

Drivers of potential future conflict are seen to be systemically interconnected. For example, a combination of environmental pressure and the global socio-economic divide could accelerate migratory pressures by a large factor over the next decades. We have noted the catastrophic rise in levels of human displacement, now exceeding those of any period since 1945. If unchecked, the pressures of climate change and poor economic performance could weaken states, making populations more vulnerable and reducing capacity to manage conflicts.

Everything depends on whether these issues are handled cooperatively now. We have emphasized that conflict resolution needs allies. This is one area which naturally links conflict prevention and environmental concerns, in recognizing the urgent need for proactive measures to avert future calamities.

Putting all this together, the question is: Can existing economic and political structures contain and manage these enormous systemic stresses, particularly at a time when the revolution in communications is making the huge discrepancies between the resources available to the haves and the have nots increasingly obvious? Will the mobile phone and the internet perhaps even put global access into the hands of the most disadvantaged for the first time in history, once literacy levels, the cheapness of the technology, and the interest of providers in increasing the global market make this possible? Given the threat of political convulsion in the state system at great power and regional levels, or a possible future economic collapse (as at one time threatened in 2008), it is not hard for pessimists to envisage the possibility of a break-up of the institutions of the international system as we have known them, a decisive reversal of direction for what we have called the 'arrow of history', and the onset of a chaotic and warring global anarchy.

The Conflict Resolution Response

But none of this is inevitable. Unlike some forms of realist and Marxist theory, conflict resolution has always insisted that, although human conflict is inevitable, large-scale human violence is not. It is not only human behaviour but also institutional development that is subject to human choices. Future survival, as always, depends on a capacity for second-order social learning – adaptation to changing circumstances. Fully aware of some recent ominous trends – in line with the founders of the field who based their analysis on hard-headed statistical evidence and clear recognition of the powerful array of countervailing dangers that existed in their day – we do not conclude on a pessimistic note. In the end, Miall (2007) sees the critical factor to be the development of some kind of *political community* at a level which contains the competing interests in question. Michael Howard has criticized premature hopes for a cosmopolitan future because '[t]he establishment of a global peaceful order depends on the creation of a world community sharing the characteristics that make possible domestic order' (2000: 105). But transformative cosmopolitan conflict resolution does not assume a prior 'thick' form of world community that evidently does not yet exist. It points, rather, to the undoubted gains that have been made in a multiplicity of 'thin' forms of political association at many levels over the past half century (see chapter 11). It argues that these can and must be retained and built upon. And it proposes a broad direction in which the 'arrow of history' needs to move if the worst of upcoming dangers are to be averted and the human family as a whole is to be able to look ahead to the future with *hope* – the prerequisite for community – and not *despair* – the incubator of violence.

Recurrent failures are not surprising. Cosmopolitan conflict resolution is in its infancy. The political, economic, psychological and ideological forces that generate violence are deeply rooted in human institutions, human historical memory and, in the view of some, human nature. But the achievements of the period from 1945 to the present day – the period in which conflict resolution has emerged as a global enterprise – have, as this book demonstrates, been remarkable. It has been extraordinary that, unlike the League of Nations, the United Nations has retained membership of all major states – even surviving the advent of Maoist China – and presided over a dramatic decline in the incidence of interstate war. It has been equally notable that the imperial era has been brought to an end with a fourfold increase in state membership. The world trade system now includes Russia, India and China. Regional organizations are linked actively into this global system. There have been striking gains in overall human welfare according to a number of measures, despite gross inequalities and exceptions, and there is no reason why over the next decades these may not be spread wider.

In the face of the biggest threats to the maintenance and strengthening of these human gains, we are happy to endorse the view of Philip Bobbitt – even though, as noted in chapter 11, he looks more to interstate cooperation than to international institutions for a containing framework:

> We cannot begin the 21st century in the way we began the 20th, with powerful states determined to overthrow the international system, tossing away the rule book for international behaviour ... All these rules were ratified in the Peace of Paris, a collective name for a series of agreements among which are the Moscow Declaration, the Copenhagen Declaration and the Charter of Paris, by which the long war of the 20th century was ended ... The current crisis is not a replay of the events that destroyed the international order in 1914. Today we do not have an old order whose enervation invites assaults from global ideological movements. Rather we have a new international order whose stability is being tested in its youth. Russia – and China – must be integrated into an international community whose problems include dealing with global networked terror, ethnic and religious cleansing, climate change, and the proliferation of weapons of mass destruction, none of which can be treated successfully without their participation. There is room in the nascent international order of information-driven market states for considerable variation. The managerial model of the EU market state, the entrepreneurial model of the US, and the mercantile model of China are all possibilities still in the process of creation. It is imperative that the competition among these various models be played out according to common, agreed-upon rules ... What cannot be countenanced are models that depend upon overthrowing a pluralist international order. (Bobbitt, 2014)

In short, this book has shown how, in relation to all four of the 'types' of upcoming conflict considered above, there are now rich resources for containment, settlement and even transformation, although the record is bound to be patchy in terms of success and failure in applying them in particular cases. As for the other deep drivers of future conflict, here conflict resolution joins hands with all the other cosmopolitan enterprises committed to combating and overcoming inequalities and injustices worldwide, so that as fair a wind as possible can be given to the life hopes and aspirations of the many – indeed the countless – future generations that we hope will inherit from us not just a clearer understanding of what is required for human survival and human flourishing in a world that will go on being irredeemably conflictual, but also some of the norms, techniques, tools and institutions to make sure that this remains predominantly non-violent.

Conflict Resolution: The Next Generation

Before the final conclusion we can sum up our central argument by remind-ing readers of the work of the first four generations of contributors to the conflict resolution field, described in chapter 2 and exemplified in the rest of the book. We can then end by identifying some of the main tasks – oppor-tunities as well as challenges – facing the current generation – generation five (see table 20.1).

In chapter 2, under *precursors*, we concentrated on the generation between the world wars in the 1920s and 1930s. We suggested that many contributory streams from the interwar period would feed into the formal inauguration of the field after the Second World War. At higher levels of conflict we noted how international relations, as a distinct discipline area initiated in the 1920s, at first shared many goals and characteristics with what came to be called conflict resolution in the next generation, and how it was the takeover of IR by realists in the 1930s and 1940s that created much of the conceptual space later occupied by conflict resolution. In this sense, revulsion against the mass carnage of the First World War launched the impetus that finally led to the creation of the conflict resolution enterprise.

The next generation, the *founders*, will always hold a special position of influence in the conflict resolution field. This was the time in the immediate aftermath of the Second World War when the distinctive features of the field were defined and exemplified. We have suggested that seven characteristics in particular marked it out and continue to make it distinctive from other areas of study (Rogers and Ramsbotham, 1999; Woodhouse, 1999a). The new formal conflict resolution enterprise was to be multi-level; multidisciplinary; transcultural; it was to focus on the challenge of non-violent conflict transfor-mation; it was to be both analytic and normative; it was to be both theoretic

Table 20.1 Conflict resolution: five generations

Generation 1	Precursors	1925–1945
Generation 2	Founders	1945–1965
Generation 3	Consolidators	1965–1985
Generation 4	Reconstructors	1985–2005
Generation 5	Cosmopolitans	2005–

and applied; and it was to incorporate a range of approaches and method-ologies in which statistical analysis would inform responses ranging across the 'objectivist' (rational actor/bargaining), 'subjectivist' (communications/ problem-solving), 'structuralist' (institution-building) and 'transformative' (dialogical and discursive) spectrum. In this way, a major challenge was laid down to the deterrence-based security arrangements that held sway during the Cold War period.

The third generation of *consolidators*, continuing to labour under the con-straints of the Cold War, achieved three main things. First, they elaborated and filled in what had up until then been lacunae in the field, ranging from clearer conceptualization of the deeper levels of cultural and structural peace-building, through more cogent comparative study of peacemaking (negotia-tion, mediation, problem-solving), and on to engagement with the challenge of various aspects of peacekeeping. At the heart of this was analysis of the sources of prevailing patterns of intractable conflict, deep-rooted conflict and protracted social conflict. Since major conflict formations are both com-plex and systemic, so must also be the approaches and methodologies used to anticipate, settle and resolve them. The second main achievement was to begin a constructive dialogue with decision-makers on both sides of the iron curtain, so that, building on existing diplomatic expertise, conflict resolution approaches could begin to contribute to a strengthening of periods of détente and softening of periods of renewed confrontation. The third main achieve-ment was to encourage the geographical spread of conflict resolution centres and organizations throughout the world. In this way, the enterprise enhanced its international credentials and attained the critical mass required to make a significant contribution when the Cold War unexpectedly came to an end, ushering in the main challenges for the next generation.

With the advent of Mikhail Gorbachev in the Soviet Union in 1985, the geo-political landscape suddenly changed. This initiated the period that formed the background for the work of the fourth generation of post-Cold War conflict resolvers, whom we have called *reconstructors*. As conflict resolution became better known and more widely invoked by aid and development work-ers, governments, international organizations and journalists, its increased prominence exposed it to raised expectations and sharper criticism. This book has attempted to trace the way in which the field has responded. Emphasis has been placed on greater sophistication in understanding how to bring to bear and coordinate appropriate approaches at different stages of conflict – contingency and complementarity – and how to dovetail peacekeeping, peacemaking and peacebuilding resources. There has been better awareness of the importance of integrating grassroots, middle-level and elite support in conflict transformation, as well as in overcoming gender and culture blind-ness. At the same time, those working in the conflict resolution field, like others, have had to grapple with the question of how to respond to spoilers, criminals and those who rely on terrorist methods. Great efforts have been made to think through the conflict resolution implications of the use of military force. And direct critiques of the conflict resolution field from a number of realists, political economists and critical theorists have been listened to and, it is hoped, constructively learned from.

So, what is the task for the fifth generation? We suggest the title *cosmopolitans* because, in our view, it is the 'culture question' that is, in the end, the decisive one, lying as it does at the heart of the enterprise of cosmopolitan conflict resolution. We conclude by stressing two features.

The first feature is the the need for the younger fifth generation to develop new tools and approaches that reflect upcoming technological and other challenges and opportunities that were not evident or available to previous generations. As described in chapter 17, the work of the fifth generation will take place in a world that is changing rapidly, most especially under the impact of global information communications technology (ICT). It has been a constant concern of peace researchers and peace activists throughout the modern era that new scientific and technological knowledge has frequently been appropriated to advance the military power of states and also the lethality and efficiency of military systems in general. In the early years of the twenty-first century the same phenomenon seems to be about to repeat itself, as the massive information-processing capacity of new information and communication technologies is applied to the revolution in military affairs, where precision-guided and automated weapons systems threaten a new era of automated war. The field of peace and conflict studies is also being radically affected by the impact of ICT in such a way that traditional distinctions between national, international and local levels of activity are being eroded and the basis for a global partnership for peacebuilding is being constructed. The internet opens up a uniquely global or cosmopolitan space, which peacemakers can use as a potent tool and environment within which to educate, advocate and problem-solve. Who can tell what forms the World Wide Web, still in its infancy but developing at astonishing speed, may ramify into over the next century? It seems likely that it will be the locus for political struggles of all kinds in which the balance between defence (shutting it down and controlling it) and emancipation (circumventing restrictions) will ebb and flow. So, taking note of this and even looking beyond it, this is the time for a younger generation of pioneers to emulate the achievements and creativity of the founders of the conflict resolution field and to build a new future on potentials and technologies of which the founders were not able to dream in their own day. This quality of creativity and innovation has been defined by Tatsushi Arai as 'unconventional viability', a process of using multidisciplinarity and new ways of knowing in order to 'shape the future, or more precisely the present–future link, beyond the conventional realities of conflict' (Arai, 2011: 1–3). It is an exciting time in which to be working, and there are many indications that new sources of knowledge and the qualities of creativity called for by Arai are indeed enriching theory and practice.[2]

The second feature is the need for the younger fifth generation to exemplify the underlying contemporary requirement for human solidarity. As we look ahead towards the third decade of the twenty-first century, we see the number one priority as ensuring that conflict resolution is indeed truly international, as its founders intended. If the central goal of transforming potential violence into non-violent change is not shared cross-culturally, then there is no international, let alone cosmopolitan, conflict resolution field. We hope that the next generation will come from all parts of the world and will draw from their own cultures in pushing forward shared human understanding of the costs of failure to manage conflict non-violently and of the benefits to be gained by strengthening non-violent conflict resolution capacity within and between societies. Chapter 15 emphasized the creativity and richness of the resources that are available across cultures and religions for the task of reducing violence and increasing solidarity. Islamic and Buddhist teachings were illustrated there. The same applies elsewhere – for example, in the African concept of *ubuntu*, where 'a person is a person through other persons' (Appiah, 2006), or in the Chinese idea of *tian xia* (cosmopolitanism), based on *ren* (human-heartedness) and *li* (right living) (Chun, 2009) (see Reading 71). In *The Cosmopolitan Vision* (2006), Ulrich Beck sees the essence of cosmopolitanism as acknowledging 'otherness' – the otherness of nature; the otherness of the object; and the otherness of other rationalities.

We saw in Chapter 3 that, according to UNHCR, there were 59.5 million people forcibly displaced at the end of 2014 compared with 51.2 million a year earlier. This has swamped the resources of areas of first settlement and is now even challenging the cohesion of the European Union. In recent history this can only be compared to the immediate post-Second World War period, when, for instance, among many other examples, 14 million refugees fled during the partition of India in 1947. This rising tide of human misery exemplifies the virulence of the threat posed by transnational conflict as described in Chapter 3. And it emphatically underlines the importance of a properly cosmopolitan conflict resolution response that links alleviation to addressing the root causes at every level, as set out in Chapter 11. Only a concerted international effort can do this.

Summing up the main thrust of this book, we can look back to chapter 2, where we noted Holsti's classification of the efforts to evolve a 'peaceful postwar order' after successive convulsions that ended in 1648, 1713, 1815, 1918 and 1945/1990 (see table 2.1, p. 42). Most of these treaties embodied some of Holsti's six prerequisites for peace, but none of them satisfied the seventh and eighth preconditions – that is, mechanisms and institutions to manage peaceful change and for anticipating future conflict-generating issues. In chapter 11 we suggested that, up to now, the 'arrow of history' can still be seen to be pointing in a direction favourable to conflict resolution. The existing post-1945 system – adapted after 1990 – has been remarkably successful in surviving the advent of nuclear weapons, the Cold War, the communist revolution in China, decolonization (which quadrupled the number of UN member states), the end of the Cold War, the onslaught of religious extremism, and the transition from a bipolar world, through a brief unipolar moment, and on to the more multipolar world of today. Can it continue to survive and adapt in the face of the latest manifestations of transnational conflict as described in this book? Or will this seventy-year system – perhaps the most successful of all Holsti's systems – also eventually founder? This is the greatest challenge facing the next generation of cosmopolitan conflict resolvers.

In the end, therefore, it is an awareness of shared humanity that underpins the global enterprise of cosmopolitan conflict resolution. And the task of the next generation of workers in the field is to push forward the widening of the circle of recognition towards the culminating point when it is acknowledged in all parts of the world – particularly by young people – that subordinate identities, whether of family, clan, ethnic group, nation, state, class, gender, culture or religion, do not cancel out the deepest identity of all – humanity – even in the most intense political conflicts.

RECOMMENDED READING

RELEVANT EXTRACTS IN *THE CONTEMPORARY CONFLICT RESOLUTION READER*

Reading 19: F. Stewart, Horizontal Inequalities: A Neglected Dimension of Development

Reading 65: S. Wolff, Governing (in) Kirkuk: Resolving the Status of a Disputed Territory in post-American Iraq

Reading 71: W. Dietrich et al., Peace Studies: A Cultural Perspective

Reading 73: D. Held, Cosmpolitanism after 9/11

Notes

CHAPTER 1 INTRODUCTION TO CONFLICT RESOLUTION

1 Technically, where one party's gain is the other's loss, we should refer to *constant-sum* conflicts and, where both can lose or both can gain, to *non-constant-sum*. However, although it is less precise, the zero-sum and non-zero-sum language has passed into general usage.

2 This has not been the end of the story. Further competitions have been held with slight variations in the conditions, allowing for the possibilities that players might make mistakes in detecting another player's move. Here a population of Tit-for-Tat players do badly because, after making a mistake, they get locked into mutual defection, and a somewhat nicer strategy, called 'Generous', which forgives the first defection and then retaliates, outperforms Tit-for-Tat. Generous in turn allows even nicer strategies to spread, reaching at the limit the ultra-nice 'Always Cooperate', which, however, can then be invaded by the ultra-nasty 'Always Defect'. If the players are allowed to remember the outcomes of previous moves, other strategies do well, especially one called 'Simpleton', which sticks to the same strategy if it did well last time and changes if it did badly.

3 A caveat here: the term 'problem-solving' in conflict resolution is often misinterpreted and confused with the use of the term by Robert Cox in a famous 1981 article, in which he pejoratively contrasts uncritical 'problem-solving' with a critically aware analysis of interest, ideology and power.

CHAPTER 2 CONFLICT RESOLUTION: ORIGINS, FOUNDATIONS AND DEVELOPMENT OF THE FIELD

1 We are indebted to Ronald Fisher for a correction to the text of the third edition here.

2 Sorokin was a professor of sociology in Russia, but left for the USA in 1922 following a dispute with Lenin. He founded the Department of Sociology at Harvard in 1930, and the third volume of his four-volume *Social and Cultural Dynamics*, published in the late 1930s, contained an analysis of war, including a statistical survey of warfare since the sixth century BC. Both Wright and Richardson referred to Sorokin's work, but he had a limited influence otherwise. Richardson was born into a prominent Quaker family in Newcastle in the north of England in 1881. He worked for the Meteorological Office, but served from 1913 to the end of the war with the Friends' Ambulance Unit in France. His experience in the war, his background in science and mathematics, and his growing interest in the new field of psychology all combined to lead him to research into the causes of war. He took a second degree in psychology in the late 1920s, and he spent much time in the 1930s developing his arms race model. During the Second World War he decided to retire from his post as principal of Paisley Technical College in order to devote his time to his peace research. He compiled a catalogue of all conflicts he could find information on since 1820, and by the middle of the 1940s he had collated his various studies. These were not published, however, until after his death, when Quincy Wright (with whom Richardson had entered into correspondence in his later years) and other academics succeeded in having them issued posthumously in two volumes (*Arms and Insecurity* and *Statistics of*

Deadly Quarrels) in 1960. Philip Quincy Wright (1890–1970) was a professor of political science at the University of Chicago from 1923 and was appointed professor of international law in 1931. He produced his monumental *A Study of War* (1942) after sixteen years of comprehensive research, which was initiated in 1926.

3 *Essays in Peace Research*, published in six volumes between 1975 and 1988, and *Papers in English*, published in seven volumes in 1980, represent the main body of his thinking. Good synthetic statements by Galtung about his general view of the scope and priorities for peace research appear in 'Twenty five years of peace research: ten challenges and some responses' (1985). For a critical account of Galtung's work, see Peter Lawler (1995).

4 The best general account of Quaker mediation remains Yarrow (1978). See also the work of other Quakers who have worked in the Quaker tradition or who applied and developed Curle's approach: Curle (1981), Bailey (1985), Williams and Williams (1994) and McConnell (1995).

5 In TRANSCEND, the 'lose–lose' end of the non-zero-sum axis is reinterpreted as often more benign than victory for either party along the zero-sum 'win–lose' axis. For example, in the Israeli–Palestinian conflict, win–lose means either Israeli or Palestinian victory, whereas lose–lose may mean the 'negative transcendence' of takeover by the United Nations as well as the 'positive transcendence' of forms of shared sovereignty.

6 Robin Vallacher, Andrzej Nowak, LanBui-Wrzosinska, Andrea Bartoli, Larry Liebovitch, Naira Musallam and Katharina Kugler.

CHAPTER 3   STATISTICS OF DEADLY QUARRELS

1 See, for example, the following three geographically referenced datasets:
UCDP – Geo-Referenced Events Dataset (GED): www.ucdp.uu.se/ged/
ACLED – Armed Conflict Location and Event Data: www.acleddata.com/
SCAD – Social Conflict Analysis Database: https://www.strausscenter.org/scad.html.

2 The Geneva Declaration on Armed Violence and Development was first adopted by forty-two states in June 2006 prompted by initiatives from the Swiss government and UNDP. By 2014 the declaration had been endorsed by 100 countries. See www.genevadeclaration. org.

3 All COW datasets can be accessed at the COW website at www.correlatesofwar.org.

4 See also ISI, ISIL and ISIS. In this book we use 'IS' without implying acceptance of any overtones that there may be. The Arabic acronym *Daesh* is also used.

5 The director of the Center for Systemic Peace is Monty G. Marshall. Full information about methodology and sources used can be found at the center's website, at www.systemicpeace.org/warlist.htm, and in detail in the center's annual global reports, at www.systemicpeace.org/globalreport.html.

6 Gurr distinguishes seven types of politically active communal group (national peoples, regional autonomists, communal contenders, indigenous peoples, militant sects, ethnoclasses, dominant minorities) which have four 'general orientations to, and demands on, the state' that may lead to conflict: access, autonomy, exit and control (1995: 3–5). All of these can be distinguished from the 'irredentist' claims of one state on territory beyond its borders on the basis of identity (e.g. Pakistan's claims in Kashmir), which would be classed as a form of interstate conflict.

7 One of the problems here is defining regions in the first place. Geographical regions do not always coincide with the most important political groupings (for example, Arab North Africa is often included in the Middle East), some countries are difficult to 'place' (is Turkey in the Middle East? is Greece in the Balkans? is Afghanistan in Central or South Asia?), and sub-regions often emerge as the most significant loci for analysis (the Caucasus, the Greater Horn of Africa).

CHAPTER 4 UNDERSTANDING CONTEMPORARY CONFLICT

1 For example, the 'seven main approaches' listed by Paul Wehr in terms of the central propositions: that conflict is innate in social animals; that it is generated by the nature of societies and the way they are structured; that it is dysfunctional in social systems and a symptom of pathological strain; that it is functional in social systems and necessary for social development; that it is an inevitable feature of competing state interests in conditions of international anarchy; that it is a result of misperception, miscalculation and poor communication; and that it is a natural process common to all societies (1979: 1–8). Each of these will carry its own implications for conflict resolution.

2 Needless to say, most theories escape such neat classification. For example, twentieth-century realist theories of interstate war have tended to combine explanations in terms of the international anarchy (contextual) and the security dilemma (relational), whereas classical realists emphasized 'fallen' human nature (internal). Frustration-aggression theories, on the other hand, have usually combined scarce resources (contextual) and a tendency to aggression in some/all individuals or societies when frustrated (internal).

3 For example, compare five well-supported interpretations of the Cold War: the orthodox western view that the Cold War was caused by Soviet aggression, the revisionist view that attributed it to the global ambitions of capitalist imperialism, the neo-realist view that interpreted it in terms of normal interpower rivalry in a bipolar world, the neo-liberal view that saw it as a dangerous dynamic generated by mutual worst-case security preoccupations, and the 'radical' view that it was an 'imaginary war' generated by the interest of elites on either side to maintain control within their own blocs (Kaldor, 1991).

4 The same is true of the Bosnian conflict, where the common outside view that this was a three-way squabble between Croat, Serb and Muslim factions was passionately rejected, albeit on very different grounds, by most of those directly involved.

5 As Holsti himself notes, the incidence of interstate war per year per state decreased from 0.035 for the period 1918–41 to 0.005 for the period 1945–95, although this is to some extent offset by the fact that the average number of states rose from thirty to 140 in the two periods (1996: 24).

6 For example, Richardson compared the frequency, duration and costs of wars between dyads of states with such variables as alliance groupings, geographical proximity, population and culture. Since then a flood of material has been produced: see Luard (1986); Levy (1989); Midlarsky (1989); Holsti (1991); and Vasquez (1993).

7 Although many, including major contributors such as David Singer (1996), see progress still being made, some commentators conclude that the overall results of attempts at statistical analysis of interstate conflict have been disappointing. After a careful survey of some of the main hypotheses, for example, Holsti finds that, '[i]n a significant proportion of the systemic studies of war, there is no verdict' (1991: 5), while, for Dougherty and Pfaltzgraff, '[u]p to the present time, the statistical techniques have produced no startling surprises, and few conclusive or unambiguous results' (1990: 347). Many of the claimed positive 'external' correlations have been challenged, such as whether rigid alliance systems produce war (Singer and Small, 1968), whether bipolar or multipolar balances of power are more stable (Waltz, 1979), at what point in a transition of power between a rising and falling hegemon war is most likely (Organski, 1958), or whether arms races increase the probability of war (Wallace, 1977). The same is true of 'internal' correlations, such as those said to support the theory that 'lateral pressure' from population and economic growth breeds war (Choucri and North, 1975) or that democracies do not fight wars. In an elaborate study of 236 variables relating to internal attributes of eighty-two nations, Rummel found no significant quantitative correlation with foreign conflict behaviour (1970). In addition, some of the more generally accepted conclusions seem

rather obvious, such as that great powers fight more wars, or that alliance membership increases the chance that a state will become involved in war if its partner does.

8 Instead of Waltz's 1959 'system', 'state' and 'individual' levels (still used in some recent accounts, such as Crocker et al., 2001: pt 1), we recommend a five-level model, comprising two 'international' levels (global and regional), one 'state' level divided into functional sectors, and two 'social' levels (identity group and elite/individual).

9 De Waal here contrasts 'Schmittian' (centrally organized force) and 'Hobbesian' (anarchic struggle of 'all against all') conflicts.

10 As with almost all classical or neo-classical approaches in the security field, however, the theory was substantially adapted in the 1990s in an attempt to account for the wider range of determinants now seen to be relevant (Buzan et al., 1997). In particular, the emphasis on the military and political sectors was expanded to include environmental, economic and societal sectors (introducing the concept of cross-sectoral 'heterogeneous' security complexes); local causes were seen to have global effects and vice versa; states were no longer regarded as necessarily the main referents, with 'societal security' introduced as a major theme (ibid.: ch. 6); and 'micro-regions' were recognized as sub-units within the boundaries of a state. The concept of security itself was taken to be intersubjective and socially constructed (ibid.: ch. 2). It remains to be seen whether greater sophistication has been bought at the expense of conceptual clarity and predictive power.

11 For example, the Tigris (Iran, Iraq, Syria, Turkey), the Jordan (Israel, Jordan, Saudi Arabia, Syria) and the Nile (Burundi, Democratic Republic of the Congo (Zaire), Egypt, Eritrea, Ethiopia, Kenya, Rwanda, Sudan, Tanzania, Uganda).

12 For example, most major armed conflicts are found in countries low down on the United Nations Development Programme's annual *Human Development Index* (which measures education, health and standard of living) or the World Bank's *World Development Report* – only one country (Colombia) in PIOOM's 1996 list of high-intensity conflicts was among the top fifty countries in the UNDP *Human Development Index* for that year, whereas seven were among the lowest twenty-five (Jongman and Schmid, 1997). Similar conclusions are included in the UN High-Level Panel report *A More Secure World* (2004).

13 The term 'Arab world' is rejected across the region by non-Arabs, including Berbers, Kurds, Assyrians, Maronites, Copts, etc., many of whom trace their origins back to pre-Arab populations.

CHAPTER 5 PREVENTING VIOLENT CONFLICT

1 The other two 'Romes' were the capital of the Latin western half of the empire, Rome itself, and the capital of the Greek eastern half of the empire, Constantinople (formerly Byzantium).

2 See, for example, Weiss (2014).

CHAPTER 6 CONTAINING VIOLENT CONFLICT: PEACEKEEPING

1 For peacekeeping in general, Charles Hunt (2015) has argued that it is important to understand how peace operations are monitored and evaluated, and that, based on field research in Liberia, enhancing the relationship between field-level evaluation and organizational learning results in more effective UN peace operations.

2 For early pioneer efforts in this respect, see Frye (1957) and Clark and Sohn (1966). The literature on enhanced UN capability (including rapid reaction and standing forces) is now well developed. For proposals and efforts to develop some form of permanent UN capability in the early 1990s, see Johansen (1990); Carver (1993); Urquhart (1993); Conetta and Knight (1995); Cox and Legault (1995); Kaysens and Rathjens (1996); Schwartzberg

(1997); Rosenblatt and Thompson (1998); Langille (2000a, 2000b); Mendlovitz and Fousek (2000); Heidenrich (2001).

3 Readers may follow developments at the UN News website, www.un.org/apps/news, and at the Department of Peacekeeping Operations, www.un.org/en/peacekeeping/about/ dpko/; also the website of the International Peace Institute, whose Brian Urquhart Center for Peace Operations provides up-to-date information and analysis, at www.ipinst.org/ program/center-for-peace-operations.

CHAPTER 7 ENDING VIOLENT CONFLICT: PEACEMAKING

1 See the Uppsala Conflict Data Program's Peace Agreement Dataset, at www.pcr.uu.se/ research/ucdp/datasets/ucdp_peace_agreement_dataset/.

2 Even major international wars may be episodes in long-term violent conflicts: about half of the international conflicts that occurred between 1816 and 1992 were the result of 'enduring rivalries' between rivals who constituted only 5 per cent of the dyads in conflict; civil conflicts too may have an episodic character.

3 In his study of ninety-one civil wars in the period 1945–92, Licklider (1995) found fifty-seven that had ended; of these, fourteen ended in negotiation and the other forty-three in military victory. Heraclides (1998), in a study of the outcomes of seventy separatist armed conflicts of the period 1945–96, found outright victory by the incumbent state in 25 per cent of cases, outright victory by the separatist movement in 7 per cent, some form of accommodation in 29 per cent, unresolved or frozen conflict in 21 per cent, and ongoing violence in 17 per cent.

4 Although such massive changes are difficult for agents to bring about deliberately, they illustrate the links between conflict resolution and the wider issues of international governance, international economic and political relationships, and the international, regional and economic orders.

5 Curle makes this personal change the basis for his theory of peacemaking: see Curle (1971, 1986; Reading 49).

6 Fisher and Keashly (1991) suggested that conflict resolution attempts should be appropriate to the stage of a conflict and argued for a 'contingency approach', in which the attempt suited the conflict stage – for example, conciliation at an early stage when communications are poor, consultation when the conflict has escalated and relationships are breaking down, arbitration or power mediation when hostility is under way, and peacekeeping when the parties are attempting to destroy one another (Keashly and Fisher, 1996: 244–9). Webb argues that the case of Yugoslavia demonstrates that the type of sequencing and coordination Fisher and Keashly urge is unattainable in international conflicts and that their model is too formulaic and schematic, but he accepts the case for the complementarity of a variety of third-party methods (Webb et al., 1996).

7 Although, arguably, responsibility for the failures lies mainly with the nation-states (Parsons, 1995).

8 For reviews of the UN's post-Cold War role as a conflict manager, see Berridge (1991), Parsons (1995), Findlay (1996) and Beardsley (2012).

9 The EU concept defines mediation as

> a way of assisting negotiations between conflict parties and transforming conflicts with the support of an acceptable third party. The general goal of mediation is to enable parties in conflict to reach agreements they find satisfactory and are willing to implement. The specific goals depend on the nature of the conflict and the expectations of the parties and the mediator. A primary goal is often to prevent or end violence through cessation of hostilities or cease fire agreements. In order to ensure peace

and stability in the long-term, mediation should be cognisant of and, as appropriate, address the root causes of conflict.

Dialogue is defined as 'an open-ended process which aims primarily at creating a culture of communication and search of common ground, leading to confidence-building and improved interpersonal understanding among representatives of opposing parties which, in turn, can help to prevent conflict and be a means in reconciliation and peace-building processes.'

10 The UN has not been able to impose settlements (Parsons, 1995). Boutros Boutros-Ghali retracted his advocacy of coercive peacemaking one year after making it (Boutros-Ghali, 1992, 1993).

11 There is also an increasing process of learning between peace processes. For example, parties from Northern Ireland visited South Africa in June 1997 and returned with ideas that helped to overcome the hurdle of decommissioning as a precondition to negotiations.

12 In 1984, Hendrik van der Merwe, a conflict researcher and director of the Centre for Intergroup Studies in Cape Town, had pioneered contacts with the ANC leadership in Lusaka with the help of the newspaper editor Piet Muller. Others were also active – for example, the Foundation for International Conciliation engaged in a facilitated mediation over features of a constitution that might be widely acceptable in 1985–6 (see Miall, 1992: 78–80).

CHAPTER 8   POSTWAR RECONSTRUCTION

1 During this period the relevant literature varied in the sub-set of intervention, reconstruction and withdrawal operations covered. Some placed the spotlight on peace implementation operations (Crocker et al., 1996; Hampson, 1996; Stedman et al., 2002). Others concerned UN peace operations (Bertram, 1995; Ratner, 1995; Durch, 1996; Ginifer, 1997; Durch et al., 2003). Others again were broader studies of how civil wars end (Licklider, 1993; Doyle and Sambanis, 2000) or of various forms of 'post-conflict' peacebuilding (Lake, 1990; Kumar, 1997; Griffiths, 1998; Cousens and Kumar, 2000; Reychler and Paffenholz, 2001; Lund, 2003; Woodward, 2003; Paris, 2004). All of these were in turn distinct from the parallel literature on humanitarian intervention, which included a different dataset: 1991 Iraq, 1990–6 Liberia, 1992–5 Bosnia, 1992–3 Somalia (Unified Task Force), 1994 Rwanda (Operation Turquoise) and 1999 Kosovo (Ramsbotham and Woodhouse, 1996; Wheeler, 2000; Chesterman, 2001; Holzgrefe and Keohane, 2003).

2 The term 'Clausewitz in reverse' and its explanation comes from Ramsbotham (2000: 172). With his usual perspicacity, Clausewitz himself was well aware of this – in the sentence immediately following his famous observation that war is simply 'a continuation of political intercourse, with the addition of other means', he adds that the 'main lines along which military events progress, and to which they are restricted, are political lines that continue throughout the war into the subsequent peace' (Clausewitz, [1832] 1976: 75).

CHAPTER 9   PEACEBUILDING

1 The decision was implemented under a joint UN General Assembly and Security Council resolution (A/Res/60/180 and S/RES/1645 (2005)) on 20 December 2005.

2 For the variety of conceptions of peacebuilding, see Lund (2003). For critiques of the orthodox liberal peace and advocates of the justice-emancipatory tradition, see Richmond (2005); Mac Ginty (2006, 2013); Kaldor (1998); Lederach (2005); for advocates of peacebuilding as statebuilding, Berger and Scowcroft (2005); for advocates of liberal-democratic peacebuilding or institutionalization before liberalization, Paris (2004);

Fukuyama (2004); Zaum (2007); and for critics of liberal peacebuilding as imperial state, Chesterman (2004a); Chandler (2006).

3 For a review of research on this, see Conflict Prevention and Reconstruction (CPR) Unit CPR and Related Publications on Conflict and Development at www.worldbank.org/en/topic/fragilityconflictviolence.

4 On this, see also the developing debates and practices around civilian peacekeeping and non-violent peace forces in Wallis (2010) and Schweitzer (2010).

CHAPTER 10 RECONCILIATION

1 Conflict managers have an inclusive approach; a goal of reconciliation; a pragmatic focus; an emphasis on process; a recognition of particular norms and cultures of the societies in conflict; an assumption of moral equivalence; and the idea that conflict resolution is negotiable and that outside actors should be politically neutral. Democratizers have an exclusive approach; a goal of justice; a principled focus; an emphasis on outcomes; an insistence on universal norms endorsed by the international community; an insistence on moral accountability; and the conviction that justice is not negotiable and that outside actors cannot be morally neutral (Baker, 1996: 567).

2 The TRC distinguished four kinds of truth: factual or forensic truth, personal or narrative truth, social or dialogical truth, and healing and restorative truth (Boraine, 2000: 151–3).

3 Hicks distinguishes between dignity and respect, which she sees as sometimes 'inaccurately linked to it' (2011: xv). *Dignity*, both in ourselves and in others, is our inherent due as humans. *Respect*, on the other hand, has to be earned and can, therefore, be forfeited.

CHAPTER 11 TOWARDS COSMOPOLITAN CONFLICT RESOLUTION

1 Institutionalism ranges from the minimalist conception of regime theorists (Krasner, 1983), for whom international law is hardly more substantial than it was for Morgenthau, through to more substantial concepts akin to those of the 'English School' (Keohane, 1989). Liberal theorists see individuals rather than states as the fundamental subjects of international as of domestic law. Barker (2000: ch. 3) offers a lucid account.

CHAPTER 12 ENVIRONMENTAL CONFLICT RESOLUTION

1 Michael Klare and Adil Najam draw this analogy in their report 'Food and water security and increasing potential for conflicts over resources', Annex 4, in Weiss et al. (2009).

2 In England, the main regime used for controlling the commons was 'stinting', which allocated a certain number of animals in relation to the peasant's holding, or rent. Manorial courts enforced sanctions against over-grazing. Another was the system of 'levancy and couchancy', which allowed a peasant to put any number of animals on the commons so long as they could be over-wintered on the peasant's own holding. In either case, rights to the commons were related to property rights in non-common land (Winchester and Straughton, 2010).

CHAPTER 13 GENDER IN CONFLICT RESOLUTION

1 Oppositional thought itself (including the construction of sexual identities as opposites) is here subverted by the 'semiotic transgression of the thetic' when the gender critique exposes this violence in its very heartland (Kristeva, 1986). In Freudian terms, this is the pre-Oedipal challenge to the whole of phallocentric western philosophy (Irigaray, [1977] 1985).

2 References to 'women', 'gender', 'gender balance', 'gender sensitivity', 'gender-based violence', 'widows', 'girls', 'sexual violence', named forms of sexual violence such as 'rape', references to international legal instruments that specifically address women, and agreements in which a women's organization had been a signatory were all coded (Bell and O'Rourke, 2010: 952).

CHAPTER 15 CULTURE, RELIGION AND CONFLICT RESOLUTION

1 Mead's four-page essay 'Warfare is only an invention – not a biological necessity' (1940) has been talismanic here – taken up, for example, by UNESCO in 1950 and repeated in 1986 in the 'Seville Statement on Violence', which challenged as 'scientifically incorrect' the idea that war was an evolutionary predisposition in human beings (Seville Statement on Violence, 1986).
2 Anthropologists who have critiqued Chagnon's work include his teacher, Marshall Sahlins, and Brian Ferguson.
3 Galtung distinguishes between world cosmologies, where a cosmology is defined as 'collectively held subconscious ideas about what constitutes normal and natural reality', held by the major Occidental, Oriental and Indic civilizations, where the Occident includes Judaic, Christian and Islamic traditions, the Orient includes Buddhist, Sinic and Nipponic traditions, and the Indic (Hindu) constitutes the 'vast in-between, whether seen as cross-roads or cradle of the other two' (1996: 211).
4 Avruch is thinking here of examples such as Edward Hall's (1976) distinction between 'high-context' and 'low-context' cultures, as outlined earlier in this chapter, or of Blake and Mouton's (1964) 'managerial grid', along the lines illustrated in figure 1.4, when applied to different cultures.
5 We are indebted to our colleague Rhys Kelly for invaluable insights on this topic.

CHAPTER 16 CONFLICT RESOLUTION IN ART AND POPULAR CULTURE

1 We are grateful to Peter van den Dungen for his expertise, guidance and advice in writing this section on peace museums.
2 For an interview with Fatoumata Diawara and her singing of *Mali-ko*, see www.youtube. com/watch?v=cqzCoQmETlg and www.youtube.com/watch?v=eUO66d8WvCY&src_vid=el wA7SHM8_U&feature=iv&annotation_id=annotation_32324.
3 On the Olympic Truce in general, see Briggs et al. (2004) and the website of the International Olympic Truce Foundation and the International Olympic Truce Centre, at www.olympictruce.org; for the UN's role and its website on Sport for Development and Peace, see www.un.org/wcm/content/site/sport/; for UNICEF, see the site for Sport and Peace at www.unicef.org/.
4 See Joan Laporta's open letter at www.fcbarcelona.cat/web/Fundacio/english/nacions_ unides/convenis/unicef/continguts/carta_laporta.html. Laporta, the president of FC Barcelona, has been very committed to developing the social solidarity and peace related activities of the football club. In 2009 he was involved in signing a partnership agreement with the Open University of Catalunya (UOC) and with UNESCO to endow a chair in sport social coexistence and conflict resolution (see UOC *Campus for Peace* journal, at www.uoc. edu/portal/_resources/EN/documents/campus_pau/memoria_0708_eng.pdf).
5 See Goals for Peace Bucaramanga, at www.goalsforpeace.com/, also Cardenas (2015). On football and peacebuilding in English football, see Woodhouse (2014).
6 The Japan Foundation has supported important early work on the connections between cultural activities and projects in conflict resolution and peacebuilding, and some of the

ideas which guided the writing of this chapter were stimulated by a round table held by the Foundation in London in November 2009.

CHAPTER 17 CONFLICT RESOLUTION, THE MEDIA AND THE COMMUNICATIONS REVOLUTION

1 These workshops have been carried out in Burundi by the Burundi Leadership Training Association, linked to the French negotiation training centre IRENÉ, led by Aurelien Colson, and a former US ambassador to Burundi, Howard Wolpe. The techniques used are described in Lempereur and Colson (2010) and on the ESSEC Business School's IRENÉ website, http://irene.essec.edu/.

2 See *The World in 2014: ICT Facts and Figures* (ITU, 2014) and the fascinating Internet Live Stats, showing real-time activity in internet use, at www.internetlivestats.com/.

3 For an excellent discussion of feminism, power and excluded groups on the internet, see Nayar (2004: ch. 12).

4 See Internet World Stats, at www.internetworldstats.com/usage.htm.

5 See Sutherlin (2014).

6 For an excellent survey and analysis of these issues, see Kersley (2014).

7 See Leadbeater (2010). See also the reports of the Global internet Society, which works 'for open and sustainable access for all', at www.internetsociety.org/doc/global-internet-report.

8 For examples, see free online courses in conflict and peace studies at http://gmutant.gmu.edu/resolve/?p=1305 and the MOOC list at https://www.mooc-list.com/, together with an informative blog about MOOCs generally at http://moocs.com/index.php/about/.

CHAPTER 18 LINGUISTIC INTRACTABILITY: ENGAGING RADICAL DISAGREEMENT WHEN CONFLICT RESOLUTION FAILS

1 There are conflict resolution programmes that do address the issue of radical disagreement, as discussed in Ramsbotham (2010). These include Jay Rothman's ARIA methodology during the 'antagonism' stage (1997), Guy and Heidi Burgess's 'constructive confrontation' (1996, 1997), Johnson et al.'s 'constructive controversy' (2000), Barbara Bradford's 'managing disagreement constructively' (2004), Bernard Mayer's 'staying with conflict' (2009), and Myrna Lewis's website www.deep-democracy.net. See also Coleman (2011) and Mitchell (2014).

2 This is not quite the same as Chantal Mouffe's idea of agonism. In Mouffe's conception of *agonistic pluralism*, the raw antagonism and violence characteristic of human society in general (the 'political') is domesticated and tamed within the democratic *agon* so that 'enemies' become 'adversaries', who thereby gain a respect for each other as well as for the democratic 'rules of the game' that define the space of democratic 'politics' (1999: 755). Whereas what we call *agonistic dialogue* is precisely verbal exchange between enemies – it still includes the antagonistic. Agonistic dialogue is the dialogue of intense political struggle in general without trying to distinguish yet between domesticated and undomesticated varieties.

3 The directors of the ORG EU project were Gabrielle Rifkind (ORG Middle East programme) and Ahmed Badawi; the Palestinian track was created and guided by Husam Zomlot and facilitated by Ahmed Badawi; the Israeli track, co-sponsored by Tzav Pius, was led by Avner Haramati, Mario Schejtman and Ofer Zalzberg, with workshop methodology devised and conducted by Adam Kahane assisted by Shay Ben Yosef and Tova Averbuch. In the second phase, funded by the Norwegian government, the UK government and the United States Institute for Peace, the Israeli Strategic Forum was facilitated by Orit Gal, Moty Crystal, director of NEST Consulting, and Amira Dotan; and the Palestine Strategy

Group was directed by Khaled Hroub, with Husam Zomlot and Hani Masri as co-directors, in partnership with Badael in Ramallah. In the third phase, the Israeli Strategic Forum has been directed by Chris Langdon and Gabrielle Rifkind and managed by Sharri Plonsky for ORG and by the Van Leer Institute, Jerusalem, under the direction of Anat Lapidot-Firilla and Yoni Mendel and managed by Eran Hakim. The Palestine Strategy Group has been managed by Sara Hassan and directed by Husam Zomlot in partnership with Mazarat, Ramallah, directed by Hani Masri and co-directed by Khalil Shaheen. The Palestinian Citizens of Israel Group has been directed by Refqa abu-Remaila and Marzuq Halabi. Oliver Ramsbotham has been chair of ORG and consultant on strategic thinking throughout, and Tony Klug has been Middle East consultant throughout.

CHAPTER 20 CONFLICT RESOLUTION AND THE FUTURE

1 In his *History of the Peloponnesian War*, the Greek historian Thucydides (c.460–c.395 BCE) famously concluded that 'what made the war inevitable' was 'the growth of Athenian power and the fear which this caused Sparta'.

2 Scholars and scholar-practitioners are engaging, for example, with the work of geographers of conflict (ISA, 2015); with the findings of neuroscientists (Fitzduff, 2015); with those working in the field of cognitive linguistics and cognitive psychology (Language in Conflict, at www.languageinconflict.org/; Kahneman, 2012); with the innovations of technologies for peace and the emergence of digital humanitarians (www.digital-humanitarians.com) and digitial peacebuilders (Peacegeeks, at http://peacegeeks.org); with the use of cultural studies and the creative arts, deepening our understanding of John Paul Lederach's 'moral imagination' (Creative Visions Foundation, at http://creativevisions.org/history/; the Songstream Project, at www.thesongstreamproject.org); and, finally, with those developing new frameworks for peacebuilding, for countering violent extremism and for post-conflict reconciliation that are flexible, adaptable to context, and locally owned or influenced, while reflecting the values of inclusive and non-violent cosmopolitanism (Schori Liang, 2015; Breen Smyth, 2014; Byrne, 2011; Cochrane, 2015; Gagnon and Brown, 2014; Korostelina and Lässig, 2014; Christie, 2014; Aggestam and Björkdahl, 2012; Roberts, 2011; Dudouet et al., 2011; Renner and Spencer, 2012; Richmond, 2011; Cox, 2009; Sweetman, 2009).

References

This list includes some references retained from earlier editions of *Contemporary Conflict Resolution* where these are seen to enhance the usefulness of the book as a comprehensive survey of the field.

Aall, P. (1996) Nongovernmental organisations and peacemaking, in C. Crocker and F. Hampson, eds, *Managing Global Chaos: Sources of and Responses to International Conflict*. Washington, DC: US Institute of Peace Press, pp. 433–42.

Abdi, D. (2010) Citizens' peace: peacebuilding in Wajir, north eastern Kenya, in P. van Tongeren, M. Brenk, M. Hellema and J. Verhoeven, eds, *People Building Peace: 35 Inspiring Stories from Around the World*. Utrecht: European Centre for Conflict Prevention, pp. 243–9.

Abi-Ezzi, K. (2008) The case of Gilad Atzmon, in O. Urbain, ed., *Music and Conflict Transformation: Harmonies and Dissonances in Geopolitics*. Tokyo: I. B. Tauris/Toda Institute, pp. 93–103.

Abu-Nimer, M. (2003) *Nonviolence and Peacebuilding in Islam*. Gainesville: University Press of Florida.

Abu-Nimer, M. (2010) Conflict resolution in an Islamic context: some conceptual questions, in Q. Huda, ed., *Crescent and Dove: Peace and Conflict Resolution in Islam*. Washington, DC: United States Institute of Peace Press, pp. 73–92.

Achcar, G. (2013) *The People Want: A Radical Exploration of the Arab Uprising*. Berkeley: University of California Press.

Ackermann, A. (2003) The idea and practice of conflict prevention, *Journal of Peace Research*, 40(3): 339–47.

Adams, D. (1989) The Seville Statement on violence: a progress report, *Journal of Peace Research*, 26(2): 113–21.

Adger, N., et al. (2014) Human security, chapter 12 in *Climate Change 2014: Impacts, Adaptation, and Vulnerability*, Working group II contribution to the IPCC Fifth Assessment Report.

Adler, E., and Barnett, M., eds (1998) *Security Communities*. Cambridge: Cambridge University Press.

Agger, I. (1995) *Theory and Practice of Psycho-Social Projects under War Conditions in Bosnia-Herzegovina and Croatia*. Zagreb: ECHO/ECTF.

Aggestam, K. (1999) *Reframing and Resolving Conflict: Israeli–Palestinian Negotiations 1988–1998*. Lund: Lund University Press.

Aggestam, K., and Björkdahl, A., eds (2012) *Rethinking Peacebuilding: The Quest for Just Peace in the Middle East and the Western Balkans*. Abingdon: Routledge.

Agha, H., and Mulley, R. (2001) Camp David: the tragedy of errors, *New York Review of Books*, 48(13), 9 August.

Ahmed, S., and Potter, D. (2006) *NGOs in International Politics*. Bloomfield, CT: Kumarian Press.

Albin, C. (1997) Negotiating intractable conflicts: on the future of Jerusalem, *Cooperation and Conflict*, 32(1): 29–77.

Albin, C. (2001) *Justice and Fairness in International Negotiation*. Cambridge: Cambridge University Press.

Albin, C. (2005) Explaining conflict transformation: how Jerusalem became negotiable, *Cambridge Review of International Affairs*, 18(3): 339–55.

Albin, C. (2009) Peace vs justice, in J. Bercovitch et al., eds, *The Sage Handbook of Conflict Resolution*. London: Sage, pp. 580–94.

Alcock, A. (1970) *A History of the South Tyrol Question*. London: Michael Joseph.

Allan, S., and Zelizer, B., eds (2004) *Reporting War: Journalism in Wartime*. London: Routledge.

Anderson, B. (1983) *Imagined Communities*. London: Verso.

Anderson, M. (1996a) *Do No Harm: Supporting Local Capacities for Peace through Aid*. Cambridge, MA: Development for Collaborative Action.

Anderson, M. (1996b) Humanitarian NGOs in conflict intervention, in C. Crocker and F. Hampson, eds, *Managing Global Chaos: Sources of and Responses to International Conflict*. Washington, DC: US Institute of Peace Press, pp. 343–54.

Anderson, M. (1999) *Do No Harm: How Aid Can Support Peace – or War*. Boulder, CO: Lynne Rienner.

Anderson, M. (2004) *Experiences with Impact Assessment: Can We Know What Good We Do?* Berlin: Berghof Research Center for Constructive Conflict Management.

Anderson, M., Chigas, D., and Woodrow, P. (2007) *Encouraging Effective Evaluation of Conflict Prevention and Peacebuilding Activities: Towards DAC Guidance*. Paris: Organization for Economic Cooperation and Development.

Annan, K. (1997): UN secretary-general's reform announcement: part II measures and proposals, 16 July, *Conflict Resolution Monitor 2*. Bradford: Department of Peace Studies, pp. 34–6.

Annan, K. (1998) Report on the Causes of Conflict and the Promotion of Durable Peace and Sustainable Development in Africa, UN document A/52/871–S/1998/318, 13 April.

Annan, K. (1999) Report of the secretary-general to the Security Council on the protection of civilians in armed conflict. UN document S/1999/957, 8 September.

Annan, K. (2005) *In Larger Freedom: Towards Development, Security and Human Rights for All*. UN document A/59/2005.

Anstee, M. (1996) *Orphan of the Cold War: The Inside Story of the Collapse of the Angolan Peace Process 1992–93*. Basingstoke: Macmillan.

Anzai, I., Aspel, J., and Mehdi, S., eds (2008) *Museums for Peace: Past, Present and Future*. Kyoto: Ritsumeikan University.

Aoi, C., de Coning, C., and Thakur, R., eds (2007) *Unintended Consequences of Peacekeeping Operations*. Tokyo: UN University Press.

Appiah, K. (2006) *Cosmopolitan Ethics in a World of Strangers*. London: Penguin.

Appleby, R. (2000) *The Ambivalence of the Sacred: Religion, Violence and Reconciliation*. Lanham, MD: Rowman & Littlefield.

Arai, T. (2011) *Creativity and Conflict Resolution: Alternative Pathways to Peace*. Abingdon: Routledge.

Archibugi, D. (2008) *The Global Commonwealth of Citizens: Toward Cosmopolitan Democracy*. Princeton, NJ: Princeton University Press.

Archibugi, D., Held, D., and Kohler, M. (1998) *Re-imagining Political Community: Studies in Cosmopolitan Democracy*. Cambridge: Polity.

Arend, D. (1998) Do legal rules matter? International law and international politics, *Virginia Journal of International Law*, 38.

Armstrong, K. (2001) *The Battle for God: Fundamentalism in Christianity, Judaism, and Islam*. London: HarperCollins.

Arthur, C., (2011) What's a zettabyte? By 2015 the internet will know, *The Guardian*, 29 June.

Ashe, F. (2010) *Gender, Nationalism and Conflict Transformation*. London: Routledge.

Ashford, O. (1985) *Prophet – or Professor? The Life and Work of Lewis Fry Richardson*. Bristol: Adam Hilger.

Askandar, K. (1997) ASEAN as a conflict management organization. PhD thesis, Bradford University.

Asmal, K., Asmal, L., and Roberts, R. (1996) *Reconciliation through Truth: A Reckoning of Apartheid's Criminal Governance*. Capetown: Mayibuye Books.

Assefa, H. (1999) The meaning of reconciliation, in P. van Tongeren, M. Brenk, M. Hellema and J. Verhoeven, eds, *People Building Peace: 35 Inspiring Stories from Around the World*. Utrecht: European Centre for Conflict Prevention, pp. 37–45.

Atran, S. (2010) *Talking to the Enemy: Faith, Brotherhood and the (Un)making of Terrorists*. London: HarperCollins.

Aubert, V. (1963) Cooperation and dissensus: two types of conflict and of conflict resolution, *Journal of Conflict Resolution*, 7(1): 26–42.

Augsburger, D. (1992) *Conflict Mediation across Cultures*. Louisville, KY: Westminster/ John Knox Press.

Austin, A. (2004) Early warning and the field: a cargo cult science?, in A. Austin et al., eds, *Transforming Ethnopolitical Conflict: The Berghof Handbook*. Berlin: VS Verlag für Sozialwissenschaften.

Austin, A., Fischer, M., and Ropers, N., eds (2004) *Transforming Ethnopolitical Conflict: the Berghof Handbook*. Berlin: VS Verlag für Sozialwissenschaften.

Autesserre, S. (2014) *Peaceland: Conflict Resolution and the Everyday Politics of International Intervention*. Cambridge: Cambridge University Press.

Avant, D. (2009) Making peacemakers out of spoilers: international organizations, private military training, and statebuilding after war, in R. Paris and T. Sisk, eds, *The Dilemmas of Statebuilding: Confronting the Contradictions of Postwar Peace Operations*. London: Routledge, pp. 104–26.

Avruch, K. (1998) *Culture and Conflict Resolution*. Washington, DC: US Institute of Peace Press.

Avruch, K. (2012) *Context and Pretext in Conflict Resolution: Conflict, Identity, Power, and Practice*. Boulder, CO: Paradigm.

Avruch, K., and Black, P. (1987) A generic theory of conflict resolution: a critique, *Negotiation Journal*, 3(1): 87–96, 99–100.

Avruch, K., and Black, P. (1991) The culture question and conflict resolution, *Peace and Change*, 16(1): 22–45.

Avruch, K., and Mitchell, C., eds (2013) *Conflict Resolution and Human Needs: Linking Theory and Practice*. London: Routledge.

Avruch, K., Black, P., and Scimecca, J. (1991) *Conflict Resolution: Cross Cultural Perspectives*. Westport, CT: Greenwood Press.

Axelrod, R. (1984) *The Evolution of Cooperation*. New York: Basic Books.

Azar, E. (1980) The conflict and peace databank (COPDAB) project, *Journal of Conflict Resolution*, 24(1): 143–52.

Azar, E. (1986) Protracted international conflicts: ten propositions, in E. Azar and J. Burton, *International Conflict Resolution: Theory and Practice*. Brighton: Wheatsheaf, pp. 28–39.

Azar, E. (1990) *The Management of Protracted Social Conflict: Theory and Cases*. Aldershot: Dartmouth.

Azar, E. (1991) The analysis and management of protracted social conflict, in J. Volkan et al., eds, *The Psychodynamics of International Relationships*, vol. 2. Lexington, MA: D. C. Heath, pp. 93–120.

Azar, E., and Burton, J. (1986) *International Conflict Resolution: Theory and Practice*. Brighton: Wheatsheaf.

Bacharach, M. (2006) *Beyond Individual Choice: Teams and Frames in Game Theory*, ed. N. Gold and R. Sugden. Princeton NJ: Princeton University Press.

Bailey, S. (1982) *How Wars End: The United Nations and the Termination of Armed Conflict 1946–64*, 2 vols. Oxford: Clarendon Press.

Bailey, S. (1985) Non-official mediation in disputes: reflections on Quaker experience, *International Affairs*, 61(2): 205–22.

Baker, P. (1996) Conflict resolution versus democratic governance: divergent paths to peace, in C. Crocker and F. Hampson, eds, *Managing Global Chaos: Sources of and Responses to International Conflict*. Washington, DC: US Institute of Peace Press, pp. 563–72.

Baker, P. (2001) Conflict resolution versus democratic governance, in C. Crocker et al., eds, *Turbulent Peace: The Challenges of Managing International Conflict*. Washington, DC: US Institute of Peace Press, pp. 753–64.

Balderston, R., and Balderston, M. (1888) *Ingleton: Bygone and Present*. London: Simpkin & Marshall; cited by A. Winchester, 'Ingleton Common', online at 'Contested Common Lands', http://commons.ncl.ac.uk/, and in 'Ingleborough and Scales Moor, North Yorkshire', in C. P. Rodgers, E. A. Straughton, A. J. L. Winchester and M. Pieraccini, *Contested Common Land: Environmental Governance Past and Present* (London: Earthscan), pp. 111–36.

Ball, N. (1997) Demobilizing and reintegrating soldiers: lessons from Africa, in K. Kumar, ed., *Rebuilding Societies after Civil War: Critical Roles for International Assistance*. Boulder, CO: Lynne Rienner, pp. 85–106.

Ball, N. (2001) The challenge of rebuilding war-torn societies, in C. Crocker et al., eds, *Turbulent Peace: The Challenges of Managing International Conflict*. Washington, DC: US Institute of Peace Press, pp. 719–36.

Ball, N., and Halevy, T. (1996) *Making Peace Work: The Role of the International Development Community*. Washington, DC: Overseas Development Council.

Bandura, A. (1973) *Aggression: A Social Learning Analysis*. Englewood Cliffs, NJ: Prentice-Hall.

Banks, M., ed. (1984) *Conflict in World Society*. Brighton: Harvester.

Banks, M. (1987) Four conceptions of peace, in D. Sandole and I. Sandole-Staroste, eds, *Conflict Management and Problem Solving: Interpersonal to International Applications*. London: Frances Pinter, pp. 259–74.

Bar-Siman-Tov, Y., ed. (2004) *From Conflict Resolution to Reconciliation*. Oxford: Oxford University Press.

Barber, B. (1984) *Strong Democracy*. Berkeley: University of California Press.

Barber, B. (2001) *Jihad vs. McWorld*. New York: Ballantine.

Barker, J. (2000) *International Law and International Relations*. London: Continuum.

Barnett, J., and Adger, W. (2007) Climate change, human security and violent conflict, *Political Geography*, 26: 639–55.

Bartoli, A. (2009) NGOs and conflict resolution, in J. Bercovitch et al., eds, *The Sage Handbook of Conflict Resolution*. London: Sage, pp. 392–412.

Bashir, B., and Goldberg, A. (2014) Deliberating the Holocaust and the Nakba: disruptive empathy and binationalism in Israel/Palestine, *Journal of Genocide Research*, 16(1): 77–99.

Baumann, M., and Siebert, H. (2001) Journalists as mediators, in L. Reychler and T. Paffenholz, eds, *Peace-Building: A Field Guide*. London: Lynne Rienner, pp. 319–21.

Baxter, P., and Ikowba, V. (2005) Peace education: why and how?, *Forced Migration Review*, 22: 28–9.

Beardsley, K. (2011) *The Mediation Dilemma*. Ithaca, NY: Cornell University Press.

Beardsley, K. (2012) UN Intervention and the duration of international crises, *Journal of Peace Research*, 49(2): 335–49.

Beardsley, K., and Greig, M. (2009) Disaggregating the incentives of conflict management: an introduction, *International Interactions*, 35(3): 243–8.

Beardsley, K., Quinn, D., Biswas, B., and Wilkenfeld, J. (2006) Mediation style and crisis outcomes, *Journal of Conflict Resolution*, 50(1): 58–86.

Beber, B. (2012) International mediation, selection effects, and the question of bias, *Conflict Management and Peace Science*, 29(4): 397–424.

Beck, U. (2006) *The Cosmopolitan Vision*. Cambridge: Polity.

Bell, C. (2008) *On the Law of Peace: Peace Agreements and the Lex Pacificatoria*. Oxford: Oxford University Press.

Bell, C., and O'Rourke, C. (2010) Peace agreements or 'pieces of paper? The impact of UNSC Resolution 1325 on Peace processes and their agreements, *International and Comparative Law Quarterly*, 59(4): 941–80.

Bellamy, A. (2008) Conflict prevention and the responsibility to protect, *Global Governance*, 14(2): 135–56.

Bellamy, A. (2009) *Responsibility to Protect: The Global Effort to End Mass Atrocities*. Cambridge: Polity.

Bellamy, A. (2011) *Mass Atrocities and Armed Conflict: Links, Distinctions, and Implications for the Responsibility to Protect*. Stanley Foundation Policy Analysis Briefs, www.stanleyfoundation.org/resources.cfm?id=445.

Bellamy, A., and Williams, P., eds (2004) *Peace Operations and Global Order. International Peacekeeping*, 11(1) [special issue].

Bellamy, A., and Williams, P. (2010) *Understanding Peacekeeping*, 2nd edn. Cambridge: Polity.

Bellamy, A., Williams, P., and Griffin, S. (2004) *Understanding Peacekeeping.* Cambridge: Polity.

Benedict, R. (1934) *Patterns of Culture.* New York: Houghton Mifflin.

Benhabib, S. (1992) *Situating the Self: Gender, Community and Postmodernism in Contemporary Ethics.* Cambridge: Polity.

Bercovitch, J., ed. (1991) International mediation, *Journal of Peace Research,* 28(1) [special issue].

Bercovitch, J., ed. (1996) *Resolving International Conflicts: The Theory and Practice of Mediation.* Boulder, CO: Lynne Rienner.

Bercovitch, J. (2006) Mediation success or failure: the search for elusive criteria, *Cardozo Journal of Conflict Resolution,* 7: 601–15.

Bercovitch, J. and Gartner, S. (2006) Is there method in the madness of mediation? Some Lessons for mediators from quantitative studies of mediation, *International Interactions,* 32: 329–54.

Bercovitch, J., and Jackson R. (1997) *International Conflict: A Chronological Encyclopedia of Conflicts and their Management, 1945–1995.* Washington, DC: Congressional Quarterly.

Bercovitch, J., and Jackson, R. (2009) *Conflict Resolution in the Twenty-First Century: Principles, Methods, and Approaches.* Ann Arbor: University of Michigan Press.

Bercovitch, J., and Rubin, J., eds (1992) *Mediation in International Relations: Multiple Approaches to Conflict Management.* London: Macmillan.

Bercovitch, J., Kremenyuk, V., and Zartman, I. W., eds (2009) *The Sage Handbook of Conflict Resolution.* London: Sage.

Berdal, M. (1996) *Disarmament and Demobilisation after Civil Wars,* Adelphi Paper 303. Oxford: Oxford University Press, for the International Institute of Strategic Studies.

Berdal, M., and Keen, D. (1998) Violence and economic agendas in civil wars: some policy implications, *Millennium: Journal of International Studies,* 26(3): 795–818.

Berdal, M., and Malone, D., eds (2000) *Greed and Grievance: Economic Agendas in Civil Wars.* Boulder, CO: Lynne Rienner.

Berdal, M., and Wennmann, A. (2010) *Ending Wars, Consolidating Peace: Economic Perspectives.* London: Routledge for the International Institute for Strategic Studies.

Berger, S., and Scowcroft, B. (2005) In the wake of war: getting serious about nation-building, *National Interest,* 81(fall): 49–53.

Berling, J. (2004) Confucianism and peacebuilding, in H. Coward and G. Smith, eds, *Religion and Peacebuilding.* New York: State University of New York Press, pp. 93–110.

Berman, M., and Johnson, J., eds (1977) *Unofficial Diplomats.* New York: Columbia University Press.

Bermant, G., Kelman, H., and Warwick, D., eds (1978) *The Ethics of Social Intervention.* New York: Halsted Press.

Berners-Lee, T. (2000) *Weaving the Web: the Original Design and Ultimate Destiny of the World Wide Web by its Inventor.* New York: HarperCollins.

Berridge, G. (1991) *Return to the UN.* London: Macmillan.

Berridge, G. (1995) *Diplomacy: Theory and Practice.* New York: Prentice-Hall.

Bertram, E. (1995) Reinventing governments: the promise and perils of United Nations peacebuilding, *Journal of Conflict Resolution,* 39(3): 387–418.

Betts, R. (1994) The delusions of impartial intervention, *Foreign Affairs*, 73(6): 20–33.

Betz, M. (2015) Capacity-building, institutional change and theories of change: creating an enabling environment for journalists in post-conflict environments, in J. Hoffmann and V. Hawkins, eds, *Communication and Peace: Mapping an Emerging Field*. Abingdon: Routledge, pp. 219–32.

Bhabha, H. (1994) *The Location of Culture*. London: Routledge.

Bilgin, P. (2014) Dialogue of civilisations: a critical security studies perspective, *Perceptions*, 19(1): 9–24.

Bilmes, L. J. (2013) *The Financial Legacy of Iraq and Afghanistan: How Wartime Spending Decisions Will Constrain Future National Security Budgets*, Harvard Kennedy School, Faculty Research Working Paper Series, RWP13-006 (March).

Birnir, J. K., Wilkenfeld, J., Fearon, J. D., Laitin, D., Gurr, T. R., Brancati, D., Saideman, S., Pate, A., and Hultquist, A. S. (2015) Socially relevant ethnic groups, ethnic structure, and AMAR, *Journal of Peace Research*, 52(1): 110–15.

Black, R., and Coser, K., eds (1999) *The End of the Refugee Cycle? Refugee Repatriation and Reconstruction*. New York: Berghahn Books.

Blackburn, W., and Bruce, W., eds (1995) *Mediating Environmental Conflicts: Theory and Practice*. Westport, CT: Quorum Books.

Blake, P., and Mouton, J. (1964) *The Managerial Grid*. Houston: Gulf Publishing.

Blake, P., Shephard, H., and Mouton, J. (1963) *Managing Intergroup Conflict in Industry*. Houston: Gulf Publishing.

Bloomfield, D. (1997) *Peacemaking Strategies in Northern Ireland: Building Complementarity in Conflict Management Theory*. London: Macmillan.

Bobbitt, P. (2002) *The Shield of Achilles: War, Peace and the Course of History*. London: Allen Lane.

Bobbitt, P. (2014) This crisis is the crucial test of the new world order, *Evening Standard* [London], 21 July.

Boege, V., Brown, A., Clements, K., and Nolan, A. (2009) Building peace and political community in hybrid political orders, *International Peacekeeping*, 16(5): 599–615.

Bohm, D. (1996) *On Dialogue*, ed. L. Nichol. London: Routledge.

Böhmelt, T. (2010) The effectiveness of tracks of diplomacy strategies in third-party interventions, *Journal of Peace Research*, 47(2): 167–78.

Bojer, M. M., Roehl, H., Knuth, M., and Magner, C. (2006) *Mapping Dialogue: Essential Tools for Social Change*. Johannesburg: Pioneers of Change.

Boon, R., and Plastow, J., eds (2004) *Theatre and Empowerment: Community Empowerment on the World Stage*. Cambridge: Cambridge University Press.

Booth, K. (2007) *Theory of World Security*. Cambridge: Cambridge University Press.

Booth, K., and Dunne, T., eds (2002) *Worlds in Collision: Terror and the Future of Global Order*. Basingstoke: Palgrave.

Booth, K., and Wheeler, N. (2007) *The Security Dilemma: Fear, Cooperation and Trust*. Basingstoke: Palgrave Macmillan.

Boraine, A. (2000) Truth and reconciliation in South Africa: the third way, in R. Rotberg and D. Thompson, eds, *Truth v. Justice: The Morality of Truth Commissions*. Princeton, NJ: Princeton University Press, pp. 141–57.

Boraine, A., Levy, J., and Scheffer, R., eds (1997) *Dealing with the Past: Truth and Reconciliation in South Africa*. Cape Town: IDASA.

Border Consortium (2014) *Protection and Security Concerns in South East Burma/ Myanmar*. Bangkok: Border Consortium, www.theborderconsortium.org/media/ 54376/report-2014-idp-en.pdf.

Boulding, E. (1976) *The Underside of History: A View of Women through Time*. Boulder, CO: Westview Press.

Boulding, E. (1990) *Building a Global Civic Culture: Education for an Interdependent World*. Syracuse, NY: Syracuse University Press.

Boulding, E. (1994) *Women's Movements for Social Change: Social Feminism and Equity Feminism*. Geneva: Women's International League for Peace and Freedom.

Boulding, E. (2000) *Cultures of Peace: The Hidden Side of History*. Syracuse, NY: Syracuse University Press.

Boulding, E. (2001) A vision thing, *Peace Matters*, 34(summer).

Boulding, K. (1957), editorial, *Journal of Conflict Resolution*, 1(1): 1–2.

Boulding, K. (1961) *Perspectives on the Economics of Peace*. New York: Institute for International Order.

Boulding, K. (1962) *Conflict and Defense: A General Theory*. New York: Harper & Brothers.

Boulding, K. (1977) Twelve friendly quarrels with Johan Galtung, *Journal of Peace Research*, 14(1): 75–86.

Boulding, K. (1978) Future directions in conflict and peace studies, *Journal of Conflict Resolution*, 22(2): 342–54.

Boulding, K. (1989) *Three Faces of Power*. Newbury Park, CA: Sage.

Boutros-Ghali, B. (1992) *An Agenda for Peace: Preventive Diplomacy, Peacemaking and Peacekeeping*. Report of the UN secretary- general, A/47/277– S/24111 (June).

Boutros- Ghali, B. (1993) An agenda for peace: one year later, *Orbis*, 37(3): 323–32.

Boutwell, J., Klare, M., and Reed, L., eds (1995) *Lethal Commerce: The Global Trade in Small Arms and Light Weapons*. Cambridge, MA: American Academy of Arts and Sciences.

Bowles, S. (2004) *Microeconomics: Behavior, Institutions and Evolution*. Princeton, NJ: Princeton University Press.

Boyce-Tilman, J. (2008) Music and value, in O. Urbain, ed., *Music and Conflict Transformation: Harmonies and Dissonances in Geopolitics*. Tokyo: I. B. Tauris/Toda Institute, pp. 40–51.

Brachman, J. (2009) *Global Jihadism: Theory and Practice*. London: Routledge.

Bracken, P., and Petty, C., eds (1998) *Rethinking the Trauma of War*. London: Save the Children/Free Association Books.

Bradbury, M., and Healy, S. (2010) *Whose Peace is it Anyway? Connecting Somali and International Peacemaking*, Accord, no. 21 [series editor A. Ramsbotham].

Bradford, B. (2004) Managing disagreement constructively, collective conscious. com/Handout9-handlingdisagreement.pdf

Brahimi, L. (2000) *Report of the Panel on United Nations Peace Operations*, UN document A/55/305– S/2000/809 (August).

Brahimi, L. (2007) *Statebuilding in Crisis and post-crisis Countries*, unpan1.un.org/ intradoc/groups/public/documents/un/unpan026305.pdf.

Bratic, V. (2015) Beyond journalism: expanding the use of the media in peacebuilding, in J. Hoffmann and V. Hawkins, eds, *Communication and Peace: Mapping an Emerging Field*. Abingdon: Routledge, pp. 148–62.

Brecher, M., and Wilkenfeld, J. (1997) *A Study of Crisis*. Ann Arbor: University of Michigan Press.

Brecher, M., and Wilkenfeld, J. (2010) *International Crisis Behavior Project, 1918–2007*. College Park: University of Maryland, www.cidcm.umd.edu/icb/dataviewer/.

Breen Smyth, M. (2014) *Truth Recovery and Justice after Conflict: Managing Violent Pasts*. Abingdon: Routledge.

Briggs, R., McCarthy H., and Zorbas, A. (2004) *16 Days: The Role of the Olympic Truce in the Toolkit for Peace*. Athens: Demos.

Brinton, C. (1938) *The Anatomy of Revolution*. New York: W. W. Norton.

Broome, B. (1993) Managing differences in conflict resolution: the role of relational empathy, in D. Sandole and H. van der Merwe, eds, *Conflict Resolution Theory and Practice: Integration and Application*. Manchester: Manchester University Press, pp. 97–111.

Brown, M., ed. (1993) *Ethnic Conflict and International Security*. Princeton, NJ: Princeton University Press.

Brown, M., ed. (1996) *The International Dimensions of Internal Conflict*. Cambridge, MA: MIT Press.

Brownlie, I. (1973) Thoughts on kind-hearted gunmen, in R. Lillich, ed., *Humanitarian Intervention and the United Nations*. Charlottesville: University of Virginia Press, pp. 139–48.

Bryant, J. (2003) *The Six Dilemmas of Collaboration: Inter-Organisational Relationships as Drama*. Chichester: John Wiley.

Brzoska, M. (2004) 'New wars' discourse in Germany, *Journal of Peace Research*, 41(1): 107–17.

Buhaug, H., and Gates, S. (2002) The geography of civil war, *Journal of Peace Research*, 39(4): 417–33.

Buhaug, H., et al. (2014) One effect to rule them all? A comment on climate and conflict, *Climatic Change*, 127: 391–7.

Bull, H. (1977) *The Anarchical Society: A Study of Order in World Politics*. London: Macmillan.

Bull, H., and Watson, A. (1984) *The Expansion of International Society*. Oxford: Clarendon Press.

Burgess, G., and Burgess, H. (1997) *Constructive Confrontation: A Strategy for Dealing with Intractable Environmental Conflicts*, Working Paper 97–1, www.colorado.edu/conflict/full_text_search/AllCRCDocs/97-1.htm.

Burgess, H., and Burgess, G. (1996) Constructive confrontation: a transformative approach to intractable conflicts, *Mediation Quarterly*, 13(4): 305–22.

Burgess, M. (2006) *Comparative Federalism: Theory and Practice*. London: Routledge.

Burns, D. (2006) Evaluation in complex governance arenas: the potential of large-scale system action research, in B. Williams and I. Imam, eds, *Using Systems Concepts in Evaluation*. Fairhaven, MA: American Evaluation Society, pp. 181–95.

Burns, J. (2000) *Barça: A People's Passion*. London: Bloomsbury.

Burton, J. (1968) *Systems, States, Diplomacy and Rules*. London: Macmillan.

Burton, J. (1969) *Conflict and Communication: The Use of Controlled Communication in International Relations*. London: Macmillan.

Burton, J. (1972) *World Society*. London: Macmillan.

Burton, J. (1979) *Deviance, Terrorism and War*. New York: St Martin's Press.

Burton, J. (1984) *Global Conflict: The Domestic Sources of International Crisis*. Brighton: Wheatsheaf.

Burton, J. (1987) *Resolving Deep-Rooted Conflict: A Handbook*. Lanham, MD: University Press of America.

Burton, J. (1990a) *Conflict: Resolution and Provention* (vol. 1 of the Conflict series). London: Macmillan.

Burton, J., ed. (1990b) *Conflict: Human Needs Theory* (vol. 2 of the Conflict series). London: Macmillan.

Burton, J. (1997) *Violence Explained*. Manchester: Manchester University Press.

Burton, J. (2001) Peace begins at home, *International Journal of Peace Studies*, 6(1): 3–10.

Burton, J., and Dukes, F., eds (1990a) *Conflict: Readings in Management and Resolution* (vol. 3 of the Conflict series). London: Macmillan.

Burton, J., and Dukes, F. (1990b) *Conflict: Practices in Management, Settlement and Resolution* (vol. 4 of the Conflict series). London: Macmillan.

Bury, J. (1932) *The Idea of Progress*. New York: Dover.

Bush, K. (1998) *A Measure of Peace: Peace and Conflict Impact Assessment (PCIA) of Development Projects in Conflict Zones*. Ottawa: International Development Research Council.

Bush, K., and Saltarelli, D., eds (2000) *The Two Faces of Education in Ethnic Conflict: Towards a Peacebuilding Education for Children*. Florence: UNICEF/Innocenti Research Centre.

Butler, M. (2009) *International Conflict Management*. London: Routledge.

Buzan, B. (1991) *People, States and Fear: An Agenda for International Security Studies in the Post-Cold War Era*, 2nd edn. Boulder, CO: Lynne Rienner.

Buzan, B., Waever, O., and de Wilde, J. (1997) *Security: A New Framework for Analysis*. Boulder, CO: Lynne Rienner.

Byers, M. (1999) *Custom, Power and the Power of Rules: International Relations and Customary International Law*. Cambridge: Cambridge University Press.

Byrne, S. (2011) *Economic Assistance and Conflict Transformation: Peacebuilding in Northern Ireland*. Abingdon: Routledge.

Cahill, K., ed. (2004) *Human Security for All: A Tribute to Sergio Vieira De Mello*. New York: Fordham University Press and the Center for International Health and Cooperation.

Cain, K., Postlewait, H., and Thompson, A. (2004) *Emergency Sex and Other Desperate Measures: A True Story from Hell on Earth*. New York: Miramax Books.

Call, C. (2012) *Why Peace Fails: The Causes and Prevention of Conflict Recurrence*. Washington, DC: Georgetown University Press.

Call, C., and Barnett, M. (1999) Looking for a few good cops: peacekeeping, peacebuilding and UN civilian police, *International Peacekeeping*, 6(4): 43–68.

Camilleri, J., and Martin, A. (2014) *The UN Alliance of Civilizations in Asia – South Pacific: Current Context and Future Pathways*. Melbourne: Centre for Dialogue, La Trobe University.

Caplan, R. (2005) *International Governance of War-Torn Societies*. Oxford: Oxford University Press.

Caprioli, M., et al. (2009) The WomanStats Project Database: advancing an empirical research agenda, *Journal of Peace Research*, 46(6): 839–51.

Caprioli, M., Nielsen, R., and Hudson, V. (2010) Women after armed conflict, in

J. J. Hewitt, J. Wilkenfeld and T. R. Gurr, eds, *Peace and Conflict 2010*. Boulder, CO: Paradigm.

Cardenas, A. (2015) The use of football and other sports for peacebuilding in Colombia and Northern Ireland, PhD Thesis, Universitat Jaime I, Castellon, Spain.

Carnegie Commission on Preventing Deadly Conflict (1997) *Preventing Deadly Conflict*. Washington, DC: Carnegie Corporation of New York.

Carnevale, P., and DeDreu, C., eds (2006) *Methods of Negotiation Research*. Boston: Martinus Nijhoff.

Carney, S. (2005) *Justice beyond Borders: A Global Political Theory*. Oxford: Oxford University Press.

Carruthers, S. (2000) *The Media at War: Communication and Conflict in the Twentieth Century*. Basingstoke: Macmillan.

Carter, J. (1992) The real cost of war, *Security Dialogue*, 23(4): 21–4.

Carver, R. (1993) A UN volunteer military force: four views, *New York Review of Books*, 40(12), 24 June.

Casertano, S. (2015) Broken peaces: the Israeli–Palestinian hyperconflict, *World Affairs* (Jan/Feb), www.worldaffairsjournal.org/article/broken-peaces-israeli-palestinian-hyperconflict.

Cederman, L., Girardin, L., and Gleditsch, K. (2009) Ethnonationalist triads: assessing the influence of kin groups on civil wars, *World Politics*, 61(3): 403–37.

Cederman, L., Gleditsch, K., and Buhaug, H. (2013) *Inequality, Grievances and Civil War*. Cambridge: Cambridge University Press.

Cederman, L., Wimmer A., and Min, B. (2010) Why do ethnic groups rebel? New data and analysis, *World Politics*, 62(1): 87–119.

Chagnon, N. (1983) *Yanomamo: The Fierce People*, 3rd edn. New York: Holt, Rinehart & Winston.

Chalmers, M. (2004) *Spending to Save: An Analysis of the Cost Effectiveness of Conflict Prevention versus Intervention after the Onset of Violent Conflict*. Bradford: University of Bradford, Department of Peace Studies.

Chandler, D. (2001) The people-centred approach to peace operations: the new UN agenda, *International Peacekeeping*, 8(1): 1–19.

Chandler, D. (2004) The responsibility to protect? Imposing the liberal peace, in A. Bellamy and P. Williams, eds, *Peace Operations and Global Order. International Peacekeeping*, 11(1): 59–81 [special issue].

Chandler, D. (2006) *Empire in Denial: The Politics of State-Building*. London: Pluto Press.

Chandler, D. (2008) Post-conflict statebuilding; governance without government, in M. Pugh, N. Cooper and M. Turner, eds, *Whose Peace? Critical Perspectives on the Political Economy of Peacebuilding*. Basingstoke: Palgrave Macmillan, pp. 337–55.

Chazan, N., Mortimer, R., Ravenhill, J., and Rothchild, D. (1992) *Politics and Society in Contemporary Africa*. Boulder, CO: Lynne Rienner.

Cheah, P., and Robbins, B. (1998) *Cosmopolitics: Thinking and Feeling beyond the Nation*. Minneapolis: University of Minnesota Press.

Cheldelin, S., Druckman, D., and Fast, L., eds (2003) *Conflict: From Analysis to Intervention*. London: Continuum.

Chenoweth, E., and Cunningham, K. (2013) Understanding nonviolent resistance: an introduction, *Journal of Peace Research*, 52(3): 271–6.

Chenoweth, E., and Stephan, M. (2011) *Why Civil Resistance Works: The Strategic Logic of Nonviolent Conflict*. New York: Columbia University Press.

Chesterman, S. (2001) *Just War or Just Peace? Humanitarian Intervention and International Law*. Oxford: Oxford University Press.

Chesterman, S. (2004) *You the People: The United Nations, Transitional Administration and State-Building*. Oxford: Oxford University Press.

Chilton, P. (2004) *Analysing Political Discourse: Theory and Practice*. London: Routledge.

Chopra, T. (2009) When peacebuilding contradicts statebuilding: notes from the arid lands of Kenya, *International Peacekeeping*, 16(4): 531–45.

Choucri, N., and North, R. (1975) *Nations in Conflict: National Growth and International Violence*. San Francisco: Freeman.

Christie, D., Wagner, R., and Winter, D., eds (2001) *Peace, Conflict and Violence: Peace Psychology for the Twenty-First Century*. Englewood Cliffs, NJ: Prentice-Hall.

Christie, R. (2014) *Peacebuilding and NGOs: State–Civil Society Interactions*. Abingdon: Routledge.

Chun, S. (2009) On Chinese cosmopolitanism, *Bulletin of the Center for East–West Cultural and Economic Studies*, 8(2): 20–9.

Church, C., and Shouldice, J. (2003) *The Evaluation of Conflict Resolution Interventions*. Londonderry: INCORE.

CIC (Center on International Cooperation) (2008) *Annual Review of Global Peace Operations*. Boulder, CO: Lynne Rienner.

CIDCM (Center for International Development and Conflict Management) (2014) *Peace and Conflict 2014*. College Park, MD: University of Maryland, www.cidcm. umd.edu/pc/.

Cillers, J., ed. (1995) *Dismissed: Demobilization and Reintegration of Former Combatants in Africa*. Pretoria: Institute of Defence Policy.

Clapham, C. (1996) Rwanda: the perils of peace-making, *Journal of Peace Research*, 35(2): 193–210.

Clark, G., and Sohn, L. B. (1966) *World Peace through World Law: Two Alternative Plans*, 3rd edn. Cambridge, MA: Harvard University Press.

Clark, H. (2000) *Civil Resistance in Kosovo*. London: Pluto Press.

Clark, I. (1997) *Globalization and Fragmentation: International Relations in the Twentieth Century*. Oxford: Oxford University Press.

Clark, K. (1968) *Looking at Pictures*. London: Beacon Press.

Clark, P., and Kaufman, Z. (2009) *After Genocide: Transitional Justice, Post-Conflict Reconstruction and Reconciliation in Rwanda and Beyond*. New York: Columbia University Press.

Clausewitz, C. von ([1832] 1976) *On War*, trans. and ed. M. Howard, M. Paret and P. Paret. Princeton, NJ: Princeton University Press.

Clayton, G. (2013) Relative rebel strength and the onset and outcome of civil war mediation, *Journal of Peace Research*, 50(5): 609–22.

Clayton, G. (2014) Quantitative and econometric methodologies in the study of civil war, in E. Newman and K. DeRouen, Jr., eds, *Routledge Handbook of Civil Wars*. Abingdon: Routledge, pp. 28–40.

Cochrane, F. (2008) *Ending Wars*. Cambridge: Polity.

Cochrane, F. (2013) *Northern Ireland: The Reluctant Peace*. New Haven, CT, and London: Yale University Press.

Cochrane, F. (2015) *Migration and Security in the Global Age: Diaspora Communities and Conflict.* Abingdon: Routledge.

Codner, M. (2008) Permanent United Nations military intervention capability: some practical considerations, *Royal United Services Institute Journal*, 153(3): 58–67.

Cohen, R. (1990) *Culture and Conflict in Egyptian–Israeli Relations: A Dialogue of the Deaf.* Bloomington: Indiana University Press.

Cohen, R. (1991) *Negotiating across Cultures: Communication Obstacles in International Diplomacy.* Washington, DC: US Institute of Peace Press.

Cohen, R. (2004) Apology and reconciliation in international relations, in Y. Bar-Siman-Tov, ed., *From Conflict Resolution to Reconciliation.* Oxford: Oxford University Press.

Cohn, N. ([1957] 1970) *The Pursuit of the Millennium: Revolutionary Millenarians and Mystical Anarchists of the Middle Ages.* Oxford: Oxford University Press.

Coker, C. (2014) *Can War Be Eliminated?* Cambridge: Polity.

Coleman, J. (1957) *Community Conflict.* New York: Free Press.

Coleman, K. (2007) *International Organizations and Peace Enforcement.* Cambridge: Cambridge University Press.

Coleman, P. (2003) Characteristics of protracted, intractable conflict: towards the development of a metaframework, *Peace and Culture: Journal of Peace Psychology*, 9(1): 1–37.

Coleman, P. (2011) *The Five Percent: Finding Solutions to Seemingly Impossible Conflicts.* New York: PublicAffairs.

Coleman, P., Vallacher, R., Nowak, A., and Bue Ngoc, L. (2005) Intractable conflict as an attractor: presenting a dynamical model of conflict, escalation, and intractability. Paper given at the 18th annual conference of the International Association of Conflict Management, Budapest, Hungary, 1 June.

Collen, C., ed. (2014) *National Dialogue and Internal Mediation Processes: Perspectives on Theory and Practice.* Helsinki: Ministry of Foreign Affairs, Finland.

Collier, P. (1994) Demobilization and insecurity: a study in the economics of the transition from war to peace, *Journal of International Development*, 6(3): 343–52.

Collier, P. (2000) Doing well out of war: an economic perspective, in M. Berdal and D. Malone, eds, *Greed and Grievance: Economic Agendas in Civil Wars.* Boulder, CO: Lynne Rienner, pp. 91–111.

Collier, P. (2001) Economic causes of civil conflict and their implications for policy, in C. Crocker et al., eds, *Turbulent Peace: The Challenges of Managing International Conflict.* Washington, DC: US Institute of Peace Press, pp. 143–62.

Collier, P. (2008) *The Bottom Billion: Why the Poorest Countries are Failing and What Can be Done about It.* Oxford: Oxford University Press.

Collier, P., and Hoeffler, A. (1998) On economic causes of civil war, *Oxford Economic Papers*, 50: 563–73.

Collier, P., and Hoeffler, A. (2001) *Greed and Grievance in Civil War.* World Bank Policy Research Working Paper no. 2355.

Collier, P., and Sambanis, N., eds (2003) *Understanding Civil War: Evidence and Analysis*, 2 vols. Washington, DC: World Bank.

Collier, P., Elliot, V., Håvard, H., Hoeffler, A., Reynal-Querol, M., and Sambanis, N. (2003) *Breaking the Conflict Trap: Civil War and Development Policy.* Oxford: World Bank/Oxford University Press.

Conetta, C., and Knight, C. (1995) *Vital Force: A Proposal for the Overhaul of the UN Peace Operations System and for the Creation of a UN Legion*. Cambridge, MA: Commonwealth Institute.

Coogan, T. (1995) *The Troubles: Ireland's Ordeal 1966–1995 and the Search for Peace*. London: Hutchinson.

Cooper, N. (2001) Conflict goods: the challenge for peacekeeping and conflict prevention, *International Peacekeeping*, 8(3): 21–38.

Cooper, R. (2003) *The Breaking of Nations: Order and Chaos in the Twenty-First Century*. London: Atlantic Books.

Corbin, J. (1994) *Gaza First: The Secret Norway Channel to Peace between Israel and the PLO*. London: Bloomsbury.

Cordell, K., and Wolff, S. (2009) *Ethnic Conflict*. Cambridge: Polity.

Coser, L. (1956) *The Functions of Social Conflict*. New York: Free Press.

Cousens, E., and Kumar, C., with Werminster, K., eds (2000) *Peacebuilding as Politics: Cultivating Peace in Fragile Societies*. Boulder, CO: Lynne Rienner.

Coward, H., and Smith, G., eds (2004) *Religion and Peacebuilding*. New York: State University of New York Press.

Cox, D., and Legault, A., eds (1995) *UN Rapid Reaction Capabilities: Requirements and Prospects*. Clementsport, Nova Scotia: Canadian Peacekeeping Press.

Cox, M., ed. (2009) *Social Capital and Peace-Building: Creating and Resolving Conflict with Trust and Social Networks*. Abingdon: Routledge.

Cox, R. (1981) Social forces, states and world orders: beyond international relations theory, *Millennium: Journal of International Studies*, 10(2): 126–55.

Cramer, C. (2006) *Civil War is Not a Stupid Thing: Accounting for Violence in Developing Countries*. London: Hurst.

Cranna, M., ed. (1994) *The True Cost of Conflict*. London: Earthscan, for Safer World.

Creative Associates (1997) *Preventing and Mitigating Violent Conflicts*. Washington, DC: Creative Associates International.

Crocker, C., and Hampson, F., eds (1996) *Managing Global Chaos: Sources of and Responses to International Conflict*. Washington, DC: US Institute of Peace Press.

Crocker, C., Hampson, F., and Aall, P., eds (1999) *Herding Cats: Multiparty Mediation in a Complex World*. Washington, DC: US Institute of Peace Press.

Crocker, C., Hampson, F., and Aall, P., eds (2001) *Turbulent Peace: The Challenges of Managing International Conflict*. Washington, DC: US Institute of Peace Press.

Crocker, C., Hampson, F., and Aall, P. (2005) *Grasping the Nettle: Analysing Cases of Intractability*. Washington, DC: US Institute of Peace Press.

Crocker, C., Hampson, F., and Aall, P. (2007) *Leashing the Dogs of War*. Washington, DC: US Institute of Peace Press.

Crocker, C., Hampson, F., and Aall P., eds (2015) *Managing Conflict in a World Adrift*. Washington, DC: United States Institute of Peace Press.

Crocker, D. (2000) Truth commissions, transitional justice, and civil society, in R. Rotberg and D. Thompson, eds, *Truth v. Justice: The Morality of Truth Commissions*. Princeton, NJ: Princeton University Press, pp. 99–121.

Cronin, A. K. (2015) ISIS is not a terrorist group: why counterterrorism won't stop the latest jihadist threat, *Foreign Affairs*, March/April.

Crump, L., and Zartman, I. W., eds (2003) *Multilateral Negotiation and Complexity*. *International Negotiation*, 8(1): 1–7 [special issue].

Cunliffe, P. (2009) The politics of global governance in UN peacekeeping, *International Peacekeeping*, 16(3): 323–36.

Cunliffe, P. (2013) *Legions of Peace: UN Peacekeepers from the Global South*. London: Hurst.

Cunningham, D. E. (2006) Veto players and civil war duration, *American Journal of Political Science*, 50(4): 875–92.

Cunningham, K. G. (2014) *Inside the Politics of Self-Determination*. Oxford: Oxford University Press.

Curle, A. (1971) *Making Peace*. London: Tavistock.

Curle, A. (1973) *Education for Liberation*. London: Tavistock.

Curle, A. (1981) *True Justice: Quaker Peacemakers and Peacemaking*. London: Swarthmore.

Curle, A. (1986) *In the Middle: Non-Official Mediation in Violent Situations*. Oxford: Berg.

Curle, A. (1990) *Tools for Transformation: A Personal Study*. Stroud: Hawthorne Press.

Curle, A. (1994) New challenges for citizen peacemaking, *Medicine and War*, 10(2): 96–105.

Curle, A. (1995) *Another Way: Positive Response to Contemporary Conflict*. Oxford: John Carpenter.

Curle, A. (1999) *To Tame the Hydra: Undermining the Cultures of Violence*. Oxford: John Carpenter.

Curran, D. (2012) The Bradford model and the contribution of conflict resolution to the field of international peacekeeping and peacebuilding, *Journal of Conflictology*, 3(1): 59–68.

Curran, D., and Woodhouse, T. (2007) Cosmopolitan peacekeeping and peacebuilding in Sierra Leone: what can Africa contribute? *International Affairs*, 83(6): 1055–70.

DAC (Development Assistance Committee) (2014) *Fragile States 2013: Resource Flows and Trends in a Shifting World*. Paris: OECD.

Dahrendorf, R. (1957) Towards a theory of social conflict, *Journal of Conflict Resolution*, 2(2): 170–83.

Dallmayr, F. (2002) Dialogue of civilizations: a hermeneutical perspective, in *Dialogue among Civilizations: Some Exemplary Voices*. New York: Palgrave Macmillan, pp. 17–30.

Darby, J. (1998) *Scorpions in a Bottle: Conflicting Cultures in Northern Ireland*. London: Minority Rights.

Davidson, C., and Goldberg, D. (2009) *The Future of Learning Institutions in a Digital Age*. Cambridge, MA: MIT Press.

Davidson, S. (2007) *Impact Measurement and Accountability in Emergencies: The Good Enough Guide*. Oxford: Oxfam.

Davies, J., and Gurr, T., eds (1998) *Preventive Measures: Building Risk Assessment and Crisis Early Warning Systems*. Lanham, MD: Rowman & Littlefield.

Davies, J., and Kaufman, E., eds (2002) *Second Track/Citizens' Diplomacy: Concepts and Teachings for Conflict Resolution*. Lanham, MD: Rowman & Littlefield.

Davies, J., Harff, B., and Speca, A. (1997) *Dynamic Data for Conflict Early Warning: Synergy in Early Warning*. Toronto: Centre for International and Security Studies, Prevention/Early Warning Unit.

Davies, L. (2005) Evaluating the link between conflict and education, *Journal of Peacebuilding and Development*, 2(2): 42–58.

Davies, N. (1996) *Europe: A History.* Oxford: Oxford University Press.

Davies, S. (2013) *The Drugs Don't Work.* London: Penguin.

Dawkins, R. (1989) *The Selfish Gene.* Oxford: Oxford University Press.

Dawkins, R. (1998) *Unweaving the Rainbow: Science, Decision and the Appetite for Wonder.* Boston: Houghton Mifflin.

Dayton, B. W., and Kriesberg, L., eds (2009) *Conflict Transformation and Peacebuilding: Moving from Violence to Sustainable Peace.* London: Routledge.

de Reuck, A. (1984) The logic of conflict: its origin, development and resolution, in M. Banks, ed., *Conflict in World Society.* Brighton: Harvester, pp. 96–111.

de Reuck, A., and Knight, J., eds (1966) *Conflict in Society.* London: CIBA Foundation.

de Waal, A. (2009) Mission without end? Peacekeeping in the African political marketplace, *International Affairs,* 85(1): 99–113.

de Waal, A. (2014) Violence and peacemaking in the political marketplace, in A. Ramsbotham and A. Wennmann, eds, *Legitimacy and Peace Processes: From Coercion to Consent, Accord,* no. 25. London: Conciliation Resources, pp. 17–20.

de Waal, F. (1989) *Peacemaking among Primates.* Cambridge, MA: Harvard University Press.

de Waal, F. (1998) *Chimpanzee Politics: Power and Sex among the Apes.* Baltimore: Johns Hopkins University Press.

Dédaic, M., and Nelson, D., eds (2003) *At War with Words.* New York: Mouton de Gruyter.

Degesys, A. (2008) Transformative pedagogy in conflict resolution as an alternative route to peacebuilding – roads less explored, in T. Woodhouse, ed., *Peacebuilding and Security in the 21st Century.* Evanston, IL: Rotary Centers for International Studies.

Depledge, J. (2006) The opposite of learning: ossification in the climate change regime, *Global Environmental Change,* 6(1): 1–22.

DeRouen, K., Jr, Bercovitch, J., and Pospieszna, P. (2011) Introducing the new Civil Wars Mediation (CWM) dataset, *Journal of Peace Research* 48(5): 663–72.

Deutsch, K. (1954) *Political Community at the International Level: Problems of Definition and Measurement.* Garden City, NY: Doubleday.

Deutsch, K. (1957) *Political Community and the North Atlantic Area.* Princeton, NJ: Princeton University Press.

Deutsch, M. (1949) A theory of cooperation and conflict, *Human Relations,* 2: 129–52.

Deutsch, M. (1973) *The Resolution of Conflict: Constructive and Destructive Processes.* New Haven, CT: Yale University Press.

Deutsch, M. (2000) Cooperation and competition, in M. Deutsch and P. Coleman, eds, *The Handbook of Conflict Resolution: Theory and Practice.* San Francisco: Jossey-Bass, pp. 21–40.

Deutsch, M., and Coleman, P., eds (2000) *The Handbook of Conflict Resolution: Theory and Practice.* San Francisco: Jossey-Bass.

DFID (Department for International Development) (2002) *Conducting Conflict Impact Assessments: Guidance Notes.* London: Foreign & Commonwealth Office, Ministry of Defence.

DFID (Department for International Development) (2011) *Building Stability Overseas Strategy.* London: Foreign & Commonwealth Office, Ministry of Defence.

Diamond, L. (2010) Liberation Technology, *Journal of Democracy*, 21(3): 69–83.

Diamond, L., and MacDonald, J. (1996) *Multi-Track Diplomacy: A Systems Approach to Peace*. Washington, DC: Kumarian Press.

Diehl, P. (2008) *Peace Operations*. Cambridge: Polity.

Dietrich, W. (2010) *International Handbook of the Culture of Peace*. Basingstoke: Palgrave Macmillan.

Dixon, J. (2009) What causes civil wars? Integrating quantitative research findings, *International Studies Review*, 11(4): 707–35.

Dobbins, J., McGinn, H., Crane, K., Jones, S., Lal, R., Rathmell, A., Swanger, R., and Timilsina, A. (2004) *The US Role in Nation-Building: From Germany to Iraq*. Santa Monica, CA: RAND.

Dollard, J., Doob, L., Miller, N., Mowrer, O., and Sears, R. (1939) *Frustration and Aggression*. New Haven, CT: Yale University Press.

Donahue, W. (2009) Terrorism and conflict resolution, in J. Bercovitch et al., eds, *The Sage Handbook of Conflict Resolution*. London: Sage, pp. 437–54.

Donais, T. (2009) Empowerment or imposition? Dilemmas of local ownership in post-conflict peacebuilding processes, *Peace & Change*, 34(1): 3–26.

Doob, L., ed (1970) *Resolving Conflict in Africa: The Fermeda Workshop*. New Haven, CT: Yale University Press.

Dorn, A. (2011) *Keeping Watch: Monitoring, Technology and Innovation in UN Peace Operations*. Tokyo: United Nations University Press.

Dougherty, J., and Pfalzgraff, R. (1990) *Contending Theories of International Relations*. New York: Harper & Row.

Downs, G., and Stedman, S. (2002) Evaluation issues in peace implementation, in S. Stedman et al., eds, *Ending Civil Wars: The Implementation of Peace Agreements*. Boulder, CO: Lynne Rienner, IPA/CISAC, pp. 43–69.

Doyle, M. (1983) Kant, liberal legacies, and foreign affairs: parts 1 and 2, *Philosophy and Public Affairs*, 12(3/4): 205–35, 323–53.

Doyle, M. (1986) Liberalism and world politics, *American Political Science Review*, 80: 1151–69.

Doyle, M. (1999) A liberal view: preserving and expanding the liberal pacific union, in T. Paul and J. Hall, eds, *International Order and the Future of World Politics*. Oxford: Oxford University Press, pp. 41–66.

Doyle, M., and Sambanis, N. (2000) International peacebuilding: a theoretical and quantitative analysis, *American Political Science Review*, 94(4): 779–801.

Doyle, M., and Sambanis, N. (2006) *Making War and Building Peace: United Nations Peace Operations*. Princeton, NJ: Princeton University Press.

Drogba, D. (2008) *Didier Drogba: The Autobiography*. London: Aurum Press.

Druckman, D., ed. (1977) *Negotiations: Social-Psychological Perspectives*. Beverly Hills, CA: Sage.

Druckman, D. (1986) Four cases of conflict management: lessons learned, in D. Behdamane and J. MacDonald, eds, *Perspectives on Negotiation: Four Case Studies and Interpretations*. Washington, DC: US Department of State, Foreign Service Institute, Centre for the Study of Foreign Affairs, pp. 263–88.

Druckman, D. (2009) Doing conflict resolution through a multi-method lens, in J. Bercovitch et al., eds, *The Sage Handbook of Conflict Resolution*. London: Sage, pp. 119–42.

Druckman, D., and Green, J. (1995) Playing two games: internal negotiations in the Philippines, in I. W. Zartman, ed., *Collapsed States: The Disintegration and Restoration of Legitimate Authority*. Boulder, CO: Lynne Rienner, pp. 299–331.

Dudouet, V. (2005) Nonviolence and conflict resolution: towards complementarity. PhD thesis, University of Bradford, Department of Peace Studies.

Dudouet, V., ed. (2014) *Civil Resistance and Conflict Transformation: Transitions from Armed to Nonviolent Struggle*. Abingdon: Routledge.

Dudouet, V., and Schmelzle, B., eds (2010) *Human Rights and Conflict Transformation: The Challenges of Just Peace*. Berlin: Berghof Research Center for Constructive Conflict Management.

Dudouet, V., Giessmann, H., and Planta, K., eds (2011) *Post-War Security Transitions: Participatory Peacebuilding after Asymmetric Conflicts*. Abingdon: Routledge.

Duffey, T. (1998) Culture, conflict resolution and peacekeeping. PhD thesis, University of Bradford, Department of Peace Studies.

Duffield, M. (1997) Evaluating conflict resolution: contexts, models and methodology, in G. Sorbo, J. Macrea and L. Wohlgemuth, eds, *NGOs in Conflict: An Evaluation of International Alert*. Bergen: Christian Michelson Institute, pp. 79–112.

Duffield, M. (2001) *Global Governance and the New Wars: The Merging of Development and Security*. London: Zed Books.

Duffield, M. (2007) *Development, Security and Unending War: Governing the World of Peoples*. Cambridge: Polity.

Dugan, M. (1996) A nested theory of conflict, *Women in Leadership*, 1(1): 9–20.

Dukes, F. (1993) Public conflict resolution: a transformative approach, *Negotiation Journal*, 9(1): 45–57.

Dukes, F. (1996) *Resolving Public Conflict: Transforming Community and Governance*. Manchester: Manchester University Press.

Dukes, F., Priscolish, M., and Stephens, J. (2000) *Reaching for Higher Ground in Conflict Resolution*. San Francisco: Jossey-Bass.

Dunn, D. (1995) Articulating an alternative: the contribution of John Burton, *Review of International Studies*, 21: 197–208.

Dupuy, K. (2008) Education in peace agreements, *Conflict Resolution Quarterly*, 26(2): 149–66.

Durch, W., ed. (1996) *UN Peacekeeping, American Policy and the Uncivil Wars of the 1990s*. Basingstoke: Palgrave.

Durch, W., ed. (2007) *Twentieth Century Peace Operations*. Washington, DC: US Institute of Peace Press.

Durch, W. J., Holt, V. K., Earle, C. R., and Shanahan, M. K. (2003) *The Brahimi Report and the Future of UN Peace Operations*. Washington, DC: Stimson Center.

Dwyer, L. K., and Cagoco-Guiam, R. (2011) *Gender and Conflict in Mindanao*. San Francisco: Asia Foundation.

Dyer, G. (2010) *Climate Wars: The Fight for Survival as the World Overheats*. Oxford: Oneworld.

Eck, K. (2005) *A Beginner's Guide to Conflict Data: Finding and Using the Right Dataset*, UCDP Paper 1. Uppsala: Uppsala Conflict Data Program; http://infoglue.uu.se/digitalAssets/18/18128_UCDP_paper1.pdf.

Eck, K. (2012) In data we trust? A comparison of the UCDP GED and ACLED conflict events datasets, *Cooperation and Conflict*, 47(1): 124–41.

ECP (Escola de Cultura de Pau) (2009) *Alerta 2009*. Barcelona: Autonomous University of Catalunya.

Edelstein, D. (2009) *Foreign Militaries, Sustainable Institutions, and Post-War State-Building*. London: Routledge.

EEAS (European External Action Service) (2015) *EUCAP Sahel Mali*, http://eeas.europa.eu/csdp/missions-and-operations/eucap-sahel-mali/index_en.htm.

Ehrlich, P., and Ehrlich, A. (2013) Can a collapse of global civilization be avoided? *Proceedings of the Royal Society*, 280(1754), doi: 10.1098/rspb.2012.2845.

El Fadl, K. A. (2005) *The Great Theft: Wrestling Islam from the Extremists*. New York: HarperCollins.

Elshtain, J.-B., ed. (1992) *Just War Theory*. Oxford: Blackwell.

Emmerij, L., Jolly, R., and Weiss, T. (2001) *Ahead of the Curve? UN Ideas and Global Challenges*. Bloomington: University of Indiana Press.

Encarnacion, T., McCartney, C., and Rosas, C. (1990) The impact of concerned parties on the resolution of disputes, in G. Lindgren, G. Wallensteen and K. Nordquist, eds, *Issues in Third World Conflict Resolution*. Uppsala University, Department of Peace and Conflict Research, pp. 42–96.

Engel, U., and Porto, J., eds (2010) *Africa's New Peace and Security Architecture: Promoting Norms, Institutionalizing Solutions*. Farnham: Ashgate.

Enloe, C. (1988) *Does Khaki Become You? The Militarization of Women's Lives*. London: Pandora Press.

Enloe, C. (1993) *The Morning After: Sexual Politics at the End of the Cold War*. Berkeley: University of California Press.

Enloe, C. (2000) *Manoeuvres: The International Politics of Militarizing Women's Lives*. Berkeley: University of California Press.

Esman, J. (2004) *An Introduction to Ethnic Conflict*. Cambridge: Polity.

Esty, D., Goldstone, J. A., Gurr, T. R., Surko, P. T., and Unger, A. N. (1998) The state failure project: early warning research for US foreign policy planning, in J. Davies and T. Gurr, eds., *Preventive Measures: Building Risk Assessment and Crisis Early Warning Systems*. Lanham, MD: Rowman & Littlefield, pp. 27–38.

Etzioni, A. (1964) On self-encapsulating conflicts, *Journal of Conflict Resolution*, 8(3): 242–55.

Evans, G. (1994) Peacekeeping in Cambodia: lessons learned, *NATO Review*, 42(4): 24–7.

Falk, R. (1985) A new paradigm for international legal studies: prospects and proposals, in R. Falk, F. Kratochwil and S. H. Mendlovitz, eds, *International Law: A Contemporary Perspective*. Boulder, CO: Westview Press, pp. 651–702.

Falk, R. (1995) *On Humane Governance: Toward a New Global Politics*. Cambridge: Polity.

Falkenmark, M. (1990) Global water issues confronting humanity, *Journal of Peace Research*, 27(2): 177–90.

Farah, A. (1993) *The Roots of Reconciliation*. London: Action Aid.

Faure, G., and Rubin, J., eds (1993) *Culture and Negotiation: The Resolution of Water Disputes*. London: Sage.

Fazal, T. (2014) Dead wrong: battle deaths, military medicine and exaggerated reports of war's demise, *International Security*, 39(1): 95–125.

Fearon, J. (1998) Commitment problems and the spread of ethnic conflict, in D. A. Lake and D. S. Rothchild, eds, *The International Spread of Ethnic Conflict: Fear, Diffusion, and Escalation*. Princeton, NJ: Princeton University Press.

Fearon, J. (2004) Why do some civil wars last so much longer than others? *Journal of Peace Research*, 41(3): 303–20.

Fearon, J., and Laitin, D. (2003) Ethnicity, insurgency, and civil war, *American Political Science Review*, 97(1): 75–90.

Fearon, J., and Laitin, D. (2004) Neotrusteeship and the problem of weak states, *International Security*, 28(4): 5–43.

Fearon, J., and Laitin, D. (2011) Sons of the soil, migrants, and civil war, *World Development*, 39: 199–211.

Feldman, L. (2012) *Germany's Foreign Policy of Reconciliation: From Enmity to Amity*. Lanham, MD: Rowman & Littlefield.

Feldman, N. (2003) *After Jihad: America and the Struggle for Islamic Democracy*. Basking Ridge, NJ: Farrar, Straus & Giroux.

Fetherston, A. B. (1994) *Towards a Theory of United Nations Peacekeeping*. London: Macmillan.

Fetherston, A. B. (1998) Transformative peacebuilding: peace studies in Croatia. Paper presented at the International Studies Association annual convention, Minneapolis, March.

Fetherston, A. B. (2000) Peacekeeping, conflict resolution and peacebuilding: a reconsideration of theoretical frameworks, in T. Woodhouse and O. Ramsbotham, eds, *Peacekeeping and Conflict Resolution*. London: Frank Cass, pp. 190–218.

Fetherston, B., and Kelly, R. (2007) Conflict resolution and transformative pedagogy: a grounded theory research project on learning in higher education, *Journal of Transformative Education*, 5(3): 262–85.

Filardo-Llamas, L. (2011) Discourse worlds in Northern Ireland: the legitimisation of the 1998 Agreement, in K. Hayward and C. O'Donnell, eds, *Political Discourse and Conflict Resolution*. London: Routledge, pp. 62–76.

Findlay, T. (1996) Armed conflict prevention, management and resolution, in *SIPRI Yearbook 1996: Armaments, Disarmament and International Security*. Stockholm: International Peace Research Institute.

Firer, R. (2008) Virtual peace education, *Journal of Peace Education*, 5(2): 193–207.

Fischer, M. (2011) Transitional justice and reconciliation: theory and practice, in B. Austin, M. Fischer and H.-J. Giessman, eds, *Advancing Conflict Transformation*. Opladen: Barbara Budrich.

Fisher, Roger, and Shapiro, D. (2005) *Building Agreement Using Emotions as You Negotiate*. London: Random House.

Fisher, Roger, and Ury, W. (1981) *Getting to Yes*. Boston: Houghton Mifflin.

Fisher, Roger, Kopelman, E., and Schneider, K. (1994) *Beyond Machiavelli: Tools for Coping with Conflict*. Cambridge, MA: Harvard University Press.

Fisher, Ronald (1990) *The Social Psychology of Intergroup and International Conflict*. New York: Springer.

Fisher, Ronald (1997) *Interactive Conflict Resolution*. Syracuse, NY: Syracuse University Press.

Fisher, Ronald, ed. (2005) *Paving the Way: Contributions of Interactive Conflict Resolution to Peacemaking*. Lanham, MD: Lexington Books.

Fisher, Ronald, and Keashly, L. (1991) The potential complementarity of mediation and consultation within a contingency model of third party intervention, *Journal of Peace Research*, 28(1): 29–42.

Fisher, S., and Zimina, L. (2009) Just wasting our time? Provocative thoughts for peacebuilders, in B. Schmelzle and M. Fischer, eds, *Peacebuilding at a Crossroads? Dilemmas and Paths for Another Generation*. Berlin: Berghof Research Center for Constructive Conflict Management, pp. 11–35.

Fisher, S., Abdi, D., Ludin, J., Smith, R., Williams, S., and Williams, S. (2000) *Working with Conflict: Skills and Strategies for Action*. London: Zed Books.

Fitzduff, M. (1989) *A Typology of Community Relations Work and Contextual Necessities*. Belfast: Community Relations Council.

Fitzduff, M. (2015) *An Introduction to Neuroscience for the Peacebuilder*. Washington, DC: Peace and Collaborative Development Network.

Floyer Acland, A. (1995) *Resolving Disputes without Going to Court*. London: Century Business Books.

Follett, M. P. (1942) *Dynamic Administration: The Collected Papers of Mary Parker Follett*, ed. H. Metcalf and L. Urwick. New York: Harper.

Foreign Affairs (2015) *China Now*, 94(3) [special issue].

Forrest, J. (2006) *The Making of a Terrorist*, 2 vols. Westport, CT: Praeger Security International.

Forsythe, D. (1977) *Humanitarian Politics: The International Committee of the Red Cross*. Baltimore: Johns Hopkins University Press.

Fortna, V. (2008) *Does Peacekeeping Work? Shaping Belligerents' Choices after Civil War*. Princeton, NJ: Princeton University Press.

Foucault, M. (1977) *Language, Counter-Memory and Practice: Selected Essays and Interviews*, trans. D. Bouchard and S. Sherry. Ithaca, NY: Cornell University Press.

Francis, D. (1994) Power and conflict resolution, in International Alert, *Conflict Resolution Training in the North Caucasus, Georgia and the South of Russia*. London: International Alert.

Francis, D. (2002) *People, Peace and Power: Conflict Transformation in Action*. London: Pluto Press.

Francis, D. (2010) *From Pacification to Peacebuilding: A Call to Global Transformation*. London: Pluto Press.

Francis, D. (2015) *Faith, Power and Peace*. London: Quaker Centre; www.quaker.org.uk/swathmore-lecture-2015.

Franck, T. (2003) Interpretation and change in the law of humanitarian intervention, in J. Holzgrefe and R. Keohane, eds, *Humanitarian Intervention: Ethical, Legal and Political Dilemmas*. Cambridge: Cambridge University Press, pp. 204–31.

Frazier, D., and Dixon W. (2006) Third-party intermediaries and negotiated settlements, 1946–2000, *International Interactions*, 32(4): 385–408.

Frazier, D., and Dixon, W. (2009) Third party intermediaries and negotiated settlements, in J. Bercovitch and S. Garner, eds, *International Conflict Mediation: New Approaches and Findings*. London and New York: Routledge.

Freire, P. ([1970] 2000) *Pedagogy of the Oppressed*. New York: Continuum.

Fry, D., and Bjorkqvist, K., eds (1997) *Cultural Variation in Conflict Resolution: Alternatives to Violence*. Mahwah, NJ: Lawrence Erlbaum Associates.

Frye, W. R. (1957) *A United Nations Peace Force*. New York: Oceana.

Fukuyama, F. (2004) *State-Building: Governance and World Order in the 21st Century*. Ithaca, NY: Cornell University Press.

Gadamer, H. ([1960] 1975) *Truth and Method*. New York: Seabury Press.

Gagnon, C., and Brown, K., eds (2014) *Post-Conflict Studies: An Interdisciplinary Approach*. Abingdon: Routledge.

Gakuin, A. (2009) *Fostering Peace through Cultural Initiatives*. Tokyo: University of Tokyo, Joint Research Institute for International Peace and Culture.

Galama, A., and van Tongeren, P. (2002) *Towards Better Peacebuilding Practice: On Lessons Learned, Evaluation Practices and Aid and Conflict*. Utrecht: European Centre for Conflict Prevention.

Galtung, J. (1969) Conflict as a way of life, in H. Freeman, ed., *Progress in Mental Health*. London: Churchill.

Galtung, J. (1975) Three approaches to peace: peacekeeping, peacemaking and peacebuiding, in *Peace, War and Defence: Essays in Peace Research*, vol. 2. Copenhagen: Christian Ejlers, pp. 282–304.

Galtung, J. (1975–88) *Essays in Peace Research*, 6 vols. Copenhagen: Christian Ejlers.

Galtung, J. (1980) *Papers in English*, 7 vols. Oslo: Peace Research Institute. [See also a comprehensive bibliography of Galtung's publications at www.transcend. org].

Galtung, J. (1984) *There are Alternatives! Four Roads to Peace and Security*. Nottingham: Spokesman.

Galtung, J. (1985) Twenty-five years of peace research: ten challenges and some responses, *Journal of Peace Research*, 22(2): 141–58.

Galtung, J. (1987) Only one friendly quarrel with Kenneth Boulding, *Journal of Peace Research*, 24(2): 199–203.

Galtung, J. (1989) *Solving Conflicts: A Peace Research Perspective*. Honolulu: University of Hawaii Press.

Galtung, J. (1990) Cultural violence, *Journal of Peace Research*, 27(3): 291–305.

Galtung, J. (1996) *Peace by Peaceful Means: Peace and Conflict, Development and Civilisation*. Oslo: PRIO.

Galtung, J. (2004) *Transcend and Transform: An Introduction to Conflict Work*. London: Pluto Press.

Galtung, J. (2008) Interconnection, in O. Urbain, ed., *Music and Conflict Transformation: Harmonies and Dissonances in Geopolitics*. Tokyo: I. B. Tauris/Toda Institute, pp. 53–60.

Galtung, J., and Jacobsen, C. (with contributions by Brand-Jacobsen, K., and Tschudi, F.) (2000) *Searching for Peace: the Road to TRANSCEND*. London: Pluto Press.

Gandhi, R. (2004) Hinduism and peacebuilding, in H. Coward and G. Smith, eds, *Religion and Peacebuilding*. New York: State University of New York Press, pp. 45–68.

Ganesan, N. (2014) The Myanmar Peace Centre: its origin, activities, and aspirations, *Asian Journal of Peacebuilding*, 2(1): 127–41.

Gannett, K. R., Kaufman, Z. A., Clark, M. A., and McGarvey, S. T. (2014) Football with three 'halves': a qualitative exploratory study of the football3 model at the Football for Hope Festival 2010, *Journal of Sport for Development*, 2(3): 47–59.

Gantzel, K., and Schwinghammer, T. (2000) *Warfare since the Second World War*. London: Transaction.

Gartner, S., and Bercovitch, J. (2006) Overcoming obstacles to peace: the contribution of mediation to short-lived conflict settlements, *International Studies Quarterly*, 50(4): 819–40.

Gartner, S., and Melin, M. (2009) Assessing outcomes: conflict management and the durability of peace, in J. Bercovitch et al., eds, *The Sage Handbook of Conflict Resolution*. London: Sage, pp. 564–79.

Gartzke, E. (2007) The capitalist peace, *American Journal of Political Science*, 51(1): 166–91.

Gastrow, P. (1995) *Bargaining for Peace: South Africa and the National Peace Accord*. Washington, DC: US Institute of Peace Press.

GCPP (2003) *The Global Conflict Prevention Pool: A Joint UK Government Approach to Reducing Conflict*. London: FCO.

Geller, D., and Singer, D. (1998) *Nations at War: A Scientific Study of International Conflict*. Cambridge: Cambridge University Press.

Gentili, A. ([1598] 1964) *De jure belli libri tres*. New York: Oceana.

Gesser-Edelsburg, A. (2011) Entertainment-education: dilemmas of Israeli creators of theatre about the Israel–Palestinian conflict in promoting peace, *Journal of Peace Education*, 8(1): 55–76.

Ghani, A., and Lockhart, C. (2008) *Fixing Failed States: A Framework for Rebuilding a Fractured World*. Oxford: Oxford University Press.

Giddens, A. (1987) *The Nation State and Violence*. Berkeley: University of California Press.

Giddens, A. (2009) *The Politics of Climate Change*. Cambridge: Polity.

Gienanth, T., Hansen, W., and Koppe, S. (2012) *Peace Operations 2025*. Berlin: ZIF.

Ginifer, J., ed. (1997) *Beyond the Emergency: Development within UN Peace Missions*. London: Frank Cass.

Gizelis, T.-I. (2009) Gender empowerment and United Nations peacebuilding, *Journal of Peace Research*, 46(4): 505–23.

Gizelis, T.-I., and Olsson, L., eds (2015) *Gender, Peace and Security: Implementing UN Security Council Resolution 1325*. Abingdon: Routledge.

Glasl, F. (1982) The process of conflict escalation and roles of third parties, in G. B. J. Bomers and R. B. Peterson, eds, *Conflict Management and Industrial Relations*. The Hague: Kluwer Nijhoff.

Gleditsch, N., ed. (1997) *Conflict and the Environment*. Dordrecht: Kluwer Academic.

Gleditsch, N. P., Wallensteen P., et al. (2001) *Armed Conflicts 1946–2000: A New Dataset*. Department of Peace and Conflict Research, Uppsala University, and the International Peace research Institute, Oslo.

Gleditsch, N., Wallensteen, P., Eriksson, M., Sollenberg, M., and Strand, H. (2002) Armed conflict 1946–2001, *Journal of Peace Research*, 39(5): 615–37.

Gleditsch, S. K., Metternich, N., and Ruggeri, A. (2013) Data and progress in peace and conflict research, *Journal of Peace Research*, 51(2): 301–14.

Gleick, P. (1995) Water and conflict: fresh water resources and international security, in S. Lynn-J ones and S. Miller, eds, *Global Dangers*. Cambridge, MA: MIT Press, pp. 84–117.

Goertz, G., and Levy, J. (2007) *Explaining War and Peace: Case Studies and Necessary Conditions and Counterfactuals*. London: Routledge.

Goldblatt, D. (2007) *The Ball Is Round: A Global History of Football*. London: Penguin.

Goldstein, J. (2012) *Winning the War on War: The Decline of Armed Conflict Worldwide*. New York: Plume.

Goldstone, J. (2008) *Using Quantitative and Qualitative Models to Forecast Instability*, Special Report no. 204. Washington, DC: United States Institute of Peace, www.usip.org/files/resources/sr204.pdf.

Goldstone, R. (1997) War crimes: a question of will, *The World Today*, 53(4): 106–8.

Goldstone, R. (2000) *For Humanity: Reflections of a War Crimes Investigator*. New Haven, CT: Yale University Press.

Goodall, J. (1986) *The Chimpanzees of Gombe: Patterns of Behaviour*. Cambridge, MA: Harvard University Press.

Goodhand, J. (2006) *Aiding Peace? The Role of NGOs in Armed Conflict*. Boulder, CO: Lynne Rienner.

Goodhand, J., and Klem, B. (2005) *Aid Conflict and Peacebuilding in Sri Lanka 2000–2005*. Colombo: Asia Foundation.

Goodwin, D. (2005) *The Military and Negotiation: The Role of the Soldier Diplomat*. London: Routledge.

Goodwin-Gill, G., and Cohn, I. (1994) *Child Soldiers: The Role of Children in Armed Conflicts*. Oxford: Clarendon Press.

Gopin, M. (2000) *Between Eden and Armageddon: The Future of World Religions, Violence and Peacemaking*. Oxford: Oxford University Press.

Grant, J. (1992) *The State of the World's Children*. New York: UNICEF.

Grau, A. (2013) Political activism and dance: the Sarabhais and nonviolence through the arts, *Dance Chronicle*, 36(1): 1–35.

Gray, A. (2008) Reconciliation in South Africa, in O. Urbain, ed., *Music and Conflict Transformation: Harmonies and Dissonances in Geopolitics*. Tokyo: I. B. Tauris/Toda Institute, pp. 63–7.

Gray, C. (2002) World politics as usual after September 11: realism vindicated, in K. Booth and T. Dunne, eds, *Worlds in Collision: Terror and the Future of Global Order*. Basingstoke: Palgrave, pp. 226–34.

Graybill, L. (1998) South Africa's Truth and Reconciliation Commission: ethical and theological perspectives, *Ethics and International Affairs*, 12: 43–62.

Greene, O., and Marsh, N., eds (2011) *Small Arms, Crime and Conflict: Global Governance and the Threat of Armed Violence*. Abingdon: Routledge.

Grenier, Y., and Daudelin, J. (1995) Foreign assistance and the market-place of peacemaking: lessons from El Salvador, *International Peacekeeping*, 2(3): 350–64.

Grieg, J. M., and Diehl, P. (2012) *International Mediation*. Cambridge: Polity.

Griffiths, A., ed. (1998) *Building Peace and Democracy in Post-Conflict Societies*. Halifax: Dalhousie University.

Grix, J., and Lee, D. (2013) Soft power, sports mega-events and emerging states: the lure of the politics of attraction, *Global Society*, 27(4): 521–36.

Grotius, H. ([1625] 1925) *The Law of War and Peace*, trans. F. Kelsey. Oxford: Clarendon Press.

Guatemalan Commission for Historical Clarification (1999) Memory of Silence Report, http://shr.aaas.org/guatemala/ceh/report/english/toc.html.

Guéhenno, J.-M. (2015) Ten wars to watch in 2015, *Foreign Affairs*, 2 January, http://foreignpolicy.com/2015/01/02/10-wars-to-watch-in-2015/.

Gulliver, P. (1979) *Disputes and Negotiations: A Cross-Cultural Perspective*. New York: Academic Press.

Gurr, T. (1970) *Why Men Rebel*. Princeton, NJ: Princeton University Press.

Gurr, T. (1993) *Minorities at Risk: A Global View of Ethnopolitical Conflict*. Washington, DC: US Institute of Peace Press.

Gurr, T. (1995) Transforming ethnopolitical conflicts: exit, autonomy or access?, in K. Rupesinghe, ed., *Conflict Transformation*. London: Macmillan, pp. 1–30.

Gurr, T. (1998) *Peoples versus States*. Washington, DC: US Institute of Peace Press.

Gurr, T. (2000) *Peoples versus States: Minorities at Risk in the New Century*. Washington, DC: US Institute of Peace Press.

Gurr, T., and Harff, B. (1994) *Ethnic Conflict in World Politics*. Boulder, CO: Westview Press.

Gutmann, A., and Thompson, D. (2000) The moral foundations of truth commissions, in R. Rotberg and T. Thompson, eds, *Truth v. Justice: The Morality of Truth Commissions*. Princeton, NJ: Princeton University Press, pp. 22–44.

Habermas, J. (1982) A reply to my critics, in J. Thompson and D. Held, eds, *Habermas: Critical Debates*. London: Macmillan.

Habermas, J. (1984) *Reason and the Rationalization of Society*, vol. 1 of *The Theory of Communicative Action*, trans. T. McCarthy. Cambridge: Polity.

Habermas, J. (1992) *Postmetaphysical Thinking*. Cambridge, MA: MIT Press.

Hachemer, P., ed. (2014) *Conflict Barometer 2013*. Heidelberg: Heidelberg Institute for International Conflict Research, http://hiik.de/de/downloads/data/downloads_2013/ConflictBarometer2013.pdf.

Hall, E. (1976) *Beyond Culture*. New York: Anchor Books.

Hall, L., ed. (1993) *Negotiation: Strategies for Mutual Gain*. London: Sage.

Halliday, F. (2002) *Two Hours that Shook the World: September 11, 2001: Causes and Consequences*. London: Sage.

Halpin, E., Trevorrow, P., Webb, D., and Wright, S., eds (2006) *Cyberwar, Netwar and the Revolution in Military Affairs*. London: Palgrave Macmillan.

Hampson, F. (1996) *Nurturing Peace: Why Peace Settlements Succeed or Fail*. Washington, DC: US Institute of Peace Press.

Hampson, F., and Malone, D., eds (2002) *From Reaction to Conflict Prevention: Opportunities for the UN System*. Boulder, CO: Lynne Rienner.

Hannum, H. (1990) *Autonomy, Sovereignty and Self-Determination: The Accommodation of Conflicting Rights*. Philadelphia: University of Pennsylvania Press.

Hansen, W., Ramsbotham, O., and Woodhouse, T. (2004) Hawks and doves: peace-keeping and conflict resolution, in A. Austin et al., eds, *Transforming Ethnopolitical Conflict: the Berghof Handbook*. Berlin: VS Verlag für Sozialwissenschaften, pp. 295–320.

Harbom, L. and Wallensteen, P. (2009) Armed conflicts 1948–2009, *Journal of Peace Research*, 46(4): 577–87.

Hardin, G. (1968) The tragedy of the commons, *Science*, 162 (13 December): 1243–8.

Harding, J. (1994) *Small Wars, Small Mercies: Journeys in Africa's Disputed Nations*. London: Penguin.

Harris, I. (2004) Peace education theory, *Journal of Peace Education*, 1(1): 5–20.

Harris, P. (2010) *World Ethics and Climate Change: From International to Global Justice*. Edinburgh: Edinburgh University Press.

Harris, P., and Reilly, B., eds (1998) *Democracy and Deep-Rooted Conflict: Options for Negotiators*. Stockholm: Institute for Democracy and Electoral Assistance.

Harris, S., and Lewer, N. (2005) Post-graduate peace education in Sri Lanka, *Journal of Peace Education*, 2(2): 109–24.

Harvey, D. (2003) *The New Imperialism*. Oxford: Oxford University Press.

Harvey, R. (2003) *The Fall of Apartheid: The Inside Story from Smuts to Mbeki*. Basingstoke: Palgrave.

Hasenclever, A., and Weiffen, B. (2006) International institutions are the key: a new perspective on the democratic peace, *Review of International Studies*, 32(4): 563–85.

Hashmi, S. (1993) Is there an Islamic ethic of humanitarian intervention? *Ethics and International Affairs*, 9: 55–73.

Hawkins, V. (2015) Peace and the absence of journalism, in J. Hoffmann and V. Hawkins, eds, *Communication and Peace: Mapping an Emerging Field*. Abingdon: Routledge, pp. 51–61.

Hayes, R., Kaminski, S., and Beres, S. (2003) Negotiating the non-negotiable: dealing with absolutist terrorists, *International Negotiation*, 8: 9–24.

Hayward, K., and O'Donnell, C., eds (2010) *Political Discourse and Conflict Resolution*. London: Routledge.

He, Y. (2007) *The Search for Reconciliation: Sino-Japanese and German–Polish Relations since World War II*. Cambridge: Cambridge University Press.

Healey, J., ed. (2013) *A Fierce Domain: Conflict in Cyberspace, 1986 to 2012*. Vienna, VA: Cyber Conflicts Studies Association/Atlantic Council [Kindle edn].

Heathershaw, J. (2008) Unpacking the liberal peace: the dividing and merging of peacebuilding discourses, *Millennium: Journal of International Studies*, 6(3): 597–622.

Hegre, H. (2003) Development and the liberal peace: what does it take to be a trading state?, in G. Schneider, K. Barbieri and N. P. Gleditsch, eds, *Globalization and Armed Conflict*. Lanham, MD: Rowman & Littlefield, pp. 205–31.

Hegre, H. (2004) The duration and termination of civil war, *Journal of Peace Research*, 41(3): 243–52.

Hegre, H., Ellingsen, T., Gates, S., and Gleditsch, N. (2001) Towards a democratic civil peace? Democracy, political change and civil war 1816–1992, *American Political Science Review*, 95(1): 33–48.

Heidenrich, J. G. (2001) *How to Prevent Genocide: A Guide for Policymakers, Scholars and the Concerned Citizen*. Westport, CT: Praeger.

Held, D. (1995) *Democracy and the Global Order: From the Modern State to Cosmopolitan Governance*. Cambridge: Polity.

Held, D. (2004) *Global Covenant: The Social Democratic Alternative to the Washington Consensus*. Cambridge: Polity.

Held, D. (2010) Cosmopolitanism after 9/11, *International Politics*, 47(1): 52–61.

Held, D., and McGrew, A., eds (2007) *Globalization Theory*. Cambridge: Polity.

Held, D., McGrew, A., Goldblatt, D., and Perraton, J. (1999) *Global Transformations*. Cambridge: Polity.

Hendrick, D. (2009) *Complexity Theory and Conflict Transformation: An Exploration of Potential and Implications*, Working Paper 17. Bradford: University of Bradford, Department of Peace Studies, Centre for Conflict Resolution.

Heraclides, A. (1998) The ending of unending conflicts: separatist wars, *Millennium: Journal of International Studies*, 26(3): 679–708.

Herbst, J. (2003) *New Order in Sight? The African Union, NEPAD, and the Future of a Continent*, Adelphi Paper no. 36. London: IISS.

Herbolzheimer, K., and Leslie, E. (2013) *Innovation in Mediation Support: The International Contact Group in Mindanao*. London: Conciliation Resources.

Herman, J. (1992) *Trauma and Recovery*. New York: Basic Books.

Hewstone, N., and Brown, R., eds (1986) *Contact and Conflict in Intergroup Encounters*. Oxford: Blackwell.

Hicks, D. (2011) *Dignity: The Essential Role it Plays in Resolving Conflict*. New Haven, CT: Yale University Press.

HIIK (Heidelberg Institute for International Conflict Research) (2009) *Conflict Barometer 2009*. Heidelberg: University of Heidelberg, Department of Political Science.

HIIK (Heidelberg Institute for International Conflict Research) (2011) *Conflict Barometer 2011*, http://hiik.de/en/konfliktbarometer/pdf/Conflict Barometer_2011.

Hilbert, M., and López, P. (2011) The world's technological capacity to store, communicate, and compute information, *Science*, 332(6025): 60–65, www.sciencemag.org/content/332/6025/60.

Hinsley, F. (1963) *Power and the Pursuit of Peace*. Cambridge: Cambridge University Press.

Hinsley, F. (1987) Peace and war in modern times, in R. Väyrynen, ed., *The Quest for Peace: Transcending Collective Violence and War among Societies, Cultures and States*. London: Sage.

Hirst, C. (2009) Can we know what peace we build? The need for and challenge of evaluation for the peacebuilding community and the potential for theory-based evaluation. Unpublished paper, University of Coventry.

Hoehne, M. (2010) Political representation in Somalia, in M. Bradbury and S. Healy, eds, *Whose Peace is it Anyway? Connecting Somali and International Peacemaking*. Accord, no. 21: 34–87.

Hoffman, M. (1987) Critical theory and the inter-paradigm debate, *Millennium: Journal of International Studies*, 16(2): 234–62.

Hoffman, M. (2004) Peace and conflict impact assessment methodology, in A. Austin et al., eds, *Transforming Ethnopolitical Conflict: the Berghof Handbook*. Berlin: VS Verlag für Sozialwissenschaften, pp. 171–91.

Hoffman, M. (2009) What is left of the 'liberal peace'? *Connect*, 21(2): 10–11.

Hoffmann, J., and Hawkins, V. (2015) *Communication and Peace: Mapping an Emerging Field*. Abingdon: Routledge.

Holbrooke, R. (1999) *To End a War*. New York: Modern Library.

Holland, T., and Martin, J. P. (2014) *Human Rights Education and Peacebuilding: A Comparative Study*. Abingdon: Routledge.

Hollis, M., and Lukes, S., eds (1982) *Rationality and Relativism*. Oxford: Blackwell.

Holsti, K. (1991) *Peace and War: Armed Conflicts and International Order 1648–1989*. Cambridge: Cambridge University Press.

Holsti, K. (1996) *The State, War, and the State of War*. Cambridge: Cambridge University Press.

Holzgrefe, J., and Keohane, R., eds (2003) *Humanitarian Intervention: Ethical, Legal and Political Dilemmas*. Cambridge: Cambridge University Press.

Homer-Dixon, T. (1991) On the threshold: environmental changes as causes of acute conflict, *International Security*, 16(2): 7–16.

Homer-Dixon, T. (1994) Environmental scarcities and violent conflict: evidence from cases, *International Security*, 19(1): 5–40.

Homer-Dixon, T. (2001) *Environment, Scarcity and Violence*. Princeton, NJ: Princeton University Press.

Hopmann, P. (2001) Disintegrating states: separating without violence, in I. W. Zartman, ed., *Preventive Negotiation*. Lanham, MD: Rowman & Littlefield, pp. 113–64.

Hörnle, J. (2009) *Cross-Border Internet Dispute Resolution*. Cambridge: Cambridge University Press.

Horowitz, D. (1985) *Ethnic Groups in Conflict*. Berkeley: University of California Press.

Horowitz, D. (1991) Making moderation pay: the comparative politics of ethnic conflict management, in J. Montville, ed., *Conflict and Peacemaking in Multiethnic Societies*. New York: Lexington Books, pp. 451–75.

Howard, M. (1976) *War in European History*. London: Oxford University Press.

Howard, M. (2000) *The Invention of Peace: Reflections on War and International Order*. London: Profile Books.

Howard, R. (2015) Conflict sensitive journalism: (r)evolution in media peacebuilding, in J. Hoffmann and V. Hawkins, eds, *Communication and Peace: Mapping an Emerging Field*. Abingdon: Routledge, pp. 62–75.

HSR Project (2013) *Human Security Report 2013: The Decline in Global Violence: Evidence, Explanation, and Contestation*. Vancouver: Simon Fraser University, www.hsrgroup.org/human-security-reports/human-security-report.aspx.

Hughes, R. (2010) A treaty for cyberspace, *International Affairs*, 86(2): 523–41.

Human Rights Watch (1995) *Slaughter among Neighbours: The Political Origins of Communal Violence*. New Haven, CT: Yale University Press.

Human Rights Watch (2014) *The Power These Men Have Over Us: Sexual Exploitation and Abuse by African Union Forces in Somalia*, www.hrw.org/reports/2014/09/08/power-these-men-have-over-us.

Hume, C. (1994) *Ending Mozambique's War: The Role of Mediation and Good Offices*. Washington, DC: US Institute of Peace Press.

Hunt, C. T. (2015) *UN Peace Operations and International Policing: Negotiating Complexity, Assessing Impact and Learning to Learn*. Abingdon: Routledge.

Huntington, S. (1996) *The Clash of Civilizations and the Remaking of World Order*. New York: Simon & Schuster.

ICISS (International Commission on Intervention and State Sovereignty) (2001) *The Responsibility to Protect*. Ottawa: International Development Research Centre.

ICRC (International Committee of the Red Cross) (1996) Annex VI: The Code of Conduct for the International Red Cross and Red Crescent Movement and NGOs in Disaster Relief, *International Review of the Red Cross*, 310, https://www.icrc.org/eng/resources/documents/misc/code-of-conduct-290296.htm.

IEP (Institute for Economics and Peace) (2014a) *The Economic Cost of Violence Containment*. New York: IEP, http://economicsandpeace.org/wp-content/uploads/2015/06/The-Economic-Cost-of-Violence-Containment.pdf.

IEP (Institute for Economics and Peace) (2014b) *Global Peace Index*. New York: IEP, www.visionofhumanity.org/sites/default/files/2014%20Global%20Peace%20Index%20REPORT.pdf

IEP (Institute for Economics and Peace) (2014c) *Global Terrorism Index*. New York: IEP, www.visionofhumanity.org/sites/default/files/Global%20Terrorism%20Index%20Report%202014_0.pdf.

IEP (Institute for Economics and Peace) (2015) *Global Peace Index*. New York: IEP, http://economicsandpeace.org/wp-content/uploads/2015/06/Global-Peace-Index-Report-2015_0.pdf.

Ignatieff, M. (2000) *Virtual War: Kosovo and Beyond*. London: Chatto & Windus.

IISS (International Institute of Strategic Studies) (1997) Chart of armed conflict, in *Military Balance*. London: IISS.

Ikenberry, G. J. (2014) The illusion of geopolitics: the enduring power of the liberal order, *Foreign Affairs*, May/June, https://www.foreignaffairs.com/articles/china/2014-04-17/illusion-geopolitics.

International Journal of Conflict Engagement and Resolution (2013) Taking stock of the field: past, present and future, part 1, 1(1); part 2, 1(2).

International Rescue Committee (2003) *Mortality in the Democratic Republic of Congo: Results from a Nationwide Survey*. New York: IRC.

IOC (International Olympic Committee) (2007) *Olympic Charter*. Lausanne: International Olympic Committee.

IPCC (Intergovernmental Panel on Climate Change) (2014) *Climate Change 2014: Impacts, Adaptation, and Vulnerability. Assessment Report 5: Summary for Policymakers*.

Irani, G. (1999) Islamic mediation techniques for Middle East conflicts. *MERIA Journal*, 3(2).

Irigaray, L. ([1977] 1985) *The Sex Which is Not One*. Ithaca, NY: Cornell University Press.

ISA (International Studies Association) (2015) Spaces and places: geopolitics in an era of globalisation, *International Studies Review*, 17(1) [special issue].

ISS Africa (Institute for Security Studies Africa) (2014) *Peace and Security Council Report, no. 58*, www.issafrica.org/publications/peace-and-security-council-report/peace-and-security-council-report-no-58.

ITU (International Telecommunications Union) (2014) The world in 2014: ICT facts and figures, www.itu.int/en/ITU-D/Statistics/Documents/facts/ICTFactsFigures2014-e.pdf.

Jabri, V. (1996) *Discourses on Violence: Conflict Analysis Reconsidered*. Manchester: Manchester University Press.

Jabri, V. (2007) *War and the Transformation of Global Politics*. Basingstoke: Palgrave Macmillan.

Jackson, R. (1990) *Quasi-States, Sovereignty, International Relations and the Third World*. Cambridge: Cambridge University Press.

Jackson, R. (2000) *The Global Covenant: Human Conduct in a World of States*. Oxford: Oxford University Press.

Jacoby, T. (2008) *Understanding Conflict and Violence: Theoretical and Interdisciplinary Approaches*. London: Routledge.

Janis, I. (1973) *Victims of Groupthink*. Boston: Houghton Mifflin.

Japan Foundation (2008) *The Role of Cultural Initiatives in Peacebuilding*. Tokyo: Japan Foundation.

Jarstad, A., and Sisk, T., eds (2008) *From War to Democracy: Dilemmas of Peacebuilding*. Cambridge: Cambridge University Press.

Jegen, M. E. (1996) *Sign of Hope*. Uppsala: Life and Peace Institute.

Jervis, R. (1976) *Perception and Misperception in International Politics*. Princeton, NJ: Princeton University Press.

Jervis, R. (1982) Security regimes, *International Organization*, 36(2): 357–78.

Johansen, R. C. (1990) UN peacekeeping: the changing utility of military force, *Third World Quarterly*, 12 April, 53–70.

Johansen, R. C., ed. (2006) *A United Nations Emergency Peace Service: To Prevent Genocide and Crimes against Humanity*. New York: World Federalist Movement.

Johnson, D. W., Johnson, R. T., and Tjosvold, D. (2000) Constructive controversy: the value of intellectual opposition, in M. Deutsch and P. Coleman, eds, *The Handbook of Conflict Resolution: Theory and Practice*. San Francisco: Jossey-Bass, pp. 65–85.

Johnston, D., and Sampson, C. (1994) *Religion, the Missing Dimension of Statecraft*. Oxford: Oxford University Press.

Joint Research Institute for International Peace and Culture (2009) *Fostering Peace through Cultural Initiatives*. Tokyo: Ayoama Gakuin University.

Jones, B. (2002) The challenges of strategic coordination, in S. Stedman et al., eds, *Ending Civil Wars: The Implementation of Peace Agreements*. Boulder, CO: Lynne Rienner, IPA/CISAC, pp. 89–115.

Jones, D. (1999) *Cosmopolitan Mediation? Conflict Resolution and the Oslo Accords*. Manchester: Manchester University Press.

Jordan, T. (1999) *Cyberpower: The Culture and Politics of Cyberspace and the Internet*. London: Routledge.

Jordanger, V. (2008) Healing cultural violence, in O. Urbain, ed., *Music and Conflict Transformation: Harmonies and Dissonances in Geopolitics*. Tokyo: I. B. Tauris/Toda Institute, pp. 128–46.

Juergensmeyer, M. (2000) *Terror in the Mind of God: The Global Rise of Religious Violence*. Berkeley: University of California Press.

Kacowicz, A. (1995) Explaining zones of peace: democracies as satisfied powers? *Journal of Conflict Resolution*, 32(3): 265–76.

Kahane, A. (2007) *Solving Tough Problems: A Creative Way of Talking, Listening and Creating New Realities*. San Francisco: Berrett-Koehler.

Kahneman, D. (2012) *Thinking, Fast and Slow*. London: Penguin.

Kaldor, M. (1991) *The Imaginary War: Understanding the East–West Conflict*. Oxford: Blackwell.

Kaldor, M. (1998) Reconceptualising organised violence, in D. Archibugi, D. Held and M. Kohler, eds, *Re-imagining Political Community: Studies in Cosmopolitan Democracy*. Cambridge: Polity, pp. 91–110.

Kaldor, M. (1999) *New and Old Wars: Organized Violence in a Global Era*. Cambridge: Polity.

Kaldor, M. (2003) *Global Civil Society*. Cambridge: Polity.

Kaldor, M. (2006) *New and Old Wars: Organized Violence in a Global Era*, 2nd edn. Cambridge: Polity.

Kaldor, M. (2012) *New and Old Wars: Organized Violence in a Global Era*, 3rd edn. Cambridge: Polity.

Kaldor, M., and Vashee, B., eds (1997) *New Wars: Restructuring the Global Military Sector*. London: Pinter.

Kalyvas, S. (2006) *The Logic of Violence in Civil War*. Cambridge: Cambridge University Press.

Kapila, M., and Wermester, K. (2002) Development and conflict: new approaches in the United Kingdom, in F. Hampson and D. Malone, eds, *From Reaction to Conflict Prevention: Opportunities for the UN System*. Boulder, CO: Lynne Rienner.

Kaplan, R. (1994) The coming anarchy, *Atlantic Monthly*, 273(February), 44–76.

Karatzogianni, A. (2006) *The Politics of Cyberconflict*. London: Routledge.

Karlsrud, J., and Rosén, F. (2013) In the eye of the beholder? UN and the use of drones to protect civilians, *Stability: International Journal of Security and Development*, 2(2): 1–10, http://dx.doi.org/10.5334/sta.bo.

Karp, A. (1994) The arms trade revolution: the major impact of small arms, *Washington Quarterly*, 17(4): 65–77.

Kathman, J. (2013) United Nations peacekeeping personnel commitments, 1990–2011, *Conflict Management and Peace Science*, 30(5): 532–49.

Katsch, E., and Rifkin, J. (2001) *Online Dispute Resolution: Resolving Conflicts in Cyberspace*. San Francisco: Jossey-Bass.

Katz, N., and Lawyer, J. (1985) *Communication and Conflict Resolution Skills*. New York: Kendall Hunt.

Kaufmann, C. (1996) Possible and impossible solutions to ethnic civil wars, *International Security*, 20(4): 136–75.

Kaysens, C., and Rathjens, G. (1996) *Peace Operations by the United Nations: The Case for a Volunteer UN Military Force*. Cambridge, MA: Committee on International Security Studies.

Keashly, L., and Fisher, R. (1996) A contingency perspective on conflict interventions: theoretical and practical considerations, in J. Bercovitch, ed., *Resolving International Conflicts: The Theory and Practice of Mediation*. Boulder, CO: Lynne Rienner, pp. 235–61.

Keating, T., and Knight, A., eds (2004) *Building Sustainable Peace*. Edmonton: University of Alberta Press and United Nations University Press.

Keegan, J. (1993) *A History of Warfare*. New York: Alfred A. Knopf.

Keen, D. (1995) *The Benefits of Famine*. Princeton, NJ: Princeton University Press.

Keen, D. (1998) *The Economic Function of Violence in Civil Wars*, Adelphi Paper 320. London: IISS.

Keen, D. (2008) *Complex Emergencies*. Cambridge: Polity.

Kelly, G. (1955) *A Theory of Personality: The Psychology of Personal Constructs*. New York: W. W. Norton.

Kelly, R. (2002) Liberating memory. PhD thesis, University of Bradford.

Kelman, H. (1992) Informal mediation by the scholar/practitioner, in J. Bercovitch and J. Rubin, eds, *Mediation in International Relations: Multiple Approaches to Conflict Management*. London: Macmillan, pp. 191–237.

Kelman, H. (1996) The interactive problem-solving approach, in C. Crocker and F. Hampson, eds, *Managing Global Chaos: Sources of and Responses to International Conflict*. Washington, DC: US Institute of Peace Press, pp. 500–20.

Kelman, H. (1997) Social-psychological dimensions of international conflict, in I. W. Zartman and J. Rasmussen, eds, *Peacemaking in International Conflict: Methods and Techniques*. Washington, DC: US Institute of Peace Press, pp. 191–237.

Kelman, H. (1999) Transforming the relationship between former enemies: a social-psychological analysis, in R. Rothstein, ed., *After the Peace: Resistance and Reconciliation*. Boulder, CO: Lynne Rienner, pp. 193–205.

Kelman, H. (2004) Reconciliation as identity change: a social psychological perspective, in Y. Bar-Siman-Tov, ed., *From Conflict Resolution to Reconciliation*. Oxford: Oxford University Press.

Kelman, H. (2005) Interactive problem solving in the Israeli–Palestinian case: past contributions and present challenges, in R. Fisher, ed., *Paving the Way: Contributions of Interactive Conflict Resolution to Peacemaking*. Lanham, MD: Lexington Books, pp. 41–63.

Kelman, H., and Cohen, S. (1976) The problem-solving workshop: a social-psychological contribution to the resolution of international conflicts, *Journal of Peace Research*, 13(2): 79–90.

Kemp, W. (2001) *Quiet Diplomacy in Action: The OSCE High Commissioner on National Minorities*. The Hague: Kluwer Law International.

Kennan, G. (1984) *American Diplomacy*. Chicago: University of Chicago Press.

Kennedy, P. (1993) *Preparing for the Twenty First Century*. London: HarperCollins.

Keohane, R. (1989) *International Institutions and State Power: Essays in International Relations Theory*. Boulder, CO: Westview Press.

Keohane, R., and Nye, J. (1989) *Power and Interdependence*. Glenview, IL: Scott, Foresman.

Kerman, C. (1974) *Creative Tension: The Life and Thought of Kenneth Boulding*. Ann Arbor: University of Michigan Press.

Kersley, E., ed. (2014) *New Ways of War: Is Remote Control Warfare Effective?* Remote Control Digest, Oxford Research Group, www.oxfordresearchgroup.org.uk/sites/default/files/Remote%20Control%20Digest.pdf.

Khrychikov, S., and Miall, H. (2002) Conflict prevention in Estonia, *Security Dialogue*, 33(2): 19–208.

King, C. (1997) *Ending Civil Wars*, Adelphi Paper 308. Oxford: Oxford University Press for the IISS.

Kingma, K. (1997) Demobilization of combatants after civil wars in Africa and their reintegration into civilian life, *Policy Sciences*, 30(3): 51–165.

Kingma, K. (2001) Demobilizing and reintegrating former combatants, in L. Reychler and T. Paffenholz, eds, *Peacebuilding: A Field Guide*. Boulder, CO: Lynne Rienner, pp. 405–15.

Kinloch, S. (1996) Utopian or pragmatic? A UN permanent military volunteer force, *International Peacekeeping*, 3(4): 166–90.

Kiss, E. (2000) Moral ambition within and beyond political constraints: reflections on restorative justice, in R. Rotberg and D. Thompson, eds, *Truth v. Justice: The Morality of Truth Commissions*. Princeton, NJ: Princeton University Press, pp. 68–98.

Klein, N. (2005) Allure of the blank slate, *The Guardian*, 18 April.

Knight, H. (2014) Articulating injustice: an exploration of young people's experiences of participation in a conflict transformation programme that utilises the arts as a form of dialogue, *Compare: A Journal of Comparative and International Education*, 44(1): 77–96.

Koh, H. (1997) Why do nations obey international law? *Yale Law Journal*, 106: 2599–659.

Korostelina, K. V., and Lässig, S., eds (2014) *History Education and Post-Conflict Reconciliation: Reconsidering Joint Textbook Projects*. Abingdon: Routledge.

Körppen, D., Schmelzle, B., and Wils, O., eds (2008) *A Systemic Approach to Conflict Transformation: Exploring Strengths and Limitations*. Berlin: Berghof Research Center for Constructive Conflict Management.

Kouchner, B. (2001) A first-hand perspective from Kosovo, *UN and Conflict Monitor*. London: United Nations Association.

Kovick, D. (2005) *The Hewlett Foundation's Conflict Resolution Program: Twenty Years of Field-Building*. Menlo Park, CA: Hewlett Foundation.

Krain, M. (2005) International intervention and the severity of genocides and politicides, *International Studies Quarterly*, 49(2): 363–87.

Krasner, S. (1983) *International Regimes*. Ithaca, NY: Cornell University Press.

Krasner, S. (2004) Sharing sovereignty: new institutions for collapsed and failing states, *International Security*, 29(2): 85–120.

Krause, K. (1996) Armaments and conflict: the causes and consequences of 'military development', in L. van de Goor et al., eds, *Between Development and Destruction: An Enquiry into the Causes of Conflict in Post-Colonial States*. New York: St Martin's Press, pp. 173–96.

Krause, K., Muggah, R., and Gilgen, E., eds (2011) *Global Burden of Armed Violence 2011: Lethal Encounters*. Geneva: Geneva Declaration Secretariat, www.geneva-declaration.org/measurability/global-burden-of-armed-violence/global-burden-of-armed-violence-2011.html.

Kreimer, A., Eriksson, J., Muscat, R., Arnold, M., and Scott, C. (1998) *The World Bank's Experience with Post-Conflict Reconstruction*. Washington, DC: World Bank.

Kressell, K., and Pruitt, D., eds (1989) *Mediation Research*. San Francisco: Jossey-Bass.

Kreutz, J. (2010) How and when armed conflicts end: introducing the UCDP conflict termination dataset, *Journal of Peace Research*, 47(2): 243–50.

Kriesberg, L. (1973) *The Sociology of Social Conflicts*. Englewood Cliffs, NJ: Prentice-Hall.

Kriesberg, L. (1982) *Social Conflicts*. Englewood Cliffs, NJ: Prentice-Hall.

Kriesberg, L. (1991) Conflict resolution applications to peace studies, *Peace and Change*, 16(4): 400–17.

Kriesberg, L. (1992a) *International Conflict Resolution*. New Haven, CT: Yale University Press.

Kriesberg, L. (1992b) *De-escalation and Transformation of International Conflict*. New Haven, CT: Yale University Press.

Kriesberg, L. (1997) The development of the conflict resolution field, in I. W. Zartman and J. Rasmussen, eds, *Peacemaking in International Conflict: Methods and Techniques*. Washington, DC: US Institute of Peace Press, pp. 51–77.

Kriesberg, L. (1998a) *Constructive Conflicts: From Escalation to Resolution*. Lanham, MD: Rowman & Littlefield.

Kriesberg, L. (1998b) Reconciliation: conceptual and empirical issues. Paper given at the International Studies Association annual convention, Minneapolis, March.

Kriesberg, L. (2001) Mediation and the transformation of the Israeli–Palestinian conflict, *Journal of Peace Research*, 38(3): 373–92.

Kriesberg, L. (2009) The evolution of conflict resolution, in J. Bercovitch, V. Kremenyuk and I. W. Zartman, eds, *The Sage Handbook of Conflict Resolution*. London: Sage, pp. 15–32.

Kriesberg, L., and Dayton, B. D. (2011) *Constructive Conflicts: From Escalation to Resolution*, 4th edn. Lanham, MD: Rowman & Littlefield.

Kriesberg, L., Northrup, A., and Thorson, S., eds (1989) *Intractable Conflicts and their Transformation*. Syracuse, NY: Syracuse University Press.

Kristeva, J. (1986) *The Kristeva Reader*, ed. T. Moi. Oxford: Blackwell.

Kritz, N., ed. (1995) *Transitional Justice: How Emerging Democracies Reckon with Former Regimes*, Vol. 1: *General Considerations*. Washington, DC: US Institute of Peace Press.

Kronenberger, V., and Wouters, J., eds (2004) *The European Union and Conflict Prevention: Policy and Legal Aspects*. The Hague, T. M. C. Asser Press.

Kumar, K., ed. (1997) *Rebuilding Societies after Civil War: Critical Roles for International Assistance*. Boulder, CO: Lynne Rienner.

Kumar, K., ed. (1998) *Postconflict Elections, Democratization and International Assistance*. Boulder, CO: Lynne Rienner.

Kumar, R. (2009) *Negotiating Peace in Deeply Divided Societies: A Set of Simulations*. London: Sage.

Kung, H., and Kuschel, K.-J., eds (1993) *A Global Ethic: The Declaration of the Parliament of the World's Religions*. New York: Continuum.

Kurki, M., and Wight, C. (2007) International relations and social science, in T. Dunne, M. Kurki, and S. Smith, eds, *International Relations Theories: Discipline and Diversity*. Oxford: Oxford University Press.

Kuttab, J. (1988) The pitfalls of dialogue, *Journal of Palestine Studies*, 17(2): 84–108.

Kydd, A. (2003) Which side are you on? Bias, credibility and mediation, *American Journal of Political Science*, 47(4): 597–611.

Kydd, A. (2006) When can mediators build trust?, *American Political Science Review*, 100(3): 449–62.

Kydd, A., and Walter, B. (2002) Sabotaging the peace: the politics of extremist violence, *International Organization*, 56(2): 263–96.

Kymlicka, W. (2007) *Multicultural Odysseys: Navigating the New International Politics of Diversity*. Oxford: Oxford University Press.

Kymlicka, W., and Bashir, B., eds (2008) *The Politics of Reconciliation in Multicultural Societies*. Oxford: Oxford University Press.

LaFree, G., Dugan, L., and Kim Cragin, R. (2010) Trends in global terrorism, in Hewitt et al., eds, *Peace and Conflict 2010*. Boulder, CO: Paradigm, p. 22.

Lake, A., ed. (1990) *After the Wars: Reconstruction in Afghanistan, Indochina, Central America, South Africa and the Horn of Africa*. New Brunswick, NJ: Transaction.

Lake, D., and Rothchild, D. (1996) Containing fear: the origins and management of ethnic conflict, *International Security*, 21(2): 41–75.

Lake, D., and Rothchild, D., eds (1997) *The International Spread and Management of Ethnic Conflict*. Princeton, NJ: Princeton University Press.

Lakoff, G., and Johnson, M. (1980) *Metaphors We Live By*, Chicago: University of Chicago Press.

Lambrinidis, S. (2002) The Olympic Truce: an ancient concept for the new millennium. Speech to the International Olympic Academy conference, Athens.

Langille, H. P. (2000a) Conflict prevention: options for rapid deployment and UN standing forces, in T. Woodhouse and O. Ramsbotham, eds, *Peacekeeping and Conflict Resolution*. London: Frank Cass, pp. 219–53.

Langille H. P. (2000b) *Renewing Partnerships for the Prevention of Armed Conflict: Options to Enhance Rapid Deployment and Initiate a UN Standing Emergency Capability*. Ottawa: Canadian Centre for Foreign Policy Development.

Langille, H. P. (2014), *Improving United Nations Capacity for Rapid Deployment*, Providing for Peacekeeping no. 8. New York: International Peace Institute.

Langille, H. P., Faille, M., Hammond, J., and Hughes, C. (1995) A preliminary blueprint of long-term options for enhancing a United Nations rapid reaction capability, in D. Cox and A. Legault, eds, *UN Rapid Reaction Capabilities: Requirements and Prospects*. Clementsport, Nova Scotia: Canadian Peacekeeping Press.

Laqueur, W. (1999) *The New Terrorism: Fanaticism and the Arms of Mass Destruction*. Oxford: Oxford University Press.

Laqueur, W. (2004) *No End to War: Terrorism in the Twenty-First Century*. New York: Continuum.

Larsen, K. S., ed. (1993) *Conflict and Social Psychology*. London: Sage.

Last, D. (1997) *Theory, Doctrine and Practice of Conflict De-escalation in Peacekeeping Operations*. Clementsport, Nova Scotia: Lester B. Pearson Canadian International Peacekeeping Training Centre.

Laue, J. (1981) Conflict intervention, in E. Olsen and M. Micklin, eds, *Handbook of Applied Sociology*. New York: Praeger.

Laue, J. (1990) The emergence and institutionalisation of third-party roles in conflict, in J. Burton and F. Dukes, eds, *Conflict: Readings in Management and Resolution*. London: Macmillan, pp. 256–72.

Laue, J., and Cormick, C. (1978) The ethics of intervention in community disputes, in G. Bermant et al., eds, *The Ethics of Social Intervention*. New York: Halsted Press, pp. 205–32.

Lawler, P. (1995) *A Question of Values: Johan Galtung's Peace Research*. Boulder, CO: Lynne Rienner.

Lawrence, F. (2008) Music and empathy, in O. Urbain, ed., *Music and Conflict Transformation: Harmonies and Dissonances in Geopolitics*. Tokyo: I. B. Tauris/Toda Institute, pp. 13–25.

Leadbeater, C. (2010) Let's open up cloud computing, *The Guardian*, 22 January.

Lea-Howarth, J. (2006) Sport and conflict: is football an appropriate tool to utilise in conflict resolution, reconciliation or reconstruction? MA thesis, University of Sussex.

Leatherman, J., DeMars, W., Gaffney, P., and Väyrynen, R. (1999) *Breaking Cycles of Violence: Conflict Prevention in Intrastate Crises*. West Hartford, CT: Kumarian Press.

Lederach, J. P. (1994) *Building Peace: Sustainable Reconciliation in Divided Societies*. Tokyo: United Nations University Press.

Lederach, J. P. (1995) *Preparing for Peace: Conflict Transformation across Cultures*. Syracuse, NY: Syracuse University Press.

Lederach, J. P. (1997) *Building Peace: Sustainable Reconciliation in Divided Societies*. Washington, DC: US Institute of Peace Press.

Lederach, J. P. (1999) *The Journey toward Reconciliation*. Scottdale, PA: Herald Press.

Lederach, J. P. (2001) Civil society and reconciliation, in C. Crocker et al., eds, *Turbulent Peace: The Challenges of Managing International Conflict*. Washington, DC: US Institute of Peace Press, pp. 841–54.

Lederach, J. P. (2003) *The Little Book of Conflict Transformation*. Intercourse, PA: Good Books.

Lederach, J. P. (2005) *The Moral Imagination: The Art and Soul of Building Peace*. Oxford: Oxford University Press.

Lederach, J. P., and Lederach, A. J. (2011) *When Blood and Bones Cry Out: Journeys through the Soundscape of Healing and Reconciliation*. Oxford: Oxford University Press.

Lederach, J. P., and Moomaw Jenner, J., eds (2002) *A Handbook of International Peacebuilding: Into the Eye of the Storm*. San Francisco: Jossey-Bass.

Lederach, J., and Wehr, P. (1991) Mediating conflict in Central America, *Journal of Peace Research*, 28(1): 85–98.

Lederach, J., Neufeldt, R., and Culbertson, H. (2007) *Reflective Peacebuilding: A Planning, Monitoring, and Learning Toolkit*. London: International Alert.

Lee, J. R. (2009) *Climate Change and Armed Conflict: Hot and Cold Wars*. London: Routledge.

Leetaru, K., and Schrodt P. A. (2013) GDELT: Global data on events, location, and tone, 1979–2012. Paper presented at the annual meeting of the International Studies Association, San Francisco, 3–6 April, http://gdelt.utdallas.edu/data/documentation/ISA.2013.GDELT.pdf.

Leitenberg, M. (2003) *Deaths in Wars and Conflicts between 1945 and 2000*. Cornell University Peace Studies Program Occasional Paper no. 29, www.cissm.umd.edu/papers/files/deathswarsconflictsjune52006.pdf.

Lempereur, A., and Colson, A. (2010) *The First Move: A Negotiatior's Handbook*. Chichester: Wiley.

Lentz, T. F. (1955) *Towards a Science of Peace, Turning Point in Human Destiny*. New York: Bookman Associates.

Levy, J. (1989) The causes of war: a review of theories and evidence, in P. Tetlock et al., eds, *Behaviour, Society and Nuclear War*. Oxford: Oxford University Press, pp. 209–333.

Levy, L. R. (2004) The internet and post-conflict peacebuilding: a study with special reference to Kosovo. PhD thesis, University of Bradford, Department of Peace Studies.

Lewin, K. (1948) *Resolving Social Conflicts*. New York: Harper & Brothers.

Lewis, B. (2002) *What Went Wrong? The Clash between Islam and Modernity in the Middle East*. London: Weidenfeld & Nicolson.

Lewis, I. (2002) *A Modern History of the Somali Nation and State in the Horn of Africa*, 4th edn. Oxford: James Currey.

Lichbach, M. (1989) An evaluation of 'does economic inequality breed conflict?' studies, *World Politics*, 41(4): 431–71.

Licklider, R., ed. (1993) *Stopping the Killing: How Civil Wars End*. New York: New York University Press.

Licklider, R. (1995) The consequences of negotiated settlements in civil wars 1945–1993, *American Political Science Review*, 89(3): 681–90.

Lidén, K. (2009) Building peace between local and global politics: the cosmopolitical ethics of liberal peacebuilding, *International Peacekeeping*, 16 (5): 616–34.

Lidén, K., Mac Ginty, R., and Richmond, O. (2009) Introduction: beyond northern epistemologies of peace: peacebuilding reconstructed?, in K. Lidén et al., eds, *Liberal Peacebuilding Reconstructed*, *International Peacekeeping*, 16(5): 587–98.

Lie, T., Binningsbrø, H., and Gates, S. (2007) *Post-Conflict Justice and Sustainable Peace*, Post-Conflict Transition Working Paper No. 5, World Bank Policy Research Working Paper 4191 (April).

Lijphart, A. (1968) *The Politics of Accommodation: Pluralism and Democracy in the Netherlands*. Berkeley: University of California Press.

Lijphart, A. (1977) *Democracy in Plural Societies*. New Haven, CT: Yale University Press.

Lillich, R. (1967) Forcible self-help by states to protect human rights, *Iowa Law Review*, 53: 325–51.

Lind, J. (2010) *Sorry States: Apologies in International Relations*. Ithaca, NY: Cornell University Press.

Linklater, A. (1998) *The Transformation of Political Community*. Cambridge: Polity.

Little, A. (2014) *Enduring Conflict: Challenging the Signature of Peace and Democracy*. London: Bloomsbury.

Livingston, S. (2011) *Africa's Evolving Infosystems: A Pathway to Stability and Development*. Washington, DC: National Defense University Press.

Lopez Vinader, M. (2008) Music therapy, in O. Urbain, ed., *Music and Conflict Transformation: Harmonies and Dissonances in Geopolitics*. Tokyo: I. B. Tauris/Toda Institute, pp. 147–71.

Love, M. (1995) *Peacebuilding through Reconciliation in Northern Ireland*. Aldershot: Avebury.

Lovelock, J. (2006) *The Revenge of Gaia*. London: Penguin.

Loyn, D. (2015) Not as bad as you think: Afghanistan is more stable than for decades – but we'll have to pay to keep it that way, *Prospect*, March: 50–4.

Luard, E. (1986) *War in International Society: A Study in International Sociology*. London: I. B. Tauris.

Lucas, E. (2008) *The New Cold War*. London: Bloomsbury.

Lund, M. (1995) Underrating preventive diplomacy, *Foreign Affairs* (July/August): 160–3.

Lund, M. (1996) *Preventing Violent Conflicts*. Washington, DC: US Institute of Peace Press.

Lund, M. (2003) *What Kind of Peace is Being Built? Taking Stock of Post-Conflict Peacebuilding and Charting Future Directions*. Ottawa: International Development Research Centre.

Lupel, A. (2014) In Colombia, peace needs to be made with extreme right as well as FARC, *IPI Global Observatory*, 9 July, http://theglobalobservatory.org/2014/07/colombia-peace-with-extreme-right-and-farc/.

Luttwak, E. (1999) Give war a chance, *Foreign Affairs*, 78(4): 36–44.

Lynch, C. (2002) Implementing peace settlements: multiple motivations, factionalism and implementation design. PhD thesis, Dublin City University.

Lynch, J. (2015) Media in peace and conflict studies, in J. Hoffmann and V. Hawkins, eds, *Communication and Peace: Mapping an Emerging Field*. Abingdon: Routledge, pp. 16–33.

Lynch, J., and Galtung, J. (2010) *Reporting Conflict: New Directions in Peace Research Journalism*. Brisbane: University of Queensland Press.

McAdam, D., Tarrow, S. G., and Tilly, C. (2001) *Dynamics of Contention*, Cambridge: Cambridge University Press.

McCalin, M. (1995) *The Reintegration of Young Ex-Combatants into Civilian Life: A Report to the International Labour Office*. Geneva: ILO.

McCloskey D. (2010) *Bourgeois Dignity: Why Economics Can't Explain the Modern World*. Chicago: University of Chicago Press.

McCloskey, D. N. (2015) Measured, unmeasured, mismeasured, and unjustified pessimism: a review essay of Thomas Piketty's *Capital in the Twentieth Century*, *Erasmus Journal of Philosophy and Economics* (forthcoming), 55 pp., www.deirdremccloskey.org/docs/pdf/PikettyReviewEssay.pdf.

McConnell, J. (1995) *Mindful Mediation: A Handbook for Buddhist Peacemakers*. Bangkok: Buddhist Research Institute.

MacDonald, J., and Bendahmane, D., eds (1987) *Conflict Resolution: Two Track Diplomacy*. Washington, DC: Center for the Study of Foreign Affairs.

McGarry, J., and O'Leary, B., eds (1993) *The Politics of Ethnic Conflict Regulation*. London: Routledge.

Mac Ginty, R. (2006) *No War, No Peace: The Rejuvenation of Stalled Peace Processes and Peace Accords*. Basingstoke: Palgrave Macmillan.

Mac Ginty, R. (2012) Against stabilization, *Stability: International Journal of Security and Development*, 1(1): 20–30.

Mac Ginty, R., ed. (2013) *Routledge Handbook of Peacebuilding*. Abingdon: Routledge.

Mac Ginty, R., and Richmond, O. P. (2013) The local turn in peacebuilding: a critical agenda for peace, *Third World Quarterly*, 34(5): 763–83.

Mack, A. (2002) Civil war: academic research and the policy community, *Journal of Peace Research*, 39: 515–25.

Mack, A. (2014) Measuring peacebuilding performance: why we need a data revolution, in A. Ramsbotham and A. Wennmann, eds, *Legitimacy and Peace Processes: From Coercion to Consent*, Accord, no. 25. London: Conciliation Resources, pp. 109–12.

McKay, S., and Mazurana, D. (2004) *Where Are the Girls? Girls in Fighting Forces in Northern Uganda, Sierra Leone, and Mozambique: Their Lives before and after War*. Montreal: International Center for Human Rights and Democratic Development.

Mcloughlin, C. (2012) *Topic Guide on Fragile States*. Governance and Social Development Resource Centre, University of Birmingham, www.gsdrc.org/docs/open/CON86.pdf.

MacMillan, M. (2001) *The Peacemakers: The Paris Conference of 1919 and its Attempt to End War*. London: John Murray.

Mak, T. (1995) The case against an international war crimes tribunal for former Yugoslavia, *International Peacekeeping*, 2(4): 536–63.

Malpas, J., Arnswald, U., and Kertsche, J., eds (2002) *Gadamer's Century: Essays in Honour of Hans-Georg Gadamer*. Cambridge MA: MIT Press.

Mancini, F., ed. (2013) *New Technology and the Prevention of Violence and Conflict*. New York: UNDP and International Peace Institute.

Mancini, F. (2014) 2014 Top 10 issues to watch in peace & security: the global arena, *IPI Global Observatory*, http://theglobalobservatory.org/2014/01/2014-top-10-issues-to-watch-in-peace-a-security-the-global-arena/.

Mani, R. (2002) *Beyond Retribution: Seeking Justice in the Shadows of War*. Cambridge: Polity.

Mansbach, R., and Vasquez, J. (1981) *In Search of Theory: A New Paradigm for Global Politics*. New York: Columbia University Press.

Mansfield, E., and Snyder, J. (1995) Democratization and the danger of war, *International Security*, 20(1): 5–38.

Mansfield, E., and Snyder, J. (2005) *Electing to Fight: Why Emerging Democracies Go to War*. Cambridge MA: MIT Press.

Maoz, Z., Mintz, A., Morgan, T., Palmer, G., and Stoll, R., eds (2004) *Mutiple Paths to Knowledge in International Relations*. Lanham, MD: Lexington Books.

March, A. (2009) *Islam and Liberal Citizenship: The Search for an Overlapping Consensus*. Oxford: Oxford University Press.

Marshall, D. (2000) *Women in War and Peace: Grassroots Peacebuilding*. Washington, DC, US Institute of Peace Press.

Marshall, M. (2014) *Major Episodes of Political Violence, 1946–2014*. Vienna, VA: Center for Systemic Peace, www.systemicpeace.org/warlist/warlist.htm.

Marshall, M., and Cole, B. (2009) *Global Report 2009: Conflict, Governance and State Fragility*. Fairfax, VA: George Mason University, Center for Systemic Peace; www.systemicpeace.org/global%20Report%202009%20Executive%20Summary.pdf.

Martin, G. (2003) *Understanding Terrorism: Challenges, Perspectives, and Issues*. London: Sage.

Martin, H. (2006) *Kings of Peace, Pawns of War*. London: Continuum.

Maslow, H. (1954) *Motivation and Personality*. New York: Harper Bros.

Mayer, B. (2009) *Staying with Conflict*. San Francisco: Jossey-Bass.

Mazurana, D., Roberts, A., and Parpart, J., eds (2005) *Gender, Conflict, and Peacekeeping*. Lanham, MD: Rowman & Littlefield.

Mazurana D., et al., eds (2013) *Conflict, Gender and Peacekeeping*. Lanham, MD: Rowman & Littlefield.

Mead, M. (1940) Warfare is only an invention – not a biological necessity, *Asia*, 40: 402–5.

Mead, W. (2014) The return of geopolitics: the revenge of the revisionist powers, *Foreign Affairs*, May/June, http://www.foreignaffairs.com/articles.

Mearsheimer, J. (1990) Back to the future: instability in Europe after the Cold War, International Security, 15(1): 5–56.

Melander, E., Möller, F., and Öberg, M. (2009) Managing intrastate low-intensity armed conflict, 1993–2004: a new dataset, *International Interactions*, 35(2): 58–85.

Mendlovitz, S., and Fousek, J. (2000) A UN constabulary to enforce the law on genocide and crimes against humanity, in N. Reimer, ed., *Protection against Genocide: Mission Impossible?* London: Praeger, pp. 105–22.

Mepham, D., and Ramsbotham, A., eds (2006) *Darfur: The Responsibility to Protect*. London: Institute for Public Policy Research.

Meron, T. (1993) The case for war crimes trials in Yugoslavia, *Foreign Affairs*, 72(3): 122–35.

Merrills, J. G. (2005) *International Dispute Settlement*, 4th edn. Cambridge: Cambridge University Press.

Mertus, J. (1999) *Kosovo: How Myths and Truths Started a War*. Berkeley: University of California Press.

Messer, E., Cohen, M. J., and D'Costa, J. (1998) *Food from Peace: Breaking the Links between Conflict and Hunger*, Food, Agriculture, and the Environment Discussion Paper 24. Washington, DC: International Food Policy Research Institute; www.ifpri.org/2020/dp/dp24.pdf.

Miall, H. (1992) *The Peacemakers: Peaceful Settlement of Disputes Since 1945*. London: Macmillan.

Miall, H., ed. (1994) *Minority Rights in Europe*. London: Pinter/Royal Institute of International Affairs.

Miall, H. (2003) Global governance and conflict prevention, in F. Cochrane, R. Duffy and J. Selby, eds, *Global Governance, Conflict and Resistance*. Basingstoke: Palgrave, pp. 59–77.

Miall, H. (2004) Conflict transformation: a multi-dimensional task, in A. Austin et al., eds, *Transforming Ethnopolitical Conflict: the Berghof Handbook*. Berlin: VS Verlag für Sozialwissenschaften, pp. 67–90.

Miall, H. (2007) *Emergent Conflict and Peaceful Change*. Basingstoke: Palgrave Macmillan.

Midlarsky, M., ed. (1989) *Handbook of War Studies*. Boston: Unwin Hyman.

Minow, M. (1998) *Between Vengeance and Forgiveness: Facing History after Genocide and Mass Violence*. Boston: Beacon Press.

Minow, M. (2000) The hope for healing: what can truth commissions do?, in R. Rotberg and D. Thompson, eds, *Truth v. Justice: The Morality of Truth Commissions*. Princeton, NJ: Princeton University Press, pp. 235–60.

Misgeld, D., and Nicholson, G. (1992) *Hans-Georg Gadamer on Education, Poetry and History: Applied Hermeneutics*, trans. Lawrence Schmidt and Monica Reuss. Albany: State University of New York Press.

Mitchell, C. (1981a) *The Structure of International Conflict*. London: Macmillan.

Mitchell, C. (1981b) *Peacemaking and the Consultants' Role*. London: Gower.

Mitchell, C. (1991) Classifying conflicts: asymmetry and resolution, *Annals of the American Academy of Political and Social Science*, 518: 23–38.

Mitchell, C. (1993) Problem-solving exercises and theories of conflict resolution, in D. Sandole and H. van der Merwe, eds, *Conflict Resolution Theory and Practice: Integration and Application*. Manchester: Manchester University Press, pp. 78–94.

Mitchell, C. (1995) *Cutting Losses: Reflections on Appropriate Timing*. Fairfax, VA: George Mason University Press.

Mitchell, C. (1999) The anatomy of de-escalation, in H.-W. Jeong, ed., *Conflict Resolution: Dynamics, Process and Structure*. Aldershot: Ashgate, pp. 37–58.

Mitchell, C. (2000) *Gestures of Conciliation: Factors Contributing to Successful Olive Branches*. Basingstoke: Macmillan.

Mitchell, C. (2014) *The Nature of Intractable Conflict*. Basingstoke: Palgrave Macmillan.

Mitchell, C., and Banks, M. (1996) *Handbook of Conflict Resolution: The Analytical Problem-Solving Approach*. London: Pinter/Cassell.

Mitchell, C., and Webb, K., eds (1988) *New Approaches to International Mediation.* Westport, CT: Greenwood Press.

Mitchell, G. (1999) *Making Peace.* New York: Alfred Knopf.

Mitchell, S., Gates, S., and Hegre, H. (1999) Evolution in democracy–war dynamics, *Journal of Conflict Resolution*, 43(6): 771–92.

Mitchels, B. (2003) Trauma, therapy and conflict. PhD thesis, University of Bradford.

Mitchels, B. (2006) *Love in Danger: Trauma, Therapy and Conflict Explored through the Life and Work of Adam Curle.* Oxford: Jon Carpenter.

Mitrany, D. (1943) *A Working Peace System: An Argument for the Functional Development of International Organization.* New York: Oxford University Press.

Montville, J., ed. (1991) *Conflict and Peacemaking in Multiethnic Societies.* New York: Lexington Books.

Montville, J. (1993) The healing function in political conflict resolution, in D. Sandole and H. van der Merwe, eds, *Conflict Resolution Theory and Practice: Integration and Application.* Manchester: Manchester University Press, pp. 112–28.

Morgan, A. (2013) *Music, Culture and Conflict in Mali.* Copenhagen: Freemuse.

Morgenthau, H. (1973) *Politics among Nations: The Struggle for Power and Peace*, 5th rev. edn. New York: Knopf.

Morris, B. (2002) Camp David and after: an exchange, 1: An interview with Ehud Barak, *New York Review of Books*, 40(10).

Mouffe, C. (1999) Deliberative democracy or agonistic pluralism? *Social Research*, 66(3): 745–58.

Moynihan, D. P. (1993) *Pandaemonium: Ethnicity in International Politics.* Oxford: Oxford University Press.

Msabaha, I. (1995) Negotiating an end to Mozambique's murderous rebellion, in I. W. Zartman, ed., *Elusive Peace: Negotiating an End to Civil Wars.* Washington, DC: Brookings Institution, pp. 204–30.

Muasher, M. (2014) *The Second Arab Awakening and the Battle for Pluralism.* New Haven CT: Yale University Press.

Muggah, R. (2013) *Stabilization Operations, Security and Development.* London: Routledge.

Muggah, R. (2014) The United Nations turns to stabilization, *Global Observatory* [International Peace Institute], http://theglobalobservatory.org/2014/12/united-nations.

Munck, R. (1986) *The Difficult Dialogue: Marxism and Nationalism.* London: Zed Books.

Münkler, H. (2005) *The New Wars.* Cambridge: Polity.

Murithi, T., and Dower, N. (2008) *The Ethics of Peacebuilding.* Edinburgh: Edinburgh University Press.

Muscat, R. J. (2002) *Investing in Peace: How Development Aid Can Prevent or Promote Conflict.* Armonk, NY: M. E. Sharpe.

Nadler, A., Malloy, T., and Fisher, J. D., eds (2008) *The Social Psychology of Intergroup Reconciliation: From Violent Conflict to Peaceful Coexistence.* Oxford: Oxford University Press.

Nagda, A., Gurin, P., and Lopez, E. (2003) Transformative pedagogy for democracy and social justice, *Race, Ethnicity and Education*, 6(2): 165–91.

Naughton, J. (1999) *A Brief History of the Future: How the Internet was Born.* London: Weidenfeld & Nicolson.

Nayar, P. (2004) *Virtual Worlds: Culture and Politics in the Age of Cybertechnology*. London: Sage.

Nells, W. (2006) Bosnian education for security and peacebuilding, *International Peacekeeping*, 13(2): 229–41.

Neumaier, E. (2004) Missed opportunities: Buddhism and the ethnic strife in Sri Lanka and Tibet, in H. Coward and G. Smith, eds, *Religion and Peacebuilding*. New York: State University of New York Press, pp. 69–92.

Newman, E. (2004) The 'new wars' debate: a historical perspective is needed, *Security Dialogue*, 35(2): 173–89.

Newman, S. (1991) Does modernization breed ethnic conflict? *World Politics*, 43(3): 451–78.

Nhat Hanh, T. (1987) *Being Peace*. Berkeley, CA: Parallax Press.

Nordås, R., and Gleditsch, N. (2007) Climate change and conflict, *Political Geography*, 26: 627–38.

Nordstrom, C. (1992) The backyard front, in C. Nordstrom and J. Martin, eds, *The Paths to Domination, Resistance and Terror*. Berkeley: University of California Press, pp. 260–74.

Nordstrom, C. (1994) *Warzones: Cultures of Violence, Militarisation and Peace*. Canberra: Australian National University, Peace Research Centre.

Nordstrom, C. (1995) Contested identities, essentially contested powers, in K. Rupesinghe, ed., *Conflict Transformation*. London: Macmillan, pp. 93–111.

Nordstrom, C. (1997) *Girls and Warzones: Troubling Questions*. Uppsala: Life and Peace Institute.

Northrup, T. (1989) The dynamic of identity in personal and social conflict, in L. Kriesberg et al., eds, *Intractable Conflicts and their Transformation*. Syracuse, NY: Syracuse University Press, pp. 35–82.

Nye, J. (1993) *Understanding International Conflicts: An Introduction to Theory and History*. New York: HarperCollins.

Nye, J. (2002) *The Paradox of American Power: Why the World's Only Superpower Can't Go it Alone*. Oxford: Oxford University Press.

Nye, J. (2004) *Soft Power: The Means to Success in World Politics*. New York: Public Affairs.

Öberg, M., Möller, F., and Wallensteen, P. (2009) Early conflict prevention in ethnic crises, 1990–98: a new dataset, *Conflict Management and Peace Science*, 26(1): 67–91.

Obermeyer, Z., Murray, C., and Gakidu, E. (2008) Fifty years of violent war deaths from Vietnam to Bosnia: analysis of data from the world health survey programme, *British Medical Journal*, June: 1482–6.

OECD (Organization for Economic Cooperation and Development) (2014) *How Was Life?* Paris: OECD.

OECD (Organization for Economic Cooperation and Development) Development Assistance Committee (2014) *Fragile States 2013: Resource Flows and Trends in a Shifting World*. Paris: OECD.

O'Flaherty, M., and Gisvold, G., eds (1998) *Post War Protection of Human Rights in Bosnia and Herzegovina*. Boston: Martinus Nijhoff.

O'Leary, B., and McEvoy, J. (2010) *Power-Sharing in Deeply Divided Places*. Philadelphia: University of Pennsylvania Press.

O'Leary, R., and Bingham, L., eds (2003) *The Promise and Performance of Environmental Conflict Resolution*. Washington, DC: Resources for the Future.

Organski, A. (1958) *World Politics*. New York: Knopf.

Osgood, C. (1962) *An Alternative to War or Surrender*. Urbana, IL: Urbana University Press.

Ostrom, E. (1990) *Governing the Commons: The Evolution of Institutions for Collective Action*. Cambridge: Cambridge University Press.

Ottaway, M. (1995) Eritrea and Ethiopia: negotiations in a transitional conflict, in I. W. Zartman, ed., *Elusive Peace: Negotiating an End to Civil Wars*. Washington, DC: Brookings Institution, pp. 103–19.

Outram, Q. (1997) 'It's terminal either way': an analysis of armed conflict in Liberia 1989–1996, *Review of African Political Economy*, 73: 355–71.

Paffenholz, T. (2005) Critical issues when implementing PCIA, in *New Trends in Peace and Conflict Impact Assessment*. Berlin: Berghof Foundation, www.berghof-foundation.org/publications/handbook/dialogues/.

Paffenholz, T., and Reychler, L. (2007) *Aid for Peace: A Guide to Planning and Evaluation for Conflict Zones*. Baden-Baden: Nomos.

Paine, T. ([1776] 1986) *Common Sense*. Harmondsworth: Penguin.

Palmer, G., D'Orazio, V., Kenwick, M., and Lane, M. (2015) The MID4 data set: procedures, coding rules, and description, *Conflict Management and Peace Science*, forthcoming, www.correlatesofwar.org/data-sets/MIDs.

Pankhurst, D. (1998) Issues of justice and reconciliation in complex political emergencies. Paper given at the British International Studies Association annual conference, Leeds, December.

Pankhurst, D., and Pearce, J. (1997) Engendering the analysis of conflict: perspectives from the South, in H. Afshar, ed., *Women and Empowerment*. London: Routledge, pp. 155–63.

Pantham, T. (1992) Some dimensions of universality of philosophical hermeneutics: a conversation with Hans-Georg Gadamer, *Journal of Indian Council of Philosophical Research*, 9: 132.

Paris, R. (1997) Peacebuilding and the limits of liberal internationalism, *International Security*, 22(2): 54–89.

Paris, R. (2004) *At War's End: Building Peace after Civil Conflict*. Cambridge: Cambridge University Press.

Paris, R. (2009) Understanding the 'coordination problem' in postwar statebuilding, in R. Paris and T. Sisk, eds, *The Dilemmas of Statebuilding: Confronting the Contradictions of Postwar Peace Operations*. Abingdon: Routledge, pp. 53–78.

Paris, R., and Sisk, T., eds (2009) *The Dilemmas of Statebuilding: Confronting the Contradictions of Postwar Peace Operations*. Abingdon: Routledge.

Parker, A. M. S. (2009) Cyberterrorism: the emerging worldwide threat, in D. Canter, ed., *The Faces of Terrorism: Multidisciplinary Perspectives*. Chichester: Wiley-Blackwell, pp. 245–56.

Parry, C., and Parry, W. (1994) *Tim: An Ordinary Boy*. London: Hodder & Stoughton.

Parsons, A. (1995) *From Cold War to Hot Peace: UN Interventions 1947–1995*. London: Penguin.

Patterson, I. (2007) *Guernica and Total War*. London: Profile Books.

Peace Direct (2004) *Unarmed Heroes: The Courage to Go Beyond Violence*. London: Clairview.

Pearce, J. (2005) The international community and peacebuilding, *Development*, 48(3): 41–9.

Pearson, L. (1957) The four faces of peace, Nobel Lecture, 11 December, www.nobel prize.org/nobel_prizes/peace/laureates/1957/pearson-lecture.html.

Peck, C. (1998) *Sustainable Peace: The Role of the UN and Regional Organizations in Preventing Conflict*. Lanham, MD: Rowman & Littlefield.

Peck, C. (2009) UN mediation experience: practical lessons for conflict resolution, in J. Bercovitch et al., eds, *The Sage Handbook of Conflict Resolution*. London: Sage, pp. 413–34.

Peirce, C. S. (1958) *The Collected Papers of C. S. Peirce*, Vol. 5. Cambridge, MA: Harvard University Press.

Perrigo, S. (1991) Feminism and peace, in T. Woodhouse, ed., *Peacemaking in a Troubled World*. Oxford: Berg, pp. 303–22.

Petito, F. (2011) In defence of dialogue of civilisations: with a brief illustration of the diverging agreement between Edward Said and Louis Massignon, *Millennium: Journal of International Studies*, 39(3): 759–79.

Pettersson, T., and Wallensteen, P. (2015) Armed conflicts, 1946–2014, *Journal of Peace Research*, 52(4): 536–50.

Pfetsch, F., and Rohloff, C. (2000) KOSIMO: a databank on political conflict, *Journal of Peace Research*, 37(3): 379–89.

Piketty, T. (2014) *Capital in the Twenty-First Century*. Cambridge, MA: Belknap Press of Harvard University.

Pillar, P. R. (1983) *Negotiating Peace: War Termination as a Bargaining Process*. Princeton, NJ: Princeton University Press.

Pinker, S. (2002) *The Blank Slate*. London: Penguin.

Pinker, S. (2011) *The Better Angels of our Nature: Why Violence Has Declined*. New York: Viking.

Poehlman-Doumbouya, S., and Hill, F. (2001) Women and peace in the United Nations, *New Routes: A Journal of Peace Research and Action*, 6(3): 1–6.

Pogge, T. (2002) *World Poverty and Human Rights: Cosmopolitan Responsibilities and Reforms*. Cambridge: Polity.

Polak, F. (1961) *The Image of the Future*. New York: Oceana.

Ponzio, R. (2007) The United Nations Peacebuilding Commission: origins and initial practice, *Disarmament Forum* [UNIDIR], 2: 5–16.

Posen, B. P. (1993) The security dilemma and ethnic conflict, in M. Brown, ed., *Ethnic Conflict and International Security*. Princeton, NJ: Princeton University Press, pp. 103–24.

Post, J., Ruby, K., and Shaw, E. (2002) The radical group in context: (1) an integrated framework for the analysis of group risk for terrorism; (2) identification of critical elements in the analysis of risk for terrorism by radical group type, *Studies in Conflict and Terrorism*, 25: 73–126.

Pouligny, B. (2005) Civil society and post- conflict peacebuilding: ambiguities of international programmes aimed at building 'new' societies, *Security Dialogue*, 36(4): 496–510.

Pouligny, B. (2006) *Peace Operations Seen from Below: UN Missions and Local People*. London: Hurst.

Powell, J. (2014) *Talking to Terrorists: How to End Armed Conflicts*. London: Bodley Head.

Pruitt, D. (1981) *Negotiation Behaviour*. New York: Academic Press.

Pruitt, D., and Carnevale, P. (1993) *Negotiation in Social Conflict*. Pacific Grove, CA: Brooks/Cole.

Pruitt, D., and Rubin, J. (1986) *Social Conflict: Escalation, Stalemate and Settlement*. New York: Random House.

Pruitt D. (2007) Readiness theory and the Northern Ireland conflict, *American Behavioural Scientist*, 50(11): 1520–41.

PSG (Palestine Strategy Group) (2008) *Regaining the Initiative: Palestinian Strategic Options to End Israeli Occupation*. London: Oxford Research Group, www.palestine strategygroup.ps.

Pugh, M. (2000) *Regeneration of War-Torn Societies*. Basingstoke: Macmillan.

Pugh, M. (2004) Peacekeeping and critical theory, *International Peacekeeping*, 11(1): 39–58.

Pugh, M. (2007) Peace enforcement, in T. Weiss and S. Daws, *The Oxford Handbook on the United Nations*. Oxford: Oxford University Press, pp. 56–82.

Pugh, M., Cooper, N., and Turner, M., eds (2008a) *Whose Peace? Critical Perspectives on the Political Economy of Peacebuilding*. Basingstoke: Palgrave Macmillan.

Pugh, M., Cooper, N., and Turner, M. (2008b) Conclusion: the political economy of Peacebuilding – whose peace? Where next?, in M. Pugh et al., eds, *Whose Peace? Critical Perspectives on the Political Economy of Peacebuilding*. Basingstoke: Palgrave Macmillan, pp. 390–7.

Putnam, R. (1988) Diplomacy and domestic politics: the logic of two-level games, *International Organization*, 42(3): 427–60.

Rabin, Y. (1996) *The Rabin Memoirs*, 2nd edn. Bnei Brak: Steimatzky.

Raiffa, H. (1982) *The Art and Science of Negotiation*. Cambridge, MA: Harvard University Press.

Raiffa, H., Richardson, J., and Metcalfe, D. (2002) *Negotiation Analysis: The Science and Art of Collaborative Decision Making*. Cambridge, MA: Harvard University Press.

Raknerud, A., and Hegre, H. (1997) The hazard of war: reassessing the evidence for the democratic peace, *Journal of Peace Research*, 34: 385–404.

Ramsbotham, A., and Zartman, I. W. (2011) *Paix sans frontières: Building Peace across Borders*, Accord, no. 22, London: Conciliation Resources, www.c-r.org/accord/cross-border.

Ramsbotham, O. (1997) Humanitarian intervention 1990–5: a need to reconceptualize? *Review of International Studies*, 23: 445–67.

Ramsbotham, O. (1998) Islam, Christianity and forcible humanitarian intervention, *Ethics and International Affairs*, 12(8): 81–102.

Ramsbotham, O. (2000) Reflections on UN post-settlement peacebuilding, *International Peacekeeping*, 7: 167–89.

Ramsbotham, O. (2004) Intervention, reconstruction and withdrawal operations 1989–2004. Paper presented at Wilton Park conference on postwar reconstruction, December.

Ramsbotham, O. (2006) Cicero's challenge: from just war to just intervention, in G. Beestermoller et al., eds, *What We're Fighting For: Friedensethik in der Transatlantischen Debatte*. Stuttgart: Kohlhammer, pp. 113–37.

Ramsbotham, O. (2010) *Transforming Violent Conflict: Radical Disagreement, Dialogue and Survival*. London: Routledge.

Ramsbotham, O. (2013) Is there a theory of radical disagreement?, *International Journal of Conflict Engagement and Resolution*, (1)1: 56–82.

Ramsbotham, O. (2015) Hans-Georg Gadamer, hermeneutic dialogue and conflict resolution, in F. Sleap and O. Sener, eds, *Dialogue Theories II*. London: Dialogue Society.

Ramsbotham, O. (forthcoming, 2017) *When Conflict Resolution Fails: Engaging Radical Disagreement*. Cambridge: Polity.

Ramsbotham, O., and Schiff, A. (forthcoming) Principled negotiation, strategic negotiation and the Kerry initiative, *Negotiation Journal*.

Ramsbotham, O., and Woodhouse, T. (1996) *Humanitarian Intervention in Contemporary Conflict*. Cambridge: Polity.

Ramsbotham, O., and Woodhouse, T. (1999a) Options for the development of codes of conduct for conflict resolution. Paper presented at Codes of Conduct conference, Soesterberg, Netherlands, April.

Ramsbotham, O., and Woodhouse, T. (1999b) *Encyclopedia of International Peacekeeping Operations*. Santa Barbara, CA: ABC-CLIO.

Randle, M., ed. (2002) *Challenge to Nonviolence*. Bradford: University of Bradford Press.

Rapoport, A. (1960) *Fights, Games and Debates*. Ann Arbor: University of Michigan Press.

Rapoport, A. (1988) Experiments with N-person social traps, II, *Journal of Conflict Resolution*, 32(3): 473–88.

Rapoport, A. (1989) *The Origins of Violence*. New York: Paragon House.

Rapoport, A. (1992) *Peace: An Idea whose Time Has Come*. Ann Arbor: University of Michigan Press.

Rapoport, A., and Chammah, A. (1965) *The Prisoner's Dilemma: A Study in Conflict and Cooperation*. Ann Arbor: University of Michigan Press.

Rasmussen, D., ed. (1990) *Universalism vs. Communitarianism: Contemporary Debates in Ethics*. Cambridge, MA: MIT Press.

Rasmussen, J., Lewis, J., and Zartman, I. W., eds (1997) *Peacemaking in International Conflict: Method and Techniques*. Washington, DC: US Institute of Peace Press.

Rasmussen, M. V. (2003) *The West, Civil Society and the Construction of Peace*. Basingstoke: Palgrave.

Ratner, S. (1995) *The New UN Peacekeeping: Building Peace in Lands of Conflict after the Cold War*. Basingstoke: Palgrave.

Rauchhaus, R. (2006) Asymmetric information, mediation and conflict management, *World Politics*, 58(2): 207–41.

Rawls, J. (1999) *The Law of Peoples*. Cambridge, MA: Harvard University Press.

Regan, P., Frank, R., and Aydin, A. (2009) Diplomatic interventions and civil war: a new dataset, *Journal of Peace Research*, 46(1): 135–46.

Reimann, C. (1999) *The Field of Conflict Management: Why Does Gender Matter?* Bonn: Arbeitstelle Friedensforschung.

Reimann, C. (2002) *All You Need is Love – and What about Gender? Engendering Burton's Human Needs Theory*, Working Paper 10. University of Bradford, Department of Peace Studies, Centre for Conflict Resolution.

Rejic, D. (2004) The news media and the transformation of ethnopolitical conflicts, in A. Austin et al., eds, *Transforming Ethnopolitcal Conflict: The Berghof Handbook*. Berlin: VS Verlag für Sozialwissenschaften, pp. 319–21.

Renner, J., and Spencer, A., eds (2012) *Reconciliation after Terrorism: Strategy, Possibility or Absurdity?* Abingdon: Routledge.

Renner, M. (2002) *The Anatomy of Resource Wars.* Washington, DC: Worldwatch Institute.

Reno, W. (1999) *Warlord Politics and African States.* Boulder, CO: Lynne Rienner.

Reno, W. (2011) *Warfare in Independent Africa: New Approaches to African History.* Cambridge: Cambridge University Press.

Reychler, L., and Paffenholz, T., eds (2001) *Peacebuilding: A Field Guide.* Boulder, CO: Lynne Rienner.

Reynal-Querol, M. (2002) Ethnicity, political systems and civil wars, *Journal of Conflict Resolution*, 46(1): 29–54.

Rice, E. (1988) *Wars of the Third Kind: Conflict in Underdeveloped Countries.* Berkeley: University of California Press.

Richards, P., Bah, K., and Vincent, J. (2004) *Social Capital and Survival: Prospects for Community-Driven Development in Post- Conflict Sierra Leone.* Washington, DC: World Bank, pp. 6–7.

Richardson, L. (1960a) *Arms and Insecurity.* Pittsburgh: Boxwood Press.

Richardson, L. (1960b) *Statistics of Deadly Quarrels.* Pittsburgh: Boxwood Press.

Richmond, O. (2005) *The Transformation of Peace.* Basingstoke: Palgrave.

Richmond, O. (2008) *Peace in International Relations.* London: Routledge.

Richmond, O. (2011) *A Post-Liberal Peace.* Abingdon: Routledge.

Ricigliano, R. (2011) Afghanistan: planning for systemic impact, in N. Ropers and D. Korppen, eds, *The Non-Linearity of Peace Processes: Theory and Practice of Systemic Conflict Transformation.* Berlin: Berghof Foundation for Peace Support.

Rieff, D. (1994) The illusions of peacekeeping, *World Policy Journal*, 11(3): 1–18.

Rigby, A. (2001) *Justice and Reconciliation: After the Violence.* Boulder, CO: Lynne Rienner.

Rigby, A. (2008) 'Tennis for peace anyone?': sport and conflict transformation. Paper presented at IPRA conference, Leuven, July.

Roberts, A. (1990) Law, lawyers and nuclear weapons, *Review of International Studies*, 16(1).

Roberts, A. (2008) Proposals for UN standing forces: history, tasks and obstacles, in V. Lowe et al., eds, *The United Nations Security Council and War.* Oxford: Oxford University Press, pp. 99–130.

Roberts, D. (2009) The superficiality of statebuilding in Cambodia: patronage and clientism as enduring forms of politics, in R. Paris and T. Sisk, eds, *The Dilemmas of Statebuilding: Confronting the Contradictions of Postwar Peace Operations.* Abingdon: Routledge, pp. 149–70.

Roberts, D. (2011) *Liberal Peacebuilding and Global Governance: Beyond the Metropolis.* Abingdon: Routledge.

Rodgers, C. P., Straughton, E. A., Winchester, A. J. L., and Pieraccini, M. (2010) *Contested Common Land: Environmental Governance Past and Present.* London: Earthscan.

Rogers, C. (1980) *A Way of Being.* Boston: Houghton Mifflin.

Rogers, P. (2007) *Towards Sustainable Security: Alternatives to the War on Terror.* London: Oxford Research Group.

Rogers, P. (2010) *Losing Control: Global Security in the Twenty-First Century*. London: Pluto Press.

Rogers, P., and Ramsbotham, O. (1999) Then and now: peace research – past and future, *Political Studies*, 47(4): 740–54.

Ropers, N. (2008a) Systemic conflict transformation: reflections on the conflict and peace process in Sri Lanka, in D. Körppen, B. Schmelzle and O. Wils, eds, *A Systemic Approach to Conflict Transformation: Exploring Strengths and Limitations*. Berlin: Berghof Research Center for Constructive Conflict Management, pp. 11–41.

Ropers, N. (2008b) *Space for Peace: The Work of the Berghof Foundation for Conflict Studies in Sri Lanka 2001–2008*. Berlin: Berghof Research Centre for Constructive Conflict Management.

Ropers, N., and Anuvatudom, M. (2014) a joint learning process for stakeholders and insider peacebuilders: a case study from southern Thailand, *Asian Journal of Peacebuilding*, 2(2): 277–96.

Rose, H., and Rose, S., eds (2001) *Alas Poor Darwin: Arguments against Evolutionary Psychology*. London: Vintage.

Rosenau, J., and Earnest, D. (2006) Signifying nothing? What complex systems theory can and cannot tell us about global politics, in N. Harrison, ed., *Complexity in World Politics: Concepts and Methods of a New Paradigm*. New York: State University of New York Press.

Rosenblatt, L., and Thompson, L. (1998) The door of opportunity: creating a permanent peacekeeping force, *World Policy Journal* (spring): 36–42.

Rosoux, V. (2009) Reconciliation as a peace-building process: scope and limits, in J. Bercovitch, V. Kremenyk and I. W. Zartman, eds, *The Sage Handbook of Conflict Resolution*. London: Sage.

Ross, D. (2004) *The Missing Peace: The Inside Story of the Fight for Middle East Peace*. New York: Farrar, Straus & Giroux.

Ross, M. (1993) *The Culture of Conflict: Interpretations and Interests in Comparative Perspective*. New Haven, CT: Yale University Press.

Rotberg, R. (2000) Truth commissions and the provision of truth, justice, and reconciliation, in R. Rotberg and D. Thompson, eds, *Truth v. Justice: The Morality of Truth Commissions*. Princeton, NJ: Princeton University Press, pp. 3–21.

Rotberg, R. (2004) *When States Fail: Causes and Consequences*. Princeton, NJ: Princeton University Press.

Rotberg, R., ed. (2006) *Israeli and Palestinian Narratives of Conflict: History's Double Helix*. Bloomington: Indiana University Press.

Rotberg, R., and Thompson, D., eds (2000) *Truth v. Justice: The Morality of Truth Commissions*. Princeton, NJ: Princeton University Press.

Rothchild, D., and Hartzell, C. (1999) Security in deeply divided societies: the role of territorial autonomy, *Nationalism and Ethnic Politics*, 5(3/4): 254–71.

Rothchild, D., and Roeder, P. (2005) Dilemmas of state-building in divided societies, in P. Roeder and D. Rothchild, eds, *Sustainable Peace: Power and Democracy after Civil Wars*. Ithaca, NY: Cornell University Press, pp. 1–25.

Rothman, J. (1992) *From Confrontation to Cooperation: Resolving Ethnic and Regional Conflict*. Newbury Park, CA: Sage.

Rothman, J. (1997) *Resolving Identity-Based Conflicts in Nations, Organizations, and Communities*. San Francisco: Jossey-Bass.

Rothman, J., and Alberstein, M., eds (2014) Deepening the definitions of success and failure, *International Journal of Conflict Engagement and Resolution*, 2(1) [special issue].

Rothstein, B. (2005) *Social Traps and the Problem of Trust*. Cambridge: Cambridge University Press.

Rothstein, R. L., ed. (1999) *After the Peace: Resistance and Reconciliation*. Boulder, CO: Lynne Rienner.

Rouhana, N., and Korper, S. (1996) Dealing with dilemmas posed by power asymmetry in intergroup conflict, *Negotiation Journal*, 12(4).

Rousseau, D. (2005) *Democracy and War: Institutions, Norms and the Evolution of International Conflict*. Stanford, CA: Stanford University Press.

Rowe, N. (2008) Dance education in the Occupied Palestinian Territories: hegemony, counter-hegemony, and anti-hegemony, *Research in Dance Education*, 9(1): 3–20.

Rubin, B., and Jones, B. (2007) Prevention of violent conflict: tasks and challenges for the United Nations, *Global Governance* 13(3): 391–408.

Rummel, R. J. (1970) *Applied Factor Analysis*. Evanston, IL: Northwestern University Press.

Rupesinghe, K., ed. (1995) *Conflict Transformation*. London: Macmillan.

Rupesinghe, K. (1996) *General Principles of Multi-Track Diplomacy*. London: International Alert.

Russett, B., and Kramer, M. (1973) New editors for an 'old' journal, *Journal of Conflict Resolution*, 17(1): 3–6.

Russett, B., and Oneal, J. (2001) *Triangulating Peace: Democracy, Interdependence, and International Organizations*. New York: W. W. Norton.

Sahnoun, M. (1994) *Somalia: The Missed Opportunities*. Washington, DC: US Institute of Peace Press.

Said, E. (1995) *Peace and its Discontents*. London: Vintage.

Said, E. (2002) *The End of the Peace Process: Oslo and After*. London: Granta.

Sakwa, R. (2014) *Frontline Ukraine: Crisis in the Borderlands*. London: I. B. Tauris.

Salem, P. (1993) In theory: a critique of western conflict resolution from a non-western perspective, *Negotiation Journal*, 9(4): 361–9.

Salem, P., ed. (1997) *Conflict Resolution in the Arab World: Selected Essays*. New York: American University of Beirut.

Saleyhan, I. (2014) Climate change and conflict: making sense of disparate findings, *Political Geography*, 43: 1–5.

Salehyan, I., et al. (2012) Social conflict in Africa: a new database, *International Interactions*, 38(4): 503–11.

Sandole, D. (1999) *Capturing the Complexity of Conflict: Dealing with Violent Ethnic Conflicts of the Post-Cold War Era*. London: Pinter.

Sandole, D. (2007) *Peace and Security in the Post-Modern World: The OSCE and Conflict Resolution*. London: Routledge.

Sandole, D., and Sandole-Staroste, I., eds (1987) *Conflict Management and Problem Solving: Interpersonal to International Applications*. London: Frances Pinter.

Sandole, D., and van der Merwe, H., eds (1993) *Conflict Resolution Theory and Practice: Integration and Application*. Manchester: Manchester University Press.

Sardar, Z., and Ravetz, J., eds (1996) *Cyberfutures: Culture and Politics on the Information Superhighway*. New York: New York University Press.

Sarkees, M., and Schaffer, P. (2000) The correlates of war data on war: an update to 1997, *Conflict Management and Peace Science*, 18(1): 123–44.

Saunders, H. (1999) *A Public Peace Process: Sustained Dialogue to Transform Racial and Ethnic Conflicts*. New York: Palgrave.

Saunders, H. (2009) Dialogue as a process for transforming relationships, in J. Bercovitch, V. Kremenyuk and I. W. Zartman, eds, *The Sage Handbook of Conflict Resolution*. London: Sage, pp. 376–91.

Savun, B. (2008) Information, bias, and mediation success, *International Studies Quarterly*, 52(1): 25–47.

Schaap, A. (2005) *Political Reconciliation*. London: Routledge.

Schäffner, C., and Wenden, A., eds (1995) *Language and Peace*. London: Routledge.

Schelling, T. (1960) *The Strategy of Conflict*. Cambridge, MA: Harvard University Press.

Schiff, A. (2014) On success and failure: readiness theory and the Aceh and Sri Lanka peace processes, *International Negotiation: A Journal of Theory and Practice*, 19(1).

Schmelzle, B. (2005) *New Trends in Peace and Conflict Impact Assessment (PCIA)*. Berlin: Berghof Foundation.

Schmelzle, B., and Fischer, M., eds (2009) *Peacebuilding at a Crossroads? Dilemmas and Paths for Another Generation*. Berlin: Berghof Research Center for Constructive Conflict Management.

Schmid, A. (1997) Early warning of violent conflicts, in P. Schmid, ed., *Violent Crime and Conflicts*. Milan: International Scientific and Professional Advisory Council of the United Nations Crime Prevention and Criminal Justice Programme.

Schmid, A., and Jongman, A. (1988) *Political Terrorism: A New Guide to Actors, Authors, Concepts, Data Bases, Theories and Literature*. Amsterdam: North-Holland.

Schmid, H. (1968) Peace research and politics, *Journal of Peace Research*, 5(3): 217–32.

Schnabel, A., and Carment, D., eds (2004) *Conflict Prevention from Rhetoric to Reality: Opportunities and Innovations*, 2 vols. Lanham, MD: Lexington Books.

Schori Liang, C. (2015) *Cyber Jihad: Understanding and Countering Islamic State Propaganda*, Policy Paper 2, February. Geneva: Geneva Centre for Security Policy.

Schuett, O. (1997) The International War Crimes Tribunal for the Former Yugoslavia and the Dayton Peace Agreement: peace versus justice? *International Peacekeeping*, 4(2): 91–114.

Schwartzberg, J. E. (1997) A new perspective on peacekeeping: lessons from Bosnia and elsewhere, *Global Governance*, 3(1): 1–15.

Schweitzer, C., ed. (2010) *Civilian Peacekeeping: A Barely Tapped Resource*. Wahlenau, Germany: Sozio-Publishing.

Schweller, R. (2014) *Maxwell's Demon and the Golden Apple*. Baltimore: Johns Hopkins University Press.

Sebenius, J. K. (1984) *Negotiating the Law of the Sea*. Cambridge, MA: Harvard University Press.

Sen, A. (2009) *The Idea of Justice*. London: Allen Lane.

Serbe, G., Macrae, J., and Wohlgemuth, L. (1997) *NGOs in Conflict: An Evaluation of International Alert*. Fantoft-Bergen, Norway: Christian Michelsen Institute.

Seville Statement on Violence (1986) http://portal.unesco.org/education/ec/ev.php-URL_ID=3247&URL_DO=DO_TOPIC&URL_SECTION=201.html.

Sewall, S., Raymond, D., and Chin, S. (2013) *Mass Atrocity Response Operations: A Military Planning Handbook*, http://carrcenter.hks.harvard.edu/files/carrcenter/files/maro_handbook.pdf

Shadid, A. (2002) *The Legacy of the Prophet: Despots, Democrats, and the New Politics of Islam*. Boulder, CO: Westview Press.

Shain, Y., and Linz, J. (1995) *Between States: Interim Governments and Democratic Transitions*. Cambridge: Cambridge University Press.

Shank, M., and Schirch, L. (2008) Strategic arts-based peacebuilding, *Peace and Change*, 33(2): 217–42.

Shapcott, R. (2001) *Justice, Community and Dialogue in International Relations*. Cambridge: Cambridge University Press.

Sharp, G. (1973) *The Politics of Nonviolent Action*. Boston: Porter Sargent.

Shearer, D. (1997) Exploring the limits of consent: conflict resolution in Sierra Leone, *Millennium: Journal of International Studies*, 26(3): 845–60.

Sherif, M. (1966) *In Common Predicament: Social Psychology, Intergroup Conflict and Cooperation*. Boston: Houghton Mifflin.

Shlaim, A. (2014) *The Iron Wall: Israel and the Arab World*. London: Allen Lane.

Shue, H. (1980) *Basic Rights: Subsistence Affluence and US Foreign Policy*. Princeton, NJ: Princeton University Press.

Siebert, H. (2014) National dialogue and legitimate change, in A. Ramsbotham and A. Wennmann, eds, *Legitimacy and Peace Processes: From Coercion to Consent, Accord*, no. 25. London: Conciliation Resources, pp. 36–9.

Simmel, G. (1902) The number of members as determining the sociological form of the group, *American Journal of Sociology*, 8: 158–96.

Singer, D. (1996) Armed conflict in the former colonial regions: from classification to explanation, in L. van de Goor et al., eds, *Between Development and Destruction: An Enquiry into the Causes of Conflict in Post-Colonial States*. New York: St Martin's Press, pp. 35–49.

Singer, P., and Friedman, A. (2014) *Cybersecurity and Cyberwar: What Everyone Needs to Know*. Oxford and New York: Oxford University Press.

Singer, D., and Small, M. (1968) Alliance aggregation and the onset of war 1815–1945, in D. Singer, ed., *Quantitative International Politics: Insights and Evidence*. New York: Free Press, pp. 247–86.

Singer, D., and Small, M. (1972) *The Wages of War, 1816–1965: A Statistical Handbook*. New York: Wiley.

SIPRI (Stockholm International Peace Research Institute) (1997) *SIPRI Yearbook: 1997*. Oxford: Oxford University Press.

Sisk, T. (1997) *Power Sharing and International Mediation in Ethnic Conflicts*. Washington, DC: US Institute of Peace Press.

Sisk, T., and Reynolds, A., eds (1998) *Elections and Conflict Management in Africa*. Washington, DC: US Institute of Peace Press.

Sites, P. (1990) Needs as analogues of emotions, in J. Burton, ed., *Conflict: Human Needs Theory*. London: Macmillan, pp. 7–33.

Skaar, E. (1999) Truth commissions, trials – or nothing? Policy options in democratic transitions, *Third World Quarterly*, 20: 1109–28.

Skjelsboek, I., and Smith, D., eds (2001) *Gender, Peace and Conflict*. London: Sage.

Sleap, F., and Sener, O., eds (2013) *Dialogue Theories I*. London: Dialogue Society.

Sleap, F., and Sener, O., eds (2015) *Dialogue Theories II.* London: Dialogue Society.

Slim, H. (2005) Violent beliefs, *RUSI Journal*, April: 20–3.

Slye, R. (2000) Amnesty, truth and reconciliation: reflections on the South African amnesty process, in R. Rotberg and D. Thompson, eds, *Truth v. Justice: The Morality of Truth Commissions.* Princeton, NJ: Princeton University Press, pp. 170–88.

Smith, A. (1986) *The Ethnic Origins of Nations.* Oxford: Blackwell.

Smith, C. (2013) *Palestine and the Arab–Israeli Conflict*, 5th edn. Boston: St Martin's Press.

Smith, D. (2004) *Towards a Strategic Framework for Peacebuilding: Getting their Act Together.* Oslo: International Peace Research Institute.

Smith, D. (2008) Systemic conflict transformation: reflections on utility, in *Berghof Handbook Dialogue no. 6.* Berlin: Berghof Foundation.

Smith, D. (2014) *State of the World Atlas.* Oxford: New Internationalist.

Smith, D., and Vivekananda, J. (2007) *A Climate of Conflict: The Links between Climate Change, Peace and War.* London: International Alert.

Smith, K., and Meyer, C. (2013) *The EU and the Prevention of Mass Atrocities: An Assessment of Strengths and Weaknesses.* Budapest: Budapest Centre for the International Prevention of Mass Atrocities.

Smith, R. (2002) *Picasso's War.* London: Simon & Schuster.

Sommers, M. (2002) *Children, Education and War: Reaching Education for All (EFA) Objectives in Countries Affected by Conflict.* Washington, DC: World Bank.

Sorokin, P. A. (1937) *Social and Cultural Dynamics*, 4 vols. New York: American Book Co.

Spagat, M., Mack, A., Cooper, C., and Kreutz, J. (2009) Estimating war deaths: an area of contestation, *Journal of Conflict Resolution*, 53(6): 934–50.

Spears, I. (2012) The false promise of peacebuilding, *International Journal*, spring, 295–311.

Sponsel, L. (1996) The natural history of peace: the positive view of human nature and its potential, in T. Gregor, ed., *A Natural History of Peace.* Nashville: Vanderbilt University Press.

Stanca Mustea, C. (2013) Peace and reconciliation: how culture makes the difference, www.unesco.org/new/fileadmin/MULTIMEDIA/HQ/CLT/images/Peace ReconciliationENG.pdf.

Starkey, B., Boyer, M. A., and Wilkenfeld, J. (1999) *Negotiating a Complex World: An Introduction to International Negotiation.* Lanham, MD: Rowman & Littlefield.

Starkey, B., Boyer, M. A., and Wilkenfeld, J. (2005) *Negotiating a Complex World: An Introduction to International Negotiation*, 2nd edn. Lanham, MD: Rowman & Littlefield.

Stavenhagen, R. (1996) *Ethnic Conflicts and the Nation-State.* Basingstoke: Macmillan.

Steans, J. (1998) *Gender and International Relations.* Cambridge: Polity.

Stedman, S. (1991) *Peacemaking in Civil War: International Mediation in Zimbabwe, 1974-1980.* Boulder, CO: Lynne Rienner.

Stedman, S. (1995) Alchemy for a new world order: overselling 'preventive diplomacy', *Foreign Affairs*, 74 (May/June): 14–20.

Stedman, S. (1997) Spoiler problems in peace processes, *International Security*, 22(2): 5–53.

Stedman, S., Rothchild, D., and Cousens, E., eds (2002) *Ending Civil Wars: The Implementation of Peace Agreements*. Boulder, CO: Lynne Rienner, IPA/CISAC.

Stein, B., Cuny, F., and Reed, R., eds (1995) *Refugee Repatriation During Conflict: A New Conventional Wisdom*. Dallas: Center for the Study of Societies in Crisis.

Stephan, M. J., and Chenoweth, E. (2008) Why civil resistance works: the strategic logic of nonviolent conflict, *International Security*, 33(1): 7–44.

Stern, J. (2003) *Terrorism in the Name of God: Why Religious Militants Kill*. New York: HarperCollins.

Stern, N. (2007) *The Economics of Climate Change: The Stern Review*. Cambridge: Cambridge University Press.

Stewart, E. (2008) Capabilities and coherence? The evolution of European Union conflict prevention, *European Foreign Affairs Review*, 13(2): 229–54.

Stewart, F. (2002) Horizontal inequalities as a source of conflict, in F. Hampson and D. Malone, eds, *From Reaction to Conflict Prevention: Opportunities for the UN System*. Boulder, CO: Lynne Rienner.

Stewart, F., and Fitzgerald, V. (2001) *War and Underdevelopment*. Oxford: Oxford University Press.

Stewart, J., ed. (2006) *Bridges Not Walls: A Book about Interpersonal Communication*. 9th edn, New York: McGraw-Hill.

Stewart, J., and Thomas, M. (2006) Dialogic listening: sculpting mutual meanings, in J. Stewart ed., *Bridges Not Walls: A Book about Interpersonal Communication*, 9th edn. New York: McGraw-Hill, pp. 192–210.

Stoll, R. (2004) Multiple paths to knowledge? Integrating methodology and substance in the study of conflict management and conflict resolution, in Z. Maoz et al., eds, *Multiple Paths to Knowledge in International Relations*. Lanham, MD: Lexington Books.

Stromseth, J. (2003) Rethinking humanitarian intervention: the case for incremental change, in J. Holzgrefe and R. Keohane, eds, *Humanitarian Intervention: Ethical, Legal and Political Dilemmas*. Cambridge: Cambridge University Press, pp. 232–72.

Suganami, H. (1996) *On the Causes of War*. Oxford: Clarendon Press.

Sugden J. (2008) Anyone for football for peace? The challenges of using sport in the service of co-existence in Israel, *Soccer & Society*, 9(3): 405–15.

Suhrke, A., and Samset, I. (2007) What's in a figure? Estimating recurrence of civil war, *International Peacekeeping*, 14(2): 195–203.

Suliman, M., ed. (1999) *Ecology, Politics and Violent Conflict*. London: Zed Books.

Summerfield, D. (1996) *The Impact of War and Atrocity on Civilian Populations: Basic Principles for NGO Interventions and a Critique of Psychosocial Trauma Projects*. London: Overseas Development Institute.

Sumner, W. G. (1906) *Folkways*. Boston: Ginn.

Sundberg, R., and Harbom, L. (2011) Experiences from the Uppsala Conflict Data Program, in K. Höglund and M. Öberg, eds, *Understanding Peace Research: Methods and Challenges*. London: Routledge.

Susskind, L. (1987) *Breaking the Impasse: Consensual Approaches to Resolving Public Disputes*. New York: Basic Books.

Sutherlin, G. (2012) A voice in the crowd: broader implications for crowdsource translation, *Journal of Information Science*, 20(10): 1–4.

Sutherlin, G. (2014) The Myth of the Universal User: The Impact of a Cultural Variable in ICT Design for Conflict Contexts, PhD thesis, University of Bradford.

Svensson, I. (2007) Bargaining, bias and peace brokers: how rebels commit to peace, *Journal of Peace Research*, 44(2): 114–63.

Svensson, I., and Wallensteen, P. (2010) *Going Between: Ambassador Jan Eliasson and the Styles of International Mediation*. Washington, DC: United States Institute of Peace Press.

Sweetman, D. (2009) *Business, Conflict Resolution and Peacebuilding: Contributions from the Private Sector to Address Violent Conflict*. Abingdon: Routledge.

Swing, W. (2003) The role of MONUC in the DRC's peace process, *Conflict Trends*, 4: 25–9.

Tajfel, H., ed. (1978) *Differentiation between Social Groups: Studies in the Social Psychology of Intergroup Relations*. London: Academic Press.

Taylor, C. (2002) Understanding the other: a Gadamerian view on conceptual schemes, in J. Malpas et al., eds, *Gadamer's Century: Essays in Honour of Hans-Georg Gadamer*. Cambridge MA: MIT Press, pp. 279–98.

Thakur, R. (2001) Research note: Cambodia, East Timor and the Brahimi Report, *International Peacekeeping*, 8(3): 115–24.

Theisen, O., Gleditsch, N. P., and Buhaug, H. (2013) Is climate change a driver of armed conflict?, *Climatic Change*, 117(3): 613–25.

Themnér, L., and Wallensteen, P. (2014) Armed conflict, 1946–2013, *Journal of Peace Research*, 51(4): 541–54.

Thucydides (1954) *History of the Peloponnesian War*, trans. R. Warner. London: Penguin.

Thussu, D. K., and Freedman, D., eds (2003) *War and the Media: Reporting Violent Conflict 24/7*. London: Sage.

Tilly, C. (1978) *From Mobilization to Revolution*. Reading, MA: Addison-Wesley.

Tilly, C., and Tarrow, S. (2006) *Contentious Politics*. Boulder, CO: Paradigm.

Toft, M. (2010) *Securing the Peace: The Durable Settlement of Civil Wars*. Princeton, NJ: Princeton University Press.

Tonge, J. (2014) *Comparative Peace Processes*. Cambridge: Polity.

Tooby, J., and Cosmides, L. (1992) Psychological foundations of culture, in J. Barkow, L. Cosmides and J. Tooby, eds, *The Adapted Mind: Evolutionary Psychology and the Generation of Culture*. Oxford: Oxford University Press.

Touval, S., and Zartman, I. W., eds (1985) *International Mediation: Theory and Practice*. Boulder, CO: Westview Press.

Transnational Institute (2015) *Linking Women and Land in Myanmar: Recognising Gender in the National Land Use Policy*. Amsterdam: TNI.

Trappl, R., ed. (2006) *Programming for Peace: Computer-Aided Methods for International Conflict Resolution and Prevention*. Dordrecht: Springer.

Turnbull, C. (1978) The politics of non-aggression, in A. Montagu, ed., *Learning Non-Aggression: The Experience of Non-Literate Societies*. Oxford: Oxford University Press, pp. 161–221.

Tutu, D. (1999) *No Future without Forgiveness*. London: Rider.

Twiss, S. (1993) Curricular perspectives in comparative religious ethics: a critical examination of four paradigms, *Annual of the Society of Christian Ethics*, pp. 249–69.

UK MOD (Ministry of Defence (2004) *The Military Contribution to Peace Support Operations*, Joint Warfare Publication 3-50, 2nd edn. Swindon: Joint Doctrine and Concepts Centre, https://www.gov.uk/government/publications/jwp-3-50-the-military-contribution-to-peace-support-operations-second-edition.

UK MOD (Ministry of Defence) (2014) *Global Strategic Trends – Out to 2045*, 5th edn. London: Ministry of Defence.

Umana, I., de Leon, B., and Tager, A. (2014) El Salvador: negotiating with gangs, in A. Ramsbotham and A. Wennmann, eds, *Accord*, no. 25. *Legitimacy and Peace Processes: From Coercion to Consent*. London: Conciliation Resources, pp. 95–9.

UNAoC (United Nations Alliance of Civilizations) (2012) About us, www.unaoc.org/about/.

UNDPKO (UN Department of Peacekeeping Operations) (2007) *United Nations Peacekeeping Operations Principles and Guidelines (Capstone Doctrine Draft 3)*. New York: United Nations.

UNDPKO (2008) *United Nations Peacekeeping Operations Principles and Guidelines*. New York: United Nations.

UNDPKO (2015a) *Peacekeeping Fact Sheet Archive*, www.un.org/en/peacekeeping/resources/statistics/factsheet_archive.shtml.

UNDPKO (2015b) MINUSCA: United Nations Multidimensional Integrated Stabilization Mission in the Central African Republic, www.un.org/en/peacekeeping/missions/minusca/.

UNDPKO and DFS (Department of Field Support) (2009) *A New Partnership Agenda: Charting a New Horizon for UN Peacekeeping*. New York: United Nations, www.un.org/en/peacekeeping/documents/newhorizon.pdf.

UNGA (United Nations General Assembly) (1998) *Declaration of a Programme for Action on a Culture of Peace*. New York: United Nations.

UNGA (United Nations General Assembly) (2005) *World Summit Outcome*. UN Document A/RES/60/1, 16 September.

UNHCR (United Nations High Commissioner for Refugees) (2009) *Annual Report*, www.unhcr.org/4a2fd52412d.html.

UNHCR (2013) *Global Trends 2012: Displacement, the New 21st Century Challenge*. New York: United Nations, www.unhcr.org/51bacb0f9.html.

UNHCR (2014) *Global Trends 2013: War's Human Cost*. New York: United Nations, p. 7, www.unhcr.org/5399a14f9.html.

UNHCR (2015) *Global Trends 2014: World at War*. New York: United Nations, www.unhcr.org/558193896.html

UN High-Level Panel (2004) *A More Secure World: Our Shared Responsibility: Report of the High-Level Panel on Threats, Challenges and Change*. New York: United Nations, www.un.org/en/events/pastevents/a_more_secure_world.shtml.

UN High-Level Panel (2013) *A New Global Partnership: Eradicate Poverty and Transform Economies through Sustainable Development*. Report of the High-Level Panel of Eminent Persons on the Post-2015 Development Agenda. New York: United Nations, www.un.org/sg/management/beyond2015.shtml.

UNIDR (UN Institute for Disarmament Research) (1996) *Managing Arms in Peace Processes: The Issues*. Geneva: UN Institute for Disarmament Research.

United Nations (1995) *Supplement to an Agenda for Peace*, A/50/60– S/1995/1. New York: United Nations.

United Nations (1996) *The Blue Helmets: A Review of United Nations Peace-Keeping*. New York: United Nations.

United Nations (1998) *Report of the General Assembly*, A/Res/53/13. New York: United Nations.

United Nations (1999a) *Report of the Independent Inquiry into the Actions of the United Nations During the 1994 Genocide in Rwanda*, S/1999/1257. New York: United Nations.

United Nations (1999b) *The Fall of Srebrenica: Report of the Secretary-General to the UN General Assembly*, A/54/549. New York: United Nations.

United Nations (2000) *We the Peoples: The Role of the United Nations in the Twenty-First Century*. New York: United Nations.

United Nations (2001) *The Prevention of Armed Conflict: Report of the Secretary-General*, A/55/985– S/2002/574. New York: United Nations.

United Nations (2002a) *Report of the Policy Working Group on the United Nations and Terrorism*, A/57/273. New York: United Nations.

United Nations (2002b) Secretary-general's statement to the Security Council on 'Women, Peace and Security', 22 October, www.un.org/sg/statements/?nid=133.

United Nations (2004) *Report on the Rule of Law and Transitional Justice in Conflict and Post-Conflict Societies*. New York: United Nations.

United Nations (2011) *Preventive Diplomacy: Delivering Results*. Report of the Secretary-General, S/2011/552, 26 August.

United Nations (2012) *Strengthening the Role of Mediation in the Peaceful Settlement of Disputes, Conflict Prevention and Resolution*. Report of the Secretary-General. New York: UN.

United Nations (2014) *The World Population Situation in 2014*. New York: United Nations.

UN News Service (2014) Rebuilding Timbuktu: UN agency working with Mali 'to keep culture significant', 27 June, www.un.org/apps/news/story.asp?NewsID=48158.

UNOCHA (UN Office for the Coordination of Humanitarian Affairs) (2015) *Fragmented Lives: Humanitarian Overview 2014*. East Jerusalem: OCHA, www.ochaopt.org/documents/annual_humanitarian_overview_2014_english_final.pdf.

UNODC (UN Office on Drugs and Crime) (2013) *Global Study on Homicide 2013*. New York: United Nations, www.unodc.org/gsh/en/index.html.

UNPBC (United Nations Peacebuilding Commission) (2007) *Monitoring and Tracking Mechanism of the Strategic Framework for Peacebuilding in Burundi*, UN document PBC/2/BDI/4, 27 November.

UNRISD (1995) *Rebuilding War-Torn Societies*. Geneva: UN Research Institute for Social Development.

UNSC (1993) *Security Council Resolution 819 on Bosnia and Herzegovina*, S/RES/819. New York: United Nations, 16 April.

UNSC (2007) *Security Council Resolution 1769 on Sudan*, S/RES/1769. New York: United Nations, 31 July.

UNSC (2014) *United Nations Peacekeeping Operations*, S/PV.7275, 9 October. New York: United Nations, www.un.org/en/ga/search/view_doc.asp?symbol=S/PV.7275.

UNSG (2014) Secretary-General's remarks at Security Council open debate on trends in United Nations peacekeeping, 11 June, www.un.org/sg/statements/index.asp?nid=7769.

Uppsala Conflict Data Program (2015) *UCDP Conflict Encyclopedia*, Uppsala University, www.ucdp.uu.se/database.

Urbain, O., ed. (2008) *Music and Conflict Transformation: Harmonies and Dissonances in Geopolitics*. Tokyo: I. B. Tauris/Toda Institute.

Urquhart, B. (1993) A UN volunteer military force, *New York Review of Books*, 40(11): 3–4.

Ury, W. J. (1993) *Getting Disputes Resolved: Designing Systems to Cut the Costs of Conflict*. Cambridge, MA: Pon Books.

Ury, W. J. (2000) *The Third Side*. London: Penguin Books.

US Department of State (2002) *Patterns of Global Terrorism 2001*. Washington, DC: US Department of State, http://go.usa.gov/QbC3.

USDOD (United States Department of Defense (2005) *Military Support for Stability, Security, Transition and Reconstruction Operations*, Directive No. 3000.05. Washington, DC, 28 November.

US Office of the President (2002) *The National Security Strategy of the United States of America*. Washington, DC: Office of the President of the United States.

Van Crefeld, M. (1991) *The Transformation of War*. New York: Free Press.

Van Crefeld, M. (2000) *The Rise and Decline of the State*. Cambridge: Cambridge University Press.

van de Goor, L., Rupesinghe, K., and Sciarone, P., eds (1996) *Between Development and Destruction: An Enquiry into the Causes of Conflict in Post-Colonial States*. New York: St Martin's Press.

van den Dungen, P. (1996) Initiatives for the pursuit and institutionalisation of peace research, in L. Broadhead, ed., *Issues in Peace Research*. University of Bradford, Department of Peace Studies, pp. 5–32.

van den Dungen, P. (2008) Museums for peace: past, present, and future, in I. Anzai, et al., eds, *Museums for Peace: Past, Present and Future*. Kyoto: Ritsumeikan University, pp. 17–25.

van den Dungen, P., and Wittner, L. (2003) Peace history: an introduction, *Journal of Peace Research: Special Issue on Peace History*, 40(54): 363–75.

van der Merwe, H. (1989) *Pursuing Justice and Peace in South Africa*. London: Routledge.

van der Stoel, M. (1994) The role of the CSCE high commissioner on national minorities in CSCE preventive diplomacy, in S. Carlson, ed., *The Challenge of Preventive Diplomacy*. Stockholm: Ministry for Foreign Affairs.

van Evera, S. (1994) Hypotheses on nationalism and war, *International Security*, 18(4): 5–39.

van Tongeren, P., ed. (1996) *Prevention and Management of Conflicts: An International Directory*. The Hague: Dutch Centre for Conflict Prevention.

Vasquez, J. (1993) *The War Puzzle*. Cambridge: Cambridge University Press.

Vasquez, J. (1995) Why global conflict resolution is possible: meeting the challenge of the new world order, in J. Vasquez, J. Johnson and L. Stamato, eds, *Beyond Confrontation: Learning Conflict Resolution in the Post-Cold War Era*. Ann Arbor: Univeristy of Michigan Press, pp. 131–53.

Väyrynen, R. (1984) Regional conflict formations: an intractable problem of international relations, *Journal of Peace Research*, 21(4): 337–59.

Väyrynen, R., ed. (1991) *New Directions in Conflict Theory: Conflict Resolution and Conflict Transformation.* London: Sage.

Väyrynen, T. (2004) Gender and UN peace operations: the confines of modernity, in A. Bellamy and P. Williams, eds, *Peace Operations and Global Order, International Peacekeeping*, 11(1): 125–42.

Villa-Vincencio, C., and Verwoerd, W. (2000) Constructing a report: writing up the 'truth', in R. Rotberg and D. Thompson, eds, *Truth v. Justice: The Morality of Truth Commissions.* Princeton, NJ: Princeton University Press.

Volkan, J., Montville, J., and Julius, D., eds (1990) *The Psychodynamics of International Relationships*, vol. 2. Lexington, MA: D. C. Heath.

von Hippel, K. (2002) The roots of terrorism: probing the myths, *Political Quarterly*, 73, Supplement 1, August, pp. 25–39.

Walch, J. (1999) *In the Net: An internet Guide for Activists.* London: Zed Books.

Waldmeier, P. (1998) *Anatomy of a Miracle: The End of Apartheid and the Birth of the New South Africa.* London: Penguin.

Walker, N. (ed.) (2003) *Sovereignty in Transition.* Oxford: Hart.

Walker, T. (2008) Two faces of liberalism: Kant, Paine and the question of intervention, *International Studies Quarterly*, 52(3): 449–68.

Wallace, M. (1977) Arms races and escalation: some new evidence, *Journal of Conflict Resolution*, 23: 3–16.

Wallensteen, P. (1984) Universalism vs. particularism: on the limits of major power order, *Journal of Peace Research*, 21(3): 243–57.

Wallensteen, P., ed. (1988) *Peace Research: Achievements and Challenges.* Boulder, CO: Westview Press.

Wallensteen P., ed. (1998) *Preventing Violent Conflicts: Past Record and Future Challenges.* Uppsala University, Department of Peace and Conflict Research.

Wallensteen, P. (2002a) Reassessing recent conflicts: direct vs. structural prevention, in F. Hampson and D. Malone, eds, *From Reaction to Conflict Prevention: Opportunities for the UN System.* Boulder, CO: Lynne Rienner.

Wallensteen, P. (2002b) *Understanding Conflict Resolution.* London: Sage.

Wallensteen, P. (2007) *Understanding Conflict Resolution*, 2nd edn. London: Sage.

Wallensteen, P. (2011a) *Understanding Conflict Resolution: War, Peace and the Global System*, 3rd edn. London: Sage.

Wallensteen, P. (2011b) The Uppsala Conflict Data Program, 1978–2010: the story, the rationale and the programme, in P. Wallensteen, *Peace Research: Theory and Practice.* London: Routledge, pp. 111–24.

Wallensteen, P. (2011c) *Peace Research: Theory and Practice.* London: Routledge.

Wallensteen, P. (2013) Toward quality peace, *Peace Policy*, 25 November, http://peacepolicy.nd.edu/2013/11/25/toward-quality-peace/.

Wallensteen, P., and Axell, K. (1995) Armed conflict at the end of the Cold War, 1989–93, *Journal of Peace Research*, 30(3): 331–46.

Wallensteen, P., and Sollenberg, M. (1997) Armed conflicts, conflict termination and peace agreements 1989–96, *Journal of Peace Research*, 34(3): 339–58.

Wallensteen, P., and Svensson, I. (2014) Talking peace: international mediation in armed conflicts, *Journal of Peace Research*, 51(2): 315–27.

Wallis, T. (2010) Civilian peacekeeping, in N. Young, ed., *The Oxford International Encyclopedia of Peace.* Oxford: Oxford University Press.

Walter, B. (1997) The critical barrier to civil war settlement, *International Organization*, 51(3): 335–64.

Walter, B. (2002) *Committing to Peace: The Successful Settlement of Civil Wars*. Princeton, NJ: Princeton University Press.

Walter, B. (2011) *Conflict Relapse and the Sustainability of Post-Conflict Peace*. Washington, DC: World Bank, https://openknowledge.worldbank.org/handle/10986/9069.

Walter, B. (2014) Why bad governance leads to repeat civil war, *Journal of Conflict Resolution*, doi: 10.1177/0022002714528006.

Walton, R., and McKersie, R. (1965) *A Behavioral Theory of Labor Negotiations: An Analysis of a Social Interaction System*. New York: McGraw-Hill.

Waltz, K. (1959) *Man, the State and War*. New York: Columbia University Press.

Waltz, K. (1979) *Theory of International Politics*. Reading, MA: Addison-Wesley.

Waltz, K. (2002) The continuity of international politics, in K. Booth and T. Dunne, eds, *Worlds in Collision: Terror and the Future of Global Order*. Basingstoke: Palgrave, pp. 348–53.

Ward, H., Grundig, F., and Zorick, E. (2001) Marching at the pace of the slowest: a model of international climate-change negotiations, *Political Studies*, 49: 438–61.

Wardlaw, G. (1982) *Political Terrorism: Theory, Tactics, and Counter-Measures*. Cambridge: Cambridge University Press.

Watson Institute (2014) *The Economic Costs of War in Iraq, Afghanistan and Pakistan*. Providence, RI: Watson Institute for International Studies, Brown University.

Webb, K., Koutrakou, V., and Walters, M. (1996) The Yugoslavian conflict, European mediation and the contingency model: a critical perspective, in J. Bercovitch, ed., *Resolving International Conflicts: The Theory and Practice of Mediation*. Boulder, CO: Lynne Rienner, pp. 171–89.

Webel, S., and Galtung, J., eds (2007) *Handbook of Peace and Conflict Studies*. London: Routledge.

Weber, T. (1999) Gandhi, deep ecology, peace research and Buddhist economics, *Journal of Peace Research*, 36(3): 349–61.

Weber, T. (2001) Gandhian philosophy, conflict resolution theory, and practical approaches to negotiation, *Journal of Peace Research*, 38(4): 493–513.

Wehr, P. (1979) *Conflict Regulation*. Boulder, CO: Westview Press.

Wehr, P., and Lederach, J. (1996) Mediating conflict in Central America, in J. Bercovitch, ed., *Resolving International Conflicts: The Theory and Practice of Mediation*. Boulder, CO: Lynne Rienner, pp. 55–74.

Weinstein, J. (2005) *Autonomous Recovery and International Intervention in Comparative Perspective*, Working Paper 57. Washington DC: Center for Global Development.

Weinstein, J. (2006) *Inside Rebellions: The Politics of Insurgent Violence*. Cambridge: Cambridge University Press.

Weiss, A. (2014) Is Putin really cornered?, *International New York Times*, 9 August.

Weiss, C. (2015) Barely begun: women as peacemakers, peacekeepers and peacebuilders in law and practice, in C. Bailliet and K. Larsen, eds, *Promoting Peace through International Law*. Oxford: Oxford University Press, pp. 274–96.

Weiss, T. and Daws, S., eds (2007) *The Oxford Handbook on the United Nations*. Oxford: Oxford University Press.

Weiss, T., Kanninen, T., and Busch, M. (2009) *Sustainable Global Governance for the 21st Century*. Dialogue on Globalization Occasional Papers no. 45. New York: Friedrich Ebert Stiftung and Ralph Bunche Institute for International Studies.

Wennmann, A. (2011) *The Political Economy of Peacemaking*. London: Routledge.

Wheeler, N. (2000) *Saving Strangers: Humanitarian Intervention in International Society*. Oxford: Oxford University Press.

Whitehead, B. (2008) We shall overcome, in O. Urbain, ed., *Music and Conflict Transformation: Harmonies and Dissonances in Geopolitics*. Tokyo: I. B. Tauris/Toda Institute, pp. 78–92.

Whitfield, T. (2007) *Friends Indeed? The United Nations, Groups of Friends and the Resolution of* Conflict. Washington, DC: US Institute of Peace Press.

Whitman, R. G., and Wolff, S. (2010) The EU as a conflict manager? The case of Georgia and its implications, *International Affairs*, 86(1): 87–107.

Whitman, R. G., and Wolff, S., eds (2012) *The European Union as a Global Conflict Manager*. Abingdon: Routledge.

Whittaker, D. (1999) *Conflict and Reconciliation in the Contemporary World*. London: Routledge.

Whyte, J. (1990) *Interpreting Northern Ireland*. Oxford: Clarendon Press.

Wiener, N. (1948) *Cybernetics: Control and Communication in the Animal and the Machine*. New York: John Wiley.

Wiener, N. (1988) *The Human Use of Human Beings: Cybernetics and Society*. New York: Plenum Press.

Wight, M. (1977) *Systems of States*, ed. H. Bull. Leicester: Leicester University Press.

Wilkenfeld, J., et al. (2005) *Mediating International Crises*. London: Routledge.

Wilkinson, P. (2006) *Terrorism versus Democracy: The Liberal State Response*. Oxford: Oxford University Press.

Williams, M. (1998) *Civil–Military Relations and Peacekeeping*, Adelphi Paper 321. London: ISS.

Williams, P. (2007) From non-intervention to non-indifference: the origins and development of the African Union's security culture, *African Affairs*, 106(423): 253–79.

Williams, S., and Williams, S. (1994) *Being in the Middle by Being at the Edge: Quaker Experience of Non-Official Political Mediation*. London: Quaker Peace and Service.

Wilmshurst, E., ed. (2012) *International Law and the Classification of Conflicts*. Oxford: Oxford University Press.

Wils, O., Hopp, U., Ropers, N., Vimalarajah, L., and Zunzer, W. (2006) *The Systemic Approach to Conflict Transformation: Concepts and Fields of Application*. Berlin: Berghof Foundation for Peace Support.

Wilson, E. (1998) *Consilience: The Unity of Knowledge*. New York: Knopf.

Wilton Park Conference (2003) *Transforming War Economies: Challenges for Peacemaking and Peacebuilding*, report of the 725th Wilton Park Conference, 27–9 October. New York: Wilton Park and International Peace Academy.

Winchester, A., and Straughton, E. (2010) Stints and sustainability: managing stock levels on common land in England, *Agricultural History Review*, 58(1): 29–47.

Wischnath, G., and Gleditsch, N. P. (2011) *Battle Deaths – Comparing the UCDP and PRIO Data*. Oslo: PRIO Centre for the Study of Civil War, www.prio.org/People/Person/?x=3463.

Woocher, L. (2009) *Preventing Violent Conflict, Assessing Challenges*. Washington, DC: US Institute of Peace Press.

Wood, E. (2003) *Insurgent Collective Action and Civil War in El Salvador*. Cambridge: Cambridge University Press.

Woodhouse, T. (1986) To live our lives so as to take away the occasion for war: some observations on the peaceful economy, in G. Chester and A. Rigby, eds, *Articles of Peace*. Bridport: Prism Press, pp. 70–89.

Woodhouse, T., ed. (1991) *Peacemaking in a Troubled World*. Oxford: Berg.

Woodhouse, T. (1999a) Peacebuilding from below, in J. Perez de Cuellar and Y. S. Choue, eds, *World Encyclopaedia of Peace*, vol. 4. New York: Oceana, pp. 293–6.

Woodhouse, T. (1999b) *International Conflict Resolution: Some Critiques and a Response*, Working Paper 1. University of Bradford, Department of Peace Studies, Centre for Conflict Resolution.

Woodhouse, T. (2014) More than a game: a case study of football in the community initiatives in England, in C. Solanes et al., Deporte y resolución de conflictos. Barcelona: UOC, www.editorialuoc.cat/deporteyresolucindeconflictosepub-p-1266.html?cPath=1.

Woodhouse, T., and Ramsbotham, O., eds (2000) *Peacekeeping and Conflict Resolution*. London: Frank Cass.

Woodhouse, T., and Ramsbotham, O. (2005) Cosmopolitan peacekeeping and the globalization of security, *International Peacekeeping*, 12(2): 139–56.

Woodrow, P. (2006) Advancing practice in conflict analysis and strategy development: interim progress report. Draft paper, Reflecting on Peace Practice Project, CDA Collaborative Learning Projects.

Woodward, S. (2003) *On War and Peacebuilding: Unfinished Legacy of the 1990s*. New York: City University of New York.

World Bank (2003) *The Role of the World Bank in Conflict and Development: An Evolving Agenda*. Washington, DC: World Bank.

World Bank (2009) *State and Peace-Building Fund: Progress Report*, 21 May. Washington, DC: World Bank.

World Bank (2011) *World Development Report 2011: Conflict, Security and Development*. New York: World Bank, http://go.worldbank.org/QLKJWJB8X0.

World Bank (2015) Fragility, conflict, and violence, www.worldbank.org/en/topic/fragilityconflictviolence.

World Education Forum (2000) *The Dakar Framework for Action: Education for All: Meeting our Collective Commitments*. Paris: UNESCO.

Wright, Q. (1942) *A Study of War*. Chicago: University of Chicago Press.

Yankelovich, D. (1999) *The Magic of Dialogue: Transforming Conflict into Cooperation*. New York: Simon & Schuster.

Yarrow, C. H. (1978) *Quaker Experiences in International Conciliation*. New Haven, CT: Yale University Press.

Yassine-Hamdan, N., and Pearson, F. (2014) *Arab Approaches to Conflict Resolution: Mediation, Negotiation and Settlement of Political Disputes*. London: Routledge.

Yawnghwe, H. (2014) Burma – national dialogue: armed groups, contested legitimacy and political transition, in A. Ramsbotham and A. Wennmann, eds, *Legitimacy and Peace Processes, Accord*, no. 25. London: Conciliation Resources, pp. 44–9.

Young, O. (1967) *The Intermediaries: Third Parties in International Crises*. Princeton, NJ: Princeton University Press.

Youssef, H. (2009) *Conflict Management in the Middle East: Regional Solutions for Regional Problems*. Beirut: Korber-Stiftung.

Zartman, I. W., ed. (1978) *The Negotiation Process: Theories and Applications*. Beverly Hills, CA: Sage.

Zartman, I. W. (1982) *The Practical Negotiator*. New Haven, CT: Yale University Press.

Zartman, I. W. (1985) *Ripe for Resolution: Conflict and Intervention in Africa*. New York: Oxford University Press.

Zartman, I. W., ed. (1995a) *Collapsed States: The Disintegration and Restoration of Legitimate Authority*. Boulder, CO: Lynne Rienner.

Zartman, I. W., ed. (1995b) *Elusive Peace: Negotiating an End to Civil Wars*. Washington, DC: Brookings Institution.

Zartman, I. W. (1995c) Negotiating the South African conflict, in I. W. Zartman, ed., *Elusive Peace: Negotiating an End to Civil Wars*. Washington, DC: Brookings Institution, pp. 147–76.

Zartman, I. W. (1997) Toward the resolution of international conflicts, in I. W. Zartman and J. Rasmussen, eds, *Peacemaking in International Conflict: Methods and Techniques*. Washington, DC: US Institute of Peace Press, pp. 3–22.

Zartman, I. W. (2000) Mediating conflicts of need, greed and creed, *Orbis*, 24(2): 255–66.

Zartman, I. W., ed. (2001) *Preventive Negotiation*. Lanham, MD: Rowman & Littlefield.

Zartman, I. W. (2005) *Cowardly Lions: Missed Opportunities to Prevent Deadly Conflict and State Collapse*. Boulder, CO: Lynne Rienner.

Zartman, I. W. (2006) *Negotiating with Terrorists*. Leiden: Martinus Nijhoff.

Zartman, I. W. (2008) Ripeness revisited: the push and pull of conflict management, in C. Hauswedell, ed., *Deeskalation von Gewaltkonflikten seit 1945*. Essen: Klartext, pp. 232–44.

Zartman, I. W., and Faure, G. O. eds (2005) *Escalation and Negotiation in International Conflicts*. Cambridge: Cambridge University Press.

Zartman, I. W., and Kremenyuk, V., eds (2005) *Peace vs Justice: Negotiating Backward and Forward-Looking Outcomes*. Lanham, MD: Rowman & Littlefield.

Zartman, I. W., and Rubin, J. (1996) *Power and Asymmetry in International Negotiations*. Laxenburg, Austria: International Institute of Applied Systems Analysis.

Zaum, D. (2007) *The Sovereignty Paradox: The Norms and Politics of International Statebuilding*. Oxford: Oxford University Press.

Ziring, L., Riggs, R. E., and Plano, J. C. (2000) *The United Nations: International Organization and World Politics*. London: Harcourt.

Index

Note: abbreviations used in the index are explained on pp. xxi–xxviii

CPSIA information can be obtained
at www.ICGtesting.com
Printed in the USA
BVHW01*1704100618
518641BV00014B/149/P